I read Tim Griswold's From Shasta
thoroughly enjoyed Tim's account c
rustic and rural beginning in the Sha ~~....~~ *California, by*
skill and determination, Tim became a world traveler and mover and
shaker in the computer and information technology world.

I found two stories unfolding in From Shasta to Shanghai. The secondary
story was the exciting evolution of computer and information technology
from the early 1960's to the present. The primary and most interesting
story was Tim's personal journey through this technical evolution. Rather
than attaching himself to any particular wave of technology and tumbling to
obscurity as more advanced waves of technology arose, Tim managed to
surf the technology for an enduring and successful career. Tim's key to
success was to push himself to learn as much as he could and take
advantage of every opportunity he could find or create. Tim managed to
learn from his misadventures as well as his successful work and business
ventures. He shares his experiences and insights derived from his military
service and his years in large corporations such as IBM and ITT as well as
his consulting work. From a country boy to positions of power and
influence circulating in the higher burnings of the internet and telecom
industry, Tim's journey was not always easy and includes the peaks, dips
and curves life throws at us but it is a fascinating and informative journey.

Tim shares his personal life and observations along the way making this
far more than a technical journal. It's the story of an amazing man of
modest beginnings forging his way into a world of business and
technology to a level few achieve.

Chuck Nelson

From Shasta to Shanghai
MY JOURNEY TO ITHAKA
2nd Edition

I was raised in the Shasta Valley, part of Siskiyou County California. With an area approximately the size of the State of Connecticut and a population of less than 45,000, it remains one of the least populated parts of America.

Shanghai China, with a metro area population greater than 35 million, is the largest city in the world. It is the birthplace of my wife and stepdaughter, and the home of my extended family. In a sense it is my second home. By any measure, the distance between these two locations could not be greater. This book tells of my journey from Shasta to Shanghai.

From Shasta to Shanghai

This book is dedicated to
all those who taught me,
and any that I might in some small way teach.

Table of Contents

In words far more eloquent than I could ever assembly, Cavafy reminds us that it is about the journey, not the destination. I understand that I share a love for this poem with the late First Lady Jacqueline Kennedy Onassis. She had it read at her funeral. I would ask the same.

Ithaka

C. P. Cavafy

As you set out for Ithaka
hope the voyage is a long one,
full of adventure, full of discovery.
Laistrygonians and Cyclops
angry Poseidon—don't be afraid of them:
you'll never find things like that on your way
as long as you keep your thoughts raised high,
as long as a rare excitement
stirs your spirit and your body.
Laistrygonians and Cyclops,
wild Poseidon—you won't encounter them
unless you bring them along inside your soul,
unless your soul sets them up in front of you.

Hope the voyage is a long one.
May there be many a summer morning when,
with what pleasure, what joy,
you come into harbors seen for the first time;
to buy fine things,
mother of pearl and coral, amber and ebony,
sensual perfume of every kind—
as many sensual perfumes as you can;
and may you visit many Egyptian cities
to gather stores of knowledge from their scholars.
Keep Ithaka always in your mind.
Arriving there is what you are destined for.
But do not hurry the journey at all.
Better if it lasts for years,
so you are old by the time you reach the island,
wealthy with all you have gained on the way,
not expecting Ithaka to make you rich.

Ithaka gave you the marvelous journey.
Without her, you would not have set out.
She has nothing left to give you now.

i

And if you find her poor, Ithaka won't have fooled you.
Wise as you will have become, so full of experience,
you will have understood by then what these Ithakas mean.

Source: C. P. Cavafy: Collected Poems
(Princeton University Press, 1975)
Trans. Edmund Keeley and Philip Sherrard

I suggest that you go online to
www.youtube.com/watch?v=1n3n2Ox4Yfk,
and listen to Sean Connery's recitation of the poem. It is well
worth the effort.
Or, simply search YouTube for "Ithaka by Sean Connery."

Preface

The most dynamic time in history

I grew up in a pre-technology world. Of course that is not completely accurate, life-altering technologies have arisen throughout history. The wheel, the compass, the printing press, sailing ships, production lines, automobiles, and airplanes are but a few examples. However, to those living in the 21st century, these "stone age" technologies that revolutionized life on earth, would most likely not even be mentioned. Instead most would focus on the technologies that have arisen during my lifetime: jet aircraft, atomic power and weapons, television, computers, satellites (providing GPS and communications for example), the internet, and a plethora of smart devices so compact, affordable, and ubiquitous that almost every citizen of the world can own and operate multiple smart devices that interconnect and interact globally. These are the devices that inform their daily life.

I would argue that the last 70 years have been the most dynamic period in human history. Almost all of the technologies that you have come to depend on have come into existence, or at least into affordable formats, during my lifetime. As you will read, I have had more than a little involvement in the evolutionary process for many of these technologies.

Pure Dumb Luck or Cosmic Revenge

This book tells the story of my American Dream. What it is, and how I have achieved it. Specifically, it covers my path, the critical decision, and what caused me to choose the branches I took. Was it predestined, something I did consciously or deliberately, was it pure dumb luck, or was it cosmic revenge? What follows is my attempt to answer these questions.

I have lived a blessed life. That is not to say a charmed life; there was never a silver platter, not even a tin plate. Why then do I consider it blessed? It is because I can truly say that I have lived the American Dream! I started with nothing and from nothing, but I have lived the life I wanted. I have traveled the world, and in the process, have learned an incredible amount about a great number of things. I have loved a great deal of the work I have done. I have experienced the love to three good women. I have made some money, and I have lost some money. I am proud of what I have done, but above all, I am humbly thankful for the life God has allowed me to live.

A real-life Huck-Finn

At the time of my birth in 1945, my father and his brother ran a herd of Angora goats in the mountains west of Red Bluff, in Northern California. We spent summers in a one room A-frame high on the side of Mount Bully Choop. We wintered in a small house in the foothills.

We didn't have a phone, television, electricity, running water, or indoor plumbing. We didn't even have mail service, but there were hills, valleys, and old mines to explore. There were a million trees to climb. We had dogs to protect us with kid goats for pets. We learned early to be on the lookout for rattlesnakes everywhere, and bear, usually near the wild blackberries that we picked for mom to make pies and jam.

This Huck-Finn life only lasted a few years for me, the youngest. Synthetic products such as nylon and rayon destroyed the mohair (the fleece from Angora goats) market, and by 1950 Dad had to find other work to support his family. Two of the skills he had learned managing the goats provided his primary of income until well after I left home.

Shearing both Angora goats and sheep was a backbreaking but essential skill that Dad used to supplement his income from the goat business. Trapping was also an important skill for any owner of goats, as several predators enjoyed dining on them. To combat this, Dad as well as his brother Charley, became quite accomplished trappers.

As the Angora market withered, Dad moved to trapping for the California Department of Fish and Wildlife to protect the deer and rancher's livestock. Trapping brought our family from the Red Bluff area to the Shasta Valley in Siskiyou County early in the spring of 1951. Trapping didn't pay all that well, and Dad continued to supplement his income by shearing sheep each spring.

The Shasta Valley was only slightly more civilized, with a few, but not many, more people. It was still rural, still isolated. Our living situation was only slightly better; there was still no indoor plumbing, but we did have electricity and later a phone. We could see the moon and stars through cracks in the roof as we lay in bed at night, but our beds were actually indoors. Dad's profession provided an excellent opportunity to work, not just out of doors, but in the wild. In many ways, our life was more akin to the 19th than the 20th century. For my siblings and me, this was a unique chance to live and learn in a world that few of our peers and none of our children would ever have the opportunity to experience.

Life in the Shasta Valley was too limited for my American Dream. We knew very little, could see very little, and opportunities were extremely limited. If asked, most would have predicted that I would become a: farm laborer, mechanic, machinist, or lumberjack. If I were fortunate, I might rise to a position with the County or the State. That future was shared by most of my classmates.

Two weeks after graduation I join the Air Force. From there, I moved to IBM where I spent 15-years, first fixing but later selling large mainframe computers. In the mid-1970s I managed the installation of the then largest computer network in the world.

My work with the Air Force and IBM both required extensive domestic travel; that shifted to international when I joined ITT to run their global service operation. For 20 years, first, with ITT and later Verisign, but also as an independent consultant, I typically spent at least two weeks a month outside of the country.

I have seen the Southern Cross from Sydney, the midnight sun in Helsinki, circumnavigated the earth, and crossed both the Pacific and Atlantic more times than I can remember. While it has been an incredible adventure, it is not as "romantic" as it sounds; think of it as a lot of very long bus rides. Most gratifying, though, has been the opportunity to explore different lands, learn different cultures, and build life-long friendships around the world.

A standard joke was that IBM stood for "I've Been Moved"; it was certainly true in my case, but moving didn't stop when I left IBM. Over the years, we lived in 37 different homes in 16 states, as far west as Hawaii and as far east as Connecticut. If you count temporary assignments of 45 days or more, that jumps to 52 houses or apartments in 21 states and two foreign countries.

In 2010, after ten years in Virginia, I retired in Henderson, Nevada. I am as busy as ever, primarily building The Foundation For Caregivers, a nonprofit I started after Sharon, my second wife, passed away. I continue to do a few international consulting projects when they interest me; most involve strategic development. In my spare time, my wife and I have gutted our 75-year old house and doubled its size. We did the work ourselves.

You have to step back and see

Life is like a Monet masterpiece. If you stand too close, you only see the individual spots of color and the lines left by his brush. They are a medley of dots and colors that are more interesting than artistic. Close, you lose perspective. When you stand back, you can see the magnificence of his work; the blending of colors, the harmony, the sweep, the totality. In life, as with art, it is only with the benefit of distance that you can see the real beauty of the Creator's masterpiece.

I have found writing to be cathartic, not the writing so much as the process of putting things in perspective, creating order out of the chaos of living. Time has provided the distance I needed to see more of the beauty of life. Looking back, I can see the significance of some decisions and in most cases the logic, or illogic, much clearer than at the time. I can now see how events or decisions, often separated by 20 or more years, are inextricably linked. I see my life as a tapestry, the threads of which, are only now apparent. I find it reassuring and visible proof of God's hand in my life.

I am a cancer survivor. I have married three times, one ending in divorce and one from death due to cancer. My wives, first white, second black, and third Asian, have helped me amass a multicultural, multi-ethnic progeny that includes one son, four daughters, and three grandchildren. Along the way, I earned a BS in Business from Charter Oak College in Connecticut and an MBA from Regis University in Denver.

What does it take to live the American Dream?

Before we get to living the American Dream, let me define the term. For me, the American Dream can be summarized in a single word: *mobility!* It is the idea that I could achieve success and prosperity through hard work, determination, and initiative. The freedom to go anywhere and achieve financial success at whatever level I was willing to purchase with my efforts. I asked that nothing be given, but nothing withheld. For me, it was never about being rich or famous; it was about the freedom to choose and the ability to reap reasonable rewards of my efforts.

Am I lucky to have lived the American Dream? In many ways incredibly lucky, but these two quotes from James Collins, the author of Good to Great and Built to Last, tell why I believe luck has little to do with it.

*"Greatness is not a function of circumstances.
Greatness is largely a matter of conscious choice
and discipline."*

*"Whether you prevail or fail depends more on
what you do to yourself then on what the world
does to you."*

I make no claim to greatness, quite the contrary; I am the ultimate "every man." I started about as far down the ladder as you can start, but I aimed high. The truth is that we are all, including you, living your version of the American Dream. You might be asking: how can that be; my life is terrible? But you need to be honest with yourself, have you made a conscious choice to do great things? Are you disciplined? Have you invested in yourself? Do you have character? Do you do the right thing even when there is higher cost or sacrifice involved? You should note that these factors are not about age, wealth, education, gender, or the color of your skin. They say nothing about how others see or treat you; these are all choices that you control, not something that others have done to you.

The American Dream is not free. You cannot get there without paying the price of admission. Did you drop out: of school, of work, of parenting, of marriage, of responsibility? Did you just give up or settle for what is, instead of striving for what could be? Do you do what is easy, or what is right? Do you walk away when the going gets complicated? Are you making smart choices, or do you follow the crowd? Did you cover your body with tattoos? Dye your hair purple? Poke holes everywhere in your body, or blow your mind with drugs to escape, to show that you are a rebel, or was it just to follow the crowd? Do you complain about everything? Do you step up for the inconvenient assignment? Do you take the overtime when offered? Do you consistently give more than expected? Are you a problem, or a problem solver? Do you see difficulties as problems to be avoided, or opportunities to learn and to grow?

Without a doubt, the answer to at least some of these is yes. Take heart; you can recover; you just have to work harder. The American Dream is not a bowl of Ramen, it takes more than water. It requires work, sacrifice, and time. You will make mistakes and have false starts. There will be plenty of pain along the road, and it will not always be pretty.

With few exceptions, the life you live is, to a large extent, the life you have been willing to purchase with your blood, sweat, and tears. If your life isn't what you wanted, look in the mirror and figure out what you need to change to make it what you want.

Here are some of the things you should consider:

Curiosity – I once considered naming this book "The bear went over the mountain" after the children's nursery rhyme. This verse talks of curiosity, "...to see what he could see." At first glance it appeared to be the story of my life, always climbing mountains to see what I could see. Regrettably, when I carefully examined the story, I discovered that the message was not intended to encourage curiosity, quite the opposite, its goal was to stifle it. "...the other side of the mountain was all that he could see." The message is that curiosity is futile, stick to your knitting, there is nothing out there worth seeking.

That lesson is 100% wrong. In fact, on the other side of the mountain, there are more mountains, there are valleys, rivers, villages, and cities. There are oceans to cross, places worth seeing, people worth meeting, and things worth doing. On the other side of the mountain there is a life worth living, but to find it, you must be eternally curious, and you must be willing to climb mountains.

Curiosity will enlarge your American Dream.

Integrity – Hopefully you will reach a point in your life, and hopefully at a young age when you realize that it all boils down to one thing, your integrity. Are you a man or woman of your word? When you say that you will or will not do something, do you keep your word? Do you "walk the talk?"

You can be rich or a beggar, you can be beautiful or ugly, you can live in a mansion or on the streets. In the end, we will die, and all that you have accumulated will mean nothing. It will come down to how you chose to live your life, to your integrity ...your word.

None of us are perfect, none of us will keep our word 100% of the time, but when you fail, do you recognize it as a failure? Do you strive to do better? Do you guard your word carefully to make sure that you don't say things that you don't mean, or make commitments that you can't keep?

The quality of your American Dream will depend on your integrity.

Humility – You may, and you should be the cause of your world, but no matter how good you are, how smart you are, or how rich or successful you might be, you are not the cause of THE world. That is God's work, and if you are not utterly humbled by the majesty of what He has done, you are a fool. It is by His grace that you are here, by His grace that you were born into the circumstances that you were, by His grace that you have had the opportunities you have, and you should never forget that. You are no better in His eyes than the beggar, the cripple, the lame, or the insane; you are just another soul struggling to grow more fully in His eyes.

Humility will add richness to your American Dream.

Grace – Grace is an unearned kindness. As God has given you infinite grace, you need to give grace to others. It is not possible for you to give unlimited grace, you are a deeply flawed human, not God. But you should never let perfection get in the way of your best. The people you meet on the street, or who serve your dinner at home or in a restaurant, are no different than you. They too are deeply flawed humans in desperate need of grace, grace that you can give by showing them respect, by appreciating what they do, by thanking them for serving, helping, or teaching you, by valuing the time they give to you.

Grace will add dignity to your American Dream.

Goals – If you don't know where you are going, any road will get you there. This quote has been attributed to everybody from Lao-Tzu to Lewis Carroll, who had the Cheshire Cat in Alice in Wonder Land speak those words to Alice. No matter who you credit, those words speak to the folly of living a life without goals. Goals are necessary to set a direction and measure progress. Goals are the reference point for your decisions.

Without goals, you will spend your life wandering in the woods. You will get somewhere, but it is unlikely to be the American Dream that you would want.

Discipline – You may think there is time to do something, to change, to get better, or to learn, but when you reach some stage in later life, you will look back and realize that time has passed so quickly. You will accomplish little if you don't have the discipline to start and to proceed. Of course, discipline depends entirely on both integrity and goals. If you don't have a destination in mind, you will never start, and you will most likely stop when the going gets tough.

Without discipline, you will rationalize all of the reasons why that wasn't what you meant; it wasn't what you actually said, or circumstances have changed, so you don't really need to do it.

Without discipline, your American Dream will never bloom.

Courage – Finally, you must have the courage to take chances. Nothing worth having is free, there will be risks, occasionally terrifying risks. Don't take stupid risks; Las Vegas is full of people who do that. Work to mitigate the risks, use judgment, think through the alternatives, consult with those you trust, and most importantly, make sure the anticipated outcome is worth the risk.

Don't run from risks, or you will spend your life running.

It is my hope that you enjoy reading as much as I have enjoyed first living, and then writing my story. In the process, I hope you also learn a few things and that you gain at least some insight into the personal and professional worlds I have lived in and influenced on my journey from Shasta to Shanghai. Most importantly, I hope to inspire you to examine your journey to Ithaka.

The Early Years

I was born in Sisters Hospital on Main Street in Red Bluff California on January 18, 1945, at 1:50 p.m. I am the youngest of four children, with two sisters and one brother.

I can't say that I remember much of my early years, so I ask my siblings to fill in the blanks. My Dad had written his life story, and this provided a lot of insight and information on his life. I also had an old document that Mom had prepared for me when I joined the Air Force. As part of my security clearance review, they wanted to know every detail of my life. That process started with her filling out a Form DD 398. That document proved very helpful as it listed everywhere I had lived, along with dates, up to the point where I joined the Air Force.

Mom took this project very seriously, and so she put in every detail she could remember. To my surprise, I discovered that I had lived in the hospital for 12 days after my birth. I had never heard about this 12-day stay until I was starting to research this section.

It took some digging, but I was finally able to get to the bottom of my extended hospital stay. It is hard to say how much is fact, and how much has grown with the telling; it makes a good story in any case.

As a result of my entry into this world, Mom came within inches of dying. Back in those days, they keep new mothers in bed much longer than they do today, but 12 days was way beyond normal. There were some serious complications. "Childbed Fever" was the all-encompassing term in those days. Childbed Fever usually meant the mother had died of an infection, probably the result of unsanitary conditions related to childbirth. That was the same term listed as the cause of death for my Dad's sister Mabel; she died after giving birth, approximately ten years earlier.

During the last year of World War II, most of the qualified medical personnel were off taking care of the wounded. In Mom's case, old Doc Frye, who was apparently known to as the "town drunk," delivered me because Doctor Woods, the "good doctor," was overseas tending the troops.

It seems Mom always had long, protracted deliveries, and the story was that Doc Frye had a fishing trip to go on and probably a bottle to help keep him warm. Fishing in January seems strange, but in any case, immediately after my birth, he left her in the hands of inexperienced nurses. Their primary role being to see that the placenta had passed and that she was "stable." It didn't, and she wasn't.

When Dad came in from the goat ranch to see his wife and new baby, Mom was running an extreme fever from the rotting afterbirth still inside her. As the story goes, she was "out of her head," and she didn't even recognize Dad. Dad started yelling for a nurse. His getting upset got Mom upset, and she tried to get out of bed. Her sudden movement stirred the afterbirth, and it finally started passing. The nurse arriving upon a bloody scene, panicked and said: "Oh my God, she's having another baby!"

Dad, who was never one to delve too deeply into emotional subjects, later commented that we four children would all have been 'left motherless' had it not been for a brand-new medical miracle called penicillin. They got things cleaned up and shot Mom full of this wonder-drug. With God's assistance and penicillin, she pulled through.

So my 12-day hospital residency was because my mother came very close to winding up in the morgue. This story was undoubtedly embellished over the years, but that is the version I was able to piece together 70 years later.

— ■ —

When I did go home, it was the "Henderson Place," an old ranch house about 45 miles west of Red Bluff. Amusingly, I now live in Henderson, NV; it is funny how things repeat themselves. No one seems to be quite sure why the ranch was called the Henderson Place. The assumption is that somewhere along the line someone named Henderson had at least lived there, if not owned it.

Tom, Betty, Barbara, & Tim with dead coyote
Henderson Place 1946

— ∎ —

Before GPS, a lot of country navigation involved references to the names of different houses or farms. Almost without exception, they took on the name of the owner, frequently dating to the time of homesteading. For those of you who may have missed that chapter in your American history class, back in the 18th and 19th centuries, even early in the 20th century, the Government had millions of acres of land that they wanted people to develop. At first, they saw this as a revenue source for the Government, but over time it became a land-grant program. The Homestead Act of 1862, there were just 32 States at that point, opened homesteading to virtually anyone who was willing to work extremely hard, to live on, and improve the land. The reward was ownership of 160 acres after five years. It makes interesting reading for anyone curious about how this country developed.

– ■ –

As for directions, they went something like this. "You go down about a half mile, and the Smith Place will be on your left. Turn right and go up to the Houston Ranch. If you get to the house, you will have gone too far. You need to take that little dirt road, well it is more of a path, about 200 yards before you get to the ranch house. It's the one on the left without a gate. Follow it up over the hill and down a bit to the river where you will see the old school house. Just past that is the Griswold Place." I like these directions much better than the lady nagging me to 'turn left at the next light.' I suppose it is just what you are used to.

– ■ –

Much of the following few paragraphs were lifted, with some editing, from my sister Betty's, somewhat romanticized writings on the Henderson Place. I was too young to remember much, but I have visited a few times as an adult. It was interesting trying to piece all of this together. The mind can play tricks when it comes to long ago events. I remember some things as if they were yesterday, but when I examine the facts, I find that I was too young to remember all that much. I don't know if I "remember," if I am taking from an old photograph or possibly something someone said. My "memory" may come from something completely unrelated. It is entirely possible that I have incorporated it as thought I remembered. Undoubtedly there is a lot of fiction embedded within what I believe are the facts.

The Henderson Place is now called Wild Horse Mesa, a romanticized marketing name since the area has nothing to do with wild horses, and there is no mesa; the name looks good on brochures. It remains a barren and dry foothill area covered with chaparral, buckeye, and scrub oak. There are a few evergreens that we always called digger pine. Betty's version is much more colorful.

According to Betty, to understand how beautiful the Henderson Place could be, you had to be there during a "good" spring. I have no idea how often "a good spring" came along. I suspect the frequency is on a par with a century plant blooming. I also suspect that Betty's memory is as fungible as mine. Supposedly, when a miracle spring does happen, it could last from the end of February to the middle of May. Betty recalls acres and armloads of

4

wildflowers in the little swales with decent soil and moisture. Incidentally, a "swale" is a low area of land, especially one that is moist or marshy. There is absolutely no part of the Henderson Place that could be considered moist or marshy; like I said, my sister tends to the romantic side. Swale is one of those words that is "regional," only used in some parts of the country, and one that has gone out of fashion over the years. There are several similar words such as a creek, gulch, gully, and ravine that all mean roughly the same thing but, like swale, they are seldom used any longer.

For Betty, April was the month to roam those hills. The blooming brush, the thick, sweet perfume of Chaparral and Buckeye, the delicate apple blossom scent of Manzanita, with the incessant hum of honeybees in the still, not quite sultry air, made for a sensory delight. We moved away from the Henderson Place in the fall of 1947 when I was about 18-months old, so I don't recall any of this.

Betty remembers there being seasons at the Henderson Place. I remember just two, winter being cold and summers being mercilessly hot and dry with maybe a pleasant week or two at each end. We both agree that when you see it dried up in the summer heat, and over-run with Star Thistles, beautiful isn't precisely the word that comes to mind. Terms like Death Valley and Hades seem more appropriate, but according to Betty, come April, Redbud bushes paint the hills with splashes of scarlet pink, and there are numberless varieties of wildflowers that grace every hillside. Again, this is not exactly the way I remember it.

The actual house melted into the dust years ago, but back in the day, it was quite small with a kitchen/eating area that wrapped around into the living area. There was one bedroom where our parents slept. The kids slept outside on a covered porch that ran around three sides of the house. When we were tiny, we slept on a cot inside. As soon as we were old enough, I suspect that was about the time we stopped nursing; we moved outside with the older kids.

On moonlit nights, we could see our breath. It did require a few more quilts during the winter. Of course, this was all we knew at that age, but what kid would miss a chance for a "sleep out" at any age? There is something special about having no walls and the quiet of the night surrounding you.

I suspect we were feeling a bit "tough" and self-assured compared to our "city" cousins. No indoor bedroom ever quite equaled the Henderson Place porch, even in winter.

Betty remembers waking to the sounds of wild birds as well as our rooster crowing. I don't recall that, but given that we slept outside and we always had an abundance of animals, I don't doubt that her memory is correct.

The toilet was an outhouse down a path a fair distance from the house. We seldom had a flashlight to guide us along the way, so it seemed like a mile when it was dark and cold. Another important rite of passage was reaching the point of not being afraid of the dark – especially when one had to make a trip to the outhouse. I didn't achieve that milestone for some years after we left the Henderson Place.

Our water was hand pumped from a cistern that was fed by a small spring nearby. The pump was outside, near the kitchen. As I recall, the water had a lot of Sulphur with a pungent odor. Betty remembers it as being "sweet."

We had no electricity and of course, there was no phone. The sun delineated our life. We did have kerosene lanterns that extended the evenings, but the work days were long for Mom and Dad, and kerosene was expensive, so there was no staying up late.

Our life was carefree and innocent. We enjoyed near total freedom, spending our days wandering the foothills, exploring the almost always dry creek bottoms, and, much to Mom's chagrin, sliding down an embankment on pieces of shale. I remembered the embankment more like a large hillside, but on return visits, I discovered it to be quite short. There was a lot of loose shale, with the bigger pieces at the bottom. We would haul a piece to the top that was big enough to sit on, and slide down the hill as if we were sledding on snow. You couldn't hang on to the edge because it would rip up your fingers, so you just sat on the rock as it slid along. It was pretty bumpy, and we seldom made it all the way to the bottom without falling off. Those involuntary separations frequently resulted in cuts, bangs, and bruises. I think Mom's principal concern was that these rides often led to tears in our clothes. A torn pant leg or sleeve meant more work for her, and since jeans were one of the few things we bought in a store, tears meant spending more money. She probably figured that if we hurt ourselves enough, we would stop our foolishness.

We weren't unchaperoned; Dad always had some excellent herd dogs that he used to manage the goats. These dogs are naturally protective of the innocent. That included us kids, so we always had one or more of these dogs watching over us as we explored. About the only danger, we had to be concerned about was an abundant supply of rattlesnakes.

We learned very early how to avoid rattlers and to kill them when possible. Rattlesnakes aren't predators in the sense of seeking out and killing people or animals, but they were a danger to adults, kids, dogs, and goats. Killing them was part of protecting our lives and livelihood.

As the youngest, I would try to follow, but more frequently, I would get a piggy-back ride on Betty's shoulders. By the time I came along, our folks were past any "novelty" aspect of parenting. They were busy with the goats and dealing with the financial strain brought on by the dwindling mohair market; much of my early upbringing fell to my siblings. As a result, I undoubtedly had more freedom at a younger age than my older siblings.

— ■ —

Life had its dangers. We were a long way from any medical help, and so our various cuts and scrapes were "tended" and left to heal. There was a trash dump near our house, and while it was supposed to be off limits, it held a trove of treasures, and we would try to dig out anything that might somehow be useful or turned into a toy. We were almost always barefoot, and at one point I stepped on the broken bottom of a bottle and cut my foot quite severely. No tendons weren't damaged, but I definitely should have had some stitches; the doctor was too far away. That scar stayed with me for decades.

— ■ —

Western Tehama County was, in many ways, the Appalachia of the West. It wasn't green and lush like the real Appalachia. I never heard of any moonshiners, but they were probably there, just out of sight. The area was dirt poor and populated with people who seldom had more than an 8th-grade education. They went to town only for the necessities that they could not obtain by growing, producing or bartering. That was limited to things like shoes, jeans, tobacco, and flower; they had little need of what a town could offer.

Texie at the Henderson Place

Old cars tended to be left to decompose where they died an irreversible death. That was partly of necessity as these derelicts were often a source of parts to keep other vehicles running, and scraps used to construct other necessities. For kids, they were an endless source of entertainment. We could kneel on the rusted springs of what had once been a seat, and pretend drive for hours.

There was one old truck we called "Poppin Johnny." It hadn't reached the dead and gone stage, but as I recall, it looked like it had. It was used each year to haul hay in from the field, our belongings up Mt. Bully Choop when we took the goats up in the summer, and to bring the mohair sacks down after shearing. It was a slow lumbering beast that would backfire at random times. That is where it got its moniker.

The breaks weren't very good. That was pretty much true of all cars and trucks back in those days. When it was being used to haul things like mohair down from our camp on Bully Choop, they would chain a log to the back end to act as a break. Without that, Poppin Johnny may well have run down the hill and most likely off the side of the very narrow twisting mountain road. Of course dragging a log along also helped smooth out some of the ruts washed into the roadway by melting winter snows and occasional rains.

8

Tim, Barbara, Tom & Betty 1947,
kid goat (not Lassie) Poppin Johnny is on the right

I asked my siblings what they recalled about these derelict vehicles and got an avalanche of conflicting versions of Johnny and other vehicles, as well as how they were all used. The stories, all told with absolute sincerity, often conflicted with what other siblings recalled, and occasionally even conflicted with other versions and other stories from the same sibling. I almost started a "range war" with the debate about all of these conflicting stories. It would seem that my memory might not be the only one that has been enhanced, embellished, or faded over the years.

Like many automobiles, Johnny's radiator tended to fall short of cooling the engine under constant strain, something like hauling a load up Bully Choop. The result was steam pouring out of the radiator cap. There was a requirement to carry ample water to add periodically along the way. Four-wheel drive was rare before the WWII jeeps, so when it came time to get up a particularly steep stretch of road, it was often necessary to turn around and back up the hill as the reverse gear was always the lowest, and therefore, the most powerful gear. Reverse allowed you to move slowly up with less chance of spinning the wheels.

I remember Poppin Johnny, not riding in it, only sitting on the hillside near the

9

house at the Henderson Place. As I recall, it didn't have a driver's side door, maybe no doors at all, and the hood over the engine compartment was also missing. My siblings would probably tell you I am confusing it with a different derelict, or maybe that was later in Johnny's life. In those days, the hoods consisted of 4 sections; all hinged together so that you could raise up either side kind of like a bird's wing. Someone had removed Johnny's hood, it may have been lost, or it may have simply been left against a tree somewhere just to make it easier to service the engine. It wasn't to access the radiator when it boiled over. Like many cars and most work vehicles, the radiator cap in that era was not under the hood. The top of the radiator was exposed so that it was easier to see when it was boiling over and for adding water whenever necessary.

Dad kept Poppin Johnny parked on a hillside so that he could coast-start it when needed. Johnny sat for long periods, and the battery wouldn't hold its charge. Coasting it down the hill and popping the clutch was a way to start the engine. It may have been a crank-start engine without a battery operated starter motor. I think it was a 1928 Model Ford, and most vehicles produced after 1920 had electric starters. I just don't remember.

Poppin Johnny was a forbidden fruit; there was a real danger of it somehow breaking free of the wheel blocks and crushing some or all of us on its uncontrolled tear down the hill. But we all know that forbidden fruit is the best tasting, and so Poppin Johnny was an occasionally visited adventure.

Both Betty and Tom recalled other old, sometimes derelict trucks that may or may not have been fused into my memory. They undoubtedly contributed to my memory of "driving" Poppin Johnny. Betty recalls Johnny being visible from the house, which meant we would have experienced the unpleasant effects of a swat with Dad's razor strap had Mom caught us playing in Johnny. Mom was almost always the deliverer of such, often deserved, pain. She was never one to say "wait till your father gets home." She was, whenever called for, both qualified and willing to administer swift and sure punishment. Incidentally, contrary to today's popular myths about spankings, they were both efficient and durable, but not in the sense of damaging our fragile egos, but rather in ensuring that we learned our lessons.

– ■ –

There was a rather long dialogue amongst my siblings concerning one particular wood saw. It was never quite settled as to whether the saw sat on the ground, mounted on the bed of a pickup, or on a trailer made from the back half of an old truck. Despite all of this uncertainty as to the exact configuration, I will try to describe what our collective wisdom recalls. Besides being interesting, it illustrates the kind of ingenuity that country folks were prone, or maybe required to have. When you lived out in the boonies, there was always something that needed to get done, and there was never any money or anyone to pay to do something. When something needed doing, you either figured it out, or it didn't get done. Sometimes, these situations came down to survival. This kind of creativity, tenacity, and independence became a part of each of us. It has had a lifelong effect on my work and my willingness to undertake tasks for which I have no more qualification than a willingness to figure it out.

With the previously stated caveat regarding an amalgamation of my three siblings' often conflicting memories, and probably at the risk of once again raising disputes from all three when they read this version, I will describe the saw.

We burned wood to cook and to heat the house, so gathering firewood was an ongoing requirement. We gathered some wood in the form of branches, but other wood that was chopped down with an ax as chainsaws were not readily available in those days. Chopped trees would typically be cut to fit the trailer or truck. That was not a size that fit inside of the stove. We required a lot of wood, and chopping with an ax was slow work; a power saw was a solution to the shortage of time for wood gathering. Dad and Charley rigged up a large circular saw to cut the wood. I think some of the key components came from an abandoned sawmill. As I remember, the blade was probably 20" in diameter. Even today, I can recall the way the blade would "sing" as the teeth flew through the air.

Looking back, the actual source of power is unclear. We didn't have electricity, so it was probably a small gas-powered motor like a Briggs & Stratton or an old Waukesha engine, which were both common in those days. Another alternative was a wide, flat belt wrapped around the rear wheel of a pickup jacked off of the ground. In those days, there was no such thing as a limited slip differential, so one wheel off the ground would spin freely. That was a common way to drive machines. However, I don't think that was how our saw worked. Most agreed that the saw was either mounted on a trailer or the back of a pickup. Undoubtedly it would be removed and placed on the ground much of the time, as we never had the luxury of dedicating any vehicle to a single task like wood chopping.

Dad and Charley built a "wood feeder deck" rigged up on a pivot. This deck was a wooden bench-like contraption with a bottom and one side in a 90-degree configuration, kind of like an "L" laying on its back. There were open ends so that the pieces of wood could fit in from either side. Like many things, the deck was constructed from flotsam and jetsam collected from around the ranch, old mines, trash dumps, derelict vehicles, or wherever and whenever they happened across some piece of something that looked like it might have some use some day. We collected a lot of these odds and ends, but you would be amazed at what got constructed or repaired with some piece of discarded steel or a scrap of wood. Nails were never too bent or too rusty not to be of use. Any nail no matter how mangled would get beat straight and used to hold down something. Looking back, I marvel at how Dad was able to drive one of these half-rusted, doglegged rejects as good as a new nail.

With this kludged together saw, an armload of small logs, Manzanita sticks worked very well for this, were placed on the deck with about 18" of the ends extending beyond the blade. The deck tilted (via the pivot) allowing the logs to come in contact with the spinning saw. The saw could cut off several pieces of firewood at once, or "in one fell swoop" ...as our father was fond of saying. I still have no idea what a "fell swoop" might be, but Dad apparently meant it to be in a single action. The logs slid along the deck in increments appropriate for the size of the stove. At that point, the deck would be tilted for another cut. Viola! Another armload of firewood cut to just the right length would fall to the ground for us kids to load up in our little red Radio Flyer wagon.

There was no safety equipment what so ever, so you had to be careful, or you could lose a finger, an eye, an arm, or your life. That was true of all of the machinery we dealt with, and much of what we did every day even past my high school years.

It is funny, as much as these old vehicles played a role in our young lives, Dad never mentioned any of them in his own life's story. I don't know if it is because he had forgotten them, or if these vehicles were just such an everyday part of his life that he didn't think to mention them. Of course, maybe it is our memories that have dramatically enlarged both the reality and the significance. Unfortunately, he is no longer here to ask.

— ■ —

It was our job, literally from the time I was big enough to carry one small stick, to take the wood to the house. "chores" were constant; I can't remember a time when each of us was not responsible for several on any given day. The garden was always in need of watering, weeding, or picking. Fruits and vegetables needed to be cleaned and canned for winter. Wood was gathered, chopped, not by us until we were a few, but not all that many years older, and carried to the house. There was always a need for kindling to start the fire, and you were never too young to gather that. Clothes needed to be hung out to dry or brought in and folded. Mom ran the washing machine. It was an old wringer type washing machine driven by a small Briggs & Stratton gas motor. There were no sensors for things like hands or arms, and that set of wringers would squeeze the blood and smash a bone as surely as it squeezed the water out of the clothes.

We went to town only a couple times a year, so mom baked all of our bread; this was almost a daily chore. The girls helped as soon as they could stand on a chair. Dad's work with the goats was incredibly physical, walking and climbing hills all day long. Even in the winter, there was water to be hauled, and an endless list of things needing repaired, built or tended. He would have a healthy appetite when dinner time came. Fortunately, mom was an incredible cook. Dad had a bit of a sweet tooth, an affliction I inherited, so she made lots of cookies, cakes and pies along with our bread.

Remember everything was cooked or baked with a wood stove so it was not simply setting the dial to 400° and waiting for the bell to ding. Getting the oven temperature right and keeping it there was a learned skill.

Pies required fruit or something like that as a filling, so we would pick blackberries down by the creek as soon as they started ripening. We probably ate as many as we picked. We would come home with a bucket of berries, along with purple fingers and faces. Bear liked blackberries as much as we did, so we had to be alert for large furry competitors.

— ■ —

We butchered our meat, goats, deer, bear, and an occasional a steer. I can tell you from personal experience that a bear that has been eating acorns and berries taste excellent. However, if the bear had been dining on fish, the taste was not so good. In the spring, young Jackrabbits made a tasty meal, and in the fall gray tree squirrels, not the ground living "digger" squirrels, made great stews, but they were harder to acquire. When we were older, we raised more beef and a few hogs as well as chickens and turkeys. We would also hunt deer

13

and later elk as they provided a much larger supply of meat for the freezer.

Dad was a trapper, and so we experimented with a few other "exotic" meat. I can attest that, despite whatever Hollywood might tell you, porcupines and raccoons are not edible.

– ■ –

While I am on the subject, I will jump ahead 60+ years, and tell a story involving my Chinese stepdaughter Ashley. We were out in La Jolla, California on a sightseeing trip about two years after she had come to live in America. Her English wasn't all that good, and sometimes I didn't realize when we were not communicating. One evening we were standing on a bluff overlooking the Pacific, and she was fascinated by the many squirrels running around the face of the cliff and begging from the tourists. Later that evening we went to a restaurant, and I ordered calamari as an appetizer. Calamari was a new treat for her, and she was enjoying it. She asked what it was and I said "squid," which drew a blank stare. I tried to relate what we were eating to the fact that squid came from the ocean like we had seen earlier that day as we stood on the bluff.

It got lost in translation. To Ashley's ear, squid and squirrel sounded pretty close and my relating them to the bluff and the ocean made her think we were dining on squirrel. It didn't stop her eating, but each time she popped a piece in her mouth, she would say "poor baby." It took a while for me to figure out what she was thinking. Once we got the critters straight, we all had a good laugh.

– ■ –

Mom always said bear lard made the flakiest pie crusts. For those of you who don't know, lard is animal fat that has been rendered (cooked) so that the oil separates from the tissue. The resulting oil becomes solid when cooled. As with most country people, we never bought cooking oil; lard was the alternative. Fresh or canned (we did all of our own canning) berries or fruit, usually peaches or apples were the usual pie fillings. On special occasion, she would use mincemeat. They were a special treat. We canned mincemeat, a combination of cooked meat, usually venison (deer meat), suit (fat), nuts, citrus, and spices.

We always had animals, both livestock as well as pets. They needed to be fed, watered, cleaned up after daily, and on occasion, slaughtered, plucked, skinned, or something. The little refrigeration we had couldn't keep meat cold very long, and it certainly couldn't freeze anything, so slaughtering critters for dinner was a routine task. The larger animals, deer, goats, steers, etc. were quartered and hung from the porch rafters to cool at night. Night hanging also kept the fly's off. During the day they would be wrapped in blankets. This process aged the meat nicely, but it couldn't be maintained very long, so we had to consume it quickly.

— ■ —

Just to put things in perspective, Mom was raised only a few miles from the Henderson Place. Her family ran a small store and post office. She told how horse-drawn wagons, and later trucks, hauled ice to their store from Red Bluff 50 miles away. At the store, they had a cellar dug into the ground, there they covered the ice with straw and a canvas to keep it frozen. Mom was only 25 when I was born, so you can see that any level of "refrigeration" was a relatively new thing.

— ■ —

The cows were brought in from the field and milked twice a day. The animal's lives depended on us doing our chores, and our lives depended upon the meat, milk, and eggs they produced to feed our family. Warm or cold, sick or healthy, the chores had to be done every day without fail.

Shearing Crew
Dad, John Linton, Walt Lesher & Frank Griswold
At Love cabin goat camp 1941

Dad and Charley were busy from sun up to sun down, and often late into the night or early in the morning, especially during kidding and shearing seasons. Mom had a ton of things to do to keep everyone fed, clothed, and safe, so many of the smaller tasks fell on our shoulders. By the time Betty reached 6 or 7, she was responsible for slaughtering the chickens. Beheading was a chore that fell to each of us as we grew older.

— ∎ —

When it came time to shear the goats, everyone got involved. Dad and Charley, sometimes with a hired crew, did the actual shearing, but everyone had to be fed, and working as they did, they had huge appetites. Of course, there was a constant need for drinking water. A good part of our job was keeping a steady supply of goats in need of shearing. Goats were moved from a big pen into a smaller pen where they could be "wrangled" to individual shearers. Any time a shearer didn't have a goat in front of him, was wasted time and lost money.

Once shorn, the mohair had to be placed in a sack and tamped down so you

16

could get a good full bag. Mohair sacks are 40" by 90" wool sacks that were cut in half crosswise. One end of the open piece was then sewed shut. These were placed through an old Ford Model T (if I remember correctly) tire rim that had all of the spokes removed. The burlap was then folded down over the tire rim, and large nails were used to "pin" the two pieces of burlap together forming an open loop at one end of the bag. The sack was then lowered down through an opening in a deck that was not quite as large as the tire rim, and arrangement that allowed almost 4' of the bag to hang free. A wool sack used the same setup, but they used full-length bags. For wool, the deck and stand are nearly 8' off the ground.

When the shearer finished, the mohair was tossed into the sack. A "tamper" got in the sack and walked around the edge of the bag using one foot to push the mohair down so that the maximum amount of mohair could be in each sack. When filled, a bag would weigh around 300 pounds. The tamper would get out, and they would use a pole and fulcrum to raise the bag up to remove the nail-pins. You had to be careful that the bag didn't slip and pinch your finger between the rim and the deck. After it was released, it would be lowered down and sewed shut. A new bag was then hung, and the process would start all over again.

A shearer would typically shear around 100 goats each day. The shearer's received payment for each goat sheared, so a tally had to be kept for each shearer. The small pens usually held six goats. As the last goat was being sheared, the other five would be let out, and five new goats would be brought in. That made for and easy counting system. A shearing crew of 4 or 5 could shear 4,000 goats in a little more than a week.

I was the youngest, and undoubtedly the least useful for most of the work that was taking place. As I got a bit older, I could be tossed in the sack with no fear that I was going to wander off to get in trouble. I don't remember how old I was when I started tamping, but I remember doing it.

Kid Angora goats, bummers, goat shed in background

When we moved down from the mountains, the chores didn't stop. Things like better refrigeration allowed us to freeze meat and some vegetables for the winter, but chickens and egg gathering, cow milking, animal feeding, wood gathering, garden tending, and many other chores were part of my daily life until I joined the Air Force.

— ■ —

We witnessed the wonder of birth multiplied many times over. New puppies were common, as there was a constant need for working dogs. Each spring we usually had at least 100 baby chicks. Some of these became "laying hens" providing eggs; the rest were fryers for our dinner table. Spring, in fact, it was more like mid-winter, "kidding season" brought thousands of baby goats each year, and a new crop of "bummer" kids.

Some mother goats, they are called "does" or "nannies," don't bond with their kids. Of course, a few does would die in the process of giving birth. Every kid that died was a loss of mohair, and that was a loss of money, a loss we could ill afford. Feeding the bummers from a bottle, was the responsibility of the older kids.

Tim with Lassie 1946

These little critters would become quite socialized. They looked at us as their mother and often became our little friends. In most cases, as they grew, they came to realize that they were goats, and they would disappear into the main herd. There was one exception, a young bummer doe that continued, even after she was full grown, to think of us kids as her family. We called her Lassie. It was probably because of the books about Lassie (the dog), but it could have been because girls, or "gurdles" as my Scottish Grandmother would say, were typically called lassies. In any case, Lassie followed us faithfully wherever we went. Even when forced to join the rest of the goats,

19

she would quit the herd at every opportunity in search out her rightful family. I don't think she ever did figure out she was a goat.

Family

I never knew either of my grandfathers. Dad's father died when he was only 6, leaving his mother with nine children to raise. One brother was even younger than Dad. Mother's father also passed away before I was born.

My father was born on December 29, 1913, in Red Bluff. He came of age at the start of the Great Depression that began in 1929. As the depression deepened, life grew increasingly difficult. Money was always hard to come by; the Depression made it harder. Like many young men of his generation, Dad was only able to complete 1½ years of high school before he had to drop out to work full time.

His first "regular" job was herding Angora goats for $15 a month, plus room and board. "Room" consisted of a tent on a hillside near the goats, and "board" consisted of whatever he cooked, often beans, over the campfire, it wasn't much, but it was a living.

Angora goats became something of a "family affair." Dad's brother Charley, as well as a distant cousin, Kay Montgomery, were also involved in goat herding at a young age. Kay was married to Dad's sister Mabel. She is the one I mentioned that died in childbirth. Bill Linton, who ultimately became Dad's brother-in-law, also worked herding goats. Bill's father, William D. Linton Jr., had been one of the first to bring Angora goats to the area. That was soon after he purchased what we knew as the Linton Place in 1903.

In 1932, when he was just 19, Dad, Charley, and Kay leased goats from the Adams Brothers. As a result of that contract, each year they would own half of the kids that were born and three-quarters of the mohair produced. In the spring of 1933, they owned about 600 kid goats. Their herd ultimately grew to 4,000.

William Linton Jr. married Elizabeth McPhee (my grandmother) a few years after he bought the ranch. It was just a few miles from the Henderson Place. In the fall and winter of 1934, Dad lived in a little shed on the Linton Place so that he could take care of the goats that wintered there. He met one of the younger Linton girls, Jean. She was only 14 at the time. They married on her 18th birthday, June 5, 1938. They were happily married for 64 years until Mom passed away a few days after her 82nd birthday in 2002. They had four children, my sisters Betty and Barbara, my brother Tom, and then me.

The Great Depression

The Great Depression, at least on paper, began with the stock market crash of October 29, 1929, and lasted until 1939, when World War II kicked American industry into high gear. Without a doubt, it was the deepest and the longest-lasting economic downturn in the history of the Western industrialized world.

The Depression poured more salt in the farmer's existing wounds. They had suffered an extended drought and falling prices throughout much of the 1920s. The Great Depression just made things worse. Lack of opportunity in rural areas resulted in the mass migration from farms to places such as California and the North. It got so bad that farmers couldn't find workers or afford to harvest their crops. Many were left rotting in the fields while people elsewhere starved.

By 1940, many of the woes of the Great Depression ended with the surge of jobs brought on by demand for war materials. That provided employment and security for those living in or near cities. It had little benefit or effect on those in rural America, where the effects of the Depression lasted into the early 1950s.

While life was difficult at best, my parent's families lived in the country. There was never much actual money, but there was seldom a lack of food. They raised vegetables as well as chickens for eggs, and livestock for meat and milk. Their circumstances were not the exception, before, during, and after the Great Depression, many rural people lived that way.

Angora Goats

Not many people can say that their father was a goat herder. Of course, he was much more than that, but herding goats was a major part of his life, especially when he was young.

The Angora goat is an ancient breed that originated in Asia Minor. Mohair, the fleece of the Angora goat, is one of the oldest fibers known to man. Biblical references dating to the time of Moses, show mohair was used in the most sacred of dwellings; the sanctuary of God had eleven curtains of goat hair as a covering.

Angora goats are very picturesque animals with both sexes having horns. Smaller than sheep, a mature buck usually weighs around 200 pounds; does weight around ½ of that. The horns of a mature buck can reach two feet or

21

more in length. They come back and away from the head, and usually, have a pronounced spiral. The horns of the female are usually no more than ten inches, with only a very slight tendency to spiral.

The Angora is among the most delicate of our domesticated animals. They are more susceptible to damage from internal parasites than are sheep. They are extremely fragile at birth, with the young requiring protection during their first few days if the weather is cold or damp. Although the mature goat in full hair is a relatively hardy animal, it cannot withstand cold, wet rains immediately after shearing.

Several Angora Bucks

Europeans began importing mohair in the sixteenth century, after a Dutchman, in 1550, learned of the Angora goats in Turkey. The name Angora was a corruption of the word Ankara, and so they became known as Angora goats.

Angoras were a major part of the Turkish economy. At one point, an Angora graced the back side of the Turkish lira. The Sultan of Turkey banned, under penalty of death, the export of both raw fleece and goats. As a result, mohair remained difficult to obtain and prohibitively expensive. It became a status symbol that only aristocrat and landlords could afford. Demand was such that wars were fought over these precious animals and their fiber.

Despite the prohibition, several attempts were made to import Angora goats to Europe. However, each attempt failed due to the delicacy of the animals. Charles V, king of France, first brought Angora goats to Europe around 1554. A few animals were presented to Queen Victoria (she reigned from 1837 to 1901), but none of these animals survived. The Angora goat did not reach the UK until 1981.

In 1838, with the export ban still in place, Sultan Mahmud II of the Ottoman Empire sent twelve neutered rams and one female to Port Elizabeth in South Africa. The rams had been castrated as the Sultan wanted to protect the country's mohair empire. However, the ewe was pregnant and gave birth to a male offspring in route to Africa. That established the mohair industry outside of Turkey. Today, South Africa is the 3rd largest mohair producer in the world. Only the United States and Turkey produce more.

Angoras were first introduced to the United States in 1849 when Sultan Abdülmecid I, gave Dr. James P. Davis seven adult goats in appreciation for his services and advice on the raising of cotton. Over time, more goats were imported. However, the Civil War destroyed most of the large flocks in the South.

– ■ –

Angora goats "browse" rather than "graze," and they tend to eat as high as they can reach by standing on their hind legs. This characteristic allows goats to adapt to grazing areas where sheep do not do well. This characteristic helped to establish Angora goats in the Southwest, particularly in Texas, where there were sufficient grass and shrub to sustain them. At first, the herds were decimated by predators. States and counties responded by placing a bounty on mountain lion, wolves, coyotes, and bear. After that, the goats flourished.

By the 1920s Texas alone had over 2,000,000 Angora goats. By that time, the United States had become the third largest exporter of mohair in the world. Texas remains the biggest producer, but the West Coast established a significant Angora population as well.

While goat meat is quite edible, even considered superior to lamb in some places, it has never become a popular consumer product. Therefore, the most valuable product of the Angora is the mohair. The word mohair derived from the Arabic word Mukhaya meaning "cloth of bright lustrous goat hair." In medieval times, mukhaya became mockaire and this later morphed to today's mohair. Goats are typical sheared twice a year, producing approximately 5.3 pounds of mohair per shearing.

Mohair is a silky fiber that lacks the microscopic scales that wool has. Therefore, mohair is less prone to be a scratchy irritant. Beauty and durability are mohair's big selling points. Mohair takes and holds dye so easily that brilliant colors can be applied. The reflective quality of mohair further enhanced the luster. Mohair is durable and able to maintain its character under adverse conditions. It is also warm, insulating, and lightweight. It has moisture wicking properties that carry moisture away from the skin of the wearer.

Mohair became a valuable product in global commerce early in the nineteenth century. Durability and beauty fed the demand. Vast quantities of mohair were shipped to textile mills around the world. In the late 19th, and well into the 20th century, every train, carriage, and automobile seat in the world was covered with mohair cloth.

As I said earlier, mother's father William Linton, Jr. established a herd of Angora goats in Tehama County shortly after he bought his homestead in 1903. That was during the period of rapid growth of the Angora industry in America. The brush and shrubbery in the area proved to be appropriate for Angoras, and his herd flourished. That herd, along with others were ultimately the source of the Angora herd owned by Dad and Charlie.

Following the economic collapse of the Great Depression, the development of synthetic fibers sounded the death knell for many of the large herds in the US.

— ∎ —

The goats had to be tended, protected from predators, and moved from camp to camp so that they would not over-graze the brush. Each spring, the herd was walked from the Henderson Place up the side of Mt. Bully Choop to a place near the Cleveland mine, where they leased grazing rights from the government. The distance of this trip was about 10 miles as the crow flies but probably 14 by the time you added all the ups and downs as well as the paths around various obstacles.

Mt. Bully Choop

The journey up Bully Choop took a few weeks as the goats would walk, eat, and rest along the way. The herders had dogs that would help keep the herd together and moving in the right direction. There were several established campsites along the way. One was called "Rattlesnake Camp." You can guess why. Some had small buildings and a few even had corrals. Each site had to have water for the goats. This journey was reversed each fall when the goats were brought back down to be "wintered" at the Henderson as well as the Linton Places.

— ■ —

Near the Cleveland mine, they built an A-frame cabin that was our summer home when we were young. Even after we moved down from the mountains, we would come back to help Charley at shearing time. We would live in either the Henderson Place or the cabin near the Cleveland mine, wherever the goats were. These were always great times, and I do remember at least some of these trips.

The Cleveland mine cabin, our home for the summer months, had even more limited amenities. There was a wood cookstove that also provided heat. The A-frame provided a sleeping area for Mom and Dad. The rest of us slept outside on beds made by nailing two poles to trees with a canvas sling for a mattress.

There was a little creek running past the cabin and wild blackberry bushes providing fruit to eat as well as for Mom's pies jam. There was a gnarled old apple tree someone had planted years earlier. It occasionally produced a few, usually odd shaped apples if the bear or birds didn't get them first.

Down the road from the cabin was a cedar tree that had been bent over and then bent upright again. It had probably been struck by lightning many years earlier. That was our "favorite tree" serving as a horse to ride or whatever our imaginations could conjure up. As I remembered it, the crook was about 3 feet off the ground, the perfect height for a pretend horse.

We went back just a few years ago. The A-frame had melted into the forest; we could only find hints of its existence. We did find one tree in the area with an elbow, but it was very near ground level. It may be that our tree had been chopped down at some point or more likely, that our memories were not quite as accurate as we thought.

As at the Henderson Place, we were allowed to roam unsupervised other than the watchful eye of Poncho, our protector dog. We had to be on the lookout for timber rattlers, a slight variation of those at lower elevations, and of course bear. There were mountain lion in the area, but I don't remember them causing us any worry. We were always under Poncho's protective eyes.

Of course, there were no modern conveniences: phone, electricity, indoor plumbing, etc. but we did have a battery-powered vacuum tube radio that we listened to occasionally. The signal wasn't very strong so Dad had rigged and antenna from the radio, out a window and up into a nearby pine tree. We didn't use it much because the batteries were expensive. I remember we came back to the cabin one time, I think we had made one of our rare trips into Red Bluff, but I am not certain. While we were gone, lightning struck the antenna tree, and part of the juice ran down the antenna wire and exploded the radio as well as the battery. It is a wonder it didn't start a fire.

— ■ —

Growing up, I had always thought that Dad had received a draft deferment during WWII because mohair, which was used in blankets, flight jackets, and other items was considered a critical war material. I learned many years later that the deferment was actually because of his shearing skills. They needed sheep shearers to get the wool off of the sheep. It was the wool that was the

26

more critical war material. At one point, they were going to ship him to Australia to help with the shearing. He made it as far as San Francisco, but they turned him back. Apparently, they had found sufficient shearers to meet the need.

By the early 1940s, mohair from their herd, could not support all of the growing families. Kay had remarried, to Florence, one of Jean's sisters, and they moved to Red Bluff in search of a reliable income. To feed his growing family, Dad started working what was called the "shearing circuit," which began close to the Mexican border in early spring and moved north as the weather warmed. The circuit ended in Montana.

Another challenge for the goat business, and by this time they had nearly 4,000 head, was the loss of animals to the various predators: coyotes, bobcats, mountain lion, and bear. That was not unique to the goat business; predators are a universal problem for all who owned livestock. Predators were also killing deer each year.

The County wanted to encourage the elimination of as many coyotes as possible, so they had a bounty of $10 for each coyote killed. $10 was a huge sum at that time; it would equal approximately $175 in 2016 dollars. To combat the predator problem, and to supplement their income, both Dad and Charley learned to trap. For both men, their shearing and trapping skills proved invaluable throughout most of their working years.

— ∎ —

Life was not simple or easy. The work never ended and the money was never plentiful. There were only two paydays a year when the mohair sold, and the folks had to budget their meager income to cover the entire year. We never starved, or anything like that, we had the abundance of our garden, our livestock and nature's bounty to eat. We were, in today's terminology, off the grid, so there were no monthly bills. We were very nearly self-reliant. There were no luxuries and no toys beyond whatever we could make from a stick or an empty thread spool.

Store-bought things were a rarity. The only store-bought present I remember during this time was a toy bus that I got for my 5th birthday. It was maybe 12" long and 5" high. It had a flywheel that would cause it to continue to move once you got the wheels started. The bumpers were designed so that when it hit something, it would reverse directions. I remember that bus being something akin to my private car. It was my treasure for several years. Most of our gifts were strictly practical things like shirts (homemade), or underwear.

We did buy our jeans and shoes, but shoes were seldom worn unless it was cold. Most everything would get handed down until it either wore out or we couldn't squeeze into it any longer. Mom made all of our things like shirts for dad and the boys, blouses, and skirts for the girls. Most of my sister's blouses came from flour sacks. At that time Mom would buy flour in 25-pound bags; remember she made all of our bread and desserts from scratch, so we used a lot of flour. Nothing came prepackaged in those days, and even if it did, we couldn't afford it. Flower came in a cotton bag. The cloth was specially designed and printed so that you could open the ends and the single side seam and have a nice sized piece of fabric to make clothes. As I recall, it took two sacks to make one blouse. That wasn't unique to our family; the flower company used cloth for that very reason. It was all part of the Depression Era frugality that we grew up with, and it lasted well into the 1950s.

— ∎ —

Doctors were almost unattainable in the event of a real emergency, and so Mom and Dad both had to have some good sense and decent medical skills to care for four rambunctious kids who saw nothing wrong with sliding down a hill on a rock or walking barefoot through a trash dump full of broken glass. We all gained some scars to verify our stupidity as well as our bravery.

There were no neighbors for miles, even in the winter. We never went to church, occasionally to Grange, but that was mainly after we moved down from the Henderson Place. I suppose it is only logical that I would grow up to be an independent loner.

— ∎ —

A few years ago, I took Kellie and Ashley up Bully Choop to the Forest Service Lookout at the top. The road was only slightly improved, still steep, winding, and severely rutted. These were the roads I grew up riding and driving, so they don't bother me. Kellie and Ashley grew up in Shanghai where every street and alley is level and paved. She was terrified by the fact that her side of the car was often so close to the edge that she couldn't see any dirt beside us. It seemed like miles of nothing but open air, almost like we were flying, but of course, we were bouncing along with dust everywhere and we didn't have wings.

We made it all the way to the top and visited the lookout station. This trip was part of a family reunion, so all of the siblings and spouses were there. We went up to the lookout, and we were able to review their old visitor's log dating back to the 1920s and 1930s. In those record books, we found Dad's, Charley's, Kay's, Bill's, and Johnny's signatures. Johnny was Mom's brother; he died in WWII. We signed our names as well, so maybe 90 or 100 years from now our grand or great grandchildren will visit and see that their ancestors were here once as well.

Cow riding 1947
Betty, Barbara, Tom & Tim with cousin Virginia Nelson

I came late in the "goat" game, and the annual shearing circuit was in the past when I arrived. The up and down the mountain trek only lasted for the first two years of my life. Dad and Charley had been at it since they were teens, and my siblings lived this life much longer than I did, so, of course, they remember it in much greater detail. There are many things that I do remember, mostly snippets rather than complete stories. Some of my "facts," as well as my memories, have clearly been "plagiarized" from the stories I grew up with, as well as my siblings' memories and writings. That is unfortunate, but I make no apology because it is the only way I can adequately describe the unique way I came into this world.

A Nomadic Life

The word nomad comes from a Greek word that means 'one who wanders for pasture.' Traditionally, pastoral nomads follow a fixed annual or seasonal pattern of movement and living. That describes my family's lifestyle perfectly, as they yearly moved the goat herd from the foothills to mountain and then back. Their purpose was to find pasture.

Nomadic life has existed throughout history. However, since about 1950, at least in America, it has not been necessary to herd livestock from place to place to find pasture. My parents were part of the last generation of pastoral nomads.

As a young man, I was told the "path to success" was to find a job with a "good company," and stay there until they ushered you out of the door with a gold watch. That had been the success path since the beginning of the industrial revolution, and it remained the predominate mindset throughout the 20th Century.

You will discover in the following chapters, that a gold watch was never part of my American Dream. Apparently, somewhere during my first 18-months, the "Nomad virus" invaded my body. Years later, I moved from a fulfilling Air Force career to an incredible IBM career that included many moves, job changes, and promotions; I choose to keep moving. I cannot tell you how many people told me I was crazy to leave IBM after 15 years: "you have it made," "why would you ever leave?" But I left, not because I was unhappy with IBM, but because I correctly believed that there were other "pastures" for my skills; other opportunities to further expand my knowledge, experience, and marketability.

Organizational mobility is the hallmark of a 21st Century career; it is the anthem of white-collar workers globally. Technology, transportation, globalization, and the ability to market one's talents, in essence, to "brand" oneself, have forever changed the relationship between professional workers and the organizations that utilize their services. By today's standards, my career appears "normal," but in the last half of the 20th Century, it was anything but normal. I was a pioneer, a "corporate nomad."

In the Introduction, I defined my American Dream with one word, *mobility*. For corporate nomads, the American Dream is within reach. You still have to work to achieve optimum results, but for the greatest number of people in history, the opportunity is available.

Farewell Huck-Finn

In September 1947 after the completion of fall shearing, when the goats came down the mountain, we moved to Dibble Creek for the winter. One of the main reasons for this move was so that my older siblings could start attending public school. In the following summers, we would live on Bully Choop with the goats at least part of the time. Money was very tight, and for a couple of years, Dad worked construction as well as shearing in the Red Bluff area. In June of 1950, we moved to the Red Bank area. Both of these communities are west of Red Bluff.

— ■ —

When I was 2, both Tom and I had our tonsils out on the same day. In those days, doctors had concluded that tonsils were a rather useless appendage, and so if you ever had anything that even remotely looked like and inflamed tonsil, out they came. I don't remember any of this of course, but I have heard the story so many times that it seems like I do.

We went to the hospital in Red Bluff, and I went to surgery first. Mom and Tom were out in the waiting room. They used ether in those days, and apparently, I was what you might classify as less than cooperative when it came time to put me to sleep. There was no way they were going to put something that smelled that bad over my face. I started screaming, kicking and trying my best to get off the table. To hear Mom tell it, I sounded like it was ten kids screaming. They had to wrap me in a blanket and hold me down to administer the ether. All the while, I was screaming at the top of my very abundant lungs. They finally got me subdued long enough to put me under, and the tonsils came out with no problem. All this time, Mom had no doubt about who was raising such a racket in the other room. Apparently, Tom started to worry and asked what was happening. Mom had to lie and tell him some child must have been injured. I bet when Tom came in for his operation they were prepared for another battle, but it didn't happen. He took his medicine without a problem.

We stayed a few days in town, with Kay and Florence I would imagine, but I don't recall. The best part about a tonsillectomy was the store-bought ice cream and Jell-O, things we never got in the mountains.

Tim 1948

A New Life as a Trapper

Dad started working as a trapper for the U.S. Fish and Wildlife Service in March of 1950. In the summer of 1950, he was assigned to work further west of Red Bluff in the mountains that straddled: Tehama, Glen, and Mendocino counties. Dad's job was to protect the deer herds.

Barbara, Betty & Tim 1947
Coyote hides at the Henderson Place

It was in this area that the "Towser and the Cheese" story happened. You can read about that in a later section as it was a favorite story for my daughter Katie.

There was a family, including some children, that lived and worked in the lookout station on Anthony peak. We would stop and visit, usually, two times a week when Dad would check his traps in that area. Sometimes we would bring them items that they needed from "civilization." This was high mountain country. In a gulch on the north side of the mountain, there was a big bank of snow that lasted all summer, and we would use that to make homemade ice cream together when we visited.

When Dad's western mountain area trapping assignment finished, we moved onto the Dee Campbell Ranch where they had an extra house that we rented. My three older siblings enrolled in the Red Bank school.

Red Bank School where I started

That was before they had kindergarten in the rural areas, and I was only 5½, so I was not supposed to start until the next fall. The school at Red Bank was originally a one-room school. During the summer of 1950, they were anticipating a sudden flood of new students as a result of what we now call the post-war "baby boom." They put a partition across the single classroom and hired a second teacher so they could split the classes into 1st through 4th and 5th through 8th grades. Apparently, they were not math majors because they were two years ahead of the real baby boom.

When school started, they realized that they didn't have enough students to justify the two teachers and so they sent an urgent note home asking for any child 5 or older to come to school. The plan was to treat their first year as a kindergarten. The goal being to fill the classroom. I was supposed to attend and then repeat the same course the next year.

I was thrilled, the girls had been home schooled while we were in the mountains, and they, as well as Tom, had started regular school at Dibble

34

Creek the previous year. I hated to be home alone all day, and I can imagine that Mom was none too happy having to entertain me.

Life took over from there. At the end of January, Dad transferred from the U.S. Fish and Wild Service to the California Fish and Game Department. His first assignment was in a town called Shillings, west of Redding. It had been called "Whiskeytown" at one time, and that was a much more appropriate name. Remember this area was all part of the Appalachia of the West, and I am guessing, pure speculation, that this area had its share of moonshiners.

The only house for rent was a dump, and the school was horrid. The teacher was only a high school graduate studying to become a teacher. She wasn't yet licensed. It was a rough town, and many of my classmates were already smoking. That inevitably leads to fights over cigarettes during recess. To prevent the bullies from robbing cigarettes from the little kids, the teacher would hold their cigarettes and then pass them out one at a time at recess.

God moves in mysterious ways. A few years later the government built the Whiskeytown Reservoir, and water completely obliterated that horrid community. Fire may have been more appropriate, but water achieved the same result.

Shasta Valley

In early March of 1951, only a couple months after his assignment to Whiskeytown, Dad was transferred to the Shasta Valley about 100 miles further north. He drove up in advance and found a place to rent near Gazelle. By that time, he got back; Mom had us all packed and ready to go. She could not wait to get out of that town. We drove north on the 10th of March.

Dad's Fish & Game pickup with Mt. Shasta
in the background. ~1954

The Shasta Valley is in Siskiyou County, which borders Oregon on the north; it is approximately the size of the state of Connecticut, but thinly populated with less than 30,000 at that time. The Valley and the County are dominated by Mt. Shasta (14,179 ft.), one of the highest mountains in California. Mt. Shasta is also one of the most spectacular as the Shasta Valley in only at 2,500 ft., and the surrounding mountains and are much lower than Shasta. That provides nearly 12,000 ft. of rise from the valley floor. As a result, Mt. Shasta appears much taller than it is.

The Shasta Valley lies in the middle of the county on the west side of the mountain. It has long been the main north/south route from Central California to the Pacific Northwest. In pioneer days, what was called the Siskiyou Trail followed Native American trails and took its name from the mountain range that runs along the California-Oregon border. In the late 1800s, the Southern Pacific Railroad built a line that followed the same path. The rail line was called "The Road of a Thousand Wonders." There were many summer resorts and lodges for hunting and fishing in this unspoiled region. Tourism remains the primary industry today.

Gazelle Mercantile ~1952
Photo provided by Janna Carter

In 1910, California voters authorized the highway that would ultimately become U.S. Highway 99, known simply as "99" to locals. By 1920 the road was constructed. It was not paved through the mountains until 1933. By 1950 small towns that serviced the highway travelers had developed every 15 or 20 miles along the route. Gazelle was typical. It had a mercantile, a Post Office, two gas stations, a couple of motels, and a few restaurants. There were several ranches in the area and so Gazelle also had a school, a grange, and at least one church. Highway 99 still exists for local use, but most traffic is now carried on Interstate 5.

Gold was discovered along the Siskiyou Trail, in 1851. A boom town sprang up. A tent-city grew quickly, and Yreka was incorporated in 1857. It became the County Seat when Siskiyou County was formed. It remains the largest town with 7,000 residents. Poet Joaquin Miller described Yreka in 1854 as a bustling place with *"... a tide of people up and down and across other streets, as strong as if a city on the East Coast."*

Since 1941, there has been a push to create a new state called Jefferson. It would consist of several Northern California and Southern Oregon counties. At one time Yreka was proposed as the State Capitol.

My older siblings, Betty, in particular, consider the Henderson Place and Mt. Bully Choop "home." For me the Shasta Valley is home.

— ■ —

The house we rented belonged to Simon (Si) Koppes who also owned the Montague Creamery. It was an old two-story wood structure built in 1905. The rent was $20 per month. We lived in this home until I joined the Air Force. The house sat on one edge of an 1800-acre dry (no irrigation) ranch. The house, as well as the ranch in general, needed a lot of TLC. Dad constantly fixed fences, work on the house, the barn, and the corrals. Over time, he put on a new roof, and ultimately resided the house with shingles. It seemed that almost anything Dad wanted to do to make our lives and the property better was ok with Si. He was always willing to discount the rent in trade for Dad's labor.

Mount Shasta with the Koppes Place on the left 1952

The morning after we arrived, it was 9° outside as well as inside; we were used to sleeping out of doors, so it wasn't all that unusual. We were just happy to be away from Whiskeytown. Spring would soon arrive, and a hot summer would follow. There was a small wood stove in the kitchen that Mom used for cooking, but it wasn't big enough to heat the house. Dad eventually found a big wood stove; I think he bartered for it, to heat the living room. It had a tough time competing with the wind that penetrated the house from all sides. Even after the shingle siding was installed, it couldn't do more than create a halo of warmth in that part of the downstairs.

There was never any heat upstairs. In the winter, we would take big river rocks, the kind that had been tumbled smooth from years of rolling along the stream bed during storms, and put them under the wood stove. When they were good and hot, we would wrap one in a towel or a blanket and carry it up to put at the foot of our bed. It didn't keep the room warm, but having warm feet for several hours made a difference.

Like most of our previous homes, there was no indoor plumbing or phones when we first got there. It did have electricity, but barely. The wires were not inside of the walls, just two wires clamped between a set of porcelain insulator bars that held them about 2" apart and slightly away from the wall. The wire was wrapped with a combination of rubber and fabric. Age, plus the constant heating and cooling had turned the coating brittle and so there were bare wires in places. There were no circuit breakers, just old screw-in fuses.

That was typical of many houses where electricity was an afterthought added long after the house was built. The Rural Electrification Act of 1936, provided federal loans for the installation of electrical systems serving isolated rural areas. Before that, most farms away from town didn't have electricity. One of Dad's first projects was to rewire the whole house. Even with the new Romex wire inside of the walls, he still used fuses. I think Dad's motivation was fear, and rightfully so, of a fire starting from the old wiring.

It was a funny house and a fun house in many ways. It had no insulation at all, and the old tongue and groove siding had dried and cracked over the years. I think it had only seen paint one time, and that was many decades earlier. The dividing wall between the upstairs bedrooms was only wood up to about half way, and the rest was cardboard nailed to the 2 x 4s. There were no ceilings on the upper floor, which had two bedrooms plus a large open landing area. I could lay in bed and look up between the rafters to see stars through the roof, or look sideways and see headlights from the occasional car that came down the country road.

– ■ –

The wind was endless in the Shasta Valley, and it came right through the walls. Day and night, summer and winter, the wind would start or stop without warning. I suppose it had something to do with the fact that relatively high mountains surrounded the valley and that the high altitude air currents would react to the mountains and the temperature. Whatever the reason, the wind, except on a simmering summer's day when we would have liked to have some, seemed to be ever-present.

Our old house, it was called the Koppes Place, of course, seemed to anticipate the wind. Like a wave of water, a gust of wind creates a slight vacuum in front as it travels along. The old house would lean as the vacuum came, only to be pushed back in the opposite direction when the wind arrived. Each lean was accompaniment by creeks and groans. The wind was seldom steady, more like a series of waves with the old house leaning back and forth, creaking and groaning as each gust approached and then hit.

– ■ –

Tumbleweeds were another constant. Even during the dry years, there always seemed to be just the right amount of moisture to grow a bumper crop of tumbleweeds. A tumbleweed grows to be an almost perfectly round bush, usually, a couple of feet across, but they can be tiny or huge. They all end up as dry, round balls of stalky weed that will roll and tumble as the wind blows. That is nature's way of spreading the seeds for next year's crop.

There were fences on both sides of the road that ran past our house. The road came straight at us from east to west, then made a 90-degree corner and ran north to south. The dry land on the west side of the north-south leg always grew an abundant crop of tumbleweeds. With the roadside fences acting as catchers, the fall and early winter winds would fill the gap between the fences with a river of round dry bushes from the top of one fence to the top of the other. This tumbleweed river would be 40' to 50' across and sometimes as much as 8' deep.

Tumbleweeds are very light weight and almost explosive if you touch a match to them. They burn very fast and super-hot, almost like gasoline. The County would come each year to clear the road, but often it would fill again in a couple of days or even overnight. Most everyone knew that you could not drive through these weeds; a hot exhaust pipe or a cigarette could ignite a fire that you could not outrun. Despite this, every once in a while someone would try driving through. Inevitably they would get stuck, and the car burned in the middle of the tumbleweed river. I don't recall anybody being killed in one of these fires, but it was only through luck because once the fire started, it would burn the whole river of weeds.

— ■ —

We had the run of the ranch. There were jeep roads, along with cow and deer trails that led up, over and around every hill. We rode our bikes all over the foothills that made up the bulk of the 1800-acre property. There were 3-speed bikes in those days, but we never had any of those fancy machines. We salvaged our bikes from trash dumps. As with the old cars and trucks on the Henderson Place, our bikes were built and rebuilt with parts from a half a dozen other bikes, all derived from similar sources. We would tear them down clean them up and reassemble them at regular intervals, in part because it was fun, but mainly because these old relics tended to break frequently with the rough riding we gave them.

We never had spray paint, but we would buy little ¼ pint cans of paint in whatever color we thought might look good: black, white, red, orange, whatever we could find. We used clothespins to affix old playing cards to the frame so they would clack as the spokes slid past. Puncher vines, I think they are officially called bullheads, were everywhere, so we were constantly patching and re-patching tires.

We would ride up the hills as far as we could peddle, and then get off and push the bike to the top. The thrill, of course, was riding down as fast as we dared. There were ruts from the rain, rocks, sticks and debris along our path. Occasionally a jack rabbit would jump and run at the last possible instant, thereby scaring the bejesus out of us. More than once our perceived capabilities surpassed the facts on the ground, and we would come home with all kinds of bumps, bruises, and abrasions. Somehow, we all made it through childhood without a single broken bone or none that I am aware of. However, given the way some of my old bones can ache when the weather turns cold, I wonder if these pains might reflect some tumble from one of our downhill sashays.

There was one "killer" hill. It was so steep that we had to lock the brakes and slide, skid, and slip our way down the hill like a skier trying to keep from going too fast. These were coaster bikes, so you only had brakes on the rear wheels. They engaged when you pedaled backward. On the killer hill, it wasn't about speed; it was about balance. Success was getting all the way down without falling off or having to lay the bike down.

— ■ —

There was an old water ditch that ran across our killer hill. It was called the China Ditch. Dug in the 1850s, it was designed to bring water from the Shasta River near Weed to the Yreka area for use in placer mining. Placer mining is where they use water to wash the dirt away, hopefully, to find gold that is heavier and left behind. The ditch was quite a physical as well as an engineering feat. The straight-line distance was about 25 miles, but the ditch had to follow the terrain with a slight downslope, so it was probably closer to 50 miles; all hand dug. It was called the "China Ditch" because the miners had imported Chinese laborers to construct it.

There hadn't been any water in the ditch, at least not in this part, for decades. Over the years, dirt had gradually filled in most of the ditch, so it was almost a level bench instead of a dip. That ditch ran across the face of our "killer hill" about 2/3 of the way up the slope. The ditch made a convenient breakpoint where we would stop to catch our breath before we took the second leg of the hill. The second leg was not quite as steep as the upper 1/3.

– ■ –

Our cousin Nick Linton came up from Red Bluff one summer, and we went out riding the hills. When we came to the killer hill, Nick took it straight-on. I think he wanted to show us what wusses we were. Nick didn't make it very far before he was going way too fast. When he hit the China Ditch, he lost it. The bike went sideways, and Nick kept on going down the hill, sans-bike. Fortunately, he wasn't seriously injured, but there was not much of his skin or scalp that wasn't scraped, scratched, and oozing blood. There may have been a broken arm, or maybe even a concussion in there somewhere. We got him home where his mom was still visiting before she drove back to Red Bluff. Nick had been planning on staying a couple of weeks, but his mom decided that one day had been more than enough. I don't know if Aunt Arla ever quite forgave us for what I am sure she felt that we had done to Nick.

– ■ –

Tom and I would trap coyotes so that we could collect the bounty. We were always trying to raise a few bucks for the scalps, so we kept the population pretty thin. If I remember correctly, the bounty was $3.

In the spring and early summer, we usually carried a gun, either a 22 rim-fire or Dad's old 25-20. The 22 uses a special shell that had a primer (the thing that causes the shell to fire) built into the rim. That meant that we had to buy the ammunition instead of reloading our own. The 25-20 used standard cartridges that allowed us to replace the primer. Those we could reload, along with all of the other ammunition that we used.

Dad used a lot of ammunition in his work, and we used more for hunting, target practice, and just shooting rocks and cans. Dad started reloading his ammo before I was born. Both Tom and I were quite accustomed to reloading. The process took several steps, but it wasn't terribly complicated. Of course, it was a bit dangerous, as we were working with gunpowder, which is highly explosive. The girls may have also done this, but I don't recall.

The first step was to resize the casing as it would expand slightly when the bullet fired. That step also removed the old primer. The next step was to insert and seat a new primer. Each step used one tool. It was a hand press bolted to a table. The press had different attachments for each stage of the process. The next step was the only tricky part. That was to put the proper amount of powder into the cartridge. It was tricky because we were working with a high explosive, and we had to be pretty accurate in our measurement. You didn't want too little, but you definitely did not want too much. Once the powder was in, the final step was to put a new bullet in the casing. You used the same hand press device but with a different attachment at the top.

For most ammunition, we bought the bullets premade. For Dad's pistol ammunition, he usually used a 38-caliber Smith and Wesson; we would melt lead and pour it into a mold to cast hollow point bullets. I believe we made lead bullets for the 25-20 as well. There was an additional step to fill the grooves in the lead bullets with a wax substance that lubricated the barrel as the bullet fired. This step also ensured that the bullet was appropriately sized. Other than that the process was the same.

— ∎ —

Carrying a rifle wasn't for protection, there weren't any dangerous animals other than rattlesnakes, and we were accustomed to them. In fact, there were not really that many rattlesnakes, and we worked hard to keep the population to a minimum whenever we could. Despite what you might think from watching too many Westerns, hitting a snake with a bullet is pretty difficult. They are tiny targets and always moving; that makes them tough to hit.

We carried a rifle primarily to shoot jack rabbits. There were jack rabbits all year around, but in the spring and early summer there were young ones, and they made good eating, so part of our bicycle adventures was to hunt rabbits for our dinner table. A head shot was ideal as you didn't spoil any meat. A young rabbit's head is about the size of the circle you make by pressing your thumb and index finger together, so you had to be a pretty good shot to hit that at 30 to 100 feet or more.

Ground, or digger squirrels were a year-around target. They were not for eating. We shot them because they dug holes in the ground and cows could break a leg if they stepped in one. There wasn't much else to shoot, an occasional deer, but not many. I don't remember ever hunting deer on the Koppes Place. There were some quail, but for some reason, our family was never much into bird hunting. We did shoot sparrows with our Beebe guns, but that was mainly just plinking to keep the population down. Sparrows are kind of like grasshoppers; they will grow and multiply very fast, and they can consume a lot of seeds and grains that would otherwise grow into grass for the cows.

I read many years later that Chairman Mao in China saw the sparrow population as taking food from the people. He started a campaign where people were to go out into the streets and fields and beat on pots and pans to make the sparrows keep flying until they dropped from exhaustion. Apparently, it was successful in significantly reducing the sparrow population. It is hard to imagine that there can be that many people available to do something like that. I have been to China, and there are in fact that many people.

— ■ —

There was a large barn near the house and a shed that we converted into a chicken coop. A coop is where the chickens go to sleep at night, and also nests to lay their eggs. Mainly you want to keep them protected from the various varmints: coyotes, fox, cats (including house cats), skunks, weasels, and any number of hawks and eagles, who enjoy a chicken dinner.

We used the barn to store hay for our cows. There was enough space to milk the cows as well as house some young animals, baby chicks for example before they were old enough to live out of doors. On the outside of the north end of the barn was an area where the cows loved to congregate to get out of the hot sun. There was an accumulation of cow manure in that area; it was well over a foot deep. Most of the time it was deep powder, but when we had our rainy season, it turned to liquid poop and smelled accordingly. As soon as the cows started milling around each spring, it would turn back to powder.

— ■ —

Weather forecasting at that point was still pretty rudimentary. The radars weren't capable of showing all of the weather patterns, and there were no satellites to take pictures of storms forming out at sea. About the only tool they had was barometric pressure, so it was more guesswork than science. Any prediction beyond what you could see coming over the horizon was pretty much a guess.

One of the few tools the forecasters did have were weather balloons. They had developed a ruggedized bundle of instruments and a radio, all packaged in a relatively small configuration. They attached a helium balloon and let these packages float up and away, busily transmitting things like temperature, humidity, and air pressure. I doubt they could measure much more. Once they reached altitude, the balloons would burst, and a parachute would bring the package back to earth.

There were no locator beacons or GPS systems; they had to rely on random people finding these packages and returning them to the Weather Service. To assist that effort, they made the disposable parachutes very colorful orange and white umbrellas. Since Dad was out in the woods all of the time, he would occasionally find these packages and ship them back to the Weather Service. Like almost everything that he came across, he figured there might somehow be a use for the parachutes so that he would bring them home.

Tom and I got to thinking that these parachutes might work for us. We figured that, even though we were heavier than the weather package, in my case, a lot heavier, the parachute would probably significantly slow our fall so that we would not be hitting the ground too hard. The logical place to try out our theory was at the north end of the barn. It wasn't too high, maybe 12', and there was a foot of powdered cow manure in case we guessed wrong.

I don't remember if only one or if both of us jumped, probably only one, and probably Tom as he was both lighter and a bit braver, or maybe stupider, depending on your frame of reference. In any case, we quickly learned that our logic was flawed. The parachute didn't have time to open in that short jump; it provided no benefit whatsoever. No bones were broken, but our egos suffered a mighty blow. We accepted defeat and didn't try to find a higher perch.

– ■ –

Heights were never a serious problem for any of us. We always had trees to climb, and we frequently had barns at various homes. Rafters were usually slightly larger than a 4 x 4. They ran across from wall to wall at a maybe 10' or 12', and there was usually some straw or loose hay below. We would take turns walking the beams. Away from the barns, there seemed always to be a log somewhere. It may just run up or around a hillside, or ideally, it may cross a creek. In our eyes, these were always inviting us to try. I don't remember anyone ever getting seriously hurt. I would like to say that we didn't take foolish risks concerning heights, but I suppose that too is a matter of perspective.

About a mile or so from the house over a low gap in the ridge was an old orchard. Long abandoned, it had not been pruned or tended in years, possibly decades. Dad pruned back the trees that were still alive, and they started producing some decent crops. The dead trees became firewood. There was one apricot tree that was a particularly good producer. It provided an abundance of fresh apricots almost every year. With these, Mom made apricot pies, plus some incredible apricot/pineapple jam that I remember to this day. There were also a few apple trees, but they never did produce much of a crop.

— ■ —

There was a small spring about a quarter of a mile north along the ridge that ran up toward the orchard. It wasn't very big, but it was easy to spot because it left a green patch on the dry hillside. It produced water year around. We dug it out and, buried a 55-gallon drum to collect the water. We ran a steel pipe along a slightly downhill path to a small ridge that jutted out just above the barn. I don't remember if the water tank was there before, or if dad found one somewhere, but in any case, there was a big water tank where we collected the spring water. The tank was at least 30' higher than the house and yard. We ran a line down and put a water troth for the cows but continued the line on down to the barn, the garden, and the yard.

The yard was never all that much, but we did have some grass, and the hollyhocks grew like weeds. Our primary focus was the garden. Getting a garden set up was a high priority as it was a major source of our food. There was plenty of land, and there was plenty of cow manure for fertilizer. At first, the issue was water, but that was solved once we got the pipe running from the spring north of the house.

— ■ —

We did have a well for drinking water. It was old and out in the open near the house. When we arrived, it had a tired old wood cover that let almost anything in that wanted in, dirt, dust, critters, whatever. The first section of the well was hand dug for 70'. It was probably 4' across. It had never produced much water and someone had run a drill down and added 20' of drilled well below the hand dug section.

The water wasn't bad most of the time, but every once in a while it would start tasting foul. We discovered that critters like squirrels and snakes would fall in and drown. When that happened, it didn't improve the flavor. On the plus side, when I got older and traveled all over the world, I never got a case of Montezuma's revenge. For that, I thank those squirrels and snakes who gave their all to create my high-resistance intestines. Despite the possibility of this future benefit, one of the first things Dad did, after cleaning out all the dead critters, was pour a cement slab and put an animal-proof cover on the well. He then built a pump house on the slab and insulated it so that the house and the water stayed cooler in the summer and didn't freeze in the winter. It made a perfect place to store potatoes in the winter. From then on, we had decent drinking water.

I can't help but smile when I recall our, less than optimal water supply. Throughout history, life was never antiseptic; ingesting a bit of dirt and germs has always been part of the human condition. We developed antibodies that made us more resilient. Today, everything is: antiseptic, purified, sanitized, and sterilized. I sometimes think that we are making our lives so antiseptic that we have become vulnerable to the slightest impurity. Of course, there is a medicine for that. Maybe Eisenhower should have warned us about the pharmaceutical-industrial complex along with the military-industrial complex.

– ■ –

A bathtub and toilet entered our house about seven years after we moved into the Koppes Place. Before that, baths were always a bit of a challenge. We used a large galvanized bath tub. It was about 2′ in diameter and maybe 18″ deep. We would take baths in the kitchen where we had the wood stove Mom used it to heat pots of water. It also provided us a warm room to bathe in. Baths were a once a week process, as it took quite a bit of time to heat the water for each one of us to bathe. It was such a relief when we finally did get an indoor bathroom with an actual water heater. A toilet was even more important because that meant that we didn't have to 'walk the path' to the outhouse day and night. We didn't have a shower, so baths were only easier, not that much more frequent.

– ■ –

The main reason for tapping the spring was for the livestock and the garden. The well never had lots of production capacity, especially in dry years, and it could have never handled the demands of a large garden. I don't know if there was a reason we didn't use the spring water for drinking, maybe it was just that the well was sufficient, and once we critter-proofed it, we didn't need to use the spring water.

I am probably exaggerating all these years later, but as I recall, the garden was at least 100' by 40'. I know that we used Dad's work jeep like a tractor to plow the garden. One year, as we were plowing, the steering tie rod broke and suddenly the steering wheel had no control over where the tires pointed. Having one wheel down in the plow trench was probably putting additional stress on this critical part, but we couldn't help but think of what would have happened if it had broken as Dad was coming down a steep curvy road, something that he did every day.

Aside from the plowing and planting part, the garden was primarily Mom's domain. The girls worked a lot with her in watering, picking, freezing and canning vegetables that helped feed the family all year. The primary crops that I can recall were: tomatoes, cucumbers, beans, corn, zucchini, lettuce, and carrots. I am sure there were others, but I don't remember. We ate a lot of these fresh, but a lot were either canned or frozen for later use.

We never raised potatoes. They probably would have grown well, as potatoes were raised commercially in the area north and east near the Oregon border. In those fields, the harvesting machines used to dig up potatoes couldn't reach areas near the fence. They left an undug area about 10' wide. Each fall we would drive to the fields and dig up 600 to 800 pounds of potatoes that we hauled in gunny sacks. We stored these in the pump house and used them all winter and summer until the next crop. I don't remember what we paid for a sack of potatoes, or if the farmers even charged. Dad did so much trapping all over the Valley; he was well known and liked. The farmers and ranchers were always appreciative of Dad and his work that saved their livestock. They probably gave him the potatoes.

— ■ —

We had some "city" cousins who would visit from time to time. They weren't actually from a city, but any village bigger than Gazelle, which was home to no more than 100 people, was a city to us. They were, by our standards, quite picky about what they would eat. The two biggies I remember were zucchini and raw milk. Zucchini was a "squash" and therefore inedible in their opinion. Mom solved that by changing the name to "whiffle weed." Getting them to drink raw (straight from the cow) milk took a bit more finesse. Mom would buy a quart of commercial homogenized and pasteurized milk. As our picky cousins used the milk, Mom would refresh the carton with raw milk. In just a few days, they would be drinking raw milk from the commercial milk carton. They never did catch on.

In case you don't know they homogenize milk by spinning it so fast that the fat (the cream) molecules are broken down so small that they don't recombine and rise to the top as they normally would. You pasteurize milk by raising the temperature to just below boiling to kill any possible bacteria that may be in the milk …you cook it. The result is what you buy in a grocery store. Milk straight from the cow tastes entirely different.

— ■ —

Mom used to say that corn was not fresh unless you put the water on to boil before you walked to the garden to pick the corn. Remember we used a wood cooking stove, so it took a while to bring water to a boil. We grew quite a bit so that we could eat it fresh as well as have enough to freeze for the winter. We always had lots of tomato plants, and so tomatoes were an all-summer staple. Mom also canned stewed tomatoes for winter. We used tomatoes in salads, ate them by the slice, and ate them like apples with a bit of salt. If you have never tasted fresh tomatoes from the garden, you cannot comprehend how different garden tomatoes taste when compared to the red cardboard you buy at the grocery store. Store-bought tomatoes are bred to pick green and ripen in-route to the grocery store. They are bred to be firm and not bruise in shipping. Real tomatoes taste entirely different.

One of our favorites was fresh tomato sandwiches. We would take two slices of Mom's homemade bread, slather on some mayonnaise, lay on some fresh lettuce, an abundant slice of fresh onion, and then a good thick slice of fresh tomato. Sprinkle with some salt and pepper, maybe some seasoning salt, and you have one delicious sandwich. We seldom had bacon because we didn't cure the pork bellies, we sliced it and cooked it uncured.

When we rode with Dad on his trap lines, Mom would send all of the fixings for a fresh tomato sandwich at lunch. If you put the tomato slice on the bread too early, it would get soggy. Mom would send the tomato whole and unsliced. Dad always carried a large pocket knife. I think each of us carried one most of our young lives. His served a lot of purposes, the principal one being to scalp each coyote and bobcat he killed. Scalping is to cut off the ears with a chunk of the skin connecting them. It was necessary to prove that he had killed these animals each month but also to prevent someone else from turning the scalps in for the bounty. At lunchtime, Dad would open the blade and wipe it on his pant leg, which itself was none too clean, and slice the tomatoes for the sandwiches. I never thought much about it at that time, but today when my wife insists I not pet the dog while I am at the dinner table, I cannot help thinking about Dad's multipurpose unsanitary knife. Chalk up another one for Montezuma's revenge prevention.

Very little went to waste. When the fall frost would come, we would pick the remaining green tomatoes and Mom would make Green Tomato Relish. She and the girls would also make both Dill and Bread & Butter pickles. These were "canned," actually put in vacuum sealed jars so that we could use them year around.

– ■ –

We always had at least one milk cow. She often produced more milk than our family needed. We would sell the excess to Si Koppes' dairy as a way to supplement our income. Most of the time we sold whole milk, but from time to time, we would just sell the cream.

We made our butter by churning the cream. If you let the un-homogenized milk sit in the refrigerator overnight, the cream will rise to the top. It can be skimmed off with a cup or a spoon. Of course, the cream can be turned into lots of useful and fattening goodies; butter is just one. Mom used a lot in her baking, which tasted great but didn't help my waistline one bit.

The process of turning cream into butter is the opposite of homogenization. Instead of spinning it fast to break the modules apart, you turn it slow to combine the fat modules to turn it into butter. It tends to work better if you let the cream warm to room temperature. A butter churn has paddles that look something like a big mixer with wooden "blades." These fit into a square-sided jar that held about 2 quarts of cream. You turn the paddles until it transitions from cream to butter. That usually took ½ hour. It can be shorter or quite a bit longer. If you churn too fast, you get whipped cream, too slow, and it takes longer. You drain off the more or less clear buttermilk for use in any number of recipes. In our case, most of this went to the dogs or hogs. You add a bit of salt to the butter and put it in the refrigerator ready for use. We never bought butter or margarine; we always made our own.

— ■ —

Tom and I used "David Slings" a lot, mainly to herd the cows. A David Sling refers to David's weapon in the biblical legend of David and Goliath. They consist of two pieces of, usually leather, filament about the size of a good sturdy shoelace. We tied one end of each string to a leather pouch. That pouch had a couple of small slits in it so that it would cradle around a rock. The other end of one line would have a loop that you put around your middle finger. The end of the other line would be clean. You pinched that line between your thumb and index finger. The lines were usually about 2' or 2½' long, depending on the height of the user. You wanted to maximize the length, because the longer the strings, the greater the range. After you had the lines held tight, you placed a rock about the size of a golf ball in the pouch. You would swing the sling around your head a couple of times and release the loose string to fire the rock.

With practice, we could send a rock the distance of a football field with little effort and decent accuracy. If a cow on the other side of the herd decided to head off in the wrong direction, we would try for a slight overshoot to turn her back toward the herd. If that failed to get her attention, a rock bounced off her rump usually did the trick.

— ■ —

In the spring, Si Koppes would bring cows to graze when the grass would green up. When it had all dried and had been grazed down, he would load them up and take them elsewhere. When Si wanted to pick up his cows, he would stop by, or call us, after we had a phone. Tom and I would go round up the cows and put them in the corral. Our reward, actually we got it far more often that we earned it, was a gallon of ice cream. Mom would sometimes fuss that he was spoiling us, but he would just grin. Si liked our family and especially us kids. In many ways, he was like the grandfather we never had.

Simon (Si) Koppes

Si was a stocky man, and you could tell that when he was younger, he had been quite muscular, probably from lifting milk cans. He was a gentleman with a thick accent. His shoulders hunched as he grew older. Of course, at my young age, he always seemed older. He couldn't turn his head very far or even straighten up to his full height. He had a walrus mustache, and his glasses were perpetually down at the tip of his nose. His eyes, which seemed always to be sparkling, looked over the glasses and under his equally bushy

54

eyebrows. The cartoon version of Geppetto from the Pinocchio movie is a good likeness of Si.

Si had an old Dodge pickup that he talked to like a team of horses. You could hear him mumbling "whoa" and clicking his tongue to "get her going." Of course, the pickup didn't work as a team of horses, so when he came to the place he was as likely as not to run into things. With his stooped shoulders and inability to turn his head, he would just back up until he would hit something. Watching him try to back the pickup and trailer up to the cattle chute to pick up or drop off an animal was a terrifying thing. Tom got in the habit of running out and asking if he could drive. Tom was pretty young, but he was still far better than Si. The old man would smile and hand Tom the keys.

— ■ —

I don't remember when we got out first phone. I don't think it was too long after we moved in. It was a "party line" meaning that several people shared the same phone line. I think there were eight houses on the line, but I am not sure. Each house had a distinct ring pattern. Ours was two longs and a short. Since it was a single shared line, you had to check to see if someone else was using the line before you could use it. Anyone could listen in on any call, and several of our neighbors did so with regularity. As they would pick up to listen the signal would get weaker and weaker until it was hard to carry on a conversation.

All phones were rotary dial at that time. I explain how rotary-dial systems work in my section on ITT so that I won't go into detail here. You could dial other people who were on the same exchange, in other words, they had the same 3-digit prefix. For any long distant calls, or to call someone in a nearby community, you had to ask the operator to connect you. If the phone line went down, it was usually out for a few days.

— ■ —

There was one movie theater in Yreka. We went once every month or two. We went to see the movies, but also to catch up on the news. There was only one screen, and one showing per night. There were sometimes matinées on Sunday, but I don't remember ever going to one. They usually played two movies each evening, and almost all of the movies were in black and white. The "feature" would usually be about an hour and 15 minutes. The first movie would be a "short." It was 25 to 30 minutes. A cartoon always separated the movies. They would change movies about every two weeks. There was no rating system then; all movies were "PG" by today's standards. In fact, most of today's PG movies would have been considered too violent and too vulgar to have been allowed in the theater.

They did show previews of coming movies, but usually only two, three at the most. There would be a "newsreel," which was typically 10 -15 minutes in length. That was our primary source of news from outside of the Shasta Valley. The Newsreel would have pieces from all over the world. I can remember short sections concerning the Korean War. Those pieces would be at least 60-days old by the time we saw them. They could easily be four months old, or even older. The newsreels were always in black and white, with a serious sounding announcer reading the news. It was just a voice-over; you never saw the reader.

— ■ —

We got our first television in 1958, about the time my sisters graduated and moved off to San Francisco. I don't remember if we got the TV before or after they left. There was no cable anywhere, and all broadcasts were black and white. We had an antenna mounted on the roof. There was only one channel. The signal came out of Redding, which is about 100 miles to our south. It only broadcast part of the day, shutting down at 10 p.m. The signal was feeble. It bounced off of the side of Mt. Shasta generating at least one "ghost" copy close beside the primary image. It was like looking at a gray 3-D image without the glasses.

— ■ —

Dad was always a big baseball fan. He liked to listen to the games on the car radio as he worked his trap lines. All radios, including those in a car or truck, were built with vacuum tubes. They were enormous. A regular car radio, while somewhat smaller than a home radio, would still be bigger than a shoebox. When you turned it on, it would take 60-seconds or more for the circuits to "warm up" before you would start hearing anything other than a buzz. All radios were AM (Amplitude Modulation). There was no FM (Frequency Modulation) at that time, and of course no digital.

AM has a much greater range as the signal can be bounced off of different layers in the atmosphere so that you can receive a high powered station hundreds and even thousands of miles away. I can remember listening to a

San Francisco station (300 miles) late at night, and occasionally we could pick up a station out of El Paso, Texas (1500 miles). I think their antenna was located in Mexico so that they could broadcast at a much higher power than the U.S. allowed. It was only possible to receive these distant stations at night.

Dad liked the San Francisco Giants. I think it was just because they were the closest and their games were the primary team on the local radio. I can remember a few of the players, Willie Mays and Willie McCovey, are two that come to mind. I remember thinking it was a bit strange to have two "Willies" on one team. I didn't know anybody named Willie. There were several Bills in my school of course, but every kid named William was called Bill, so I probably didn't make the connection.

If he had the time, he watched the games on TV. It was just a gray mess as far as I was concerned. The cameras weren't very good, so the players looked more like ants on a gray field than actual people. With the weak signal, you could not see the ball. If someone hit it, the cameras would follow the ball, but all we saw was a gray screen. I thought it was an insane waste of time, but Dad liked to watch.

Many years later, I was living in Westlake Village west of LA, when Mom and Dad came for a visit. I took Dad and Brian who was probably about ten then, to the opening day game at Dodger Stadium. The LA Dodgers were playing the San Diego Padres. I was never a baseball fan, but I enjoyed watching Dad and Brian watching the game. It was Dad's first experience watching a professional team play in a big stadium, and he was like a kid. Screaming at every strike, but especially when someone hit the ball. He was not a Dodgers or Padre's follower, but that made no difference. He talked about that game for years, and I know this was a memory he truly cherished. For me, it was an honor to be able to give him the gift of his first real pro game.

— ■ —

I remember the smell of the saw mill; there were several in the Shasta Valley. All over Northern California, the trees were cut from the forest and hauled on logging trucks to the closest sawmill. Big dusty logging trucks were always a frightening thing to meet on a narrow mountain road. They were very noise, they seemed always to be going too fast, and they never quite fit the narrow winding roads.

When you were driving one-lane mountain roads, the "rule" was that the car going uphill had the right of way. It was too easy for a car backing downhill to lose control and go over the edge. It was much safer for a car to slowly back uphill. This rule didn't apply to logging trucks. For them, you had no choice; you just had to get out of their way. The challenge was to get them to slow down or stop so Dad could pull the jeep up an embankment or half over the edge to let one of these big behemoths past. Fortunately, logging trucks tend to pulverize a dirt road, turning it into a dust-bowl. They also made a lot of noise. Because of these factors, you usually knew when you were on a road where logging trucks were likely, and you often heard them well before you saw them.

When the trucks reached the mill, they dumped the logs into a big pond. The pond water had a distinct musty smell. The water would keep the wood from drying out and splitting before it reached the blades. The sawmill usually had a way of feeding the logs up a ramp directly from the pond into a large circular saw that trimmed the bark off of first one side and then the other. The log was then flipped on its side so that they could trim the two remaining sides. The log was cut into ever-smaller pieces as it proceeded through the mill. These were then cut into the desired lengths.

The sawdust and the pieces of mostly bark from the first few cuts fell onto a conveyor that dropped them into a massive "beehive" burn tower. These burners were round cones maybe 40' high. Each mill had one of these burners with a conveyor belt feeding the scraps to the fire. To keep embers from flying out to light other fires, they had a dome-shaped screen covering the top. These towers looked like giant rusty salt shakers. Smoke rose from these beehives 24/7. At night the towers and the screens would glow red hot from the burning wood. Some of the heat from the burn tower was used to dry the lumber. The rest went up in smoke.

The pine smoke has a very distinct smell that would permeate the air for miles around. If there was little wind, the smoke from several sawmills could cover the entire valley. The smell was not necessarily unpleasant, but it was very distinct. If you light a fire in your back yard and use fresh-cut pine scraps, you will find that it smells different from a fire that is burning other kinds of wood. The smell of one of those backyard or beach pinewood fires still takes me back to my youth.

Back in those days, the mill either burned or sold as firewood, anything not made into standard boards or posts. Today sawdust and scrap wood become engineered wood products like particle board, and OSB (Oriented Strand Board). Most bark becomes mulch for gardens. There are no burners today, and little goes to waste.

— ■ —

For several years leading up to the summer of 1954, the entire family had been working and saving to buy a new car. As I recall, the one we had was a worn out 1941, Chevrolet. It looked much older, and Dad was probably spending endless hours keeping it running.

Our new 1954 Ford

Shortly after we arrived, Dad started shearing sheep in the Shasta Valley every spring. The money from his shearing went into the "new car fund." He found that Costello and Deter, the saw mill in Yreka, would pay us to stack the tailings into cords. A "cord" of wood is a stack that is 4' wide, 4' tall, and 8' long. That is a lot of wood. I don't remember what they paid us to stack it, or what they charged when they sold it, but any pay was better than none. We would go to the mill and stack wood almost every evening, and all that we earned went to the car fund. By 1954, we had enough, when added to the trade in value of our old car, to make a significant down payment on a new Ford

Fairlane. It cost about $1,800.

Mom and Dad went back and forth between the Ford dealers in Weed and Yreka. Mom wanted to get more for our old car than they wanted to give. Mom and Dad were willing to stay the course. They drove back and forth from one dealer to the other until she got them to step up to her goal. Our new Ford was shiny and green. I remember Dad asking Mom what color car she wanted and her answer was any color as long as it is green.

— ■ —

They still had to borrow money to pay for the car. The folks went to visit Mr. Ernest Smith, the president of Scott Valley Bank in Fort Jones. They gave them a loan with no problem. This was the beginning of a long relationship between Scott Valley Bank and the Griswold family. I know that the folks continued to use them for their banking needs even years later when they moved to Alaska.

Banking was a very personal business based almost entirely on relationships in those days. I got my first car loan through SVB. Several years later while I was still in the Air Force living in Caldwell, Idaho, I bought another car. The dealer, of course, wanted to finance my vehicle. They make a lot of money off of the loans. I told him I would pay cash and he couldn't believe that I had that kind of money. I explained that I didn't, but I had a good banker. He asked me to how it worked. I said the deal was simple. I would write him a check and the bank would make it good. I would drive down to Fort Jones California (that was about 400 miles away) sometime in the future, and we would catch up on the paperwork. He couldn't believe such a causal relationship was possible, so I had him speak to Mr. Smith at SVB who of course confirmed the arrangement. The guy just shook his head, and we did the deal.

I know Tom had a similar relationship with SVB, but I don't know if either of the girls ever worked through the bank in that way.

— ■ —

The summer of 1954, the Fish and Game assigned Dad to work on the Northern California coast inland from Crescent City. I think the assignment was for two months, Dad's job was primarily intended to protect some Reeves Pheasants they had transplanted to the area. Reeves Pheasants are a native of China. Looking back, it is a bit strange the Fish and Game department was introducing a foreign species into the environment. I suppose they thought this was a suitable habitat for this species, and that the pheasants would make good game birds for hunting. A few years later, as the environmental movement took hold, there was increasing pressure to allow only native species to populate any area. I don't know it the project worked, or if the birds died out.

For the summer, the Fish and Game furnished a small trailer plus we had some tents. We set up our camp at Gasquet (pronounced gas-kee), a wide spot in the road about halfway between the Oregon border and Crescent City.

It was an idyllic kind of summer. We were camping in the Six Rivers Grassy Flats Forest Service campground that sat on a small tabletop area surrounded on two sides by the Smith River. The river was cold, but not too cold for a bunch of dry country kids to play in. I couldn't swim, so it was more wading and splashing for me. I didn't learn to swim until many years later when I was stationed in Mississippi with the Air Force. I wouldn't go so far to say I was ever much of a swimmer, but I can at least get around a pool without drowning.

– ■ –

Once, I don't remember at what age, but it was while I was still in elementary school, all four of us were playing in an irrigation sump that was near the intersection of Old Westside and Pumphouse roads. That was a mile or so from our house.

A "sump" is a pit that a farmer digs for temporary storage of irrigation water. It is a kind of mini reservoir. Sumps are usually 12' to 14' deep, 15' or 20' wide and 40' to 60' long. A nearby irrigation ditch filled this sump. The sump acts as a buffer so that they have irrigation water for their fields when they need it most.

It was definitely not all that smart to play in a sump; they are deep with steep sides making entry and exit difficult; also the water can be quite dirty and stagnant. I imagine that with today's laws, any sumps that still exist must be securely fenced to keep foolish kids out. Back then, there were no fences or at least no kid-proof fences, and so we were over at the sump one hot summer's day floating on inner tubes and swimming. I fell or got knocked off of the inner tube I was floating on and started sinking like a rock. Fortunately, one or more of my siblings managed to drag me out. I was spitting greenish sludge for several minutes. My eyes, nose, and throat burned for hours. I don't think we ever told Mom, but it was a long time before I ventured back in the water that was over my head.

— ■ —

Dad's work at Gasquet was in a much more confined area, and so he was not putting in his regular long summer days. That gave the family weekends to explore the redwoods, the beaches, and the dense coastal forest. I had never seen the ocean. Most of my life, all of 9 years at that point, had been spent in arid areas. The nearby river and lush green forest were almost as exciting as the ocean.

We were able to go to the beach often. We could play in the surf, walk and run on the hard wet sand, look for all kinds of ocean critters: starfish, clams, mussels, sea anemones, urchins, etc. We collected washed up sea shells, agates, sticks and any other fascinations we could find in the backwater areas, or piled up against the rocks. We had cookouts and picnics almost every weekend. Dad rigged an A-frame net to catch smelt, a tiny fish, about 4 or 5 inches long, that came up on the beach to spawn. We enjoyed both the catching and eating.

At the campground, it seemed like every night was a hotdog or hamburger feast. We didn't have our garden to tend or to feed us, and we didn't have our freezer full of things that we had hunted, or raised and slaughtered. We got to buy "regular" items such as bread and potato chips at a nearby store. There was ample time to fish and the Smith River had some nice sized trout that made for great fishing and eating.

We had a Border Collie named Texie that had been with us for many years. She was a wonderful dog with only one eye as an eagle had clawed out her other. She was super at herding us kids and watching over us. You could trust Texie to guard pretty much anything you left at the campsite. If you left a steak out on the table, Texie would never touch it. It turned out her only vice was fish. Mom sat some trout out on the table one evening getting ready to build a campfire to fry them. Texie got up on the table and chowed down on the fish.

— ■ —

After our summer at Gasquet, we took our first family vacation. We drove our new Ford up to Craters of the Moon National Monument in Southeast Idaho, over to Teton Park in Wyoming, on up through Yellowstone Park then up nearly to the Canadian border and Glacier National Park in Montana. We drove across to Seattle to visit some relatives and finally south to home. That was long before Interstate highways. Those were voted in by Congress two years later. It would be decades before the transcontinental network was even close to being complete.

Almost all of the highways at that time were narrow two-lane roads. They often followed section lines (a section is 1 mile square) with 90 degree turns every few miles. Today "beltways" are built to allow traffic to avoid cities. In those days, highways were often routed miles out of their way so that they could zigzag through town to maximize the exposure. Highways were the lifeblood of these towns; gas stations, grocery stores, and motels lined the streets.

All of that made travel slow. Today you can easily drive 500 or even 600 miles in a single day. Back then, things were much slower. Speed limits were normally just 55 mph on the open roads, and 25 and sometimes 15 in every small town. You would be doing good to make 250 miles in a full day of driving.

Like every vacation, this was a camping vacation. We didn't stay in hotels or eat in restaurants. In the evening we would find a campground, or more often just pull off the road into a gravel pit or over a ridge on some tiny dirt path and set up camp for the night. We never went to a restaurant, and there were no fast-food places other than a few Dairy Queens. Mom would cook dinner and breakfast on a two-burner Colman gas stove that we carried.

Mom cooking breakfast next to
our Rambler 1960

After breakfast in the morning, we would pack up the car and head down the road. At noon, we would stop at a small store, there were no supermarkets in those days, and buy a loaf of bread, some bologna or other lunchmeat, and a small jar of mayonnaise. Lunch meat did not come prepackaged in those days. We call it "deli service" today, but back then it was just regular business to slice the lunchmeat as the customer's requested it. We added a little mustard and some lettuce, and maybe a tomato if we could find a good one at the store or a roadside farmer's stand. We usually got a bag of chips and something to drink, often a can of v8 tomato juice, which Dad particularly liked. We would find a small park or some area off the road and have a picnic lunch.

These foods were delicacies. Store-bought anything was a rarity; store-bought bread was something to be treasured. It was so soft and spongey. Of course, it had no taste, but who cared, it would just melt in your mouth.

My cousin David Montgomery, Kay and Florence's youngest son, would stay with us for a week or two almost every summer. For David, it was just the opposite; homemade bread, jam, and ice cream were special treats. To us they were what we normally had, so store-bought was unique.

Riding in the front seat was cherished. It was a throne worthy of a king and occasionally worthy of a good squabble. The Ford had a bench seat in front, as did almost all cars back then. Mom always sat in the middle next to Dad, so that left the right window seat with the window all to yourself; no siblings were crowding you, it was heaven. We all wanted that place in the car; we had to take turns. We kept careful track of who was next and when it would be their turn. If we had those little pocket timers back then, I am sure we would have been monitoring the seconds of each rotation. If we had smartphones, we would have mapped out the changing stations like pony-express stops, a day in advance. I can imagine that our parents remembered our seat monitoring with less relish.

— ■ —

During the spring and fall, Tom and I often rode our bikes to school. It was about 5 miles, but mostly flat so it was an easy ride. We rode our bikes everywhere. Sometimes to Gazelle to Carter's Mercantile. Ann Carter was a classmate of mine when we were in the Gazelle school. Her parents owned the Mercantile. The Mercantile was relatively small, and it never had a lot of anything and not a wide variety of the things that they did have, but they stocked an assortment of groceries as well as odds and ends of the things the tourists or local ranchers would typically need. They had things like coveralls, maybe blue jeans but I don't recall, work shirts, ammunition, and a small drug store. They were also the gas station, so they had grease and oil available. They stocked a few tools, but again, not that many. With a pair of pliers, a crescent wrench, a screwdriver, a hammer, and of course baling wire, you could fix almost anything. Where I came from, duct tape never quite measured up to baling wire. I still keep a small roll in my garage.

Soda bottles had a cash redemption value even back then. I think it was 1¢ each. That was a significant reward as a new bottle only cost about 10¢. A candy bar or pack of gum was a nickel. So if we could gather up a few bottles that tourists had pitched out the window, we could turn them in and get a treasured bottle of coke.

We seldom bought soda of any kind, but we made our root beer in the summer time. The recipe was pretty simple. To 1 bottle of Hires Root Beer Concentrate, 4 pounds of sugar, and ½ teaspoon of yeast. Mix this with about 5 gallons of water in a vat, we used our multipurpose galvanized bathtub, then bottled it in used quart beer bottles. We had a bottle capper to crimp the caps on the bottles. Once we had the bottles sealed, we would store them in a small hollow we had dug under the side porch. That kept them out of the sun and at a relatively constant temperature, not too cold and not too warm. They were ready to drink in about a week to 10 days.

Sometimes we would let them stay too long or get too hot, and a bottle would explode. One explosion often took out the surrounding bottles in the process. The Root Beer tasted pretty good over ice. If you chilled it well before drinking, it was even better.

Gazelle Elementary

When we moved to the Shasta Valley, it was the middle of the school year, and I immediately started in the Gazelle Elementary school. It was a two-room school, but a larger one with more students. Since I was already in the 1st grade, I just continued and went on to the 2nd grade the next year. That is the reason I graduated from high school when I was 17.

We didn't have a school bus, but the school district paid a private individual to use her car to act like a small school bus. The lady's name was Mrs. Stone. She and her husband lived about half way between our house and the school.

Mrs. Stone had two separate routes that she drove every morning and evening. The 4 Griswold kids were the bulk of one route. Mrs. Stone drove a relatively nice car, a Desoto if I remember correctly. In the afternoon, she did her first run up Callahan Canyon before she took us home. That schedule brought her the closest to her home after she dropped us off.

One afternoon Mrs. Stone came around the corner headed back to the school to pick us up after her Callahan Canyon run. She was driving rather fast, as I recall that was pretty standard for her. There was a girl that rode with us. She was closer to Betty's age, and I don't remember her name. This girl said, in a normal voice, "here she comes like a bat out of hell." There was no way Mrs. Stone could have heard her, but somehow she did. Boy oh boy did she light into that girl when she stopped to pick us up. Maybe she not only drove like a bat, but she could also hear like one.

Gazelle Elementary 1952
Photo provided by Janna Carter

— ∎ —

I was selected to play the part of the Littlest Angel in the Christmas play for the 1951 school year. I don't remember much about the play itself, but there was supposed to be a gift exchange after the show. For some reason whoever drew my name didn't come or didn't bring a gift, so I was left empty handed. It must have been quite traumatic for my fragile ego, or I wouldn't remember it at this late date. Maybe it was the beginning of my recognition that fame has a downside.

Gazelle Elementary was relatively uneventful in my school life. I transferred to Grenada in the middle of my 4th grade. I remember a few classmates, primarily because we later attended high school together. We touched base again when we were planning our 50th high school reunion in 2012.

Gazelle 3rd Grade Mrs Osborn
Jerry Eiler, Janna Carter, ?,
Sheila Franklin, Tim Griswold
& Artie Baumann 1952
Photo provided by Janna Carter

Grenada Elementary

In February of 1954, in the middle of my 4th grade, we transferred from
Gazelle to Grenada Elementary School. The School District had built a new
school in Grenada, which was about the same distance from our house to the
north as Gazelle was to the south. They realigned the school districts and

moved us to the new Grenada school when the new school was ready.

Grenada was a mile or more off of 99, and it was a bit larger than Gazelle. It was more of a "farm community," developed around the needs of the local farmers rather than the tourists driving up and down 99. It was still a small town, maybe 100 people.

Betty and Barbara had been placed in the same grade when they transitioned from homeschool to public school. They were four years ahead of me and so they started high school in Yreka in the fall of 1954. Tom and I continued at the Grenada Elementary school.

Tim, Betty, Tom, Barbara 1954

The Grenada Elementary school was new and much bigger. We rode a real school bus that would turn around at our house. We were the first ones to board every morning and the last ones to be dropped off in the evening. The school had four classrooms, actually 5 with the kindergarten class. Each room held two grades: 1-2, 3-4, 5-6, and 7-8. There was even a gym. Our class was still pretty small. I don't remember if any kids joined or left over the next four years, but the graduating class in the spring of 1958 had 12 students.

— ∎ —

I don't remember many special events during elementary school. We had school plays at Christmas and maybe at other times. The school was pretty small, so I am sure I had a part in a few of these, but I don't recall any. We didn't have any music or sports, so other than recess; it was all class work.

Tim 1958

In the 8th grade, we each had to memorize and recite the Gettysburg Address in front of the class. I was always terrified of speaking, but I tackled this assignment with everything I could muster. I would recite the Address over and over as I did my chores, milked the cow. Any poor beast that couldn't object to my droning on became my audience. When it finally came time to say it in front of the class, I aced it. I think I was the only one. It helped me get past a few of public speaking jitters, but it didn't cure my fear.

My classmates stayed together through our high school years. One, in particular, remains a good friend to this day. Chuck Nelson had been in the Big Springs school. He had transferred to Grenada a year earlier than my transfer. After high school, I lost track of almost all of my classmates, but several of us reconnected in the run-up to our 50th reunion in 2012.

I had heard bits and pieces about Chuck over the years. I knew that he had gone into law enforcement and at least for a while had been in the FBI. Other than that, his whereabouts was a mystery. I found him before the reunion, and we reconnected and rekindled our long dormant friendship.

Arlene Sears was another classmate. We were friends, and I suppose you could call us competitors. Come graduation from the 8th grade; Arlene was the valedictorian, and I was salutatorian. I don't remember being aware or ever thinking about such things at that age. Given my terror of public speaking, had I known, I might well have deliberately flunked a course or two just to avoid having to speak at graduation. Arlene didn't make it all the way through high school with us. She dropped out to get married and so I lost track of her as well until the 50th.

Hi-Ho Hi-Ho, off to Work I Go

We each started working as soon as we could find someone to hire us. There were farms nearby, and both Tom and I started moving sprinkler lines for Frank Bortolazzo & Sons in 1956 when I was 11. That was primarily summer work, but it began with the growing season. That was before school got out for the summer, and it extended well into the fall.

The Bortolazzo's owned several alfalfa fields near our house. They had to be watered frequently as there was never enough rain to produce a decent crop. Today they use big wheeled self-propelling sprinkler pipes that either take them in a circle or down a field. In those days, it was all brute force. Of course calling what I was able to do at 11 "brute force," is more than a little disingenuous.

A "sprinkler line" consisted of a row of 50 or more 30' sections of 4" aluminum pipe. At one end of each pipe was a 2' riser and a rotating sprinkler head at the top. The pipe sections clipped together with a mechanism that latched when you pushed one pipe inside of the other. There was a small plate on the receiving end to make it easier to mate the pipes. They came apart by pushing, twisting, and then pulling. They weren't very heavy, maybe 30 pounds per section, but they were often full of water, so you had to raise one end to empty the water. Most of the time, when you tried to drain the pipe, the water would flow into the next section of pipe as you had to do the lift-twist-pull thing to get the pipes apart. That meant that you were lifting the same water over and over again, and it could be quite cumbersome. Even when it was empty, the length made it awkward to manage, especially an 11-year old.

There was a larger underground line that brought the water from the sump to the field. That would usually run down the edge or the middle if it were a big field. It had heads that would stick up out of the ground every 40' or so. When it came time to move the line, which was twice a day, we would unhook the line from the riser and move the hooking mechanism to the next riser, and reinstalled it. Then we used the twist-pull process to disassemble the entire line one piece at a time. As we took it apart, we would walk each section over the 40 feet and hook it up in the new position. We would proceed down the line, moving one piece at a time.

Of course, when it was time to move it, the area where the line was currently setting was wet from having just run for 8 to 10 hours. Swarms of mosquitos were attracted to the moisture, and they had nothing to eat except for Tom and me. They would get in our nose, ears, and eyes. Especially in your mouth if you were foolish enough to open it. It was usually a bit muddy as well. So we would walk back and forth from wet to dry to wet with swarms of mosquitos biting on us all the while. Since we were unable to let go of the pipe that we were carrying, they pretty much had a free banquet, at least until we got the pipe hooked up and started smashing them. Then immediately it was back for another pipe and another swarm of mosquitos.

There was no mosquito repellent at that time, so by the time we finished moving the line, and that usually took from an hour to an hour and a half. Our arms and faces had countless mosquito bites and hundreds of little splotches of our blood where we had been able to victimize our victimizers. The good news is that I got enough mosquito venom that even to this day, I seldom even get a bump if one bites me.

In fields that had been recently mowed, the alfalfa was short, the work was easier, and the mosquitos were fewer. When it was close to time to cut it again, the alfalfa would be about knee high. We would be slogging through wet hay along with the mud and mosquitos.

It wasn't a particularly difficult job. The lines had to be set straight, and at a consistent distance from the old line. We occasionally got out of alignment, and we had to go back and reset them to get them where they needed to be.

Once we had the line in the new position, we would get on our bikes and ride to the sump, which was usually a half mile or so away, and set the timer and turn on the pump. We did this twice a day seven days a week. For a month or so in the spring and fall, we would not move the lines in the morning on school days. In the morning there wasn't time because we had to milk the cow, feed all the animals, eat breakfast and then catch the bus to school. One of the Bortolazzo brothers made the morning move. The water would finish by the time we got home, so after a short break, we would make the evening move. As soon as school was out, we took over the morning moves as well.

This process went on all summer. For this work, we got the princely sum of 75¢/line move. We split that so we netted 75¢ each day when we made two moves. That amounted to $22.50 each month. It may not seem like very much, but it didn't matter to us back then. In 2016 dollars that would be $200/month. Not bad wages for an 11-year old.

– ∎ –

During the summer we worked more and made more. As soon as school was out and we had a full day to work, our assignment expanded. The Bortolazzo's had more land near Highway 99 about 3 miles from our house. They had other sprinkler lines for us to move over there, and frequently other work for us. They let us use an old Model A Ford pickup to drive back and forth. We all knew how to drive because that was part of growing up in the country. We didn't have licenses. Tom was older, 13 or 14 by then, so he was the designated driver. It wasn't that it was too far to ride our bikes, it was that we would be wasting too much time traveling south to do one line, then north to do another, then back home to repeat the process later in the day.

The old Model A was in rough shape. You had to make sure you didn't drop anything as the floorboards were rusted/rotted out and you could look down and see the road as you drove along. If you drove slow, you could see the oil dripping from the engine. It leaked and burned so much oil that, even with the short trips, we had to add a quart about every other day.

I don't think I did any tractor driving that first summer, but by the second summer, at age 12, I was driving a tractor to rake the hay into windrows. The alfalfa grew quickly to about 12" or 14" in height, at which point it would start blooming. Right at the peak of the bloom, they would cut the hay with a big mower that was attached to the power takeoff on the tractor. We weren't allowed to drive the mowers as that was considered too dangerous. I suppose they were more dangerous than the rake, but not by all that much, either one could kill you pretty quickly.

When cut, the hay would lay flat where it fell. In about 3 days it would be partially dried out; then I would come along with a rotating rake pulled behind a tractor and rake the hay into windrows. About two days later, I would use the rake to turn these windrows over again for a final drying. A day or so later the baler would come along and scoop up the alfalfa and make bales. We didn't drive the hay balers because of the danger. They were temperamental beasts that required constant watching and fixing to keep the bales the right size and neither too tight nor too lose.

We had to line the bales up so a truck with a special chute could come by and pick them up and move them out and make way for the next crop. This water, cut, rake, rake, bale, remove cycle was repeated for three crops each year.

I liked the raking as I enjoyed driving the tractors. It was power, control, and freedom, all in the hands of a kid. I hated aligning bales. They usually weighed about 125 pounds. That was probably close to what I weighed. I have never had a lot of upper-arm strength, so lining them up required sliding, dragging, or rolling the bales; there was no way I could lift and carry even a 100-pound bale.

— ■ —

I remember moving a tractor from the Bortolazzo's north fields where they lived, to the fields near our house. I think I was 14 at the time. I had to drive down Highway 99 a half mile and then on a dirt road the rest of the way. This was before Interstate 5, so 99 was a busy road. I was driving an old John Deere tractor with a massive flywheel that was used to stabilize the engine as the tractor drove or as various attachments were activated or deactivated. The flywheel was solid steel; it probably weighed 100 or more pounds. It was perhaps 20" across and 3" wide.

You also used the flywheel to start the tractor engine. You would turn on the ignition and set the throttle and then spin the wheel by hand to start the motor.

It worked like cranking a car in the old days. The engine provided a lot of resistance, so it was a little hard for me to get it to spin. Once I got the hang of it, it wasn't bad.

On this particular trip, I was towing a hay rake, and I had just left Highway 99, maybe a quarter of a mile up over a slight rise then down the other side. I was standing as I was driving, which was more comfortable than sitting in the bouncing steel seat. It was probably a bit of an ego trip as well as it felt like I was grown up driving on the road as opposed to just in the fields. Suddenly the flywheel, which was probably spinning at 800 or 1000 rpm just a few inches from my foot, slipped off of the end of the shaft. The centrifugal force carried it up beside where I was standing, maybe 6" from my side. There was a loud humming sound coming from the spinning flywheel as it passed my ear. It had to be loud for me to hear it over the noise of the tractor. It continued up and over the top of the tractor about 10' above my head. All of this had a slow-motion feel. The tractor started shaking like it was going to tear itself apart, so I was scrambling to shut it down while at the same time trying to figure out what the heck was taking place. As the engine started to slow, I looked out in front of the tractor about 40' where the wheel hit the ground throwing up dirt and rocks. It bounced a couple of times as it was flying down the road. It drifted across the road, down and then up the side of the ditch, under a barbed wire fence breaking the bottom strand. At that point, it disappeared. It was about 200 yards out and down in knee high alfalfa. A fence line and weeds were blocking my view. I could see pieces of alfalfa flying and the track it was making, but it was hard to see the actual flywheel.

I got the tractor completely stopped and started walking down the road to try and find the missing wheel. I traced its path through the alfalfa and under another fence. It crossed Pumphouse Road, took out the bottom wire on another fence and then into another hay field. About 200' feet out in this field it smacked into a big oak tree and left a 2" dent in the tree. The wheel had traveled well over a quarter of a mile on its own. It was laying there at the base of the tree.

I tried to lift it to roll it back but couldn't get it to move so I left it and walked back to the Bortolazzo's farm to tell them what took place. Thank heavens I had been standing. If I had been sitting, my knee would have been angled out over the flywheel, and it may well have taken off my leg on its trip up and over the tractor. Thank God I was off of Highway 99 because there was lots of traffic there. On the dirt road, there were no cars, animals, or people in its path. It could have easily killed anyone it hit. Like I said, raking hay wasn't as dangerous as mowing, but it could still kill you.

— ∎ —

Time of day was a critical issue for most hay work. The alfalfa had to be relatively dry to cut clean. Wet hay stuck to the mower and caused jams. That meant mowing started no earlier than 10 a.m. as you had to wait till the dew dried off. Raking had to happen while the hay was moist or the leaves and blossoms wouldn't be knocked off. That meant while the dew was on the hay, so starting about 4 a.m. and ending by 9 or 10 a.m. Baling was like raking, an early morning thing.

Once I started raking hay, I had to be in the fields no later than 4 a.m. I couldn't do that on school days, but every Saturday and Sunday I would be out there. Of course, as soon as summer hit it was every day. We would adjust the sprinkler line moving so that it fell after the raking and then late in the evening.

If I remember; we got 50¢ per hour for our tractor work. The money was not just for fun; it was our responsibility to pay for everything that we could. That meant any fun things of course, but we didn't have a lot of time for fun. We bought our school clothes, Christmas gifts, and saved for expenses during the entire school year. There wasn't much left over after that.

— ∎ —

In this age of plastic trees that often rotate and even play music, high-tech lighting and a plethora of "artificial enhancements" to Christmas and Christmas trees in particular, it might be worth a moment to understand what our trees and decorations were like. Trees were usually pines we chopped down and brought home. We never bought one on a lot, in fact I don't recall any tree lots back in those days. They probably had them in the cities, but where I grew up everyone went out in the woods and chopped their own. On occasion we would use a juniper tree that we would simply find somewhere on the Koppes ranch. While not quite as attractive as a pine, the smell of the juniper was a pleasant alternative.

Decorations were strictly traditional. We did, at least in the later years, have lights, but these were the big kind that were about 1½" long. They only came in 5 colors as I recall. Of course this was a huge improvement in safety over the candles that some had used in earlier days. We had a scant few ornaments that we had collected over the years. There were never more than a couple dozen. I don't remember ever buying any, so they were all at least as old as I was. They were very fragile and one wag of a dog's tail meant that a year seldom passed without at least a few ending up in the trash. Those we had were usually missing substantial portions of their colored coating. There were aluminum ice cycles that we would carefully hang on the tree and also carefully remove and store for the next year. We did buy additional ice cycles from time to time. There were no garlands or strings of glittering anything. Each year we would create our own decorations by stringing popcorn on thread and draping it around the tree. As you can imagine this was a rather laborious process; you had to use a needle and long thread poking individual pieces of popcorn and sliding them along the thread. You had to be careful as it was quite easy to break the popcorn as you were sliding it down the thread. On the plus side, you could eat the broken pieces.

Popcorn garlands were a long-standing tradition as most people would put their trees outside, in part because of the fire hazard and in part because houses were a lot smaller in the past. The popcorn attracted birds and squirrels so it made a bit of a festive environment. Of course if the tree was inside the birds and squirrels were replaced by mice, or an occasional dog taking a bite of popcorn. If a dog decided to chow down, that would invariably end up with a tree crashing to the floor.

In addition to the popcorn garlands, we would create long chains of colored paper links. For these, we would get come construction paper and cut it into ribbons that were about ½" wide and 4" or 5" long. We would loop these in a circle with each loop passing through the pervious loop forming a long chain. We didn't have staplers, so we glued each loop with a small dab of glue. You had to pinch the ends together and hold them until the glue dried before you could make the next loop. The glue we used was a smelly white paste that was about the only glue available back in those days.

It was a slow process and the "chains" never lasted from year to year, so like the popcorn garlands, the process was repeated each year. At our house, there was always a bit of a competition to see who could make the longest chain and if any chain would break after the glue dried.

While our trees were not nearly as glitzy as trees today, the process of decorating was a family affair that spanned several days. I am not sure I would like to revive that tradition.

Just because I was working and making money didn't relieve me from my chores at home. When I started the 8th grade, Tom was starting high school, and the girls were in their senior year. Their bus left about an hour before mine, and so I had responsibility for all of the morning chores for that school year. To make up for it, they had all the evening chores. There was more to do in the evenings, the biggest task being the firewood. There was only one cow to milk, but chickens, a hog, turkeys, rabbits, and of course the dogs to feed. There was no time to sit around, it was chores, breakfast then onto the bus.

We would have a coyote in a steel cage from time to time. The purpose was to collect urine. Coyotes are like dogs in that they like to pee on every bush, but particularly where some other coyote had already peed. For trapping, urine was the attraction, but not just any urine, it had to be coyote urine. Since wild coyotes weren't inclined to volunteer samples, we got coyote urine by putting a coyote in a cage with a metal floor so when he peed it would flow down to a collection tank.

When we did have a coyote in the cage, it was our job to feed and water him, clean his cage, and collect the donations. Of course, a wild coyote in a steel cage was not exactly willing partners in this endeavor. In fact, they were usually quite unhappy about the whole process, so you had to be careful when cleaning and feeding.

We would fill gallon jugs for storage, a process that required many weeks of collection. Dad would later put the urine in smaller bottles with a sprinkle top so he could "bait" his traps appropriately. The correct term is "settings." The trap was the steel device that locked onto the coyote's foot. It was attached to a 4 or 5-foot chain, which was hooked to a small piece of scrap iron, something like a 6" piece of railroad track. To catch a coyote, Dad created a "setting" where he buried all of this, hopefully exactly where the coyote would stand to pee on the bush that he had carefully sprinkled a small amount of the collected urine. The "art" was to figure out exactly where the coyote would put his foot and locate the setting right there. Urine was the pièce de résistance when it came to trapping.

Dad had other bait that he created from various animal parts. It stank to high heaven, and the creation process was not pleasant. Dad did this on his own, so I won't go into how he made his secret sauce. In most circumstances, the combination of secret sauce and urine was alluring enough to get the coyote to let down his guard and ignore any lingering human scent that would otherwise cause the coyote to seek some other bush. While collecting urine was every bit as disgusting as it sounds, it was, like many other tasks on a ranch, something you dealt with because it had to be done.

— ■ —

After you wash all that out of your mind's eye, maybe I should explain how you milk a cow. Of course on a big dairy farm it is different, they use machines, but we used our hands. Milking is a cooperative process. The cow has milk that the human wants while the human has grain that the cow wants. So you trade a cow meal for a bucket of milk.

The problem is that the cow might finish dinner before the bucket is full, and so there needs to be a bit of forced cooperation to ensure that we get our way. To do that you had to get the cow to put her head in a "stanchion." A stanchion is like a fence inside of the barn. It had two upright 2 x 4s with one hinged at the bottom. The cow would put her head between the bars to eat some grain, hay, or another treat that you put out for her. Once she did, you pulled the pivoting board over and locked it against her neck in a way that allowed her to move her head up and down to eat, but that didn't allow her to back out of the stanchion. Cows are reasonably bright animals, unlike some farm critters, turkeys and sheep being at the bottom of the brains-curve. None the less, cows never seemed to catch on to this stanchion game. Of course, maybe they actually wanted to get rid of that heavy load of milk hanging between their hind legs.

Now that she was secure, I would sit on a one-legged stool by her hip. These single leg stools looked like the letter "T." Some people use a three or four legged stool, but I always preferred a single leg. A cow, even one that is locked in a stanchion, can move pretty fast. I found it easier to move over or around a single leg stool as opposed to one that stays put when you stood to jump back.

The single leg also allowed you to lean against the cow as you milked. The seat would stay with you. Of course, if you leaned too far and if the floor was wet or slippery, you had to be careful that the stool didn't pop out from under you leaving you in a rather unpleasant position on your butt in cow poop, possibly with a startled cow stepping on various parts of your body. Since barn floors are often wet and slippery this was a real danger.

Once balanced on the stool, you put your head in front of her knee and against her stomach behind her ribs. This position allowed easy access to her udder and teats, but it also allowed you to feel her muscles flex if she started to shift or move. You washed the nipples and usually rubbed on some bag balm; that is an ointment that looked like an extra thick Vaseline. Bag-balm made it a bit easier to milk, but mainly it was to protect her teats from drying out in the wind. Incidentally, you can still buy bag-balm at Costco from time to time. You have to ask for it at the pharmacy, but you will find no better hand lotion if you are working out in cold or wet areas.

Placing your head on her belly just in front of her knee also helped to keep her from swinging her foot forward and kicking or stepping in the bucket that you placed directly beneath her udder. It didn't prevent her from stepping or kicking, but it gave you a warning as she flexed her muscles.

You grasp one teat in each hand and pinching your thumb and index finger together near the top of the teat to seal it so that the milk wouldn't flowing back up into the udder. You could then either slide this pinched thumb and finger combination down forcing the milk out or as I preferred, close your fingers into a fist one finger at a time so as to force the milk down and out. Both methods worked, it was just a matter of preference.

You continued this process emptying all four quadrants of the udder. It was important to "strip" the last of the milk out because the cow would regulate milk production based on how much was used. If you left some milk behind, production would quickly decrease.

Along the way, you would undoubtedly get swatted by her tail. Flies and cows are like bread and butter. They just go together. Of course, the flies vastly outnumber the cows. The cow's primary defense mechanism is their tail. They swish it constantly to chase away flies. As you milk, your head is right in line with the path that tail usually takes. You got used to this, and it keeps the flies off of you as well, but if the cow had been eating fresh green grass, they frequently got a bit of the scours, that's diarrhea for the uninitiated. That invariably got on their tails and subsequently transferred to the back of your head, neck, and shoulders with each fly swat.

You had to be on constant lookout for any sudden move to urinate or take a poop. There was seldom a lot of warning, but if you paid attention, you might feel the cow's stomach muscles move against the top of your head. Of course, not all movement equaled an impending disaster, so you had to use judgment and be quick about getting the bucket as well as yourself out of the line of fire. Our cow usually gave anywhere up to about 2 gallons of milk at each setting, so it took a bit of time to go through this ritual.

— ■ —

You may not know it, but cows have personalities. Some are calm; some are skittish. Some cows like the milking process, others, not so much. Some cows have "attitude." We had one we named Bossy because she was. She liked to push around any other cows in the area. She would always claim the highest spot on any mound or hump in a pasture. She would come down to graze, but as soon as she finished and started chewing her cud, she would climb to the top of the raised area and chase away any other cow that might consider challenging her. Bossy didn't mind the milking process, but she never really let you forget that she was the boss.

People say cows have two stomachs. In fact, they have four, but who is counting. The idea of two comes from the way a cow eats. They will graze on grass or hay, eating up to 50 pounds at a setting. As they graze, they roll their food into small balls called a "cuds," which they swallow and store in their first stomach. After the cow is through grazing, she will move away from the grass and regurgitate these cuds one at a time and chew them to break them down to a digestible consistency. The process takes 50 or 60 chews on each cud. She then swallows that cud into her second stomach and starts on the next one. After this second chewing, the cud proceeds from stomach to stomach being gradually broken down and digested.

— ■ —

The milking process didn't end with collecting the milk. We then took the milk to the house and ran it through the strainer and separator. The strainer was a piece of fine cloth that would remove any chunks of debris that might have fallen in the bucket. Hopefully, there were none. The separator had a large bowl mounted on top of a machine with a set of spinning disks. You had to crank it up to speed then turned the valve to let the milk enter the spinning disks. The disks were designed to separate the heavier milk from the lighter cream, depositing them in separate containers. It wasn't perfect; it got about

98% of the cream out of the milk. That gave you real creamy drinking milk as well as cream for butter or to sell.

Of course, cleaning was the last step of the process. On school days, Mom would take on the separation process and the cleanup. When we were in the fields, Mom, or the girls, when they were still at home, would cover the morning chores. When we weren't working or going to school, those were just part of the job.

I mentioned my friend Chuck Nelson a bit earlier. Chuck wrote a marvelous book about his younger years. It is called "Life at The End of a Dirt Road" ISBN: 1425922112. I highly recommend reading it as you will get a good idea of what it was like to grow up in our time. In that book, Chuck wrote a description of milking that will bring tears to your eyes. At least it will if you have ever sat your butt on a stool and filled a pail of milk. He generously allowed me to reprint that portion as an Appendix. It will give you a good idea of why you should pick up his book.

– ■ –

When Dad started shearing sheep in the Shasta Valley, I think that was the spring of 1953, when I was 8. Tom and I were expected to assist him in this work. We couldn't shear of course, but we were there to wrangle the sheep into position, tie the wool, and tamp the wool into the sacks. Wrangling sheep is not a terribly difficult process, but there are a few tricks. You would never suspect it by looking at one, but sheep have a reverse gear. Really, they do! You stand beside one, put one hand on her flank to hold her against your legs. Then you put your other hand under her nose and jaw. You must be careful not to get bitten in this process. Sheep aren't meat eaters, but they are incredibly stupid and a misplaced finger between a nervous sheep's teeth, can still get nibbled. You raise the nose up while holding the sheep against your leg and she will start backing up. When you get her to the correct place, you raise the nose a bit more and twist just slightly, and she will sit down. All you have to do then is grab her front legs, tip her back, and drag her on her rump into position for Dad to start shearing. It is pretty simple once you get the hang of it.

It wasn't easy when you came to a big ram that weighed at least twice what I weighed. They had a stiff neck and a bad attitude. For some reason, they were never willing to cooperate with some kid trying to back them up, and they were strong enough to put up a real battle.

Another issue was "toe pops." As you worked with the sheep or tamped the wool, your shoes became very slick with lanolin from the wool. When a sheep would step down on your foot, as frequently happened while you were doing the backup dance, their sharp pointed toes would invariably slide on the slick leather and pop off of the edge of your shoe making it feel like they were ripping your little toe off in the process. I never lost any toes, or even broke any bones, but it sure did hurt.

Tom was stronger. He usually got the pen and wrangling job while I got the tamping job. As I explained in the previous chapter a wool sack is almost 8' long and about 3' across. It was suspended in a tower so that it did not touch the ground. As Tom tossed the fleeces in, it was my job to compact them down so that a full sack would weigh between 450 or 500 pounds.

To start, I would toss in half a dozen fleeces then jump in on top. At that point, I would be down at the bottom of the sack with no way out. I couldn't reach the top and probably wouldn't have been able to pull myself out if I did somehow reach it. I just had to keep on packing in the wool, with Tom tossing new fleeces on top of my head. I would gradually work my way back to the top. A typical sack would hold about 22 to 25 fleeces. It took 2 or more hours to complete. Of course, this varied by the kind of sheep, some have more wool than others, and the density of the wool. Cold winters made the sheep grow more wool than they did during a warm winter.

All of these ranchers knew Dad as their trapper, but also as their shearer. By extension they knew Tom and I. They expected us to come and help and most paid us quite well for our day's work. The days were fairly long, usually 8 to 10 hours, and we would get about $2; occasionally they would give us $3 each. That was truly a bonus. These ranchers had their hired hands of course, but they knew that we knew how to work with Dad, to feed him the sheep at the right pace, to take care of the wool, and to get it sacked properly. They had other work for their regular crews, so they were glad to see us come. We would often eat lunch and sometimes dinner with the rancher.

One Spring we were shearing at the Prather Ranch. Morley Prather was a longtime friend. We had been there several prior years. For some reason, Tom and I made a bet about who could get the most fleeces in a wool sack. I don't remember why we decided to bet, or what the wager was, but I won with 43 fleeces in a single wool sack. Our contest wasn't a secret; everyone was watching and cheering us on. When I finished, the sack was so tight and full that it probably weighed close to 1000 pounds. The next year when we came to shear, Morley laughed and told us there would be no betting this time. It seems that when they got the sacks to the train station to load, that one burst at the seams and spilled wool everywhere. It took them three sacks to get it all back together.

Growing Up

There were some snow-fed lakes in the Trinity Alps west of Scott Valley. They were fairly high up and would freeze over in the winter. It would be late spring or early summer before they were open again. Each year the Fish and Game would stock these lakes with trout from the fish hatchery. Stocking was usually done from an airplane as they were in a wilderness area, and not accessible by any form of motor vehicle. Many of them were a 2 or 3-hour hike from the nearest road. These lakes were very serene. They were pleasant places to drop out and fish, even if you never caught a thing.

Every year Dad would gather a bunch of kids, sometimes the three Hettema girls, Mike Auman, our cousins David Montgomery and or Nick Linton. Usually at least one father would come along: Harold Hettema was the most frequent. We would journey for 4 or 5 days to one of these backcountry lakes for some high mountain camping and fishing. These became known as "Dad's Famous Fishing Trips." It seemed that there was always something larger than life that took place.

On one trip, I don't remember who else was with us; we went in a little too early and the lake we were planning on fishing was still frozen over. When we discovered the ice-bound lake, we started looking for alternatives. On the map, it seemed like a reasonable hike over a ridge to another lake that had better sun exposure. We thought it would be open and fishable, and it was. However, it turned out that the ridge that looked so simple on the map was far from simple. We were engaged in some serious climbing and working our way down steep inclines that bordered on cliffs. Darkness caught up with us before we could finish our descent into the new valley. We wound up sleeping on ledges with cliffs at our feet. No one was hurt, and we did catch some fish in the new lake.

We always tried to pack enough food based on the assumption that we wouldn't catch any fish to supplement our meals. On one trip, we came close to being skunked fishing wise, and Dad had underestimated just how much teenage boys eat when setting around a campfire. We had enough, but we were cutting back for the last couple days.

These trips were always fun, and it was great to see Dad in his element. Along with the fishing, he was teaching us life lessons. We will all remember the climb over the ridge or the running low on food, more than we will ever remember the actual fishing.

— ■ —

Sometime after we moved to the Shasta Valley, we started getting involved in Square Dancing. At first, the club didn't want any children, and there was a bit of a kerfuffle. Eventually, they either relented, or someone else started a new club where kids were welcome. We started a kid's club within the main club. There were dances once a month at a grange hall north of Yreka. There were also frequent jamborees within a hundred-mile radius that we attended on occasion.

Square dancing was good clean family fun, and it was a treat to travel the jamborees. Our family never stayed overnight; we had animals to tend, and so we would always drive back home after the dance. These would be late night trips, usually through some pretty desolate country. For some reason, I was never one to sleep in the car. I am not sure what the reason was, but I suspect I was afraid I would miss out on something. Because they knew that I would stay awake while the other kids slept, I usually got the prized right front seat on the return trips. I could watch the trees fly by, and the night sky with the moon and stars. These were always fun.

— ■ —

We traveled with Dad as he ran his trap lines whenever we could. It was not only because we enjoyed the time and the adventure, but we could also speed Dad's work. Every farm and ranch had locked gates, and of course, every lock was different. Dad carried a set of keys like a jailer. There had to be a hundred different keys on that loop. Somehow Dad could keep track of which key was for which gate.

Betty, Barbara, Tim & Tom with bobcat 1953

On any day, he might have to open and close a dozen gates as he entered and left various farms and ranches as well as gated Forest Service areas. When he worked alone, this meant getting out to open the gate, getting in and driving thru, then out again to close the gate. This process was cut in half if we did the gate. Once we could reach the peddles, Dad would frequently let us drive at least through the gate, but often in the fields beyond. As we improved, he let us drive even rougher roads. In this way, we all were quite accomplished drivers by the time we were old enough to drive legally. At that point, the minimum age was 15½ for farm kids.

We also learned the ins and outs of setting traps and finding the animals. Dad used a short chain attached to the trap and a piece of scrap iron. That allowed the coyote to drag the trap into the bushes. That cut down on the number of stolen traps, but it meant that you had to hunt them when you arrived. That was a major part of the dogs' work, but it sometimes took a while.

We would often spend a couple of summer weeks visiting with Uncle Charley. This would be during the short breaks between hay mowing cycles. At first, it was when he had the goats up on Bully Choop, but later we would go over to Garberville where he lived near the coast. These were always fun visits. Charley was a very gentle man. He was not a disciplinarian, and we probably got away with far more than we should. Grandmother Griswold always lived with Charley. She was not what you might call a sweet and gentle grandmother. We got along all right, but she was better at a distance. Despite this, our summer visits were a nice break from the seemingly endless chores that awaited us back home.

– ■ –

During the summer of 1956, Dad was assigned to tag deer in the McCloud Flats area. The job was to snare a deer by the legs, hold it down and check its general health, was it a male or female, if male how many points on the antlers, if a female, did it have any fawns and estimate its age by examining the teeth. He had to put a tag in one ear, and fasten on a collar with a piece of colored plastic visible from a distance. The Fish and Game wanted to know when and where these deer were shot or died, so there were instructions to return the tags when found.

This was dangerous work. Deer aren't accustomed to being approached by humans. Deer are big and strong with sharp horns and hooves. When you snare them, and then come up to them in the dark, they tend to panic; to fight for their lives. They don't like to be held down, and they kick and bite if they get the opportunity. For safety, there were supposed to be two adults doing this work. For some reason, Dad wound up working alone.

I went with him one week. Most of the work was at night when the deer would come into a watering hole for a drink. A bell was attached to the snare. When it rang, we had to go quickly so that the deer wouldn't hurt itself. We would be sound asleep when the bell would start ringing. We would rush to the spot to hog tie the deer. My job was to hold the flashlight, as Dad wouldn't let me near these panicked animals.

There was a spot near our campsite with a spring and pond at the foot of a cliff. That was the watering hole the deer were headed to when they would get snared. I would crawl out on a ledge of rock at the top of the cliff that was maybe 30' above the pond. I had binoculars so I could watch as the various animals came to water. It was almost like they had worked out a schedule so that no predators would be there while the squirrels were drinking, and no squirrels would be there when the bobcat came to drink. It was all choreographed and quite harmonious.

A fascinating thing for me was the number of different bird species and all of their colors and songs. You hear birds all the time in the woods, but you don't get to see all that many because they are up in the trees or brush and they fly away if you get close. I spent hours out on that ledge.

At the campsite, some frustrated hunter had nailed a bunch of bones to a tree in the shape of a big bird. Someone, maybe the creator, had written Big Butted Bird across the bones.

The daytime was peaceful as the deer seldom came in for a drink during daylight hours. Dad loved to tell stories but seldom got personal or even parental. I can't ever remember him giving me "personal or life advice"; trapping, hunting, building a fence, fixing a motor, or digging a well, yes, but never any explanations about life. My parents' idea of parenting was to set an example. We were expected to just "absorb" any necessary lessons by watching. This deer trapping assignment was probably the only time he and I ever had anything close to any "father/son" talks. It was the only time I can recall when he was not busy or distracted with all the other things in life or a gaggle of kids on a fishing trip. He was relaxed, or maybe as close as he ever got to being relaxed. We had one-on-one time and he talked more than I can ever remember talking; sadly, 60 years later, I don't remember what we discussed.

Discipline in our family came in two forms. First, you were expected to be disciplined in your work, to do what needed doing when it needed to be done, without questions or complaints. Whether it was feeding the dogs, milking the cows or bringing in firewood. Completing the task wasn't something to be negotiated or slipped around; it was expected, just do it. Interestingly, this was never something that was talked about or that there was an established punishment if we failed to do our work. I don't recall any time when there was a problem, a spanking, or even a discussion about chores. We knew our responsibilities, and we did them, it was as simple as that.

Big Butted Bird

— ■ —

There were never a lot of rules. No one ever told us 'you have to be to bed by a certain time.' Whether we were getting up at 3:30 a.m. to go to rake hay, or at 5:30 to milk the cows on a school morning. Mom would come to the foot of the stairs and call once, and not too loudly, you came with one call. It was

89

never stated, but it was clearly understood that Mom got up to make us a hot breakfast and pack our lunch; no matter what time or for what reason. We were to respect the fact that she did and we were to respond quickly and pleasantly. The unstated and unwritten understanding was "God help you if you didn't." No matter if you had been asleep for 8 hours or 8 minutes, we just did. No one ever volunteered to find out exactly what it was the God would need to help us through if we didn't.

I remember one-time Tom and I went coon hunting with Carl Hellwig. Carl was a bit older than we were and had some hounds that he liked to use to hunt raccoons at night. We drove over to Scott Valley and spent the night chasing the dogs who were chasing the raccoons through the woods. It was a lot of fun but not something that I wanted to do more than once. We got back to the house a bit after 3 a.m. We just ate breakfast and went to work. Like I said, there were no bedtime rules; we were expected to manage our lives.

Alcohol and cigarettes fell under a similar self-discipline rule. However, this one was clearly articulated so there would be no doubt or confusion. If any of us ever wanted a drink, no matter what age, they would buy the first 6-pack, but we must sit and drink every can in front of them and drink them at one setting. The same applied for cigarettes. They would buy the first pack, but we must sit and smoke them in front of them. They knew of course if we did we would get very sick and never want another. The clearly stated threat was: God help you if we find you are sneaking around behind our backs. Again, no one wanted to learn why God's assistance would be required.

In the decades that followed, none of us ever got into any serious drinking. Other than Tom taking up smoking while he was serving in the Navy, none of us ever took up smoking. I think it had to do with the fact that we knew we could, but we also knew they didn't want us to start. Finally, we knew there would be swift and sure punishment if we tried sneaking.

— ■ —

Pets were a constant in our lives. We always had dogs, but these were working dogs first and pets second. They were either herding goats or working dogs that Dad used for his trap line work. We never had "house" dogs. A dog had to be able to pull its own, or it was gone. We had chipmunks for years. These were actually Golden Mantle Ground Squirrels, a slightly bigger version of the same thing. They made great pets. We could hold them and feed them.

They seldom tried to run away. They had a big cage with a wheel that they could run in for exercise. They had a little house for their nest. We watched them have babies over the years. We learned early on not to give them rice to eat. They liked to stuff food in their cheeks, and rice would swell up when it got wet; we had to dig it out of their overextended cheeks.

We had a horny toad, I think it was technically a horned lizard, but horny toad always sounded better. I don't recall that we gave him a name. He didn't do much, just sit in the sun and catch flies and eat the grasshoppers we gave him. He moved pretty slow, so he was easy to catch if he ever got loose.

Magpies

We had magpies in a cage next to the garden. We raised them from babies. It was a big area, probably 10' x 10'. We taught a few to say "hello." They were beautiful birds, but not all that social in my experience. We tried raising pet coyotes from tiny puppies, but they never became domesticated. They were always wild and always an inch from biting you. Sometimes, less than an inch. One of our "pet" coyotes bit my arm, and I carried the scars for many years. We eventually gave up on the idea of a pet coyote.

Dad with coyote pup

We picked up a baby burrowing owl somewhere. We called him "Hoot-Mon." We brought it home and asked Mom if we could keep it. Bless Mom's heart, she always said yes. He turned into a pretty decent pet. He would fly around our house and land on your shoulder, arm, or head wherever it felt like. That could be surprising to a guest who was not expecting an owl to suddenly land on their head and flex its talons as Hoot-Mon was prone to do. He was about 6" tall, and had an unusual ability to camouflage himself. He could land somewhere on a deer hide or a work shirt and ruffle his feathers and settle into it in a way that made him almost invisible.

Griswold's with Lee Ann Michale
and Faye Baby 1958

We had a pet deer that had been hit by a car. I remember her hanging in a sling in our living room for weeks or maybe months while her injuries healed. We called her Faline (from the Disney movie) or Faye Baby of course. By the time she was healthy enough to walk, she had bonded with humans in a way that meant that she could not survive in the wild. We kept her for a while, and she would follow us everywhere like a dog. I am not sure, but I think we gave her to the Medford Zoo.

In general, you are not allowed to keep wild animals, but because Dad worked for the Fish and Game, he was frequently in a position to rescue animals that would have otherwise starved to death. We only kept Faye Baby long enough to get her back on her feet.

Dad brought home and orphaned bear cub one time. He was relatively small, but he was still a very wild bear. There was no way to domesticate him and he eventually went to the Medford zoo as well. I think it was sooner rather than later in his case.

Tom and I were riding our bikes home from working one morning when we spotted several baby skunks playing in a field. We caught one and held him by the tail so he couldn't squirt. Mom said we could keep him, but there was one nonnegotiable condition. We had to get his scent glands removed so he didn't stink and couldn't squirt. We took him to the vet for the removal, but the vet declined. He said there was no way he would do that in his office. He was afraid he would never be able to get rid of the smell. He made us a deal. He gave us some ether, a scalpel and told us how to go about the removal.

We came home and took him to the barn for his surgery. Mom put her foot down hard on any in-kitchen operating room. Flower proved to be a friendly and loving pet. He liked to lay in your lap, or behind your shoulders. He loved climbing your pant leg, fortunately with his back to your leg, not his claws. After he had grown a bit older, being a male, he decided that every shoe was a potential mate and proceeded to act accordingly. We didn't tolerate that for long. Once again, we got out the ether and scalpel and this time extracted his manhood. He seemed to be fine, but he disappeared a few weeks later. We knew he had not died under the house. If he had, we would have surely smelled him. We assumed that his dignity had suffered too much and that he decided to revert to the wild.

Flower's disappearance remained a mystery for 50 years. We all went back to the Shasta Valley for a family reunion in 2012. We stopped by the Koppes Place; it had long ago burned to the ground. The only thing that remained was the old pump house. While we were there, we got to talk with a neighbor who still lived in the same house. She told us her dad had shot Flower when he caught him snooping around their house. He later figured out that he was our pet skunk, but he never told us.

I am sure we had other pets that I have forgotten. We never had any snakes, which was just as well as I have never been a fan of snakes. Cats were also absent from our house. Despite the fact that we lived in the country where there were both field mice and kangaroo rats, cats were not something that anybody ever seemed to want. We are all dog people.

— ■ —

On October 4, 1957, the Russians launched Sputnik, the first earth-orbiting satellite. That shocked the world; how could the Russians beat us to space? Sputnik initiated the space race that shaped much of our lives and public discourse for the next three decades. Sputnik got me suddenly interested in space. I remember starting high school the next fall, thinking that I wanted to become an astrophysicist. That dream quickly evaporated when I discovered that my math acumen wasn't anything close to what was needed.

Sputnik was tiny, about 2' across, and in a relatively low orbit. You could see it, or the sun shining off of it, as it passed overhead at night. The transit schedule appeared in the newspaper, and we talked about it at school. We would all go outside at night to watch to see if we could spot this awesome and somehow threatening thing up above our heads. It only lasted a few months as it dropped out of orbit and burned up January 4, 1958. None the less Sputnik was a pivotal event in our history.

— ■ —

Dad was a good teacher. He was not overt about the teaching process, I am not even sure he was aware that he was teaching, but it seemed he was always pushing me, and I think all of my siblings, to learn more. It was not about formal education. I don't remember either Mom or Dad ever even talking about my attending college. It was about turning every experience into a learning opportunity. I will always be grateful for this.

Many years later, after Mom had passed, I ask Dad about the lack of pressure or pushing for education. His response was simple. "you're the one we never worried about." I took this as a compliment, but I have occasionally wondered how their "worry" manifested itself vis-à-vis my siblings. Maybe they did treat them differently, but I was never conscious of it. Of course, maybe I was just too oblivious.

— ■ —

When we were hunting or just driving down a mountain road on the trap line, Dad would ask if I saw anything different on that hill or valley. My usual answer was "no." He would stop and teach me how to look and how to see things that were out of place. A color that was incorrect a shadow that looked wrong, any clue for some incongruity. After a while, I learned to see the leg of a deer showing from under a bush 200 yards across a valley. It was the one thing that didn't quite fit, the gray was the wrong hue, or there was a white streak where it didn't belong. You had to train both your eyes to see and your mind to process what you saw.

I grew up to be an incredibly good computer service technician for IBM, and I often credited Dad's observational teachings for my success. I could walk into a computer room full of moving tape drives, chattering disk drives, rattling printers, and blinking lights, and "see" what was out of place at the instant the red light popped up on the console of the computer. One particular tape had just moved, a disk drive was retracting its heads, or maybe a pattern was visible in the console lights. Whatever it was, Dad's long ago training would click in, and I could sense what was not right.

— ■ —

Dad was an excellent trapper. He worked differently from most trappers. Most would set a cluster of several traps hoping a coyote would wander into one of them. Dad thought about how the coyote would think, how they would approach an area, and most importantly, where they would stand to hike their leg to take a pee. Instead of setting a bunch of traps relying on blind luck, he would figure out just where the coyote would put his foot when he hiked his leg, and that was where he would set one trap. I understood Dad's genius, but for me, it was like "ok, so what's next?" The idea of just finding another place where another coyote would hike its leg was not going to float my boat.

— ■ —

I saw hints of Dad's own frustration at the smallness of the Shasta Valley and trapping. He talked at one time about immigrating to Australia and trapping Dingo's, which were devastating the sheep and cattle. I know he and Mom spent a fair amount of time investigating the possibilities, but it never worked out. For a time, he studied Television repair with the thought of opening a shop I suppose. For some reason, he never did follow through on that. After I left home, they bought some land and built their home. In his mid-50s they sold it and moved to Alaska to start a new adventure. While he wasn't in an educational or financial position to reach much higher, this searching continued for the rest of his life.

— ■ —

My parents were most definitely children of the Great Depression; they were both smart and wise, but they were not so much overt "teachers" as "doers." A lot of my learning was from example rather than "lessons." I don't recall all that many expressions or rules, but they did exist. It seems to me that the most powerful ones were unstated but clearly understood. They probably remained unstated because they never thought it necessary to put them into words. They were pretty direct about most everything, including discipline. I don't think either had heard of, much less read The Prince. A simple application of the razor strap was a graphic and immediate lesson of right vs. wrong, reward and punishment, no wasting time, no need to be subtle or clever, screw Machiavelli … whack … point made, discussions ended. I must say that I don't recall a single instance where the whack was unearned.

Oft-repeated verbal expression taught many lessons. The first that comes to mind is: "fool's names and fool's faces are often seen in public places." That applied to no-no's such as graffiti on the bathroom walls, but it had widespread applicability and subtle force. It discouraged any untoward seeking of advancement or recognition. It was their way of saying: "Just who the heck do you think you are?" or "you are getting too big for your britches." "Fool's names" was a convenient catchall smack-down. It is unquestionably applicable in today's' Facebook/Twitter/Instagram world. Unfortunately, it has apparently been forgotten. Not by me.

Another unstated "rule" that shaped much of my early life, and not always for the better, was: "to be a man you get a job, get married, and have kids." No one ever said anything about finding the right person to marry or waiting till you had a chance to figure out what life was about; they may have been implied, but I missed whatever subtly may have been present.

In looking back, it seems to me that much of our family's thinking was extracted from, or at least represented by the Reader's Digest. For years, I carried, both physically and mentally, one classic Reader's Digest Griswoldism that said: "It is better to be small and shine than to be great and cast a shadow." That one sentence epitomizes the Griswold ethos. Of course, no one bothered to point out that we all cast a shadow, nor did anyone say that you can be great and still shine.

Together these spoken and unspoken lessons went a long way to defining our lot in life: do your best, mind your place, and don't make waves. I am sure that part of this came from their childhood experience enduring the poverty of the Great Depression, but I think it is also very deep in our Scotch-Irish heritage. I thank God I was the last of the litter. By then our parents had either learned, or they were too tired to care. Most likely, they just assumed that the message was clear by that point. Whatever the reason, these isms were not quite as inculcated into my being. I was eventually able to slip out from under some of the most constraining ones. It did take time.

I remember looking at the hippies and finding myself unable to comprehend how or why they could live the way they did. The concept of an irresponsible, unaccountable, unproductive life was completely foreign to me; it still is, but at the same time, seeing them made me aware that my ethos was self-limiting. While I never considered following their path, the mere fact that they existed encouraged me to examine and ultimately alter at least some of my self-imposed limitations.

— ■ —

The world outside was beginning to touch my life. We grew up between, born during WWII; I was technically neither a child of the depression nor a post-war baby boomer; I benefitted and suffered from both, but in my case at least, fit with neither. It was an idyllic time; crime rates were low and families were strong. The valley we lived in was barely touched by the outside world, but it was beginning to leak in via a weak television signal from Redding. It bounced off the side of Mt. Shasta collecting an abundance of snow along the way. We had a "party-line" phone shared amongst eight households. At least one neighbor always listened in (yes there were "hackers" way back then), so the news spread quickly. There was no Internet, Google, mobile phones or text messages. The newsreels we saw were at least two months old. Yet somehow we survived.

— ■ —

Much of my character was formed by the time I finished elementary school. I learned a lot, but I don't remember the schools being the primary educators or shapers of my being or beliefs. It was more family and circumstance that were directing and shaping me.

I understood that I thought differently from my siblings as well as my family. All of us were smart, as were both of our parents, so it was not a matter of smart or stupid. It was more about where my mind was focused. The outdoors was a big part of our family's life. It was evident that for both Betty and Tom, it would be a significant part of their life going forward. While I loved the outdoors, I found it to be a bit too confining for my taste. It may sound strange to say that the outdoors was limiting, but for me, it was synonymous with "local," and I wanted a life that was much larger. I wanted to see the world, to travel and experience different things.

I was a loner then, and I still am. I was a fat, more accurately stated, I was obese, and fat kids were shunned by society back them. That certainly encouraged my tendency to prefer to be alone. I also learned fairly early that I could "read" people pretty well, and understand far more about them and their thinking than the words they spoke. Somewhere along the line, I learned that this knowledge was not always appreciated when shared with others; I learned to keep these observations to myself.

I liked to read; it was the only immediately available way to satiate my curiosity. I enjoyed reading about distant places and different ways of seeing the world. I don't remember if there were historical novels back then, if there were, I hadn't discovered them. I liked biographies and history books as they exposed me to unknown things.

I discovered Mahatma Gandhi. It was only a few years after his death and the freedom of India, so it may well have been something that I found in a Life magazine, on a newsreel, or some school assignment. Maybe it was a book a librarian recommended; I don't recall. I became passionate about learning of his life and his philosophy. I read everything about Gandhi that I could find I was deeply interested in how he was able to win India's freedom from British dominance, and how his methods compared to our own Country's struggle nearly 200 years earlier.

High School

In many ways, elementary school just blended into high school. The bus ride was longer, and there were far more kids, but it was still just school. I moved about the campus to go from class to class instead of sitting all day in a single room with a single teacher. My sisters had graduated and left home so it was just Tom and me. Otherwise, life was much the same. The days began and ended with chores. Spring weekends were spent helping Dad with his shearing, followed by field work, followed by full-time field work as soon as school was out. School somehow seemed secondary to work and chores. Growing up was just something that came along for the ride. It was a part of the process, but not the primary focus.

Yreka High School ~1960

Yreka Union High School was the largest school in the County. Yreka itself had less than 4,000 people, but they brought in students from the surrounding area, some so far away that they stayed in town during the week. The school itself had approximately 600 students. Our class had 128.

They had been in the process of building a new school for some time. The old school, which dated back at least 50 years, was already overcrowded and they saw a tidal wave of Baby Boomers close behind me. Most of the old school buildings had been condemned years earlier. Of course, that never stopped them from using them, even after the new buildings started to come online. The main building of the original school, the gym, and some other facilities remained in use well past my high school years.

As a result of the old and new, we had two campuses about two blocks apart. They had laid out the classes so that the upper-class courses were primarily in the new buildings. The gym and several of my classes were in the old buildings. As my schedule worked out, it seemed I had to crisscross the two campuses between each class. They extended the break between classes to accommodate these sprints, but there wasn't a lot of time to spare to go to your locker and get different books.

— ■ —

Exploding into puberty, we were all trying to figure out who we were. As in

100

all schools, there was a social "bell curve." The jocks, cheerleaders, and children of the rich …the "beautiful people," were of course at the top of the curve. The Indians, the Native American kind, were at the bottom of the curve. The rest of us, the unwashed masses, fell in between.

I was definitely on the lower end of the curve, only marginally above the Indians. I was fat. I was the son of a trapper and sheep shearer. I didn't have a car, I rode the bus, and I milked cows every morning before school. Lacking a shower, and with a limited wardrobe, my cologne of choice, or more accurately of necessity, was Eau de Barnyard. I wasn't into sports, and I liked reading more than socializing. I was poor, and I was country. Few of them knew it, but I even Square Danced. I was undeniably not cool. In truth, there were probably a number of Indians who were higher up the curve than me.

In 1972, when we returned for our 10-year reunion I found that the bulk of the unwashed masses had gone out and done something. Many of the men had served in the military, most in Viet Nam. Some had gone to college, and several had moved out of the Shasta Valley. Based on those present at the reunion, most had done something meaningful with their lives. The beautiful people, the highly envied at the top echelon of the bell curve, had almost all gone to college, many had not finished, and most had returned to Yreka to take meaningless jobs awaiting their parents' retirement or death when they would be able to take over the family business. One was driving a cement truck; another was stacking shelves at the local Safeway. Almost without exception, the least enviable people in the room were the formerly beautiful people. They were failing, simply because they never had to learn to succeed.

— ■ —

I was an average student in high school. Maybe slightly above average grade wise, but I was never seriously motivated to get better grades. I don't know why, probably boredom. It wasn't that the courses were too difficult, or even that I didn't have time to study. My study time was limited, but never seriously impacted by either work or chores. In most cases, my classes didn't seem relevant so I didn't put in the time that I could or should have.

There may well be a lesson here that the education industry, and it has become an industry. It is the equivalent of the old axiom: "when the only tool you have is a hammer; every problem looks like a nail." In the case of education, when the only acceptable outcome is college attendance, then every class is tailored, and students are measured against that goal. Unfortunately, that goal does not reflect reality. Not every student sees college as the next logical step in their life and for those students, a curriculum designed solely for that outcome lacks relevance.

Without exception, the teachers I admired, could relate to, and learn from, were the teacher who could associate their teaching to the real world. I liked the vocational classes, drafting, metal shop and auto shop best as they were obviously relevant, but these were typically teachers who had worked for some years before they decided that they wanted to become teachers. They understood the "real" world and could tie what they were teaching to how we would be living in a few short years. Conversely, the teachers that I struggled to understand were the ones who had gone from high school to college and then back to teach high school. They had no experience, and they were teaching what was often incorrect information written by others who were equally inexperienced and clueless.

Despite my frustrations with the quality and value of my classes, high school did, almost by accident, set my direction.

— ∎ —

When I reached my senior year, I had run out of classes that I wanted to take. I enrolled in Shorthand 1 and Art 1 for lack of anything better. Very shortly after the school year started, they set up a special experimental program called Work Experience Education Program (WEEP). The course was pretty insignificant; it didn't even make the Year Book, and the Year Book Committee was always scrounging for anything to fill out a few more pages. As I recall, there were 8 or 10 of us in the program. To get in, we had to have enough credits so that we could forfeit 2 class periods for WEEP, which was noncredit.

Mr. Warren Tormey, a former teacher, and local businessman was the program coordinator. We spent a couple of weeks taking tests designed to help us discover our "ideal career path." I think they were the State Employment Battery. They asked questions like "Would you rather: a) drown b) be shot in the head or c) be killed by your best friend with a stick?" Some choice; there was never a "none of the above" option. After a couple of weeks, we each received a few dozen IBM cards with various holes punched out to represent our skills, interests, and aptitudes. I am not sure how they could figure this out based on our death preferences, but someone apparently thought they could.

The object was to put all the cards in a stack and find places where the holes lined up allowing you to see through the entire stack. You then took the column and row number and looked up the corresponding career path. Most "careers" were gender specific and pretty typical for that era: secretaries and teachers for the girls, mechanics, and clerks for the guys. We had a few good laughs imagining ourselves in some of our "optimum" careers. We soon discovered that each of us, regardless of gender, had one thing in common; we were all "qualified for military service."

The WEEP program allowed us to work two hours each day at various jobs in town. We rotated every 6 or 7 weeks. Mr. Tormey drove us to and from work each day in his car. These trips gave him a chance to ask questions and provide feedback. He was teaching us, but we never thought of it as such.

My first "job" was at the Dentz machine shop on the south end of town. Mr. Dentz offered me an apprentice machinist position after I finished high school. I declined. Next, I worked as jailer's assistant. My supervisor was my girlfriend's father. Mainly I was taking meals to the inmates. I don't think that career was one of the holes in my IBM cards. These jobs only accelerated my desire to get out of town and to find a different job.

The last job changed my life. At the US Forest Service, they gave me a stack of green-and-white-striped computer printouts and sat me at a drafting table. They taught me how to use numbers from the printouts to plot points and create a topographic map. Once completed, I had to calculate how much dirt needed to be moved from ridges to valleys to build a logging road.

That was an aha moment; suddenly all those years of meaningless math classes had a purpose, and computers were the key! That lead me to the Air Force because they had the best computer schools and that lead me to IBM because they had the best computers.

Today computers are so ubiquitous that few could imagine a school or career that didn't include computers in some way, but in 1962 that was not the case. Computers were few and far between. They were enormous and mysterious, locked away in air cooled chambers where few could see or touch them. They used vacuum tubes not microchips, not even transistors. They didn't have operating systems; programs consisted of a stack of IBM cards that were complete in themselves. These computers didn't give exact answers; you ran important jobs three times and took the average answer. Believe it or not, we put men in space using these computers.

In 1962 computers were about the last thing someone in Yreka would ever consider for a career. I tried to explain what I was planning to do, but my parents, like most at that time, could not understand what computers were or how they could be useful. I think they thought it would pass.

Of course, it didn't, and over the years my children and others would ask how I got started in computers. My standard answer was "the Air Force," which is technically correct. As time passed, I began to examine and connect the earlier dots that led to the path that resulted in the career. It became clear that the pivotal event was the US Forest Service assignment and Mr. Tormey's WEEP class. Without that class, I may have never taken those first steps down the path that led to a lifetime of opportunity, travel, and experience that I, the son of a goat herder and trapper, could have never imagined.

I got into WEEP because it was a cool way to get out of a couple of classes and off the campus. I didn't consider it all that important or even begin to fathom what was taking place. I certainly didn't recognize the contribution Mr. Tormey was making to my life. He was not like any of my math or English teachers. Mr. Tormey never told us what to do or how we should think or do something. In fact, I never really thought of him as a "teacher"; he was a friend and adviser. He treated us like adults. I don't recall him ever raising his voice to anyone or directing us to do anything. There were many discussions but no tests; he just quietly led us to reach our conclusions. To me, the highest compliment I can pay him is to say that he was a mentor.

But I never told him. In 2011, when I started catching up with classmates, and thinking about our reunion I mentioned the WEEP class to Edna (Buker) Campau who was a good friend and also in the program. She asked if I had ever thanked Mr. Tormey …can someone please tell me why women always know how to recognize a guy's stupidity? Unfortunately, I had failed to do that.

I contacted his son Robert, who was also our classmate. I told him how his father had impacted my life. He said his father had passed away a year earlier at age 98. I know Robert appreciated my words, but his dad deserved to hear them himself. He had earned the honor of knowing how his work had changed my life. I sincerely regret my negligence.

All of the other classes and years run together. Nothing stands out as truly significant or meaningful. Gym class was a pain. If there had been an LAES (Last At Ever Sport) trophy, I would have most likely swept the title all four years. I was too fat, slow, and clumsy. I didn't even have the strength to be a good blocker on a football team. I understood early on that my path out of the valley was dependent upon my brain and not my brawn. Sports were not relevant, so I didn't feel like I was missing anything.

— ■ —

I did like to watch the football games and at least some of the basketball games. I don't remember attending any other sports events at our school. I suppose there were, but I wasn't really into games. I had "school spirit" in that I wanted our team to win, but that wasn't the reason I went. I think it was more the one opportunity that I had to feel like a carefree high school student. It was the only time when there was nothing to do, just relax and let life happen.

I did take a year of Spanish. It was my freshman year. Maybe I just wasn't quite ready or maybe I didn't have, or take the time to devote to learning what was a hard subject for me, but in any case, I barely made it through the class with a passing grade. I often tell people that they gave me a passing grade on the condition that I didn't try to take the second year of Spanish. That isn't entirely accurate, but it does reflect how I struggled in that class.

I have traveled a great deal and worked in foreign countries with people who often spoke little or no English. I have always found that I was able to communicate quite well, even if I didn't understand or speak their language. There are several reasons, patience being high on the list, but also watching and listening will help you understand much of what is said. Finally, non-verbal communications, facial expressions, hand motions, etc. are a major part of communications. These tend to be fairly universal and after you pick up on their meaning, understanding the gist of a conversation is not that difficult.

I find business communications are easier. Those discussions usually center around universal concepts: delivery times, price, quality, quantities, etc. Whenever the conversation drifts off to personal chatter, it is much harder to follow.

— ■ —

Work and chores went on. From moving sprinkler pipes at 11, I graduated to driving a tractor pulling a rake, and later to pulling a mower or a baler. By the time I had my driver's license at 15½, I was driving a grain truck, first alongside the harvester as it collected wheat, and then over to the grain elevators at Montague to unload. The truck had a detachable 5th wheel trailer. I would pull into the dump area at the grain elevator, and unhook the trailer. They had a crane that would lift the front end of the trailer and pour all of the grain out the tailgate. They would set it back down, and I would have to move the truck a little to reattach the 5th wheel. Once I had it hooked up and the tailgate re-secured, it was back to the field to get another load. We would work from 10 a.m. to 9 or 10 p.m. every day.

I only drove the truck for a couple of weeks. I switched to driving a D6 Caterpillar pulling the harvester; the money was better. There was a lot more dust as the Cat added its dust with a cloud of dust and wheat chaff created up by the harvester. I had to wear goggles to see, and a handkerchief to breath. By the end of the day, I was caked with dust and sweat.

A Caterpillar doesn't have a steering wheel or brakes. It had two poles that look kind of like an old-fashioned handbrake on a car, except that they were longer and vertical. One pole controlled each track. You pushed forward to move that track forward and pulled back to move it backward. The middle was neutral. To go straight you pushed both forward the same amount, to turn you could move one to neutral and the other forward. If you wanted to turn sharp, you did a push/pull, and the Cat would do a pirouette.

Pulling the harvester was a bit tricky because the harvester was off to the side, not straight behind the Cat. You had to keep the harvester aligned with the edge of the wheat. If the harvester were too far in, you would miss some wheat, too far out and you were wasting time and fuel. Cornering had to be gradual to keep the harvester aligned, but also not to cut too sharp and catch the hitch on the side track. The Cat provided a slow bone-jarring ride that was extremely noise. At the end of the day, you felt like you had earned your pay.

When I went to work for IBM a few years later, they tested my hearing. I remember the audiologist telling me I had "farm boy" ears. All those years of shooting guns and working around noisy machines undoubtedly took their toll.

– ■ –

Tom bought a 175cc motorcycle for transportation. As soon as I got my license, I ordered one as well. There weren't any motorcycle dealers in our area, so we ordered them from Sears. Believe it or not, Sears back then was much like Amazon today. They had a catalog that came out a couple of times each year. It was about 1½" thick. At one point you could even buy a kit house from Sears. They sold Puch Motorcycles from an Austrian manufacturer. When mine arrived, they had sent me a 250cc instead of the 175cc that I had ordered. Obviously, I was pleased with their upgrade.

After graduating, Tom worked for a while at the Fish and Game warehouse in Yreka before he joined the Navy. He rode his motorcycle to work each day. There was a neighbor dog that liked to chase him whenever he first got on Highway 99. Dogs that chased cars and bikes were a common thing. These were "ranch dogs" that spent the majority of their lives laying in the shade near the house. Chasing a passing car or bicycle was probably a welcome respite from an otherwise dreary day.

In the case or a car, the chase was dangerous for the dog as they could easily be run over. In the case of a bicycle, the danger was to the rider. A dog could startle the rider, bump a wheel, or more commonly could bite an ankle; any of which could easily result in a crash.

Necessity is called the mother of invention, so we developed our anti-dog weapon. In those days, gas stations had a bell to tell the attendant when someone drove up. The electronics was pretty simple. They had a ½" rubber tube across the drive. The tube had two wires on the inside. When a car drove over the tube, it would short out and ring the bell. These tubes were quite durable but still flexible.

Tom and I would get a piece of this tubing from the dump and cut a piece that was about 18" long. We would attach a leather lanyard to one end that we could loop around our wrist. We then slid the piece of tubing down inside of the bicycle's handlebar. Whenever a chase dog got close, we could draw our arm back in a quick sweeping motion, grabbing the tube as it came out of the handlebar. With a continuous downward swing, a well-aimed shot would slap the offending dog in the face.

It was low-tech but quite effective; you usually only had to smack a dog in the face one time to get him to back off. It didn't break them of the chasing habit, but those that insisted on chasing would keep their distance, and that was all that was required to be safe. More often, they would just stand at the roadside and bark. I don't think we were the actual inventors of this dog defender, but I have no idea who came up with the original idea.

Our weapon was necessary for bicycles where the dog could outrun the rider. For motorcycles, the solution was just to outrun the dog.

— ■ —

One afternoon we were both heading to Yreka and as we pulled onto Highway 99, Tom was maybe 50 or 75 feet in front of me. As usual, the offending dog came wheeling out of his driveway to go after Tom. He didn't see me coming. I saw him, but it was too late to swerve or stop, and I ran right over him. I think it was more of a side blow because he wasn't hurt and I didn't crash. He had already run back home by the time I got turned around. Tom said the dog never chased him again. I guess he didn't know what hit him but he didn't want seconds.

— ■ —

Motorcycles were rare in that area. As far as I can remember, we had the only two in the county. You never saw any on the highway like you do today. The cops loved to stop us for any reason. I think it was more a novelty than anything. I only got one ticket, and in all honesty, I didn't deserve that one. I stopped at a stop sign but didn't put my foot down. With the wide tires and a lot of years on a bicycle, it was relatively easy to balance for several seconds without falling over. The cop said I didn't stop. There wasn't a lot I could do; the fine was only $5. I suppose it is justice for all the times I could have gotten a ticket but didn't.

— ■ —

Today we hear a lot about "barn-finds," old cars that have sat around in some barn and warehouse unused and unnoticed for decades. Because Dad was out in the woods and wilderness all of the time, he used to come across old cars abandoned 30 or 40 years in the past. A lot of these cars were from the 1920s and often they only had a few hundred miles on the odometer. Dad told me that back in the 1920s the government had purchased the timber rights from the Native Americans in the area. Many would use the money to buy a new car. Usually a Ford Model A. They knew nothing about cars or driving. They would drive along until the car ran out of gas and not understanding why it stopped, they would simply walk away and leave it. "Easy come, easy go."

He would also find old barns and buildings from long-abandoned farms. Often these were back in the woods and trees had taken over the properties. I remember one old barn that had a 1930s vintage Ariel Square-Four motorcycle leaning against the wall. It looked like someone had just driven it into the barn and leaned it against the wall. No dents or bangs, just a lot of dust. The garage was way off of any road somewhere in the southern end of Scott's Valley. I never knew who owned the place, and I have no idea where it was after all these years. I do occasionally wonder if anyone ever recovered that old cycle. Restored, it would be worth a lot of money.

— ■ —

I was riding my cycle to work one morning on a dirt road. I heard a strange rattle and reached back to check if my lunch pail was slipping. It was, and so I glanced over my shoulder. That was a mistake. I allowed the wheel to get into the soft dirt at the side of the road and there was no way to get it to steer back onto the road. It just ran along the barbed wire fence ripping up my leg until I could get it stopped. I got off and shut the gas valve. The front fender was bent, and one rear strut was broken. I was standing there looking at it and swearing under my breath when I felt something wet on my ankle. I looked down and saw that my pant leg was half gone. It was like someone had taken scissors and cut down the middle front of the leg to the bottom seam, around to the back, leaving the seam intact, then back up to just below my pocket and back to the front. The cloth was completely gone, along with a good chunk of my leg.

Fortunately, the barbed wire had not quite reached the bone, and it had miraculously not cut any tendons. Close, but only flesh. I was in shock, and so it didn't hurt at all; the bleeding was not as bad as it could have been. I was more pissed at myself than anything. I walked a quarter mile to the nearest farm and called Dad. He and Tom came. Tom drove the cycle back home, and Dad took me to the hospital for stitches. I was stove up for a couple of days, then back on the cycle and back to work. I still have the scars.

That incident brought home the reality that these things could easily kill me. I always loved riding and continued until two years later when I came home on leave from Mississippi. I was headed to Idaho and knew that it was time to let my motorcycle days go. I sold it for nearly as much as I paid for it. I have ridden a few times since, but never really thought I wanted to buy another one.

With the motorcycle, I had more flexibility to take other jobs and multiple jobs. The summer between my junior and senior year, I worked for two different farmers and put in long hours. Come August; I went to the bank with two checks totaling more than $750. That was a lot of money back then. It would be many years before I again made that much in a month.

— ■ —

I didn't date much in high school. I was not what you might consider a catch for any girl. I had slimmed down, but I certainly hadn't gotten any "cooler." Dating was never really very comfortable because I didn't' have a car. That meant that the only option was to use Dad's work truck, which was usually either an International Scout or a Ford Bronco. It was always filled with traps and bait that smelled rather strong to use a polite word. Even washing the rig and cleaning it out, hardly made it into a "chick magnet." I had to find a pretty tolerant girl to put up with being taken out in either of those rigs.

In those days, "nice girls" would never get on a motorcycle. Even if they had wanted to, their fathers would have undoubtedly said no, so having "wheels" didn't increase my dating opportunities. I got turned down a lot. I knew that I would be moving on as soon as I graduated, so dating was not the primary focus of my life at that stage. I did have a girlfriend and we dated for some time during my senior year. She sent me a "Dear John" letter shortly after I headed off to Basic Training in the Air Force.

I was good friends with her sister and her fiancé, later husband, and I knew her folks quite well. I stopped to see her parents when I was in the area for our 10th reunion. Her parents, in particular, her dad, always liked me. I remember sitting on the front porch talking and having a drink. When her mother went inside, her father leaned forward and laughed quietly. He told me it was a good thing we broke up because his daughter was now "as big as a bus." I was married myself by that time. I just smiled. How was I supposed to respond to that?

— ■ —

My sisters had left for San Francisco right after they got out of high school. That was the same time I was graduating from Grenada Elementary. The Summer after my freshman year, I went to San Francisco to visit Barbara. Betty had moved up to the Redding area by that time. I don't remember how I got to and from San Francisco. It might have been by bus, but I don't think so. I think the folks drove one way and I rode the other way with Barbara.

I remember touring around San Francisco and Oakland with Barbara. We saw all of the tourist things, the Golden Gate Bridge, China Town, the San Francisco Zoo, and the Japanese Tea Garden. I also remember you could get a basket of prawns and French fries much like you get chicken strips today. That was quite a change as the only fast food place in Yreka was an A & W Root Beer stand on the south side of town.

At the Zoo, there was a big gorilla. The poor thing had a cage that was maybe 12' wide and 10' deep. Along the back wall was a "house" where he could go in and close a sliding metal door. The poor critter was bored out of his skull. He would go into his house and start banging on the steel door with the side of his clenched fist. Each blow would cause the door to slid down just a little. He would sit there bang, bang, bang, with the door gradually hiding him. As the door slid down it worked like a drum getting ever-louder; you could hear it all over the park. People would come to see what the racket was. They would get right up against the bars, which was a double cage with maybe a 6" gap between the inner and outer bars. When the crowd was all pressed in against each other, and the door was maybe a couple of inches from the bottom, he would slip his fingers under the door and slam it up with a terrific bang. At the same time, he would leap across the cage and hang himself on the inside bars with his face level with the gawking tourists. He would let out a mighty growl. Of course, all of this happened in a split second. It never failed. The crowd would scream and fall all over themselves trying to get back. He would walk around for a bit while the crowd gradually thinned; then he would go back inside and start all over again.

— ■ —

Hunting was a big part of Dad's life. He liked deer hunting but became interested in Elk hunting as well. Of course, there were no elk in California, so we applied for permits to hunt in Colorado. We got four or maybe five hunting permits; I don't remember exactly. Our cousin David Montgomery accompanied us, and we drove to south-central Colorado to hunt. Poncho, our dog, was with us as well.

Colorado elk hunt Poncho, Mom,
David Montgomery and Tim 1960

Three teenage boys plus a dog in one car got pretty gamey by the time we had been in the back seat a couple of days. We stopped at a campground in Western Colorado one night, and Mom insisted that we each take a bath in the river. It was October, and there was ice around the edges; Mom would not relent, so we bathed, but rather quickly.

Over the years, we made another trip to Colorado, and the folks made a trip to Idaho, all to hunt elk. They didn't get anything on the Idaho trip so, Dad, Tom and I took a quick trip a few weeks later for a second try. I don't remember if we shot anything, but I do remember that we were almost snowed in.

Our hunting was always for the meat. Of course, the antlers were nice trophies as well, but that was secondary to stocking our freezer. I was never much of a hunter. I am not opposed to hunting as long as it is primarily for the meat and not just to put a set of horns on your wall. In any case, it was never really something that I got excited about doing. After I left home, I never did hunt again.

112

I can't leave my Shasta Valley years, without talking a bit about the smells and sounds of life. In my travels, one of the things I often noticed was the smell that accompanies certain locations. Some are hard to describe or even remember, but others are easy to categorize. For example, the smell of kimchi seems to be everywhere in Korea. I mentioned the smell of the beehive wood burners and millponds at the saw mills in a previous chapter. Other scents remind me of my youth. The first would be the smell of freshly mown alfalfa. It has such a distinct smell that is nothing like any other crop. If I am driving down a highway and catch that scent, I instantly remember working in the fields.

Barnyards have a distinct smell, and it is not just the manure, well mostly, but not exclusively. There are a wide variety of animal smells that create a hodgepodge of odors. Individually, baby animals: puppies, lambs, and calves all have their distinct smells. Chickens and rabbits, cows and their milk. Hay has a musty smell. It all blends into an odor that becomes quite familiar. Going back now, I might well find the fragrance, while memorable, far less tolerable.

Different kinds of forests have different smells as well as different sounds. Pine trees have a very pleasant scent, and the sound of even a light wind across the trees is very relaxing. Nothing smells quite like juniper, either the trees or when the wood burns. Oak has a distinct musty smell. The Redwood forests always feel a bit damp and musty. The smell of fresh cut wood is also distinct as is the sound of the wind in different venues from open grassland to thick forests. It whispers, rattles, and whines, all depending on the vegetation. You learn all of these when you live amongst them. I doubt I would still be able to distinguish the difference after all these years away.

Of course, there is the smell of a thunderstorm and the first rain on a hot, dry summer's day. I think the smell is the ozone created by the lightning, but let's not get too technical. Once the rain stops, particularly if it is a short and sudden downpour, there is the musty smell from the wet ground. These are just a few of the many things my city-slicker friends missed.

— ■ —

By graduation, much of my core character was defined and established. I was disciplined and conditioned to always be aware of my surroundings. I was considerate of others and respectful of authority as well as my elders. I knew how to think. I was both curious and restless, and certainly not afraid of hard work. I had a career direction, and while I did not yet have a clear understanding of my path, I knew my next step. I was both capable and willing to take on challenges. All of these characteristics would serve me well throughout my life.

The last of the Innocents

In early June 1962, when we stood to receive our diplomas, the world was a quiet and peaceful place. The Korean War was a decade gone, and the biggest worry seemed to be the immoral impact of Rock and Roll. Our parents questioned whether our generation would survive this scourge.

We didn't know it, but we were standing at the juncture of two tectonic plates, one geopolitical, and one social, and they were already starting to shift. Viet Nam, a tiny spec of land half a world away, was the home of a decades-old conflict simmering but still invisible. A war that would take half a hundred thousand lives, devastate a huge piece of my generation, and forever reshape how our citizens viewed war. It would begin in earnest, just two years in the future. In fact, like undetected cancer, it had been quietly churning along for nearly a decade.

We had worried about "the bomb," a nuclear attack had seemed a real possibility since the early 1950s. What we didn't know was at that very moment, Russia was busily installing missiles in Cuba, just 90 miles from our shore. In just four short months the Cuban Missile Crisis would bring us to the brink of thermonuclear war, closer than at any moment in history.

The Civil Rights movement was also nearing a tipping point. It had been centuries in the making, but it had officially begun eight years earlier with the landmark Brown vs. The Board of Education decision. There had been many milestones since, including the Rosa Parks' initiated bus boycott of 1955. In June of 1962, unbeknownst to us, it was about to burst onto the national scene with the forced integration of Ole Miss just three months in our future.

Tim Graduation 1962

Society itself was changing. Our graduation marked the end of one generation and the beginning of another. Those that followed would forever be known as Baby Boomers. They created a tidal wave of hippies and war protestors that would soon change the political landscape, culminating in Woodstock just six years on. These long-haired miscreants would forever alter the world with their lifestyle built around sex-drugs-and-rock-and-roll.

The suffrage movement, which had brought women the right to vote just 40 years earlier was about to spawn a second social transformation that is often called Women's Liberation or Feminism. The goal was to free women from oppression and male supremacy.

As we stood to celebrated our own liberation that early June day in 1962, we had no inkling of any of these major geopolitical and social issues that would soon wash over our generation. We were truly the last of the innocents.

Looking back, I mourn the loss of innocence. Growing up in the Shasta Valley at that time, we were free to roam, to explore, to take chances, swim in the irrigation ditches, hunt coon in the middle of the night, spear a few frogs, to learn, and to grow up. We could be gone all day or even all night, and no one would ever worry. Today we always worry about where our kids are, about drugs, crime, and everything else. Where is there space for kids to be kids, to make mistakes, to learn, and to grow up?

U.S. Air Force Period 1962 – 1967

We spent the summer of 1954 in the Six Rivers National Forrest campground near Gasquet. While there, I was fascinated to discover an unusual carnivorous plant the Darlingtonia Californica. It is also called a cobra lily because of its resemblance to a cobra about to strike. The flower uses its beauty and fragrance to attract insects. The insect must crawl through a small hole to reach the nectar. Once inside they are trapped as the lily carefully hides the tiny exit hole by curling it underneath and offering multiple translucent false exits. Inside, the walls of the flower are covered by a lubricating secretion and downward-pointing hairs. The insect exhausts itself trying to leave via the fake doors. Eventually, it would tire. The slippery walls and hairs force the prey downward preventing its escape.

I came to see the Shasta Valley as similar. It is beautiful, tranquil and inviting. It appears safe and protected, an escape from the hassle and hubbub of city life, but it was also a trap. It is restrictive and confining, but there is a price to be paid for the beauty and safety. The price was more than I was willing to pay. Escape is not easy, but I desperately wanted out of the small world of my youth. I wanted to do something, to see the world.

My decision was not a spur-of-the-moment thing. I had decided early in my high school years to join the military as soon as I graduated. My sister Barbara was attending Chico State College, now California State University, at Chico, but for me, the idea of spending more years sitting at a desk listening to teachers, who, in my estimation were pretty clueless as to how the world worked, was not a path I wished to follow.

I wasn't opposed to more education, in fact, I wanted, and will continue to learn as long as I live. However, I wanted it to be both practical and applied learning as opposed to the abstract and often impractical education from teachers who had knowledge, but lacked wisdom or experience beyond their classroom studies. As you will read in the part about my ITT years, while I returned to traditional education institutions to obtain a Bachelors' and later a Master's Degree, I never returned to the actual classroom. For business, I needed the credentials, but as far as I was concerned, there was little to be gained from attending classes; I chose a different approach.

From the outset, I eliminated the Army and Marines as they could not lead me in the direction I wished to go. I never considered the Coast Guard. I don't think I was even aware that it existed. I saw my options as either the Navy or the Air Force. The Navy appeared, at least in theory, to offer a better opportunity to see the world, but I felt that spending months looking out a round window at a lot of water so that I could spend 24 hours on shore leave in a foreign port was not my idea seeing the world. I know that they don't have windows, but that fact only made it worse. If you weren't on the deck, you were spending your life inside a can. The Air Force, with bases all over the world, seemed like a better option. Maybe I wouldn't get to as many places, but when I went, I would spend enough time to get to know a bit about the country. My intention was to make a career of the military. I later abandoned that dream; we will get to that in a bit.

For me, the biggest draw was the educational opportunity. My naïve analysis at the time led me to conclude that the Air Force had better technology training than the Navy. Ultimately, I focused on computers, but initially I was just looking at the broad sweep of "technology," which I am not sure I could have defined at that time.

The Navy may well have had equal tech opportunities, but they focused on ships, and the Air Force focused on airplanes. That clinched it. I always have, continuing to this day, been both fascinated and in awe of airplanes and anything that flies. Think about it, a chunk of wood will float almost indefinitely. How can you not be awestruck by an agglomeration of aluminum, motors, and computers that can weigh a 1 million pounds, lifting off from Hong Kong, climbing to a height of 4 or 5 miles, fly for 8,000 miles, and then land in Chicago 16-hours later?

Leaving Home

We lived in the country on an old dryland ranch in the northernmost part of California. We were about 40 miles south of the Oregon Border and about 12 miles south of Yreka. There were not a lot of events, exciting or otherwise that took place in Siskiyou County. The only thing that I can remember was the annual County Fair held in August of each year. For me, the Fair was about as exciting as watching cows graze.

In my eyes, everything happening in the world was taking place somewhere else. I read a lot, but the things I learned didn't touch my life. For me the most exciting event was my leaving home to join the Air Force. I had planned to take this step for years. I could not wait; I was only 17½ and 2-weeks out of high school when I joined. I think that I slipped in about a month earlier than I was supposed to. If I remember, the rules were that I had to be 17.5 years of age. In fact, I was a month short of that when I enlisted.

Leaving home had nothing to do with my family, we got along fine, it was just that it was time. My siblings had all completed high school and left home; it was now my turn. I think my folks were as happy to see me go as I was to go. In any case, there was no resistance, in fact, not even any comment regarding my plan. They could finally have their life after nearly 25 years of raising kids. Early one morning I had Dad drive me to Weed, a town about 15 miles south of our house, so that I could catch the Greyhound bus to Redding, the closest Air Force recruiting office. He handed me a $20 bill and told me to take care of myself. Short and straightforward.

I got to Redding, and someone from the Air Force met me at the bus station. After the testing and signing a lot of papers, we all rode the Greyhound to Oakland where we checked into a hotel for the night. The next day we were taken to the San Francisco airport, and along with other recruits, we flew to Los Angeles, and then to San Antonio. We probably stopped in Dallas for a plane change, but I don't remember that.

It may be difficult for anyone today to comprehend, but here are a few relevant facts about my "worldliness," or more accurately my lack of worldliness. Of course, I had camped out, shot a lot of rifles and pistols, and done some hunting and fishing. I had traveled by car to several states, something that many of my classmates had not done. I had worked in the fields since I was 11 and assisted Dad in his work trapping and shearing sheep since I don't know when. We rented a house on a ranch, so there were always chores: milking the cow, feeding all the animals: dogs, rabbits, chickens, pigs, turkeys, and calves. The mix and quantities changed from time to time, splitting wood and bringing it to the house, etc., etc., etc. Work was part of my life as far back as I can remember.

At 15½ I bought a motorcycle. I had a reliable income working on farms in the area, and more freedoms than my elder siblings. By the time I grew up, I think that the folks had realized that the odds were good that we would survive our stupidity.

Tim's motorcycle 1963

I was always a loner, and pretty independent, but I was unquestionably overly confident given how naïve I was to the ways of the world. Until I left home, I had never eaten in a restaurant, never slept in a hotel or motel, and never been on an airplane, or a train. I had not even been on a bus other than a school bus. Believe it or not, I had never even sat in a barber's chair; Mom had always given me haircuts. Leaving home changed all of that instantly. Other than riding on a train, I did all of those things within the first 72 hours.

Getting the training I wanted

I knew that I wanted to learn computers and radar if it were possible to do both. I was not able to figure out which path would fulfill my desire. Remember this was long before the Internet and so research was both painstaking and very limited. I gave up trying to break it down and decided that what I would specifically look for was the longest electronics oriented training the Air Force offered. I assumed the "longest" had the greatest possibility of covering the broadest array of equipment.

The recruiting posters said that you could "choose your specialty." In military speak, it is called your MOS (Military Occupational Specialty). Each MOS had a training path, so choosing your MOS controlled your training, and your training dictated you career. Of course, it was impossible, with the limited information available in Yreka, to find anything that broke down any of this. It also turned out that there was a bit of a lottery involved in the MOS selection process.

When I enlisted, I took a rather lengthy set of aptitude and intelligence tests covering a lot of different subjects. You took the test before signing the enlistment papers. I think they wanted to know if you were able to rub two sticks together before they let you join. Of course, that is just a guess. Your scores on those tests determined your place in the MOS selection queue. I scored highest that day, so I got to choose first. You listed the 3 MOSs you preferred. I had no idea which MOS lead to which training so I ask a recruiter which would provide the longest training in computers and or radar. Fortunately, and unlike some of the horror stories I have heard about recruiters, this guy was honest. He gave me three numbers to enter.

I assume all of the recruits for a particular period were pooled and their requests were then matched against the demand for people in various MOSs, but here again, I will never know. I will also never know if the MOS where I eventually landed, was one that I entered. There was far too much going on at that point for me to keep track of such details.

Basic Training

Air Force Basic Training was kind of like Boy Scout training amplified only slightly. Much of it was pretty routine for me. You got up early, you did PT (Physical Training), marched a lot and attended classes. There were all the standard things like classroom studies, shooting, only M1 rifles as I recall, obstacle courses, a couple of night marches, but nothing too outrageous, not even too strenuous. For me, the only real challenge was doing the proper number of pushups. As I said earlier, I have never had much in the way of upper arm strength, and pushups were a challenge even when I was in the best of shape. Basic was a lot tougher on the "city kids."

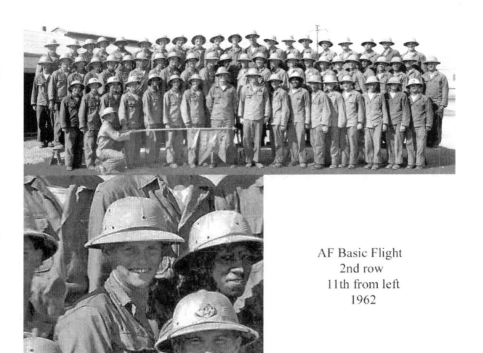

AF Basic Flight
2nd row
11th from left
1962

We had one Indian, a Navaho kid from Arizona. We called him Chief of course. He was as nice a guy as you can imagine, but he was completely out of shape; pudgy and soft. Everyone in the squad tried to help Chief pass the physical tests. We would work with him on sit-ups and pushups. We would try to get him to exercise, but in the end, they busted him out of the service as he was unable to do any pushups and not enough sit-ups.

Of course, not everyone in the "flight" as it was called, were "kids." I was only 17½, and there were a couple of others my age. Most were at least 18, or 19, and a few were in their early 20s. Those from the cities had no idea what was coming their way. Rising at 3:30 a.m. was pretty much what I was used to; it was a real shock to city dwellers.

One of the first lessons I learned was "don't stand out." We arrived at San Antonio airport at about 10 p.m. There were a bunch of new recruits from all over. They gathered us up and put on blue AF buses headed to Lackland Air Force Base. When we arrived, they split us into groups of 45 or 50, and our TI (Training Instructor) was waiting for us. He asked, or maybe I should say he yelled questions like who had been in ROTC or an Eagle Scout. They became our "Squad Leaders," a blessing from the nether world as it turned out. They were supposed to get everyone to do what the TI wanted, but they were as clueless as the rest of us. They often were on the receiving end of the wrath that people felt toward the TI but dared not express.

We marched, a term I use very loosely, to our barracks. 3:30 came almost instantly; very early, and thunderous. The barracks were WWII era 2-story wooden structures. No air conditioning, only big noisy fans at both ends. They were firetraps, to put it mildly. The TI lived in the barracks for the first 2-3 weeks. That was to make sure we were sufficiently aware of the rules, and it gave the squad leaders time to learn what to do in an emergency.

We arrived early on a Saturday morning. Regular airmen and civilians didn't work weekends, but of course, weekends were just part of Basic Training, just two more days of the week. The absence of any support personnel meant that we were not issued our uniforms until the following Tuesday in our case. We had all assumed, or been told by our recruiters, that we would be issued uniforms immediately, and that there would be no place for our "civilian" clothes, so most of us had arrived with nothing much more than the clothes we were wearing.

Late June in San Antonio is sweltering. I wore a pair of loafers with spongy soles. The pavement was so hot the soles had melted by Tuesday. I was pretty much marching on my bare feet. I wore a couple of pair of socks, but the soles of my feet blistered from the heat and the marching. We were a rag-tag looking group in all kinds of civilian clothes struggling to get everyone on the same foot at the same time. We were also a pretty smelly group by the time we got our uniforms and toiletries. And yes, there was one guy who brought his golf clubs. I can only imagine what his recruiter had told him.

"Lights out" was at 9 p.m. There was supposed to be no talking after lights out, and usually that was the case as we were exhausted by the time we turned in. Lights were on at 3:30 a.m., but that turned out to be another fiction. We were supposed to get up, dress, brush our teeth, and do whatever else was needed, then be in formation at 3:45. Our "area" (bed, footlocker, etc.) was supposed to be ready for inspection when we left the barracks.

You have undoubtedly heard about bedding so tight you could bounce a quarter off the covers. That was in fact, part of the requirement. Footlocker inspection required that every item inside the footlocker had to be correctly placed, and properly prepared. Razors were to be clean and dry. Toothbrushes spotless and all properly laid out. Underwear and socks had to be rolled and tucked into themselves so that the sergeant could bounce them off the wall without them coming unrolled. Believe me, they tried. The fact that I didn't need to shave was a significant advantage; it saved time and my razor was always perfect.

The floors, the bathroom, and the showers had to be spotless as well, dry like nobody lived there. Needless to say, it was impossible to do all of this in 15 minutes. We needed more time. The solution was obvious. It was boiling with no air conditioning. We chose to sleep on the tile floor with just a towel under us. That kept the floor shiny, and it was cooler than sleeping on the bed. It had other benefits. You didn't mess up your bed, so you only had to stretch the blankets to make sure they were tight. That was easier from under the bed. I could just reach up through the wire mesh and pull the blanket edges. You could easily do this in the dark before "lights on." We all became quite adept at brushing our teeth, making sure our area was in order and getting dressed, quietly, with nothing more than the light from the "Exit" signs. Shoes were the very last thing because you wanted to protect the shine on the floor. Walking in our socks helped. Life in the dark of night quickly took on order.

Discipline and order, especially following orders, didn't come naturally to a lot of the guys. Guys like me who came from the farm and those who had been in sports were accustomed to the rigors of basic training. Those who had lived like regular "civilians" had a steep learning curve. The TIs were accustomed to this and instantly identified those who needed to be blessed with the TI's attention. For the rest of us, it was simply a matter of staying out of the line of fire. Don't draw attention, just do what you are told when you are told. In many ways, Basic Training was an adventure. Of course, it would have been much different had I been on the receiving end of the TI's attention.

We ran a lot of fire and gas drills to make sure we could get out of the building safely. I am not sure why we needed gas drills as there was no gas in the building, but it had the added advantage of requiring us to leave the building with the lights off. The first person to the light switch was supposed to cover it with his hand and stay there until everyone was out. I was upstairs, and as you can imagine, on more than one occasion, bodies were piled at the foot of the stairs. There were also times when someone would forget to cover the switch resulting in a "lights-on," and a theoretical explosion. Of course, we would have to repeat the exercise, usually after about 30 minutes so that many were back asleep at the start of the next drill. I don't remember precisely, but I think we were required to empty the building in 90 seconds. We all had to assemble in formation across the street in that time. There were ample opportunities to fail and of course any failure lead to yet another drill.

— ■ —

There were several incidents of interest after the TI had stopped sleeping in the barracks. One recruit was from New York and was supposedly a nightclub singer. He was always bragging about how he had performed here or there. Of course, none of us could argue with him. One night after we had been there a while, people pressed him to sing for us. He sounded decent, but we were supposed to be quiet, so his singing pissed off the night duty officer. That earned us 18 fire and gas drills over the next few hours. It was impossible to get any rest, and there was always a reason we failed the test so we knew another one would follow. Sometimes they would be immediate, sometimes spaced out twenty or thirty minutes. We tried just sitting on the floor ready to run when the alarm sounded. He caught on quickly and sent guards in to make sure we were actually in bed with our shoes on the floor. Just for kicks, he told us we failed the last drill, and so we returned to our barracks thinking one more would follow. Everyone was exhausted, and we laid there half asleep and half awake, waiting for the bell that never came.

Come 3 a.m., we had to pay the price for actually having slept in our beds; they had to be made up ready for inspection when we fell out at 3:45 a.m. Needless to say, there was no more singing after lights-out, but on the plus side, we didn't have any more fire or gas drills through the rest of Basic training. Over the years I have heard others tell similar stories, so I think the singing was just a convenient excuse to administer a night of torture.

— ■ —

On one Saturday night after an unusually long day of marching, one airman started complaining that he was very ill. He lay in bed moaning and begging for a doctor. The squad leader notified the Duty Officer, he called an ambulance. We learned the whole story later.

When he got to the base hospital, a doctor was called in from home. When the doctor arrived, he leaned over the bed and asked: "Son, what's the problem?" The airman replied, "Doc, you got to help me, my feet are killing me." They busted him out of the Service shortly after that incident.

We also had the "queer" barracks in our squadron. That was the barracks where they placed people scheduled for discharge. The upper floor was reserved specifically for gays who were not allowed to serve at that time. The lower floor was for everyone else, guys like my Navaho friend and the sore foot guy for example. People who were living in the barracks waiting for discharge paperwork were not considered "airmen" and therefore security and safety guards had to be posted to make sure there were no fires. Guards came from different flights in the squadron. You had to stand guard for a 4-hour shift.

I did one shift, and it was one too many. The rules were that you were not, under any circumstances, to go upstairs alone. An armed Duty Officer would come every 2 hours. Together you would do a safety and security check upstairs as well as downstairs. Upstairs was not a pretty sight, and not something a naïve 17-year old should have had to witness. It took a lot of years before I could wash that out my mind's eye.

— ■ —

One of the official rules was that PT (Physical Training) be suspended if the temperature was over 90°. There was a red flag at the corner of the field to let the TI know. Of course, this was South Texas in the heart of summer; the Heat Flag never came down day or night in all the time I was there. But what would basic training be without PT and marching? The solution was to do PT before the sun came up. I suppose that was at least part the reason we had to be up and out by 3:45 a.m., but if not for the heat, I am sure they would have found another reason.

— ■ —

As I said earlier, the secret to success, or at least to minimizing harassment, was to avoid standing out. Flights were organized by height with the tallest in front. You didn't want to be the tallest or the shortest as this made you a target of opportunity for the TI at all times.

When we marched on the streets, which was all the time, there were two "road-guards" in front and two in back. The front guards' job was to run ahead and block traffic at cross streets as we marched through. At that point, the rear guards would double-time to the front of the flight. Of course, after we had passed the guards that were out had to run back to the rear of the flight and get back in sync at the proper distance. These poor souls were constantly harangued for not being fast enough, not yelling loud enough, not in the right position, failing to synchronize quickly, or just because.

One of our road-guards was a tiny black kid. He must have had to stand on his toes to reach the 5' 2" height minimum. Not only was he short, his voice was also high and squeaky. The road guards had to shout something; I don't recall what it was, at each cross street. I am sure the TI chose him because of his squeaky voice. It gave the TI endless opportunity to harangue him. That came to a head one day at the mess hall. Some might call it a "dining hall," but the military always called them "mess halls." I am not sure of the reason. Maybe it was because the word "dining" elevated the nature of the process far above what was warranted. Of course, it possibly referred to what they shoveled on your tray …a mess. As we entered, we had to "sound-off" with our number. It started with "one sir," "two sir" and proceeded from there. Our diminutive road-guard was number 38. When he squeaked out "38 sir" our TI lit into him, calling him a girl and several other names. He made the poor kid stand aside and continue to scream "38 sir" as everyone passed. By the time everyone had entered the mess hall, the poor kid's voice was completely shot. You could barely hear him. As I said, anonymity was safer.

— ■ —

You need to understand that the purpose of basic training in any military unit is to remove as much of your personality as possible and to replace it with what and how the military wants you to think, believe, and act. There are varying degrees of this process; you might call it brainwashing, depending on the branch of the service. The Air Force probably being the least, and the Marines the most severe. The Marines are often called "jarheads." The nicer version holds that this refers to the style of haircut. However, it is inconceivable that a bunch of marines would relate to each other based on the style of their haircuts. The derogatory definition, which is much more likely to reflect the origination of the term, is derived from the process of unscrewing the top of their heads, emptying out everything, and replacing it with a Marine brain. Kind of like refilling a jar. Incidentally, to a fellow Marine Jarhead is a term of honor, but some take it as a sign of disrespect from someone other than a Marine. So don't go calling a Marine a Jarhead unless you can run very fast.

This reshaping of the individual is the nature of military service the world over, and it is critical as it trains the individual to follow orders, think and function as a team. In war, that can be the difference between life and death, not only for you but those around you.

127

Before you go think "oh that is terrible," consider the actual purpose of all education, but college education in particular. Is it not the case that the sole purpose of college is to change the way you see and react to the world? Is it not their desire to warp your mind to their version and world view? I might point out that by comparison, colleges are very inefficient. The military can accomplish in 3 months what a college takes four years to achieve. Also, the military produces a much higher quality brain and citizen than most colleges today.

— ■ —

Parades were yet another reason to march in the sun. Several flights were graduating each week, and so there was a ceremony every Saturday. It was a great opportunity to get everyone dressed up and out marching. The graduation ceremonies were held on the flight line where there was lots of concrete to march and stand on. Of course, there had to be speeches, endless, meaningless speeches, by people who apparently had nothing better to do with their lives. I suppose the speakers thought they were imparting some wisdom on these young, malleable minds. However, for those of us standing on hot concrete, the speeches were just so much blah-blah-blah. Each week these things filled up several hours.

All the time they were blah-blahing, we had to stand in formation at "parade rest." Parade rest is a formal position in which you remain silent and motionless with your left foot 12" to the left of your right foot and with your weight resting equally on both feet. Your hands were clasped behind your back with the palms to the rear. No scratching of the nose, no matter how much it itched; no wiping away the sweat that was streaming down your forehead, into your eyes, and dripping off of the end of your nose. You stood still dressed in your blues; that is a blue suit complete with tie and jacket, as opposed to our usual green fatigues. Of course, a tie and jacket, along with the hot sun make it even hotter than usual.

One lesson you learned quickly was that when standing at parade rest in the sun at 110° or more, you never locked your knees. Locking your knees restricts the blood flow and in the heat, if you did, you would soon pass out. Those who made that mistake were easy to identify, they would naturally fall forward hitting the concrete face first, usually breaking at least their nose. The sound of an unconscious body hitting concrete gives a very distinct and unpleasant "thud." You were not to move or look around even if it was the guy next to you. The medical teams always had work to do at the Saturday

128

parades.

— ■ —

The time passed quite quickly. There was little time to think or even to mark the days. Mail call was daily during the week, with letters and occasional "care packages" of candy and cookies from family. In those days, there was no FedEx, Priority Mail, bubble wrap or Styrofoam peanuts, so cookies were usually dried out and reduced to small chunks and crumbs by the time they arrived. They were so bad I sometimes wondered if the guys in the mail room were using the boxes as footballs before they sent them along. None the less, the packages were welcomed. We would all gather around and consume whatever arrived, as there was no place in our areas to keep anything like food.

A high percentage, myself included, got "Dear John" letters from their girl back home. It got to some of the guys, but others were running a "pool" betting on who would get the next one.

Right at the end of Basic, we did get one Saturday off with a pass to go into San Antonio. Most headed to the bars. A few of us went sightseeing; the Alamo and the River-Walk were the most interesting. I think there were only four of us that made that choice. There were some sore heads come 3:30 a.m. Sunday, and a lot of barfing during PT.

Keesler AFB

We transferred to Kessler before the completion of Basic training. As I recall, we had completed eight weeks at Lackland, with another four weeks at Keesler. At Keesler, we did part time Basic and part time KP (Kitchen Patrol). Those who were completing their Basic training provided the weekday KP at all of the mess halls. The students on the base provided weekend KP. As I remember, we had to do 2-weeks of KP during the 4-week basic training extension. Completion of Basic Training brought a promotion to Airman Third Class, one lonely stripe on each sleeve. I am not sure that this looked any better than a bare sleeve.

At Keesler AFB 1963

The trip was a long bus ride from San Antonio, Texas to Biloxi, Mississippi. Thank heavens it was on a chartered Greyhound and not a hot, noisy old blue Air Force bus. Biloxi is right on the Gulf Coast about 90 miles east of New

Orleans. I moved from scorching San Antonio, to sweltering Biloxi. I also transferred from the South to the Deep South; that came as a shock. 1962 was the tipping point for the Civil Rights Movement. Prior to 1962, it was in the very early stages and not yet visible outside of the Deep South where segregation and Jim Crow Laws were very real. Not on base, there everything was integrated, but once you left the confines of the base, you immediately knew that you were in the South. Drinking fountains were marked for "White" or "Colored." We were nearly 100 years past the Civil War, but it was still very visible in the civilian parts of the South. In the community theaters, the "colored" section was the balcony. They played Dixie before the movie, and everyone stood with their hands over their heart. I had a black roommate, and we were good friends, but off base, we could not associate with each other.

There was a good deal of racial tension in the civilian community. The Ole Miss riot began September 29, 1962. That was only a few weeks after I reached Keesler. It was the result of the forced (by the Federal Government) integration of the University of Mississippi, known affectionately as Ole Miss, at Oxford, Mississippi. Segregationists were protesting the enrollment of James Meredith, a black US military veteran. Two civilians died during the first night. One was a French journalist. Nearly 70 people were wounded. By the end of the conflict one-third of the US Marshals assigned to the campus were injured. From that point forward, segregation was no longer a secret known only to southerners.

— ■ —

The Cuban Missile Crisis began just two weeks later, on October 16, 1962. Keesler had a couple of runways, but its primary mission was as the center for electronics training for the Air Force. Normally, there was little air traffic and very few airplanes. When the Missile Crisis started, there were suddenly dozens of planes and lots of traffic. They all disappeared a couple of weeks later when the Crisis we resolved. That period was very intense, as it looked like we were about to enter into World War III.

For the benefit of those who didn't live through the Missile Crisis, or for those of you who may have missed it in your history classes, it is worth spending a couple of minutes understanding just how close we came to WWIII at that point.

C47 from my barracks window
at Keesler AFB Mississippi 1962

The Cuban Missile Crisis began when an American U2 spy plane took pictures of Russian missiles being installed on the Island of Cuba. President Kennedy responded to the discovery by quarantining Cuba with a naval blockade. He also threatened air strikes and even an invasion. Soviet Primer Nikita Khrushchev's initial response was provocative, and as Russian cargo ships approached the naval blockade tensions were extremely high. Ultimately, Khrushchev backed down, turned his ships around, and agreed to remove the missiles. The crisis ran from the 16th through the 29th of October, 1962. For those 13 days, we were quite literally a hair's breath away from nuclear war. Incidentally, my brother Tom was in the Navy, and he was on a ship that was part of the blockade.

Keesler is on the Mississippi Gulf Coast, only six hundred miles from Cuba. It was within easy striking range for US aircraft, but also for Cuban/Russian aircraft. Keesler quickly became a staging area for what was nearly a war. The base was on high alert and locked down. We heard little through most of the crisis, but the TV news was available, and no one could stop the rumors. The rapid buildup made it all the more ominous. We were all very aware of the potential for nuclear war.

It turned out that in addition to electronics training, Keesler was in the business of training the Vietnamese Air Force using old WWII fighter bombers. We saw these men frequently. They wore green fatigues or flight suits with no rank or insignia showing their country of origin. They were tiny little guys with very high voices, and they usually held hands while walking. You can imagine what most of us assumed. None of us knew anything about Viet Nam. We had never heard of the place. We were not yet officially in the war, so it was not in the news. I doubt that any of us would have been able to find Viet Nam on a map.

— ∎ —

A funny thing happened somewhere in the middle of my basic electronics training. They asked if I wanted to study Chinese. The assignment was in Turkey. The job was classified, but I already had my Top Secret Clearance. It was pretty obvious that my job would be listening to, and translating Chinese radio traffic. I declined. In part because I enjoyed electronics, and in part because I knew that learning foreign languages was not a skill I had or was ever able to develop. The irony is that forty-five years later I married a Chinese wife. Speaking the language would have been a plus.

— ∎ —

I received the Outstanding Student Award for the Basic Electronics training, which ended just in time so that I was able to travel home on leave at Christmas. With my salary, $28/month, there was little opportunity to build up enough to pay round trip airfare. The good news was I did have enough for a ticket on Greyhound. I think it was less than $50. Can you imagine traveling from Mississippi to extreme northern California and then back to Mississippi, a 5,000-mile trip, for less than $50? The bus ride was 72-hours each way, so that consumed a total of 6 days out of my 14-day leave.

My classes were from 4 p.m. to Midnight. A classmate named Cliff Roberts lived in San Francisco. He and I caught the westbound Greyhound out of Biloxi at about 2 a.m. Fortunately, it wasn't crowded, and we were both able to find empty seats where we could get some sleep. This December night was dark and foggy, which is common along the Gulf Coast. We had traveled only a few miles to Pass Christian, MS when a beer truck with no tail lights pulled out in front of us. We were traveling at 50 or 60 mph when we hit. The bus driver and the passenger in the right front seat died in the crash. Fortunately, no one else was severely injured. The accident crushed the front exit and the throttle jammed so the engines were running away. Roberts and I climbed out

133

a window. He headed back down the highway to stop traffic while I was able to kill the engines.

After about an hour Greyhound sent another bus to take the passengers to New Orleans. We were asked to give statements, but we didn't have much to offer as we were both asleep at the time the accident occurred. They offered a medical checkup, but we both declined. All I had was a cut on the side of one shoe. We both felt the most important thing was to get on the next westbound bus. They gave us a release to sign, and I think we each got $100. That was 4-months pay, an excellent Christmas present. Of course, after about 24-hours every bone and muscle in my body ached.

They held the Los Angeles Express bus for us. Being considerate, they reserved the right front passenger seats, the location with the best view, but it also happened to be the location of the second fatality on our previous bus. The fog was so thick that there was probably only a couple hundred feet of visibility. This was before Interstate highways, and buses were required to stop at all railroad crossings. Of course, the driver was familiar with the road, so he knew the locations the railroad crossings. We would be tearing down the highway when suddenly he would start breaking. We could not see anything other than the gray fog coming at our face, so it made for a very tense ride. We weren't able to get out of that cursed front seat until we were halfway across Texas.

I don't think I got more than a couple hours sleep all the way home. Crossing Texas took an eternity. We joked that each sunrise; we could see where you would be that night. It seemed endless. We took a northbound bus out of LA, and Roberts switched to a San Francisco bus at Fresno. Once again, it was foggy when I left Fresno. Almost immediately I knew something was wrong; I could tell we were headed south instead of north. You couldn't see the side of the road, and there was no sky visible, but I have always had a good sense of where north is. I guess it comes from growing up in the mountains. I became concerned because I knew that we were going south. I finally ask the guy next to me where he was going. He said Redding, which is also north of Fresno. I became increasingly agitated and finally got up to ask the driver if we were on the right bus. I made it halfway up the aisle when the bus stopped and then turned north. He had driven south to pick up Highway 99 northbound. I walked back to my seat, and the Redding passenger asked me how in the heck I had known we were going south. The only thing I could say was I grew up in the mountains.

I finally got to Siskiyou County close to sunrise. There had been a recent snowstorm, but the bus driver was willing to let me off at Pumphouse Road about a mile from home. I walked home to be greeted by our dog. I was excited to be home, but everything had changed in the seven months since I had left. There was no longer a cow to milk; most of the other livestock was also gone. The folks were planning to buy some land to build a house, something they had never mentioned when I was at home. They were getting rid of a lot of stuff that had collected over the past 20 years. The downside was I was facing another 72-hour bus ride to get back to Mississippi. Fortunately, that trip, although very long, was uneventful.

— ■ —

When I got back from leave, I started "sets" training. The Automatic Tracking Radar equipment. Our mission was Secret. We were not allowed to "mix" with the non-classified students. Each day, we were taken off-base to a secure location for training. Our class started at 4 p.m. and ended at midnight. We rode a bus back and forth to the site. By the time we got back to our barracks, it was close to 1 a.m. In theory, we were supposed to go to the mess hall for breakfast and then go to sleep. I didn't like eating and then going to sleep, so I usually skipped breakfast.

There were a couple of us with birthdays around the same time in January. One night after class, we decided to steal a desert from the mess hall to celebrate. Our only choice turned out to be a pie. Now a mess hall pie is not like what you get at the local restaurant. They are feeding thousands at every meal, so they size things accordingly. They baked pies in pans that were 20" wide and 30" long. We stole half a pineapple pie. We took some plates and silverware to eat with. We also took a partially emptied 3-gallon box of milk. We got it all back to our barracks and had our little birthday party with enough pineapple pie to feed 30 or 40 people. Of course, there were only a few of us, so everyone had all they could eat, actually far more than we should have eaten. So much pineapple pie, that to this day, I don't like it. I am not even a big fan of pineapple.

— ■ —

We all had security clearances, and we were not supposed to talk to anyone about what we were studying. We received frequent lectures about the sensitivity of our training and the equipment. One of our classmates was a bit older. He was married and on his second 4-year tour in the Air Force. One night he came to class and told us his wife had seen a movie called "B-58 Hustler." In that film, they showed an actual bomb run against one of our radar sites. The shot was from the inside of the cockpit of a B-58. All of this was supposed to be highly classified.

Ultimately, our equipment and training were declassified. It took a while for the paperwork to catch up with reality. Once that happened, they held a press conference. Press people were invited to our facility to look at the equipment and take pictures. It was a bit surreal given how they had pounded the secrecy into our heads.

Everyone used flash bulbs at that time. They were the big jobs, about the size of a ping-pong ball. The guy who came to take pictures had both pockets of his suit jacket stuffed with bulbs. He started taking lots of pictures, and he would just eject the spent bulbs onto the ground. Of course, that meant we would have to pick them all up after he left. The combination of his arrogant approach, his condescending attitude towards the students, and then his dumping the spent bulbs, pissed off more than a few of us. I don't remember who did it, but someone got into a radar van and turned on the search radar. It was a megawatt radar, think of it as a supersized microwave oven with the door open and a focused beam of RF energy. It could light fluorescent bulbs half a mile away. He swept the radar across the visiting press guy, and every one of the bulbs in both pockets went off at once. His jacket was dazzling for a couple of seconds, and then smoke started curling out of the pockets. He peeled off his jacket and stomped on the smoldering bulbs in the pockets. No one said a word and whoever it was that turned on the radar, shut it off and slipped out of the van during all of the confusion. Our press guy said nothing as he made a speedy departure.

— ∎ —

Because the equipment was classified, we were not allowed to bring materials back to our barracks to study. Our alternative was to take a bus to the off-site location at 1 p.m. so that we had a few hours to study before class. I did this most days. This scheduled meant that we didn't have to participate in most Squadron activities. We got out of mowing lawns, painting buildings, and general cleanup.

Even with our "squadron duty" exemption, weekend KP was still something we had to do one weekend day every 6 or 8 weeks. You had to be there early in the morning as breakfast was served beginning a 5 a.m. Most of the work was pretty routine, but there was one area, the "clipper" room, that everybody hated. The trays and dishes went to the clipper room for cleaning. When they started coming in, they piled up fast. There was always leftover food, and the dishes would start sliding with food falling all over the place. It was hot, smelly, and wet. Water was everywhere; by the end of the day, your shoes would be wet all the way through. Of course, you would smell like an over-ripe trash dump.

Most of the airmen were young and single. They wanted to go party on weekends, but being GIs getting paid all of $28, once per month, meant that most of the time they had no money. Of course, the weekend after payday was the designated party weekend. Several of us that were not into partying soon discovered that we could sell our time to airmen who got assigned KP on a party weekend. The going rate was $5 to cover their shift, but if you were so unlucky as to get chosen for clipper room, it was $7.50. Most of us who sold ourselves to cover KP duty quickly learned to volunteer for the clipper room. You got used to it, and the money was good. Remember we only made $28/month, so picking up $7.50 was like a 25% raise. There was an added advantage; you had money to go party the next weekend when the others were broke. There was less competition on those weekends. Incidentally, beer was 10¢.

— ■ —

Cockroaches loved the heat and humidity. Three inches was typical for a Mississippi cockroach. The Clipper room was always wet, and there were bits and pieces of food no matter how well you cleaned. Hordes of cockroaches made their home in the clipper room. When you came in at 4 a.m. and turned on the lights, you would see hundreds of cockroaches. They would quickly disappear behind equipment, into cracks or wherever they could. It was a bit creepy to see how many there were and how quickly they could all disappear.

The clipper room had a piece of garden hose that was 6 or 8 feet long. The hot water was kept very near the boiling point to help sterilize things. The room was all cement, including the walls. The floor sloped to a drain in the middle. All of this was designed so you could wash the place down after each meal service.

When we started our shift, we would sneak into the room with the lights off. You would crunch as you stepped on cockroaches; turn on the hot water and let it run till it was scalding, then spray down the room in the dark. When you turned on the lights, you would see dozens of cockroaches floating down to the drain. You had to shovel them into the trash.

— ■ —

Several of us hung out together and one guy, Jim Longley, brought his car back when he went home for Christmas. Occasionally we would just stay in Biloxi, but there was not a lot to do. Mississippi was "dry" (no alcohol) at that time but not Biloxi. Bars were plentiful, with no age limit. If you could crawl up on a barstool, and you had the cash, you could drink. It was common to see the local sheriff come in to collect his payola while you were sitting drinking beer in this "dry" city.

Most weekends, we would head out to various destinations away from Biloxi. We went over to Pensacola, FL a couple of times. The beach was real nice, but it was crawling with Navy guys from Mobile, AL, so it was not a lot of fun. Mobile was the same way, so we only went there once. We hit New Orleans a few times, once for Mardi Gras. New Orleans was an unusual scene for this country boy, especially Bourbon Street during Mardi Gras, but it was too expensive to spend much time there.

Most of the time we went up to Hattiesburg. Mississippi Southern University was in Hattiesburg, and there was also a large nursing school. It was far enough from Keesler and Mobile so that there were few GIs. It was pretty cheap, and there were lots of girls. There weren't any bars, but moonshine was readily available. I was never much of a drinker, so alcohol availability didn't matter to me. One of my classmates wound up marrying a girl from Hattiesburg.

Tim at Hattiesburg MS 1963

Moving to my Next Assignment

When I completed electronics training early in June of 1963, I was assigned to a remote radar site located near Vale, Oregon. I was also given leave time before reporting to my new assignment. I could not face the idea of another long Greyhound ride, so Floyd Weaver and I decided that we would hitchhike home. We also wanted to avoid the long dreary trip across Texas, so we chose to go north to St. Louis, and then head west.

The obligatory portrait 1963

There was no north/south Interstate at that time, and so we traveled mainly on State roads through Hattiesburg, and Jackson MS, up to Memphis TN and finally to St. Louis MO. From there we turned west. It was night as we traveled two-lane roads up through Mississippi, one of the poorest parts of America. We could see shacks in the cotton fields near the road. The walls were every bit as bad as the old Koppes Place. I could see the TVs inside of the houses we passed.

We rode with a classmate as far as Memphis. We hitched in uniform, and it was a great experience. Most of our rides were relatively short but one covered hundreds of miles. We were warned not to get out in East St. Louis if we valued our lives. We heeded that advice. That was 50+ years ago; I can only imagine how bad it is today.

We agreed on some rules, first never accept a ride if either of us were uncomfortable with the driver, we only had one instance where we turned down an offer. Second, one of us had to stay awake at all times. That became a problem because we had worked all day before leaving and by the middle of the next night we had gone more than 40 hours with no real sleep. We were somewhere west of Topeka Kansas when it started raining about 2 a.m. There was no Interstate in that area, and we were in some pretty desolate country. We decided that it was time to take a break. It took a while, but we finally found an open motel and crashed for the better part of a day, not only to rest but to wait out the rain.

Along the way we met some very friendly folks, a lot were retired or military families. I kept a diary but foolishly gave it to my girlfriend who didn't return it when we broke up. I do remember one ride. A mother and daughter picked us up on the west side of St. Louis and gave us a ride clear to Kansas City. They had a brand new Nash Rambler with a console mounted air conditioner. I had never seen a car with air conditioning before that. They had a Pekingese dog that would lay in front of the AC. There was dog hair swirling around the car.

The girl was probably 15 or 16 and both she and her mother were a bit ditzy. She was in a private all-girls school and had no understanding of life. They were headed south from Kansas City, and so we parted company at a truck stop on the east side of the city. They wanted to buy us lunch. We tried to decline politely, but they insisted. I will never forget the girl's comment. "Daddy will be so proud that we picked up two service men to protect us." Floyd and I had many good laughs about that one over the years.

— ∎ —

Hitching across Kansas and Eastern Colorado was slow, mostly short rides with farmers. As we approached Denver, the majestic Rocky Mountains began to grow on the horizon. I have always loved the mountains and of course Texas and Mississippi don't have any. Up to that time, I wasn't conscious of just how much I had missed seeing mountains, but seeing the Rockies grow up over the horizon nearly brought tears to my eyes. We learned that it was illegal to hitchhike on the Interstate Highways in Colorado. We had a ride all the way to Denver and considered trying our hand at catching another ride from an on-ramp, one that would take us past the area where there was Interstate developed. Several days of standing by the road and hopping from one short ride to another had significantly lowered our enthusiasm to ride our thumbs for several more days. We were thinking we needed to catch another night's sleep before starting the next leg, and we weren't looking forward to hitching through Utah and Nevada in the summer heat. We decided it was time to catch a flight to San Francisco.

At San Francisco, I said goodbye to Floyd as he lived near Bakersfield. I crashed for the night then hitched on north to Yreka. Floyd was assigned to a sister radar site at St. George, Utah. We crossed paths several times over the next few years, but I lost track of him after I left the Air Force.

— ■ —

My leave was pretty uneventful, but "home" had changed so much I didn't fit in. All the livestock had been sold or slaughtered as the folks had bought a piece of land where they were starting to build their home. At that point, they were living in a tent on the new property while they were building the garage. They planned to live in the garage while they built the house. I had space in a separate tent that they used for storage.

The folks showed me the house plans, and Mom asked if I recognized them. They seemed familiar, but I couldn't place where I had seen them. It turned out that I had drawn them as a project in a drafting class when I was a sophomore in high school. Of course at the time, I never imagined anyone would build the house I had drafted, but apparently, the folks liked it, so they decided to build it.

I rode with Dad on his trap line for several days and visited a few friends. I soon became so bored that I decided to report to my new assignment early. I did buy my first car, a red 1960 Ford Falcon, and I sold my motorcycle. The Falcon was not what you would call a well-built car. The engine soon proved that it was not up to the long distance trips and that made up the bulk my driving.

Tim & Tom at Koppes Place 1963

Vale Bomb Plot

In early July of 1963, I became part of the Strategic Air Command. Specifically, I became part of Detachment 5, 1st Combat Evaluation Group, at that time the site was located on a mountain top in the high desert about 10 miles west of Vale, Oregon.

— ■ —

For those of you unfamiliar with the state of the world in the early 1960s, I will take a bit of time to explain life in the hottest part of the Cold War, and our role in that war as well as the Viet Nam war.

After WWII, the West, in particular, the United States, United Kingdom, France, Canada and Australia aligned in opposition to the Eastern Block lead by the Soviet Union. The rest of Western Europe was part of the "West" as well, but in truth, they were relatively insignificant other than to be the presumed physical battlefield in the event of another war.

While it was called a "cold" war, it was often a hair's breath away from becoming a "hot" war. Everyone assumed "hot" meant nuclear with missiles and bombers flying from both sides. The stakes were extremely high. The two sides were restrained by what was called the "MAD" (Mutually Assured Destruction) policy. The short, but very real story is that if the missiles ever flew, we would completely annihilate each other and probably most of those living on the earth.

This was not a game; it was very real, and the leaders of each side held a finger over the "launch" button at all times. The closest they came to hitting the button was the Cuban Missile Crisis, which I wrote about earlier. Few know exactly how close war was, but it was scary-close. Understanding this MAD policy lays the foundation for my AF work.

— ■ —

One of the more flamboyant Air Force Generals was Curtis LeMay. He was considered a brilliant and creative tactician. His basic philosophy was "go big!" If you are going to use military force, use overwhelming force; deliberately use too much. In the end, you will save lives. He believed the way to prevent an attack was to build an incredibly powerful, well-armed and well-trained Air Force. SAC (Strategic Air Command) was the Air Force Unit responsible for any atomic attack. LeMay became SAC commander in 1948. At that time, any attack would include bombers. The land-based ICBMs (Inter Continental Ballistic Missiles) were developed in the early 60s. The sea-launched SLBMs, which were controlled by the Navy, were coming online in the mid-60s. They became the third leg of what was known as the nuclear triad.

When he first took command of SAC, LeMay ordered a mock attack on Dayton, Ohio. To his dismay, most of the bombers missed their target by more than a mile. One result of the failed test run on Dayton was to establish what ultimately became the 1st Combat Evaluation Group (CEVG).

The Combat Evaluation Group and Radar Bomb Scoring (RBS), were a little-known, but critical part of the Cold War. During the formative years of SAC,

145

in particular, before 1961, bomber crews suffered from high accident rates, low bombing accuracy and a lack of command standardization. In 1949, the 3908th Strategic Evaluation Squadron was established to standardize and instruct aircrew across SAC. On Aug. 1, 1961, the 3908 SES was combined with 1st Radar Bomb Scoring, a World War II era ground-based radar bomb scoring group. I joined that unit two years later. This combined group had a three-fold mission; to create command standardization, to provide radar bomb and electronic warfare scoring, and to provide contingency combat support. CEVG & RBS were LeMay's pet project. He used them as a cudgel to drive his essential "go big" philosophy.

With headquarters at Barksdale Air Force Base, LA, the 1CEVG had permanent detachments in more than ten states. The CEVG also had locations in Korea, Guam, and Germany. Each of these sites provided entirely different terrains, creating realistic situations that allowed the SAC bomber crews to train for nearly any mission.

Throughout the Cold War, 1/3 of all SAC bombers were in the air or on 15-minute standby at all times. 1/3 were in training, and 1/3 were down for maintenance. The mission of RBS (Radar Bomb Scoring) was to train and evaluate the bombing and electronic warfare capabilities of the SAC bomber crews. Each crew had to complete a specific number of successful bomb runs each quarter.

— ■ —

At each RBS site, there was a variety of radar and electronic warfare equipment modified specifically to track, test and evaluate the bomb crews. Our systems were "tuned" to emulate Russian air defense systems. While the equipment was "state-of-the-art," at the time, the "art" was all-vacuum-tube equipment. That was similar to commercial computers, which were mostly vacuum tube based as well. Solid-state systems entered the market around the time I completed my Air Force tour, but the old equipment remained mission critical well into the late 1960s.

Vacuum tubes were not too reliable under the best circumstances, and the older the systems, the greater the frequency of failure. That presented a serious problem when it came to evaluating the bomber crews. Thousands of dollars and days, if not weeks of planning preceded each mission. If equipment failure caused the mission not to be scored, it was all a waste. LeMay's solution was for RBS operators to be qualified technicians. We were trained on every piece of equipment: radars (search, tracking, fire control, etc.), (analog) computers, radios of all frequencies, and on every operational position on the site. The only exception was the electronic jamming equipment, which fell under a different MOS. The Automatic Tracking Radar Specialist MOS (30353) was the only MOS that included such a broad array of equipment. That is the reason the training was as long and complicated as it was.

— ■ —

Normally, there were about 40 technical people assigned to each RBS site. We operated on three shifts with ten men per shift. Two shifts were operations, scoring bomb runs, while one shift was for maintenance. The other ten men were away on TDY assignments. All crewmembers rotated through both maintenance and operations. We all had to be able to repair any device at any point during the day or night. The goal was to minimize the outage should any device fail.

The equipment was mobile, mounted in truck vans. Each of the roughly 13 RBS (they activated and deactivated a few sites from time to time) sites were located in areas that had similarities, primarily geographic, to target locations in Russia. Each radar site could score both high and low altitude bomb runs. The high-altitude runs were at 35 to 40 thousand feet, from multiple Initial Points (IPs or approach points).

Each site had a low-level route where the bombers would follow the terrain to avoid radar detection. The low-level routes were hundreds of miles in length. These are called "oil-burner" routes because jet engines are less efficient at low altitude and usually left a thick trail of smoke when on the low-level route. Remember, B-52s have eight engines, so there was a lot of opportunities to burn oil. The low-level route for the Wilder bomb plot location, more about Wilder later, started in Central California, went south, then east, crossing over the Sierra Nevada Range. It then ran up the eastern slope of the Sierra Nevada mountains, swung east across the high desert and then followed the Owyhee mountains across southeastern Oregon bringing the bomber in on a set of targets along the Snake River.

Radar at RBS Site Vale, Oregon 1963

Low-level flying was all manual flying, usually at 2,000 feet above the terrain with radars off. On occasion, they would run the low-level route at 500 feet. B-52s are not small, and they don't pop up and down like a fighter. Flying a low-level route at 2,000 feet was tough enough, you cannot imagine the physical endurance and abuse to the airframe as well as the crew to do terrain following at 500 feet for several hundred miles. They trained as if their life depended on it, and in fact, all of our lives did.

The B-52s ran the low-level route at just under 400 mph. We got an occasional B-58 on the range, and they ran the low-level route at 500 feet and Mach .92; that is 700 mph. I can testify that, with the radar available at that point, it is almost impossible to track a B-58 traveling 700 mph at 500 feet. The radar paint is so small and mixed in with so much ground clutter that it is nearly invisible. You can also imagine how a B-58 roaring over your head at 500 feet and 700 mph could scare the bejesus out of some unsuspecting hunter or tourist wandering out in the hills. At that speed, you won't hear the plane until it has passed.

– ■ –

The range was a circle with a 75 nautical mile radius from our site. The ceiling was 50,000 feet. All military aircraft were supposed to clear onto and off the range, even when just passing through. I recall one time a B-36 called in to clear across the range. Everyone was surprised that one of those old bombers was still in the air. We were even more surprised when the aircraft commander called back and said: "never mind, we are above your range at Angels 56" (that is 56,000 feet).

That was the one and only B-36 I ever came across. The B-36 was a remarkable aircraft designed in 1941; it had a 10,000-mile range; 40 hours of flying time, without refueling. It could also carry a heavier payload than the B-52. In fact, it held the payload record until the 747 was developed two decades later. The B-36s had six 28-cylinder Pratt and Whitney engines providing 22,800 horsepower. Some later versions included four additional outboard jet engines that brought them up to 40,000 hp. That was supposed to give them a service ceiling of 55,000 feet, which was well above any fighters of that era. Apparently, they could go higher.

We had another strange incident one morning at the end of the maintenance period. The date was in early 1964. We always locked onto some available plane, usually a commercial jet, flying by to test the radars as well as the plotting equipment. I happened to be working on the backup plotter that morning when the radar operator asked me to run a plot on a test airplane. The plotting equipment automatically generated 3-second time hacks, little blips in the plot line. The time marks allowed us to calculate ground speed. These hacks were normally a bit over ¼" apart for a bomber traveling at normal speed. The hacks for our test plane were close to 1" apart. At first, I thought the plotter was acting up but after the other radar and plotting equipment showed the same result, we became very curious about what we were tracking.

The aircraft was coming up out of Nevada, and it was maneuvering, not flying a straight line. We calculated that it was traveling at close to 2,200 miles per hour. We ran north/south lines on the plots, marked them with locations, date and time, and sent them off to Barksdale (our headquarters) asking what the heck this was. It took only a few days before we got a very brief and very specific response. "Track what you are supposed to track and leave other things alone!" We never did know what we had locked onto, but years later, when I learned of the SR-71 Blackbird, I suspect that is what it was. Blackbirds were beyond standard classification at that time; no one was supposed to be aware of them. We certainly weren't.

— ■ —

When an aircraft started a bomb run, either high or low level, they would notify us that they were inbound and at which IP (Initial Point). Once the RBS site picked up the plane on the radar, we began playing the role of an enemy target. First, when the radar locked-on to the aircraft, the Electronic Warfare Officer on the plane had only a few seconds to detect the lock-on and jam it. In theory, failure meant that the aircraft would have been blown out of the sky by a missile. The electronic warfare officer had to concurrently identify and jam several other signals created by our electronic warfare team at the RBS site.

We would terminate the electronic warfare (EW) testing after 30 or so miles and then track the aircraft as they did simulated bomb drops, usually on two designated targets. While they were making their run, we continued producing different jamming signals to block the radar navigator's image of the target area. The purpose was to test the ability of the radar navigator to hit the target under adverse conditions.

The primary scoring radar would lock on to the bomber and plot the course of the aircraft. When the bomber was 10 seconds from the mock bomb drop, the radar navigator transmitted a high-pitched tone. The navigator would drop the tone at the point where the simulated weapon would have been released. Our plotting equipment used this "tone drop" to indicate the precise point of actual bomb drop.

Once the mock weapon was released, the RBS crew determined the ground speed, the aircraft track, and the wind direction. With that, we could calculate the location a real bomb would have exploded. We would give the aircrew their results in encrypted form. We also sent them back to their Wing.

We scored the crew on both their response time, their ability to jam our signals with sufficient power to prevent us from tracking them (during the electronic warfare period) and the accuracy of their bomb drops. If we were able to track them during the EW test, if they were slow to respond (timeliness as well as the strength of jamming) to the barrage of test signals we sent out, or if they failed to drop the bombs accurately, they failed the run.

A failed run had significant repercussions. Any failed run had to be repeated successfully two times to maintain their readiness status. Our scores were a critical component of the aircrew's rating. If I remember correctly, the crew designations were A, T, and S, Sierra being the top rating. They were the best. They seldom blew a bomb run. One failed bomb run would cost them their Sierra designation.

Some of the bomb runs were under extreme conditions. There would be a special safety/training officer on board to watch over things and evaluate the crew. The aircraft would take off with the windows blacked out, in the blind. Climb to altitude and refuel, still in the blind. At some point, the radars would be turned off and all navigation equipment shut down simulating a massive equipment failure. That didn't end the flight. B-52s included a periscope on the top. The Navigator had to rely on celestial navigation. They would complete their bomb run several (8-10) hours later. The entire mission was in the blind. There was no allowance for the added complexity of their flight; the scoring accuracy requirement remained the same. They seldom missed.

The aircrew would tell us which IP they were entering so that we didn't inadvertently pick up a commercial airliner and blast him with all kinds of jamming. Once we had a Navy crew make a bomb run with an IP of Boise. That was the one, and only time Boise was used as an IP. It was not a problem for us, but as it turned out, the IP was in line with all of the radio and TV antennas on the mountain behind Boise. Our jammers knocked all of the commercial stations off the air. Fortunately, it was only jamming, and no equipment failures resulted, but they were off the air for nearly 10 minutes.

— ■ —

I remember late one evening while we were still at the Vale site; we gave a

151

failing score to a Sierra Crew. We were able to track them through their jammer. In the real world, that would mean that we could have launched a missile and wiped them out of the sky before they reached their target. The bomb crew was so pissed they landed at Mt. Home Air Force Base. That was about 100 miles from our radar site; they grabbed a staff car and drove to our site. They arrived at about midnight demanding to be let on the site to inspect our equipment. We had no officers on site at that hour. Our team leader, a crusty old Master Sergeant, named Adams, grabbed an M1 carbine, walked out to the gate, and told the Colonel if he tried to come on the site he would shoot him. The Colonel and his crew left.

Of course, that wasn't the end of it. There was an investigation, and SAC sent a team to monitor a few bomb runs. The MPS-9 radar was a fixed-frequency radar. The magnetron could not be easily adjusted to change the frequency. However, we discovered that you could change the receiver to pick up a "sideband" signal that was an echo pulse at a slightly different frequency from the primary radar signal.

When we locked on a plane, the electronic warfare officer would immediately turn on the jammer based on the primary signal frequency. We would then shut down the magnetron and watch to see if the jamming continued against the now dead radar. If they continued to jam, that meant the EW officer was getting lazy and not monitoring the radar signal. We would turn the magnetron back on and then tweak the receiver, so it picked up the sideband signal. With that, we could track the airplane.

The SAC inspection team, which primarily consisted EW officers, watched us bag a nice big B-52. They could clearly see that we were able to track their plane, but they screamed "foul." They claimed the MPS-9 was a fixed frequency radar and therefore, we were not playing by the rules. Our commander looked at him smiled and said "We are the Russians; we can do whatever the hell we can make our equipment do. If you think it will protect your precious bomber to tell the real Russians that they can't change the frequency of their radar, then have a good flight." Nothing more was said, but within 24 hours SAC changed their procedures so that they never got caught sleeping on our MPS-9 signal again.

— ■ —

Strategic Air Command crews were not the only ones who used the training sites. Navy, Marines, National Guard, NATO and Korean Forces were all allowed to use our radar scoring system to gauge crew readiness, the accuracy of their bomb drops, and electronic warfare countermeasures. At our site at least, aircraft from these other services were rare, and the few that did, mostly Navy, couldn't hit the broadside of a barn if it had a big red bullseye painted on it.

— ■ —

I remember one Navy bomber called IP late one night, and we searched and searched but could not locate any aircraft anywhere close to where he said he was. We did find one lone airplane at the correct altitude, but it was about 30 miles away from the intended IP. We locked on, but before we started jamming his radar, we ask him to make an "ID" turn. That would be a simple "S" turn so we could be sure we had the right aircraft. His response was comical. He replied, "Roger that, which way would you like me to turn ...please." He was asking us to help him get back to where he was supposed to be. We gave him a hint, but he still missed his intended target by several miles.

Each site had about 15 targets, which could be a power plant, a bridge, a dam, or just coordinates on a map. The SAC aircrews flew against these fixed targets so often that their training value gradually diminished. They became good at hitting them, damn good.

The RBS Express

All of our equipment was mounted in vans, and therefore semi-mobile. To combat the familiarity problem, we moved every few years. Each bomb plot was selected to the mirror, as closely as possible, a target area in Russia.

I first joined Detachment 5 when it was at Vale, Oregon. A few months later, we moved the site to Wilder, Idaho. The move occurred while I was on TDY at Wamsutter, Wyoming, so I didn't get to set up the new location.

Wilder was a far more attractive place. The site sat on a bluff overlooking a sweeping bend in the Snake River, which was probably 300' lower in elevation. There was farmland to our north and east, and across the River south and west on the Oregon side were orchards as well as other farmland. The Owyhee Mountains were south and west while the Sawtooth mountains behind Boise were to the east and north. This location had the advantage of being closer to towns (Nampa and Caldwell Idaho) where we could find apartments. The Vale site was a long way from anywhere, and so we had to ride a bus about 60 miles to and from the site each day.

Changing the "fixed" site locations was not sufficient to keep the training as fresh as desired, so the 1st CEVG created the RBS Express, an RBS site mounted on a train. There were three RBS Express trains, each train was an entirely self-contained facility, as they were intended for remote locations. The train had all the necessities: lodging, maintenance, and scoring equipment. The RBS Express began running routes in February 1961.

Each RBS Express consisted of 21 cars, 17 support, and 4 radar/EWS cars. The radar cars were flatbed cars with the radar vans mounted on them. There was a separate generator car just for the radar section. The generator cars had four huge diesel generators that could produce enough electricity to power a good-sized town. The other 16 cars, called the "live-aboard" section, consisted of a separate generator car, a dining car, two day-rooms, supplies, admin, and 4 Pullman sleepers. There was also a boxcar for maintenance parts and equipment.

Live-aboard on RBS Express 1966

The Pullman cars were extensively modified Army Hospital cars. Each was self-contained. All had grain paneling with private 3 x 7-foot roomettes. The beds were a bit narrow, only about 24" wide, a standard twin bed is 39", but the designers had worked hard to maximize the functionality. Each roomette had a huge picture window with blackout curtains so night workers could sleep. There were built-in wall closets with a locking entrance door. The foot of the bunk could be folded up and over the top part of the bed creating a writing table. There was a laundry box with a padded top that served as the stool when you were using your desk. The only problem was that pyramid-shaped hinges were required to allow the lower section of the bed to fold up and over the upper part. The top of the hinges stuck up above the mattress about 1 inch. It turned out that these hinges were strategically located right at your knee, so when you rolled over in the narrow bunks, your knee would invariably bang into one of the hinges.

At the center of each Pullman car, there were several toilets, showers and even a laundromat with stacked washer/dryers. These cars were all interconnected so we could walk through the whole "live-aboard" section. The Commander had the very last room on the tail of the train. It was two rooms with the wall knocked out between them.

Of course, to display the proper Air Force image, the live-aboard section was painted Air Force Blue, with the SAC emblem on each car. The roof was silver. The radar vans were white with the SAC shield, and the undercarriages were all black. This color scheme was quite striking, especially when you came upon the RBS Express sitting out on some desolate stretch of track with nothing else for miles around. It did, however, create an issue with the cold and sun combination.

The train cars in the live-aboard section had heaters and air conditioners of course. When the sun hit the big blue slab side of the train, it would heat it up turning on the AC. At the same time, in the winter, a cold wind would invariably be blowing so the other side of the train would be freezing. If your compartment were on the shady side, you would freeze while those on the sunny side roasted. Come afternoon the roles would reverse. While the train was at Wamsutter Wyoming, it sat east to west. With the sun relatively low and further south in the winter. As a result, the south side was always hot, and the north side was always cold. While we were at Wamsutter, everyone was always suffering from a cold. We were dealing with the freeze/cook cycle, confined in relatively close quarters, and having to go out into the frigid wind every time we needed to move from the live-aboard section to the radar side of the RBS Express. Colds were inevitable.

RBS Express Wamsutter WY 1964

The whole purpose of the RBS Express was to keep providing fresh new targets. For that, the trains would move to a new location about every six months. We would tear down the antennas and jack up the vans on air shocks to minimize vibration damage. There were hoists mounted on the bed of the flat cars. That made lifting the antennas off and on relatively simple.

157

A conventional locomotive would hook up and pull the train to its new location. We weren't allowed to ride on the train during the actual move. That probably would have required a ticket or something. I used to joke that I had spent more time on a train than almost anybody, but had never moved an inch. When the train arrived at the new location, the conductor would park it precisely on a pre-surveyed mark showing longitude and latitude. This was always on a siding or spur line, not the main track. The targets were already selected and mapped in relation to that location. We would usually be there when the train arrived. It required about 12 hours to set up the radars. After that, we were open for business.

— ∎ —

Three different RBS detachments would supply a scoring/maintenance crew and some support people. Total staffing for the train would be about 30 RBS personnel at one time plus about 10 others that were not from any RBS site. These included a couple of cooks, a medic who also ran a small PX that was open a couple of hours a day, and a few other support personnel, mainly to keep the diesel generators running properly. They came from various SAC bases. It was considered choice duty for them as they had a tiny team to cook for and take care of, and they didn't have to put up with any of the usual "military" hassles that they would have back at their regular base. As a result, we always had excellent support staff, especially the cooks.

We had free access to the kitchen whenever the cooks were not on duty, so if you wanted to fry up some eggs at 3 a.m. you could. Most of our food was purchased in the local communities and from restaurant supply vendors. We were always out in the boonies, so this was a real boon for the suppliers and we got top quality stuff.

TDY tours were from 6 weeks to 3 months. Of course, the frequent TDY assignments was disruptive, particularly to those who were married, but these extended stays at secluded sites allowed us to go places in the country that we would not have otherwise seen. We also had the opportunity to meet people, civilians as well as RBS crews from other fixed sites. Over a few years, I got to know most all the people in the entire squadron.

We held at least one "open house" at each location. The local population, most who never had contact with the military or the Air Force, could visit to see what we were about and to meet the crews. There was occasional friction when too many young men came to small towns and went out on a Saturday night, but in many cases, the communities would "adopt" the RBS teams, inviting individuals to their homes, churches, and other community events during holiday seasons. Remember, much of this time was during the Viet Nam War when many in the military were experiencing open hostility from civilians, some even being spat upon when they were out in public in uniform. We had a very different experience, especially when we were on the RBS Express.

– ∎ –

The trains received a steady stream of first-run movies. They would send a couple of new films every two weeks. I was usually one of the projectionists, and so I got to see the movies so many times I would know all the "punch" lines and be sick of them by the time we got some new movies. Hud, with Paul Newman, was the big movie while we were at Wamsutter. I had seen it at least 20 times by the time a new movie came to replace it. When I went back to Nampa, Idaho after that assignment, my girlfriend had been waiting to see Hud until I got home. I took her, but I slept through the whole movie. Many years later when we were living in Connecticut, I met Paul Newman at a party. He got a kick out of my story.

Fortunately, there was an extensive library of old movies, including many WWII and Korean War USO tours with Bob Hope, Bing Crosby, and others. When everyone got tired of the latest flicks, we would watch these.

Over my nearly four years with Detachment 5, I did 6 RBS Express tours. There were two tours at Wamsutter, Wyoming. Wamsutter has a population of 68 today. At that time, it was just a spur line on the train track and a couple of houses about a mile away. I never saw a soul, so I am not even sure that anyone lived in either house. At Wamsutter, the radar portion of our train sat on a spur that ran diagonally from the main line. The live-aboard section was on a siding right next to the main line.

The whole site was located squarely on top of the Continental Divide. That was ideal for the Radar as we had a clear 360° view, but it meant that approaching trains, from either east or west, would be grinding uphill to reach the top of the Divide. The grade wasn't steep, but it was long. The railroad would pop an additional 4 or 5 big diesel engines at the back of the train as pushers. That meant that a long freight train might have 10 or 12 diesel engines pulling and pushing to get over the top of the divide. The add-on pushers would be switched out twenty or thirty miles after they crossed over

159

the divide and then they would push another train headed the other direction. These big engines caused the ground and the tracks to vibrate as much as a half mile ahead of the slowly advancing train. As this was the main east/west rail route across the middle of the US, the traffic was constant, and the vibration shook the whole live-aboard section as each train slowly climbed the grade. It was tough to sleep.

– ∎ –

My first tour at Wamsutter was in the winter. On that trip, I concluded that it doesn't snow in Wyoming, it snows in Utah, and the wind blows it all the way across Wyoming. The days would be cold but sunny with a wind blowing from the west. It was strange, maybe because we were on top of the Continental Divide, but the wind didn't blow in your face, just below your knees. I suppose it was a case of high pressure on the Western slope and low pressure on the Eastern slope. The air, in the form of wind, would flow across the Divide like water flowing over the lip of a bathtub. As a result, there would be snow blowing about a foot above the ground to the point where you had a hard time seeing the ground at times.

We parked our cars near the train, and most of the time they just sat there waiting till we went home. I remember opening the hood of my little Ford Falcon one day and seeing the snow packed solid and frozen all the way to the underside of the hood. The wind had blown the snow up into the engine compartment until it gradually filled up. The sun would shine on the hood and warm the top of the snow so that it would melt and then refreeze as the water moved down away from the warm metal. We had to get heaters and blankets to melt the snow before we could start our cars. Fortunately, it warmed up by the end of that tour.

We were at Wamsutter on April 17, 1964, when the first Ford Mustangs hit the showrooms. For those who are not fans of the Mustang, I don't know how that can be, but ok, I will accept that there are a few who are not, the introduction of the Mustang was a huge event. For a bunch of young men trapped on a cold train sitting on top of the Continental Divide, the new "pony" car was a huge deal. The nearest Ford dealer was located about 70 miles west in Rock Springs. Several of us piled into a couple of cars and drove there for the launch. We collected all the brochures we could get our hands on and hung pictures on our walls. I doubt the dealer was all that happy to see us, as none of us could afford to buy one, but we could dream.

I did two tours at Joseph City, Arizona. That was another busy track, but not as bad as Wamsutter, primarily because it was nearly level. J City was another wide spot in the road located between Winslow and Holbrook AZ. The Eagles had a hit song called "Take it easy" that was popular while we were at J City. One of the lines was *"Don't let the sound of your own wheels drive you crazy."* We changed the lyrics to *"Don't let the sound of train wheels drive you crazy."* It became the RBS Express theme song.

Our site commander was a Mormon, which worked well since there are a lot of Mormons in the Eastern Oregon and Idaho areas. He was able to work with local property owners and merchants to smooth out things that could have been more difficult without his aid. He was a Lt. Colonel and a bit eccentric. I remember the first time I came on site to report in at Vale. I saw a man in khakis (most everyone typically wore green fatigues) crawling around under the radar vans, which were all up on jacks so about 4 feet off the ground. The guy was apparently policing (cleaning up) the area. It turned out that guy was our commander. I guess life running an RBS site was boring.

He was apparently quite wealthy, and he worked hard to support the crew. Before moving to the Idaho area, the site was at a World War II Army gun emplacement at the mouth of the Columbia River near Astoria, Oregon. Apparently, the Army, as well as the Navy, were using the old bunkers as warehouses to store a lot of "off-the-books" equipment, including some household appliances, stoves, refrigerators, etc. Our colonel decided that his men could use some of this stuff to help furnish apartments and otherwise make life a bit easier for his troops. When the RBS site moved to Idaho, it was in another location before a second move to Vale; the colonel hired two big moving vans and filled them up with booty from the bunkers.

The Navy was none too happy about losing so much of their booty, so they sent two flatbed trucks over to the Idaho warehouse the colonel had rented. They loaded all they could carry and hauled it back to Astoria. When I joined the site a year later, he still had the warehouse, and there was a lot of stuff in it. I went there a few times to see if there was anything that I needed for our apartment.

The stuff that was left was mostly very old military electronic equipment dating back to WWII or maybe the Korean War. Most of it was not compatible with our equipment, but there were hundreds of vacuum tubes that we all used to keep our personal TVs working. The colonel was paying for storage space out of his pocket. He eventually got tired of paying for the warehouse. He didn't want to sell the stuff, so he gave most of it away to whoever wanted it. After clearing out anything that was even slightly useful, there were still some huge cathode ray tubes (for radars and sonars I would guess) that were not compatible with any civilian equipment or any of our gear. He had us set them out on a sage brush covered hillside near our site at Vale. We used them for target practice. I doubt that anyone had much use for these parts, but it did seem like a big waste. It was undoubtedly hard on the environment.

— ■ —

The officers from each site did TDYs as well, and so our commander was the RBS Express Commander for one of my Joseph City, AZ tours. Joseph City, of course, was named after the founder of the Mormon Church, so again he fit right in. Joseph City is just south of the Painted Desert. Our commander worked through the LDS Church and set up a breakfast steak-fry out in the desert. Several of the locals participated, acted as guides, and provided their pickups; the Air Force supplied the steaks, and they were excellent steaks as you might imagine. We had a great early morning cookout and spent the day exploring the desert. For some reason, none of the locals brought their daughters along for the festivities.

— ■ —

While we were at Joseph City on my second tour, four of us decided to sign out a staff car and drove over to the Grand Canyon. We had done the Petrified Forest and the Meteor Crater on other side trips, but the Grand Canyon was the biggie. We left early Saturday morning, but it was close to 9 a.m. when we arrived. We wandered around taking in the sites. After lunch, we decided we wanted to hike down the trail a bit to see what it was like below the rim. A couple of the guys were the gung-ho type and suggested that we walk to the bottom of the canyon. The Bright Angel trail is 7.8 miles. We were all young, and in pretty good shape, so 8 miles one way didn't seem too unreasonable. We got started a bit late in the day, but going down was no problem. The 4,460-foot drop in elevation made it all downhill. Climbing back up turned out to be a big problem for one of the guys. Fred Villanueva was a bit heavier and not in the best shape. At about the halfway point he was ready to sit down and not go any further. The two gung-ho guys challenged each other to see who

162

could reach the top first, so they took off. I was left to convince Fred to keep walking. It grew dark, fortunately not too cold, but the only light was from the stars. Surprisingly, down below the rim, with no surface light, the Milky Way gave enough light to navigate the trail. I didn't know there were so many stars.

I pushed, prodded, promised, and refused to leave Fred even though he kept telling me to leave. We didn't get to the top until nearly 11 p.m. Fred made it to the car before he collapsed. We piled in and drove back to J City. I never will forget how long that walk was or how many stars there were in the sky that night.

— ■ —

Floyd Weaver, the guy I had hitchhiked cross country with, was at J City for one of my tours. Another friend Clayton "Clay" Pett, a Mormon from Idaho was also there. Neither Clay nor I drank and we were sitting in the dining car late one Saturday night drinking coffee and talking when Floyd came back from a long night in Holbrook. Floyd went back into the kitchen and got a raw egg and a table knife. He came back and sat down beside me. As Clay and I were talking, Floyd started chipping away at the top of the egg.

There is an old wives' tale that a raw egg will prevent a hangover, so I knew what he was doing. Floyd was chipping the top off so he could suck the egg out. Apparently, Clay, who was sitting across the table, had never seen this before. As we talked, Clay was staring at Floyd's chip-chip-chip as if he was discovering gold. Floyd finally got a nice round hole cleaned away, and as Clay watched in horror, Floyd tipped his head back and emptied the egg down the hatch. Clay lost it. He started gagging and made a run for the door where he soon lost his dinner. He came back looking rather green. I was laughing till tears were running down my cheeks. Floyd just sat there in complete confusion. I reconnected with Clay a couple of years ago, and I ask him if he remembered the incident. He said he most certainly did.

— ■ —

I did one tour in Ree Heights South Dakota. This location was flat as well, but there were few trains on the main track. The siding was ancient, and so the live-aboard section had a 6″ list from side to side. Six inches doesn't sound like a lot, but it makes it hard to walk down narrow halls without hitting the side. It also makes it hard to sleep without rolling out of bed, and banging your knee on the pyramid hinge, or rolling up against the picture window, which would be either hot or freezing, depending on the weather and time of

163

day.

The Inspector General visited the train at Ree Heights. They did a lengthy report on the living conditions, saying that the combination of the list and the noise made it unlivable. The solution was typical government. They simply changed the name from "live-aboard" to "exist-aboard." Problem solved!

Each of the RBS Express locations was unique in some way but also the same in that they were towns in name only. There were seldom more than a dozen citizens. Whoever selected the RBS Express locations seemed hell bent to incorporate miserable weather conditions with the experience. It seemed we always went to the cold areas in the dead of winter and the hot areas in the summer. I suppose that is logical, as the weather in Russia tends to fall in this same cold or boiling pattern.

— ■ —

Ree Heights, population 62, is a "town" that had burned to the ground more than once over the years. It had a unique magnetic high, a little North Pole, located about 3 miles from the train. A B-52 is as big as a barn and impossible to miss on the radar at 3 miles, but when it passed through that magnetic high, it would completely disappear from our radar screen. Our radars had periscopes attached to the masts so we could see the airplane we were tracking. We could manually track the aircraft using the periscope. As we followed the plane, it would first disappear off the radar, but then as it emerged from the intense magnetic field, it would suddenly pop back up on the radar again. It was quite something to watch.

For the first few weeks of my tour at Ree Heights, we participated in a research project called Operation Great Dane. They were testing the impact of the magnetic field on various electronic equipment. During that time a specially equipped prop plane flew patterns at different angles and altitudes across the magnetic field. They had a repeater of some kind on the aircraft so between that and our periscope; we could track them through the field. Our job was to run plots on all of their passes. As they passed through the area, they would call out numbers that we annotated on the plotting papers. Later, there was a thick volume published on this research. I saw it at some point. Interestingly, I can't find any reference whatsoever to Operation Great Dane anywhere on the Internet. I don't know if it is still so classified as to be kept out of the system, or if it is so insignificant as to be lost to history. Maybe I will never know.

RBS Express at Ree Heights SD 1966

Tour with the Army

I also did a TDY with the Army in Seattle. It included both Army and National Guard locations. It was a 4-month tour in the late winter and spring of 1965. There were several Nike anti-aircraft missile sites located around the city. The Army operated some of the sites; others were National Guard. Obviously, their purpose was to shoot down approaching bombers should the time come. They practiced tracking civilian aircraft, but this was a one-sided training exercise. Someone decided that SAC should run practice bomb runs against various targets in the Seattle area to give the Nike Sites a chance to track real bombers. The sites had different equipment than we had at the RBS sites, so this allowed the aircrews to practice a different set of electronic warfare tests along with different locations.

I was assigned to work with Sgt. Gustafson from our RBS site. Our job was to ensure that the bomb runs were correctly scored. Remember how critical these bomb runs were to the flight crew. They were also very costly, so they didn't want to waste money. I think the Air Force didn't trust the Army not to attempt to make themselves look better than they were. In my humble opinion, this was a very real fear as the Nike crews were not very good when it came to tracking a real bomber.

This assignment was somewhat interesting as I got to live with my new wife

165

in Seattle for several months, a rarity for TDY assignments. I also got to work in close collaboration with the Army and to deal with controlling when the SAC crews were allowed to practice electronic warfare.

There were some Russian "fishing trawlers" that cruised up and down our West Coast just within international waters. These boats were actually "elint" (electronics intelligence) platforms monitoring any and all electronic signals they could find. For obvious reasons we did not want to run electronics warfare tests while they were listening. We could still make the practice bomb runs, just not play the electronic warfare games. The Coast Guard was monitoring the trawlers locations, and they would alert us whenever they were within range of our tests.

— ■ —

The Nike sites had a "secret" radar. They were not supposed to use it or turn it on when there was an elint trawler anywhere near. It was their "best-and-final" backup in case of a real attack. It was supposed to be unknown, even to the SAC bomber crews.

At that time, SAC was still flying a few old B-47s. They had one variant, the EB-47, which were ECM (Electronic Counter Measures) aircraft. These e-birds carried every electronic warfare tool in our arsenal. They featured a pressurized module in the bomb bay. It contained 13 separate jammers that were under the control of two electronic warfare officers (EWOs). B-47s normally only had one EWO. EWOs were also known as "Ravens." The name "Raven" being a reference to the black birds, which referenced "black ops," meaning classified operations. While most jamming system of that era were "broadband," blanketing a broad range of frequencies in hopes of jamming radars operating anywhere within that range, these jammers could be selectively tuned to specific radar frequencies by the Ravens. That permitted much higher jammer power on the specific frequencies that represent the greatest threats.

The EB-47s did not even carry bombs. Their role was to fly in with the bombers to wipe out any radar signals, thus clearing an electronic path for the primary bombers as they dropped the heavy weapons. However, a radar jammer tends to announce its presence and location by the radio signals it emits, so EB-47 crews were perfectly aware that they were unlikely to return from an operational mission into the USSR. If they could cover for the B-47 and B-52 bombers, however, it was viewed to be worth the sacrifice.

166

The EB-47 crews needed their training runs just like any SAC crew. We had one e-bird make a run against one of the Nike sites. During the electronic warfare portion of the bomb run, the aircrew really punished the Nike site. Their jammers were so intense; they inverted the images on the Nike radar screens. They were so fast at attacking the signals that the site couldn't even come close to finding and tracking the bomber. The Nike crew got pissed and decided, against all their rules, to turn on their secret radar to track the "old" B-47. They hit the switch and turned the radar toward the inbound bomber. Before the radar had even picked up the aircraft, the Ravens hit their secret radar and inverted its scopes as well. The Nike crew immediately shut down their radar and looked at each other in astonishment. It seemed the EB-47 had a few secrets of its own, and there was no way they were going to let some Army puke track their bird. I laughed when the Nike crew told me what had taken place. I never told them it was an e-bird.

In truth, the EB-47s were used to overfly the Soviet Union on some occasions during this period. They were taking pictures, and gathering signals intelligence of their own. You have to admire those guys; the B-47 was relatively fast for its day but not faster than a MiG, and it could only reach 40,000 feet so anytime they entered enemy airspace they had to rely more on their ability to block any electronic tracking. Their lives depended on it. As far as I know, none were ever shot down. Their existence and capabilities were highly classified, and not published until decades later.

– ■ –

Working with the Army was a fascinating experience. I can't speak for today, but at that time, the Air Force was laid back in comparison to the Army. RBS sites were several levels more relaxed than the "real" Air Force. In the AF you never salute indoors. On the RBS sites you only saluted (even outdoors) an individual officer one time during a day, and if you forgot, no one got upset. When we were traveling to a TDY assignment, we often carpooled with one of our lieutenants or a captain. The rules were simple; once the car door closed we were all equals. We shared driving, expenses, etc. When we go to the other end, he was an officer again, but not in the car.

You always showed respect and appropriately addressed any officer, of course, but the environment was not real military by most standards. As an example when I worked as a "controller" responsible for all communications within the radar site, and with all aircraft on the range, I never used a "sir" when speaking with the aircrews, which were all officers of course. I was in

167

charge of the range and in general terms we were on equal footing. Respectful, professional and courteous at all times, but no discussions of rank cluttering communications with unnecessary chatter.

By comparison, the Army was quite uptight about rank and saluting. Most of the officers at the Nike sites tolerated our more casual style, but I did have one run-in with a new lieutenant. I usually worked at the Nike sites, but one day I had to come to Ft. Lewis for an early morning meeting. As I was walking up to the building for my meeting, a young Army lieutenant was approaching the building with his arms loaded down with books and other items. It looked like it may have been his first day. I said "good morning sir, may I assist you?" he responded negatively, and I held the door so he could enter first. When we got inside, he was obviously pissed and called me to attention while he proceeded to ream me out for not saluting an officer. He was in full tilt; I suspect trying to impress his new bosses. He went on for several minutes and finally ask what I had to say for myself. I replied simply "Sir, in the Air Force, we are instructed not to salute an officer when he is unable to return the salute. We are to show appropriate respect and to provide any necessary assistance, but we are not to inconvenience the officer."

His loud ass chewing had caused all work to stop, and all eyes were on us waiting to see what would take place. He stood silent for several seconds then dismissed me without further comment. The room remained silent for several additional seconds before the usual commotion resumed. There were some smirking faces, both officers and enlisted. I had several free beers that evening as the word quickly spread. Like I said, it was a fun assignment.

Beefeater

The naming standard for the RBS sites was to go by the name of the nearest community. For example, the site near Vale, OR was called "Vale Bomb Plot," but for some reason, Wilder was the exception. Wilder went by the code name of the low-level route, "Beefeater." I don't remember anyone ever calling it "Wilder Bomb Plot," it was always just called Beefeater.

We had an excellent crew and good officers. Beefeater was always considered the best of the RBS sites. We lived like civilians. We rented apartments and drove to work. There were no military facilities beyond the site and its equipment. I don't remember there even being so much as a military car. We never had inspections, and there was no kitchen so no KP. There weren't any of the usual military routines. We didn't have a PX, but we did have a medic, his primary job was giving vaccinations and passing out cold medicines when necessary. That was about it. I only recall putting on my blues one time; that was when I reported for duty at the Vale Bomb Plot. As I recall, that was the only time after I left Keesler. When people ask what I did, I told them I "worked for the government."

Mountain Home Air Force Base was about 75 miles from Wilder. Mountain Home was a SAC base with B-47s when we were at Vale, but as the B-47s were phased out, it became a TAC (Tactical Air Command) fighter base with F4 Phantoms. We could go to Mt. Home to access the PX and for non-emergency medical support, but otherwise it was not part of our existence. The only time we lived as if we were in the military was when we were on TDY assignments, and even then, it was a pretty casual existence. It was a very pleasant way to live.

The only hassle was dealing with a place to live. We received "separate-rations" (a food and housing allowance) as we had to live in the civilian economy. However, when we went on TDY we lived on the train and ate in the dining car, so we didn't get separate-rations during that time. That meant that we had to move out of our apartments, store our stuff, and then find a new place after the assignment. Fortunately, the local population was reasonably accommodating. Those of us who were single would typically have 3 or 4 roommates. At any given time, at least one would be away on TDY, so we could usually get by with no more than a few occasional nights sleeping on the couch. For those of us who were married, it became a much bigger hassle as our housing costs continued while our very limited income went down during every TDY.

— ■ —

We lived and worked remote, so it was rare to actually go to a base, but whenever we were on a SAC air base; the flight crews treated us very well. As I said earlier, for a time, Mt. Home AFB was a SAC base with a wing of B-47s. Whenever we went on TDY, we would go to Mt Home to pull travel funds for the assignment. One time we were on the base standing in line at the pay window. One of the guys with me, I don't remember his name, was short, not more than the 5'2" minimum. He was cocky as all get out, always cracking a joke or acting bigger than he was. He had a terrible "short man's complex." Like most airmen, we wore "unit caps," in our case; they were black with gold "RBS" embossed on the front.

It was lunchtime, and the window wasn't open. We were back 10 or 15 places in this unmoving line. A Major in a flight uniform walked up to the front of the line causing everybody to move back. Rank does have its privileges, so there were no objections. The Major turned around to see if anyone was grousing about his jumping the line and wouldn't you know, my short friend leaned out of the line and made it obvious that he was staring at the Major's nametag. At the same time, my friend tipped his hat ever so slightly. The Major looked at him like he was going to say something, then noticed at his hat. He immediately got out of line and walked back to where we were and stepped in line right behind me. He wanted to compare the process from our side of the fence. We had a good visit while we waited for the pay window to open.

Because we were not part of the base, no one, other than the aircrews, had any idea who we were or the meaning of RBS. After the window had opened, we got our money we said goodbye to the Major, and headed for our car. Three guys stopped us and asked who the heck we were and why the Major showed so much deference to a couple of lowly airmen 2nd classes. We explained, and everyone had a good laugh.

– ■ –

Money was always tight while I was in the Air Force. Even without the separate-rations issue, it was hard to live on the meager wages we received. After I got married, we usually went to Mt. Home every couple of months to stock up on groceries as well as other necessities from the PX. I remember that a jar of Gerber's baby food was 9¢ at the PX, about ½ of the price at the local stores. Fortunately, gas was cheap.

I usually took on a second part-time job to make ends meet. I painted houses, mowed lawns, occasionally drove a tractor, or whatever I could find. There was a guy (maybe a company but I don't remember) that built concrete cattle feed bins for the potato farmers. The farmers often fed cattle on their property during the winter as a second source of income. Of course, the cows helped fertilize the potato fields as a bonus. The work was mostly during the winter. It was dirty and cold work, but my boss was willing to accommodate my rotating shift and frequent TDYs, so I was able to work whenever I was available. That was a real plus because it was a scheduling hassle for both of us.

When we would get to a farm in the morning, we would go to the potato cellar and grab a nice big spud. We would wash them, wrap them in aluminum foil. We would dig a hole and place our potatoes under an inch or so of dirt. We set a good-sized fire over the spuds. The fire helped keep us warm, while it cooked our lunch. By noon, we would have a hot baked potato. Add some salt and pepper plus a good-sized piece of fresh butter, and it was an excellent way to supplement whatever else we had brought for lunch. It was not good for the waistline, but a piping hot baked potato sure hit the spot on a cold winter Idaho day.

Cheap Gas

I remember when gas was 10¢ per gallon. At Wilder, I had to commute from Nampa to Wilder each day. We would purchase $1 gas coins each payday so we would be sure to have enough to get to work through the month. Each of these "coins" would buy 10 gallons of gas. The trick was to make sure you had sufficient room for all that you could buy for a dollar; there were no refunds. Every once in a while, there would be a "gas war," and you could get 12 gallons for one coin.

We usually carpooled to save money. One of the guys, Sgt. Fred Hurst owned a 1963 Split Window Corvette. Needless to say, he was the envy of all. Those who carpooled with Sgt. Hurst scored nearly as high on the totem pole, even if we were like sardines in the back seat. He was a pretty cautious driver, but we did get an occasional fast ride home in the middle of the night. One time, the fog was so thick one of us had to walk the car part of the way home. The driver couldn't see the road at all so one person got out and walked the edge of the road so Fred could drive. Fortunately, the dense fog only lasted a mile or so before it thinned to the point where he could see.

Fred was one of the gung-ho guys I mentioned earlier who raced out of the Grand Canyon. If I remember correctly, he left the Air Force to become a Baptist minister.

The Oriental Way

There was one crusty old Chief Master Sargent at our site. Of course, he went by the name "Chief." I don't remember his actual name. That is a shame, but it was 50 years ago. I do remember at least part of his story. He had enlisted in the Army Air Corp in WWII. That was before the Air Force was a separate branch. I don't remember the specifics of what he did during the war, in fact, I don't remember him ever talking about it, but everyone was aware of at least some of his history. He was awarded a "battlefield commission" to 2nd

Lieutenant. That recognition that was typically considered second only to the Congressional Medal of Honor. From there he received three additional "spot-promotions" and finished the war as a Major. By any measure, that represents an incredible honor and achievement. There was a total of just 25,000 battlefield commissions out of more than 16 million who served during WWII. I was not able to determine how many made it all the way to Major, but I suspect there were very few.

After the war, all branches of the service wanted to "realign" their ranks so that all officers had to be college graduates and had to have completed the Officer Training Course. The solution for those who stayed in the service, but didn't meet the criteria, was to move them back to the enlisted ranks. In his case as a Chief Master Sargent. A high percentage of the enlisted men who stayed in were also lowered in level because those who reenlisted were predominately those who held a higher rank. Most military organizations remained top-heavy 18 years later. That is in part why promotions were all about time in grade and time in service.

Fortunately, when he retired, Chief would receive his retirement pay based on his highest honorably held rank; he would retire as a Major. He was a super nice guy. As you can imagine, he had pretty much seen it all. He was very relaxed, and at ease in any situation. He seemed to make his schedule and work on whatever interested him. He also appeared to have a good deal of money. He was single, I think he had lost his wife, but I don't remember for sure. Our commander, a Lt. Colonel, treated him as an equal. He and the Colonel were always betting on games and chatting like lifelong friends.

The Chief liked being a mentor to a few of the younger airmen and he took me under his wing. He taught me some valuable life lessons. Specifically, I learned how to deal with stress and with stressed out individuals. Don't sweat the small stuff, and compartmentalize your problems. He called it the "oriental" way. If you had a problem, work on it until it was solved, or you came to a point where you were unable to proceed due to some unknown, or some external dependency. Put it back in its compartment and don't worry about it. Of course, don't forget it, but don't waste energy or time if you can't solve it right now. Take out a different problem and work on it until it was resolved or until you couldn't make further progress, then put it away and proceed to the next. He taught me that those who try to solve a bunch of different problems simultaneously usually wind up solving none. Work on them serially, and you will get far more done with far less stress.

As for dealing with stressed out people; his lesson wasn't quite as clear. However, I have taken what he started and constructed my approach. The main thing is to accept that "there is no such thing as an irrational act." Think of the crazy man talking to the lamppost. It sure looks irrational to any sane observer, but the key thing to remember is that for that man, it is entirely rational. No one and that includes a certifiably insane person will act in an irrational way. Their actions may appear completely irrational to you, but they are rational to the individual performing the act. Therefore, the challenge is always to try to figure out what the rationale of the other person is. If you can do that, you can understand their actions; you can empathize with them. By not rejecting them or their actions out of hand, you can communicate with then and deal with their stress or whatever the problem is that is driving their actions. Understanding their rationale will defuse the situation and lead you to success in your dealings with that person.

Bomb Comp

The RBS system standardized bomber flying techniques and identify weakness in training, but the 1st CEVG did not exist just to train weak flyers; it also identified the best flyers. Beginning in 1961, the 1st CEVG assumed the responsibility of scoring the International Bomb Comp. Bomb Comp used the same methods that we used to score any other bomb run. The winner of the competition, the best bomber crew in the free world, received the prestigious Fairchild Award.

The last TDY I did was at the 1966 Bomb Comp. Bomb Comp was often called the World Series of Bombing. It was a tournament for the best bomber crews from the US, the United Kingdom, Canada, and Australia. After missing a few years, there had been an abbreviated Bomb Comp in 1965. I was not involved in that one. The 1966 Bomb Comp was a full-scale event that included 35 B-52 wings, two B-58 wings, and three RAF crews, one each from England, Canada, and Australia. They were flying Vulcan bombers.

174

There were 40 aircraft and flight crews in total. The B-47s were all mothballed by then, and this turned out to be the last year that the B-58s participated. There were no Bomb Comps during the Viet Nam War, and by the end of that war, the B-58s had been decommissioned.

— ■ —

The B-52s, which at that time had been flying for nearly 15 years, remain the Air Force's primary heavy bomber 50 years later, in 2016. In fact, the B-52s are projected to remain a critical part of the fleet until 2040, an incredible lifespan of 90 years. The B-52s have been continuously upgraded, but in a world where technology is obsolete after 18 months, that speaks to the design, flexibility, and durability of these remarkable aircraft.

— ■ —

Each competing Bomb Comp crew flew two missions consisting of on-time takeoff, night celestial navigation, two low altitude bombing runs, and one high altitude bombing run, each with two releases. There was airborne refueling and other parts to the Bomb Comp, but we were not involved in those areas. Two RBS Express trains provided traditional RBS scoring. Each was moved to a new location so that none of the crews had any experience with the range.

The RBS staff were handpicked from all of the RBS sites. As with the bomber crews, the RBS staff were the best individuals. To be selected was a significant recognition. I was the Plotter for the RBS Express located in Wendell, Idaho.

I normally worked as the site Controller as it was usually the most critical position responsible for coordinating all site activities. As with most jobs, they started you at the easiest position, which was a backup radar operator. As you learned and demonstrated your proficiency at different positions, you took on more complex roles. The controller was the top dog. It typically took 5 or 6 years to master all that was necessary to become the Site Controller. Besides being proficient at every position (operations and maintenance) on the site, the controller had to know the regulations backward and forward and have the gravitas to enforce them with aircrews who all out-ranked the controller.

Controllers had to be able to multitask; all communications within the site, and between the site and the aircrews took place through the controller. He had to listen to operators in two radar vans, the recorder, the plotter and the backup plotter in a second computer van, the electronic warfare crew in yet another van, and up to 8 aircraft on the range at any time. Some aircraft would be conducting bomb runs, while others were either entering or leaving the range. The controller had to monitor four different radio sets at all times. The controller ruled the site; I enjoyed being the controller.

— ■ —

Having the ability to monitor and participate in multiple conversations simultaneously was a necessary skill, but it did have some drawbacks in social settings. I could be in a room full of people and without even thinking about it, I would follow virtually every conversation in the room. I occasionally got in trouble when I elected to participate in conversations that I was not part of physically. It was such a routine part of the controller's job that I was usually not even aware that I was doing it until it was too late. It is a learned skill, and unfortunately, I have long since lost this ability. I suppose it is better for my social life.

— ■ —

In the case of Bomb Comp, the controller's role was a much-diminished function, to the point of being probably the least important position on the crew. For Bomb Comp, we knew in advance exactly which aircraft was next in line and when it would arrive. The crews were all top notch, so there was never an issue of rules violations. Even if there were, the controller could not intervene unless there was a safety issue. Since all the bomb runs were identical and the encrypted scores were not transmitted to the crew, as they were normally, communication was quite limited. In addition, there was no other air traffic on the range. It was enter-drop-exit. The controller's role was mostly just saying hello and good-bye.

For Bomb Comp, the plotter and the recorder were the most critical positions. Typical runs were at 15-minute intervals. For the competition, they used 8-minute intervals. The two (simulated) bomb releases were about 3 minutes apart. That meant that the plotter only had about 2 minutes to score both releases and set up for the next run. Normally, you would have about 12 minutes, which even then could be somewhat hectic if there were a long series of back-to-back runs. On an 8-minute cycle with 40 aircraft in a row, there was no time for mistakes or to even catch your breath. There was also additional pressure because it was all done with a bunch of strange officers crowded into your workspace watching your every move. With 40 bomb runs in less than 6 hours, and with no breaks; the Plotter's life was intense.

Calculating and plotting the actual bomb release is a rather complicated process. It considered the flight characteristics of the bomb, burst altitude, and even the Coriolis effect. That is a measurement of how far the earth moves during the time the bomb was falling. The Recorder was responsible for running all the calculations based on tracking and speed data provided by the Plotter. He then provided the adjustment data to the Plotter who would then plot the actual flight path of the (simulated) bomb. Once the theoretical impact point had been identified, the plotter could score the drop by measuring the range and azimuth from the actual target. The plotter/recorder team had to be very close; communications had to be flawless. There was no time for second guessing, or making mistakes. All the while, the observers, who probably only had a vague idea of all that was taking place, loved to lean in close as the plotting board was where all the visible action was.

While participation was an honor, the actual RBS crewmembers were anonymous to the aircrews. We never gave names, rank, home site, or any form of identification. Our job was to score the process, not to be mainline participants.

At the end of one long night, after I had scored the last run, the Controller needed a bathroom break and so I sat in for him. The only task was clearing the last few planes off the range as they reached the 75 nautical mile point. As I said earlier, we generally didn't include any "sirs" in our communications. To do so would have just added unnecessary radio traffic. However, I had developed a "signature" style as a controller at Beefeater Bomb Plot. The only time I said "sir" was as the aircraft signed off our range. My standard exit was "Good day (or night) and good flying to you and your crew sir."

On this night, as one of the last aircraft requested exit clearance I replied with my standard 'good night and good flying' line without even thinking. The pilot immediately responded "Ah, goodnight Beefeater." As the pilots' communications were broadcast throughout the radar train, the fact that I had been identified came as a shock to the observers. I didn't own up to my signature line as the "tell" because I didn't want to lose it. I only said they must have recognized my voice. Most of the RBS crew knew instantly how the aircraft had identified me, but the observers remained clueless.

Close only counts in horseshoes

The full story is that "close only counts in horseshoes, hand grenades, and A-bombs."

No history of the 1st CEVG and RBS would be complete without at least a brief mention of their involvement in the Viet Nam war. I was scheduled for discharge June 20, 1966, but my tour was extended nine months due to manpower shortages. That did not provide enough time for me to go to Viet Nam, but over time, most of my friends at Beefeater and the other RBS sites did.

That war was long before GPS, Tomahawks, and precision guided bombs. B-52s, usually with their radar turned off due to the threat of SAMs (surface to air missiles), were dropping uncontrolled "dumb" bombs from 40,000 feet. A bomb that missed by 200 feet would not only fail to destroy the intended target; it could easily kill our troops. You don't have to be a navigator to figure out that to get an uncontrolled bomb to hit a target 8 miles away, you have to know precisely where to release it. That is impossible with no radar and no GPS.

To remedy this, SAC used the 1st CEVG to direct aerial bombing raids, under the code name Combat Sky Spot. During the 7-year period from March 1966 until August 1973, more than 3,000 RBS personnel operated multiple Sky Spot locations, 24 hours a day. They directed more than 300,000 USAF, Navy, and Marine sorties, including reconnaissance and rescue. They also directed 150,000 tactical air strikes, as well as 75 percent of all B-52 strikes, including Arc Light sorties Linebacker II missions.

Like many who went to Vietnam, Sky Spot suffered causalities. Civilian surveyors and builders, as well as airmen, died in building Sky Spot locations. Unfortunately, once built, the radar sites located in South Vietnam, Thailand, and (secretly at Station Lima-85) in Laos, were vulnerable. The Sky Spot sites were high-value targets, as hostile Vietnamese realized that by destroying a relatively undefended radar site, U.S. air power became inaccurate and ineffective. As a result, the casualty rate among Sky Spot personnel was, for a time, the highest of any military unit in Viet Nam.

Technology

Technology is at the base of my entire career, and so it is important to keep track of how these technologies evolved over the years.

The Air Force equipment I initially trained on was WWII vintage, vacuum tube, analog computers. About a year before I left the Air Force, a new system was introduced. That was a modern digital system with solid-state technology. This transition was consistent with the technology evolution taking place in the civilian world.

The impact of this new technology was significant. Before that time, a minimum of three people, the radar operator, the recorder, and the plotter, were involved in the scoring of the bomb drop. The recorder made the calculations, and the plotter physical scored the rum. The new system replaced the recorder and the plotter. The radar operator locked on to the aircraft, and the computer did all the tracking, calculating and scoring. While I was there, we still did the manual procedure as a backup, but it was evident that these functions would soon disappear.

– ■ –

Just a brief lesson on the difference between analog and digital computers, as this transition is significant. An analog computer determines a value based on the amplitude of a signal. In simple terms, a value of 1 V (volt) could represent a 1; a 3 V could represent a 3, and so on. It was easy to design Vacuum tube circuits that produced and recognized these steps in voltage, but the tubes didn't always provide a precise voltage. Was a 1.5 V value a 1 or a 2, who could know? Vacuum tubes were also slow to transition from one voltage to another. That restricted the speed of the computer. Finally, they were big, and they consumed a lot of electricity, so they produced a lot of heat.

A digital computer works strictly on binary conditions. A circuit is like a switch. It is either on equaling a 1, or off equaling a 0. Transistors work mostly on the off/on condition, they are much smaller, more reliable, they consume less electricity thus producing less heat, and they transition from off to on much faster. As transistors were made smaller and smaller, millions fit on a single ½" square silicone chip.

Initially, these early systems did not have any error checking. Users had test programs that they ran periodically to make sure the computer was producing accurate results. In some cases, they would run a program three times and take the average answer.

It may be hard to believe, but early in the space program, rockets were designed using these computers. In fact, the first men were sent into orbit using these same computers. How would you like to ride on top of a zillion tons of high explosives being shot into space where no one had ever been before, all designed and controlled by computers that were so flakey that you had to run a program three times and take the average answer? Now that takes guts!

Spare Time

The aircrews did their qualification testing early each quarter. That gave them time to retest if necessary. It also got the monkey off their back so to speak. That meant that our work was frontloaded each quarter and trailed off to almost nothing by the end of the quarter. We were not given any advance schedule of activities, so we had to be there even if there were no aircraft on the range.

Many of the guys filled the hours playing Pinochle or Crazy Eights. I certainly did my share of card playing, but I quickly became bored with cards. Someone had to monitor the radios at all times, so I volunteered and used the time to study the Ops Manuals. Learning the rules lead to quick advancement to the position of Controller. I continued to babysit the radios even after becoming the controller. That gave me the opportunity to study other things without being considered a complete "nerd."

— ∎ —

The Air Force offered self-study "extension" courses in electronics and other subjects. These were free of course, and I completed more than 20 during my AF years. I also purchased a commercial course from Cleveland Institute of Electronics. This course guaranteed that I would pass the examination for a First Class FCC License.

An FCC license is required to work on anything that transmitted over the airways. A 3rd Class license is simply for radio operators. It is pretty straightforward and just tests to make sure you know what you can and cannot do with your equipment, as well as what you cannot say on the air.

The 2nd Class license examination required considerable knowledge of electronics. Aircraft and ship owners are required to have a technician with a 2nd Class license sign off on their equipment any time there has been an issue or maintenance performed. There is also a Radar Endorsement, which is, of course, specific to radar equipment. The 1st Class license is the top level. It requires more in-depth transmitter knowledge. Every commercial radio and TV station is required to have at least one 1st Class licensed technician.

I studied for months and finally drove to Portland Oregon to take the exam. I took all of the examinations in a single setting. That was a mistake; I should have taken the tests over multiple days, but the FCC only gave the exams once a quarter and so I would have had to come back a few months later; I couldn't afford the time or expense. Collectively the tests amounted to more than eight hard hours of exams. I received a 2nd Class License with Radar Endorsement but missed out on the 1st Class license. I was a bit frustrated, but in the end, I never had a job that required any license, so I suppose it didn't make any difference. The course I had taken guaranteed a 1st Class license, so I did get my money back.

Radar Games

It turns out that animals are pretty sensitive to things like RF energy, even if it is a mile away. People won't feel it, but birds and antelope can. At Wilder, the site sat on a bluff overlooking the Snake River. Below us, and out a little less than a mile, there was a small island in the river. The island was a private duck hunting club. Through the periscope on the radar, which had a 20x magnification, we could easily see the hunters crouched in their duck blinds waiting for the birds to come down to land.

We would turn off the radar and watch for incoming ducks or geese. We could follow them down until just before they got into shotgun range. At that point, we would switch on the radar and hit the birds with a healthy dose of RF energy. They would immediately spook and fly away. The hunters would stand up and look around to see who had moved and caused the birds to spook. They never did figure out what we were doing.

— ∎ —

Antelope are incredibly curious, but also incredibly stupid. Hunters frequently plant a pole in the ground and tie on a piece of colored ribbon. The antelope will become obsessed with trying to figure out what the fluttering ribbon is. They were always cautious and so would not approach the flag directly. They would swing back and forth gradually getting closer and closer until the hunter had a good shot. Scratch one antelope.

At Wamsutter, we did the same thing, but without a gun. We would plant a flag out a half-mile or so from the train and watch the antelope through the periscope with the radar turned off. Just when the antelope was ready to stick out their nose to sniff the ribbon, we would kick on the radar. The antelope would immediately spook and run away. We would shut off the transmitter, and after running a few hundred feet, the antelope would stop, flick its tail a few times and then start his back and forth path, returning to the flag. The antelope seemed to never tire of trying to figure out what that ribbon and the strange feeling were.

The Kennedy Assassination

President John F. Kennedy was assassinated November 22, 1963, in Dallas, TX. I was working that day at the Vale bomb plot when we received the news of Kennedy's assassination. There was an aircraft inbound for a bomb run, and they suddenly aborted their run and told us they were leaving the range immediately. At the time, we didn't know why. Within a few minutes, we received notification. The military was placed on the highest alert level because no one knew if the assignation was part of a greater plot and potentially the start of war. Remember, this was just one year after the Cuban Missile Crisis.

In reality, we were just a flyspeck of a bomb plot in the middle of the high desert in eastern Oregon. Our mission was to train and evaluate SAC aircrews for exactly what they were now preparing to do. Should the assignation of our president be the first step in a new war, their job was to penetrate Soviet airspace and wipe the Soviet Union off the face of the earth. All available bombers were now on alert, and most were flying to their assigned positions surrounding the Soviet Union. Their bomb bays were filled with very real nuclear weapons and locked in a safe on each aircraft was their designated targets. The crew would not know their specific targets until they received the proper launch codes from now President Lyndon Johnson. No one was thinking about making any practice bomb runs.

We were on alert but had absolutely nothing to do and no responsibility in the greater drama that was unfolding around us. We sat and listened to the radios, which were totally silent. We played cards and went home at the end of our shift. Work-wise, it was a big non-event. That continued for several days before things returned to normal.

The Beatles

The Beatles' made their historic first appearance on the Ed Sullivan Show on February 9, 1964. A lesser known fact is that their first North American appearance on prime time television was actually on the Jack Parr Show in January 1964, but that appearance had little impact on the American audience. The Ed Sullivan show blew the top off the music world.

You couldn't be alive and not be aware of The Beatles, but I must admit I never really understood or much appreciated them or their music. It never really connected for me.

Some things I missed

Many things that began during my Air Force time didn't reach full force until years later. I wasn't quite a "baby-boomer" as I was born in 1945, but close. The boomers begat the "hippie" movement with free love, sex, drugs, and rock & roll that consumed a sizable part of what became known as the boomer generation. I didn't understand the music, never tried drugs, and I was married and had no interest in the "sexual revolution" that was taking place. I never felt disenfranchised, misunderstood, or rebellious.

The anti-war movement was just starting. Over the years that followed, there were many college protests, street riots, draft-dodgers, etc. The Kent State shootings took place several years after this period. I didn't understand the protests, and I didn't support them. I had too many friends whose lives were on the line; I was not about to protest what they were doing.

In 1972, Jane Fonda traveled to North Viet Nam and was filmed laughing and clapping on an anti-aircraft gun. She was supporting the North Vietnamese and condemning Americans. These photos were used extensively for propaganda purposes. At the very time, she was cavorting with the enemy; there were American POWs nearby being tortured and held in deplorable conditions. The army she was praising was killing our soldiers. Many, myself included, saw this as giving aid and comfort to the enemy, an act of treason. Fonda earned the name "Hanoi Jane, the American traitor." She has apologized many times, but "sorry" does not excuse treason or the deaths she helped bring about. For most of us who proudly served our country, she will forever remain Hanoi Jane, the traitor.

Marriage and Family

My Air Force period began when I was just 17½ and ended just after I turned 22. These are very formative years in anyone's life, and I was no exception. I established my career foundation during these years. I also built my family. I got married to a local Idaho girl in 1964 when I was 19, and she was 18. I became a father at 20 and again at 22, just two weeks before I left the Air Force.

I am not one to look back and say I: could have, would have, should have, but

I do look back and try to evaluate the crucial decisions I made in my life so that I can make better decisions in the future. A mistake that many people make is to say, "if I had it to do over again I would have done it differently." That ignores the "butterfly effect." A different choice on even a minor decision would have set my life on a different path, and I would not be the person I am today. I am extremely happy with where I am today and equally satisfied with the road my life has taken. That said, I can still realistically evaluate my decisions and see where I made errors in judgment, and I certainly made many judgment errors during the period that I was in the Air Force.

My marriage was one of the more severe judgmental errors I made in my life. I am not saying it was a mistake, or that I would make a different choice, but I can now clearly see that my decision was based on my lack of judgment and lake of discernment. I do not mean to disparage Jane, she was, and as far as I know, still is, a good person. She may, or may not view her decision as an error in judgment, but that is up to her to decide. The judgment error, as far as I am concerned, was mine.

The family I was raised in was rare. I never saw my parents argue or even disagree. I am sure they must have at various points, but it was never visible to me. Maybe they had worked it all out before I was old enough to recognize friction, but they clearly understood their different roles in the marriage and rearing of the children. They always worked smoothly as a team to accomplish their goals. I naïvely assumed that all marriages worked this way. My naïveté is laughable because I could clearly see that the families of our neighbors and friends at school were not like mine.

I also naïvely believed that to "to be a man" you grew up, got married and had children. That was one of those Reader's Digest type Griswoldism from childhood. I grew up, got married and had children. Unfortunately, because I just assumed that marriages worked the way my parents' marriage worked, it never dawned on me that the key to a successful marriage was to choose the right partner. Again, I naïvely assumed that my partner would have the same values and goals as I did. In retrospect, I was unbelievably dumb to make these assumptions; but I did.

I will talk later about how our marriage progressed and ultimately ended. Suffice it to say I built the marriage on invalid assumptions based on my naïveté. I believed that a marriage between two good and decent people would somehow just naturally come together and work.

184

Planning My Exit

One of my personal goals has always been to be "second to none" in my job. Specifically, to be the best there was at whatever I did for a living. I did achieve this in my short Air Force career. Unfortunately, in the Air Force, at least at that time, your rank and therefore your pay was never about how good you were or how hard you worked, it was all about time in grade and time in service. In the RBS system, there were a relatively large number of older NCOs (Non-Commissioned Officers), some even from WWII and the Korean War era. It didn't help that the RBS assignment was such a unique and pleasant version of military life that it encouraged reenlistment. This glut of "old guys" clogged the upper ranks. It was tough for young airmen to gain rank.

While rank came with time in grade and time in service, responsibilities came with effort and expertise. I had advanced to hold the most critical position of Controller far faster than normal and my skills and dedication had been recognized through several commendations and my selection for the most demanding role for the 1966 World Bombing Competition. Unfortunately, that was where it ended. NCOs that were not as capable or as hard working were clogging the system while making far greater income. I saw all of this very much like being in a union; you just had to show up. In time, you would receive your reward. It was all about time. There were exceptions; on the downside, they could kick you out if you screwed up, but upside opportunities were few. This "union like" atmosphere drove me crazy, and as a result, I have avoided working for a union all my life.

As the time neared to leave the Air Force, the Viet Nam war was starting to crank up, and RBS crews began rotating to Tan Son Nhut Air Base in Viet Nam to guide real bombing missions instead of to the RBS Express. My Air Force tour was extended for nine months when RBS staffing became critical. The 9-months was not sufficient to do a tour in Viet Nam, but I did receive an additional stripe as a consequence of the extension. The extension also conveniently covered the medical cost of our second child, and it meant that Uncle Sam would ship my household goods when I did leave the AF.

— ■ —

As exit time neared, I had no idea how easy or difficult it would be to get a job. I had never actually been in the position of looking for a job. I had almost no savings so making a rapid transition was critical. My strategy was to "darken the sky" with resumes. Knowing that my FCC license was important to airlines, I applied to United as well as Alaskan Coastal (later Alaska) airlines. I also applied to Raytheon, Burroughs, National Cash Register, and IBM. There were many others that I no longer remember.

United was one of the first to respond, and after a couple of interviews, they offered me a job working at San Francisco International with a starting salary of $750 a month. That was a huge sum since I was making $275 at that time. The United offer was a union job. I remember asking about opportunity and the recruiter laid out a schedule of time and pay steps. I ask what would be the opportunities for rapid advancement if I were excellent at my job. He repeated the same time/pay schedule. That was not the answer I wanted to hear, but having an actual offer in my pocket gave me a distinct advantage in dealing with other opportunities. I ultimately got offers from all of the companies I listed above.

I remember that the most impressive interview was with Burroughs. I went to their office in Boise, and after some written tests and an interview, I was taken back to the shop area where there was an old calculator, probably about 1910 vintage. It had cast iron legs that stood almost chest high. It was designed for use while standing at a bank teller window. It was 100% mechanical. He lifted the cover off the monster and showed me the inner workings. He pressed one button and turned the crank, which caused the machine to print a number on the paper roll. He turned to me and said "I will be back in 5 minutes. Tell me how it does that." I have had interviews where I had to spend the day with a physiatrist, but I have never had an interview that was quite as technical or specific as the Burroughs interview. It also told me what kind of equipment they wanted me to work on, mechanical. Even though they offered me a job in the Seattle area, I knew that Burroughs was not where I wanted to work.

I negotiated for weeks with Alaskan Coastal. It wasn't a union shop at that time, and the salary was very high $900. The location was in Juneau. At that point, I had a romantic vision of living and working in Alaska, so the opportunity was very attractive. The sticking point was getting my household furniture to Juneau. The AF would pay to take my belongings to Seattle, but no further. There are no roads into Juneau, so my stuff would have to go by ship from Seattle. I didn't have much furniture, but I had even fewer funds to ship my stuff. I wanted Alaskan Coastal to pay the freight, and they were resisting. We seemed to reach an impasse, and I had other offers so I could be a demanding. They didn't respond to my demand, so I let it slide.

I was also talking with IBM, which was my preferred employer. I had spoken to them about factory work in either San Jose or Boulder. The decision deadline was rapidly approaching, and I didn't yet have an offer in hand. I had been dealing with a guy in San Jose. We were down to the final negotiations when I got a call from him, and he asked if I preferred Boulder or San Jose, but he also asked if I had considered the Field Engineering Division. I knew nothing of the Field Engineering Division or the Customer Engineering job. When he described their role, I said I was more interested in this work than factory work. He said he would talk to the Denver Branch and see what they could do.

He said I would need to interview with a Field Engineering Manager. I explained to him that I was down to the wire and that I had to tell the Air Force where to ship my goods on Monday, one week before my actual discharge. This was Tuesday, less than a week to go. I was working a shift where I didn't get off work until 6 p.m. and Boise, the nearest IBM office, was more than an hour away. He hastily arranged an interview for Thursday at 8 p.m.

I drove home from the site, picked up my wife, and drove to Boise for the late evening interview. I didn't even have time to change out of my fatigues. After we had talked, the manager told me he would get back to me. I said no, I need a decision tonight. That must have seemed rather brazen coming from the mouth of a 22-year-old, in fatigues. I explained why, and he asked me to wait outside the office for a minute. He called me back after a few minutes and offered me a job in the Denver North Branch Office starting at $500 per month. We shook hands, and I was hired.

In those few minutes, my transition from the airman to civilian was complete, but as Lucy would say, I did have some "splaining" to do to my wife who was waiting in the car with our children. She was glad to be out of the house and to be participating albeit indirectly, in the decisions that would affect the next phase of our life. Jane was glad that she at least knew where we would be moving. However, as we drove home, she had a hard time understanding why had I rejected an opportunity paying three times what we were currently making, that also included great travel benefits, for one that paid only twice as much. More importantly, what did this new job mean for our young family? I really couldn't answer the second question, but for me, it was the simplest life-changing decision I ever made. As it turned out, it was also one of the best. It was not about the money. In fact, no job I have ever taken was about the money. It was the perfect job, for the perfect company, in the location I wanted to live and work. Explaining was one thing, but ultimately it came down to her accepting what was essentially my decision based on intuition.

Over the next week, I informed United and others that I had accepted another offer. I didn't contact Alaskan Coastal as I had not heard from them in some time and assumed the opportunity had never fully materialized.

About two months after I started with IBM, I was attending training in Rochester, MN when a cable from Alaskan Coastal caught up with me. In essence, it said, "Where are you?" As far as I could determine, they had accepted my final requirements and sent an official offer letter. Somehow, that letter never reached me. In retrospect, I see God's hand in this. I was infatuated with the idea of living and working in Alaska. Had I accepted their offer, my life would have undoubtedly been dramatically different. IBM was the right decision at the time, and He made it simple by removing the Alaskan Coastal temptation.

Conclusion

I remember my Air Force time fondly. The training and experience were excellent; it provided the foundation for the remainder of my career. I didn't get outside of the US, other than a weekend in Vancouver while I was on the TDY in Seattle, but I did a lot of traveling all over the West, much of the South, and the Midwest. I had discipline before joining, but the AF reinforced my self-discipline. I grew up while serving, and while I would hardly say I became "worldly" at that young age, the many experiences I had helped me mature. The alternative to my AF time would have been either college or working in the civilian world. The Air Force was, at least for me, the best use of my time at that age.

The benefit of looking back 50+ years is that you can see patterns that were not visible at the time. I see first in my leaving the Shasta Valley to join the Air Force, and then in my decision to leave the Air Force, an underlying desire to move up the food chain as it were. I didn't like being in a position where I was just responding to decisions made by others, and working with products and processes designed by others. I didn't want to be the tail wagged by the dog; I wanted to be involved in the designing and making process. I wanted to be the dog.

The IBM Years 1967 – 1981

My years at IBM were an adventure, both fun and challenging. IBM expanded the technical foundation I began in the Air Force, but it also established my business acumen and credentials. The skills, education, and experience I gained at IBM shaped the entirety of my career and in many ways my life. I often refer to this period as my "IBM University" years.

A layered Computing Architecture and the IBM Gold Rush

I joined IBM in the "gold rush" period. IBM had introduced their revolutionary System/360 in 1964. The S/360 was a disruptive technology that revolutionized what would become known as the IT (Information Technology) industry. The success of the S/360 broke IBM out of the pack of computer companies driving it to become the dominant manufacturer and the 5th largest company in the world for a period. The common phrase at the time was "IBM and the Seven Dwarfs" referring to Burroughs, Sperry Rand, Control Data, Honeywell, General Electric, RCA, and NCR. At the start of the decade, they were all fairly evenly matched. By 1965, IBM held 65% of the market.

The layered computing architecture introduced with the S/360 was the core of that revolution. That architecture was a phenomenal accomplishment that has withstood the test of time and continues to dominate computing more than 50 years later.

Before the S/360, computers of various sizes all worked independently and differently. Memory as well as disk and tape storage were very expensive, with very little capacity, and still quite slow. A computer with 2K, 2,000 bytes or characters, of storage, was considered a large machine. An 8K memory module was about the size of a file drawer and could cost as much as $2 million. That was in 1965 dollars; it would be more than $15 million today. Just to put that in perspective, 2K is roughly the equivalent of a single typed page. Today, you can store 256 GB (billion bytes) on a device the size of your thumbnail at the cost of less than $50.

I recently heard this rather startling comparison. A singing birthday card requires 24K, the equivalent of 12 mainframe computers of the 1960 era. Taking that one step further, the computer that was on the Apollo 17 spacecraft that navigated the last Apollo spaceship from the earth to land on the moon and then return to earth had just 24K of memory. Apollo 17 was launched December 7, 1972.

As an aside, it was the high cost and minimum size of storage that spawned what would become known as the Y2K problem more than a quarter of a century later. What became known as the Y2K problem had to do with how programmers used dates in applications. Since all years started with "19", there was no reason to include those two unnecessary bytes that occurred over and over in programs and data. A simple 2-digit number like "67" was understood to represent 1967. Because memory was so small and expensive, programmers used shortcuts like this to save space.

No one anticipated that programs written in the 1960s and 1970s would still be in use at the turn of the Century. Worse yet, over the years, even after memory became more plentiful and less expensive, some programmers, out of habit, continued to use this 2-digit date shortcut to represent dates. In all these programs, when the year 2000 came, it looked as if "1999" rolled over to become "1900."

Since most computer applications use the date to sequence information, two-digit years would sequence the year 2000 data earlier than a 1999 data. Even something as simple as calculating a person's age would come up with a negative. That could generate all kinds of errors, false reports, and potential system crashes. That is what became known as the Y2K bug.

As the new Century approached, companies and governments all over the world panicked. The new Century didn't officially begin until the 1/1/2001, but most people think it started at 1/1/2000. It was impossible to know how many programs had 2-digit dates, and even programs with 4-digit dates often relied on data generated from other programs that may have 2-digit dates. Many people thought all computers would crash, airplanes would fall out of the sky, electric generators would shut down, ATMs would quit working, or maybe spit out cash, traffic lights, and even some cars would stop working. A new dark age would decent upon the world, all because of the missing 2-characters of the date field.

From roughly 1995 until the date rollover, almost all application development stopped. The only new software applications were those that replaced ones known to have Y2K issues. All the IT industry talked about was Y2K. A whole new sub-industry called "remediation" sprang up around the Y2K problem. The Media became obsessed with apocalyptic visions. Billions of dollars were spent trying to go through every line of code in every program and update it to handle the new year.

I can remember watching the year 2000 change starting with Australia and proceeding around the globe. We were all watching and listening to news reports to see if the end of the world would be upon us. In the end, we survived with very few severe outages. There were some, but mainly outside of the US.

– ■ –

A lesser-known "crisis" was the date system on all of the GPS (Global Positioning System) satellites. These were all running on a 10-digit clock system, which counted the number of seconds from January 6, 1980. That clock address space gave a total of 1023 weeks that ended on August 21, 1999. At that point, the clock would roll over to 00. For some reason, this situation never caught the fancy of the media and so not as many people were even aware of this impending crisis. The GPS systems were repaired in time. August 1999 came and went, and no airplanes fell out of the sky. That gave the tech world some hope that we would also survive the Y2K rollover.

– ■ –

Jumping back to the early 1980s, just to show you how easy it is to misjudge the future, when Microsoft introduced DOS (Disk Operating System) for the IBM PC, Bill Gates famously insisted that there would never be any reason to have a computer with more than 64K of memory. His engineers "hard-coded" this addressing limitation into the OS and it was a huge problem when it became apparent that 64K was not nearly enough memory addressing space.

Gates also famously resisted considering the Internet as a serious game changer for a long time and this cost Microsoft dearly as it tried to catch up. Even the most visionary often miss what in retrospect seems obvious.

– ■ –

A similar addressing problem still plagues the Internet. IPv4 (Internet Protocol Version 4) has a 32-bit addressing space. That is more than 4 billion potential device addresses on the Internet. As huge as this number seems, it is not nearly enough for all of the devices currently on the Internet. A new version IPv6 was developed to deal with the addressing issue. Unfortunately, it is extremely difficult to alter something as fundamental as the addressing structure within a global network of billions of devices without bringing the whole thing crashing down. As a result, the Internet is still struggling with how to maintain cross-compatibility as it transitions to IPv6, which has a theoretical maximum addressing space of 2^{128}. That is more than 340 undecillion, for those of you who are counting. That is supposedly enough to give an IP address to every grain of sand on every beach in the world. Hopefully, we won't run out of addresses soon.

— ∎ —

Returning to the pre-1964 computer era, in those days of tiny memories, programs were all standalone. They were punched into a deck of IBM cards that were fed into a card reader and loaded (read by the card reader) into the computer. There was no "operating system" (OS) resident on the computers. Therefore, these card decks had to include the instructions on how the computer was to handle everything from reading the cards, processing the data, to printing or writing the results to a tape drive. It even had to handle error conditions. Remember, all of this had to be able to execute (run) within the 2,000-character space available. Many systems were even smaller.

In most cases, the data, also in punched cards, would follow the program itself, so the stack of cards could become massive. If there were a lot of cards, it would read a few, process that data, then read a few more. As you can imagine, it was hard to load all of the data into this small storage area to do anything like sorting more than a few cards. If a sort was needed, there were standalone sorters that could be used to get the cards in the correct sequence.

There was no cross-platform compatibility; a program developed for one machine type would not run on any other machine type, even if the same vendor manufactured both.

Some of the slightly older computers had large "plug-boards" with the "program" hard wired into the board using jumper cables. These boards were swapped into the computer, and then the data to be utilized by that application would be read in by the card reader.

— ∎ —

The S/360 was revolutionary in many ways. Most significantly, it created a model independent architecture for the entire S/360 line. That meant that the OS was common across all models of S/360. Cross-compatibility meant that an application developed on one S/360 Model could, at least in theory, run on any model of S/360. In fact, this was not entirely accurate, as the Model 20, the smallest version, did not use the same OS as the other S/360 models.

Furthermore, some programs required specific memory sizes or I/O (Input/Output) devices meaning that the program would not run if those resources were not available. Finally, some programs were so big and required so much actual computation that they would overwhelm a smaller model S/360. However, even with those exceptions in mind, programmers could develop and test an application on one model knowing that it would also operate in a different "production" environment.

Without trying to provide a complete systems architecture or computer science course here, the key to this cross-compatibility was the layered architecture developed for the S/360. The "layering" separated the software into component layers that had defined functionality and standardized interfaces between them so that the adjacent layers could operate independently, knowing that they could hand off specific functions to the adjacent layers without being concerned about how those adjacent layers went about completing their tasks and responsibilities. The layered architecture (short version) consisted of hardware/firmware, OS, I/O, applications, and data.

The layered architecture meant that the programmers no longer had to worry about how the computer did the routine work, things like reading from the card reader, printing a page or dealing with an error condition. They also didn't have to worry about how a specific instruction would execute on a particular model. That was all handled by the S/360 layered architecture. They could just instruct the OS to "read," and the OS would manage all the intricate steps required to read a card, and if necessary deal with any errors. They didn't have to worry about the model of the card reader, or even if the data were being "read" from a card reader, a tape drive, or a disk drive. They simply wanted data, and the OS would go about the task of getting that data. That had tremendous productivity and cross compatibility benefits.

The hardware and the "firmware," called ROS (Read Only Storage or ROM Read Only Memory), are the guts of the actual computer. Firmware is the non-destructive, meaning that it doesn't go away when you power off the computer, code that tells the hardware circuits how to execute the various instructions that the computer was capable of running. The OS works in conjunction with ROS to provide a complete computing environment.

That meant that the lowest layer, the hardware, and firmware, could be swapped out as the technologies evolved. That protected the customers' investment in software while allowing them to take advantage of the efficiencies and power as new technologies became available.

IBM took a huge risk, quite literally betting the company on the S/360 with its layered architecture. The bet paid off, and the S/360 revolution begat the "gold rush" that followed.

— ■ —

One primary reason to have an OS was to manage the computer resource efficiently. Remember, on prior systems, the computers ran only one application at a time. That was very inefficient. When a program needed to print something, it would tell the computer to "print." Depending on the size of the print output, that could take hours. During that time, the computer couldn't be used for anything else.

The OS allowed multiple applications to be running on the computer at any time. In those days, these programs were not running simultaneously, but they were sharing the computing resource like slices of time. When we start talking about virtual systems, multiprocessor, and "multi-core" computers, it is possible for more than one program to be running simultaneously, but those capabilities were years away in 1967.

Using the printing example, when Application "A" told the computer to print, the computer would turn that process over to a "channel" that had dedicated hardware and firmware that could get the data from memory and send it out to the printer. Once it handed that task off, remember the I/O (Input/Output) layer, it would switch to Application "B" and do whatever it needed to do next. When Application B needed to wait for something, maybe to get data from a tape drive, the computer would hand that off to a different channel and then it would call Application "C" and start working on whatever it wanted to do.

Does this remind you of the "Oriental way" of dealing with problems that the old Chief Master Sargent taught me back in my Air Force days? It should.

— ■ —

Any knowledgeable computer person would tell you these are very simplistic and not entirely accurate examples, but (at the duckies and birdies level) they illustrate how the OS was able to utilize the computing resource more efficiently. The OS has very sophisticated mechanisms to manage resources. For example, the OS can limit the time any one application has control of the computer so that it doesn't hog the system.

In truth, this OS and the layered architecture require considerably more computer power and far more memory than would be needed if the individual programs operated directly with the hardware as they had before. However, the tradeoff is that the programming process is more efficient because the programmer doesn't have to worry about how the work gets done. At the same time, the use of the valuable computing resource is far more efficient because it is now shared, thus eliminating the wait time. That made it more efficient to solve complex problems, and in many cases, it was required even to make solutions possible. Of course, as hardware and memory became more powerful, smaller, and cheaper, the inefficiencies of this layered architecture became irrelevant when compared to the advantages it offered.

– ∎ –

IBM was one of the very first system vendors to recognize that a family of compatible systems that were able to execute the same software would allow customers of all sizes and in all markets to build scalable solutions for their businesses. You will read later how ITT attempted to duplicate IBM's success with their System/12 telephone switch product line. You will also learn about my involvement in that effort.

Over the years, there have been a lot of additional complexities added to each layer of this architecture, but the underlying layered architecture developed for the S/360 more than 50 years ago has withstood these changes. It continues to dominate the IT industry today. It has been a hallmark of IBM's approach to the market, and it remains at the heart of IBM's success.

– ∎ –

About now you might be saying something like "it is nice that you know all this esoteric stuff, but why do I care?" The answer is that this layered architecture and OS are not some abstract things that doesn't affect you. Everything you touch today has a computer in it. Your watch, your phone, your PC, your tablet, your radio, and your refrigerator, to name a few computerized devices that you use every day. Your car has a dozen or more computers that control every operation. Every one of these computers is based on a family of compatible computers, Intel for example, and every computer has an OS that uses a layered architecture. Incidentally, almost every one of these tiny computers is more powerful than the typical mainframe computers back in the late 1960s. If not for IBM's development, the technologies you depend on today would not exist.

You can download an application onto your smartphone or your tablet, which may be manufactured by different vendors, use different internal computers, and be manufactured several years apart. Did you ever wonder how an application could have such versatility? The answer lies in the layered architecture developed by IBM a half century ago.

Think about an Android phone. It may be manufactured by LG or Samsung or someone else, but it is running an Android OS. It may be a single, a dual, or a quad processor, but still, it is running Android. The applications you are running may have been written for version 3.2, but they work perfectly on version 4.5. They can run on your tablet, which also uses the Android OS. All of this is only possible because Google developed Android as a layered OS.

James Collins, author of many books including Built to Last, Good to Great, and How the Mighty Fall, has written that "the System/360, along with Ford's Model T and the Boeing 707 jet, were the three most important business innovations of all time."

I am writing in 2016, and things will undoubtedly have changed by the time you read this. However, I can say with confidence that even if you are reading this in 2116, the computers in your life will have an OS with a layered architecture based on the IBM approach.

A Computer Perspective

It can be easy to miss the thread that runs from the IBM S/360 mainframe of 1964 to your smartphone. It is equally easy to forget how far computers have come. Here is a brief review of what has taken place during my lifetime.

In 1951 a UNIVAC I, the largest computer at that time could execute 2,000 instructions per second. In 1972, roughly 20 years later, the IBM System/370 Model 158 was considered the benchmark. It could perform 1 MIPS (Million Instructions Per Second). In 2014, the Intel processor found in many $1500 PCs, could perform 238,310 MIPS.

As of 2016 the fastest supercomputer in the world could perform 93 PFLOPS (Peta Floating Point Operations Per Second). A "peta" is a quadrillion or a thousand trillion. A floating-point operation is far more complicated than the basic instructions measured in IPS or MIPS.

But speed is nothing without memory. In 1962, a computer with 2,000 bytes of storage, the equivalent to one typed page, was considered large. By 1968, a large computer might store 1,000,000 bytes (MB). The memory alone cost $3 million, the equivalent of $21 million today. It required an air-cooled cabinet about the size of a refrigerator. In 2016, a 256 GB micro SD card is not much larger than your thumbnail and cost less than $50. Incidentally, that 93 PFLOPS supercomputer has 1.5 PB (quadrillion bytes) of storage. At this rate, personal computers will be in this range by 2030.

We need to save all of that data. In 1956 IBM began shipping the IBM 305 RAMAC (Random Access) system. The heart of the system was the 350 disk storage unit. The 350's cabinet was 60 inches long, 68 inches high, and 29 inches wide. It contained fifty 24-inch disks spinning at 1200 RPM. The capacity was 5 MB (million bytes). The 305 leased for $3,200/month; that is $1.6 million in 2016 dollars over 60 months. In 2016, a 5 TB (trillion bytes) disk drive costs $140 and fits in your shirt pocket.

IBM Field Engineering Division 1967-1978

I joined the Denver North Branch of the Field Engineering Division (FED), arriving the 3rd of April 1967. I came straight out of the Air Force. My wife and I, along with our two small children age 18-months and 2-weeks lived in Nampa, Idaho, a medium sized town with about 20,000 people at that time. I had lived four months in Seattle on a TDY assignment while in the Air Force. Other than that brief assignment, I had never spent any time in a city. Coming to Denver was exciting, but a bit scary because I had no idea where to live or even where to start looking. We found an extended-stay hotel just a few blocks from the IBM Denver office and rented a room thinking that we would start looking for a place to live as soon as I knew a bit more about my work location.

I arrived at the Denver IBM building early just to make sure I didn't get lost. As I got on the elevator, the very first time, "Daddy Warbucks" stepped on with me. Daddy Warbucks refers to "Annie." Google it if you don't recall. A rather distinguished looking gentleman, tall with a shiny bald head, and dressed impeccably, or at least compared to what I was accustomed to seeing. He immediately stuck out his hand, said "Hello Tim, my name is George Mahalik. Welcome to IBM." I had no idea who he was or how he could have possibly known who I was. Later that morning I was formally introduced to Daddy Warbucks. George was the Branch Manager.

I was a bit shocked that someone recognized me. In retrospect, it would seem rather easy. At the time I was too young and probably too nervous even to be aware of just how different I must have looked getting on that elevator the first day. I was all of 22 years old, just barely, and I had a fresh, clean face. Truth be told, I could barely manage to grow enough beard to require shaving at that time. I had a military haircut and military bearing. I was wearing a brand new suit, shirt, tie, and shoes. Probably not all that comfortably as it was a new experience for me. Aside from my look, you need to remember, this was 1967, a couple of years before Woodstock. At that point most young people had scruffy beards, long hair, tie-dyed shirts, and spent a good part of their days and nights smoking marijuana, dropping acid or doing any number of things to destroy their mind and body. I must have been easy to spot in any crowd. I also would guess that George was the person on the other end of the phone during my rather unorthodox interview/hire process. He would have been the only person with the authority to say "hire him." As the Branch Manager, he was also undoubtedly aware that this would be my first day. Given all of that, identifying the kid on the elevator was probably not all that difficult. The only thing I will never know is if his entry into my elevator was purely coincidental, or if he somehow timed it. Never the less, I was forever impressed that he took the time to make himself aware of these things and to reach out to welcome me.

— ∎ —

The Field Engineering Division (FED) was responsible for service of all IBM punch card and computing equipment. I soon learned that there was also an Office Products Division (OPD) that sold and serviced devices used in the office. That consisted mainly of typewriters but later expanded to include copiers. I was more than happy not to be in the OPD.

I found an abundance of paperwork awaiting me. Like the Air Force, IBM always had an abundance of paperwork. There were also several self-study courses awaiting my arrival. They were a mix of electronics and device specific courses intended to prepare me for the FE Basic Training course. I felt right at home. The electronics courses were very elementary, and I remember skipping the reading and just taking the quizzes. I covered a couple weeks' worth of classes in one morning. The device training was more interesting. These were mostly electromechanical devices, primarily IBM card punches, verifiers, and card sorters. This equipment was called Unit Record Equipment.

Unit Record machines had become as ubiquitous in industry and government during the first two-thirds of the twentieth century as computers would become in the last third. They allowed large volume, sophisticated data-processing tasks to be accomplished while electronic computers were still in their infancy.

Data processing required moving the punched cards through various unit record machines in a carefully choreographed progression. This sequence from machine to machine was meticulously planned and documented with detailed flowcharts. All but the earliest machines had high-speed mechanical feeders to process cards at rates from 100 to 2,000 per minute. Punched holes were sensed with mechanical, electrical, or, later, optical sensors.

They told me that I would be traveling to Rochester, MN in a few weeks to attend an 8-week basic training course. That covered all of the traditional Unit Record equipment: keypunches, verifiers, sorters, along with information (probably better classified as indoctrination) about IBM, and how we were to conduct ourselves. In my case, a 6-week class on the 1050 Teleprocessing System followed basic training. Again, a pattern similar to my Air Force experience.

– ■ –

You may wonder about my use of the gender-specific "he" in this narrative. At that time, it was exclusively men. In the Air Force, there were no female airmen in any of my classes, at the RBS site, or involved in any of my TDY assignments. Even the administrative staff were all male. At IBM all CEs were men at that time. There were secretaries in the Denver Branch, but none in the Boulder sub-office. Most of the keypunch operators and a few of the computer operators were women, but other than that, it was an all-male environment.

– ■ –

Initially, IBM only leased their computers with the OS and maintenance bundled into the lease. At about the time I joined, there was an antitrust suit brought against IBM. The main issue was this bundling, which the Justice Department viewed as a constraint of trade. As the Justice Department (of the US Government) started to move forward with the antitrust suit, IBM spent a lot of time and money educating field personnel about the legal actions and exactly what we could and could not do and say. A major part of our legal training also covered union activities. What we could and could not do and how to deal with customers who were unionized. IBM settled the suit in 1969. That brought about a significant shift in both software and service. That legal insight proved to be very useful later in my career.

IBM Basic

There wasn't any reason to leave my family in a hotel in Denver while I went to live in a hotel in Rochester, so I took them with me. We drove of course and rented an upstairs furnished apartment over a home. The owner was also an IBMer. He liked to rent to the guys coming for Basic as the money was good and the source was reliable.

Basic training was just that. Most of my classmates were ex-military with significant electronic training and experience. Little time was spent on electronics training as it was unnecessary. There were quite a few devices to cover, but also an extensive company orientation process. As we were the primary IBMers that interfaced with the customers from day to day; our company knowledge, our dress, conduct, and competence were considered equally important.

The company motto was "IBM Means Service." That and "Think" signs were everywhere. The message of the indoctrination was very clear. We were the face of IBM, and we were to represent our company with integrity and honor. As most of us were ex-military, we were disciplined and knew how to follow orders. We were also happy to be working for IBM, so there were very few problems. We learned quickly, and we followed instructions.

IBM had some "Company Songs." There was even a songbook. Unfortunately, I didn't keep a copy. These were sung to simple tunes, and they had been around for decades. One I recall was "Ever Onward IBM."

> There's a thrill in store for all,
> For we're about to toast,
> The corporation known in every land.
> We're here to cheer each pioneer
> And also proudly boast
> Of that "man of men," our friend and guiding hand.
> The name of T. J. Watson means a courage none can stem;
> And we feel honored to be here to toast the "IBM."
>
> EVER ONWARD -- EVER ONWARD!
> That's the spirit that has brought us fame!
> We're big, but bigger we will be
> We can't fail for all can see
> That to serve humanity has been our aim!
> Our products now are known, in every zone,
> Our reputation sparkles like a gem!

We've fought our way through -- and new
Fields we're sure to conquer too
For the EVER ONWARD IBM

EVER ONWARD -- EVER ONWARD!
We're bound for the top to never fall!
Right here and now we thankfully
Pledge sincerest loyalty
To the corporation, that's the best of all!
Our leaders we revere, and while we're here,
Let's show the world just what we think of them!
So let us sing, men! SING, MEN!
Once or twice then sing again
For the EVER ONWARD IBM

Once a week we were all ushered into an auditorium to hear about our company's history and to sing a few IBM songs. In retrospect, I can't help but think of the songs the Chinese sang to Chairman Mao. Yes, it seemed rather hokey, but it was part of our acculturation. Just as Air Force Basic reshaped the thinking of the many individuals coming from diverse backgrounds and molded us into a cohesive unit that could function well together, IBM's Basic was intended to and did accomplish the same result. We all left Basic as True Blue IBMers.

— ■ —

As an aside, several years later, we did a skit for the January kick-off meeting. In preparation for the skit, I interviewed several "old-timers" at the IBM plant in Boulder. John had just returned from service at the end of WWII. He related this interview exchange:

> **Interviewer:** *I noticed that he arrived without a hat. Do you own a hat?*
> **John:** *No*
> **Interviewer:** *You need to get a hat, IBMers wear hats.*
> **Interviewer:** *Are you married?*
> **John:** *No*
> **Interviewer:** *Do you have a girlfriend?*
> **John:** *Yes*
> **Interviewer:** *You should get married, IBMers are married.*

It wasn't quite that bad in 1967, but the underlying beliefs were still prevalent.

IBM was a very traditional company. They had a very strict dress code, "bankers attire," meaning suit, tie, and a white shirt at all times, even when working on the dirtiest piece of equipment. Incidentally, many of the 1050 systems were installed in rail yards. They were used to transmit and print various schedules, messages, and traffic directives. A few trains were still using coal, but even the diesel-electric trains produced a lot of black oily soot that made it almost impossible to work on the equipment without getting filthy.

I bought my "bankers uniform" when I came to work for IBM. They had made the requirement clear, and so I went to a men's shop in Nampa before we moved to Denver. I bought two suits plus some shirts and ties. A couple of the shirts were very pale pastel, one light blue, and one pale yellow. No one said a thing about my wearing them until my final class appraisal. At that time, the instructor told me that I would have been designated the Outstanding Student if I had not worn "colored" shirts. I was surprised that no one had said anything the first time I showed up in "color," but also a bit frustrated by the "bankers attire" definition. I explained that where I came from, bankers wore cowboy shirts with pointed pocket covers, bolo ties, and often silver collar tips. My explanation didn't move the needle, but I never forgot that lesson. It was best to remember that IBM was a very conservative company.

– ■ –

The 1050 Teleprocessing System was introduced in 1963. It communicated over analog phone lines serially, half-duplex (one direction at a time), at 75 or 150 bits per second. It is hard to imagine 15 characters per second, but that was state-of-the-art in those days.

A significant portion of the training covered the 1053 Console Printer. That was a modified version of the IBM Selectric typewriter, the one with the golf-ball type element that would tilt and rotate before being "fired" against the paper to print the character. The System/360 computer consoles used a slightly different version. It was a mechanical marvel but also a mechanical beast. It was quite a reliable printer despite all the precision moving parts.

Our training exercise was to remove every component from the frame and then reassemble the beast and make it function properly. That would have been challenging enough under normal circumstances, but the units we were working with had been stripped and rebuilt dozens of times. None of the screws would tighten properly, and the rattling and banging of the type ball tended to shake things lose. It was hard to get a unit working, even harder to keep it working, but a working printer was the "pass" criteria for the course.

Naturally, there was a good deal of friendly competition to see who would get their printer working first. When the first student completed, he called the instructor over. The instructor watched it type for a minute or so then he picked it up about 2 inches and dropped it back onto the workbench. Needless to say, there was a lot of rattling and clanking and the printer stopped working. When the second student finished, the instructor pulled the same stunt. I was the third to finish. When I called the trainer over, I picked up my ball peen hammer. He watched the printer as usual and then he asked: "why the hammer." I smiled and said, "if you drop my printer I will use it on your hand." He laughed and walked away. He didn't drop any more printers.

— ■ —

When the training was complete, I drove back to Denver. Jane didn't have a driver's license at that time, so I did all the driving. We came south to Des Moines, Iowa on Interstate 35 and then headed west on Interstate 80. That section of Interstate 80 was brand new. In fact, much of what existed of the Interstate System was brand new. Remember the whole concept of an interstate highway system came from the Eisenhower administration in 1956. Incidentally, the reason Ike wanted the coast-to-coast highway system was so that the president could more efficiently move convoys of military men and equipment if and when the need arose. To get a complete path from coast to coast required nearly two decades.

— ■ —

The interstate system changed much about life in America. Before the Interstates, there were few "long-haul" trucks. Long distance transport was via rail. You could rarely get things like bananas outside of the big port cities. On the rare occasion when you did, they would be black and bruised by the time they got to the corner grocery store. There were few supermarkets, mostly small mom & pop stores. If you lived outside of a city as we did, most of the fruits, vegetables, eggs and meat you consumed were what you raised or bartered with a neighbor. In my case, we raised all of our food; vegetables, fruit, eggs, and meat, of course, we also hunted deer for meat (venison). Mom and my sisters canned the fruits and vegetables for winter and we slaughtered, butchered and froze our chickens, beef, and pork as well as venison.

Most communities had "farmer's markets" where the town's people could get what they needed. These were real farmers who lived nearby and they sold what they grew themselves. Today's farmers' markets are, in many cases, nothing more than outdoor grocery stores. Often the "farm grown" produce comes from the same factory farms that sell to the supermarkets. It may get to you a day sooner, but it tastes no better. Back then, even things like milk and ice cream were locally produced. There were no national brands of frozen goods because there were no refrigerated trucks to haul cold items even from town to town.

The Interstate system changed all that. It was gradual of course, but soon you were able to buy bananas in Montana even in the winter. It gave birth to supermarkets, which ultimately replaced the corner groceries, which were themselves supplanted by the big-box stores like Wal-Mart. That may not sound like much today, but it was a revolutionary life-changing process that began with the Interstate System.

— ■ —

Back to our travels. It was evening when we got to Des Moines, and my plan was to avoid any morning rush-hour traffic by finding a motel west of the city. However, because this section of the Interstate had just been open a month or two, none of the infrastructures that we are accustomed to seeing today had developed. I drove late into the night trying to find a motel. Brian was about 2-years old, and Teri was just 4-months at that time. You can picture two crying babies in the back seat.

Finally, at about 11 p.m. with everyone completely exhausted, I found a little village with an old motel that had a vacancy. We checked in and immediately crashed. After a couple of hours, I was awakened by some rustling noises. I switched on the light to discover several large rats were sharing our room. We packed up and headed west.

Servicing Computers

When I returned to Denver, George asked if I would like to work out of the Boulder sub-office supporting the IBM plant. The plant was between Boulder and Longmont. I had never been to Boulder nor seen the factory, but I only had one question: "Where can I get computer training the quickest?" Jim Gilbert, soon to be my new manager, told me Boulder and I immediately accepted the assignment.

I was fortunate to have the opportunity to be assigned to service equipment at the Boulder IBM factory. It was funny because most Customer Engineers preferred to work in the commercial accounts. They considered the commercial accounts to be the "real" customers. However, working at the IBM plant provided several benefits. First, there was a greater concentration of equipment, so I didn't waste time traveling between accounts. That allowed me to support a greater quantity of machines thus gaining more experience. As an example, a big S/360 Mod 50, my primary system at that time, in a commercial account would typically have 1.5 CEs assigned full time. That meant that two systems, typically at two different accounts, would have 1 Senior CE each plus a CE that split his time between the two systems. The CE would be given the easy stuff that the senior techs didn't want to do, things like cleaning the filters.

There was no Mod 50 Senior CE for the internal (within the IBM factory) account. In fact, I was the only Mod 50 tech assigned to the Boulder Plant. Initially, I had sole responsibility for a very large Mod 50 but within six months, a second, and then a third Mod 50 were installed. I was the only technician for three large Mod 50 systems. Yes, I cleaned a lot of filters, but there was a lot more that I got to do, and any time there was a problem, I was the one to work on it, not get coffee for some Senior CE while he had the fun.

– ■ –

The second benefit of supporting the internal equipment was early access to unannounced products. The internal accounts received products and enhancements before announcement. They were needed to conduct compatibility testing. That created endless opportunities to attend "engineering" classes, which taught the equipment at a much deeper level than standard Customer Engineering training. Sometimes the people who were developing the courses for the CEs would be in the same engineering classes, but more often, I would be trained by the engineers and as an engineer, even before the course developers.

It also created numerous opportunities to work directly with the Boulder IBM engineers. Boulder IBM developed and manufactured magnetic tape drives and controllers at that time. The tape drive engineers had little expertise on the Mod 50, or later 370-155 or 158. They had to rely on me to help then diagnose interface issues, sometimes even to develop test cases for them. One of those engineers was a guy by the name of Tom Kavanagh. We crossed paths again at NBI. I will write more on that later.

The Mod 50 was a bit unique in the S/360 line. It was at the low end of the "large" systems range, but it had enough computational power and memory for the vast majority of users. All of the S/360 computers used a universal cabling system to attach I/O devices. These were called "bus (data) and tag (control signaling)" cables. The cables were almost 1" in diameter. As I recall, they had 12 shielded (wrapped with a grounded mesh) separate wires in each cable. That allowed any I/O device to be attached to any model of S/360.

The "channel" hardware on the computers managed the transfer of information as well as the control of the remote devices through these cables. The signaling was digital, either a zero value or a plus voltage, which represented a one. Most models of the S/360 were fairly forgiving when it came to the timing of the switching of the signal values on the bus and tag cables. That meant that the hardware didn't check the precise timing of the transitions from 0 to 1. That allowed for cable lengths to vary quite a bit without causing problems. It could, on occasion lead to problems if the cables were too long, or if the pair of cables were not the same length as it could result in lost data without a channel error. However, the Mod 50 was different; it was what you might call persnickety about the timings. As a result, the Mod 50 would generate channel errors when none of the other S/360 models had a problem.

That characteristic made the Mod 50 the ideal test system. If the device ran on a Mod 50, it would run on any of the S/360 computers. Conversely, if it were not tested on a Mod 50, it might work fine on all other machines, but fail when put on a Mod 50. Problem determination was an issue. The Mod 50 had a single "System Check" light. Behind that light was a group of a hundred or more "or" circuits, all feeding that one red light. That meant that when a red light came on, it could be generated by 100 or more conditions, with no indication of which one caused the failure. That made it more than a bit difficult to find out exactly what had failed.

The Boulder engineers were experts on their equipment, but not on the Mod 50. As a result, I had many opportunities to work hand in hand with the engineers to find out exactly what was causing the errors. That gave me a great deal of intense experience and knowledge about how the channel interface worked.

— ■ —

The Boulder IBM plant was scheduled to receive a S/370 Mod 155 several months before the announcement of the new System/370 generation of computers. That system was needed to test a new tape drive system scheduled to be part of the S/370 rollout. Jim Fessler and I went to IBM's Poughkeepsie NY plant for 2-months of engineering training. Jim was a good friend and another CE supporting the Boulder Plant; he was a S/360 Model 65 guy.

After engineering training, we did a 2-month stint on the manufacturing line building systems from the ground up. That was followed by a 4-month assignment to the Engineering Laboratory to support what was called C-Test.

C-Test was the final intense system test before the announcement. One of the main testing suites was the "environmental" tests. Specifically, measuring the impact of various temperature and humidity combinations to determine the break points, but also which components failed and at what temperature and humidity point.

– ■ –

They had several systems in the labs; two were in environmental chambers where they could do all kinds of torture testing based on temperature and humidity. The test centered around stressing the system based on playing with the systems timings. As you can imagine, a large system of that era had a thousand or more critical and adjustable (using jumpers) timing setting. The timing for the 155 was in the nanosecond ranges. A nanosecond is 1/1,000,000,000 of a second.

First, we set all the timings exactly at the midpoint and ran the humidity and temperature up, down, and split. At each configuration, we would run all kinds of diagnostics to see if there were any failures. Next, we set some timings long by certain amounts, test again. Then we would set different timings short, test again. On and on and on. For months, Jim and I lived in the chamber, spending shift after shift tweaking the timings, running diagnostics, identifying the failure points, then finding and replacing failing components. While they had diagnostics running on one machine, we would be tweaking the timings on the other computer. Jim went home after two months; I stayed all four. So for four months, I did nothing but timing, fixing bugs and installing engineering changes, 10 hours a day, six days a week, 100% on the Mod 155. That equaled more than 20 years of actual field experience.

Life inside the chamber was not pleasant. One day the chamber would be 95° and 95% humidity and the next day it might be 35/95. Since we were not part of the permanent Lab staff, you know who got that duty. The good news is I got to where I could time a complete system in an 8-hour shift. That was normally a 30 to 40-hour process. I also got to see almost every conceivable bug that could occur. In addition, I got my hands on several "engineering-only" tools and documentation that were technically not supposed ever to leave the factory. Since I had to support machines in the plant at Boulder, no one got upset when I took sets of tools with me on my return to Boulder. They came in very handy on more than one occasion.

We were working 10-hour shifts including Saturdays, so we were pulling down a lot of overtime. The engineers were all exempt, meaning they didn't get overtime. They were happy that we were there and willing to work long hours doing the stuff they didn't want to do. The Lab Manager signed off on our time cards each week, and we sent them back to Boulder for processing. After we had been doing these killer hours for a couple of months, the manager called us in to ask about a bill he had received from the FE Division. It had not occurred to him that we were nonexempt and that he was paying us time and a half for all these crazy hours.

Fortunately, he was not upset; he was more concerned about how many hours we were putting in, and what impact it might be having on our families. Jim's wife and my wife knew each other well from Boulder and we were living in the same apartment complex, so the wives were able to hang out together, and they were enjoying the extra money. Jim went home after two months, and so I sent Jane and the kids off to Idaho so they could visit with her family.

— ■ —

I don't think in all my years; I have ever worked in a single assignment without any travel for that long. When I finished the Poughkeepsie assignment, I had to drive back to Boulder alone. I got off work fairly late in the evening and drove across the river to Wilks-Barre, PA. Someone asked me why I didn't just stay the night and start out the next day. I remember telling him that after eight months, I just wanted to wake up in a different state. The next morning, I got up early, and I didn't stop to rest until I reached Ogallala Nebraska. That was 1,600 miles and almost 22 hours of driving. I made much better time with no one else needing to stop for food or potty breaks.

— ■ —

We had a lot of fun while we were working that assignment in Poughkeepsie. Initially, five families were going through the same training. Bob Rogers and his wife Betty were from Seattle. Jerry Spoolman and his wife Evangeline

(Vangie), were from the San Francisco Area. Tom Beauregard and his wife were from Chicago. I don't recall her name. Jim and Sharon Fessler, as well as Jane and I were from Boulder.

The others were all in Region Staff or Branch Specialists positions, and so they were in support rather than direct service roles. They only attended the first two parts, the engineering training and working on the assembly line portions before they returned to their home offices. Fessler and I stayed longer. We knew that we would all be there together for some time so we located an apartment complex near Kingston, NY where we could all rent space for our stay. The complex was outside of town in an area that was very rural and quite pleasant.

That was in 1969, so I was just 24 at the time. Jim and Sharon Fessler were close friends. I knew Bob Rogers as he was our Region Senior FE Specialists and had been in the Denver office before taking the job in Seattle. I had not met Tom or Jerry, but we all commuted and worked together, so we got to be friends quickly. The men all hung out together at work and the wives at the apartment complex. On weekends, we had barbecues and dinners together at the complex.

We formed a compact to drive the local grocery store crazy. The stores in that area of New York were a bit on what you might call the funky side. Not too clean. The best one we could find had a pet Labrador dog that had the run of the store. The first thing we did was tell the manager to get the dog out of the store. It took a while, but it got to the point where when any of us would show up they would get on the PA and tell someone to "get the dog out." Another thing we did was try to go to the same one or two checkers each time. We would always smile and tell her to "have a nice day" as we left. Telling someone in New York to "have a nice day" is about as foreign as asking them to fly, so they would just look at you with a blank expression. Again, it took a few weeks, but before long when we would approach her stand, she would start with a smile and greet us with a "how are you doing today." It was fun to see her immediately revert to her grumpy self for the next customer.

— ■ —

During the engineering training, the instructors would take every Friday afternoon to meet with the other engineers and learn what changes had been made. That gave us every Friday afternoon off.

At that time, the Poughkeepsie IBM plant had a private golf course open to

IBM employees only. It was an exquisite course that had been on the PGA Tour at one point. None of us were golfers, but it provided a fun way to get some exercise and sun, so on Friday's we would go over to the course and rent clubs for the afternoon.

I am a terrible golfer, but no one took it seriously so we just abused the balls and walked in the sunshine. We usually played 11 holes as that took us back close to the clubhouse. Invariably we would have a couple of holes where we bet a round of beer. Whoever had the highest score on that hole would buy a round for the group. Somehow, I would improve whenever there was money on the line. I lost my share, but not every time.

After we finished, we would head to a local watering hole called The Three Caballeros. It was a dive on Route 9, the main highway that ran down the east side of the Hudson River. It was the favorite watering hole for CEs when they came to Poughkeepsie. Not fancy but the beer was cold, and you were likely to run into someone you knew. It was an old, single story standalone building with a gravel parking lot. The bar was down about three steps from the street level, so you walked down and then in, kind of like walking into a basement. In today's parlance, it would be considered a "biker bar." There weren't any bikers around in those days.

Bob Rogers had a terrible reputation as a lady's man. It was reportedly so bad that when he was in the field as a CE, his wife would accompany him to work and drive him from service call to service call just to keep him in line. On the first afternoon when we headed to the Three Cabs, Bob was going on and on about how he hadn't been there in years. We thought it was a bit strange how he carried on. It was one of those "me thinks thou doth protest too much" kind of things, but we let it slide until we walked in the door. As I said, you walked down and in. Since you were coming out of the bright sun into the dimly lit bar, it took several seconds for your eyes to adjust to the darkness.

On this day, as we were standing to let our eyes adjust, we saw a barmaid across the room gradually turn our direction, to welcome the new customers. It was kind of like she was in slow motion. She had a tray of full beer glasses raised above her head. Obviously, she was taking them to a table. She turned, and when she saw us, she tossed the tray spilling beer and glasses everywhere. She screamed "Booooooob," came running across the room and jumped into his arms. The rest of us burst out laughing and simultaneously said, "so you haven't been here in years."

Jim Fessler and I were about the same age, and quite competitive but in a friendly sort of way. One of the "games" we played was trying to see if we could get the other's wife pissed at her husband. Sharon and Jane were accustomed to this and seldom fell for whatever our ruse might be. On one trip to The Cabs, Jerry Spoolman, after a couple of beers decided he was up to joining the game. Jerry was a bit older, maybe 30. I guess he wanted to be one of the boys. He foolishly bet me that I couldn't get Vangie pissed at him. He didn't need to say why. Vangie was drop dead gorgeous, but she was ...blond if you know what I mean. She was Jerry's second wife, and closer to my age. A former airline stewardess, he had met her in his travels.

We were all having a barbecue at the apartment complex the next day; sitting around a table enjoying the afternoon sun. Vangie was pouring drinks for everyone. Jerry was sitting directly across the table from me when Vangie refilled my drink I put my arm around her waist and paid her a compliment about how attractive she was. But then, I continued saying "I don't know how you ever met Jerry. When we are in the bars, he always picks the ugly girls." I was watching Jerry's face as I said this and it went from normal to white in an instant. All of the guys who had seen Jerry throw down the challenge the day before nearly rolled off of their chairs. On our Monday morning commute, Jerry told us he had a rough weekend.

– ∎ –

As with any advanced technologies, there were occasional manufacturing issues that required what amounted to a major rebuild of the computer in the field. Whenever these situations occurred, the commercial customers got priority shipment of the replacement parts. That meant that the internal systems had to suffer with whatever the problem was until parts became available. My job was to keep the computers running despite these problems.

For commercial accounts, factory teams were usually dispatched to "rebuild" the computers. The local CEs got to assist, but the factory teams did the heavy lifting. Internal machines never received factory assistance. The local CE, which would be me, was left to rebuild the internal machines on our own. That was, in part, why I received engineering-level training on new equipment. These factors combined to provide me the opportunity to learn more and hone my skills far faster than any CE working in any commercial account.

These "factory rebuilds" created some interesting opportunities. In 1968, there was a ribbon cable problem. In S/360 computers, the various circuit boards where the SLT (Solid Logic Technology) cards were plugged, were interconnected using flat (ribbon) cables that were about 1" wide. Connectors were soldered to the ends of these cables. Attaching these connectors to the cables was a manual process. The manufacturing process initially called for the technician to solder one connector on one end than to dip that end of the cable in a mild acid solution, which removed the rosin used in the soldering process. The soldered area was then covered with a thin layer of shellac to protect the joint from humidity, and then the end cap was put in place.

As you can imagine, this was a rather slow process. After several years of successfully manufacturing millions of these ribbon cables, one technician decided it would be much faster to solder cables throughout his shift, and then for the last hour or so dip and spray all of the cables he had assembled during that day. His productivity was light years beyond his coworkers. Soon he received an enormous "Suggestion Award," $250,000 if I remember correctly, and the entire line was converted over to this solder first, then mass dip at the end of shift process.

Unfortunately, whoever had designed the original process, had failed to explicitly mention that the dip-while-hot process was necessary because the mild acid solution only removed the rosin while it was still warm. On the mass-dipped cables, over time, the rosin would begin to corrode and ultimately create a high-resistant short between adjacent connections. Needless to say, these high-resistant shorts caused lots of intermittent bugs a few months after the cables were installed.

Any technician will tell you the most difficult problem to fix is an intermittent problem. With hundreds of ribbon cables in a machine, there was potential for hundreds of intermittent problems to plague the customer and the CE.

It took some time for IBM to trace the problem back to its origin, and then additional time to build, ship, and install replacement cables for all of the affected machines. I had one of the infected Mod 50s, and it took nearly six months before I received an entirely new set of cables to rebuild the machine. There were a lot of bugs to shoot during that time. The overtime from the problems on this one machine paid for my flying lessons and pilot's license. The experience also earned me the Sr. CE promotion.

About a year after the 155 started shipping, a similar problem began to develop with the MST (Monolithic System Technology) technology. MST is a microelectronic circuit family consisting of high-density monolithic circuit chips on ceramic substrates. One version, MST-2, was developed for use primarily in the middle range System/370 Models 145 and 155. That was one of the first generations of actual microelectronics, and some of the physics of this breakthrough were not yet fully understood. The problem as I understand it, was that as electrons flowed around the corners of microcircuits printed on the ceramic substrate, the circuit would very gradually physically move on the substrate. That ultimately caused lines to either break or to come in contact with parallel lines. Thus causing the chip to fail. The problem was, in many ways, similar to the Ribbon Cable problem on the S/360 systems.

These early systems became plagued with card failures. The solution was to replace every card in the machine with a newer version of the MST technology. That included the cards that contained the timing jumpers. Mass replacement of all the cards could cause their own problems, mainly bent pins, but the real issue was the need to retime the entire system after the cards were swapped. As I said earlier, timing a complete system with teams of two experienced line technicians (the people who build the machines) was scheduled to take five 8-hour shifts. In the build schedule, it was listed as taking from 30 to 40 clock hours. Of course, that was on the factory floor where there were no interruptions, and all possible tools were available. CEs were never trained to time the entire machines as this was something that was never needed in the field, except now.

By the time this problem developed, my reputation was well established. I was dispatched to several commercial accounts around the country to assist in what was called the MST-5 Migration. The first time was to the State of Oregon in Salem. I arrived on Friday of a holiday weekend. The customer was scheduled to give the system over to the technicians at 6 a.m. Saturday and they required that it be operational at Midnight Monday. Sixty-six hours was considered an exceedingly tight schedule. The customer was extremely unhappy due to the many problems they had been experiencing.

This MST-5 Migration had never before been attempted in the field, and everyone in the area was anxious. It was considered a high-risk situation. A factory technician was dispatched to "train and assist" the card replacement and timing. On Friday the local CEs plus all 155 CEs from Portland were milling around speaking in low tones. By afternoon, the backup Sr. CEs and FE Specialists had arrived from Seattle.

There was a big meeting with all the CEs, the sales team, several IBM Managers, and the customer's IT executives. There was a gaggle of folks at the meeting. The factory tech had a nice slide show about the technology changes. He proposed a staffing schedule. It was accepted without debate. The 12-hour shifts were set up to have the strongest members on the most critical shifts, in particular, the final push to get the system timed and then restored. The customer reluctantly allowed that they could live with an additional 8 hours of outage, but any loss beyond that would impact critical public services.

It was quite a show with lots of furrowed brows. I just watched without comment. At the end, they ask me if I was comfortable with the plan. I told them it was fine but that we wouldn't need all the time. They were pleased by my response and confidence, but clearly doubtful. I admit I probably appeared more than a bit cocky. I was still pretty young, 25, and by far the youngest in the room. Furthermore, not one of them had ever met me before.

I was assigned the first 12-hour shift along with the factory tech. The stated goal was to get the cards all swapped new-for-old. The second shift was to begin the timing process. Timing was scheduled to run three total shifts (36-hours) according to their plan. That left an 18-hour window as a safety margin and to fix any bugs.

The factory guy, and I arrived a couple of hours early Saturday morning to make sure everything was laid out the way we wanted. For testing, all of the cards had been placed in a system at the factory. That included timing the system so that the actual timings should be relatively close when placed in our system. The factory guy started to explain how we would power off the machine and swap all the cards then power on and fix any problems that were not obviously timing related. I told him we would do it differently. He knew a bit about my line and C-Test experience; to his credit, he allowed me to take the lead. He probably assumed I would also take the blame if it all went south.

The 155 had a clock switch that allowed the CE to turn off the clock. That froze the computer at that point. I knew that 95% of the cards could be swapped with power on. The exceptions were a few channel drivers (higher voltage cards). My many hours in the environmental lab had taught me exactly which cards could be hot-swapped.

I told him we would run a diagnostic pass and document, but not fix any problems. Once we had that completed, we would start cycling a particularly intensive test and freeze the clock. We would then swap all the cards in one board (usually about 12 cards), unfreeze and see if we had bent any pins or otherwise introduced any new failures. We proceeded to do this, avoiding the driver and timing cards until we had all the easy cards swapped. That took less than an hour, and we didn't introduce any bugs. We powered the system down, swapped all the driver cards and then retested. One of the new driver cards failed, so we swapped the old card back in and retested. Then we froze the clock and swapped all the timing cards. We were ready to start timing. We had completed the assigned goal for shift 1; it took a little over an hour and a half.

— ■ —

The way you time a machine is as a team. One person plugs the oscilloscope on the correct pin and examines the signal to determine if the timing is long, short, or correct. He freezes the machine, calls the value to the other person who is physically on the other side of the logic gate; that person pops the card and changes the jumpers to make the correction. There are dozens of sets of jumpers on each card, so you have to move the right set. There were few markings, so you have to use trial and error to find out which direction and by how much you need to move the jumpers. That is why it typically took an experienced team 30+ hours to time the complete system. More importantly, this was exactly what I had spent four long months doing in the environmental chamber in Poughkeepsie.

We moved very quickly, and the factory guy said nothing until about 5-hours in when I finally missed one adjustment and had to move the jumpers a second time. He just grunted. We finished the timing at 5 p.m., 11 hours into the first shift. Basically, other than testing we had just completed 66-hours of work. We started a more intensive set of all diagnostics.

The system was ready to turn over to the customer at 6 p.m. when the 2nd shift arrived. The crew was both happy and pissed. Glad that the system was restored, but a bit upset because they wanted to learn how to do the timing. The salesman and the customer IT manager also came in to check on our progress. They were beyond thrilled. Everyone turned to the factory guy and asked why the estimation was so far off. He just pointed to me and said, "I have worked on the 155 line for more than a year, and I have never seen anyone do what this guy can do. There is no one on the line that can do what he did."

We left the 2nd shift to run more diagnostics and make any further tests they wanted while we were treated to a great dinner and drinks by the sales team.

— ∎ —

I also went to New Orleans to do a system there. They put me up in the Howard Johnsons downtown. It turned out there was a sniper on the roof of a building nearby, and they had to evacuate the hotel for a while. The evacuation was short-lived as the police quickly removed the sniper, New Orleans style, in a body bag. Other than a meaningless chat with the police, I was unaffected as I was working at the time of the incident.

There was one rather funny incident at that same hotel. The Poughkeepsie plant had once again sent a technician to cover their you know what. He was a young guy with a family, and he brought his wife and two babies to see New Orleans. They were staying at the same hotel but on a different floor. We had planned to get together for dinner the first evening.

When I got off the elevator on his floor, a black prostitute was leaning against the wall near the elevator. That was a common occurrence in hotels, not only in New Orleans. You learn how to identify these working girls. I said nothing, just walked past her to the intended room.

When I arrived, the door was partially open, and they ask me in. It was a scene of utter chaos. I don't remember the guy's name, but he had his shirt off, and the bathroom door was open. He was brushing his teeth. The wife was changing the youngest one's very stinky diaper on the bed, and the oldest who was about 18 months was tearing around the room sans clothing. It was not a big shock; I had lived this scene many times myself traveling with small children.

Just as I closed the door and surveyed the chaos, there was a knock on the door. I automatically reached back and opened the door. The prostitute walked through the door as if she was ready for business. As she did, her eyes scanned the scene just as the stench of dirty diaper hit her nostrils. She immediately made a U-turn and walked back out without saying a word. Her stride on leaving was much faster than when she came in.

The knock and her entrance had the effect of freezing all that was happening in one of those action movie ways. Even the 18-month old terror stopped in his tracks. We all watched her prance into the room, spin and almost run out.

In that instant, her face went from a smile to something near terror. Her mouth opened, but no words came out. They weren't needed; we could all read her thoughts on her face. Just like in the movies, when the door closed, the speed in the room resumed instantly, and the chaos began again. We all burst out laughing at the same time. The whole thing took maybe 5 seconds, but it is the most memorable part of my trip.

— ∎ —

The introduction of the S/370 marked a significant shift in the work Customer Engineers performed. Up to that time, CEs, although most were not real electrical engineers, were highly trained and skilled technicians. To fix these complicated computer systems you had to have an in-depth knowledge of how they worked clear down at the circuit level. As technology became, more compact, greater and greater sections of logic could be put on a single card, and eventually onto a single chip. That meant that it was far harder to get an oscilloscope onto a particular point in the logic as it was inside of chips or layers of the card, and even if you did, you couldn't repair the card; the only fix was to replace it.

At the same time, the engineers were building very sophisticated diagnostic software and firmware (software that is hard-coded into the machine) into the devices so that they could troubleshoot the system more thoroughly and display appropriate error codes when they recognized a failure. The approach to diagnosing and fixing these new machines was to use the error codes to follow a set of MAPs (Maintenance Analysis Procedures). These were troubleshooting flow charts. You would start with an error code; follow the flow chart using diagnostics or other indicators to find out which card to replace. In theory, you no longer had to know anything about how the machine worked, and in many cases you didn't even need an oscilloscope.

Jim Fessler and I attended an early class on the 3830/3330 disk storage system. The class was the first "official" FE training on the 3330, and it was all about how to use the MAPs to diagnose and repair the systems. Initially, MAPs were effective for about 95% of the failures; that percentage gradually grew to nearly 100%, but it never did get to the point of perfection. For those problems that the MAPs missed, there was nothing that the CE could do but dig out the logic manuals and go down into the data flows, functions, and circuits to figure out what was failing. That was the old fashion way. The problem with the FE training was that it stopped at MAP training. That created a problem for me, and for Fessler to a lesser extent, as he didn't like to travel. We were the ones who got called when the MAPs failed, and the CE had no idea how the machine worked.

On the first day of class, the instructor told us he was going "to teach us a new way to fix the equipment." Fessler and I both knew where he was going, and we both knew that we weren't going there. They spent a few days going over the system logic, but mostly introducing the MAPs. Then we went into the laboratory to practice troubleshooting.

They had spent months developing their course and designing "bugs" specifically to teach us how to use the MAPs. They would pull a card and install a "defective" card that had a connection cut so that it would produce the desired error code on the diagnostics. We went along with their approach for the first two or three bugs, just enough to get comfortable running the diagnostics. Then we stopped using the MAPs. We tossed the books on a table and didn't even open them. Instead, we would read through the diagnostic software code and then develop our own code that would repeat the error. From there, we would get out the o-scope and the logic and start troubleshooting the old fashion way.

At first, the instructors thought it was funny, and it did take us a lot longer than our classmates to diagnose a problem. We were taking this approach because we knew that we were the last line of defense. When we got called, it would be because the MAPs had failed to lead the CE to the problem. We also knew our manager, and he was not about to settle for "they didn't teach us."

After a day or two of our "stubborn" refusal to use the MAPs, and despite the instructors' and ultimately their manager, insisting that we follow the intended approach, the Education Center Manager called our branch manager and told him "we weren't cooperating" with the instructors. I got a call from George Mahalik asking what was going on. I explained what they were teaching as well as how and why we were using our approach. He said he would "take care of it." By the next day, we had no more complaints or pressure from the instructors. They let us do it our way. They were not exactly supportive or happy, but at least they stopped interfering. We were learning the system in depth. At the same time, the "bugs" they were using became more complicated. It got to the point where we could diagnose and fix the machines faster than our classmates.

When we got back to Boulder, Jim Gilbert told us what had taken place. After George had talked to me, he had spoken with Jim to confirm what I had said.

Jim had backed me 100%. George called the education center manager back and "chewed his ass," to quote Jim. He told them that we were doing exactly what he wanted us to do and that if they interfered further, he would have their jobs.

The 3330 training was another one of those aha moments. It was clear where the technology was going and that "card-swapping" would become at CEs job for all equipment. We had gotten away with fighting the system this time, but that would not always be the case. Card swapping was not what I wanted to do for a living. I had "the keys to the kingdom" at that moment. I knew that my knowledge and skills would be in high demand for several years to come, but I also knew that it was time to started planning my next career move.

– ∎ –

The one and only time I ever got drunk was while I was attending that 3330 class. I don't remember when, but at some point, while I was living in Boulder Jim Fessler convinced me to try scotch. I was never much of a drinker, but for some reason, scotch was much more to my liking than whatever I had been drinking before. It was scotch from then on. The lab portion of the 3330 class was at an IBM facility in Menlo Park. That was unusual because the Ed Center was in San Jose. I think the development laboratory was in Menlo Park, but I don't recall the reason. To cut down on the commute up and down Highway 101, which was a horrid commute even then, we switched hotels from the place we had been in San Jose. On Friday after we had won our battle with the instructors, we decided we would go out and celebrate. We sat and drank and swapped war stories, probably mostly lies, and continued to drink way more than we should have.

After we returned to our motel, Jim said: "I think I am going to be sick in about half an hour." He beat his deadline by about 29 minutes. I laughed, but I was never sick. No hangover, nothing, but I reminded myself that I preferred to be in control, and drinking didn't make me happy, it just made me uncomfortable. I suppose that is why I never had any interest in any drugs. I never tried any and never wanted any.

– ∎ –

The very first S/370 155 shipped west of the Mississippi went to EDS in Dallas, TX. EDS was a service bureau ran by H Ross Perot, a former IBM salesman, and later presidential candidate. EDS was a huge customer and Perot knew every button to push inside of IBM. That is most likely why he got

219

commercial machine #2. The local CEs had been trained, but not equal to 1/100 of what I had been through, and they had 0 experience. There were some initial bugs and Perot smashed hard on several high-visibility buttons inside of IBM. As a result, I was sent to babysit the system. It was a quiet week. The local team had fixed the bugs, and the machine was running error-free. We couldn't get access to the system because it was already in production, so there wasn't even an opportunity to train the local techs.

We had a lot of talk time, and I got to try out a lot of excellent restaurants in Dallas. I also got to meet Mr. Perot. He was a funny guy, short and skinny, with a high squeaky voice. He knew how to drive IBM crazy with his demands, but he knew how to treat people well.

— ■ —

About a year after the 155 announcement, I was asked to go to Poughkeepsie for another round of advanced engineering work on what was called the 155-DAT (Dynamic Address Translation). That became the 155-II.

The S/360 Model 67 was the first production machine with a DAT. It was reintroduced in the 370 155-II and became standard in the second generation S/370s, the "8" series (148, 158, 168) machines that replaced the initial S/370 line.

Dynamic address translation is the process of translating a "virtual" memory address into the corresponding "real" address. In English, the DAT included both hardware and software. It allowed the computer to create a "fake" or "virtual" computer inside of memory, and to run a different OS and set of applications on the fake computer just as it would run on real hardware. In fact, multiple virtual computers can be running simultaneously on a single machine. Of course, it takes a lot more memory and computational power to make this magic work, but running multiple virtual machines is a common thing today.

The primary purpose of the DAT hardware and software was to create and manage multiple virtual memory spaces. It uses a combination of "real" memory, that is memory that physically exists on the computer, and "virtual" memory, which is space out on a disk drive that is "mapped" so that it looks and acts like it is part of the "real" memory. It is much slower to access of course.

If you think of a typed page, it would exist in total within the "Virtual mapped space" on the disk drive. But at least initially, it would not be anywhere in "real" memory. When the program decided it wanted to read the first sentence, it would say "go get me the first sentence" thinking that was in "real" memory. The DAT hardware would say "ok, give me a second" and it would go look at real memory to see if it had any space to store the first sentence. If it did, it would grab the phrase from the virtual drive and place it in real memory and then tell the computer that it was there.

The DAT would keep track of where it had stored the sentence. The computer might think it was at address 11111. In fact, it was located at address 12345, but the computer didn't know or care. The OS would say "go get me the data at address 11111." The DAT would know that the real location was 12345 and it would get the data and hand it to the OS. Hence the name "Dynamic Address Translation."

That is a super simplistic example and explanation. In most cases, when the DAT went to locate space to store the first sentence, it would find that all of the "real" memory was full. It would check to see what data hadn't been used for a while and it would write that data out to the "virtual address space" on the disk drive and then go get sentence one and put it in the area it had just emptied. But even that is more complicated than it may appear. The data it moved out may not be from the same "virtual" computer, so it has to keep track of who that data belonged to and made sure it wrote it out to the proper virtual address space. It also had to remember if that data had been modified or if it was unchanged. If it had changed, it had to be written to the virtual space. If it were unaltered, then it could just be overwritten and forgotten. All of this is going on millions of times each second and for several virtual machines simultaneously. So the DAT is, in fact, a complete and very sophisticated computer that does nothing but manages these multiple virtual addresses spaces completely separate and more or less invisible to the OS.

Another way to look at it is to think of it as a single computer that you could run Unix, Windows, Mac OS, and Android all on the same computer at the same time. Each of these operating systems and the application programs they are running would think that they had a complete computer all to themselves. Hopefully, this will help you to begin to understand what DAT is all about, but also how massively complex the memory management processes had to be to keep all of these data organized and the different operating systems believing they were the rulers of their world.

I went to Poughkeepsie to learn the DAT hardware and software at the engineering level, but also to find out how to take an existing installed 155 and tear its guts out and rebuild it to incorporate the DAT hardware. That was a massive change. It included physically removing and replacing a full gate (a 4' X 5' frame of computer boards, cards, and all the wires) plus several logic boards in other parts of the computer. In truth, it was an entirely new computer once the DAT was installed and operational. That process was far more complicated than just repopulating and retiming a system. Of course, the system did have to be retimed after the DAT hardware was installed. For this, I spent another six weeks in Poughkeepsie, two learning the equipment and software, two on the manufacturing line building DAT equipped systems, and two in the engineering lab.

I only converted one machine at the Boulder IBM factory. That machine was used for several months before the actual product announcement. It was used to develop and test hardware and software for the upcoming 2nd generation S/370 systems, the "8" series (148, 158, 168, etc.).

The DAT machines were an engineering bridge to the new generation, so there weren't many 155-II conversions or installations in commercial accounts. Factory teams completed the few commercial system conversions. The S/370 158 came out at about the same time as the 155-II announcement. The 158 had the DAT built in from the beginning.

I went back to Poughkeepsie for another 6-week cycle of training-building-testing on the 158 before the announcement. As you can see, I spent a lot of time in the Poughkeepsie area over the years.

– ■ –

Rocky Flats was not my primary account, but I took calls out there several times. It was a Top Secret facility. For a long time, no one knew what they did. Even the people who worked there had no idea. The entire facility, including the manufacturing plant, was underground.

I came out one Saturday to install engineering changes on some equipment. They would always search my car, search my tool bag, everything. I could not get in unless I had been requested to come and my name was on their list. No unannounced visits. I finally got in, and they escorted me to the computer room where I would be working. The computer room was 4-stories underground. It was like a bank vault, complete with the heavy metal door with the big ship's wheel to open the locking slides. The entire room had a grounded copper wire mesh built into the ceiling, walls, and floor. That was to prevent the emission of any signals from the computer room.

They told me exactly which parts of the room I could go into and which parts to avoid. I was to call if I needed the restroom or whenever I was ready to leave. Surprisingly, they didn't leave a guard in the room while I worked. When I finished, I called for my escort. He came, and we climbed the stairs to the exit. The exits were down below the surface with a sloping ramp outside of the door. For the weekend, the doors had a steel band with a lead seal.

The guard called out to the security room and told them we were leaving and which door number. He hung up and just stood there looking at the door. I ask him what the holdup was and he told me he was trying to remember if this was the right door. I asked what he meant, and he said we could only exit through certain doors and that they rotate the doors every shift, so no one knew in advance.

I ask why it was a problem, hadn't he just called and cleared our exit? Yes, he had, but they wouldn't tell him if he was going out the wrong door. So I again asked what's the problem, do we set off an alarm or something? No, there are machine guns mounted outside of each door, and if we exit from the wrong one, well you understand the consequences. I told him he was definitely going out first. Fortunately, we were at the right door.

— ∎ —

Apparently, the way they kept the workers from knowing what they were building was to compartmentalize everything. A conveyor belt would bring an assembly into a room. The employees in that room would add some components to that assembly and then put it back on the conveyor belt and send it out of the room. The next room would get it, add some more components and then send it on. As a result, only the few who handled it at the very last stages knew what this device was.

The secrecy held until 1969 when there was a fire at Rocky Flats. That released some Plutonium into the air. All hell broke loose, and the truth about what they were doing began to come out. It was then that everyone learned that they were building the triggers for nuclear warheads.

— ∎ —

At IBM, as with every job I have ever had, my goal was always to be the absolute best at whatever I did for a living. It took a couple of years, but I was able to achieve and maintain that level until I transitioned into management.

223

My rate of advancement reflected my achievement. All new Customer Engineers (CEs) start as Associate CEs. They typically advance to a full CE after 12 to 18 months. I was promoted after only six months. From CE the next step was to Senior CE. That usually requires 6 to 8 years' experience as a CE. I was promoted to Senior CE 28 months after I was hired, 22 months as a CE. A tiny percentage of the best Senior CEs advance to FE Specialist. There is no standard time, but a minimum of 5 years as a Senior CE was fairly reasonable. Of course, only a minuscule percentage ever achieve this level. I became an FE Specialists after just five years with the Company.

There was only one higher technical level available for Field Engineers. That is Senior FE Specialists. That position was extremely rare, only the best of the best can achieve this level and only when there is a position available on the Regional staff. There were no Sr. FE Specialists in the branches. As you can imagine, once an individual reached this level, they typically stay there until they retire. The opportunity to achieve this level was rare. I became a Senior FE Specialists in my 7th year with IBM.

I specialized early and took advantage of every opportunity to hone my skills, I would work on any problem or technical challenge that became available, and attend advanced training whenever possible. There simply was no better service tech when it came to the specific systems I worked on. Those being the S/360 Mod 50, S/370 Model 155, 155-II, and 158. That included the primary external components, called I/O or Input Output devices, the disk and tape storage systems.

Success, of course, was not instantaneous, it took time and lots of effort. It took a willingness to step up whenever there was a need. IBM provides 24/7 coverage. Many CEs would limit themselves to no more than two night or weekend calls per week, usually only on the systems they had direct responsibility to support. I would not turn down a call; even multiple calls in the middle of the night. There were many nights I would be called out two or occasionally even three times, so often, that my manager had to limit the number of calls. One of the nice things was that you got a minimum of 4 hours pay anytime you were called out. Time and a half rate and double time on weekends. We got our regular pay twice a month; overtime checks weekly. My weekly overtime checks were often larger than my ½ month paycheck.

I soon started getting calls outside of the Denver Branch. After my 2nd year, I would typically be called out of town a couple of times each month; two times in a week was not out of the question. These were situations where the local branch had not been able to fix a problem, and typically the regional Sr. FE Specialist had been called and was either unavailable or had also failed to resolve the problem. There were even a few situations where a factory representative was called but failed. For me, these were fun calls. The pressure was always the greatest, and I thrived under pressure. The customer was usually in dire straits because the system had been down for an extended period. The sales team were typically beginning to panic as they could see the customer tossing the equipment out, or not buying more. I was always in the hot seat. In all the calls I took, I never failed to fix the problem.

The typical call came in the middle of the night, and it usually went something like "can you travel?" My answer was always "yes." OK, be at the airport for flight #xxx on United or Continental (usually) leaving at t:tt. The dispatcher usually didn't know any details, so there was no use asking. My only question was "warm or cold," meaning the weather at the destination. I always kept a small bag packed.

I would drive to the airport, get my ticket and find out where I was going. It could be anywhere in the US, but there were a few trips outside of the country. When I got off the plane, someone would meet me and brief me on the way to the account. It might seem strange that they wouldn't find some way to pre-brief me, but for me, being kept in the dark was something of a blessing. I could travel with a clear mind and not overwork the problem until I had access to the machine. The salesman (always a man at that time) usually met me. Their briefings were more about how the customer was doing than the technical problem. Occasionally the Field Manager would be there, and that helped give me a feeling for the technical issue.

I found it interesting how often the team had fixed the problem by the time I got there. I think it was physiological as much as anything. Once the customer was told that "the expert" was on his way, they would back off to await my arrival. That relieved the pressure on the CEs, and they could concentrate on the technical, as opposed to the political problem. Quite frequently, that allowed them to resolve the problem.

— ■ —

I traveled to Chicago for a class one time. They had booked me into the Palmer House Hilton. When I pulled up in the taxi, a doorman opened the door and stuck out his hand for a tip. Another doorman grabbed my bag, carried it to the top of the stairs and again the hand for a tip. Into the lobby, another doorman, another hand, another tip. It required 5 or 6 tips before I was finally in my room.

I found this all astounding. The Palmer House was an old and very elegant hotel. It had an enormous ornate lobby, murals on the walls and ceilings, polished brass and gold that made it look incredibly opulent to this country kid. Of course, there were service people everywhere, all expecting tips for doing a minuscule amount of work. That was so unlike IBM FE, but I expected the room to be on a par with what I had seen getting to it.

As was typical of FE; we were living 2 to a room. When I opened the door, I discovered that the room was so small I could sit on the sofa, which was a sofa bed and put my feet on the front of the TV. There was a Murphy bed for my roommate. No floor space at all when the beds were made up. It was such a letdown after all the gold and glitz.

— ■ —

Finding the right person when you land at an airport is a skill, and like anything that you do often enough, you develop a 6th sense about who to approach. It was customary for the person to stick an IBM card in their suit breast pocket, inconspicuous, but effective. Unfortunately, not everyone knew this or had a card handy. In other jobs, I have had to meet unknown persons in foreign airports and train stations. I got pretty good at spotting the right person. It was usually in their eyes.

Some years after leaving IBM, I came into the Newark Amtrak Station traveling from DC. I was meeting a company, and they were supposed to pick me up at the station. When I got off the train and looked around, no one seemed to be looking for me. I walked outside of the terminal and immediately noticed a car with two men sitting in it. They were just talking to each other and not even looking out the window. There were dozens of cars of course, but this one was the one. I walked up, knocked on the window and asked if they were there to meet me. They were in total disbelief that I could identify them in a car amongst all the other cars. They had sent someone inside to meet me, and they were able to call him on his cell phone. It turned out he had been in the restroom when I came off the train. I don't know exactly how I can spot the right person, but it is usually not difficult.

Flying

I took flying lessons and got my private pilot's license while we were living in

Boulder. I have always loved airplanes and flying. The overtime I was making at IBM gave me the finances I needed to indulge in this luxury.

I particularly loved flying up into the Rockies. That gave me a unique way to combine my love of the mountains with my love of flying. Most of the time I would practice in a Cesena 150, but occasionally in a Cesena 172. When I was flying solo the 150 was big enough and a lot cheaper to rent by the hour. A 150 could barely make it over the Rockies, and you had to understand the mountains if you went there. The passes between the mountains were usually up at about 11,000 feet. That was about as high as a 150 could fly if it were in perfect condition. But the real problem was the wind that would frequently flow through the pass.

The barometric differentials were usually the highest from early December through March. During these periods, Boulder would experience frequent windstorms where the winds flowing down the face of the mountains would exceed 100 mph; 120 mph was not uncommon, and occasionally they would reach over 150. These winds were like waterfalls. The air flowing down the canyons would then churn at the bottom like a real waterfall. They were not something you wanted to experience in an airplane.

There was almost always a difference in barometric pressure from one side of the mountains to the other. The air would be flowing from the high-pressure side to the low-pressure side. That was usually west to east, but not always. It was similar to my wind experience at the RBS Express when I was on a TDY assignment at Wamsutter, WY. It would flow through the pass and then down as it followed the face of the mountain like water flowing over the lip of a dam.

Altimeters work off of air pressure, and the air pressure inside of the airflow would be different from that outside of the flow. Therefore, when an airplane entered this airflow, its altimeter would become inaccurate. That created a dangerous situation for any pilot who depended on the altimeter to tell him if he was high enough to make it through the pass.

Even when the pressure differential was small, it created a dangerous combination. As you flew into the pass, your altimeter might remain steady, even while you were caught in the downward pull of the higher pressure air flowing through the pass. You could be losing altitude while your altimeter remained constant, a life-threatening situation. A lot of "flat-landers," even experienced pilots, would not compensate for this phenomena and they would wind up smashing into the mountainside 50' or 100' below the lip of the pass.

The first rule when flying in the mountains is never to approach a pass straight on. Fly in at an angle along the face of the mountain. That way, if you get in trouble and see that you are not going to be able to make it through the pass, you can just veer off 45 or 50 degrees and be clear of the mountain. If you came straight in, you would have to turn at least 150 degrees, and there would not be enough room or time to do that as you approached the pass.

The second thing is to ignore your altimeter. Ignoring your instruments is diametrically opposed to everything a pilot is taught, but in the case of flying through a high-mountain pass, it could save your life. Instead, watch a mountain or some distant object on the other side of the pass. If the object is getting lower in your windshield, you are maintaining your altitude or possibly even gaining altitude. Both good things. If the object is getting higher in your window, that meant that you are losing altitude and it would be wise to swing away and make another try. These are simple rules that would save your life.

The last thing was to gain your altitude before you ventured into the mountains. Go out over the plains and spiral up to maximum height and then attack the mountain. Don't ever try to gain altitude while you are flying up a canyon that is also gaining altitude under your feet. It may very well have a flow of air pushing you down at the same time. That is a sure way to die.

I don't know how many people got killed because they were both stupid and cheap. Whenever a strange plane came into the Boulder airport, one of the resident flight instructors would ask the pilot if they were heading west. If they were, the instructor would suggest that they buy an hour of his time, leave the family at the airport to take a break, and take a quick trip up the mountain to learn the rules. Very few would take them up on it. I suppose they thought they were being "hustled," but the truth was that a $25 investment could have saved the lives of the entire family. Occasionally they would come back and ask for a lesson after they got the crap scared out of them.

Another common mistake was to fill up their tanks before they went over the mountains. They thought that fuel would be cheaper or they didn't want to stop until they got several hundred miles further west. Fuel weighs about 6 pounds per gallon; that adds up quickly. Weight and balance are critical in small planes, and 300 or 400 pounds of fuel could reduce both the climb rate and the maximum altitude by 500' or more. Those factors could easily be the difference between life and death when flying in the mountains.

There were even commercial pilots who did stupid things that cost them their lives. I recall one who landed a 727 in Denver then hopped into a private plane, a Cesena 182, and flew into the mountains for fun. He apparently forgot that his single engine prop job didn't have the same power. He tried flying up a canyon and wound up as roadkill.

We had a few people fly into the ground east of Denver. Many East Coast pilots never fly higher than 5000' as that is way above ground in Georgia for example, but it is about 300 feet below ground in Denver. Every once in a while, some flat-lander would fly into Denver at night and forget that he was flying into the "mile high" city. Their airplane would stay at 5000 feet until the ground got to 5000 feet, about 50 miles east of Denver. At that point, they would die.

Stupid will kill you fast in an airplane.

— ■ —

I loved flying in the mountains. I followed all the rules. I would head toward a pass never intending to go through it. As I approached, I would veer away and then point the nose down and run down the canyon and out onto the plain. I would keep the plane at maximum allowable airspeed and zoom along above the trees. When I reached the bottom, I would suddenly pop out onto the vast flat plains that ran from Boulder to the Appalachian Mountains. It was a real hoot!

I did one cross-country with the family. We flew from Boulder to Nampa, Idaho, and back. On the return, I had a hard time gaining altitude on a hot day fully loaded with fuel coming out of Rawlins, Wyoming. I was on the Eastern Slope of the Continental Divide, so the ground was getting lower as I continued east. I was gradually gaining clearance both from the lowering earth and the lowering gas tank. It was a bit unnerving in any case. When I go back to Boulder, there was a steady wind at about 50 knots blowing straight down the runway. I came in to land because I was accustomed to high winds and knew the airport well. It was more like landing a helicopter; I came in very high, about 600 feet above the end of the runway and just slowed and settled onto the runway at about midpoint. A couple of guys came out and hung onto the wings so I could taxi in without flipping over. It was a bit stressful none the less.

Mountain flying over the Rockies

While I was finishing up my paperwork, a twin Beechcraft came on the radio and asked about the conditions. Boulder was an uncontrolled airport, meaning it had no tower or controller. I got on the radio and talked to him about how he should approach. The airport was up on a plateau so the earth dropped away at the east end where he would be approaching. That meant that the air would be flowing down the runway then down over the bluff. That is very much like the mountain pass I described earlier.

I told him to come in hot, faster than normal by at least 20 knots. Come in high, at least 500' as he crossed the threshold. Normally this would be something like 50 to 75 feet. Then immediately throttle back and touch down at least 300' down the runway. Boulder had a nice long runway so he would have plenty of room. He said he understood.

It was dusk, and we watched him approach with his landing lights on. He came on a straight in approach from the east. I could see he was making a standard approach, way too low. I grabbed the mike and told him to go around and come in higher. He said nothing and ignored me. We watched as his lights disappeared below the end of the runway when he caught the downdraft. We figured he was going to crash for sure. There was a guttural roar as he firewalled his twin engines and pulled hard on the stick. The Beechcraft came roaring up over the end of the runway with the nose pointed up at about 30 degrees. I swear he was so close that there must have been grass stuck to his wheels. The only thing that saved his stupid ass was that he had a pair of huge powerful engines and he reacted quickly. We watched him climb steeply to about 1000 feet. He came back on the radio and all he said, in a very shaky voice, was that he was going to Broomfield to land. I never did find out who he was, but I bet he never tried to land at Boulder on a windy day again.

– ■ –

My friend Jim Fessler also took up flying and we would go out together on occasion. He was one of those who got the bug. He ultimately left IBM to become a commercial pilot. The last I heard, he was flying twin-engine prop jobs making hops throughout Colorado and New Mexico. Like most beginning commercial pilots, he wasn't making any money, but he was building hours. His passion cost him his marriage, but I think that was happening in any case. I suppose he continued and got into bigger planes, but I lost track of him.

– ■ –

I tried flying only one time when I moved to LA. I rented a plane at Van Nuys airport and flew out to Catalina Island with the family for a picnic. Catalina was beautiful, but it was extremely stressful dealing with all the restrictions around the big airports, especially LAX, and with all of the traffic. When I came back to Van Nuys, I found myself 12th in line to land on the left runway. There was similar congestion on the right runway.

I parked the plane and never flew again. I figured that I needed at least 4 hours in the air every month to stay safe. I couldn't afford it, I didn't have the time, and flying with all the traffic and restrictions was no fun. Better safe than sorry.

Travel

I was constantly in training and traveling. Many of the training classes were for extended periods of time, a month or more, and so I usually took my family, and we drove. We crossed the country so many times that I got tired of driving the same routes so I would throw in alternates. The northern route through Chicago, the central route through St. Louis, once across Canada, once down across the South on return from an extended stay in Kingston. Los Angeles for a month-long class. Kansas City for another month. Teri was 2-weeks old when we left Idaho to join IBM in Denver. When she was 18-months old, she had been in 42 States, and she had never been on an airplane.

We had harness type seatbelts for the kids. I modified the lap belts so they ran up and over the seatback. Each child had a sturdy harness, and the belt ran through loops on the back side. That gave them the freedom to move around and lay down, but it held them in check if I ever had to stop quickly. Fortunately, I never did. They were great travelers. They could deal with the long days because they had some freedom. We would check into a motel at night then go to a grocery store and walk them up and down the aisles to get some exercise. Brian learned to read the billboards beside the road, and he would shout them out as he recognized the various signs. He could "read" most of the major chain brands of gas, motels, and fast food places. Teri caught on to the game pretty quick as well.

We had two "splat-mats." They were plastic sheets about 3' square. We would put them under the kids' high chairs whenever we went into a restaurant. I had never before seen either the harnesses or the splat mats, and I don't think anyone else had either. I don't remember where we got them. It was interesting to see the response from the waitresses. They were so appreciative of the fact that we saved them from having to clean up two messes after we left. We got excellent service everywhere we went.

— ∎ —

On one trip across Canada, we spent the night on the Canadian side at Niagara Falls. We were no more than ½ mile from the US border. It was early spring before the tourists hit town; it was still pretty cold and gray. We went to dinner at a Chinese restaurant. There was only one other family in the place.

They were obviously from New York City with heavy accents. They had two daughters, one about 10 and the other around 15. The 10-year old was having fun and enjoying her adventure. The 15-year old was being a 15-year old. She was reading a book and totally ignoring her family. Her mother was loudly haranguing her to participate, all of which was falling on deaf ears. At one point, mom said, "If you don't shape up we will never take you abroad again."

It was all we could do not to burst out laughing. I had always thought the term "abroad" meant something like traveling to Europe. I could not conceive of it applying to being in Canada only ½ mile from the American border.

— ■ —

On that trip, we lived in Woodstock, NY for about 6-weeks. That was the spring before the famous Woodstock Festival. Woodstock was a neat little village, completely unlike what you might have heard about the famous festival. That actually took place a few miles outside of town. We lived there for the last part of the winter, and well into spring. It was quiet and rustic, the kind of place that you would see in a movie about the rural part of New York.

— ■ —

I made a lot of trips to the Mid-Hudson Valley, Kingston/Poughkeepsie area. They provided opportunities to explore New England. My cousin David Montgomery was in the Navy and stationed at New London, CT, so we went to see he and his wife a couple of times. Mystic Seaport was nearby with lots to see and explore. The Rhinebeck Airdrome was near Hyde Park. It was a fun place to go and see WWI vintage airplanes demonstrated on weekends. We drove up through Vermont, New Hampshire, Maine, and Massachusetts. We spent a weekend exploring Newport, Rhode Island. There were many mansions open for tours in Newport, but also in the mid-Hudson Valley. The best was the Roosevelt Mansion, which is a National Historic Site. We had not traveled to Europe yet, but many of these old homes were much like what I would see later when I did go to Europe.

As time went on, I spent more time in airplanes. I was traveling all over to fix computers. While I visited many cities, these were usually in-and-out, with little time to see anything other than the airport, a computer room, and maybe a hotel. It was still a fun and exciting time, even if not an opportunity to get to know the people or the places.

Life in Boulder

While we were attending IBM Basic, one of the things that our instructors cautioned us about was an unexpected situation concerning keypunch operators. They approached the subject with delicacy, but in retrospect, it was good that they talked about it.

A keypunch machine had a typewriter-like keyboard where the operator input the data. The machine ran the card through a thin slot that held it in registration while the holes were punched, one column for each keypress. The "chad" are the tiny rectangular card pieces that are punched out. They fell down a chute to a chip box located directly below the punch mechanism.

The machines had a small table that measures roughly 2' x 4'. The operator would sit with her knees under the table while she typed on the keyboard. That had the unfortunate effect of placing the chip box directly in front of and between her legs. The electronics associated with the machine were in a cabinet that was suspended below the back half of the table. That was where the CE would usually be working. With the chip box removed, there was a "window" from the back of the machine looking directly through. You can figure out what the view through this window would be. I have no idea why the designers didn't take steps to remedy this, but it remained true with every generation of keypunch equipment. Maybe somebody had a perverse sense of humor.

As you can imagine, our instructors informed us of this "situation" so that we did not do anything inappropriate while working on a machine. What they didn't warn us about was that we could also find ourselves on the receiving end of these inappropriate images.

— ■ —

I only worked on Unit Record equipment briefly while I was getting trained on the large mainframe computers. I was assigned to the Rocky Flats facility for a couple of weeks. If I remember correctly, the reason was a combination of my security clearance and the fact that their regular CE was on vacation or away at training. As I described earlier, Rocky Flats was a strange account. It was all underground, and everything was top secret. What I soon discovered was that the keypunch room, which had about 25 women working there, was a hotbed of practical jokers.

Most of these women were in their late 30s or early 40s; there were a few a bit younger and a couple quite a bit older. They came to work in the morning and went 4-stories down into the ground like a bunch of miners. They were locked in a vault and stayed there all day never being allowed above ground. The operators were busy at their keyboards punching in encrypted data that they couldn't understand or discuss once they left the room. They were apparently bored out of their minds. Who can blame them?

So in I come, all of 22 years old and about as green as can be. I was fresh raw meat for all of their frustrations, and they took great delight at yanking my chain. They all knew what was going on and they all laughed uproariously whenever they were able to embarrass me, which turned out to be fairly often. One of the first instances was when one operator deliberately removed the chip box while I was working on the backside of her keypunch. I must have turned the color of a ripe tomato.

After a couple such incidents, apparently, I wasn't responding with the desired degree of fluorescence, so on another occasion, the operator excused herself to visit the ladies room to remove a certain item of clothing before she removed the chip box. It was not sexy, it was not seductive, it was only embarrassing. Needless to say, that was the whole purpose of their torture.

On another occasion, one of the elderly ladies who worked on a verifier complained that the machine was "taking extra cycles." A verifier looks almost exactly like a keypunch; it also works very similar to a keypunch. The only difference is that instead of punching out the holes, it has sensors that check to make sure the proper holes have already been punched out. So one operator punches the card, and a different operator retypes the same data to verify that the correct holes were punched.

If an error occurs; the operator would lean over and write on the card to indicate which column was in error. I soon discovered that the cause of the "extra cycle" problem was the size of the operator's more than ample bust line. She was heavy, and her breasts were large so when she leaned over they would press down on the keys and cause the machine to think she had typed another character, hence the "extra cycle."

This was a relatively small room, and every lady in the room, except the operator of this machine, of course, was completely aware of what the problem was. In fact, I suspect that they had not only seen it before, but they were most likely guilty of taking steps to recreate the problem. I stood there a while watching this operator, all the while knowing what the problem was, and wondering how I was going to explain the cause of the problem to someone older than my mother. It was not like it is today, we didn't talk about such things in public. In the meantime, all the rest of the operators were watching, enjoying my torture and wanting to see just how I was going to handle this touchy situation, pun intended.

Fortunately, this was one of the "bugs" they had taught us in basic training. I watched the operator for a while, then asked her to give me a few minutes to try it myself to see if I could make it fail. I had one of the keypunch operators make up several cards that were simply the alphabet followed by numbers 0-9 repeated across the entire card. I sat at the verifier acting as if I could type and after the lady lost interest, I quickly turned the height adjusting knob on the chair up about 1½ inches. I went around back and pretended to "swap out a part" before I returned the machine to the operator. Problem solved, but 24 ladies were sorely disappointed that I had avoided yet another embarrassment.

In fact, these kinds of incidents were surprisingly common, and they made for some interesting shop-talk as we compared notes among the CEs. Over coffee, the CEs would exchange stories, offer solutions, and warn each other about particular operators who liked to pull these stunts. I think a lot of it was because most of us were pretty young and conservative; we were clean cut and always dressed in a suit. In the mid-1960s, most people our age were the polar opposite.

It may have simply been that it was their way to liven up an otherwise dull day. I sometimes suspected that these ladies exchanged "how to embarrass the CE" stories at their classes or over coffee. I don't know, but at least in part, we were targets because it was easy and we were frequently the only males around to tease. I can't imagine that they thought that they were advancing a relationship. However, I do know of some cases where that was the result. It never worked with me. I was too square, too busy, and too conservative to even think about finding out. Nonetheless, I surely was embarrassed on more than one occasion.

After a while, I became somewhat immune to the tactics, but every once in a while someone would come up with something new. There were even a few occasions where I was able to reverse the sting. On one such occasion, I was working at NeoData, an account in downtown Boulder. There was a very attractive young operator who was notorious for harassing the CEs. She liked to wear the micro-miniskirts that were in vogue at the time, and she had the legs to make an ultra-short dress work well. One day, I was working on the

1403 stacker. That is the mechanism on that refolds the paper after it passes through the printer. It sits relatively low, on the backside of the machine, kind of out of site from everyone. I was squatted down on my haunches when this young lady walks up very close and tells me that she is having a problem with the paper stacker tearing her stockings.

I had noticed that when she came over, another female operator, one that was a bit older and more conservatively dressed, accompanied her. I don't know why, maybe it was because I had been warned about this operator, or maybe I had been through enough of these things by then, but I sensed that this was yet another trap. So when she informed me, in her best sexy voice that her nylons, which were at that point, all of maybe 10" from my ear, were being torn by the stacker, I turned and acted as if I was looking for a hole in her stockings. I looked first at her ankle and then let my eyes slowly follow up her leg until they hit the hemline of her very short skirt, which was at about eye level. Without looking up or away, I pointed over my shoulder toward the other operator and quietly said: "she never complains." Nothing more was said, and they both beat a hasty retreat.

— ■ —

We lived in an apartment in Boulder only briefly. I had VA benefits that allowed me to purchase a house with nothing down. That was good because I had nothing to put down. As soon as I returned from another long school, this time in Kingston, NY, where I took the family along, we bought our first home. It was a small 3-bedroom brick house on 33rd St. in Boulder. It was a single story without a garage, basement, or carport. It was probably about 800 square feet. It did have two bathrooms. The yard was good-sized but in need of some serious TLC. The price was $14,500. If I remember correctly, our payments were $105/month.

First home Boulder CO 1967

For the next few years, I was constantly going off to schools and temporary assignments. Jane didn't drive. She had taken lessons while she was in high school, but for some reason, she had never taken the test to get a license. That was not a big problem while we were living in Nampa. Even though I was frequently away on lengthy TDY assignments, she had family as well as a lot of friends to help her get around. When we moved to Colorado, there was no support system and her non-driving created serious problems. With two small children, there was always a need for some item, medication, detergent, or a doctor's appointment. This was back in the days of cloth diapers, so those were at hand. Coordinating her transportation needs with my travel and long working hours became quite a hassle. It was also a constant source of worry for me whenever I was away from home. Invariably it meant that the very first thing I had to do whenever I did get home was drive her somewhere to take care of some urgent need. Exhausted, I finally told her to get a driver's license or start walking. She took the test and passed with no problem. It was such a relief knowing she could get around when I was away.

— ■ —

One winter Sunday I got very sick. After a heavy lunch of pork chops and stuffing, we went to the movies. I was uncomfortable throughout, and it got progressively worse as the afternoon turned into evening. My stomach was hurting. First I tried sitting still. Later I tried laying down. Eventually, I tried laying on the cool wood floor. Nothing seemed to help for very long. I finally told Jane I thought I needed to see a doctor. She didn't drive yet, and of course, she needed to take care of two young children. Our next-door neighbor was a young chiropractor, only a few years older than I was. He drove me to the emergency room, and they immediately moved me to surgery and removed my appendix.

I had had similar episodes over the years, but none as severe, and they always cleared up after a few hours. The doctors told me my appendix was a mass of scar tissue from these previous episodes. Because I had eaten earlier, they gave me an epidural rather than general anesthesia. I was out in either case; I awoke at about 2 a.m. and got out of bed to go to the bathroom. I didn't have any problem, but the nurse came in in a panic telling me I had to lay flat for at least 12 hours, otherwise, I would suffer migraine headaches. Fortunately, I missed that bullet; I never had any headache problems.

I only spent one night in the hospital. I didn't work for a couple of days, but I was scheduled to fly to Los Angeles on Wednesday for a class. My manager wanted to reschedule, but I was bored stiff sitting at home. In my mind, all I would be doing was sitting in class, and so I caught my plane and attended the class.

– ∎ –

We lived in that house only for a couple years and then bought a new home on Oneida St. This was a brand new home. In fact, we were the first people to buy in the development. The builder was a young guy just starting out, and he needed someone to step up and buy his first home. As an incentive, he gave us a lot of extras with our new home. We sold our old house for $18,800. We sold it ourselves, without a realtor. The new home cost $28,000.

We had a lot of fun as the neighborhood developed. We started by introducing ourselves to every person as they moved in. We organized block parties and community yard sales. This process made for a very cohesive community. Everybody knew everybody. Ernie Pierce and his wife Carol lived across the street. Ernie was IT Director for Head Ski. He and I could talk technology. We became good friends, and kept track of each other for some years after we moved out of Colorado.

Hippies

1967 was the "Summer of Love." The Summer of Love refers to a social phenomenon that occurred when more than 100,000, mostly young people, converged on the Height-Ashbury neighborhood in San Francisco. It became a pivotal moment in the hippie movement. The result was that San Francisco, specifically the Height-Ashbury neighborhood, became the melting pot of politics, war protests, music, drugs, and the total lack of sexual and social inhibition.

The rock-opera "Hair" also débuted in 1967. The opening song "Aquarius" contained the line: *"This is the dawning of the Age of Aquarius."* The song also talks about peace, love, and understanding. Other favorite songs spoke of the Hippy culture. *All we need is Love* (The Beetles), and *San Francisco (Be sure to wear flowers in your hair)* (Scott Mckenzie). The Age of Aquarius supposedly corresponds with the rapid expansion of technology, the decline of religion, and an era of peace and understanding. There is an "age" of approximately 2150 years for each of the Zodiac signs. Much has been written about the Age of Aquarius, but there is also much debate as to when the Age began, or if it has even started. In any case, the song was the embodiment of the hippie philosophy.

The Summer of Love and the supposed dawning of the Age of Aquarius defined the hippie movement and brought the counterculture into public awareness. It also exposed a fault line that was developing between the survivors of WWII, and their 20-something children. The parents, who were now middle-aged, had been shaped by the Great Depression as well as the World War. They knew hardship; they took life seriously. Their children had no understanding of this. The introduction of "the pill" (the birth control pill) early in that decade left their generation free to reject the traditions and responsibilities that constrained their parent's lives. The counter-culture they developed was the polar opposite.

The friction between generations was palpable, exacerbated by an unpopular war growing in Viet Nam. The "hippies" with their rejection of traditional values, their strange attire, long hair, weird music, and extensive use of marijuana and psychedelic drugs, were the latest in a series of groups to be feared. While the Summer of Love established the movement, Woodstock, which took place two years later during the summer of 1969, was the seminal "hippie" event.

— ■ —

Boulder Colorado experienced a smaller, but very similar Summer of Love, with a massive influx, I think most locals at that time saw it more as an invasion, of hippies. As with San Francisco, Boulder was forever changed.

During this period, a series of events and political shifts created the perfect political storm. The hippies arrived in mass beginning in 1967. In 1971, 18-year olds got the right to vote. In addition, they were allowed to vote where they attended school rather than in their home districts. At about that time there was one of those periodic apocalyptic predictions of the imminent end of civilization. In this case, a giant meteor was supposed to strike in the middle of the Pacific Ocean with force so great that it would create a new continent on the opposite side of the earth. These two events would supposedly cause massive tidal waves that would drown nearly everyone. Boulder was one of the few safe places. That was a clarion call to all free love, pot smoking, hippies. City streets and parks were suddenly treacherous. Every bush was a toilet, and every bench or green spot was a bed. They invaded summer cabins and plundered any movable object. These bearded do-nothings overwhelmed our world. Come election time, the hippies and the students; all wanted to vote in protest of the Viet Nam war. Boulder's political makeup changed overnight.

Once they achieved power, they wanted to make Boulder over in their image. They enacted all kinds of laws designed to freeze things as they were. A few of these actually benefited Boulder, many did not. One of the good things was that they annexed the land and then zoned a greenbelt around the city. That wasn't all that good for the landowners, but it did prevent the urban sprawl that has destroyed so many communities. The downside was that they enacted laws that made it almost impossible to make an addition or improvement to your property. I am sure their intentions were good, but the result was that the city began to atrophy. Construction stopped, and people couldn't fix up or even maintain their property. It was years before they began to loosen the regulations and the city started to prosper again.

It was funny to watch how the new "power players" reacted to having power. First came the stupid laws, then came their personal transition from outsider to "the establishment." Once they had the authority, just like their predecessors, their goal became to maintain it and to increase their power. Thirty years later the ruling class was mainly aging hippies who had come to power decades earlier. Having said all of this, Boulder is still a charming, albeit expensive place to live. If you are a conservative you might as well not vote, but it is still

241

a cool city.

— ∎ —

There were a lot of technology and scientific businesses located in Boulder. IBM had their factory. Beach Aircraft had a small operation located north of town. They were working on stuff with NASA and the Apollo Program. Rocky Flats, which was being run by Dow Chemical at that time was about 8 miles south of town. They were building the triggers for the nuclear warheads and bombs, but nobody knew that. The National Center for Atmospheric Research had an installation on a bluff overlooking the city, and the National Bureau of Standards ran their atomic clock at a facility near the university.

The Apollo program was in full swing while we lived in Boulder. Man first landed on the Moon on July 20, 1969. At the time, we were on a camping vacation with Jane's sister Mary. We were traveling across Wyoming on our way to Yellowstone. We checked into a hotel in Jackson Hole, Wyoming, so that we could watch the moon landing and the first steps on the Moon. I will always remember that moment.

We were also in Boulder in April 1970 when Apollo 13 had its unfortunate adventure. We had a friend who worked in the X-ray department at Beach Aircraft north of Boulder. They built some of the tanks on the Apollo ships. His job was to X-ray the welds to look for possible defects. When the explosion occurred on Apollo 13, no one knew what had happened, or why. I remember him being called to work and spending several days digging through every X-ray trying to find any welding flaws.

Moving to LA

Boulder was a wonderful place to live and work. My commute was about 10 minutes. The air was still immaculate, and many people with asthma relocated there to ease some of their symptoms. IBM was good about trying to accommodate people with medical needs, and so there was always a waiting list of individuals who wanted and needed to relocate to the area. That made for an older and more senior staff in the Boulder sub-office. It also meant that once you got there, you never wanted to leave. I was the exception. I had my eye set on advancing as far and as fast as I could, and it became very obvious that Senior CE was probably the ceiling, at least for several years, if I stayed in Boulder.

Family portrait 1969 Brian, Tim, Teri, Jane

I was young and ambitious, and a bit too full of myself at the time. I pushed hard to advance, working long hours, taking any call, any class, and any assignment. I remember as we were walking back to the CE room from the meeting where they announced my promotion to Senior CE, Sam Duffield, one of the "old-timers" in my mind, he was probably in his early 40s, casually said to me "so now you can stop pushing so hard." I am afraid I wasn't too gracious in return as I replied: "I don't intend to retire here." It probably sounded like a slap in his face as he clearly did intend to retire there; I undoubtedly projected the opinion that I saw him as already being retired. In any case, I continued to push, and after a couple of years, I started talking with my manager about looking for other opportunities.

There was an unwritten rule in IBM that you shouldn't turn down promotional "opportunities." You could get away with turning one down, but if you turned down a second opportunity, the next one would not be as good. My first opportunity came for a position as an instructor in the Washington, DC education center. I flew to Washington for an interview and spent a couple of days looking over the area. I came back thinking the location would be great, but the job would suck. I knew it was a step toward becoming an FE Manager, which I saw as my future path, but they were teaching CEs to read MAPS, and to me, that would be stone boring. When I got back, I had a good talk with Jim and George Mahalik and told them that I didn't want to take that path. They understood and almost immediately set up an interview for a position at the Field Tech Support Center in Los Angeles. I flew out and interviewed. It was only a bit more interesting, still not what I was looking for, but there were possibilities. It turned out to be an excellent move.

I did not see a clear path beyond the Support Center, but I liked the idea of moving to LA because there was so much going on with IBM in that area. There were several branches as well as the Western Region Headquarters. There was also an education center in the same building that I would be working in, so there was some room for other opportunities. In 1972, I took the job and the promotion to FE Specialists. I had been in Boulder just five years.

– ∎ –

The Tech Support Center was put in place to provide telephone support to Customer Engineers in the Western Operations area including the Midwest and everything west to Hawaii. The Center staff consisted of FE Specialists with expertise on virtually every piece of equipment in the IBM inventory. My specialties were the same as I had in the field. That included all of the peripheral equipment that could be attached to the mainframes, primarily disk, tape, and printing subsystems. The Center took incoming calls from CEs and tried to help them solve problems.

Most of the calls were pretty simple, but occasionally I would get one that was a bit unique. I remember one was a tape drive problem somewhere in New Mexico. The CE was in a remote location, not Albuquerque. He was a new CE, just back from basic training and not trained on that equipment. Unit Record equipment was all he knew. I don't remember why he was the only person available to take a call on this tape drive, but he was desperate for someone to walk him through fixing it. I spent a couple of hours on the phone, but we got it running.

In theory, we were available to fly in to provide hands-on support if necessary. In reality, that seldom happened. The Support Center staff was pretty thin, so if I were out on a call, it would leave my equipment group uncovered. There were also several intermediate layers before they could call me out.

I did go out on a few onsite calls, but it was rare. I remember one call was on a

155 at Gibraltar Savings in Los Angeles. They had been struggling with an intermittent problem that no one had been able to resolve. It didn't take long for me to find that they had a defective ROS (Read Only Storage) board. As is often the case, it was only intermittent because that particular circuit was only occasionally used. ROS is the firmware that tells the computer exactly how to boot up, and how to execute commands. On the 155, the ROS boards were large multilayer cards about 9" wide and 14" long. Each board had hundreds of lines etched into the surface on each side. These lines had tiny tabs that acted like miniature capacitors. A strobe signal sent down the line would sense the presence or absence of a tab. The result read as either a 1 or a 0 by a matrix of wires embedded under the top layer on the board.

The ROS boards were not "serviceable." These units were sealed; when one went bad, you had to get a new board. There was no schematic diagrams or information provided that would allow the CE even to scope a board. Fortunately, they were extremely reliable and seldom failed. You will recall that when I had worked in engineering, I had collected a few special tools. One was a set of schematics that showed me how to decode the ROS address and trace the logic for the circuits on the boards. I was not supposed to have this information, but when I was in Engineering, I had to use it frequently to debug problems during development. Fortunately, that information, along with a few other "factory-only" tools managed to fall into my briefcase before I left Poughkeepsie.

The problem at Gibraltar happened on a Friday before a long weekend, and there was not a replacement part closer than Poughkeepsie, NY. Poughkeepsie was closed for the weekend by the time the problem was isolated. That was early in the life of FedEx and so next day delivery wasn't reliable. Monday was a holiday, so there was no way to get a replacement part before the middle or even the end of the next week. Losing the system for that long was unacceptable.

There was general panic when everyone realized the situation. I listened for a while. I finally took the Field Manager, Sales Manager, and Account CE into a conference room and told them that I could probably put a temporary fix on the board. I made them commit to me that no one would know what I had done as I was not supposed to use my magic tricks in public. Of course, they swore their eternal silence.

I pulled the ROS board and took it into the CE area where I had a light and magnifying glass. With the crew hovering over my shoulder, I decoded the

ROS address to the correct line and, using the magnifying glass traced it until I found the crack that was causing the problem. After carefully scraping away the Mylar coating, I rubbed a soft pencil across the crack to smash it down, but also to fill in the crack with the conductive lead. When I popped it back into the computer, it worked like a champ. I was an instant hero, but my secret lasted all of maybe 5 minutes. I got calls from dozens of 155 CEs asking for the information. There was no way I would give it out. It was one of those things that could cause more problems if used incorrectly, and if I distributed it, it would have been easy to trace the source back to me.

— ∎ —

When we moved to LA, we bought a house in San Pedro. We found that houses were very expensive compared to what we had in Boulder. We looked for days and disliked 99% of what we saw and couldn't afford most of it in any case. We were particularly turned off by what we saw in the San Fernando Valley. We finally found the San Pedro house. It was in terrible shape. The yard was abandoned. Trees and shrubs were overgrown, and the grass was dead. There was a Poinsettia bush in the back yard that was as big as many trees. The house had been rented, and the carpet was stained and torn in many places. The tenants had disassembled a truck in the driveway and the engine in the kitchen. All of the kitchen cabinets were covered inside and out with black grease from the engine or tools. As I remember, we paid around $45,000. There was a lot to do to get the house livable, and we spent most of our time and money cleaning it up.

The house was in a cool location on a bluff overlooking the Pacific Ocean. Our house was not exactly "overlooking," it was a block or so back from the edge of the cliff, so there were other houses in between. Our only "ocean view" was a tiny part of Catalina Island that you could see out of a bathroom window. It was foggy most mornings. I would get up to fog, but as I drove up the hill to get on the main road to go to work, I would drive up into the sunlight.

It was fun being close to the ocean. We had the ocean smell, and there were tidal pools nearby where we could take the kids to see the starfish and other critters. Also, being that close to the ocean, we had near-constant breezes and little smog.

— ∎ —

I had bought a 1960 Austin Healey 3000 while we were living in Boulder. It was a "basket case" when I bought it. I had to tow it home because the transmission was shot. It was originally dark green, but the body was beaten pretty badly. I stripped it down to the frame and rebuilt it, transmission and all. I had it painted a cream color when I finished reworking the body. I spent so much time and money on that car that Jane called it "the blond mistress in the garage."

My 1960 Austin Healey, The *"blond mistress"* 1971

I drove it winter and summer; it was a lot of fun to drive. It was not all that reliable, but since I had completely rebuilt it, I could fix most anything that would break. The main thing was the transmission. The British engineers had designed the transmission with no rear seal. The drive shaft had a reverse thread to pump the oil back into the transmission as you drove. Of course, it would pump the oil out whenever you backed up and the threads would actually help the oil to drain out if you were foolish enough to park facing uphill. I reengineered it to accept a seal on the shaft. It wasn't foolproof, but it was a significant help.

As with other weak design areas, rather than fixing the problem, they gave you a way to check to see if you were low on transmission oil. For that, they put a dipstick on the transmission so that you could check the oil level every time you got gas. The previous owner had apparently failed to do this, and that is why the transmission was blown.

247

The thing that made the transmission hard to rebuild was keeping the needle bearings in place while I was assembling it. I was talking to my brother Tom about this problem, and he gave me a simple solution. I placed grease on the shaft and then put a rubber band around the shaft. I put the needle bearings under the rubber band and slide the assembly into place. The first time the gear turned it would chop up the rubber band that would dissolve in the grease in any case. Problem solved! Thanks, Tom.

There was another irritating problem "designed" into the car. It had an electric fuel pump located right behind the driver's seat. It had two old problem-prone side-draft SU carburetors. Aside from their tendency to flood when you were starting the car, the floats tended to stick. The engineers obviously knew of the problem. Rather than fixing it, they installed overflow tubes that ran from the float chambers straight down to dump any excess gas on the ground any time the floats stuck. Fortunately, the dump was on the side away from the exhaust pipe so starting a fire was not a serious risk.

You became accustomed to the sound of the fuel pump in normal operation it would have a brrrrrutp sound every few seconds, as it would refill the float chambers. When a float jammed, it would be a continuous brrrrrrrrr. At that point, I would have to pull to the roadside raise the hood and smack the carburetors on the side to unstick the floats.

The stock engine was an old 6-cylinder tractor engine. It was heavy and not real responsive, but the sound that came out of the exhaust was uniquely Austin Healey. It was a very deep, loud purr. You could identify an Austin Healey 3000 for miles before you saw the car. They sit low, and they were pretty small so they were not all that easy to spot. Friends would tell me they could hear me coming 5 minutes before I got there. It was an exaggeration of course, but the sound was quite unique.

I loved my Healey and took it to California when we moved to Los Angeles. I would drive it to work, which was mainly freeway driving for about 20 miles. When the oil crisis hit in 1973, they changed the speed limit to 55 mph. The Austin Healey had no springs to speak of, and no shock absorbers at all. It only had about 1″ of padding in the seats, so my butt was sitting on a stone and only about 6″ from the concrete at all times. This combination made for what you might call a "hard" ride. I was young, and it didn't bother me until the 55 mph change. It turned out that 55 mph was the resident frequency for the suspension on the 3000. It would hit each cut in the cement roadway at just the right rate to drive your butt up toward your shoulders with a bone-jarring effect. I would get to work in the morning feeling like an LA Rams linebacker had hit me. I couldn't afford to keep it as a weekend car, so I had to sell my blond mistress and get a different commute car.

Moving back to the Field

I was in the Support Center for about a year. I found it incredibly boring just to take calls and not be able actually to get involved. The Center only lasted for a few years. I think it was a combination of frustration on the part of the staff, plus it failed to decrease equipment outage, and that was the original intention and justification.

After about a year in the Center, I was transferred back to the field to solve an urgent staffing problem in the Santa Barbara, CA branch. Santa Barbara was a relatively small office with few large systems customers. There were two data centers located in Westlake Village about 60 miles south of Santa Barbara. One was an internal IBM Center; the other was a State Farm Insurance regional data center. The Oxnard sub-office managed the Westlake team.

The timing was perfect for my car change. When I first went to Westlake for an interview, I saw a Volvo P-1800 two-seater parked by the freeway with a for sale sign. I had just sold my Healey and was looking for something small and sporty to replace it. I owned a Volvo earlier and liked the way they handled so I bought the P-1800. It was a fun car, but I soon found out why the guy was selling it. Two problems would intermittently cause the vehicle not to start. The first was relatively straightforward. There were a set of fuses of course, but Volvo had used a weird fuse with cone-shaped ends that had a very small contact surface. The fuse for the fuel pump had corroded and was intermittently not making contact. No fuel, no start.

The second problem proved to be more mysterious. Periodically, as I was driving down the highway, the engine would simply shut off. After I got to the side of the road, it would not start. About an hour later, it would suddenly work again. I tried to figure it out with no luck. I took it to a Volvo dealer with equal results. In all fairness, it would never fail when I had it in for service, so there was little they could do besides guess at the cause. I finally found an independent Volvo service tech near Oxnard, and I took it to him. He kept it for a few days and discovered the problem.

One of his techs was a Navy jet mechanic at Point Mugu Naval Air Station, which was nearby. He took the car over to the base and ran some tests with the equipment he had available to service the jets. He found that there was a

249

"standing wave" (a signal or voltage level) on the spark plug leads that would gradually build up over time. When it reached a certain threshold, it would shut down the computer and the car would stop. When the voltage dissipated, the car would start again. The fix was simple, replace the carbon spark plug leads with solid copper leads as specified by Volvo. I drove that car well over 100K miles. It was a bit expensive to maintain, but after my initial problems, very reliable and a lot of fun to drive.

— ■ —

Back to the Santa Barbara branch. In Westlake Village, IBM had one very large S/360 Model 75 that was used to support the aerospace industry in Southern California. There was also a Model 50 in the same data center. State Farm had a single S/360 Model 40 in their data center. The Westlake Field Engineering operation was almost a sub-office in its right. It had three system CEs and two CEs that serviced card equipment and a few teleprocessing operations. It didn't have a dedicated Field Manager. The one FE Manager in Oxnard was not a big systems guy and his time was consumed managing several CEs servicing small accounts. Westlake had operated rather "loosely" for several years.

A crisis was brewing because IBM was planning to replace the Mod 50 with a S/370 158 in their Center and at the same time State Farm was replacing their Mod 40 with their own 158. Although the System 370 had been out for several years, Santa Barbara had no large system S/370 experience, and other than the one CE servicing the 360/75, and one for the Mod 50, not even any large S/360 experience.

I was brought in as the "Area Manager," a title that I had never heard of the before or since. It was a made-up thing to accommodate the unique situation. I had dotted line management responsibility for all (5) personnel in Westlake, and a charter to "clean up the operation and get the team up to speed to service the new 158s." It was a bit strange for IBM in that I was technically not their manager, I was an FE Specialists, but all the CEs, including the non-systems guys, reported to me. A big part of my job was covering for the systems people who I was sending away for training. They were experienced CEs and so once trained, they could easily carry the load. However, getting trained on the mainframe and all the new peripherals required several months.

Personally, I was co-managed by the FE Manager in Oxnard and Len McWilliams, the Branch Manager in Santa Barbara. Len treated me as a Field

Manager, and the FE Manager in Oxnard treated me as his equal. This hybrid arrangement allowed me to work on the equipment while managing and training the team. Strangely, it worked out quite well. The staff was very capable and wanted to take on the new systems; they just had no management support or direction, so they had been operating on their own. Although it was never officially stated, it was clear from the beginning that this arrangement was temporary. Once I had the operation working, I would be moving on. The crew was more than happy to have someone they could work with to get organized and up to speed.

It was a unique group of men. There was one charter member of the John Birch Society; he walked around with a copy of the Constitution in his pocket. One guy was in the Taxpayers Union. As a protest against taxes, he had not filed his income taxes for several years. The third guy was an aging hippie and ultra-liberal. Needless to say, there were some interesting discussions amongst the group. Remarkably, they all got along very well.

I soon discovered that the oldest member of the group, the John Bircher, was blind in one eye. That meant that he had no depth perception. I discovered this by accident when I rode in his car one day, and he scared me nearly to death as he would run up behind cars. The biggest problem was that he wasn't all that good at fixing the computer part of the computers; he loved working on the power supply problems. That was a problem because you are talking about 240 volts at 200 amps. If you get across the wrong terminals, you become a crispy critter in very short order. I talked the branch manager into training him on programming and got him transferred out of the engineering work. He was a bit unhappy about that, but there wasn't any choice.

For me, being the Westlake Area Manager was a great assignment. It was far enough away from San Pedro that IBM paid to move us to Westlake. We bought a new house in Westlake Village; it was less than a mile from the IBM location and only about 2 miles from State Farm. I got to "practice" being an FE manager without all the hassles that went along with that. I also got to work on equipment, which I always loved.

The IBM data center 158 arrived first, and we got it up and running in short order. The State Farm system was only a month or so later. It went in smoothly as well. The State Farm account was the first time I had worked extensively in a commercial account. During the installation, I had significant interaction with the sales team, but more specifically with the AAS (Administrative Account Specialist) for the account. That was all new to me

251

as the internal accounts had no equivalent. I met with the sales team regularly but only spoke with Sharon Muckleroy, the AAS on the phone, as she worked in the IBM office on Wilshire Boulevard in LA. Our interaction was primarily to order missing items, to coordinate shipments as we removed the Mod 40, and in general to manage the installation paperwork. We never met, but she was always pleasant and efficiently resolved whatever administrative problems I came across. I only mention this because several years, and several jobs later it transferred to the LA Finance Office where she worked. It is a cute story that I will cover later.

Moving to the Region Staff

After about a year, I had Westlake Village operating smoothly, and the team trained and ready to continue the operation. At that point, I was promoted to Sr. FE Specialists on the Western Region Staff in Los Angeles.

I initially came on the Region staff as the 155 and 158 expert, but at that point, the 155/158 install base was quite stable, and all of the branches had well trained and experienced Customer Engineers. The new 3890 Check Sorters were an emerging crisis, so I was immediately assigned to manage the Region's 3890 Check Sorter program. This lead to a long relationship with the banking industry and over time, I became something of an expert on the technical side of that industry.

The 3890s were installed at each of the major banks: Bank of America, Security Pacific, United California Bank, and Wells Fargo in the Los Angeles area. If I recall, correctly there were a total of 9 systems. The 3890s are huge electro-optical-mechanical monsters. On a single pass through the machine, the 3890 would read the magnetic ink on each check, OCR the amount field, microfilm both sides, write an 8-digit processing number on the back of each check, and sort the checks into 1 of up to 36 pockets. All of this took place while the paper checks were traveling through the machine at close to 60 mph. Every time there was a jam or transport problem, it would shred several checks. These monsters could process 5000 checks in less than 2 minutes.

— ∎ —

Today, paper checks have all but disappeared, but back in 1975, paper checks were the lifeblood of the banks. Everyone paid their bills and bought groceries with a check. When the checks reached the bank, it was paramount to get them processed so that the money could quickly move from the payer's account to the payee's account. Thousands of checks were processed every

252

night. The checks were ultimately returned to the customer, and so they had to go through multiple sorting passes to get to the right basket. They had to be sorted to the individual customer and stored, as they were returned with the bank statements each month.

Several laws limited the time the bank had to process the checks and get them to the customer's home bank. If they waited too long and the payer had insufficient funds, the bank would have to eat the loss. The processing window was small. If the check were an "on-us," meaning that it was within the same bank, it was all accomplished in one night. If it were drawn from a different bank, the physical check had to be processed and then quickly, hopefully the same night, but usually the next day, moved to the payer's bank so that the funds could move between the banks. That was one of the reasons the various LA banks had their check processing centers physically located very close to one another. This processing window was particularly problematic if it was an out of state bank. In that case, they had to physically send the check by air to that state for processing.

The banks were also trying to minimize what was called "check kiting." Check kiting was when a payer wrote a check without sufficient funds in their account, and then deposited the money before the physical check reached the bank. In effect, during the period from when the payee received the money until the point where the payer's account was debited, the payer was using the bank's money without paying any interest. That is technically against the law, but that was not stopping anybody. It a was common practice. It was an irritant at the individual level, but it could be a significant problem for the bank.

Companies were masters at this game. That was one of the reasons that most people were traditionally paid on Friday. The company would distribute their payroll checks, possibly several million dollars, and then move the money from an interest bearing savings account to their checking account on Monday when it was needed to clear the checks. During this time, while the bank was "lending" the money, the bank would be borrowing "short term" money from the Federal Reserve. The short term money was costing them interest on top of the interest they were paying the company for their savings account money. That may seem like minuscule amounts, but in a big bank, this could add up to millions of dollars each month. You can see why having the check sorters operational was critical.

Incidentally, eliminating most of these problems is one of the primary reasons banks have pushed so hard for electronic payment systems and debit cards as they eliminate the physical check. They also provide immediate transfer of funds from your account to the recipient's account. You cannot kite a debit card or an online payment transaction.

– ∎ –

The 3890 was "pushing the envelope" in virtually every arena: optics, magnetic ink reading, OCR, and document transport. Everything was done on-the-fly and at incredible speed. When first introduced, the machines had significant issues: reliability, engineering, training, and parts shortages. Machines were breaking almost daily, and these failures were severely impacting bank operations. The banks were remarkably tolerant. In part this was because when it was operating, the 3890 provided an enormous productivity gain. They also realized that they were working at the bleeding edge of technology. That said, there were limits to their willingness to accommodate the problems long term. There was great fear that the whole program would blow up resulting in lost customers, the loss of mainframe business, and potentially lawsuits. As a result, senior management at the highest levels of the: Field Engineering, Data Processing, and manufacturing divisions became directly involved, quite literally in every problem.

I was the point person for the 3890 program in the Western Region. These machines were used primarily at night, from 8 p.m. to 4 a.m., to process checks that had been collected at individual bank branches and transported to the Check Processing Centers. There they were sorted and then distributed out to the paying banks. I had to come into the office every morning at 6 a.m. to collect data for all 3890 service incidents for the previous 24-hours. Most days there would be 3 or more problems, almost always more on Mondays, as they would run the machines both on Friday night and Sunday night. That represented 1/3 of the machines failing daily. I first did a quick investigation and gathered the "facts" for each incident. I had to determine if there were any issues with parts, personnel, training, or machine design. I had to identify who was responsible and the next steps where appropriate. Finally, I had to assess the customer temperature and predict if we were on the path to some bigger disaster or lawsuit.

Once I had assembled the facts and identified any issues, I had to write a synopsis, a letter for each incident. These letters went out over Bill Perrin's signature. Bill was the Director and Western Region Manager for the FE Division. Each letter was a concise but detailed review, with forward-looking

254

analysis, flagging any potential issues, anything that might impact this rolling disaster.

These letters were coming in at the very top of each division, and we all know how brown stuff flows downhill. It was critical that I did not miss anything, but also that I not "cry wolf." The letters were faxed to all the division president's offices with copies to FE Western Ops HQ in Chicago. It was a tightrope to walk with zero time to debate report content.

As you can imagine, there were a lot of politics involved. Much of it right in my building. I had to do all the gathering, analysis, estimating, and report creation on my own, there was no backup, no partner or "expert" to consult. Before my reports could be sent, each had to be reviewed by my boss Dick Clark, by his boss the Tech Support Manager Bob Haberger, then by Bob's boss, the Western Region Manager, Bill Perrin. My mornings were VERY intense, as all this had to be written, approved and faxed out by 10 a.m.

My boss was a straight shooter and getting his approval was never a problem. In all honesty, he was only an observer as he had no real input to my work or the process. He did give me one of my first serious political lessons. Gary Breckenridge was the Branch Manager at the Finance Branch. His branch was the sales office responsible for all of the 3890 accounts. Dick told me to personally deliver copies of the reports to Breck, no later than 10:15 a.m. He wanted to make sure Breck wouldn't get blindsided by anything I said. It was important to keep it "unofficial" with no paper trail. That branch was about two blocks away from my office. Breck usually wanted a quick discussion after he reviewed the letters. He had a very easygoing personality, but he was a superstar in the DP Division. It became a morning ritual as he would have his door open and a cup of coffee awaiting my arrival. It was always fresh brewed, not out of a machine, the man had class.

My biggest challenge was getting Haberger and Perrin to both sign off on the same text. Haberger was an in-your-face kind of guy. For him, it wasn't just broke, it was "a f---ing disaster." And, we weren't "failing to get support from DP," it was "those idiots in sales have their heads up their a---es." Perrin was the polar opposite. If you were standing in front of him with your nose bleeding on his white carpet, he might gently push the Kleenexes across the desk; he would never tell you to wipe your nose.

At all times, Bill preferred an indirect approach to confrontation. You could bleed all over his carpet, and he would never address the issue directly. It took some time, but I became quite adept at "wordsmithing" to fit my reports in the fuzzy space between these two personalities. However, before I learned, I experienced some rather stressful mornings. After a while, I learned how to craft reports on any disaster so that the reader could see it the way that suited their personality. At that point, the game became getting all letters passed each morning without any rewrites. The 3890 crisis taught me some incredible business skills: rapid assessment, writing, and politics. These proved to be some of the most valuable lessons and skills I could have ever learned.

It was also the beginning of great friendships with Bob, Bill, and Breck. When Haberger left to become Branch Manager for Denver South, I gave him a framed poster of a big ugly Orangutan with a caption that read "When I want your opinion I will beat it out of you." A few years later, I visited him in Denver as part of the TIPS installation roadshow, and he had that poster hanging on his wall. We had a good laugh about it. He said he used it to "set expectations" whenever one of his managers came into his office. He wasn't that bad, but he liked to portray a tough-guy persona.

Systems Assurance

After the 3890s had stabilized, I became the Regional FE Systems Assurance Representative. This assignment was another fount of knowledge and experience. In the 3890 program, I learned how to quickly gather information, evaluate probable outcomes, and to wordsmith reports to say what had to be said while keeping the body count to a minimum. The SA position expanded my training on situational analysis along with learning what questions to ask, and when to ask them. How to probe, how to read between the lines and understand what needed to be done to salvage a failing project. These were the basic skills that I used decades later when I became a consultant. Managing the politics had been a part of the 3890 program. It was equally important in SA, but it would become the heart of my next assignment as Project Manager.

In SA I had a DP counterpart, a Senior Systems Engineer, Kay Holland. It was the first time I had partnered with a woman. We traveled and worked together across the Region. We were usually out of the office 3 or 4 days a week, about ½ the time flying to branches outside of LA.

Systems Assurance was a new program and approach for IBM. Our job was to audit the DP and FE office operations as well as assess customer preparedness before any major system installation. Consider it a "fire prevention" program. The goal was to assure the smooth installation and ongoing operation of the system. There was a little training in Chicago, but mostly that was an exchange of lessons learned and how-to's with other Regional SA teams. Our day to day work required leveraging the field experience we had. Kay and I had the authority to force changes or even hold up installations if necessary.

I believe that my selection as the Region SA representative was because management had seen that on the 3890 program I could thread the needle and get the job done without slaughtering any civilians. I don't remember any of the individual names but to get the SA post, I had to interview with the DP Region Manager and a couple of his management team, so DP had some level of signoff. I would guess Breck also had a say, if not sign off.

The 3890 was my first political minefield. The SA role was even more political, and it came with significantly higher risk for me personally because I was completely on my own. No one was there to correct or adjust my analysis, decisions, or preapprove my reports. I had to stand by the questions I did or did not ask in the audit meetings, the reports I generated, and the positions that I took. On occasion, I had to stand in opposition to my DP counterpart when I felt the customer or the DP branch were not sufficiently prepared for the installation. If my management didn't back me, my credibility as an SA Rep would instantly vanish.

— ■ —

Working directly with my DP counterpart was a real education in how the DP Division and offices functioned. She and I spent time before and after each audit discussing what our concerns were, what we had learned, what we may have missed, and what our position would be in our separate reports. The reports were independent, but both FE and DP Branches and Regions were copied.

Working with Kay was a great experience. We spent a lot of time together flying or driving. We were both looking to advance in the company, and we wanted to understand how the different divisions worked. We spent a lot of time discussing operations, politics, and procedures. Kay went on to become an SE Manager, and I lost track of her when I went to the Project Office. She was a tough cookie and very smart. Her one weakness was her tendency to see the FE branches as at fault in any problem, but that was a standard DP ailment. We had some interesting "debates" on this issue.

The SA role gave me direct exposure to both the DP and FE teams at every branch in the Region, and it seemed that the FE branches, not unlike Kay, always had a bone to pick with their DP counterparts. Many of them wanted to use the SA process to even scores. I had to avoid the faux problems while identifying real issues. Of course, it was not always about sales problems; the problems were sometimes on the FE side as well.

I held the SA position for a little more than a year when I was promoted to Project Manager for the Western Bancorp (WBC) Teller Item Processing System (TIPS) network.

In retrospect, I believe that this series of jobs lead directly to the Project Manager's job. No Field Manager and no one else on the Region staff had my credentials. I am sure that both Jack Leach the Project Office Branch Manager, and Bill Perrin knew that the Project Manager would have to have credibility with the FE branches as well as the DP project team. They probably assumed there would be a fair amount of politics in the process, but as much as I respect their management and vision, I don't think it is possible that they foresaw Goshawk (a second generation project). Even if they did, they could never have imagined just how political Goshawk would become. Since the Project Office was specifically established to support the LA Finance Branch of the DP Division, Breck, the DP Branch Manager, most likely had a say in my selection as well. I didn't ask at the time, and so I will never know for sure.

— ■ —

The most immediate thing that I noticed when I came on the Region staff was that for the first time, I was in an organization populated by true peers. These were all relatively young men. Of course, I was the youngest, as usual, they had rocketed up through their careers as quickly as I had. Most had been there longer and were older, but each one was a superb technician who had earned his stripes. It was truly a pleasure to work with such an outstanding set of talented professionals. Unfortunately, I never got to know most of my counterparts personally. My peers were more directly involved in supporting specific classes of equipment, while I was immediately moved into special programs that were more political and not specifically product support related.

I became friends with Rick Diederich who would later work for me in the Project Office. I am not sure why Rick and I hit it off, maybe because we were about the same age, or maybe it was just our personalities. In any case, I was able to reconnect with Rick many years later after retirement.

There were only a few educational opportunities on the Region Staff. One of the best, or maybe just the one I most remember, was the Staff Training Program (STP). It was a 2-week class for mid-level professional staff from various divisions. My class was in the San Jose area. I think they moved the classes around, but I don't remember. There was a lot of "how IBM works" stuff that helped, and even some discussion about dealing with inter-division politics, but for me, the most significant part was a public speaking session. We were given a preparation assignment before class. Specifically, we were to prepare a 5 to 7-minute speech on any subject that we wanted. I made mine on an investment I was involved in; a new toy called a "hang-up."

I was always terrified of public speaking, but I knew that this was a weakness that I had to overcome. I deliberately sought assignments where I would be forced to speak publically. I was both excited and terrified to make my presentation at the STP. As the class went on, no one mentioned the speaking assignment. I think most of us were hoping they had forgotten about it. In the middle of the 2nd week, the instructor started the day by announcing that today and tomorrow we would give our presentations. Suddenly the friendly relaxed atmosphere that had developed became very tense.

He looked around the room and pointed to me saying, "you're first." Instant terror! He told me to go outside, close the door and wait. I did. He came out and said that I was to imagine that I was working in the hold of a cruise ship on the last day of the voyage. There was an enormous, noisy farewell party going on in the main ballroom. I had just discovered a major fire in the hold of the ship, and it was my job to run into the ballroom and alert the partygoers to the problem. I was to scream "fire in the hold" at the top of my lungs. He instructed me to wait outside until he told me to come in.

He went back in, and I waited for what seemed like an eternity. I found out later that while I waited outside, he casually chatted with the class to waste time, but he also instructed my classmates that they were to remain completely passive no matter what I did. How insidious was that?

After a time, he yelled for me to come in. I did and I yelled, "Fire in the hold" at what was probably more of a squeak than a yell. Nothing, not a peep, not a smile, not even a recognition that I was in the room. My classmates were not only enjoying my torture; they were worried about what horrors would befall them when it came to their turn. I was sent outside to try again. After another

259

long wait, I was called in again with the same passive response. By the third or fourth time, I was starting to forget everything and even get a bit pissed that I was getting nowhere. My classmates were also warming to their part in my torture. They started talking amongst themselves while I screamed at the top of my lungs. Finally, after I don't know how many of these out and in cycles when I came in and did my yell, which was actually getting weaker due to my strained vocal cords, my classmates responded with shouts and cheers. Before I could say a word, the instructor turned to me and said, "Give your speech!" I did, and it went flawlessly. I was not nervous, and I was pumped up. I got a nice round of applause at the end.

The instructor thanked me and allowed me to sit. He proceeded to tell us all that we needed to learn to pump ourselves up whenever we gave a presentation. If we weren't pumped, we would come across flat. It was alright to have butterflies; you just wanted them flying in formation. I have never forgotten that lesson. To this day, whenever I go onstage to give a presentation, which incidentally I love doing, I scream "fire in the hold" in my mind. It sets me up. I walk out pumped and with a smile remembering the story.

I was learning a lot and having a lot of fun as the SA Representative. As with most promotions, I was not looking to change positions when my next boss came looking for me.

College

Up to the time, I moved to the Region staff; I had never had a lot of interest in obtaining a college degree. However, as my focus shifted from tech to business, I realized it was time to look at other educational opportunities. When I finally got into a position where I was not traveling constantly, I decided to enroll in night school and started accumulating college credits.

Night school was a world unto itself. Although I can't compare because I have never attended a single on-campus college class, as far as I can tell, night school has few similarities to attending on-campus class. My classmates were like me, trying to accumulate credits while living and working something of a normal life. Time, work, and family commitments required that we squeeze our education in when and where we could.

Classes were held at various high schools in our area. To accommodate the long commutes many of us had to live through each day, they usually ran from 7-9 p.m. Various courses were offered Monday through Thursday evenings. I frequently found myself in classes with the same individuals. We all had the same core requirements to get out of the way, and there were not many options, so we tended to fall into the same sequence of classes. Most of us would take either 2 or 3 classes a week, and by the time we finished work, commute, family obligations, classes, and studies, we were pretty exhausted by the last class on Thursday night.

I remember one course I took was "Art Appreciation." It was a required Humanities course; it was held on Thursday evenings. The class was in a high school classroom. There was no air conditioning or at least not at that hour. The classroom was hot, and we were all tired. The instructor was a young lady that taught at the main campus of the Moorpark Community College. Her approach was to turn off the lights, turn on the slide projector, and then lecture to pictures of various art pieces. You can imagine the effect of a warm classroom, the hum of a slide projector fan, and her soft, rather monotone voice on a bunch of exhausted students. It was all we could do to stay awake, and most of us failed on more than one evening.

About half way through the class she voiced a complaint that no one ever asked any questions. It was true; no one had asked a single question. Not being a dummy, the next week I decided I would ask at least one question. She was lecturing to one of Picasso's pieces. I raised my hand and asked what was probably on everybody's mind, "what makes this art, and the things my 6-year old draws, not art?" I thought it was a fair question and certainly something I wanted to know. Of course, I didn't realize that the real answer was "nothing." Picasso's was art only because somebody who somebody thought should know, had said it was art. My daughter's scribbles were not art because nobody of any significance would dare call it art.

Well, my question pissed off our teacher. Probably because she really couldn't answer it. She got defensive, loud, and eventually angry. We all just sat there while she rattled on making no sense at all. After class, I walked her to her car and apologized. I explained that I had not asked my question with any malicious intent. I simply didn't understand and wanted to know. She went away mollified, but no one asked another questions during the remainder of the course.

— ■ —

In another class on "Women's Issues," which was a subject that was starting to raise its ugly head due to the feminist movement, we were supposed to read two books on "women's liberation" and pick one to do an oral report. She gave us a long list of titles.

A friend, Beverly Pollack, was in the class as well. We had been in several classes together, but I also knew her as she worked at the State Farm location, and her husband was my State Farm Insurance agent. We talked about the idea of doing a joint review. We would both read the same book. She would give a report based on a feminine perspective; mine would on the same book based on a masculine viewpoint. Our teacher thought this was an interesting approach.

I looked the list over and, being the troublemaker that I can be from time to time, pointed out that there were no titles dealing with "men's liberation." Our teacher said that if I could find something, bring it to her for approval and she would accept it. Beverly thought that might be fun. We both searched but had no luck finding written material. I finally found one group that said we were welcome to attend their meeting and do a report on them. I called Beverly and asked if she were free on Saturday --she was. I told her we could meet with these people for a few hours and do interviews and gather information. We had both been unsuccessful in our search, so she was excited to have something. She asked me where we would meet and I told her it was a nudist colony in the Topanga Mountains. She immediately said "no way." I had to laugh, as there was no way I was going to a nudist camp either.

We finally found a professor at Cal State Northridge that had some material. Ultimately, we did our oral report on that material and our opposing perspectives. We asked the teacher for an entire class period, and to not announce the subject, just explain that we were making the opposite view approach together. When we got up, we asked everyone to take out a paper and write three characteristics that were feminine and three that were masculine. We gathered the papers and compiled two lists on the board. It turned out that both lists had only about 8 or 10 characteristics. On the feminine side was the word "consumer" while the masculine list contained "provider."

We then announced our subject "men's liberation." Two men immediately voiced strong opposition and started to leave. The teacher intervened and told them that if they left, she would flunk them for the course. Beverly and I found that we agreed more than we disagreed when we reviewed the subject. Basically what we both said was that the mistake the feminists were making was trying to be more like men. The reason it was a mistake was that men were actually in more need of "liberation" than women. Women had more latitude to change jobs, stay home to raise a family, go back to school, and present themselves in whatever manner (soft or firm, easy going or difficult, etc.) they chose, while men, being the primary breadwinners at that time, had little opportunity to shift gears. It started from the beginning; girls played with dolls, boys with guns. Girls are coddled when they got hurt; boys are told: "big boys don't cry." Girls could be "Tomboys," but there was no corollary for males; they could never be "girly" in any form. In short, finances, as well as people's expectations of men, prohibited them from changing course. By the end, the guys who were initially upset were agreeing with what we had to say.

– ■ –

Night school also ended my coffee drinking. That may sound strange, but let me explain. I started drinking coffee while I was in the Air Force at Vale. I was never an avid coffee drinker, but there wasn't anything else to drink at the RBS sites. Remember this was decades before you could get bottled water, and since coffee was what everyone drank, I fell into the habit.

When I was working as a Customer Engineer, I would "drink" a dozen or more cups a day. I use quote marks because I never actually drank most of those cups. Most computer rooms were food and drink-free areas, but whenever the mainframe was down, the company would quickly grind to a halt. When I would arrive to fix it, they would invariably assign me a "gopher," usually one of the IT department's secretaries, and her instructions were to "get him whatever he wants, but don't let him out of there until he gets it fixed." About the only exception was to go to the bathroom, and if I had asked for a bottle to pee in, I think most would have given me one. They all knew me and knew that I drank decaf coffee so they would immediately get me a cup even if I didn't ask.

I was busy and focused on the problem at hand and would usually only take a couple of sips of the coffee before I got the computer running, at which point I would be out the door to another account and another cup of coffee. I may have a dozen cups of coffee in a day, but only drink the equivalent of a couple of full cups.

When I started working in the Project Office, initially, I would spend the entire day in the office going from one meeting to another, always with a cup of coffee. For some reason, we only had regular coffee, not decaffeinated. So instead of drinking a couple of cups of decaf a day, I was drinking 6 or 8 cups of the high-test stuff.

At the end of one semester of night school, several of us went to Du-Par's Diner in Thousand Oaks, to celebrate and to try to figure out who was going to be in what classes the next semester. I probably drank another 3 cups of high-test on top of the 6-8 I had already had that day.

I went home and went to bed only to wake up a couple of hours later to use the bathroom. I went back to bed but the caffeine had taken over, and I could not get back to sleep. I got up the next morning and told my wife I was quitting coffee …cold turkey. Of course she asked why, and I told her that it didn't make sense to pay money not to sleep at night. I have not had a cup since. That was 1976.

When I told my secretary not to get me any more coffee and why, she went out and bought a dark-glazed cup along with some lemon juice. The cup was dark, so I didn't notice that the liquid inside was clear. The lemon juice gave the hot water some flavor. It also helped cleanse the caffeine out of my body. I had headaches and cravings for a couple of weeks as the caffeine cleared my system, but after that, I found that I had no desire for coffee. I no longer like the taste. For me, it is almost impossible to make ice cream taste bad, but coffee ice cream tastes bad.

— ∎ —

The staff assignments, as well as the Project Office, also finished off my marriage. For most of my married life, I traveled extensively; often up to 80% of the time. I would come home and see some of the problems that were going on, but by the time I had showered and changed my clothes, it was time to hit the road again. When I went into the various staff positions, my travel dropped down to maybe 10% and so I would be home almost every night. What I discovered was that my wife and I were at two dramatically different places in our lives.

It would be inappropriate for me to try to say what Jane thought. However, in a few words, I believe that if I had taken a job as a TV repairman at a local shop, and been at home every night, even if my income were ¼ of what I was then making, she would have been happier. At the same time, I had tasted business, travel, and many new challenges. I wanted more, more challenges, more opportunities, more experience. I was not about to stop learning and growing.

In my mind, our marriage had been a deal where she would focus on raising the kids, and I would concentrate on bringing in the income needed. In all fairness, I don't know that I had ever communicated this expectation, I just assumed we agreed. I felt that I had held up my end of the bargain, but I could see that the kids were more or less raising themselves, and I wasn't happy with the result. I saw my work moving me into ever-higher circles, and she was uncomfortable with the kind of circles we were already moving in. We had grown in different directions too long and too far to recover.

The divorce was relatively amicable. I didn't even hire a lawyer. Of course, I paid for hers. The children stayed with me. Technically, we had joint custody, so they were free to choose where they wished to live. When I remarried, and Sharon sold her house, we calculated the net present value of the alimony payments plus her half of the equity in our home and gave Jane a check for the full amount. It was a far better deal for her than waiting for a check each month, and waiting for us to sell the house. The sum was a large enough, well over $50,000, to pay cash for a house in Idaho where she ultimately chose to live. It was sufficient for a very comfortable life if she managed her money wisely.

Summary of my Pre-Project Office IBM Years

The Layered Architecture I discussed earlier was key to IBM's long success in the mainframe business; however, I think their success can be attributed to something else. IBM has always seen itself as a business partner, not just a technology supplier. The approach was never to "sell" or even to "service" hardware or software; it was always to provide solutions. My years with IBM inculcated this "consultative" approach into my subconscious. It has formed the basis of my relationships with clients, family, friends, and just people in general throughout my life.

I don't know that my time at IBM altered my fundamental beliefs so much as it filled in the blanks and firmed up my foundation. The company was built and operated on the basis of honesty, integrity, and service. It fostered innovation and rewarded both vision and effort. There were constant reminders: to think, to under commit and over deliver, to put the customer first, to operate at all times with integrity, and to tolerate, as well as to be, a Wild Duck. These were entrenched in my psyche.

Interestingly, IBM's "layered" architecture built on the Oriental Way the old Chief had taught me in the Air Force. That influenced my thinking in subtle ways. It is a bit difficult to describe without sounding cold. In fact, it is anything but cold. I learned to deal with problems, life, and relationships in separate "layers" so that I could isolate the impact between various elements. If I were busy studying college courses, for example, I could divide that work and the time spent so that it had minimal impact on my family and work.

The Project Office 1976-1978

At the beginning of 1976, I was on the IBM Field Engineering Division Western Region staff located at 3424 Wilshire Boulevard in Los Angeles, CA. I was the Regional Systems Assurance Representative when I was offered the position of Project Manager for a unique one-off project that fell outside the technical and scope-of-work boundaries of any standard Field Engineering Branch or even the Region Staff.

Tim 1976

A Project Office (PO) was established specifically to manage the installation of the TIPS (Teller Item Processing System) network for Western Bancorp (WBC). There were several significant technical and management challenges. First, we were dealing with new technology. The IBM 3600 Banking System, had only been recently introduced. It was IBM's first entry into the retail bank branch market. The 3600 was a networked terminal system designed to replace the traditional electromechanical calculators. The 3600 would revolutionize bank operations. Second, it used IBM's new SNA (Systems Network Architecture) communications protocol. SNA was a layered architecture that used the communications (phone) lines more efficiently, eliminating much of the need for dedicated telephone circuits. SNA substantially reduced communication cost, opening the door to new larger networks that were previously unaffordable. In many ways, SNA was a precursor to the Internet.

TIPS was a vast network by mid-1970 standards. If memory serves me correctly, Western Bancorp had approximately 1800 locations scattered across the 11 Western States. That made it by far, the largest SNA network in the world at that time. Finally, the customer demanded a very aggressive schedule allowing only 18 months to complete the installation.

— ∎ —

Typically, a new network would represent an incremental change to existing infrastructure, replacing an existing set of equipment or adding to an existing data center. Our project was more complicated because we were starting from scratch; there was no data center, no network, and no staff.

There were three parties involved directly in the TIPS project: the customer WBC, the IBM sales team, and the PO team. At the initial joint project team meeting, there were only six people. WBC had only two people assigned at that point. The PO consisted of only two people, Jack Leach the Branch Manager, and myself as Project Manager, and two from the sales team. The Sales team was larger as they had been working on the project for some time as part of their sales effort. They only sent two people so that they would not overwhelm everyone else. The sales team worked for my old friend Gary "Breck" Breckenridge, Branch Manager for the LA Finance Branch. That meeting started the 18-month clock.

Significance of the TIPS Network

In the mid-1970s, the banking laws were arcane and incredibly restrictive. Banking across state lines was prohibited. Therefore, it was not considered interstate commerce. This allowed individual states to make the regulations. In some cases, their laws dated back nearly a century. Some states prohibited branch banking. That meant that a bank was only permitted to have a single location. ATMs were just beginning to reach the market, and some states had included ATMs in the branch banking prohibition. For those states, it was not permissible to have a drive-up teller system or an ATM in a location that was not physically a part of the main bank building. I recall one instance where a bank installed a pneumatic drive-up teller system across an alley from the bank building. The State made them tear it out.

While interstate banking was prohibited, WBC had formed before those laws and it was grandfathered in as the only multistate banking organizations. While WBC owned banks in multiple states, they were still required to operate their banks separately; each operated under separate names. That made WBC's banks look like they were independents, rather than a single organization.

As you can see the situation was a mess with conflicting State and Federal jurisdictions fighting for control. Ultimately, banking was moved to interstate commerce so that it could be regulated consistently nationwide.

If you are under 50, I doubt that you can imagine how it was before networked teller machines appeared. Before TIPS, tellers all worked exclusively with electromechanical calculators that provided no access to the customer's actual account information. Tellers had to rely on the "pass-book" carried by the customer. Therefore, banking was based on relationships. If the teller didn't know you personally, the branch manager probably did and would most likely have to approve a transaction.

As recently as 1975, even in the smallest towns, bankers were the power brokers. They controlled access to money and thus dominated commerce and much of our individual lives. Banking was done only at the bank; there were no ATMs or debit cards. Credit cards were rare and accepted at only a few locations; you paid with cash or by check. Getting your cash was difficult; there was no such thing as "cash-back" at stores. There was no banking across state lines. Getting an out-of-state check cashed, or even accepted for payment, was next to impossible. When you traveled, even within the U.S., you had to either carry either cash or traveler's check. Finally, banks were only open Monday through Friday from 9 a.m. to 3 p.m. People had to adjust their schedules around bank hours. There were no alternatives; banks ruled, they didn't have to be responsive.

Interestingly, the banking situation had a lot to do with family structure. A much smaller percentage of women worked, in no small part because everyone had to deal with the constraints created by access to money. With no ATMs or branch banking, if you worked across town, getting to the bank during business hours was next to impossible. At the same time, banking was essential, to get cash, make deposits, and deal with the financial minutia of life. That often fell to the wife. Banking had to change to free up women's lives.

Today, we seldom write a check or set foot in a bank; no one knows their bank manager. There are even "digital" banks with no physical facilities. Our paychecks are deposited, regular bills are received, and most are paid electronically. Credit cards provide instant access to personal lines of credit, often from multiple financial institutions, not just banks. We can make purchases, manage our finances, pay our bills online, and access our cash from ATMs or in the form of "cash-back" at most stores. We can complete almost any financial transaction 24/7 from our PC, tablet, or smartphone.

It is impossible to overstate the significance of the TIPS network, and impossible to imagine what your life would be like today if these laws remained. Bank-by-phone, Internet banking, ATMs everywhere, and easy access to your credit or cash anywhere you travel, none of this would exist. All of this has revolutionized life as we know it.

— ■ —

Given the restrictive and fragmented banking environment, a significant part of WBC's motivation for the TIPS network was to give their various banks the appearance, if not the reality, as that was still illegal, of a single unified multistate bank.

WBC's management was pushing for change, and they used the TIPS network to pressure the regulators to change the laws to allow cross-state banking. While they were the only multistate banking organization and therefore critical to driving change, they could not accomplish this alone. They brought all of their different banks under a single brand, First Interstate Bank. That positioned them to take quick market advantage once the laws changed. This forced their competitors: Bank of America, Nations Bank, Chase, Wells Fargo, and others, to also pressure the regulators so that they would not be left behind. It took several years, but the laws did change.

TIPS was also significant for IBM. Up to that point, tellers used calculators manufactured primarily by Burrows or National Cash Register. The 3600 was IBM's first entry into the teller-automation arena. If it were successful it would be a disruptive technology as it not only replaced the calculators, it would bring the tellers online with real-time information about the customer's accounts. That had the potential to improve productivity and reducing bank losses. It would usher in a whole new era of "financial services." The entire industry, including the regulators, were watching.

A decade earlier, the IBM S/360 revolutionized the computing industry. The 3600 in conjunction with SNA communications protocol, another layered architecture, had the potential to transform the banking sector. I think that assigning similar names, S/360 and 3600, was deliberate. IBM was betting big and took a significant risk. If it failed, they would get a black eye in the industry, and the concept of teller automation would be set back for years. Specifically, if I failed in my mission, it would set back the effort.

TIPS was successful, and as a result, everything changed. Terminal-based item processing became the banking standard globally. Today, IBM remains a major supplier of products and services to banks, and virtually all bank systems, even devices not manufactured by IBM, use the SNA protocol. <u>Anytime you access banking services anywhere in the world, you are benefitting from the TIPS network. TIPS revolutionized banking, and I played a significant role.</u>

Incidentally, in parallel to IBM's move into the retail financial market, they were introducing checkout scanners into grocery stores. While I was not involved in that effort, I can say that this was equally disruptive to all retail sales operations. Collectively, the 3600 and the checkout scanners were IBM's first foray into retail operations. This was approximately 5 years before the IBM PC was introduced.

PO Operations

Operationally, the PO was in uncharted territory. To comprehend the significance of doing something as radical as the PO, you need to understand a bit about management inside of the FE Division. Field Engineering management was systemized to the extreme. There were rules and measurements for everything. For managers, the rules were covered, first in New Manager Training, and then "engraved" in a two-volume set of

Management Guidelines backed up by an intricate web of measurements and reporting.

Everything was documented, and the results were measured in multiple ways. Each CE had to account for every minute of their daily shift, every machine they worked on, coffee breaks, and any overtime they might work. Parts usage was recorded and tracked. A record was kept of any parts in the trunk of their car. Preventative maintenance, engineering changes, backlogs of any scheduled work, etc., everything was tracked. There were periodic employee opinion surveys designed to measure employee satisfaction but also to measure management performance. Every report was cross-matched and charted on a branch/region/division and historical basis. Absolutely nothing was left to chance, and there was scant room for anyone to fly very far out of formation.

I don't mean for this to sound as autocratic as the above description implies, there was a lot of room to excel, to hone your skills, and sufficient training to develop new skills. Any CE that had talent and was willing to put in the effort could move up the ladder, at least to the Sr. CE level, almost as fast as they wanted. The FE Division had a lot of recognition events, nights on the town for example. The Means Service Award was the highest FE award; it was a recognition of superior performance. It included a trip to the annual FE Awards Conference. The DP Division's equivalent was an Outstanding Achievement Award with a trip to the SE (System's Engineering) Symposium. The DP Division gave me and Outstanding Achievement Award for my work on the TIPS network. I attended the SE Symposium event that year, but the FE Division also invited my wife and me to attend the FE Awards Conference. As far as I know, I was the only person in the FE Division ever to receive a Systems Engineering Outstanding Achievement Award.

Suggestion Awards provided an opportunity for anyone to suggest product and process improvements. There were monetary awards as well as recognition for implemented suggestions. There were near-infinite educational opportunities and, to a large extent, employees could chart their career path. The ability to direct your path was naturally based on performance and company need, but during the Gold-Rush years, demand was high, and so choices were plentiful. For those who performed, there were generous pay raises and promotion opportunities. IBM's Field Engineering Division was a great place to work. If there was any burden, it fell on those who, for whatever reason, were more interested in coasting or wanted to "chart your own course." If you did either, it started raising flags almost immediately.

— ∎ —

All of this tracking and measurement applied to managers as well as CEs. As a result, managers were open and willing to work on problems. If not, they would be identified through the employee satisfaction surveys; these were taken very seriously. Along with the generous benefits and rewards, much of the satisfaction came from the challenging work, and the professional environment. It helped that there was broad industry recognition that IBM's Field Engineers were, unquestionably the best of the best. Overall, this system was both efficient and effective. It produced and rewarded high-quality performance, as well as a high degree of both employee and customer satisfaction.

— ∎ —

None of these measurement systems applied to the PO. We were in uncharted territory. There was no way to measure our work; we didn't use parts or have backlogs. Our "customer" was not a traditional customer in field engineering terms. We did not install or service any equipment. We used no parts, and we were not responsible for customer satisfaction. We were tasked specifically with managing a massive project and coordinating the necessary resources. We had a good Branch Manager, Jack Leach, and a very supportive Region Manager, Bill Perrin, who had trust in the team and gave us the room we needed to get the work done.

Jack and I were fortunate that we were allowed to raid the Region staff and hand pick our team. The result was a small elite group of over-achievers, willing and able to operate outside of the conventional management structure. There were no laggards; no one had any interest in coasting. We were all the type who loved a challenge, and our work was incredibly challenging. We lived "outside of the box" in every sense. That is a term I personally dislike because a box is 2-dimensional, and life is not 2-dimensional.

The PO Mission

We had three goals: get the network installed, keep it installed, and make service profitable.

Installing the Network

Our first challenge was to manage the process, coordinate resources, and get the network installed on time. As Project Manager, this was my primary responsibility.

The PO was not permitted to build a "tiger team" to go out and do the installation ourselves. That would have required building a large staff with significant travel and living expenses. More importantly, it would have interfered with traditional FE Branch responsibilities. My job was to manage the installation, to coordinate all the players and resources to get it installed on time with minimal disruption to local branch operations. The network spanned 11 states, 3 FE Regions, and dozens of branch offices. I had no actual authority over the branches or any of their resources, so I had to encourage rather than demand cooperation.

I or someone from my team visited every FE office before their actual installation. At each branch, we would present the PO's approach both for installation and ongoing network management. Initially, these presentations were primarily to management and the CEs that would be involved in the installation process. Over time, as word of our work began to spread, the presentations grew to where they often included the entire branch. It became quite a roadshow. My earlier Staff Training Program speakers training came in very handy.

Matrix management was a new concept in the mid-1970s, and it was an unheard of approach inside of IBM. That term was never applied to my work; I didn't even hear that name until years later, but in fact, that is what it was. I was learning as we moved forward. I had no safety net. There was no backup plan or alternative; failure was not an option.

The fact that we went out of our way to bring the local FE branch offices on board was a critical part of the management process. These visits gave the branches an opportunity to review our plans and processes, but to also ask any questions or voice any concerns they had. In effect, it was a "speak now or forever hold your peace," kind of thing. If they didn't push back at these meetings; they were not in a position to balk later. I don't think we could have succeeded without these face-to-face meetings. It was also extremely helpful that most of the branch management teams had already worked with me as the Regional SA representative. I don't know if Bill and Jack considered this when selecting me, but I will give them credit and assume this was a factor.

— ■ —

The Project Office was Branch 049. We were located in California, so we played on the 49er theme for several things. I remembered that my father had a hatpin in the shape of a miner kneeling and panning for gold. He sent it to me, and so I had an artist build a mold from that piece. I had several hundred of these pins made up as tie tacks since no one wore hats anymore. I also had Lucite paperweights made with the pin suspended in front of a map of the WBC States.

Once the local installation was complete, I or someone on my staff, revisited the branches. At these visits, we presented tie tacks to everyone who had participated. Managers and others who made significant contributions received paperweights. In all cases, I sent letters to each participant. These were for their personnel files. That was a real object lesson in employee motivation and matrix management. Word spread fast, and it never failed to amaze me just how much mileage you could get by recognizing and thanking people for what they had done. People will break their backs for you if they know you appreciate what they are doing, particularly if you do something that publically recognizes their contribution.

Most of the CEs and FE Managers we worked with were the "roadrunners," the guys who ran from location to location fixing small devices. As important as their work was, there was little glory compared to those who serviced the big accounts and mainframe computers. To have someone come in and publically praise them for their contribution was satisfying for them, and gratifying to me personally.

In the end, with our great team and with the help and cooperation of hundreds of CEs and FE Managers scattered across a vast area, we installed the network on time and under budget.

– ∎ –

I don't think anyone had ever thought through the facilities side of the PO. Day one, we had no physical space, no phone number, and not even a single desk to call our own. We were itinerants, working from borrowed space, initially in the IBM Aero Space Building. At another point, we briefly made our home in a conference room in the Region building on Wilshire Boulevard. There were no mobile phones in those days. We did have pagers, but even with those, tracking us down was sometimes a challenge.

Finding space, getting desks, equipment, and all the minutia of actually establishing a brand new office from scratch was also my responsibility.

Starting an all-new office inside of IBM was a rare occurrence. Usually, as a branch got too large, its territory and staff would be divided into two offices. That was not our situation. There was nothing to divide, so we were on our own. It took some time and a lot of scrounging, but I was able to establish a pretty nice office space and a truly exceptional staff.

We were constantly in meetings with the customer and sales team, or out of town visiting local FE Branch offices across the WBC network. We needed someone to be in the office on a daily basis, so one of my first battles was getting a secretary, yes, that is what they were called in those days, to cover the phones, arrange our travel, handle correspondence, and run the day-to-day business of the office.

I interviewed at least a dozen experienced administrative candidates. None would touch the PO. Part of it was that they had built their reputation in their "home" office and didn't want to derail their career path. I was completely unprepared for the responses I got whenever I would talk about our unique environment and opportunity. Most administrative people thrive on order. The open-ended, start from scratch, no rules PO environment was an absolute turn-off. I finally found one young lady, Sandy Eggum, who was a dispatcher, not an experienced secretary. When she responded: "that sounds exciting!" she got the job.

Despite her initial enthusiasm, when it came time to step out and make things happen, Sandy got cold feet. One of the first things I needed was for her to travel to Chicago for Administrative training. She had never been on an airplane or checked into a hotel on her own; she was terrified. She called me from the LA airport in tears, begging not to go; I insisted, as we had no alternative. She called again when she got to the hotel in Chicago, still terrified, but feeling a bit braver after having accomplished that much on her own. She came back after a week a changed person, full of confidence and ready to take on the many "office building" challenges we faced.

Getting telephones and a typewriter was easy. The biggest problem was obtaining an IBM Series/1 computer for our development work. At that time, no FE Branch had a computer, but it was worse because the Series/1 was from the Small Systems Division of IBM, and we were part of the big systems world. They repeatedly tried to force an IBM 3790 on us, but that machine was for data processing only; it lacked the analog interface required to connect with the Racal communications equipment. The process control functionality we would need was only available on a Series/1. That was a critical element of the network management solution we needed to develop. I don't remember what the turning point was, but we finally got the equipment.

We also needed Racal modems, which were competitive to the modems that IBM made. There was some pushback, but that one was easier to win because we needed to replicate the customer's environment and WBC had chosen Racal.

Keeping it Installed

The second challenge was to figure out a way to keep the network installed.

Today we have broadband, wireless, fiber and cable networks that are already installed at virtually every house, apartment, office, restaurant, hotel, and even in City Parks. Most commercial buildings have Ethernet, WiFi, Bluetooth, RF, and IR networks. If none of those are available, we can quickly turn our smartphone into a hotspot. There are networks everywhere; it is simply a matter of choosing one and plugging in. Often it is as simple as plugging in a box and flipping a switch.

All of this is a very recent development. Up until just a few years ago, getting a network drop installed and getting a device attached and functioning was a major undertaking, even for a highly skilled technician. Once it was working, keeping it working, while less difficult, was an ongoing challenge. In part, this was because the technology was not well developed, but also because assembling and operating a large network was a very complex undertaking involving many separate vendors.

IBM didn't charge a separate installation fee; they incorporated that cost in the overall product cost. Of course this drove the price up. Other vendors would charge an installation fee but waive it in order to get the business. As a result, on more than one occasion, once a complex network was installed and stable, the customer would begin phasing out the more expensive IBM equipment, replacing it with lower cost equivalents.

Part of the justification for the PO and the reason I had to use matrix management as opposed to a tiger-team, was to lower the cost of installation. My goal was to eliminate, to the greatest extent possible, the time-consuming redundant efforts required for installation.

Managing Profitability

Our third mission was one that nobody believed possible. We had to figure out how to make a profit on the equipment service.

IBM had a serious problem servicing networks profitably. In our case, this was exacerbated by the fact that DP had negotiated a 10% service discount as an incentive for the customer to lease and retain the IBM equipment. That made it easier to keep the equipment installed, but it had the potential to make profitability even more elusive. Bill Perrin, our Region Manager, and the individual Branches were not given any relief for this discounted service contract, and the size of the TIPS network had the potential to produce dreadful results on the various reports I mentioned earlier. As it turned out, that fear gave us leverage to invent a radical new way to service networks.

The problem was not equipment reliability or CE training; it was in part vendor identification, and in part an unintended consequence of the move to the MAPs (card swapping) service approach I mentioned earlier. It was the customer's responsibility to identify the responsible service provider. If a service request came to IBM and the problem was not the IBM equipment, the customer was supposed to pay the cost. In reality, that seldom happened.

Here again, a bit of background might be helpful for those unfamiliar with procedures and the state of technology in the mid-1970s.

— ■ —

There were hundreds of telephone lines originating at WBC's El Segundo data center. Let us follow just one. At the data center end of the phone line, there was a modem manufactured by Racal. On the data center side, the modem attached to a very complex set of equipment and software. The equipment and some of the software was from IBM. WBC developed other software, and other vendors provided still other software. Any of this could cause problems.

The job of the modem is to translate the digital computer signal into an analog signal compatible with the telephone circuit. Once transformed, the signal, which was a short message addressed to a particular device on that phone line, went out on the phone line crossing several states with drops at bank branches in a couple of dozen different locations.

In fact, with SNA, it was even more complicated as any given message was broken into several smaller "packets" sent over the phone line to the intended device. That device must reassemble the individual packets into a single message. Packets may arrive out of sequence, with errors, or not arrive at all. The SNA system needed to reassemble the original message correctly, and if one or more of the packets were missing or contained errors, the remote device communicated with the host (the computer in El Segundo) and ask for that packet be retransmitted. Once the entire message was received without error, it was ready for processing. Incidentally, this is the way the Internet works today, but we were building the TIPS network 15 years before the Internet became public.

Each "circuit" is made up of hundreds of logical paths within the telephone company's network. There is not one solid piece of copper wire that runs out from the El Segundo data center all the way to the bank location in Bozeman, Montana. The various "packets" can be routed over a dozen or more different paths to reach the desired endpoint. There it would be reassembled. This routing is done automatically by the phone company's computers. They chose paths on a packet by packet basis. Their choice would reflect traffic, errors, circuit availability or whatever was programmed into their systems. The choices were seldom the same and the path selection criteria could vary based on time of day or a number of other variables. Within each path, there were hundreds of switches and amplifiers, any of which could cause problems.

There was typically a local telephone company that took the signal from the AT&T network and carried it to the bank branch where there was another modem to turn the analog signal back into a digital data compatible with the IBM equipment. That process was repeated at each of a dozen or so bank locations hooked to a single telephone line. There was more IBM equipment attached to the modem in each of the bank branches.

Many of the telephone switches and data lines in that period were as much as 40 years old. That was typically the case in the rural locations where small "mom & pop" phone companies were locally owned and operated. This equipment was never designed to meet high-speed data communications requirements.

With all the components and vendors involved, there were hundreds of potential failure points. Of course, that was repeated for each one of the hundred or so lines leaving El Segundo.

— ■ —

One funny incident will illustrate just how unreliable the phone network could be. During the installation and testing phase, there was a problem with a phone line that ran through Roswell, New Mexico. The WBC Network Control Center (NCC) in El Segundo reported it to the local phone company in Roswell, and after repeated "resolutions," they were still having difficulties. The NCC called in the AT&T representative who had overall responsibility

279

for all of the various phone companies involved. After explaining the problem and their many attempts to get it resolved, a tech in the NCC plugged the failing line into a speaker. Everyone could hear John Denver singing his current hit. Needless to say, John was not supposed to be sharing the data line. The AT&T rep got the problem resolved. Solution unknown as the problem "went away during testing," which was the standard answer to almost every communications problem.

– ∎ –

Failures didn't have to originate from a piece of equipment. A power surge or line noise anywhere in this circuit could also cause problems. If there were a lightning strike on, or near, a phone line in the Owyhee Mountains of Nevada, line noise could propagate across the entire line, often producing red lights on multiple IBM machines connected to that line but located in banks hundreds of miles away, a bank in Bozeman Montana for example. In reality, errors would probably show up on several machines in several states. Because the red lights appeared on the IBM machines, there was a high probability that one or more service calls would go to IBM. Furthermore, since each FE branch operated more or less autonomously, none would be aware that there were similar simultaneous calls at other locations. Even if they were aware of multiple calls and suspected a line problem, they didn't have the latitude to alter their response. The customer had called for service; the CE had no choice, they had to visit the bank to investigate.

Since the lightning strike was a momentary event generating a line noise spike, the machines would be functioning correctly when the CEs arrived at the bank branches. There was no way to replicate the error. That left the CE with only the error log. This is where the unintended consequences of the card-swapping approach came into play. Following standard troubleshooting procedures, remember the MAPS I talked about earlier, the CE would replace the "most probable" card in the IBM 3600 controller. After a week or so, with no further errors, the CE could only conclude that he had, in fact, replaced the defective card and the problem would be closed. The card would be marked as "defective" and returned to the factory for repair.

In our example, this false call scenario was repeated at multiple locations serviced by this single circuit. When these "defective" cards ultimately reached the factory for repair, they would naturally pass all tests without errors. If a card did fail a test, the failing component would be replaced and retested. The rebuilt card could then be put back into the parts inventory system. However, and here is where this example gets expensive, the factory technicians knew that it was impossible to replicate and test all possible conditions, and they could not risk populating the parts system with intermittent problems. Therefore, these non-failing "defective" card, would be smashed. Making things even worse, if enough of the same cards were being returned as defective, but not failing the testing process, the engineering team would be forced to assume that their testing was insufficient and so they would expend even more resources trying to enhance the testing process, and improve the card.

All of this was a complete and costly waste of time and money; it occurred because the wrong vendor was initially identified, but that could not be known or proven. Unfortunately, this situation was not unique to the TIPS network; it was happening daily in networks all over the world. Furthermore, there was no obvious way to prevent it.

Centralized Network Management

In most networks up to that point, each end-point operated autonomously. Problems were identified by the customer staff at the end point, and service calls were placed from that location directly to the local IBM FE branch. The PO turned this upside down by centralizing network management.

We centralized problem management in a Network Control Center (NCC) at the El Segundo data center. Whenever there was a failure, the bank branch had to call to the NCC. We knew that in a network of this size, there was a high probability of hundreds of active problems at any given time. If problem management were left to individuals in the remote locations, problems would fall through the cracks. Network availability and ultimately customer satisfaction would suffer. We also realized that even with centralized management, without a computerized approach, no amount of paper and organization, we always called this the "green eyeshades and pencils" method, could prevent some mishandled problems. We concluded that we needed a computerized problem management system and since no such program was available at that time, we had to develop our own.

— ■ —

One of the things that made our network management revolution possible was the fact that WBC had selected an advanced modem from Racal that included a secondary diagnostic channel. That was a second low frequency, narrow bandwidth modem that talked directly to the remote modem and not to the

IBM equipment. This secondary channel was used for diagnostics and error reporting on a modem-to-modem basis. Racal also provided a management console for the Network Control Center in El Segundo.

For our tracking system, we used an IBM Series/1. That was ultimately interfaced with the Racal console. When completed, this allowed our system to automatically generate a problem record any time a modem failed anywhere in the network. Of course, the Racal modems would typically generate an error as a result of the lightning strike example I used above. We were therefore able to identify these types of problems quickly, and recognize that they were line, not modem related. When a bank called to report a problem on the IBM machine from a location associated with a known line or modem problem, the NCC could easily recognize that this was not an IBM hardware issue. That prevented most wrong vendor calls.

With our system and management process, for the first time, it was possible to avoid most wrong-vendor calls. Once the proper vendor was identified, that vendor would be contacted by the NCC and problem would be managed to completion using our system.

— ∎ —

Aside from dramatically reducing wrong-vendor calls, one unanticipated advantage of our approach was that the CEs had a knowledgeable professional to deal with any time they had questions, needed assistance, or needed to hand off a call to another vendor. In other networks, CEs frequently found themselves trying to deal with clueless end users. Many times the person who placed the call was a clerk or secretary with no information beyond "it has a red light." When questions arose or if it became necessary to hand the problem off to a different vendor, the CE could waste valuable time, often creating customer frustrations, when trying to find the right person and communicate the situation. The NCC made life easier. Most CEs quickly saw the advantages and the results of our computerized NCC. Cooperation was seldom a problem.

— ∎ —

Our solution opened a window of visibility to the entire network operation. Combining modem error records, end user calls, and host equipment problems, onto a single problem management system, allowed easy identification and isolation of multiple simultaneous failures. That prevented most of the very expensive "wrong-vendor" call scenarios I described above.

One of my jobs as Project Manager was to assemble and analyze quarterly reports for all equipment in the network. In that process, I would compare our network's performance with all installed similar equipment. The results were dramatic. We had fewer service calls, shorter outages, and service was profitable, even incorporating the discount.

— ■ —

We included "change-management" software in our management system. Change is a constant occurrence in a large network. Branches open, close, or move, new equipment is added, a branch is remodeled, whatever you can imagine. Changes, in particular testing, adding new systems or removing systems, frequently generate errors and outages, instability, and other service issues. By including centralized change management, we eliminated unnecessary service calls.

— ■ —

I don't know if Jack was the sole source of the vision for a centralized and automated network control center, or if he had outside assistance. Of course, it evolved and expanded as we concentrated on the issues, but I know that Jack had at least the core idea when he initially interviewed me and that was before the PO was announced. I also know that it was this vision that allowed us to fulfill missions #2 & #3 successfully. Furthermore, that vision had a much longer term impact on the PO and each of the members of the team.

Disruptive Technologies

A "disruptive technology" fundamentally alters the way something, often a business process, is done. It is "disruptive" because it obsoletes the way it was done before the introduction of that technology. Disruptive technologies often appear obvious once they arrive. Automobiles, jet aircraft, the S/360 and its architecture, the PC, the Internet, etc. They become so integrated into the new normal that we seldom think about how things were before they arrived. That certainly describes the impact TIPS had on the banking industry and our lives.

Today, centralized problem management seems obvious, but remember, this was before PCs or microprocessors, before large networks and the Internet. Up to that point, almost all computing took place inside massive data centers. For the TIPS project, we turned the process on its head. We developed the first standalone, purpose-built system, specifically to manage network service. Service desks and help desks are standard today; they all evolved from our revolutionary approach developed in 1976.

– ■ –

It is worthwhile stepping back for a moment to look at the progression of my career. I offer this because it would be easy to miss the pattern that has now become fully developed. In the Air Force, I joined RBS just two years after that organization had been formed. At that point, there were still many processes that were being "tuned." RBS was a disruptive technology within the Air Force. It revolutionized the entire concept of how SAC bomber crews, the folks that were caring for the nuclear weapons that were protecting our nation and preventing World War III, were trained.

These technologies, although I was no longer directly involved at that point, were instrumental in executing the air war over Viet Nam. The Viet Nam War became a major turning point in the prosecution of air warfare. Aerial bombardment moved from saturation bombing as seen in WWII, to increasingly precise targeting. RBS was the precursor to precision guided weapons. It was the "proof of concept" showing the need and value of precision weapons. They became an increasingly major component in all subsequent wars. This shift led to the development of precision guided bombs that were yet another, albeit much later disruptive technology.

I joined IBM in the early days of the Gold Rush period. A new disruptive technology; the concept of a layered Operating System reshaped the world of computing, and built the foundation for what would become known as the Information Technology (IT) industry that underpins industry, commerce, government, and warfare the world over. That technology remains the dominant solution 50+ years later.

I moved even closer to the starting point with the introduction of the second generation of that technology when I became deeply involved in the testing and launch of the System/370, and still closer to the next wave of the computing evolution, the DAT systems that gave birth to "virtual computing" that are ubiquitous today.

In 1976, at the age of 32, I was Project Manager for the TIPS network. I had moved to just one level below the top of the food chain when I was responsible for installing the world's largest SNA network. Both TIPS and SNA were disruptive technologies, this time in the fields of banking data communications. These technologies changed banking globally and ushered in the era of massive networks.

As you can see, with each technology, I was not only involved, I was moving up the food chain so to speak. I was becoming involved earlier, but also at more influential levels. With the centralized problem management system that we invented for the TIPS network, Jack and I were at the top of the chain. We were launching our own disruptive technology, one that would forever revolutionize the management of large networks and consumer devices of all types. Next you will read about Goshawk, which was our follow-on to the first generation system. With Goshawk, we forced IBM to rethink problem and change management.

As you read subsequent chapters, you will learn of my involvement in several other major disruptors, some successful, others not so much. I was there for the birth of the PC, Office Automation, digital telephone switches, the mobile Internet, and Internet marketing. You will learn just how difficult it can be to shepherd a disruptive technology from birth to acceptance. How, in every case, it will, at some point, become a battle to overcome inertia and the entrenched forces that will always resist disruptive change. The old ways never go quietly into the night; they will always fight tooth and nail to retain their dominance. Identifying, sometimes building the disruptors, and the battles that ensued, even when I did not succeed, were my American Dream.

Personal

I don't know if Jack initially considered other people for the Project Manager position. I jumped at the chance and never bothered to ask. In fact, I had never even considered the question until I was writing this history of the PO. If he did, I could only imagine how many traditional FE Managers might have run screaming for the door, much like the admin people I interviewed. Why would a regular FE Manager give up his territory and career path to take a lateral position while undertaking the risk to be involved in what had a high potential of being a disaster in the making? I never considered the possibility of failure.

— ■ —

There was little opportunity to provide any training to other team members. There were no project management classes available, and there was no need for equipment training. I did attend a Systems Engineering class on the 3600 so that I could better understand both the technology and the marketing side as well as the customer's expectations. I also attended a 4-day bank teller training class at WBC's CA bank. Introducing teller-automation was a radical change in a centuries old process. I needed to understand the current process and the characteristics of the end users. The training also provided a better understanding of overall bank branch organization and operations and the challenges our new system would introduce. This training made it easier to communicate with, and relate to, bank branch management. That training influenced the design of our management system. It also came in handy years later when I started Servare.

– ∎ –

I attended IBM New Manager school. That was a two-week course held at a remote hotel in the tiny town of Salisbury, Connecticut. It was right next to the New York and Massachusetts borders. There were new managers from several divisions, so it covered broad-based concepts that were not specific to the Field Engineering Division. IBM was a great training company. They invested a lot in training and had excellent courses.

It was late fall, and the leaves were already off of the trees. It was chilly, and the town was small, so there was nothing much to do other than gather together and talk amongst ourselves. I think that was part of the plan. The isolation forced individuals from different divisions to interact and learn more about other areas of the company. I remember one exercise; they asked the participants to explain what the "IBM Means Service" motto meant to them. Being in the service division, I had always taken it quite literally; it was my daily job. I was surprised to learn that individuals from each division had a very personal sense of what the motto meant and how it applied directly to them and their division, even their department. That was a powerful lesson on the importance of corporate culture.

I also remember that the chef at the hotel was a young guy who had recently graduated from the Culinary Institute of America. The CIA, located in Hyde Park, New York just north of Poughkeepsie, is one of the best, culinary training school in America. I had passed it many times during my assignments in the Mid-Hudson Valley. At that facility, they had a program where the students would prepare a special meal for a restaurant that they operated in the school. The restaurant was only open for a few meals each week, and reservations were tough to get, but when you did, the food was always great. The young guy at the hotel was an incredible chef. It was a surprise to find him out in a tiny hotel in a tiny town like that.

Goshawk

When we discovered that we would not be able to give our network management software to WBC, we were forced to sell it to them. Selling the software was a bit of a challenge in itself. The FE Division had no mechanism to sell software of any type. In our case, the software was neither a product nor software developed under contract, as FE did not do contract software development. Ultimately, we used a slight of hand and the DP branch sold the software to WBC as an SE Services contract, and then DP reimbursed the PO for the revenue collected.

If I remember correctly, we sold the system for $5,000, which was sufficient to make it legitimate, but not a real reflection of the cost of development or the value of the software. That solved the problem of allowing the customer to pay for and use the software. Unfortunately, this created an entirely new set of challenges. Part of the timing of the sale had to do with the completion of the TIPS installation process. With the network installed, there was no justification for continuing the Project Office. However, the software was not complete or fully tested when we had to sell it. We had not yet developed the module that would allow it to interface directly with the Racal controller and automatically open a problem from that system. We had not even developed the necessary database cleanup utilities, and there was no documentation. In short, it wasn't ready for sale. Unfortunately, as it no longer belonged to us and we were not Systems Engineers, there was no mechanism that would allow us to continue to work on the software, or even to maintain it. We could not even contract to perform any software updates or services. We did a few things in "the dark of night" to keep it running, but these had to be pretty minimal. The DP branch was not prepared to do any custom work on the system as they had no SEs trained on the Series/1, and no desire to divert resources from their primary work.

287

GOSHAWK

Western Region Project Office
FE 049

IBM

That ultimately led to us launching the Goshawk Project as a follow-on to the TIPS project. The original intention of Goshawk was simply to create a platform to continue and expand the work needed to operate the NCC. Over time, our goal morphed into an actual development environment leading ultimately to the announcement and release of an official IBM product called the Series/1 Systems Management Facility (SSMF). This transition amounted to the full birth of our disruptive technology. It set off a political firestorm throughout our division as well as the manufacturing division responsible for networked products.

— ■ —

As an aside, I am the one who named the project "Goshawk." The idea came from the book Shogun by James Cavell. A goshawk is a bird-of-prey that can be trained to hunt with a handler. The relevant characteristics of the goshawk are that it will take on prey bigger than itself. Most birds of prey fly into an orbit where they wait until a target to attack becomes available. A goshawk will fly directly from the handler's arm to the prey, even following it down a hole if necessary.

Our Goshawk system used a very direct and proactive approach to network management. We were taking on entrenched people and processes within the FE Division as well as several official development organizations inside of IBM. We were unquestionably attacking prey much bigger than ourselves.

The name Goshawk was more than a slight poke at the then-current mainstream approach to network problem management, which carried the code name "Orbit." Orbit was just an extension of the passive/reactive approach that had been used unsuccessfully for years. We never spent time denigrating Orbit, but we frequently talked about Goshawk's proactive direct approach. We could also document the fact that our approach produced superior results. The name was both appropriate and well recognized. It undoubtedly pissed off more than a few as well. I had people as much as 15 years later respond to that name and claim some recognition or affiliation.

— ■ —

Incidentally, Shogun became "required" reading for our staff. If you haven't read that book, put it on your 'must read' list. Read it twice. The first time for the sheer joy as it is an excellent read. The second time as the absolute best book on applied management practices you will ever read. It became standard practice to use Shogun references when referring to the political process surrounding Goshawk. Rick Diederich joined the PO a bit later. He told me years later that if he hadn't read Shogun, he would have missed ½ of the nuance of what was being discussed daily in the PO.

Mission Impossible

Development of an actual product by an FE Division team located in the field, a product in direct competition with tools under development within existing "official" IBM channels, was nothing short of a political impossibility, but we did it. The whole process was unheard of and contrary to everything IBM and the FED had ever done. Fortunately, we had gained credibility, and powerful friends, by solving the TIPS service management issues. The quarterly network service performance data carried a lot of weight as it dramatically illustrated how our approach was benefitting the customer as well as IBM. At the same time, these reports demonstrated the failure of the "business as usual" approach. It was impossible to refute the data; without that, Goshawk would have undoubtedly died in the nest.

I was deeply involved in the political morass surrounding Goshawk. In fact, I was more involved in the political process than the actual development process; most of that was managed by Jack. My team did have testing and documentation responsibility, but my primary function was to again act as the project manager. In a somewhat strange reversal of roles, I was managing Jack's project. In a sense, I was managing my manager. My team developed schedules and comprehensive Gant charts to track progress. We held reviews and managed the documentation and testing process. When necessary, it was my job to beat up on Jack and his developers when they didn't perform.

Our initial and primary goal was to develop a stable platform for the TIPS NCC. We knew from the beginning that we wanted to get Goshawk out as a field tool. We didn't know what format or even how we would ultimately accomplish that feat, but we knew that system documentation was critical to our success. I hired two outside consultants, Joan Hughes and Barbara LaPerle, to document the system. Joan was the lead and Barbara was part of her team. They were both very professional and had done tech writing for several software vendors. Joan, in particular, had a knack for seeing where there were inconsistencies in what we were developing. If you have ever worked with software developers, you know that hidden inconsistencies are part of their specialty. Her feedback helped improve the final product.

Mostly my job was to act as the project manager, to track and report progress to all interested parties. The second piece, the reporting function, was where the real politics came into play. We were challenging the status quo. That was not the way things were supposed to work, and we had some very deadly enemies, some in very high places. Many were determined to shut us down.

Each month I would fly to NY to report progress to all of our various overseers, observers, interested parties, and hostile detractors. Sending me shielded both Jack and Bill from being put on the spot and forced to answer or agree to things they didn't want to have to agree too.

As I said earlier, Bill was not one for confrontations. As FE Western Region Manager, he was legitimately (at least officially) removed from the whole process. There was no way he was going to get in the middle of any of the seemingly endless mud fights. On the other hand, Jack's personality was what you might call "(considerably) more reactive." Had he been in the meetings, he would have probably responded to the requests and pressure in a more incendiary way. I gave them an excuse for not attending. For Bill, it was "not my job, talk to the Project Office." For Jack it was "not my job, talk to the Project Manager."

As Project Manager, I could dodge the bullet when they were calling names and demanding commitments. I could legitimately respond to any request that it was "not something I could commit to." Of course, I was always willing to "carry any request back to Jack." The responses this provoked were seldom pleasant, but they had no choice. I could measure it, track it and report it, but I wasn't the developer. If Jack were there, he would have had no choice but to answer and commit.

Despite objections from senior executives in NY, my position as the Project Manager gave me legitimate status and authority to attend the HQ meetings and do the presentations, but it also meant that I was on the receiving end of all of the incoming fire and flak. On more than one occasion, I had to maintain my composure and stand my ground while Senior VPs were yelling at me. These guys were not accustomed to being challenged or rebutted by anybody, let alone a lowly 1st line manager. Thank God, I had the unconditional support of both Jack and Bill. When I was in the midst of a ton of incoming flak, I could always take solace in the fact that I would soon be on a long flight with no telephones and ready access to a few scotches. I would have time to decompress, unwind, put it all in perspective, and inevitably see the humor in the process. Goshawk was an incredible education; it toughened me up. The experience proved invaluable in my later career.

I don't want to imply that it was all doom and gloom. The entire process was exhilarating. We were gorillas challenging the old guard, changing the world, and we were winning. Goshawk did have friends, some in high places; some were pretending to be foes whenever they were in public. The key supporters that I remember were Bob Campenni and Tom Furry, my apologies to all those whom I have forgotten. We had spies in the "enemy camps," supporters who were surreptitiously feeding us the inside story and strategies of those opposed to the project.

After each trip, I would hold a debriefing with Bill and Jack. Most times we would have a conference call with one or more of our supporters to get their perspectives and to develop our strategy for the next meeting. These debriefings were far less stressful than their NY predecessors. In fact, we were all enjoying our adventure, and there was frequently a lot of humor about the process in general as well as the discomfort we were inflicting on the "old guard."

With Bill and Jack, I was treated as close to an equal as was possible. I was never excluded. I could ask any questions, make suggestions, offer strategies, and raise any objections that I wanted. While the others were all older and more senior, this was new territory for all of us. I was the one on the front line, often used as a stalking horse. I was the one receiving the incoming fire, and they treated me as an equal. I got a lot of coaching and an incredible education in the process.

As with any war, all the planning goes out the window when the bullets start flying. I was the one in the room, and it was up to me to duck, dodge, and parry to win the battles. While I fielded a lot of the incoming flak, in my mind, the real kudos go to Jack and Bill who trusted me to be the front man while they worked to develop the software and obtain the funding we needed.

— ■ —

One bright spot in these monthly meetings was that I could time my flights so that I had a chance to see a Broadway show on each trip. I would land at JFK, rent a car, drive to the same-day ticket booth in the city, and grab whatever looked interesting. I was seldom disappointed. After the show I would drive up to Armonk for the next day's meetings, a bit of pleasure certainly lessened the pain.

I was addicted to Broadway plays after a couple of visits to Chicago. The first play I saw was Hair. I will never forget sitting in the theater. The lights went down, and the music started. As the curtains began to open, I became aware that people were coming from the back of the theater, behind the audience. They were walking toward the stage row to row on the arms of the chairs. They were stark naked! Quite a shock to my naïve younger self. I also saw Jesus Christ Superstar at a theater in Chicago. The music was incredible.

The Museum and Smithsonian Projects

There are always "things" that don't fit anywhere in a traditional business structure. The PO became a convenient catchall for these one-off mini projects. As a result, a couple of fun off-topic projects fell in my lap.

IBM was completing a new building at 590 Madison Avenue in downtown NY. The plan included an extensive display of equipment along with the history of computing, and a museum of computing to be located on the ground floor. In parallel, IBM had agreed to provide equipment and some interactive "educational" software for display at the Smithsonian in Washington DC.

Charles Eames had been commissioned to plan the NY installation, and I was assigned to work with him to coordinate equipment requisitions, shipping, and any other requirements that he might have. In essence, I was on his staff. Internally I was working with IBM's Public Relations Department. It was logical not only because this work fell outside of any traditional organization, but also because his offices were in Santa Monica, a short drive from our office.

– ∎ –

For those of you who don't recognize the name, you should take some time to look him up on the Internet. Charles (1907-1978) and his wife Ray Eames were famous designers who made significant contributions to the development of modern architecture and furniture. They were contemporaries of Frank Lloyd Wright. They were "disruptors" in their own field, and they had to deal with some of the same rejections of their "revolutionary" approaches to design.

If you have ever sat in one of those single-piece plastic chairs found in virtually every cafeteria, and who hasn't, you have the Eames to thank. They also produced, I think on commission from IBM, but that was before I was involved, "A Computer Perspective," a comprehensive review of computing from the 1920s through the mid-1970s. As part of this effort, they had developed a multipage foldout that covered the history of computing from ancient times.

I met with Charles several times and visited his office/warehouse in Santa Monica. I remember him as being quite old at the time and in failing health. I must laugh because he seemed "old" to me, I was 33, and he was 71. I am that same age as I write this book. Despite his age and ailments, he was full of life, energy and ideas. He was an inspiration to meet and working with him was a pleasure. Unfortunately, he passed away later that same year.

His warehouse in Santa Monica was crammed with memorabilia. There were even some things hanging from the ceiling. One that I remember was an old canoe. It was handmade with Indian markings on an animal hide covering. I believe it was an authentic original artifact. There were thousands of similar, one-of-a-kind items that he and Ray had accumulated throughout their busy lives and extensive travels. I would have loved to explore that cave for days, unfortunately, other than one short tour; our time was spent working on the IBM NY project. I often wonder what happened to all of those treasures after he and later Ray passed.

There was a funny event that illustrates both Charles' sense of humor and his down to earth nature. The warehouse floor was concrete of course. His staff and Ray, I never had the chance to meet her, insisted that he use a wheelchair to navigate the vast space. He could walk, but with obvious discomfort. He had just received a new electric wheelchair. That was long before these motorized wonders became popular. In fact, I had never seen or heard of such a thing. We went into the warehouse where he was showing me around; I walked while he rode in his new chair. He liked his new toy but feigned frustration at being "bossed around" by the "girls." He was telling me about the chair, and being an engineer, I was quite interested in how it worked, in particular, the joystick. After a few minutes, he got off the chair and told me to "take it for a spin." I tried to decline, but he insisted. So I took a lap around Charles Eames' warehouse in his new electric wheelchair. As I was driving, Charles was shouting out what I was seeing. I still smile at the image. What a unique experience.

I met Charles in NY on one of my regular trips. We walked through the new building to make sure his design would work the way he wanted. I was not responsible for much other than being his conduit, interface, coordinator, and occasional breaker of log jams. It was not much of a "project," from my side, but it was a lot of fun. I left the PO before the NY building was complete, and he passed away at about the same time, so I never did get to see the finished product. He did give me copies of A Computer Perspective, and of his History of Computing foldout. Regrettably, I did not ask him to autograph them. I do still have the two documents.

The Smithsonian project was also a relatively small undertaking that ran in parallel with the NY Museum. That was several years before the personal computer, but IBM built a line of small 5100 workstations that could be set up to work much like the PC that was still a few years in the future. The 5100 was far more expensive, about $20,000 if I remember correctly. It was industrial-strength of course, but still basically a personal computer.

We had a young intern Chris Cole working in the PO whenever he was home from Harvard for winter and summer breaks. He was a very bright young man and a skilled programmer. I ordered a 5100, and Chris designed three or four computer games that could be played by most anyone from middle school up. They were designed to both teach a few computing basics and to introduce the novice user to the world of computing. Of course, they were nothing like even the simplest games available today, but they were quite novel at that time.

I ultimately installed Several 5100s in the Smithsonian. I managed Chris' work and went to the Smithsonian to set up the systems and get the display ready for the public. I vaguely recall that Charles Eames was involved as well, probably to design the display, but I don't remember any details.

Lessons Learned

The Project Office was truly a seminal event in my life. There were others of course, but my experiences in the Project Office profoundly altered my personal life as well as my career. There were two phases of the PO, the initial TIPS Project, and the Goshawk Project. They tend to run together and can easily be mistaken for a single project. However, they were completely separate and distinct. The initial TIPS project was relatively short lived, just 1½ years, with clearly defined parameters. The bulk of our work centered around traditional FE work. It was the scale of the project that made it unique.

By itself, the TIPS project would have just enhanced our individual resumes, and there is a good chance that the PO staff would have been absorbed back into routine FE operations. Goshawk was an unplanned extension of the PO life, and as it turned out, Goshawk changed everything. It was not only the technology; it changed the career paths of the entire PO staff. The Goshawk experience opened our eyes; it made it impossible for most of us to go back to the world we had known before.

After WWI, there was a famous song named *"How Ya Gonna Keep 'Em down on the Farm?"* In the lyrics, the sentence was expanded to say *"After they've seen Paree."* An excellent question. Once your eyes are open, it is impossible to go back to the old ways. Goshawk was an eye opener.

Any list of lessons learned would be incomplete. It is simply impossible to detail all that I learned or all the ways that it impacted my life and my career path. That said, here is my partial list.

Entrepreneurial Management

I learned that I enjoyed management; more specifically I liked unstructured "entrepreneurial" management. That was something that was fundamentally incompatible with the FE Division. I doubt it existed anywhere in IBM, then or now. The truth is, entrepreneurship rarely exists in any large organization. There can be short duration sparks such as the WebNum project I did at Verisign many years later, but the natural instinct of a bureaucracy is to kill entrepreneurship, which is the antithesis of bureaucracy.

Thinking about Leaving

I had enjoyed my career with IBM, the company was excellent to work for, the pay and benefits were good, and my career was moving very rapidly. I could see that great opportunities lay ahead. Before the PO, I had never considered leaving. Working in the PO opened my eyes to a much larger world.

I came to realize that I would eventually have to leave IBM. There simply was no place within that organization where I could manage. Furthermore, I saw very little challenge, aside from maintaining my sanity, in operating within the confines of the FE Division.

I reached this conclusion fairly early in the Goshawk phase. While I was, at some level, aware that the path I was on would lead away from IBM, one event, in particular, brought it home.

As we were embarking on the Goshawk phase, I developed, with help from Norm Nadeau, a revolutionary approach to managing IBM's networked equipment. My proposal was to extend the secondary modem channel into the IBM devices that were connected to the modem and to equip those devices with the circuitry and firmware needed to not only capture error logs but to perform diagnostics and some level of remote troubleshooting.

That was a quantum extension of the process and benefits we had already learned in the TIPS Project. In effect, this would move the NCC (Network

Control Center) from identifying and dispatching the correct vendor, to allow at least partial problem determination for the IBM devices attached to a network. That could all be accomplished through this secondary channel of the modem. It would allow for the execution, potentially even automation, of the MAPs (Maintenance Analysis Procedures) remotely. It could dramatically reduce maintenance costs and move, at least partially, the cost and responsibility of problem determination to the customer. The financial implications were staggering. That could substantially reduce problem diagnosis time and cost. It would ensure that the CE would know which card needed to be replaced when they were dispatched. They could come with all necessary parts.

While remote access and troubleshooting are commonplace today, they were unheard of 40 years ago. Unfortunately, this approach was contrary to IBM's philosophy, and it did not fit within IBM's modem architecture as they did not incorporate a secondary channel. To adopt this proposal, the company would have to license the technology from Racal (or others) and extend their secondary channel beyond the modem. That was not something that IBM did at that time.

My approach also meant that equipment service for these devices would, to a great extent, be removed from the FE Division. At that point, serviceability was under the control of the development function within the manufacturing division. FE had only serviceability review and sign off responsibility, but that was a toothless function. First it was staffed and managed by people who had no idea how to improve the overall process, and second, the development divisions had responsibility for overall product profitability, which included service. The developers drove the serviceability side, and they were focused at the individual box level, and not the network level. They could not see the forest for the trees.

If my approach had been implemented, it would have revolutionized the networking world in ways that we can only imagine. It would have solved the network management problem as well as the service profitability problem. It would have also made Goshawk IBM's primary approach to network management.

The approach would have been a major disruptive technology that would have leapfrogged IBM's competitors. It would have improved reliability, and availability, as well as reducing service costs. In retrospect, I believe it had the potential to lower the price of these networked devices dramatically.

297

Therefore, it could have potentially increased IBM's market share.

To Jack and Bill's credit, they agreed and supported my vision to the point of arranging for me to present my proposal to Dick Liebhaber, a Senior VP in the FE Division. They very well may have had to get approval from Bills boss; I do not know, but I suspect they did. Looking back, they took a considerable political risk in letting me make my pitch to an executive of that level. That was before I had my extensive experience of shepherding Goshawk through all the political fires that we ultimately went through. I was still pretty green; if I screwed up, it would have reflected poorly on both of them.

Liebhaber sat through my presentation in our conference room, and he asked some good questions. He apparently understood the proposal and probably far more about the consequences and political ramifications than I did at that time. At the end of the day, I was exhausted. The sweat had probably reached my waistband.

Dick was very complimentary and appreciative, and then he gave me a life-altering lesson that I will never forget. "Tim I understand what you are proposing, and I think it is a great concept. I appreciate the thought you have put into this, but you need to know that IBM is like a big elephant. We tromp through the jungle and our trunk swings back and forth grabbing the best opportunities, but we can't catch them all. There are whole pieces of the forest that we miss, some right under our face. They are either too small or not the right fit, but we simply can't take all the opportunities that come our way. Others are just out of our reach, and it is too difficult to move the elephant to take advantage of those." His short answer was, "no."

In retrospect, I realize that Liebhaber wasn't ready or willing to take on the totality of the "IBM system," and that would have been required. There was a standard method of developing serviceability into all new devices, including networked equipment. To adopt my proposal, Dick would have personally had to take on the status quo and do battle, not only inside the FE Division but within the product divisions. I have no idea what all was on his plate, so I won't try to judge his motivations, but it is evident that, for whatever reason, he chose not to undertake this challenge. IMHO (In My Humble Opinion), that was a strategic mistake.

– ∎ –

I went home that night and had an oversized glass of scotch and a long stare at the fireplace. I came to the realization that the flip side of what Dick had said was that there were a lot of opportunities out there. As long as they didn't threaten the elephant, IBM would look favorably on those who provided solutions.

I also understood that meant that I would have to leave IBM to pursue other opportunities. I recognized that the time was not now, I was learning too much and having too much fun. There were other skills that I could learn at IBM, but it was clear to me that the time to leave would come sooner rather than later.

Watch out for Trucks

One of Jack's oft-repeated axioms was that you always had to *"watch out for the trucks coming over the hill that are going to run over your ass."* Or more simply *"watch out for trucks."* I was already aware of the issue of unintended consequences, but more in a reactive than proactive way. Jack's message brought about a subtle but fundamental change in my thinking. Proactive "truck watching" was important in planning the network installation, managing people, and management in general. It was a critical survival skill in the political environment we found ourselves in with Goshawk.

It has also proven to have general applicability in life. Jack drilled the "trucks" message into my core beliefs to the point where it became instinctive to try to anticipate and manage the unintended consequences of my actions and decisions.

I can't tell you how often I used the same expression and incorporated it into my decision-making process. Jack probably has no idea how impactful his wisdom was. I have tried to teach others, including my children, but either I am not as good a teacher or the students are not as willing to learn. Of course, they may have learned but not been aware until some later date.

Matrix Management

The concept of matrix management was very new; I didn't even hear the term until years later. I certainly didn't read any books on the subject until much later, but it was the structure we used to install the TIPS network. I had to learn on the fly. Communications, credibility and more communications were the keys to success. This experience proved useful in many situations, ITT in particular, where I was working across borders and companies to try to implement programs.

Exposure

Exposure is good, but always remember that you can die from exposure. I was a first line manager, but I was working at levels and with people many levels above those that anyone in my position would have usually interfaced. The opportunity to move in these circles was unheard of, and it has proven unbelievably beneficial to my career.

As Project Manager, I was inside of the politics, conflicts, and the critical decisions made. That exposure was not limited to our office or even the Regional office. I was allowed to interface at the highest levels in the FE, DP, and product divisions. Through this process, I became comfortable walking into any senior executive's office, making my case and defending it if necessary. That was not a one-off opportunity, but something I did on a weekly and monthly basis.

Over the years, I have met with very high-level people including Fortune 100 CEOs, Al Gore, royalty and senior politicians in several countries. I cannot adequately express my gratitude to, and respect for both Jack and Bill for their confidence and the trust they showed by allowing me to represent them at these levels. I cannot imagine anyone even two or three levels higher up the food-chain ever having a similar opportunity.

Entrepreneurship

The PO was an in-house entrepreneurial organization. I was an entrepreneur before I ever heard the word. There was so much about the PO that was new and untried. We were operating without any guidebook or safety net. We were solving pressing problems by developing new approaches, inventing procedures, structure, and technology on the fly. These are all things that were unheard of in IBM.

Politics

I learned to deal with, and even enjoy the process of managing politics at a level that I had never seen, or ever imagined. I have since come to understand how politics play such a central role in every organization. Being able to recognize and navigate the political world proved to be both useful and profitable in my later consulting work.

Project Management

Project management was critical to the success of the TIPS installation, but also to the development of the original network management software and later the Goshawk system. There were no software packages at that time, so I had Chris Cole write a program so that we could automate the creation of Gant charts. Chris had studied project management at Harvard and had some fascinating ideas on how to incorporate risk assessment into the management process. His work was vital to our success. Disciplined project management was also a skill that I have used extensively in my post-PO professional and personal life.

I was spoiled

I didn't know this for several years, but looking back I realize that the PO experience spoiled me. I could never work long-term for another company. I just couldn't tolerate the incompetence that I witnessed in every organization that I worked for after the PO. I could do it for a while, but I found it frustrating beyond my tolerance threshold after a short time.

Project Office Success or Failure?

In a word, both. As far as completing its original charter, there can be no question that the PO was a spectacular success. We completed all assigned missions on time and under budget. The Goshawk portion was also a spectacular success. Not only did we complete the project, but we also got a product into the IBM catalog, something that was simply not possible for a field team to accomplish. There can be no question that Goshawk altered other projects inside of IBM. A "mainstream" management solution was eventually developed. I saw a demonstration of that software several years after I left IBM and noted that the screen faces were remarkably similar to the User Interface we had developed for Goshawk.

— ■ —

Unfortunately, the PO was also a colossal failure on IBM's part, specifically, it was a missed opportunity on a gargantuan scale.

With the Goshawk project, the PO became, in essence, a "skunk-works." That was not a unique concept or structure. It had been used successfully by several large companies, most notably Lockheed Martin Corporation for revolutionary programs such as the SR-71 Blackbird spy plane. Skunk-works were needed to bypass bureaucratic inertia to make things happen.

In the PO, we assembled some of the most uniquely talented individuals in the Division, if not the whole company. We proved, both with the original TIPS missions and again with Goshawk, that we could work within the enterprise to

301

solve "unsolvable" problems. The experience gained by the individuals in the PO was irreplaceable. Unfortunately, the Division and the Company failed to recognize and capture the investment they had made in the PO and our team.

Ultimately, except for Norm Nadeau, every member of the PO team left the company in fairly short order. I believe Bill Perrin should be included in the PO-induced talent exodus. Bill was a rising star in the FE division. He had unique experience and a proven record of success. Bill stuck his neck out in establishing and supporting the PO, and like everyone in the PO, he was clearly not rewarded for his efforts. He never specifically told me why he left, but the timing was suspicious.

$$- \blacksquare -$$

There is no doubt that our talents could have been harnessed to address any number of service issues, and potentially product issues as well. Instead, Division management pushed to disband the PO. Granted, making the PO a permanent "skunk-works" for the FE Division would have required creating exceptions to traditional career path guidelines: appropriate titles, salaries, and other incentive/award programs were needed, but the benefits would have been worth the trouble. Instead, IBM tragically made no effort to reward or retain any of these individuals. The talent and experience lost by that failure cannot be measured.

I see this failure as representing the overall incompetence of IBM's executive ranks at that time. Senior management's inability or unwillingness to recognize and leverage the asset that was the PO, speaks volumes about the lack of vision in the highest offices. It is not possible that senior management was unaware of the PO or our work. As mentioned earlier, Dick Liebhaber was an SVP in the FE Division reporting directly to the president of the Division. He was clearly aware of the PO. I also had many meetings with senior managers in the FE and DP Divisions as well as relevant product groups. Apparently, none of these individuals had the vision and fortitude to see the PO as an asset worth saving.

$$- \blacksquare -$$

I did not think about it at the time, but in retrospect, I see this as gross negligence on the part of each of these senior executives. Any one of them could have benefited from this investment by transferring the PO and staff en masse to their division. If Liebhaber had acted upon the idea I pitched early in the Goshawk portion of the project, we could have altered the future of IBM.

An MBA Business Case Study should be written about the PO and IBM's failure to leverage this asset. This failure proved that the real problem was not that the elephant was just hard to move. It showed that the elephant was blind. Goshawk foretold the struggles IBM experienced over the next couple decades. It was a management failure, not a people failure.

— ■ —

It was also a failure on my part because I did not take the knowledge and experience I had gained and build my own company around it. Granted, this was decades before venture capital and the whole start-up phenomenon became popular, and my experience was technical rather than business at that point, but in retrospect, I should have at least attempted to start my own company to develop the service technology components I had described to Liebhaber. I am sure I could have found the money, and there is no doubt that I could have licensed the technology back to IBM or one of its competitors. Unfortunately, the idea of spinning out my own company never occurred to me.

Wild Ducks

When I worked for IBM in Boulder, I met Ken White, the senior graphics designer at the IBM Boulder plant. He developed the "How to Stuff a Wild Duck" poster that became quite famous. It was a takeoff of Thomas Watson Jr's statements regarding Wild Ducks within IBM.

It was printed on a matte black background. The image showed a duck stuffed with mind-numbing political speak. I was blown away by the graphics, but even more so by the message. There were two different generations of the same poster. One had an outline of a duck with the words inside. The other had no outline, just the words. I still have a framed version of the poster hanging on my wall.

For me, the overarching message from the Goshawk experience was that IBM no longer valued Wild Ducks.

"We are convinced that any business needs its wild ducks. And in IBM we try not to tame them."
  T.J. Watson, Jr.

and

304

"You can make wild ducks tame, but you can never make a tame duck wild again."
T.J. Watson Jr.

"The reasonable man adapts himself to the world. The unreasonable man persists in trying to adapt the world to himself. Therefore, all progress depends upon the unreasonable man."
George Bernard Shaw

The duck was filled with a jumble of expressions:

"...Don't fight city hall. It doesn't matter. cubicles. YES, BUT. Lip service. Rules Rules Rules. You're not onboard. Remember, this is IBM. Administrivia. Work Week. Draft a memo...."

These statements and attitudes would kill any wild duck.

Post Project Office

As we neared the end of the Goshawk Project, Jack told me that he was getting pressure to move me into a traditional Field Manager's position in a local branch office. Jack knew I was not looking to go in that direction, and we both resisted for as long as we could, but as Goshawk wound down, the pressure grew. Bill Perrin finally ask me to meet him for lunch to talk about my future. As I said earlier, I had already determined that I did not want to follow a traditional IBM FE career path.

Bill and I had worked together extensively, even before the PO, and as a result of several years of working together, we were closer than would have normally been the case for a first line manager and the Region Director. I can't imagine another circumstance where the Region Director would ever meet with a first line manager to discuss his future career, but Bill was that kind of gentleman. Bill explained to me how he saw my career going forward. First a year or so as a Field Manager. Then a Headquarters stint in NY for a couple of years. After that, out to a region staff manager's position for a couple of years, then back to HQ for another round. Next out as a Branch Manager, then off to a Region position for a couple of years, then back to HQ for a couple of years. Finally, if all this worked as planned, out as a Regional Director ...10-12 years down the road, plus half a dozen cross country moves. Of course, if I screwed up or if someone somewhere along that path didn't like me, well then I could wind up in some backwater branch biding my time until I retired or got shoved out the door.

I listened patiently and asked a few questions. Then I told Bill that, with all due respect, I didn't want to be a Region Manager. He asked me why and I explained that from what I could see, he had little opportunity to manage anything. He was given his territory, his headcount, his budget, and a ton of reports. He didn't get to choose the equipment or customers; he didn't have much freedom to do what I liked doing. Surprisingly, he didn't object or even disagree. He only asked me what I wanted to do. I told him I wanted to learn how to peddle (sell). He pushed back saying that the DP Division only hired from the top 10% of the best schools and that since I didn't have a degree he was not sure there would be many opportunities for me to move to a sales position.

He agreed to let me try to find an opportunity, and if I could find a DP branch that would take me, he would let me go. No doubt he figured I was on a wild goose chase and that we could resume this discussion as soon as I had exhausted the possibilities.

Gary Breckenridge was the DP Branch Manager for the LA Finance Branch. I had worked closely with Breck and his team for many years. He knew me well, and we had done battle over some situations where sales wanted to give the customer, WBC most recently, but other banks and State Farm Insurance in previous positions, more than the FE Division was willing to give. While I was on the Region Staff, I had also worked with his team as the coordinator for the 3890 debacle, and as the FE representative on the Regional Systems Assurance Team. We had a long history and had met many times, so he was very familiar with my work and capabilities. Our many battles had been professional, and we had mutual respect for each other.

After my meeting with Bill Perrin, I called Breck and ask for a meeting. At lunch a couple of days later he asked what was up. I told him I wanted to come to work for him and learn how to peddle. He asked only one question, when? As it was approaching the end of the year, we agreed on a January 1, 1979, start date, beginning as a Systems Engineer. My move from FE to DP was that simple.

— ■ —

There were some extenuating circumstances that I was unaware of at the time, but that I am sure caused Breck to jump at the opportunity to bring on a seasoned manager with technical and political skills. He had two major accounts that were in crisis. They had lost Crocker United Factors (CUFie). CUFie had run out of patience with the IBM team who had bungled things very badly. They had specifically told the salesman never to set foot in the account again. Rumor had it that they had security physically escort him to the door, but that was never confirmed. They had canceled a large system that had been on order and sent termination letters for every lease they had. It was over! CUFie was my first account.

Turning it around was quite easy. While CUFie was beyond pissed, they didn't have a lot of choices. To transition off of their installed systems to non-IBM, or even to IBM but from a third party rental, would have been a massive and disruptive undertaking that could have cost millions plus they would have lost millions during any transition. Factoring, like most financial businesses, is a minute by minute operation. You have to be there and ready to move at the moment the customer needs money. If you can't meet the client's needs, they will take their business elsewhere, and it will be tough to get them back.

A new sales rep, Hope Kobayashi, was assigned to the account. She was a novice, but she did all the actual order writing and paper processing. She was told specifically to observe but not interfere; my job was to deal with the customer. All that I needed to do was show some real understanding, point out some of the problems they would face if they followed their stated path, do some serious handholding and win their confidence back. In the process, I had to learn the factoring business quickly, but with my now extensive banking background, that was relatively straightforward. In the first six months, I not only got all of the leases reinstated I got the canceled system back on the books and sold more than $5 million in new business.

The next basket case was Gibraltar Savings. Some brilliant sales team had convinced Gibraltar to move their legacy COBOL systems to a brand new S/370-168 running MVS (Multiple Virtual Systems). That meant rewriting every one of their critical and noncritical business software packages. That was a monumental task. It was not a bad long-term strategy, but the plan was ill-conceived and it was bringing Gibraltar to its knees. Their DP Director was beyond incompetent. He and his team, undoubtedly with the support and encouragement of the IBM team, were convinced that the COBOL programmers would be so thrilled to have the opportunity to upgrade their skills that they would line up to get trained to work in the MVS environment. Furthermore, they would individually figure out how to develop replacement applications for the legacy COBOL programs they were responsible for maintaining. That was one case that clearly should have been flagged during a Systems Assurance audit. It had occurred well after I left the SA position. I don't know who or why this was missed, but someone should have been fired over this mess.

Needless to say, it didn't quite work out as planned. Instead of rushing to upgrade their skills, the programmers rushed to find new jobs. Most of the COBOL programmers had been around for decades. They could see that Gibraltar was moving away from COBOL. That meant that they would have to learn a whole new computing environment. They not only had to learn the new environment and new skills, but they would also be starting at the bottom of the ladder competing with young kids fresh out of college. That was an unattractive "opportunity" for a bunch of senior programmers, mostly in their late 40s to mid-50s. There were lots of COBOL jobs available, and so they jumped ship. It was a problem because there was no one to develop new versions of the software, but the most immediate crisis was that there was no one to maintain the mission critical legacy systems. Many of these programs had been around for years, and there were patches on top of patches, few of which were documented. In many cases, the programs had become the personal domain of the programmers that had been working on them. As these key people left, Gibraltar was literally in danger of not being able to keep their systems operational from day to day.

Gibraltar was harder to turn around. The IBM team had definitely screwed up in letting this disaster happen. When I arrived, there was a highly incompetent customer management team that had to be addressed. That required a sub-rosa process of bypassing and eventually eliminating the Director. His team, even those who were incompetent, had no confidence in him. Eventually, the CEO became aware of the situation, and a replacement was found. IBM helped keep the pieces working while we worked to resolve the management problem. That was my primary task. It was touch and go for a time, but we finally succeeded.

– ∎ –

I never learned to code, so I wasn't really in a position to make a career as a Systems Engineer. That was never my plan in any case. While I was spending more than half of my time functioning as a salesman, it was all on-the-job training and, without a degree, as Bill Perrin had suspected, there was never an opportunity to become a legitimate salesman. That was also not my plan. I just wanted to learn sales skills. In truth, I was working more as a consultant, both to the customers and to the IBM teams. That was a great learning experience, but not something I wanted to do long term. I knew IBM, the equipment, and the politics, all I had to work on was learning to sell. I was able to accomplish that in very short order.

– ∎ –

Remember I told you briefly about working with Sharon Muckleroy when I was installing the system at State Farm Insurance in Westlake Village many years earlier. By the time I joined the DP Branch, those conversations were five years in the past. Sharon and I had never met or even spoken since, and for both of us, life and work had moved on. As it turned out, we were both divorced from our first spouses by this time.

When I came to work in the Finance Branch, I was assigned one desk in a cluster of six. I met most of the other desk "owners" and noted that the one desk-mate that I had not met was Sharon Muckleroy.

I had forgotten about our talking long before, but who can miss a name like Muckleroy. Seeing her name reminded me of our earlier conversations, but no one was sitting at the desk. A day or so later a lady sat down at the desk. She was huge; my first thought was that she was a female version of Rosie Greer. For those of you who don't know, Rosie was an enormous football player back in those days. She was nice enough but certainly not attractive to me. I made the instant decision not to remind her that we had worked together on the State Farm account.

No problem, nobody said anything, so I assumed Sharon had forgotten State Farm. A few days later, a very attractive and much slimmer woman sat down at the same desk. Ok so now I am confused. I kept to myself and a week or so went by with this musical chairs game continuing, first Rosie next a Rose. I said nothing.

I was studying several SE training manuals preparing to head off to Dallas for a class. After a couple of weeks, it appeared that the desk belonged to Rose and not Rosie. I was too busy to pay a lot of attention until once as I was passing by Rose, or more accurately Sharon turned and asked if I remembered her. We had coffee, or tea in my case and started dating after I got back from Dallas. We were married about six months later.

It turned out Rosie was named Cheryl Pryor. She had the same job as Sharon but covered different accounts. During the musical desks period, Sharon was out for training, and so Cheryl was filling in for her. After we had married, we told Cheryl the story about the confusion and we all had a good laugh.

Brian, Tim, Sharon, Tracee, Teri June 9, 1979

We were super secretive about the fact that we were dating. It wasn't a problem from any rules or regulations standpoint, but we both felt it was probably better to not have all the rumors that tend to accompany office relationships. Nobody in the office suspected. Hope Kobayashi my sales partner at CUFie worked with me every day, and of course, she knew Sharon as we all worked in the same office. She had no idea we were dating. One Friday in early June, I told Hope I was going over to the Diamond District, which was only a couple blocks from CUFie. I didn't tell Hope, but I was on my way to pick up our wedding rings as Sharon and I were getting married the next day. Hope ask if she could tag along. I said sure. Hope was blown away when I picked up the rings. Of course, she asked who the lucky girl was and could not believe it when I told her Sharon Muckleroy. Hope came to our wedding the next day. It was a small private affair with our kids, and a few guests. Angie, a longtime friend of Sharon's, was her Maid of Honor. Mike Reader, my dentist, and a good friend was my Best Man.

312

Tim & Sharon honeymoon in Tahiti 1979

Sharon and I honeymooned in Tahiti, and while we were away, Hope lived in our house to take care of the kids. Unfortunately, we lost track of her over the years.

Sharon and I decided we wanted to move our merged family out of Los Angeles. Not only to have a better quality of life, but we both had dysfunctional Ex's that lived in the area and felt it would be better for our kids if they didn't have to deal with their "other" parents. As the end of the year proached, I talked to Breck, and since I had succeeded in solving the roblems he had brought me in for, he offered me a promotion to X where the DP Division's SE Support Center was located. The SE as responsible for both field support and to interface with the various development organizations working on requirements for future e and software releases. I was in charge of data communications for on to be announced IBM Personal Computer. Of course, the PC turned o be yet another disruptive technology. Sharon took a lateral to a Branch in Dallas.

We bought a new house in Trophy Club, TX. We soon found that we disliked living in Dallas. It also turned out that Sharon found it difficult to be treated as an equal in the Dallas branch where she transferred. She worked on the EDS team, which was by far the largest customer for the branch, but there were very distinct differences in the way she was treated compared to other team members. Sharon had been hired as the first minority AAS (Administrative Account Specialist) in the LA Region many years earlier, so she was accustomed to proving herself. But this was 1980, and both female and black AAS's were common. Or at least in LA they were common, not in Dallas. Sharon was the only black and the only woman on the EDS team, and nearly the only female AAS in the office. She had far more experienced, and seniority than her peers but they wanted her to work in the background. It was never clear whether this disparity was because she was black or that she was female. It didn't make any difference; there were other things she wanted to do.

We bought an old residential building in Grapevine, remodeled it, and rezoned it. She left IBM and opened it as a Montessori school. She had all the licenses and quickly filled the small space that we had. At about that time I got recruited as the Director of Customer Support for NBI, a small, but rapidly growing office automation company in Boulder, CO. A Director position, but certainly not on a par with Bill Perrin's Region Manager Directorship at IBM. I decided that the time had come for me to leave the IBM University.

IBM Years Conclusion

I spent nearly 15 years with IBM. I had enjoyed my time with the company, and I have, to this day, nothing but respect and gratitude for the opportunity to work for the IBM. These were wonderfully fulfilling years. My skills and personality were a perfect match for that company at that time. I had incredible success. I advanced from a new-hire to the very highest technical position the Field Engineering Division had in less than eight years. I learned to function at the professional staff level on a cross-divisional basis. I became a manager and later a salesman in fact, if not in name. I played a significant role in supporting what is considered by some to be one (the System/360) of the three most important business innovations in the history of mankind.

I was in critical positions involved with the announcement and introducing new generations of mainframe computers, and radically new technologies including virtual memory, the Personal Computer, banking systems (both back office 3890s and front office teller workstations), and telecommunications technologies. I played a key role in altering how large data communications networks were installed and maintained. I traveled all over this country both by car and by plane. I learned politics, big business, and entrepreneurship. I developed expertise in project and matrix management, as well as consulting. I learned the manufacturing, finance, telecommunications, and Information Technology industries in depth. In what could only be considered frosting on the cake, I had the opportunity to work with Charles Eames in two fun projects.

I was blessed to be selected as the Project Manager. I was doubly blessed to have both Jack and Bill's trust, to be treated as an equal. In normal business conditions, there was no conceivable reason they would have allowed me to operate unsupervised at the levels I did. First line managers never go head to head with senior executives in their division, never mind other groups. The risks are just too high. I will be forever grateful.

On the personal side, I grew up. I established both my business and technical acumen; I began my college education. My family grew, struggled, and was reborn. I was prepared for the next chapter of life.

NBI

People laughingly said NBI meant "Nothing But Initials," but NBI was the complete name of the company. The three letters were not initials; they stood for nothing more than the three letters.

In the early 1980s, the big marketing buzz was "the paperless office." Of course, that never happened. NBI had developed what at the time was very sophisticated word processing software that they sold along with their proprietary hardware. Their Office Automation systems were designed for legal firms with their unique line numbering and footnoting requirements. Large legal firms as well as large corporate legal staffs tended to have more complicated documentation requirements. They also had more money available, and they wanted to squeeze more productivity out of their administrative staff. Office Automation was a logical way to gain efficiencies.

Office Automation in the form of proprietary systems turned out to be an intermediate disruptive technology. Initially, it was a replacement for the electric typewriter, and it took a big step toward killing that standard office appliance. The big advantage was memory and storage which made it possible to access stored documents and to edit all documents without retyping.

NBI's main competitors were Wang and IBM. Vydec was fairly active but mainly low-end, so we didn't run into them often. NBI was the up the coming office automation company, a "giant killer" challenging Wang and IBM. That was all before PCs running word processing software became the real disruptive technology that wiped out typewriters as well as the emerging Office Automation industry.

NBI's equipment was very expensive. A standalone word processor could cost $15,000 or more. That was a big step up from a $1,200 IBM Selectric typewriter. An NBI office network with eight workstations and a controller could run as much as $200,000. The equipment was initially standalone (with no communications to the mainframe computer), but most companies that could afford this equipment had other computing equipment and they wished to be able to communicate with their word processors.

— ■ —

Communications were by far the weakest link for all Office Automation vendors. Interestingly, it was especially true for IBM. That reflected the "elephant" nature of Big Blue. While IBM certainly had sufficient communications knowledge and engineering capabilities, those skills were primarily within the large systems and large networking products portions of the company. Office Automation was logically part of the Office Products Division (OPD). At that time, OPD sold typewriters and copiers, equipment that, back then, did not communicate with the mainframes. Within IBM, OPD was a poor stepchild. The "real" IBMers were busy fighting battles with insurgent "distributed computing" technologies from companies like DEC and HP. They were too busy fighting forest fires to become involved in OPD's brush fires. There was little interest in incorporating OPD products into an overall communications strategy.

At NBI, I was initially responsible for both the field engineering (hardware) and systems engineering (software) support centers. There was a need for discipline within the support process. Once I got the organization running smoothly, I turned my attention to other needs in the company.

NBI was a small company, and like any small company, there were many unmet needs. I quickly learned that data communications, much like our competitors, had been an afterthought at NBI. Every large customer was demanding "host communications." Specifically, the ability to upload and download documents to the host for archival storage and search purposes.

Manufacturers had opted to install cheap, off-the-shelf start/stop technology so that they could respond positively to the "communications requirement" on the RFPs. That was the same type of communications I had trained on 15 years earlier for the IBM 1050 system. It had been obsolete for more than a decade, and it was virtually useless in this environment.

To make matters worse, both our engineers and our sales teams were clueless when it came to communications. That allowed our competitors to spin all kinds of tall tales about how they could do this or that. Wang was bad, but IBM was the worst. They played on IBM's credibility. Their answer was always "we're IBM, of course we can do that." Our team was unable to challenge any of the many exaggerations and downright lies that they were confronting. They couldn't even articulate the limited capabilities that we did have.

Having just left a position with IBM where I was responsible for laying out the timeline for future communications products relating to the PC, I had specific knowledge of IBM's communications capabilities. I knew that IBM could not do what the customers were asking and that it would be several years before their host software could interface with their OA products in any useful way.

Interestingly, I had just fought this battle while I was at IBM. I was trying to get an option for more advanced communications, but some people inside of IBM were afraid the PC would cannibalize the 3270 terminal market. They pressured me to "dumb-down" the PC telecommunications. Being fresh from these battles, I was well aware of the weaknesses of IBM's current communications software. I knew which version of their host software would be compatible with the OA systems, and just how many years it would be before that version would be available.

I created a proposal and business case showing how NBI could gain a competitive advantage by adding 3270 SNA emulation. It was accepted, and Communications Planning became part of my responsibilities. That quickly consumed most of my time. I eventually had six managers with a total of nearly 80 people in my organization; some were in Europe. The communications job was primarily pounding on the engineering department, overseeing product testing, and supporting the sales teams. I was never responsible for the actual design.

The elephant aspect of IBM meant that they couldn't make any significant communications changes on their hardware in less than three years. The elephant was too big to move any faster. NBI was small and could turn on a dime. We were able to implement and start shipping 3270 SNA compatibility in less than four months.

— ■ —

Despite our now superior communications capabilities, our sales team could not explain the difference between start/stop and SNA. They could be easily brushed aside by the false statements made by the IBM and Wang reps. They couldn't get past me.

Invariably the administrative side of the prospect companies wanted the NBI equipment because of the superior usability and performance. At the same time, the IT team wanted IBM because they knew how to work with IBM and they always preferred to interface with fewer vendors.

In most companies, the IT departments viewed the administrative side of their business much like IBM DP viewed the OPD people. They would provide

319

support in name only. They didn't care that the word processors couldn't communicate with the host computers, they just didn't want to deal with another vendor. The IT departments would invariably lay out some significant technical hurdles before they would accept new vendors.

My solution was to have our sales team set up a meeting with the IT communications people in attendance. These sessions were fun. The IT techs invariably came to the meetings acting like a bunch of banty roosters. Their sole intention was to poke holes in any non-IBM vendor's plans. Our guys knew that their job was to set up the meeting, make the introductions, and then shut up.

These meetings would start with the usual pleasantries, and then I would ask the communications "geeks" a couple of simple, but leading questions. As geeks love to do, they would instantly puff out their chests and start spouting acronyms knowing that nobody but a fellow geek could even begin to follow what they were saying. What they didn't know was that I was a fellow geek dressed in sheep's clothing, in this case, a suit and tie.

The meetings always had one or two geeks sitting across from me, and the three of us would be talking techno gibberish. I would play along for a few minutes while they got further and further out into the stratosphere. Everyone else at the table just sat and watched, most not understanding a word. After the techies trotted out their usual canard about how IBM could do this or that I would come down on them like a sledgehammer. I would tell them specifically why IBM could not do that with the software version that they were currently using, and if they read IBM's published specs on the upcoming version, that they would not be able to do it then either. I would then explain how we at NBI were approaching the problem in a way that was compatible with their current software.

When I explained how we were able to communicate with their system today, it was all done in tech talk and acronyms. No one else at the table could understand a word of what I was saying, but everyone could see that I was taking the geeks to school. Their posture would visibly change. Their attitudes went from arrogance to respect. They started out as alpha-males in charge of their world, but that soon changed. Even those unable to follow the conversation could tell that instead of telling me how things worked, they were asking me how they could work. In the end, they would turn to the IT Director and tell him that we knew what we were doing and that we were able to do things now that IBM would not be able to do for the foreseeable future.

320

We won almost every one of these sales.

I didn't have to divulge any IBM confidential information, all I had to do was ask very specific questions, shoot a few holes in their BS, and speak to our capabilities. As a result, my presence was in high demand. I became involved in literally every major account sale. People always loved to visit Boulder, so some of these briefings took place at NBI headquarters. However, most of the important sales meetings were in the field. These meetings were more productive because the geeks attended. As a result, I was traveling about 80% of the time.

— ■ —

My original position at NBI did not involve the communications planning or the direct marketing support functions. These had arisen out of necessity as things do in small companies. Over a short period, they had become the major part of my work. I felt very strongly that my salary and stock options were not appropriate for my contribution.

I knew the president of NBI, Tom Kavanagh personally. He was an ex-IBMer, and I had worked with when he was in the Boulder IBM plant. He went from IBM to Storage Technology southeast of Boulder. Back when I was a CE in Boulder, I had serviced equipment, at Storage Tech from time to time and ran into Tom on several occasions. He is the one who recruited me to NBI.

Tom and I had an ongoing dialogue about my compensation. I think he believed he had me over a barrel, and since the company was in the process of going public, there were some restrictions on exactly what he could do as to stock options. However, elevating me to a VP position could have easily solved all problems. I had clearly earned it, but I was not one of the "sacred seven," and he was not willing to make the change.

— ■ —

There was a "cult" factor at NBI. The "sacred seven" were the initial team. It consisted of Tom plus all of his VPs plus a couple of individuals Tom had known forever. One was a worthless alcoholic who had been Tom's roommate in college. He was drunk before noon on most days, and no one ever gave him anything serious to do because he would inevitably screw it up, but he was Tom's friend and therefore one of the untouchable sacred seven.

The sacred seven isolated themselves from the rest of the company. It was an exclusive club with closed admission. The seven felt that they were, and

321

always would be "the company." There was no room for new blood.

However, there was a desperate need for that new blood in the senior team. NBI hired some excellent people, but they refused to let them have any real power or significant influence in how the company developed. They also refused to compensate them appropriately. This narrow, myopic view of the world contributed to the company's ultimate downfall. The good people became frustrated and left, and the hanger's on simply were there for the ride.

Four of the seven bought DeLoreans which were new and all rage at that time. They would all park them in front of the main entry in the handicapped spaces which were wider and so they could open the gullwing doors. The standard joke was that senior management was handicapped. In many ways they were.

— ∎ —

I pushed Tom and the others to consider launching a standalone DOS-compatible software word processing package targeted at PC owners. When I was at IBM, I had seen the tsunami hit when IBM announced the PC. They had 250,000 orders in the first 30 days. To me, it was clear that there was no future for standalone word processors based on proprietary hardware. Unfortunately, NBI was making lots of money off of the proprietary hardware, so Tom and the rest of the sacred seven were opposed to my idea. They took the position that "the office is not a place for a computer."

I pushed until he finally told me to shut up. That was an incredibly stupid decision that ultimately destroyed the company. I don't know if NBI could have won against Microsoft Word, but they had a huge head start, superb software, and some very loyal customers. If they had spun out the software and ultimately abandoned the proprietary hardware as I recommended, they could have focused all of their engineering and resources on building the best possible word processing software and potentially additional PC software products. I even proposed a plugin card for the PCs that would have maintained some degree of proprietary hardware in the new vision.

To me, it seemed obvious. The target market after just one month of IBM PC sales was one quarter million devices. That was far more than NBI had been able to sell in the 6 or 7 years of their existence. The price of a software package would have been far less, but the market was so vast by comparison that they had far greater revenue potential. If they had seen my vision, there is, in my opinion, a good chance that today we would all be running NBI word processing software on our PCs and Macs. At the very least, Microsoft might have acquired NBI.

— ■ —

Ignoring my recommendation was not their only mistake. Even with their commitment to proprietary hardware, they failed to invest in the next generation of standalone systems. Instead of using the cash gained from going public to invest in the next generation systems, they used much of their windfall to build a beautiful new headquarters location on the north side of Boulder, an edifice for themselves. That was after I left NBI.

The egos of the sacred seven had become so swollen from the success of their IPO that they spent endless hours arguing about the size of their offices, the convenience of their parking spots, and the thickness of their carpets. It seemed that no one was thinking about the business. It was a classic case of "Nero fiddling while Rome burned," and burn it did. Their product line became stale and by the time management realized the position they were in, the time for standalone word processors had passed and the money needed to develop a software version had been spent.

— ■ —

Working for NBI was good training, mainly in what not to do. Tom Kavanagh was adamantly opposed to putting any personal computer functionality into the word processors. For him, it was a violation of the "beauty of a specialized device." However, tables were an important part of many documents, and customers wanted to incorporate the ability to do spreadsheets (at a minimum) with their word processors.

Fireman's Fund Insurance Company was NBI's biggest and oldest customer. More than once, Fireman's had placed a significant order at a critical moment that kept NBI's doors open. Tom fought the PC add-on until Fireman's Fund finally told him personally that they would not buy another NBI word processor unless it had the ability to run VisiCalc, the preferred spreadsheet of that time. Realizing that losing Fireman's Fund would kill the company, Tom finally relented and literally over a one-week period, they re-engineered the systems to include basic PC functionality. I suspect the fast turnaround was due, in no small part, to some engineers who saw the stupidity of Tom's position, and had secretly designed the needed solution long before Tom woke up.

Ultimately, I discovered that there were some illegal activities taking place and that convinced me that I needed to separate myself from the company. It had to do with drugs. It was nothing that the company was specifically doing, but they were looking the other way while it was taking place. It had the potential of being a real headline story.

It was behind closed doors of course, but I didn't want to risk being tainted by association should criminal charges ever happen. All I had were rumors, but they were well-founded, and I had seen enough to feel that they were most likely true. It was not something I could take to the police, so I chose to walk away.

— ■ —

I made my first trip to Europe while I was with NBI. They were growing quickly in the European market and having the same issues regarding data communications. I went to Brussels and London to work with my team members in these locations and to teach classes to the sales and support staff. I also met with a few large customers. I was able to take Sharon and Tracee on this trip. We had a lot of fun, particularly in England. We took some time off to play tourists and enjoyed a short stay in Windsor. It was the first of my many European adventures.

— ■ —

When I left NBI; they slapped a lawsuit on me trying to restrict what I could do. I countersued, saying that they were trying to restrain my ability to make a living. I won, and they had to pay several thousand dollars in legal fees as well as damages. I soon discovered that suing ex-employees was their standard practice. This modus operando was part of what was wrong with the sacred seven. They played like they knew everything, but when people got fed up and walked, they wanted to stop them from succeeding or ever working in their area of specialization. It was a form of vindictive blackmail. Eventually, the word spread and good people were not willing to work for the company.

— ■ —

On the personal side, it was exciting to get back to Boulder. I have always loved Colorado and Boulder in particular. I had left Boulder approximately ten years earlier. Much had changed, both in my life and in Boulder. We rented a townhouse on East Arapahoe, not all that far from where we had last lived. We bought a 4½ acre lot on a south-facing hillside in Pinebrook Hills, a mountain subdivision close to Boulder. We started designing a 4,500 sqft solar home. Our intention was to live the rest of our lives in that home. Of course, it didn't work out that way.

Pinebrook Hills, Boulder CO 1983

The house was a challenging project. Solar homes were coming into fashion at that time, and since the home was at an elevation close to 6,000 feet, winters could be quite cold. We had deliberately selected a south-facing open lot to take maximum advantage of the winter sun. With something like 300 sunny days a year, Boulder has ideal weather for solar. Of course, it is cold in the winter, but even when cold, with the clean air and thinner atmosphere, if you can capture the sunshine in a protected area, you can gain a lot of heat.

I didn't know a lot about solar, but I liked the idea of using the sunshine to supplement our heating. I talked to several "solar architects," or at least they claimed that on their business cards, only to discover that few of them had any more knowledge than I did. I learned to ask one simple question: "Tell me about your house." If they didn't live in a solar home, the odds were good they were just guessing.

I found one guy that had built an envelope house. An envelope home is a double-walled house with a space between the walls. You insulate both walls, leaving an open space between, thus creating an air pocket. This design is quite efficient, but also quite expensive. He started designing our house, but I soon discovered that he wanted to make some architectural statement with our project. Of course, the construction costs associated with his dream would have been unnecessarily high. He wanted things like round walls and triple pane trapezoidal windows, all of which would have to be custom built. After a couple of sketches, we told him no thanks.

As I have had to do so many times in my life, I had to educate myself. I got a bunch of books and started studying solar homes. I wound up designing a 3-story super-insulated home with a lower level greenhouse. The walls were R-38 with R-50 ceilings. All entries were set up with air-lock vestibules so that you came in and removed your coat and boots then entered another door to get into the house.

Each level was stepped back so that it aligned with the slope of the hill. That provided abundant decks and allowed us to take full advantage of the winter sun. On the lowest level, I included a greenhouse with a large cement mass to absorb energy during the day and radiate heat at night. On each level, there were overhanging decks to block the sun when it was higher in the sky during the summer. This arrangement allowed us to capture the sunshine during the winter, but to shade the rooms when the sun was higher during the summer.

I incorporated an air handling system that pulled the hot air that naturally rose to the ceiling of the third floor and discharged this warm air at the back side of the bottom floor. After I had designed what we wanted, I went back to the architect and had him draw up the plans. It was still expensive to build, but nothing like what he originally had in mind. We stuck to standard shape and size for our windows. For example, we used glass from standard patio doors for the windows in the greenhouse. The code required double pane and tempered glass. Patio doors fit the bill at a much lower cost. We were also fortunate that there was a building slump at the time, so we were able to get contractors at reasonable rates. Our total construction cost, including the land, came in at just under $55/sqft. Not bad for a custom home in the mountains.

— ■ —

Shortly before we completed the house, a headhunter contacted me concerning a position at with ITT. Sharon and I were standing on the deck of our new home, holding the Certificate of Occupancy and looking out at our stunning view when I told her that I had just received a very attractive offer to become the Global Director of Product Support Technology at the ITT Programming Center in Wilton, CT. I asked her what she thought, and she smiled and said: "when do we leave." Forever nomads, we never moved a single box into the new house we had spent so much time and energy to build.

That was our third major move in less than five years: from Westlake, CA to Dallas, TX, next to Boulder, CO and now to CT. It was four moves for Sharon as she and Tracee as they had moved from their home in LA to Westlake when we got married. We moved a lot during our 25-year marriage. For us, it was part of our great adventure. I guess we both had some "gypsy" in our blood.

— ■ —

There were a few interesting personal stories during this period. I did some consulting after leaving NBI and before joining ITT. One assignment was to teach basic data communications to NCR's office automation sales staff. I conducted several classes over a few weeks at NCR's Dayton, OH facility. NCR tried to get me to join them and move to Dayton. I turned that down.

A few years later Sharon and I were in Detroit to visit her family. It was the first time I had met any of them. We discovered that her brother Ted was a student in one of my Data Communications classes at NCR. Neither of us knew we were brothers-in-law at the time.

— ■ —

We enjoyed our time in Boulder. Even with my travel, we found time to explore Colorado on the weekends. The Chautauqua in Boulder was one of our favorite places. During the summer, there were many plays and concerts to enjoy. We also enjoyed watching CU football games. Mostly they lost, but it was still fun. Pearl Street was always a fun place to hang out, meet friends for dinner, or just to have a drink in the evening.

In Rocky Mountain National Park 1982

The place we rented was a 3-bedroom townhouse with an unfinished basement. We were storing most of our stuff in boxes in the cellar, but we had set up some space as a bedroom for Brian. When Thanksgiving came, we didn't want to dig through the boxes to try to find our turkey pan, so we bought one of those large aluminum pans designed specifically for turkeys. When the turkey was ready, I used two hot mitts and picked up the pan at each end. I was turning from the oven to place the rather large bird on the table when the sides of the pan folded. The turkey along with all of the juice and vegetables slid out and fell to the floor. The turkey was sliding and spinning across the floor with Jackie, our Basset Hound, in hot pursuit. Jackie was howling and trying to get traction on the wet, oily floor while Sharon and I were laughing and trying to scramble to catch the turkey as well as keep the dog away. We were all slipping and sliding; it was complete chaos. In the end, we were able to rescue the bird, but it took a good while to clean up the floor. A Thanksgiving can't pass without me remembering and laughing about that scene.

It seemed Jackie was always up to some mischief. She was rather stout and low slung, but she could get into trouble at elevations you would never think she could reach. Teri had gathered a vast hoard of chocolate and candies at

Halloween. With diabetes, she had to be very careful about not eating too many sweets. She had placed her stash on top of a dresser in her bedroom which was on the 2nd floor.

We came home one day and as we came in Jackie came running down the stairs howling like someone was whipping her. She was banging into the stair walls and "arooooing" all the while. She ran past us and down to the basement. We were all laughing because we knew she had been up to something.

Teri went immediately to her room and discovered that Jackie had somehow gotten up onto her bed and then up on the dresser where she proceeded to consume a good bit of her candy stash. The pieces she hadn't eaten, she had chewed and slobbered on. The bag was a total loss. Teri came down the stairs almost as fast and howled nearly as loud as Jackie.

Family Transition

Our family made some significant transitions during our short time back in Boulder. Brian found his career. Up to that point, he had shunned computers. That was "something Dad did," and he wanted to be different. I had an Apple II that I used for consulting. We didn't have much space, so I kept it on a small table in our bedroom. Brian was always shy when it came to girls, but in a computer class at school he was teamed up with two girls. The team had a programming project to do, something like print "Hello" on the screen. Brian discovered that he had a knack for programming and the girls were more than happy to let him take the lead. His motivations and interests instantly changed. Very soon, we had to kick him out of the bedroom each night so we could go to bed. Brian ultimately made a career in computers. It all started as a way to impress a couple of girls.

Most people send their kids off to college; we reversed that. Brian enrolled in CU, and we got him settled in and then we moved to Connecticut. I think that he really couldn't believe that we were leaving him in Boulder.

— ■ —

Teri wanted to live a few months with her mother in Idaho while we were in the chaos of our move. She then decided she wanted to stay with friends to finish high school in Boulder. From there, life took over and she never did live at home again.

Jackie was getting too old to live through another move, and so we gave her to

329

a friend who wanted a spoiled old Basset Hound. We replaced her with an Old English Sheepdog that we named Bossley. He was a wonderful dog, but his hair was always everywhere.

We came to Boulder with a family of five and an old Basset and left as a family of three with an Old English Sheepdog.

— ■ —

There was another significant family change that didn't manifest itself for some years. I had had a vasectomy shortly after Teri was born. I was very young, but I couldn't see Jane living on birth control pills for decades. Every drug has side effects, and it just didn't seem to be the best thing for her health to keep using drugs year after year.

After Sharon and I married, we talked about having a baby, but of course there was this little problem of my vasectomy. While we were living in Boulder, we decided to try to have that reversed. I went back to the same doctor who had performed the original surgery and had him reconnect the pipes. That was a lot more painful and complicated than the original process.

We tried unsuccessfully for years and finally gave up, assuming it would never happen. About six months after we abandoned all hope and special procedures Sharon was suddenly pregnant. Katlin was born almost six years after my reversal procedure.

— ■ —

My short time at NBI had helped me further refine and expand my telecommunications knowledge. It also provided a great window into a new, but short-lived industry called Office Automation. That gave me exposure to administrative operations. Remember, the bulk of my work up to that point had involved the data processing side, and how companies used mainframes and networks in support of their operational objectives. Later, the OA industry became part of the IT world and personal computers replaced standalone word processors. That showed me how disruptive technologies can develop, and can themselves be disrupted by newer and bigger disruptive technologies. I also had a close and personal experience with management transitions that need to happen as entrepreneurial companies grow and mature. Maybe I should say how they should transition, but as NBI clearly demonstrated, often fail to take place.

ITT

ITT was a very different kind of company. In many ways, it was the polar opposite of IBM. It was the first, and at the time I was there, the largest global conglomerate. It was ranked #17 on the Forbes list of the world's biggest companies. The name at that time was International Telephone and Telegraph. Later, after it had shed most of its telephony subsidiaries, it was changed to simply ITT.

The company was founded in 1920 and immediately acquired several phone companies in Europe and Central America. In 1925, Western Electric which is a development and manufacturing subsidiary of AT&T was forced to sell off its international subsidiaries due to antitrust issues. ITT acquired those assets. It continued buying other phone companies but began to diversify into other industries in the 50s.

Harold Geneen became ITT's CEO in 1959. By all accounts, Geneen was a real SOB, to put it mildly. He was notorious for abusing everybody. He held quarterly meetings with all of his Group VPs, and he would chew them out in the foulest language possible. These were all successful business executives responsible for multibillion-dollar businesses. He was known to bring these men to tears.

ITT had a rather "colorful" past under Geneen's stewardship. Here are a few of his exploits:

- ITT was involved in the 1964 coup d'état in Brazil. Details are sketchy, but the then CIA Director went to work for ITT a few years later.

- In 1970 ITT owned 70% of the Chilean telephone company. When Allende's government tried to nationalize the company, ITT helped set up a military coup d'état.

- ITT made a larger than usual donation to the 1972 Republican convention, apparently in exchange for a favorable outcome of a legal action before the Justice Department.

If you want to learn more, read The Sovereign State of ITT.

There are several theories about how Geneen managed to buy hundreds of companies. The one I favor centers around ITT's acquisition of The Hartford Insurance Company.

Insurance companies are required to maintain huge asset reserves to back up the policies they cover. As the story goes, when ITT acquired The Hartford, someone discovered that most of The Hartford's assets were "on the books" at 1920s valuation. Geneen had them revalued to the current rates, and this freed up billions of dollars that he could use to buy companies. When that bucket of money ran dry, Geneen retired. I don't know if this is the real story, or even if it is partially correct, but it sounds good, and it sounds like Geneen.

General Hamilton replaced Geneen as CEO in 1977. Geneen moved on to become Chairman of the Board. Things didn't work to his liking, so Geneen forced Hamilton out and replaced him with Rand Araskog in 1979. Araskog was apparently a better politician, or maybe the Board was just sick and tired of Geneen's stunts. In any case, Araskog successfully forced Geneen out soon after that.

Araskog spent the next two decades unwinding the conglomerate Geneen had built. This is my speculation but founded on personal experience as well as decades of management. As a conglomerate, ITT's ROI was not acceptable. Geneen managed to mask a lot of this with a "corporate shell game," always buying and selling companies with promises of better things to come. With the acquisition money gone and performance still less than the market expected, Araskog had no choice but to trim to try to achieve better financial results. Furthermore, there was little synergy between the kinds of companies ITT owned. What do a multinational bakery, a global hotel chain, an insurance company and a handful of telephone switch manufacturing companies have in common? Ok, that was a trick question. Obviously, they have nothing in common. It is almost impossible to manage these diverse industries with the same team. Management from a bakery is not interchangeable with the administration from a switch manufacturer, so it was hard to develop or optimize the management team. Finally, as you will learn below, cross-country politics made it impossible to amalgamate even those subsidiaries that appeared to have everything in common. In my opinion, Araskog had no alternative.

– ∎ –

I joined ITT in 1984. At that time ITT owned over 1,000 companies. They could not tell you from day to day exactly which companies or even how many they held. While Araskog was busy divesting companies, some of the companies ITT owned were themselves conglomerates that were busy buying and selling companies. ITT SpA in Italy, it was called Face (pronounced "fa

332

chea") at that time, was one example.

In addition to The Hartford Insurance Co., ITT owned a number of notable companies including Sheraton Hotels and several telephone companies around the world. They owned Hostess Bakeries, the maker of both Wonder Bread and Twinkies. ITT continued its ownership of the old Western Electric subsidiaries that were manufacturing: PBXs, telephone switching systems, and handsets among other technology products.

Two of the biggest former Western Electric companies were BTM (Bell Telephone Manufacturing) in Belgium and SEL (Standard Electric Lorenz) in Germany. There were other old WE businesses in France, Spain, Italy, and the UK as I recall. These companies sometimes competed, but their main competitors were Siemens in Germany, Ericsson in Sweden, as well as North Electric and Western Electric, both in the US. These companies sold telephone switches all over the world. There were other competitors, but they were more regional at that time.

ITT and the PTTs

Outside of North America, most telephone companies were government owned rather than privately held like AT&T. In most cases, the phone service and the postal service were combined under one agency called the Postal Telephone and Telegraph or PTT. That is an artifact from the early days when the telegraph was the only electronic form of communications, and those offices were typically co-resident with the Post Offices. PTTs are the carriers; they operate like AT&T, Verizon, etc. The PTTs are not to be confused with BTM and SEL; these companies were manufacturers of switches and other devices that were sold to and used by the PTTs.

ITT owned several other technology companies in the US as well as in other countries. These companies developed and manufactured (mainly electronic) equipment for various branches of the military.

The switching business is quite complicated, and few people outside of the industry have any idea how it operates. Hopefully, I won't bore you with too many details, but it is a fascinating business, so let me try to explain it at the "ducky and birdie" level.

The ITU (International Telecommunications Union) regulates the global telephony system. It was formerly called the International Telegraph Union. The ITU is now part of the UN. One could argue that the ITU is one of the few things the UN has done reasonably well. The ITU controls virtually every aspect of the global system including all standards, radio frequencies, satellites, and most importantly, the telephone numbering system.

Remember the ITU as the "ruller" of the global telephone system; remember also its relationship with the UN. We will cross paths again a few years later when I was working for VeriSign. At that point, I had invented a disruptive technology that put me at war with the ITU. The results were predictable, but I came close to winning.

Each country has one or more networks that operate under the umbrella of the ITU's regulations. In most cases, there are multiple networks including both fixed and wireless systems. Getting all of the networks within a single country to work together can be challenging, but it doesn't end there. The global telephone network is a massive spider web, an interconnected network-of-networks that operate in each country. Initially, these were all independent, even inside of the US, for example, the networks were not compatible, and not interconnected. Over the last century, they have been fairly well integrated so that they operate together more or less seamlessly.

Interestingly, it may surprise you to learn that the biggest problem with interconnecting these networks was not the voice signals themselves, it was the billing process. When a call goes from Chicago to Tokyo, it crosses dozens of different companies' properties and switches. There is a copper wire at both ends, microwave towers, various switches, one or more under-ocean cables, possibly cell towers, each is owned by different organizations, and each wants their piece of the revenue from that call. Figuring it all out and getting everyone to agree on their piece of the pie is a huge problem. Setting up the software to manage and distribute the pennies is a monumental problem.

Some of you may recall that in the early days (the 1980s), mobile phones from one carrier, Sprint, for example, would not connect with mobile devices from a different carrier. That was not the result of a voice problem; it was a billing problem.

The system is not static. Just think about the impact of things like satellite communications, text messaging, and VoIP (Voice over Internet Protocol). All of these interconnected networks are constantly evolving, not at the same pace and not always in the same direction. Remember also that some of the companies are privately owned; some are state-owned. These companies are often direct competitors. All are located in different countries with different political systems. Many of these countries are not necessarily friendly to each other. The fact that the ITU has been able to make all of this mesh together seamelessly is a major accomplishment that benefits our lives immensely. Finally, it is funded by the companies it regulates, and the vast majority of those that benefit from the ITU have never heard of it. Like I said, it could be argued that the ITU is the only portion of the UN that is actually successful.

— ■ —

Every telephone call must pass through at least one switch that establish the path from one point to another. There are roughly three types of switches, and each type comes in several configurations. The easiest way to understand this is to dissect a telephone number. Let's look at the elements of this phone number, 1-702-555-8709. Numbers are different outside of the US, but the process is similar.

Reading from the right, the first group is the 4-digit "subscriber" number (8709 in this case). In essence, the subscriber numbers are the extensions off of the Local Telephone Switch. The "prefix" (555) is the next element. That is the address of the Local Switch itself. Each prefix represents one "local" switch.

Many phone calls are to phones that are on other prefixes, so the local switches need to be connected to a 2nd level switch that covers major regions, think Area Codes, 702 in this case. Again, not all calls are within a single area code, so there is another level switch that connects different area codes. Finally, there is yet another level that switches calls between countries. Country codes can be from 1 to 3 digits. There are currently 205 Telephone Country Codes. The U.S. Country Code is 1.

That is a very simplified but a reasonably accurate illustration of how the switching system in North America works and how this network of networks can talk to each other. There are additional complexities such as PBXs (Private Branch Exchange). These are small switches that create a private network that resides below the Local Switch level. These are usually inside of a single company. Even local customs can impact how the telephone switches are set up. As an example, for a long time, it wasn't necessary to include the Area Code if it was the same as your phone number. Today, most systems require the Area Code for all calls. Some even require the country code.

Of course, an expert could tell you where I have taken some serious liberties.

Also, it is important to remember that this example is for the North American numbering system. Like license plate numbers in California, countries have run out of number combinations and so they have added additional layers, a 2-digit City Code for example, or extended the number pool with a 5-digit subscriber number. In some cases, they expanded the prefix to 4-digits. The possible switching combinations are almost infinite. Of course, different switch configurations are needed to match those requirements.

— ■ —

The telephone switch manufacturing process is also unique. Most equipment that we are familiar with, even large mainframe computers, are manufactured as complete systems in a factory. The larger devices are then partially disassembled, shipped to the customer, and reassembled.

Before the introduction of digital switches which I will discuss later, telephone switches were manufactured on the PTT premises, not in a factory. That was required because the device was so tightly integrated with the physical phone network.

They would quite literally pour concrete and manufacture the switch on the spot where it would live for its life. Every switch was more or less customized to the customer's requirements. Switches were built, tested, and then turned over to the PTT. From that point forward, the manufacturer didn't service the switch; the PTT did that. The manufacturer's only involvement was to supply parts. That is an important fact to remember when you consider my new job as Director of Global Support Technology. My group was not servicing the switches, it was providing tools and technologies so that the PTTs and carriers could service their switches. This was a very different environment than service in IBM for esample.

— ■ —

There is another unique custom in at least the European markets. I didn't get involved in sales in other markets, so I don't know if it was the same elsewhere. Let's use Germany as an example. SEL, the ITT subsidiary, and Siemens, a competitive German company, would get an RFQ (Request for Quotation) from the Deutsche Bundespost (the German PTT) for 10 Local switches to be installed in various locations in Germany during the next year. Ericsson and other companies might also receive the RFQ, but in this example, let's keep it simple. SEL and Siemens would prepare bids that would be reviewed by the Bundespost. Let's assume that Siemens won the bid.

In America, that would mean the Siemens would sell and deliver ten switches to the Bundespost. But not in Germany. In Germany, Siemens would get an order for six switches and SEL would get an order for four switches. But here is the part that will blow your mind. Siemens would be required to provide their complete specifications to SEL, and SEL would then manufacture the four switches built to Siemens specifications. That means all of Siemens' proprietary information would have to be shared with SEL, their competitor.

The primary purpose of this bizarre arrangement was to ensure that both companies could survive and prosper to compete another day. It also brought about a strange relationship both between competitors and between the companies and the government which owned the Bundespost. This technology sharing arrangement meant that the Bundespost would only have one switch type to maintain and stock parts. That lowered both training and parts costs for the Bundespost. Finally, it created two competitive parts sources.

As an American business person, this arrangement has always been hard to wrap my head around.

Government Business Partnerships

Another thing that came as a huge surprise was the close relationships between the ITT subsidiaries and the government in their home countries. The consequences of those relationships were sometimes incredibly complex and far-reaching. In the US, the relationship between companies and the government is somewhat contentious. Of course, there are tax and incentive deals made to bring a manufacturing facility to a state for example, but still, this is minor by comparison.

As an example; BTM was Belgium's: largest manufacturer, largest employer, largest exporter, and largest tax payer. The executives at BTM had deep personal relationships with the Royal Family in Belgium. Many were, in fact, part of the royal bloodline, or at the least, more "aristocrats" than managers.

ITT was continually attempting to get the various subsidiaries to act more like they were part of the same company, to cooperate and collaborate on the development of the System/12 switching product line for example. More on this later. Whenever ITT management tried to push BTM to work more closely with SEL and others, rumors of "nationalization" would suddenly start circulating. As a result, ITT would have to back down. If you think logically, these European subsidiaries should have been merged into a single company as far back as the 1920s, but national borders and country politics prevented this. Ultimately, repeated government intervention prevented ITT from competing as it could and should have. That, of course, goes back to my earlier assessment of why Araskog had no choice but to divest many of these underperforming assets.

Like the United States, European governments track everything. Unlike the US, they actively manage the outcomes. Their balance of payments was a great concern as it is critical to the survival of their small country-by-country economies. As a result, government involvement affected many business decisions. All of this was before the creation of the Euro Zone and the European Union. That has been an unsuccessfully, in my opinion, attempt to create a "United States of Europe." Judging by the current chaos in the Euro Zone and the Union, it appears that these countries are no longer doing as good a job managing all of these factors.

Executive Lunches

The way European executives did lunch was yet another shock. Remember this was the executives and not for most line managers. I first ran into this while I was working at NBI. I saw it repeatedly at ITT, but to a lesser extent as an independent consultant. Morning meetings seldom started before 9 a.m., and they would break for coffee (or tea) and sweets at 10:30. These breaks were much more casual than their American equivalent. Lasting from 30 to 45 minutes, these were social events where people would stand around and chat about anything but the subject of the meeting at hand. In America, coffee and a treat are common at meetings, but the meeting would start earlier and continue almost immediately after a 15-minute break.

At lunch, which was usually at either 12 or 12:30, everyone would adjourn to the executive dining room. That was typically two rooms. The first would be a bar, and everyone would stand around and chat while they consumed a minimum of two hard liquor drinks. In this relaxed atmosphere, the talk would be about golf or some other non-business topic. After 30 or 40 minutes, with two drinks on an empty stomach, everybody would be thoroughly relaxed. We would then proceed into the actual dining room. Lunches were invariably a very nice spread accompanied by at least two different wines, with a desert drink capping off the meal.

How anybody got anything done after lunch is beyond me. I could barely stay awake. In most cases, nothing would get done until evening which was yet another round of drinking and eating at a nice restaurant. It was at the evening meal when deals got done. I came to believe that many of the executives were barely functioning alcoholics.

A Flat World

The ITT subsidiaries were called "Units." The choice of this designation was quite telling. Virtually every organization you deal with is some form of hierarchy: families, schools, churches, businesses, etc. ITT was not. They had somehow managed to set up a flat management structure. A lot of this had to do with the international nature of the conglomerate, but most importantly, as I discussed above, ITT management had very limited control over their subsidiaries. As long as BTM, for example, came even close to their performance numbers, there was nothing ITT could say or do. The Units functioned more as equals than subsidiaries.

It took me six months to figure out how to get work done inside this crazy flat world, and even longer to understand the scope of the challenges I faced. Under normal circumstances, given my level/title/range of responsibilities, if I told the president of a subsidiary that he had to do something related to product service/support, I would have the authority to back it up. That was not the case in ITT. They would ask me to one of their liquid lunches, smile and act very cooperative; we would discuss whatever I was requesting, and I never got any pushback. Once I was out the door, it was business as usual. Great eating, excellent liquor, friendly conversations, but they never did what I asked them or much of anything else as far as I could tell. I discovered that the executives in most of these units, aside from being aristocrats and functioning alcoholics, were typically more figureheads than managers. They weren't expected to do much aside from drinking and socializing. They liked my visits because it gave them an excuse to have a liquid lunch, and it was probably a line item in their monthly management reports. For them, it was a total win.

What I finally learned was that to get anything done, I had just to do it. I wouldn't say "you need to do this," I would say "I will send a couple of my team over to work with you and set this up." They would happily cooperate, as long as it was on my budget. Of course, once my people left, there was little likelihood that the project or program would move forward. It would atrophy and soon disappear. Back home, we joked that it was like punching a marshmallow.

— ■ —

There were other surprises. One was the open collaboration between
339

competitors, or maybe I should say, potential competitors. On one trip to Austria, they showed me a very nice Intel 386 based PBX that they were getting ready to announce. It was targeted at small to mid-sized companies. If I recall, it could handle up to 12 incoming lines. It was nicely packaged and priced. Switzerland was my next stop, and after they had completed their briefing I walked to the executive dining room with the CEO. We talked about business in general. I observed that the Swiss company did not offer a PBX; they concentrated heavily on various types of radio equipment. I suggested that he might want to look into the new Austrian PBX as a logical addition to his product line. He said that they were not interested in that line of goods. I naturally asked why not? There are many small companies in Switzerland, and the product seemed an ideal fit. He replied that a different (non-ITT) company sold PBX equipment in Switzerland. So I said suggested that the Austrian PBX would be a good entry into that market. He repeated that Company X sold PBXs. I was obviously confused, so he explained. He told me that if we started selling PBXs, then Company X would start selling radios, and they would have a competitive war. Things were very comfortable as they were.

His response caught me completely off guard. This kind of competitive collaboration is illegal in the US. I immediately switched subjects. You need to understand that when you are an American, American laws apply to you no matter where you are in the world and no matter what the local customs are, or what local laws permit. While it may be entirely legal for the Swiss company to collaborate with their competitor in this way, in fact, I don't know if it is legal, it remains illegal for me as an American business executive to be involved in any way.

— ∎ —

In many parts of the world, there are both official and unofficial procedures that amount to payoffs, bribery, or whatever you wish to call it. All of these are, of course, illegal in America. If an American businessman is caught making any payoff, no matter what local laws and customs might be, that businessman will go to jail. That is not to say that it doesn't happen, but woe unto the individual and company that gets caught. Because it is acceptable in so many situations and locations, this prohibition can make it tough for American businesses to compete. I am not saying it shouldn't be that way as it does preserve the integrity of our businesses and our government.

The customer would sometimes play quasi-legal games on the financing side. In one example where I was not personally involved, ITT could not sell

340

switches to the PTT in India because the Indian government wanted to tie the purchase and financing of jet fighters into the deal for telephone switches. Ultimately, a French company sold them the switches and the planes.

Inter-Country Battles

I discovered that in many ways, the various European countries were still fighting WWII. That was in addition to the company/government power struggle that I discussed above. The System/12 plan required ITT Units in all of these countries to come together and cooperate toward a standard product line. Various pieces of the system were apportioned out to different units. Because those Units that had already developed digital switches had been responsible for the entire system, and they had carried the whole development cost, this new structure meant that they now had to hand over critical parts of their systems to other units and other countries for development and testing. That didn't sit well with any of the units, but it is especially contentious when it came to Germany, France, and Belgium. There was also lots of resistance to the idea of having ITT Programming, a new US-based operation, having overall management responsibility.

That inter-unit friction was evident in virtually every System/12 meeting I attended. That added to the difficulty I had getting the Units to do anything that I asked them to do.

My later work as a consultant involved a lot of work in Europe. I saw considerable improvement in the inter-country cooperation, particularly after the Euro Zone was created.

Digital Switches

Digital telephone switches began coming to the market by the early 1980s. All of the phone switches before that were huge electro-mechanical monsters. As you dialed a phone number, the rotor on the handset would create a set of electrical pulses equivalent to the number dialed. If you dialed a three, it would produce three pulses for example. Each of these pulses would cause a rotary relay to move or "step" one position. The next number you dialed would cause the next "stepper-relay" to move the corresponding number of steps. In this way, as you dialed the number, you were sending the signals that created the electrical connection for the voice circuit. With digital switches, tones replaced the dial pulses generated by the handset.

A lot of these stepper-relay switching devices were manufactured back in the

1930s. Interestingly, as digital switches displaced these switches, many of the old machines from North American and Europe were shipped to Africa and installed to live for many more useful years. As antiquated as these switches were, they were a huge leap forward for an area where, before that, there was no telephone service. Using these recycled switches kept the cost down, and in these markets, the economies were so bad that any phone service had to be close to free.

ITT had introduced a couple of digital systems by 1982. One was from SEL and one from the Spanish subsidiary if I remember correctly. Additional digital switches were under development in other subsidiaries. These systems were all developed independently and were not architecturally or operating system compatible in any way.

Independent of these European development activities, ITT's Advanced Technology Center in Connecticut, had invented a novel distributed switching system technology based on a massive number of Intel 086 microprocessors, each capable of switching several lines. By 1984 they were using either a 286 or for more lines a 386. To understand this distributed switching technology, think of a tree. This technology was located out at the ends of the branches so that most switching took place without calling on central resources. It was therefore very efficient and very scalable.

– ■ –

At about this time, Araskog decided that he wanted to replicate the IBM S/360 vision of a common physical architecture as well as a common layered operating system across an entire range of digital switches. The name given this product line was the System/12. His intention was to incorporate the ATC's microprocessor-based distributed switching technology with a yet to be developed Operating System.

I think that, at least in part, this strategy came from Araskog's personal experience as Marketing Director for Honeywell from 1960 to 1966. He witnessed the introduction of the IBM System/360 and saw firsthand how it revolutionized the computer industry and propelled IBM to the position of industry leader. I believe he envisioned the System/12 product line engendering a similar revolution and benefit for ITT. Like IBM, Araskog bet the company on his vision. Unlike IBM, he failed.

The concept may have been good; the strategy was fatally flawed. There were several problems. First, various ITT subsidiaries had already developed two digital switches and were working on others. All were completely incompatible from both an architecture and operating system standpoint. None of these systems used the technology developed by the ATC. ITT should have written off these first generation digital switches, and started from scratch. They could have continued to sell the 1st generation switches while they began with a clean slate to develop a 2nd generation family of switches.

They chose a different approach. Unfortunately, either Araskog, or someone else, convinced him that it was possible to retrofit these existing switches with a common architecture, OS, and overlay the existing hardware with the ATC's new technology. This approach was neither reasonable nor logical. It was doomed to fail no matter how much money you threw at the problem, and ITT threw a lot.

The second problem was the endless inter-company and inter-country politics. Because of this, headquarters could exert only limited pressure on the subsidiaries, and smashing this atom would take far more pressure than ITT could exert.

Enter ITT Programming

The first critical step in Araskog's plan was to design an architecture for the Operating System. That was to be followed by actually developing the OS. Unfortunately, ITT had no significant software capabilities. Individual Units had developed some software, but there was no organization-wide software development organization. ITT lacked any significant software expertise, and there were no development standards. They had never developed any sizable software system, and they had never conducted a cross-company development effort. They were decades behind the state-of-the-art for the software industry. They were not even close to where IBM had been when it initiated the S/360 OS development process 20 years earlier. Araskog's solution was to establish ITT Programming and raid IBM's software centers for expertise.

ITT Programming was part of their Advanced Technology Center. The ATC was considered the equivalent of ITT's Bell Labs. A new EVP was recruited from IBM to run ITT Programming. His charter was to develop a "Programming Center of Excellence" within the ATC. That Center would have overall responsibility for the development of the OS for the System/12.

The Programming Center had architecture design responsibility and overall management responsibility. However, the bulk of the actual programming was not done by the Programming Center; that was to be parceled out to software people inside the individual subsidiaries. That required that the subsidiaries work in close collaboration to develop the massive switching system OS. It was another exercise in matrix management, where resources scattered across many different organizations in the various countries had to function as a single team. Unfortunately, there was no precedent for this, and these organizations and the people were loath to cooperate with each other, but even more resistant to having ITT Programming run things.

Just to add one more layer of complexity to the matrix, the ATC, not ITT Programming, had overall responsibility for integrating their microprocessor switching technology into new as well as the existing switches. While ITT Programming was part of the ATC, there was a lot of resentment within the ATC; they saw the Programming group as "new kids." Their work had traditionally tended toward theoretical rather than applied research. They disliked having a new organization with zero knowledge of the company or the switching business, suddenly holding all the power and a seemingly endless budget.

Developing a Programming Center of Excellence from scratch, while simultaneously developing an overall switching system architecture, was a herculean challenge. Coming primarily from IBM, none of the ITT Programming staff had any switching expertise. Furthermore, the plan required that they retrofit this yet to be developed architecture into two existing switches while altering their physical design to incorporate the new distributed switching technology. Even if you have no systems knowledge, you can see the fallacy of this approach. Those with a deeper understanding of the task will tell you it was simply impossible.

I have no idea who was talking with Araskog or if he was just refusing to hear. But for whatever reason, there was a major, and inexplicable disconnect between their concept/goal, and reality on the ground.

No Service Company

My position was Global Director of Product Support Technology inside of the ITT Programming Center at the ATC. Specifically, I was hired to design and implement a support architecture as a subset of the overall System/12 architecture. At that point, the top level architecture did not exist. At the same time, I needed to make this program fit within the operating structure of the various ITT Units as well as the existing procedures of the PTTs.

Remember that all switches before the introduction of digital switches were maintained by the PTT staff. ITT's only role had been to provide parts when ordered. The second significant technology market for ITT was military systems, primarily radar and radio equipment. Here too, ITT built the machines and turned them over to the military. Once again, their only responsibility was to provide parts when ordered. As a result, ITT was a 60-year old technology company that had no service operation. Individual subsidiary companies had service activities for their smaller product lines, but there was no cross-company or cross-country service operation and most significantly, absolutely no service function or organization for their telephone switching businesses that made up the bulk of their technology sales.

The introduction of digital switches required that I dramatically alter the way the PTTs serviced the switches. Specifically, they had to take on the responsibility of maintaining the software and coordinating with the ITT software developers to manage problems. There was a very real possibility that local PTT service staff could alter software to fix problems or add features. That could create an unmanageable environment where every switch had "custom" alterations that were incompatible with centrally generated software patches.

The PTT's were entirely hardware oriented and predominately unionized government employees. That meant that they were unfamiliar with software management procedures, and it also meant that they were resistant to change. In the best of circumstances, they were fearful of losing any part of their responsibility. They would need extensive training and new tools to work on the systems and to interface with ITT. They also needed some new managers who understood what was coming. Until I joined the project, no one had considered any of these challenges. I was standing between two organizations that had zero experience or expertise regarding software service.

Introducing digital switches required that both ITT and the PTTs leap from the dark ages to the bleeding edge of the service business. Both organizations would have to stand up state of the art service operations capable of smoothly interfacing with each other and maintaining new and therefore unstable systems at the 99.999% reliability level. That was a gargantuan challenge that had taken IBM years if not decades to understand and master. ITT, as well as the PTTs, had to have it designed and implemented from scratch, flawlessly the first time.

Coming from IBM where equipment service was at the core of their business, I found it very strange to be in a technology company with no service

345

operation, no service history, and not even a sense of service. Despite the fact that most of the Programming staff came from IBM, very few had any service knowledge. In this environment, I found it incredibly difficult to create a sense of urgency even inside of the ITT Programming Center itself. In all fairness, the Programming Center staff were overwhelmed just trying to get their arms around the architecture design challenges. Most saw service as a future problem. Without management support within my organization, it was impossible to get cooperation from management in the subsidiaries or the PTTs.

My Journey to ITT

I was surprised when I got a call from a headhunter looking to fill a position in ITT's Programming Center. We talked a bit about my background, and the position and it sounded quite exciting and challenging. Of course, at that point, I didn't know any of what I have described above. He had me forward my resume and said he would get back to me.

In truth, I didn't expect much to come of the inquiry. I had been contacted by headhunters before, and their usual approach is "do you know somebody who ___ (fill in the blank)." While they would always accept recommendations, I knew that in fact, they wanted to know if I was interested in the position. Most of the time I wasn't. The ITT search approach was different. The headhunter didn't use the standard oblique approach; he specifically asked if I was interested.

I was aware of ITT of course, but I had no knowledge of the Programming Center. I didn't even know anyone who worked for ITT. I had no contacts and no idea who had given my name to the headhunter. I learned later it was someone familiar with my work on the Goshawk Project.

The job was the Global Director of Product Support Technology responsible for ITT's global service operation. He faxed me a job description. Organizationally the position was only four levels down from the CEO. I liked the power that a position at that level should have, but I did not know how little real power it actually carried. However, one item on the job description caught my eye. The job required a Ph.D. At that time, I didn't even have a Bachelor's degree. I called the headhunter back, and he said he was aware of this but thought he could work around the issue. I figured what the heck, might as well see what comes of it.

A few days later he called and asked me to fly to New York for an interview

346

and testing. The interview was routine, but the testing was something I had never experienced. I was asked to spend a morning taking the standard psychological tests. You know the ones that asked questions like: would you rather die from a gunshot or a knife wound. The answer was neither, but that was not an available option. These tests were not all that unusual. However, spending nearly 4 hours with an actual psychiatrist that afternoon was extraordinary. It was an interesting way to spend the day. I don't remember all of it, but it appeared that they were trying to get a sense of how I would deal with some of the strange things that can fall into your lap as you travel around the world. Since I was to be a Director, I would be working mainly with Division heads and CEOs from subsidiary companies. I learned later that this level of testing was standard practice for executive level positions at ITT.

Apparently, I passed because they asked me to travel out to Connecticut for additional interviews. Those went well, and I was offered the position a week or so later after I was back in Boulder.

Trial and Error

I was the head of a good-sized organization with two levels of management under me. Unfortunately, there was no indication of the goals or expectations for ITT Programming or my group. At that point, I was completely unaware of any of the issues I described above. In truth, I was not able to completely understand the situation or my job until well after I left ITT.

There was a lot of travel starting from day one. While ITT Programming was, at least in theory, the headquarters for the entire program, we all worked remotely at the "operational" headquarters located at the BTM facility outside of Brussels, Belgium. There were critical meetings every other week, sometimes weekly, and so I would commute to Brussels at least twice a month. The Brussels meetings usually lasted a couple of days. I would use these trips to travel to other countries to visit the "Units." My goal was to understand the Units and PTTs.

On these trips, I would meet with the CEOs and senior managers of the various ITT subsidiaries. They would give me presentations on their businesses; products, markets, competitors, and service operations. These were usually "canned" presentations of course, but collectively, they gave me an excellent understanding of ITT's European market and services on a country by country basis. Of course, that was the purpose of the trips.

Too Fast and Poorly Managed

ITT Programming grew far too quickly, and it was very poorly managed. ITT Programming exploded from nothing to about 800 people in the span of 12 to 18 months. More than 90% of these people came from outside of ITT, the majority from IBM. Very few, and I include myself, understood what ITT was trying to accomplish or what the challenges were. I certainly didn't know when I first joined, and it took me more than six months to even begin to understand what they needed me to do. My boss had no idea.

A part of this reflected the newness of the ITT Programming organization as well as Araskog's apparent belief that you could solve any problem if you threw enough money at it. Our group appeared to have an unlimited budget and our senior management was completely undisciplined. In truth I never got a sense that the mission was all that important, or even understood; it was more about the appearance of productive work, and the "fun" of the project. No one ever pushed back on any proposal or the budgets I submitted. No one ever questioned why I was making a trip or who I was planning to see. Money was always available. In some ways, it felt like management's sole objective was to ride this ship as far and as high as it would go.

There was zero orientation. No one ever went so far as defining ITT Programming's roll in the System/12 strategy. In fact, I don't recall anyone ever really talking about the System at any point. It was just start attending meetings and see if you can do anything. Not specifically about service, just anything I honestly don't know if anyone above me had a clue as to what our goal was. Certainly no one below me did. It was a hot mess. I came on board and immediately started flying off to attend meetings. Of course, it was important to meet the players and to get involved, but without any orientation or even discussion of objectives, I had no idea which team I was on or where the goal posts were. There was no way to take a stand or set a direction as I was in the midst of this amorphous blob made up of small groups from 10 or 12 Units. It was all about what appeared to be, and in fact was, senseless motion. I didn't fully understand what ITT Programming's actual mission was until several years after I had left the company and had the benefit of looking back without the day to day mania going on around me.

There were ample opportunities to integrate and focus the group, but they were squandered. They held frequent and very expensive senior management conferences. The first I attended was on the island of Madeira off the coast of

Africa. It was just a couple of months after I joined. All of the VPs, Directors, and 2nd level managers from ITT Programming plus the various Unit teams we worked with were in attendance; there were at least 200 people.

They threw a lot of money at these events. Can you imagine the cost of flying all of these people to an island resort off the coast of Africa? A part of the goal was to get the players from all the Units, the ATC, and ITT Programming together to develop relationships that might lead to better cooperation across the project. In that sense, these meetings were a success. But there was so much more that could have and should have been accomplished.

The vast majority of us had less than a year with the company. It was the perfect opportunity to set the direction, lay out goals and milestones, but mostly to clarify any confusion that existed. Unfortunately, it was all about R&R. I flew to Lisbon and then to Madeira, and stayed in a 5-star Sheraton for 4 or 5 days. There were a few meetings, just enough to qualify the event as a business meeting, but most of the time we spent at the pool, touring the island, shopping in the village, or drinking port wine. A very enjoyable week, but not very productive. I don't recall a single presentation or discussion addressing the overall mission, strategy, or goals. There were not even any events or exercises to encourage cross-organization cooperation.

— ■ —

I do remember the airplane trip into Madeira. For the leg from Lisbon to Madeira, I was on a TAP (Transport Air Portugal) Boeing 727. The flight reminded me of one of those old black and white movie scenes of a bus in Morocco or someplace. The standard overhead bins were replaced with netting so people could get more in …a lot more. Some of the nets were hanging down so low they nearly touched the heads of the passengers. There was everything short of live animals in these bins. There may have even been a few animals, but I never heard one, so I guess not.

Madeira is a big rock sticking up out of the ocean. There aren't any real beaches; it is mostly just steep rocky cliffs or bluffs down to the water. In the case of the Sheraton, the pool was down close to the water, and there was an outdoor elevator that took you a couple of hundred feet from the lawn above to poolside. On the flight in, as we began our letdown over the ocean, I was watching out the window to see where we were going. I finally saw this big rock, but I couldn't see the airport.

As we got closer, I noticed a lot of the passengers were crossing themselves. I didn't think much beyond the fact that Portugal is a Catholic country. Then as we were on our downwind leg flying past the island, I spotted the airport out the window. Pylons supported much of what little there was. The runway appeared to set beside this big rock. It looked incredibly short.

We turned onto the base leg and then onto the final approach. Out the left window, there was nothing but rock, and we were getting closer and closer. Out the right window there was nothing but water; here again, we were getting closer and closer. When we crossed over the end of the runway, the pilot slammed the plane down and instantly applied full reverse thrust as well as maximum brakes. The plane seemed to stand on its nose as it shuddered, groaned, and quickly came to a full stop on the runway. I have never experienced such a brutal stop in all of my flying. We paused for several seconds, sitting still on the runway. Later I realized the pilot was probably saying a prayer. Finally, the pilot used the engines as well as the steering to turn the plane around. As he did, I discovered that my wing was hanging out over the end of the runway. There was nothing but water below. He had used every possible inch of the blacktop to stop the plane. Now I knew why everyone had been crossing themselves. We taxied back up the runway as there were no parallel taxiway along this narrow path.

Fortunately, jets require less runway to take off than to land. If I ever go back to Madeira, I will make sure I take a plane that has a shorter stopping distance than the old 727's. I found out later that for many years, Madeira had been ranked as the third most dangerous airport in the world. I did some research and found that they have added a new piece of runway to the airport. It is still on pylons, but it is almost half again as long.

— ∎ —

On the Madeira trip, as usual, I tried to make my time productive. I took one of my managers for a work assignment at Face, our Unit in Italy. When we returned to Lisbon after we left Madeira, I spent the night at a Sheraton of course. We were supposed to fly to Vienna the next morning. When we reached the airport, we learned that a mechanical problem had grounded the plane. They said that they had to fly in a part and that we would not able to get a flight to Vienna until late that evening.

We went out to the taxi line and asked several drivers if they spoke English. We found one whose English was not too bad, and we hired him for the day. He gave us a personal tour of Lisbon, one that you would never get on a tour bus. We bought our driver lunch, and he took us to his home to show us where and how the "real" people live. At the end of the day, our tab was only about $20. We each gave him $20.

Incidentally, Lisbon is a lot like San Francisco, a deep water port with a massive suspension bridge that looks much like the Golden Gate. Also like San Francisco, they have a lot of earthquakes.

Similarities to the Western Bancorp TIPS Project

I had been at ITT nearly a year when I began to see similarities between ITT's problems and those that Western Bancorp faced a decade earlier.

At Western Bancorp; the individual banks carried different brands and operated as independent organizations. One objective of the TIPS network was to create the appearance, if not the reality of a single organization. In WBC's case, appearance ultimately became a reality. ITT's Units were equally autonomous, and I believe that with vision and proper management, ITT Programming could have brought about a similar appearance of a single monolith programming operation. In retrospect, I believe that the entire ITT Programming management team was as confused about the overall objective as I was. Everyone was focused on the immediate objective, creating an architecture for the System/12 OS. No one was looking at the big picture.

ITT Programming should have implemented: training standards, advanced programming classes, software management practices, and reporting standards. With standardized practices, and by bringing programmers and managers into the Center for training, over time, individual developers, as well as managers from various Units, would have gotten to know each other and lines of communications between Units would have naturally evolved. That might have eventually helped to bring about a unified operation.

In some ways, this related back to General LeMay's problem when he took control of SAC. I believe that standardized training and practices had the potential of providing the same benefits provided by the 1st Combat Evaluation Group and RBS. Unfortunately, at ITT no one was thinking strategically.

I am not suggesting that it would have been easy, maybe not even possible given ITT's country-by-country structure. However, ITT Programming's Charter was to create a "Center of Excellence." Therefore, improving corporate-wide software skills and standardizing practices was clearly within

351

the scope of that Charter. Even if unification were never fully achieved, the potential benefits of building a corporate-wide community of software professionals would have justified the investment.

Unfortunately, I was unable to leverage my experience. As I said above, from the day I walked in the door, I was tossed straight into the fire, and it took months just to figure out what was going on. By the time I recognized the underlying problems and the possibilities presented by the creation of the Programming Center, it was too late. Senior management was invested far too deeply in the current strategy to take a step back and examine possible alternatives. I suspect they had already passed the point of no return by the time I joined ITT. Furthermore, I was too new, and not high enough in the organization to get a hearing concerning a radical new approach. It didn't help that this was way outside of my charter.

In fairness to our senior management, I was not there from the beginning of ITT Programming, and I do not know what was proposed, suggested, or demanded. All that I do know is that ITT Programming came across as a heavy-handed interloper injecting itself into long established relationships. That created resentment and resistance, rather than cooperation and collaboration.

The logical approach would have been to start by developing a few smaller projects where they could have implemented and tested cross-Unit management training and control systems. Instead, they jumped directly into the deep end of the pool. Jack Bergman's quote seemed to apply. "There's never enough time to do it right, but there's always enough time to do it over." In this case, the clock ran out before there was a chance to do it over.

The fun side of traveling

On one trip, I arrived in Zurich relatively late in the evening and just ate and went to bed. The hotel was outside of the city on a hillside. Shortly after sunrise, a loud bell close outside of my window started my day. I looked out. There was a small patio, and a large cow with a huge brass bell was grazing not 10 feet from my window. It was one of those quintessential "Switzerland" moments.

Wakeup call Zurich Switzerland 1985

— ■ —

There were no Sheratons in Milan at that time, so I usually stayed at the Grand Duomo Hotel in the center of Milan. The Grand Duomo was a very nice classic old European hotel. I made several trips to Milan and Rome while I was with ITT. I liked Italy a lot, especially the people. Unfortunately, Rome seemed filthy to me when I first visited. After several trips, I got used to the garbage everywhere and learned to love the city. I never could understand how they could treat this classic city with such disregard.

— ■ —

On one trip to Milan, I was also treated to Rosita con Funghi - rice, and with mushrooms. There is a local mushroom that they cook with rice that is to die for. I also "discovered" Grappa, which is a poor man's liquor. After smashing the grapes, they skim off the "garbage." That includes twigs, seeds, skin, and maybe some leaves. Probably other stuff, but we will ignore that. They made the "trash" into this rather robust and pungent liquor. Grappa is a traditional drink for the working class. It is barely drinkable. It is bitter, you might even say awful, but they put raisins in it overnight to draw off some of the bitterness. Once a sufficient quantity of raisins have met their death, it is not all that bad. Like so many other things, over the years, grappa has become somewhat fashionable, so it now tastes much better; at a higher price of course. I even had Grappa at Hanezawa Gardens in Tokyo one time.

I was in Milan to meet with an executive from our Italian Unit. I had assigned one of my managers Pete (I don't remember his last name) to work with Face for several weeks, and he was just finishing the assignment. We had dinner together, and the Face manager introduced us to Grappa. It didn't taste all that bad, kind of a musty taste but not bitter; the raisins had apparently done their work. As we were leaving Italy, Pete and I stopped by Duty-Free. I had a ritual of spending whatever local currency I had in my pocket as it was too expensive to convert it back to dollars. We both bought a bottle of Grappa as well as a bottle of Amaretto.

Pete told me later about his Grappa experience. He fancied himself to be something of a chef, and when he got home, his wife was at work, so he decided to cook a big celebratory dinner. Somewhere in the midst of the preparation process, Pete decided to have a glass of grappa. He took a big gulp and immediately spit most of it into the sink. He had forgotten that you were supposed to soak it in raisins overnight. He described the taste as what you would think Absorbine Jr. would taste like if you were foolish enough to drink it. For those of you who don't know, Absorbine Jr. is a vile smelling pain relief and anti-fungal rub that people used for athlete's foot. He went into the bathroom and brushed his teeth several times and repeatedly gargled with mouthwash, all to try to get rid of the taste and smell. When his wife got home, Pete gave her a big kiss. He said she pulled back and asked him what in the world that horrible smell was. Grappa took the edge off his romantic evening.

Sharon and I both tried the grappa at a later date. I did soak it in raisins, but maybe not enough. Neither of us liked the taste. Several months later Mom and Dad were visiting, and I told them the story about the grappa. Dad said he would like to try it. It turned out he liked it, so I sent the bottle home with him. I assume he drank it; he never said.

In a funny twist, Sharon and I tried the Amaretto the evening I got home. We both liked Amaretto, but this bottle tasted a bit strange. Neither of us drank more than a couple of swallows. I got a splitting headache, and Sharon got violently sick. We heard later that there was a problem where somebody had mixed antifreeze into a batch of Amaretto. I guess that must have been what we had. It is fortunate that we didn't drink more, several people died from the poison. We poured the bottle down the drain, and I have never touched

Amaretto since. It is funny how just one bad experience can forever kill the desire for some taste. Remember the pineapple pie story from my Air Force days.

— ∎ —

Travel with ITT was certainly different from any company I experienced before or after. All international travel was Business Class. Since I was an ITT corporate executive, a limo would pick me up at home and take me to the airport. In many cases, another waited when I landed. ITT owned Sheraton Hotels, and I was provided suites at their hotels, usually with flowers, fruit, and a bottle of wine in the room when I arrived. Lots of exciting travel, meals, and some incredibly insightful global business experiences. Not what you would call bad duty.

— ∎ —

I collected a lot of airline miles, and so I was able to take Sharon with me on a couple of extended trips to Europe. One trip was for another big meeting similar to the Madeira conference. This one was in The Hague. They had several special events for the wives of the executives. Sharon had a great time touring the city. She particularly enjoyed the flower auction and flower farms. She got to see a lot of the city that I never had a chance to visit. After the meeting, I rented a car, and we drove to Brussels where I spent a couple of days in meetings.

As usual, we stayed at the Sheraton where I always stayed when I was in Brussels. There was a restaurant called Chez Leon that was just off of the Grand Platz which was near the Sheraton. I loved that restaurant and would go there a couple of times whenever I was in Brussels. They had a custom of shouting out the names of their frequent guests, and they, of course, knew me on sight. Whenever I would come in they would call out "Welcome Mr. Griswold." That caught Sharon off guard the first time.

They used old wooden picnic tables like you might find in someone's back yard. Newspapers covered the tables. Chez Leon served the best mussels cooked in a cast iron pot with onions, celery, and cilantro along with other things. I think they were cooked mostly in beer. Along with a pot of mussels came a loaf of French bread and I always ordered Stella Artois which wasn't available in the US at that time. Their menu was small, but I never ventured far from my usual selection as it was so delicious. After we had eaten at Chez Leon a couple of times, Sharon insisted we try some other restaurants.

I also showed Sharon the red light district. Most of northern Europe has a much more open relationship with their ladies of the evening. It can be quite funny, or maybe shocking to our American sensibilities. It was only a block or two from the Sheraton which was near the train station. The buildings were old; they had probably been department stores in some past life. They had big display windows, but at this point, they were not showing the latest fashion; they were presenting the ladies that were available for services.

It was not romantic or sexy in any way. It was kind of sad and seedy. Most of these ladies were approaching, or even well into middle age. They looked like a typical housewife and mother. They would be sitting in chairs up in their windows reading or knitting. Men would walk up and ring the doorbell, and the woman would come talk for a few minutes. After some negotiations, the guy would go in, and the curtains would close. After a bit the man would leave and a few minutes later the curtain would be opened again, waiting for the next customer.

There were dozens of cars driving up and down the street. I suppose most were looking and laughing like we were. It put a whole new meaning to the term "window shopping."

After I had finished my meetings in Brussels, I was on vacation for two weeks. We drove south about 200 miles to Paris. We had to drive the surface streets from the north side of Paris to get to our hotel. I had not driven through that area before. Of course, this was before GPS, and not speaking French it was a bit of a hassle. I suppose today you wouldn't dare drive these streets, and you would have to speak Arabic. It is sad how Paris, and most of Europe, has become.

I was moving forward very slowly as the streets were small and very crowded with both cars and people sharing the same space. We were inching along, and Sharon suddenly started laughing. I was concentrating on not hitting any of the bodies squeezing between cars. She pointed over to the sidewalk where a dozen or more ladies were leaning against doorways and cars. All of them were topless. Apparently, we had stumbled into Paris' red light district. Like I said, the Europeans have a different attitude about prostitution. As the French would say, *"c'est la vie,"* such is life.

We had reservations at a hotel that was a former convent. A coworker had recommended it. He had said it was quaint but comfortable. It was raining when we arrived and we were not able to park very close to the hotel, so we had to drag our suitcases some distance in the rain. That is not a good way to start a vacation or hotel stay. There were no elevators or busboys in this convent, so when we checked in we had to climb several flights of stone stairs that were less than 2 feet wide. Sharon always packed her suitcases very full, and it was hard to get them up the stairs because there wasn't room to carry them beside you, and of course, you could not drag them.

When we got to our room it was pretty bleak; quaint, certainly, comfortable, hardly! There was an old metal framed bed with an ancient mattress. It had a great dip in the middle; we would be sleeping very close. We sat on the bed; an old army blanket was the only cover. Neither of us said a word for several minutes. Then almost simultaneously we both asked if the other was happy with the place. The answer was a universal NO!

We grabbed our bags and schlepped them back down to the lobby and told them we were not going to stay. For some reason, there were people lined up trying to get in, so they were happy to return our fees. We found our way to the Le Grand Hotel and checked in. Not quaint, but very comfortable. It was much more expensive, but our ten-minute stay at the convent was all we needed to have a great story to tell. It is funny how memories are made.

We spent several days in Paris enjoying all the tourist things, Notre Dame, Versailles, the Champs Elysees, the Eiffel Tower, the Louvre, the Folies Bergère, several nice dinners, and a boat ride on the Seine. I had ITT associates in Paris, and they took us to dinner at a small basement restaurant that no tourist would ever find. It was one of those local French things. The food was excellent, but what made it special was wandering through the catacombs that ran under an ordinary block of old French houses. Of course, the wine helped.

— ■ —

After Paris, we drove southeast across "mustard country" to Lake Geneva in Switzerland. It was a full day's drive through gorgeous Dijon scenery. We got hungry when we were out in the middle of nowhere. It was early afternoon when we got off the freeway and found a little village about 10 kilometers from the highway. We drove through town which was about two blocks long and came back to the only hotel in the village. The town had closed for an afternoon break, but the bar at the hotel was doing a good business.

We were greeted warmly. Like most Europeans, the locals had taken English in school, but in a small village well off the beaten path, they seldom had an

357

opportunity to speak the language. They were pleased to have us there so they could practice. We drank a glass or two of wine and asked if there was any possibility to get something to eat as we drove on. They asked what we wanted, and we said that a couple ham and cheese sandwiches, a bottle of water, a bottle of wine, and something sweet would be great. Of course, this was all negotiated using "pidgin English." They made up a sack lunch for us. We paid and left. As we were driving back to the freeway, Sharon opened the bag to see what we had. For dessert, we had two lovely chocolate tortes which turned out to be superb. Sharon laughed when she opened the first sandwich. I looked over and saw that it consisted two thick slices of French bread with a slice of brie cheese about an inch thick. We both knew that the other would be the same, but with a thick slice of ham. We got what we asked for, a ham and a cheese sandwich. They were delicious.

We stayed at the Beau-Rivage hotel in Nyon on Lake Geneva. The name means "beautiful river," but of course, we were on the lakefront, not a river. I guess water is water. It is a chain of very nice hotels, so the name had nothing to do with our location. Over the next few days we explored Lausanne and Montreux, then we drove over the mountain to Interlaken. Interlaken was cold, and there was actual a bit of snow falling. It was off season, and the hotel was empty. They gave us a room that was very fancy. The porcelain fixtures were all made to look like lions. I took pictures, but unfortunately, over the years, the images have been lost. From Interlaken, we drove to Zurich and spent a few days before we flew home.

— ■ —

On another trip, I was able to take Sharon to Vienna, Austria where we stayed for several days. I had several meetings, and I took some vacation time. Our son Brian had a college friend in Vienna and his friend kindly acted as our tour guide while we were there. We did all of the tourist things including the Schönbrunn Palace, which I like better than Versailles. We saw the Royal Lipizzaner Stallions and the opera; the Marriage of Figaro. I am not a big opera fan, but it was fun to see such a classic performed by one of the best opera companies in the world. We also met his family and had dinner with them.

On the weekend, we went to Kittsee, a town near the Hungarian border. Kittsee is on the Danube river, and so fish was naturally the specialty at the restaurant where we had lunch. I don't know what it was, but it was probably 2-feet long. The Müllers had friends who owned a local winery, so we got a private tour. We also went to the Hungarian border. The Berlin Wall was still standing, but much of the Iron Curtain was disappearing at this point, and we were able to walk across the frontier and take pictures of the empty guard towers as well as the fence that marked the border.

Wine tasting Austria 1985

From Vienna, we drove to Venice Italy. It was a beautiful drive. I remember one stretch of road starting at Tarvisio on the Italian border and running down to Trasaghis, Italy. The road followed a canyon through the mountains. It was new at that time; the canyon was steep and very winding. The road was a marvel. They had drilled something like 17 tunnels through the ridges. In many places, you would go from a tunnel straight onto a bridge then back into a tunnel. Some of these tunnels were several kilometers long. That went on for miles and miles. Unfortunately, it was almost impossible to take any pictures as there was no place to pull off and the bridges were all relatively short, so there was no time. Just in and out down the canyon.

Venice was a fun place for a few days. I have never been a big fan of "tourist towns," those places that survive mainly on the tourist trade. They usually come to resent the very business that feeds them. In one of those ironic twists of fate, I have wound up living in tourist towns more than once in my life: Vail, Colorado, Maui, Hawaii, and now in Las Vegas, actually Henderson, but

Henderson is just a bedroom community for Las Vegas which is the ultimate tourist town.

We stayed in a hotel right off of St. Marks Plaza and did all of the traditional tourist things. Several gondola rides, dinners out, everything. We particularly enjoyed boat trips to Murano and Burano to see the crafts and glass blowing. We had a lot of fun, but for me, the constant tourist traps got to be a bit much after just a few days. From there, we drove to the airport in Milan and flew home.

I always enjoyed traveling with Sharon and sharing these adventures whenever I could. I teased her because she always over packed. She did improve the more we traveled. Sharon was willing to take detours and discover the unexpected. However, she was always hesitant to try new dishes. I would always try something that seemed different or interesting. I remember once when we went to dinner in The Hague. We chose a restaurant that specialized in "game." There was venison, rabbit, wild boar, and many other types of meat that you don't ordinarily find in restaurants. It was a bit challenging because no one spoke any English. Using hand signals and sounds we were able to figure out most of the menu. I ordered sweetbreads and Sharon ordered rabbit. The meals were delicious, but as usual, when Sharon tried my selection, she immediately wanted to swap plates. That happened so many times over the years. We used to laugh because she never changed. She would always order conservatively and then wish she had been more aggressive in her choice.

— ∎ —

I will always remember the best meal I have ever had in my life. I was on a different trip from The Hague to Antwerp. I was traveling alone as usual, and I chose to drive because I had a weekend to burn between meetings. I have always preferred to go by ground whenever I had the time. You really can't see much or get to know people when you hop from airport to airport.

I left The Hague Friday afternoon, and I drove along A44 on the North Sea coast. I stopped at a hotel called the Grand Hotel Amrath Kurhaus. I didn't have any reservations; I just picked a hotel that looked nice. Winter is definitely not tourist season on the North Sea coast, so space is always available. It gets dark very early in December, and this was a cold winter weekend. When I arrived at the dining room, I was the only person there. The waiter came, and I ordered a single malt scotch, neat, of course, just the way

God made it. No ice or anything to distort the perfect taste of my favorite drink. I looked at the menu and couldn't read a word of it. Fortunately, the waiter spoke decent English. I closed the menu, and I asked him to have the chef prepare whatever he thought I would like.

Kurhaus Hotel 1985 Scheveningen The Nederlands

One of the things I have always enjoyed is the local foods. I do have a couple of rules. I won't eat anything that comes to the table alive, and I won't eat dog. These rules are not a real issue in Europe, but they do impact your dining in Asia. When I travel on business, invariably my hosts want to treat me to the local specialty. Most are decent, some are great, but some are undeniably terrible. Mud-slugs in Shanghai falls in the terrible category. A small snail soaked in a bad liquor overnight and then served, grit and all. Not a treat.

I was served an incredible meal at the Amrath Kurhaus. There were many courses, and every one was phenomenal. Throughout the entire meal, I was the only patron. At the end of the dinner, the chef came out and asked if I enjoyed his creations. I told him I had enjoyed them greatly. I ordered another scotch and one for him. We enjoyed a drink, and he told me a bit about himself and where he was training, which was in Paris. I opined that as a master chef, he probably found menus quite confining. He said that he loved it when a patron made the request that I made. It usually happened in the summer when they were busy, so he didn't have the time to be as creative.

Tonight was special because he could focus entirely on having fun and the challenge of trying to guess what would make me happy. He said that most of the dishes he had prepared were not on the menu. I thanked him, paid my tab, which was surprisingly affordable, and said good night. I have done this "make what you think I will like" a few times in my life and have always enjoyed the result. That said, none were ever as phenomenal as that feast.

— ■ —

I almost always traveled alone. Sometimes I would bring people with me, but then I would be leading them or introducing them to others. I never really thought about it at the time, but for me, I was more comfortable on my own. I suppose that is a reflection of my "loner" mentality. I found most travelers had a number of "rules" about what they would or would not do, or eat. Maybe they wanted to drink or chase women, neither of which held my interest. It just seemed to me that most people have appalling travel skills; traveling alone was so much easier.

With both Sharon and later Kellie, travel is easy. I think it came down to trust. Both knew that I know my way around almost anywhere I could take either of them. Since I had a pretty good idea of what either would and would not enjoy, they could just relax and go along with whatever I wanted to do.

— ■ —

When I traveled in Europe, it seemed people often thought I was a local. Maybe it was because I was alone and they were accustomed to seeing Americans traveling in groups. Maybe it was that I was just so relaxed that they assumed I was from wherever I happened to be. I don't know how many times people have asked for directions in a city where I had never been before, often in a language that I could not understand.

I was in Madrid one time while I was with ITT. I had some time, and I decided to check out a local department store. I was just looking around, seeing what was in the stores, and the prices. I hate to shop, but I learned over the years that you could get a good sense of the people if you visit the places the locals shop and eat. I was wearing a Dutch fisherman's cap that I had picked up in Amsterdam. A lady came up to me and started asking where I got my cap. She began in Spanish and I knew what she was asking, but gave her a blank stare in response. I wanted to see where she went with this. Europeans often speak many languages. It is partly their education system, but primarily because of the proximity to many different countries. She switched to

362

Portuguese, which I knew was Portuguese, but could not understand. From there she went to French, then German, and finally English. When she hit English, I smiled and explained that I was an American, which was the same as saying I didn't speak anything but English. She told me she thought I was a local. I told her that I had purchased the cap in Amsterdam on a recent visit. She was looking for one for her husband. We chatted a bit before she left.

Of course, I never had any problem being mistaken as local when I was in Asia. But American businessmen traveling alone in Asia seemed to be even rarer. I remember one time on a train from the Osaka airport to Kyoto. That was later when I was working with Verisign. I was alone as usual, and there was a group of 6 or 7 Americans in the same car. They were all chatting amongst themselves, completely ignoring everyone else on the train. They were far too loud and interfering with other people's space, something you should never do on a Japanese train, or anywhere in Japan. It brings out the "ugly American" feeling in locals as well as other travelers.

I didn't pay any attention to the details, but it was evident they were all from the same company and that at least the majority of them had never been to Japan before. One was sitting across the aisle from me and at some point, he introduced himself. We chatted for a few minutes, and he told me how excited he was to visit Japan. Of course, he asked me if this was my first trip and I said no, I was here at least once a month. I commented that he had quite a gaggle of folks with him and asked why so many. I don't remember his exact answer; it was some meeting; the kind I would have attended alone. He asked me where my team was and I told him that I always traveled alone. He reacted like I was a space alien. He brought his whole group over to meet this strange creature who would dare go out of his home country all by himself. I thought it was funny.

I never did figure out why so many American businessmen and women travel in groups when they go internationally, but travel single when they travel domestically. I don't know if it is fear; are they just afraid to be alone? Maybe their companies don't trust them to function on their own, but then why would they trust them domestically. I have seen this all over the world. It makes me think of an American cocoon. These clusters tend to focus inward toward their own group. I can't help but feel that this alienated their customers. In any case, they clearly missed the opportunity to learn about the people and culture. It was a double failure in my mind. It is a strange phenomenon that I never was able to unravel.

On one trip to Japan, I visited Sanyo-Haier in Osaka. I was with Koji Sasaki, but I don't remember the reason for our visit. When we arrived, they sat us in a very nice executive reception area waiting to meet the CEO. There were some gorgeous art pieces, paintings, and sculptures decorating the room. We sat there for some time, and I kept looking at one painting of a Paris street scene that was clearly a fake. I finally asked Koji very quietly if he could tell me why they would hang an obviously fake painting amongst all the other pieces. He was taken aback and asked me why I thought it was fake. I pointed out that the drives were on the right side of the cars. They drive on the right side in Japan, but not in Paris. He realized it was a fake when I pointed this out, but because everyone in Japan is accustomed to right-hand drive, it appeared natural to him.

– ∎ –

As I write this in 2016, "gender identity" has become the latest and greatest "Politically Correct" issue of the day. There is an ongoing debate about bathroom and locker room issues, with neither sex wanting to admit these gender changing or indeterminate gender individuals.

That may have been brought on in part because of Bruce Jenner, the one-time Olympic Gold Medalist (1976 men's decathlon). Later he was part of the TV personality clan named the Kardashians. He then decided to become Caitlyn Jenner, complete with all the necessary drugs and surgeries. For reasons that are beyond my interest or understanding, this has become a major news story over the past two years.

Incidentally, I met Bruce Jenner back in 1978 when he was a popular speaker following his gold medal Olympic performance. I was given an Outstanding Achievement Award by the DP Division, for my work on the TIPS network. It appeared that I was the only person in the FE Division ever to be given this award, and the FED did not know what to do with me. They decided to send my wife and me as special guests to the Field Engineering Means Service Award Conference that was held in Phoenix that year. They treated us like royalty, and the evening after his speech we had dinner with Bruce and several FE executives.

– ∎ –

Back to my ITT experience. One Monday morning Peter Barton, one of the managers reporting to me came into my office laughing and said that I was not going to believe what had happened. It seemed that one of our programming staff came to work Monday morning in a dress and announced to the world that from this day forward, he was a woman. I think his given name was Alex, but he was now to be called Alexa. Alexa had brought work to a complete stop. There were all kinds of discussions going on as to why, when, did you know, did you suspect, etc., etc. The most immediate problem was which bathroom Alexa was to use. The guys were saying no way, and I think Alexa was fearful of going into the men's room, maybe with some justification, as the American public was not anywhere close to being ready to accept even homosexuality, let alone gender changes. Of course, the women were equally as adamant that Alexa was not to be allowed in their bathroom.

I called HR and gave them a heads up and ask for immediate assistance. We did a quick huddle and located a bathroom that was a bit out of the way but that we could make Alexa's private bathroom. The bigger problem was how to deal with what we anticipated would be the ongoing strain and possible discrimination that Alexa would undoubtedly face. Ultimately, with Alexa's concurrence, we arranged for a couple of months leave with pay followed by a transfer to a new location. An assignment where Alex would be introduced from the beginning as Alexa and where it would be up to Alexa to maintain her privacy about the entire situation. We felt the 2-month break was appropriate for Alexa to deal with any personal or emotional issues surrounding the case. Of course, the transfer destination was kept secret. All in all, I think it was handled appropriately and quite humanely given we were 25 years ahead of the curve so to speak.

— ■ —

My time at ITT was exciting and challenging. I traveled extensively and collected a ton of frequent flyer miles. I learned a great deal about the telephone switching business as well as doing business in Europe. Despite my best efforts, I never felt like I was making any significant headway toward establishing a logical and sustainable service approach for the System/12. How do you design a service strategy and the necessary technology for a global company that has no service operation and no concept of service as a critical component? Part of the problem was the ongoing conflict between the telephone people and the computer people. However, it was more than just political, there was a fundamental gap between the philosophies that had developed over the years. Amidst all of the architecture battles, there was little room for a voice crying out about service. There were just too many factions all fighting to maintain their turf, and none were willing to look at the greater good or even how to logically approach service. It was a constant struggle, even to gain cooperation within ITT Programming.

I was not the only one struggling with these challenges. In fact, the whole System/12 program was flailing and bleeding money. Rumors began to circulate that ITT was looking to unload the entire switching business. Alcatel, a French company, ultimately acquired the operation including most of the ITT Programming staff. I interviewed with Alcatel, and they offered me the same position along with a relocation to Paris. I decided not to accept this offer for several reasons. First, I could not see any improved opportunity to solve the service problem. Specifically, I did not get the sense that Alcatel had any concept of service either. Their switching business, like ITT's, had never had to build a service operation. Second, I do not speak French, and neither did Sharon or Tracee, our daughter. I love Paris, what is not to love, and I really would have enjoyed a few years living on the Continent, but I had worked enough with the French to know that unless you were fluent in the language, you would quickly get run over in any French company. It would also have been difficult for the family, Tracee in particular, to move into a French speaking school system.

I had been thinking about starting my own company for some time, and this seemed like the opportune time had come to make that move. I put together my Business Plan and started looking for funding.

Small World

It is funny how small the world is. I have flown so much over the years that I ran into the same people over and over again. I would often be stuck at an airport waiting for a connecting flight. I found that I could not sit in any airport anywhere in the world for more than 30 minutes without meeting someone that I knew.

I wondered how this could be until a friend gave me an explanation. He told me I should think of the world population as an upside down wedding cake. The top layer is the biggest, something more than 90% of the total population. Those people have never been on an airplane, so you won't ever see them. The next layer flies only occasionally, and again you are unlikely to meet them twice. The next layer is business people who travel somewhat frequently, but not like I did. Finally, there is the layer that travels constantly.

This layer of the wedding cake is an incredibly small portion, only a few thousands of the billions of people in the world. Finally, there is a subset of that subset which is just a few thousand who are in the same business areas that I am in, and so they are traveling on the same circuits with me. These are the people I would bump into over and over.

Sometimes it is just because I have met so many people. One weekend when I was in Vienna, I was walking from the hotel past the Stadtpark, a charming park near the Sheraton Bratislava Hotel where I was staying. I had some time to explore, so I was walking around the city and visiting the museums. In the park, I ran into a friend and his wife. We had worked together several years earlier at IBM in Dallas.

On the Personal Side

Taking the position with ITT meant relocating to Connecticut. I had worked in New York a great deal and been to Connecticut several times, but I had never lived there. We purchased a lovely home in Weston, CT. It was on 2 acres. We found there was a lot to like about living there. Most of our neighbors worked in New York City and rode the train from Westport on a daily basis. My office, when I was not in Europe, was in Wilton, just off the Turnpike, so I was fortunate to commute on the old Connecticut Turnpike going against traffic. It was a beautiful drive.

Weston is very rural. There was a "village center" which consisted of a small hardware store, a small general store, a gas station, and a post office. There were no traffic lights and no subdivisions in the classic sense. There were a few areas where someone had purchased 30 or 40 acres and put houses on them, but with the minimum zoning of 2 acres, and with all houses in the ½ million+ range, these hardly looked like subdivisions.

I had purchased a VW convertible while we were living in Boulder and it was the perfect car for the area, particularly in the fall when it was cool, and the leaves were so colorful. On weekends we would drive around exploring. Bossley, our Sheepdog, loved to sit in the back with the wind blowing in his face. People would drive by and take pictures of him leaning into the wind. I think he liked it so much because it was one of the few times he could get the hair out of his eyes so he could see clearly.

The streets and roads of much of the State were paved versions of the old wagon trails and horse paths that followed the streams two centuries earlier. There were no GPS systems or cell phones in those days, and since trees were everywhere, it could be difficult finding your way around. We both carried Thomas Guide full multipage street map books in our cars, but even with that, I had to find Sharon and lead her home on more than one occasion. Fortunately, everybody in the town was friendly, so when she got completely lost she would just stop at a house and ask to use their phone to call me. Sharon was not the only one who struggled to find her way around, so people were used to lost residents.

The area was very friendly. The remnants of Hurricane Gloria hit in 1985. Power was knocked out for several days. Everyone had wells and septic systems, so no power meant no water. We had a swimming pool, so I went door to door on our cul-de-sac to show everyone how to get drinking water out of their water heaters. I also invited them to come to our house with a bucket to get water from the pool to flush their toilets. We all survived and we had some great bar-b-ques as the food in everyone's freezers was thawing. We had to eat whatever they had or throw it away.

College

As I said earlier, I did not have a degree when I joined ITT, even though my job description called for a Ph.D. I believe that requirement had more to do with the fact that we were part of the Advanced Technology Center where everybody had Ph.Ds. None the less, I recognized that for me to continue to advance in my career, I needed to get a degree.

ITT did provide some excellent college level classes for its executives. They were taught on college campuses by professors during off times. They were 2-week classes concentrating on a single subject. I recall a few that I attended. One was financial management for non-financial managers. It was at UNC-Chapel Hill. Another was manufacturing, taught at UC San Diego. The training was excellent, and it was usually on a subject that was new to me.

I was traveling all of the time, so attending class was out of the question. I had to find an alternate approach. After much searching, I discovered that Charter Oak College, a state institution in Hartford, would work with me to finish my degree. That was before "executive" courses and schools like Phoenix University. Charter Oak reviewed the not quite 30 units I had accumulated in night school. They considered my military and IBM classes along with the ITT training and gave me another 25 units of credit. That left me with nearly 70 units required to graduate. They said I could "test out" of any classes I wanted. That meant that if I took the exams and passed, they would give me credit. I still had to pay for the classes of course, but I didn't have to attend. Some of the tests were CLEP (College Level Examination Programs), some were classes taught at Charter Oak. Fortunately, ITT would cover the cost of the courses. I asked them how many classes I could take at once and they said there was no limit, all I had to do was take the test and pass the courses. I hit it hard and spent virtually every flying and every waking hour plus a lot that were not all that awake, studying and taking tests. Nine months later, I had my BS in Business.

Tim's graduation Hartford CT
Dad, Mom, Tim & Sharon 1984

We sent tickets so that Mom and Dad could and attend my graduation. They enjoyed Connecticut, and we had them come on another occasion before we moved back to California. They particularly loved the fall colors and the rural nature of Weston. That was before Dad had his knee joints replaced and so he had trouble walking very far, but while I was at work, he loved to take Bossley and walk our cul-de-sac. We were on a ridgetop and relatively flat so the walk was easy. Whenever we were out on a trail, his trapping instincts would kick in, and he was always pointing out raccoon and deer tracks to

Tracee.

— ∎ —

There were a lot of raccoons and they were quite a nuisance. There were also a few skunks, fortunately fewer and not as aggressive as the raccoons. Being on an older septic system, we didn't use the garbage disposal. That meant that much of our skins and trimmings went into the trash can. Raccoons would attack the trash cans trying to get at any scraps that might be inside. I built a fence around the trashcans. We would take a 2 x 4 and jam it under the top rail of the wall and across the tops of the cans. It was quite tight, but some learned how to get past that, we added bungee cords and anything else we could think of to stop them. It seemed that somehow the raccoons could still occasionally get the lids off. Whenever they did, they made a terrible mess scattering trash all over the place.

If you came out to put trash in a can any time after dark, there would invariably be at least one raccoon trying to break into the can. The raccoons were quite brazen; they would sit there and look at you as if to say "what do you want?" I kept a broom handle near the back door to chase them off. I would put the trash in, lock the lid down. They would be back on top of the cans by the time I got inside.

— ∎ —

There were a lot of interesting people living in the area. We were the only interracial couple, and so we got invited to a lot of parties. I guess that was the reason; it certainly wasn't my dynamic personality or good looks. We met a lot of people. Paul Newman and Joanne Woodward lived nearby. They were actually in Westport, but close to Weston. They had an unusual living arrangement, with two houses on their property. They each lived in a separate house. I guess they loved each other but were too independent, or maybe their egos were too big to live under one roof.

Robert Ludlum, the author, lived about a mile from our house. I had read all of his books and got to meet him a few times. He was quite old at the time but liked to talk with people who knew his work. He invited me over to his house for tea on a couple of occasions. There were lots of actors and actresses who worked on Broadway. Most were rather odd people when you got to know them, but we did get several invitations to see their plays in New York, sometimes with backstage passes.

There was a big dairy store called Stew Leonard's located in Norwalk. It was a unique store, kind of like a Whole Foods but almost exclusively vegetables and dairy products. It was a fun place to go, and their fresh veggies were the best. Connecticut was the weekend home for a lot of New York's richer families who wanted to get out of the city. They also liked to have dinner parties. Stew Leonard's recognized this opportunity; they had a lot of gourmet prepared foods that you could take home and simply heat and serve.

We got to be friends with Steve Guthman and his wife. Mrs. Guthman was a Leonard and sister to the head of the family that owned the store. Her father, who was in his 80s at that time, was a Holocaust survivor. I loved talking with him about his life and how he had been able to survive.

— ■ —

About the only thing I didn't like about CT was the weather. Springtime was beautiful, but there were millions of tiny bugs called "no-see-ums." They would drive you crazy whenever you were outside. They would fly up your nose and into your eyes and ears. In the springtime, if you went outdoors to work in the yard, you had to wear protective clothing and a mask. They disappeared in early summer, but hot, muggy weather replaced them. The falls were spectacular. Not too muggy and the leaves were beautiful. In the late fall, it would rain, and all the leaves would turn gray and fall off the trees. It seemed like the transition from colorful to gray took about 48 hours, always accompanied by rain. Everything turned gray in late October. The sky was gray, the trees and ground were gray, and the snow would turn gray very quickly. It stayed gray till the end of March. That and the lack of mountains was depressing on a day to day basis.

TriQuest

I left ITT in part because they sold the switching technology to a French company and my job was moving to France, but in part, because I was growing frustrated with working for others. I wanted to build my own business. I reached back to the centralized service management principals implemented in the Goshawk system and identified a business opportunity to apply these same management principals to the service of non-networked equipment, the unwashed masses; that populate every workplace.

I assembled a business plan around this opportunity and started looking for a Venture Capitalist that would fund such an operation. Surprisingly, I quickly located a startup VC firm in Stamford, CT that agreed to fund me. TriQuest was focused on the emerging "smart building" trend and saw my service management concept fitting nicely within their anticipated portfolio.

A smart building was envisioned to be an office building or campus in which the building owner incorporated the infrastructure that most companies would need in their offices. That would include the networking infrastructure, telephone system, PBX, video conferencing, an on-premise print shop, advanced power management, and, in some cases the actual computers and terminals that a small company would need. In some ways, it was an extension of the "executive suite" concept but applied at the macro level to a complete building or campus.

I saw significant problems with this idea. Specifically, the technology was changing too fast. It would be obsolete before it was out of the box. The IBM PC had only been on the market 3 or 4 years, but it was already revolutionizing the office. It had replaced almost all typewriters and word processors. The PC was beginning to cut deeply into the computer workstation market and was even eroding the distributed computing market. The PC had brought about the death of Wang and NBI (Office Automation), and it was hurting DEC (Digital Equipment Corporation), the leading distributed computing company at that time. Apple introduced the Macintosh after I joined TriQuest, so it had not yet revolutionized the imaging market. It was clear that change would continue, and there was no clear direction.

Data security was another issue. Hacking and even viruses were still in the future, but the tools to segregate and protect data for individual companies in a shared environment were nonexistent at that point.

Despite my doubts about the long-term viability of the smart building concept, I saw an opportunity to use the money TriQuest promised to establish my company in a way that I could support, and yet not be dependent upon TriQuest's strategy to pursue smart-buildings.

TriQuest was small, only five people at that time. It was organized and run by a rather eccentric individual named Jim Gershman. Jim had owned and operated an electric shaver company that he sold to a flamboyant pitchman named Victor Kiam. Kiam had purchased Remington Shavers from Sperry and turned the company and its products into an overnight sensation with endless TV commercials featuring Kiam telling everyone that the Remington *"shaved closer than a blade."* I don't remember the details; it may have been that Gershman came over from Sperry as part of the purchase deal. Maybe he had some guarantees. Whatever the story was, there apparently had been some serious misrepresentation on the part of Kiam, and an intense legal battle ensued. Gershman eventually prevailed and received a handsome settlement that included royalties from Remington and Kiam personally for a number of years. That gave Gershman the financial resources to start TriQuest. I do remember that the mere mention of Kiam or hearing one of his commercials would send Gershman's blood pressure up 20 points.

TriQuest had funded one company that was closely related to the smart-building business. I don't remember now exactly what they did, but Tommy Payne, a coworker at the ITT Programming Center, was CEO. The CFO at TriQuest was also an ex-ITT Programming Center Director. Both were ex-IBMers, and I knew these individuals at ITT. These relationships were critical to my getting involved with TriQuest.

TriQuest was in the early stages of raising its first capital round, and so they did not have the money at that point to fund my operation. To keep me in their group, they hired me as their VP of Technology. My job was to screen all potential funding requests to determine if they were a fit with TriQuest's defined objective.

It was a fascinating job and quite challenging. I would typically receive a dozen or more funding requests each week. Most included a business plan. I would review each plan and make the first cut to eliminate those that were outside of our scope. That immediately brought the prospects down to one or two at the most, often zero. If I felt that they were a possible fit, I would bring in the CFO to review the plan's numbers to see if they made sense to him. Usually, these two steps would bring the count down to just a couple prospects for any given month. For each one, I would write up a synopsis that covered the concept and how I saw it fitting the TriQuest strategy. Those I circulated, along with the associated business plan, to the other VPs. Ultimately we would have a group meeting to discuss any plans that made it successfully through all of the team. Most focused on some new technology or business strategy, and so there was a lot of research that went into my process.

If a business plan made it through all of these steps, I would ask the requesting company to come and make a presentation. Presentations usually happened less than one per month. We could be very selective because we had a clearly defined target market and because we did not yet have money to fund anybody. I was building a portfolio to draw from once we had our fund put together.

For me, this was another educational opportunity. I got to look at and dissect a lot of business plans covering a lot of different technologies, industries, and concepts. I worked closely with the CFO as we would debate the market, financial, and technical assumptions underpinning the plan. I learned a great deal about how to create a good plan and how to construct a reasonable financial model.

Jim Gershman

As I said earlier, Gershman was colorful. It appeared that the Remington lawsuit had shaped his thinking. He was quite open with the team, and he would brag about how and why he had organized his life in a unique manner. He was all about protecting his assets. He had divorced his wife of 30+ years, but it was a divorce in name only. Although I must say he was quite the philanderer, so he used his divorce to his advantage in every way possible. As part of the divorce agreement, he put all of his assets in her name, and they continued to live together as husband and wife. He received a monthly stipend. If someone sued him, he had nothing that the other party could touch. At worst, if he lost, he could just declare bankruptcy and not a single thing in his life would change.

He was a rather distinguished looking gentleman who had moved in high financial and social circles. He walked with a limp, slightly dragging one leg. He often used this "distinguished" persona to his advantage. He was perpetually late, especially when it came time to catch a flight. If he were in danger of missing a plane, he would have one of us scramble ahead and tell the flight crew to "hold the plane, the Senator is on his way." It never failed, and no one ever questioned if he were a Senator. I am sure if they had, he would have confidently lied his way past any inquiry.

For Jim, image was everything. He wanted to attract big investors, both individuals as well as large enterprises and so he leased very classy space at a proper address in Stamford. He leased two stretch limousines and hired two drivers who were former instructors at the Bondurant Racing School. Remember, there were only five of us so why two limousines? We could use the limos whenever we needed, including for personal use, but mainly, they were to pick up people flying into New York or to bring Wall Street executives out to our facility. He insisted that each of us drive a high-end car that the company leased. I don't think that he cared what we drove, so much as what our area of the parking structure looked like; he wanted it to appear as if we were the most successful company you could imagine. I drove a BMW 735i. It was a beautiful car and a lot of fun to drive. It was the first year of BMW's new traction control system, and surprisingly, it was completely useless in snow or on slick roads. The car was plagued with reliability issues. Others drove Jaguars or Mercedes-Benz. Jim drove a Porsche. There was expensive art throughout the office, and of course, a couple of very attractive secretaries. It didn't make any difference if they could type, or if he even had anything for them to do, it was all about image. Maybe he was right about all of these trappings, but the exorbitant costs were rapidly driving the company to the poorhouse.

— ∎ —

Jim's connections opened many doors. We met with commercial real estate companies like Coldwell Banker, Cushman & Wakefield, and finance companies including Schwab, AIG, and several other Wall Street Firms. Several of us flew to Belgium to meet with members of the royal family and ultimately with King Baudouin. There were meetings with the senior managers from several major Northern European banks including Deutsche Bank, Societe Generale, and ING. It was quite a series of drinking, eating and talking.

TriQuest ultimately received a contract to manage a $5 billion fund to be used for low-interest financing of commercial building retrofits. We were to work with major North American commercial real estate holding companies and developers. The goal was to use this low-interest money to generate business for Northern European manufacturers. Our job was to do the leg work, open the doors and do the preliminary due-diligence to qualify the client. We did not approve or process the actual loans. The various banking professionals who provided the money would process the loans.

The carrot for the developer was a very attractive interest rate; the stick was that a sizable portion, 60% if I remember correctly, of the equipment and steel purchased had to be manufactured by Northern European companies. There was some backend work as well, but that was mostly customer service and coordinating shipments from the suppliers. We were not involved directly with the banks or the loans. Our compensation for managing the fund was 2% per year. That was $100 million per year.

You can imagine our exuberance on the flight home. We could have probably made the trip without an airplane. After the initial euphoria, there was no follow-up. That wasn't precisely the funding source Jim had in mind, but he could have easily spun off a startup to manage the funds. Initially, it could have required a minuscule team, two, or maybe three of us to start, and we were already on board. Our CFO could head the company as it was primarily a financial play, and I could have easily done the sales and relationship building with the real estate companies and developers. A third person could have worked at developing the ongoing support operation, but that was not critical the first day, and we would have the money to build the necessary teams.

It would have been a tough business to develop. The 60% Northern European content clause would have been hard to achieve, but the interest rates we could offer were way below market rates, and so we could attract prospects. Supposedly, around 70% of the original cost of a building would be spent retrofitting that building every ten years. I never knew where that figure originated, or if it was accurate, but it seemed to be widely accepted. Of that, roughly 50% would be for labor, and 50% for materials. Assuming that 70% figure was correct, that meant that a $10 million building would spend about $3.5 million on retrofit materials every ten years. Again, I have no idea if this is correct, it seemed high to me, but all of those who should have known, accepted these ratios.

All of us pushed Jim to move on this opportunity, ideally to spin it off, but to at least assign someone to the project. We did get him to go as far as letting us fly out to Portland to meet with Cushman and Wakefield for a potential project in Oregon City, but we couldn't get him to move forward. No amount of prodding brought action; he seemed just to lose interest as soon as we were back in Stamford. After the project had languished for six months, the Belgium's cancelled the contract. Needless to say several of us were beyond pissed. We could have all grown very rich off of this contract over the next several years.

– ■ –

What we learned from the Belgian deal as well as several similar situations, was that Gershman was a "corporate skirt chaser." The next deal was always the best thing possible, but as soon as he had it in the bag, he forgot about it and immediately went after the next great deal. We had a small, but experienced team that could have easily taken charge of any of these deals and successfully managed them, but Jim would never let us take that step. He wanted us on the airplane with him chasing the next deal. We were his trophies. For him, it was all about the team and the appearance of a gaggle of top-notch executives to help him close the deal. There were some very heated debates, but he never gave in.

I had seen businesses that couldn't get the deals and others that were unable to execute the deals. TriQuest was able to get the deals, and our team was strong enough that I think we could have successfully implemented, but Jim had no interest in actually performing. I never could to figure out why he was this way. Maybe it just comes down to the fun of the chase.

The end was predictable. We never got the VC fund together, and we never had any deal even remotely close to the Belgian deal that he let slip through our fingers. Funding ran out and he could no longer pay salaries, rent, or the lease on my BMW. What a waste.

Lessons Learned

For me, every company has been an opportunity to learn, and I have always believed that I learned more from my failures than I ever learn from my successes. There were certainly a lot of opportunities to learn at TriQuest. I got to be good friends with Tommy Payne as well as the CFO of TriQuest. Unfortunately, I can no longer remember his name. While Tommy was managing a company owned by TriQuest rather than working within TriQuest, he was dealing with many of the same issues in his relationship with Gershman.

Tommy and his wife Barbara came to dinner one time. Billy and Barbara O'Brian were also our guests. Barbara O'Brian was our realtor and we had become good friends. On the surface, the matchup seemed like it should have worked. We were all professionals and roughly the same age and the personalities seemed like they should have been compatible. Unfortunately, the two Barbara's were more like fire and gasoline. They were extremely competitive with each other, and while they were civil, there was a lot of energy flowing between them. Tommy and Billy seemed to hit it off quite well and even to be enjoying watching their wives spar with each other. Sharon and I could only watch and keep the drinks refreshed.

Bossley, our very large and very friendly Old English Sheepdog, was not allowed on the carpets. In part, this was because he was constantly leaving a trail of long white hair, but mostly it was because he was so big that he could take over a room if we allowed him to roam. The floors throughout were hardwood, so he did have plenty of space to roam, just not on the carpets.

Both the Payne's and the Lyon's had Lhasa Apso dogs. I love dogs, but Lhasa Apsos are unquestionably my least favorite dog. Sharon had one when we got married, and that dog was a terror. When we left him in the house alone, he would pull any pillow he could find into the center of the room and pee on it. I had to constantly be on guard because he would come up behind me and try to bite me if he could. He didn't like men, any men. We finally had to get rid of him.

One of the subjects the Barbaras were sparring over was who had the smartest/cutest Lhasa. I remember the Lyon's dogs were named "Bonwit" and "Teller" after the famous fashion retailer. While they were hissing back and forth, Bossley snuck into the dining room and attached himself to Tommy's willing hand. When I noticed Bossley, I told him he had to get out. Tommy immediately spoke up and in a voice that was a couple of decibels too loud said: *"he is ok, it is great to have a real dog to pet, not like those little faggot dogs we have."* For those who might not know, "faggot" is a derogatory term for gays. Tommy's little speech hit the table like someone had dropped a brick in a punch bowl. The room went quiet as the two Barbaras were left, at least for a few seconds, speechless. Barbara Payne gave her husband a look that could have easily drawn blood. Tommy, who was a big Texas guy, about 6'5", had a grin on his face from ear to ear. Barbara Lyon shot a quick look at Billy who was laughing so hard he almost fell off of his chair. He was trying his best not to laugh out loud, and his face was beet red. Billy's face was always beet red, but at the moment, it was even redder than normal.

Both women started speaking at the same time, but they were no longer talking to each other, each had zeroed in on their husband, both of whom had had a few drinks over the evening and were enjoying watching their ever so

379

respectful wives meltdown in our dining room. Sharon and I glanced at each other. We were also having a hard time maintaining straight faces. Needless to say, the party broke up almost immediately. After they had left, we poured another drink and went out to the spa for a good laugh. Bossley got a treat. I will never forget that dinner party.

First Macintosh

Apple launched the Macintosh in 1984. I had an Apple II at home, and I had TriQuest provide a Mac for work. That was soon after the product was first released. All it had was a 400K micro floppy with 128K of memory. There was no hard drive in any Mac at that time. It was fun to use, slow and somewhat underpowered, but the lack of a hard drive made it almost useless for documents and spreadsheets.

The word processor that I was using required a full floppy just to load. Once you got the app loaded, you pulled the floppy out and put in your data disk. If you were saving versions of any document you were working on, you would quickly run out of space on the floppy and have to move to a new one. Of course, saving versions was critical because the system would crash and eat your document quite regularly. If you ran out of space while trying to save a document, it would crash. It didn't pre-check to see if there was enough room, and it couldn't split a document across multiple disks, so you had to keep the document size small enough to fit on a single disk. If you thought it might overflow, you had better put in a new floppy. The application took almost all of the storage, so there was very little room for a document in memory, about three pages max if I recall. It didn't load all of the word processing features because they would take even more memory. Whenever you tried to do certain things, it would ask you to put the application disk back into the system. If you had a document that was taking up too much memory, when you tried to bring in the additional feature it would crash. You spent more time swapping floppies and recovering from crashes, then doing actual work.

Within a few months, it became evident that they needed more storage. Apple released what they called the "Fat Mac," a 512K version that also included a hard drive. I am not certain about the size of the hard drive, but I think it was 2 MB. It wasn't all that big, and so you still had to create backups regularly to offload any less used data. Fortunately, they released a kit so I could upgrade my original Mac to Fat Mac.

When TriQuest collapsed, they shut the doors owing each of us money. Jim made the mistake of bouncing our last salary checks. Since he signed them personally, I threatened to have him arrested. Bouncing a check was not something his divorce could protect him from, so he quickly came up with the funds. It covered the bounced check, but that wasn't all that he owed. Since there was nothing to salvage and Jim was not paying salaries, everyone took their work computers as partial payment. That Fat Mac served me well for many years. I did ultimately upgrade to a larger hard drive, still minuscule by today's standards, but with the increased memory and hard drive, that was a solid and very useful system.

Moving On

We liked Connecticut, but it was too expensive to live there and try to start my company. Also, I had no business contacts in the East Coast. So we decided to move back to California.

I didn't want to use my savings to pay for a move, so I took a director's position at Western Digital in Irvine California. I was primarily involved with sales of WD chipsets and disk drives to IBM for use in their PC product line. There was nothing wrong with WD, but it was not something that I wanted to do for the long term. It was simply a way to pay the bills and to get us back to where I had contacts.

While I was with WD, I traveled primarily to IBM's Boca Raton, FL facility to negotiate product requirements for new PC versions. In parallel, I reworked my business plan and started working on developing the business using self-funding. I was only with WD for about a year. Once I had the pieces working and my first customer, I left.

— ■ —

I had sold my VW convertible when TriQuest gave me the 735i. That was a mistake, but I foolishly assumed TriQuest would succeed. I was now in needed a second car. I bought a BMW 325 when I first came to Irvine. It was less than a year old and only had 7,000 miles, so they offered me a maintenance contract that was the same as a new car. I had mixed emotions about buying the contract, but it covered everything for ten years or 100 K miles. Being in the service business, I know how lucrative those maintenance contracts are. On the other hand, I had seen the reliability issues on the 735 and suspected that the original owner of this 325 might have unloaded it because of service issues.

As with most car dealers, selling the maintenance contract was the responsibility of the finance department. I think their logic was that after you have gone around and around with the sales guy; you would be so tired of haggling that you would be more willing to buy their overpriced service contract. It was late in the evening by the time I was talking to the finance guy, and he hit me with this 100 K mile service offer at $1900. I told him I wasn't interested at that price and he asked me what I would pay for it. I told him $900, figuring he would never go there, and that it would get him off my back. To my surprise, he took my offer. He haggled a bit, but I stood my ground. I think it was one of those end of the day, end of the month situations and he wanted to get one more sale on the books.

What a blessing that service contract was. The car was a dream to drive and tended to go way faster than it felt like you were going. Unfortunately, it had a bad habit of eating very expensive parts along the way. They replaced the transmission, the blower twice, and the computer board at least once. There were AC problems, radio problems and other things that dropped off from time to time. I drove the car until it hit 98 K miles and traded it in. There was no way I could have afforded to keep it through another major service incident after the contract expired. As much as I love driving BMWs, I will never quite get over the maintenance issues that those two cars had.

Servare

When I started my service management company in 1988, I searched long and hard for a name. I wanted something that implied service, but something that would be a bit different from the plethora of companies with the overused word "service" in their name. I was also looking for something that would be simple, ideally a single word that would cause people to pause for that extra heartbeat to think about the name. Somewhere in my searching, I came across "servare" and a definition that indicated that the word meant "to serve." It sounded good, so I grabbed it.

My concept was a simple extension of the management principals we had developed a decade earlier for the Western Bancorp TIPS project and further refined in the Goshawk project. Specifically, I wanted to use a version of the central computerized problem and change tracking system we had developed to manage service for the "unwashed masses," the hundreds of devices that are installed in business offices everywhere but not attached to a network.

I was not looking to compete in the management of any equipment connected to the corporate IT network. I saw this arena as already crowded. To compete there, I would have to build a better mouse trap and assuming I could find an exploitable angle, that would take lots of time and money, both of which I lacked.

My logic was that a company could gain similar efficiencies for office equipment service if they used a centralized approach for all non-networked equipment. The list of equipment included obvious things like typewriters, copiers, and PCs, but there are many other pieces of equipment including things like elevators and air conditioners that require service when they fail. At our first and largest customer, First Interstate Bank, the list of equipment was quite extensive. Drive-up teller windows, including the sliding trays, the speaker systems, and pneumatic systems. They also had: currency counters, check encoders, calculators, standalone (non-networked) PCs, and MICR (Magnetic Ink Character Recognition) writers. The MICR machines were used to encode every check before sending them to the central processing location. Many of these machines were critical to customer operations and customer service.

New technology has replaced many of these devices, and most are in some way connected to the Internet. None the less, you would be surprised to learn how many "antique" devices like typewriters are still in use for limited and specific functions in many banks and offices. Furthermore, being connected to the Internet does not mean that they are managed.

I had assumed that most of these devices were poorly managed. I verified my assumption at First Interstate Bank (FIB). As an example, FIB had a contract with Xerox for copier service. That contract guaranteed a 2-hour response in the metro areas and 4-hour response in most other bank locations. There were a few remote offices that were on a next business day schedule. When we started managing the Xerox machines, we were able to document that their average metro area service was slightly more than 6 hours. In the second and third tier markets, it was always greater than one day, in many cases multiple days. We worked with Xerox and got their average metro response time down to less than 3 hours, but they were never able to achieve their contracted response time. As a result, FIB received a substantial rebate on their service agreement. That rebate alone was worth more than our management fee for all of their office equipment. We were charging $1/device/month for most devices, but the rates were lower on some of the seldom used/breaking machines.

Service inside First Interstate Bank was a very expensive mess that no one had ever reviewed. We found several drive-up teller (pneumatic) systems that had been paved over years earlier. FIB was still paying annual service contracts on these nonexistent systems. A service contract on one system was typically in the $3,000/year range. In another case, we found that FIB had a master service agreement for all typewriters. The branches were unaware of the agreement, and so they were calling for local service technicians and paying on an hourly basis. FIB was, therefore, paying twice for typewriter service.

We documented well over $100,000 in service savings per year even after deducting our fee. We recorded dramatic improvements in response time and lower equipment outage.

— ■ —

I started Servare out of my pocket. I talked to Chris Cole at Peregrine Systems. Remember he had worked at IBM on the Goshawk Project; he developed the software for the Smithsonian project. He and a few other Goshawk alumni had started Peregrine several years earlier. He agreed to support my effort by giving me a license to the Unix version of their management software. That was essentially Goshawk V2.0.

I became an Apple Unix Developer so that I could get cheaper hardware. I purchased a Mac II system and added a card so I could drive several Wyse terminals. It ran A/UX (Apple Unix). Chris came over to my place, and we installed his software. It was a little slow on the Mac II, but it was quite a sweet machine. I ran the business on this single machine for several years.

I stayed with Western Digital until I was able to get the system up and running and get my first customer. At that point, I left and went full time with Servare. I hired and trained several part-time operators. The job was attractive for mothers of school-age children as they could work a 4-hour shift while their children were in school. That worked well for me as I didn't have money to pay for full-time employee benefits.

We had about 12,000 devices under management and normally there would be two operators on duty. The actual management process was relatively straightforward. The biggest challenge was to create a database of all of their locations, all of the equipment at each location, and the corresponding service relationships. Finding information on any service contracts and any special terms such as guaranteed response time was a real challenge. Their purchasing department certainly didn't have their arms around service contracts. They appeared to be paying bills with no backup documents. As with the TIPS network, the bank branches were instructed to call us anytime they needed service. We opened a problem record and captured all necessary data. We then contacted the service vendor and managed the call to completion.

We generated performance reports for our customers. I trained our FIB contact on how to read and interpret the various reports. Most of the time we worked together on the analysis. That was useful because I learned what we needed to modify on the reports. For the first time, the customer could see the impact that service was having on their operations.

Over time we were able to identify specific bank equipment that needed to be replaced, or in some cases discontinued altogether. They could also see where they needed backup devices. For instance, they added another check encoder at every branch. These are the machines that imprint the colored dots that show the date and amount on cashier's check or money orders. The purpose of this imprinting is to ensure that once created it cannot be altered.

Banks charged $5 to create a cashier's check or a money order. If the encoder were down, they would lose that business. Calculating the average outage and the number of items sold each day, I was able to document the lost annual revenue. Aside from the cost, these outages meant that the branches could not meet their customer's needs.

FIB talked to the equipment provider about giving them a guaranteed response time, but Brandt wanted no part of that and gave them a prohibitively high quote. FIB determined that it was cheaper to install a second encoder in every office.

Brian Joined Servare

I needed help. I was running the entire business: I was the IT department, the service desk manager, the salesman, janitor, trainer, manager, etc. If one of the staff called in sick or had to go home because of a sick child, I filled in as one of the service desk operators. I had to open the doors in the morning and close the doors at night. The biggest problem was that I had no time or freedom to go out and sell the service to additional customers.

Brian had graduated from college and was working in New York. I convinced him that I needed him more than the nonprofit he was working for and so he came to California and took over several of my many roles.

While he was in college, he had been working with NeXT computers which he liked. He wanted to rewrite our software to run on that platform. NeXT was a relatively new company started by Steve Jobs after he was forced out of Apple. Jobs developed the NeXT using Unix. I won't go into detail, but at the time NeXT was like a Mac on steroids. Ultimately, Jobs came back to Apple and brought the NeXT OS called NeXTSTEP with him. He replaced the Apple OS with OS X which is, in fact, NeXTSTEP.

At first, I resisted making the investment to redevelop on NeXT. We were working fine on the Mac II, and I had fears that NeXT was not going to make it in the market. At one point, IBM announced that they were acquiring a license to port NeXTSTEP (the operating system) over to the PCs to replace IBM's version of PC Unix. That gave me enough confidence in the company's future to make the investment.

We became NeXT Developers to get cheap hardware, but we also gained some NeXT sales and some software development contracts along with the cheaper hardware. Brian set out to develop a GUI (Graphical User Interface) version of our management system. He also tailored the system so that it was much easier to coordinate all of the devices, locations, and contracts that came with multiple customers.

The software he developed was very efficient. Not only was it easier for our operators, it dramatically improved their productivity. We went from two operators to manage the calls to less than one operator for the same number of units.

— ■ —

Unfortunately, the economy at that time was in a recession, and I was having a difficult time finding any new clients. I was engaged in a lengthy sell cycle with McDonald's and traveled to Chicago several times to meet with them. They liked the idea because their stores are wall to wall equipment and almost every device in a store is a revenue generating unit. If the ice cream machine broke, they couldn't sell cones, shakes or sundaes. That is a lot of income on an hour by hour basis. From a small company standpoint, the problem was that McDonald's was just too slow to make a decision. They wanted endless meetings, and their decision cycle looked like it was going to take years. Skype didn't exist, so I was traveling to Chicago for every meeting. We just didn't have the resources to deal with them, and ultimately I had to walk away.

One of the lessons we learned from McDonald's, but also from others, was that big companies were very reluctant to hand over such a critical component of their operations to a tiny company with no real resources or track record. It seemed a bit twisted that they were not doing the job themselves, but were concerned about letting someone else do it.

At about this time we began to see that FIB was getting shaky. The person we had been dealing with passed away and, given the slow economy; FIB was in no hurry to replace him. That left us with no real contact, and on internal advocate. We thought that this could easily result in a nonrenewal of our contract.

Brian and I decided that our best strategy would be to commercialize the software he had developed and sell licenses so that companies could use their own staff to manage equipment service. We figured that there was potential for lucrative consulting work to go along with setup and operations. In that vein, we stopped trying to sell our service bureau approach and concentrated our very limited resources on hardening and documenting the software.

As we had anticipated, FIB did not renew the contract, but we were close to having a shippable product and so we pressed our approach. Unfortunately, just as we were getting ready to announce our software product, Steve Jobs announced that NeXT was "no longer in the hardware business."

NeXT's new strategy was to produce a version of NeXTSTEP that they intended to sell as an alternative to the DOS operating system used on IBM PCs; this was before Microsoft Windows. They announced a delivery date 18 months in the future, but like most software companies, NeXT was notorious for missing their scheduled release dates.

We were caught flat-footed, totally unprepared for this eventuality. We had no contingency plan. We had already purchased a booth at the NeXT tradeshow in San Francisco with the intention of announcing and demonstrating our product at that show. We suddenly had no platform on which to sell our software. There was no possibility that we could survive until NeXT started shipping their intended PC version.

Brian and I discussed alternatives and concluded the most logical way forward would be to raise some investor (venture) capital. The first step was to clean up our books. We had been selling a few NeXT computer systems each quarter, generating what, on the surface, looked to be a good income from sales, installation services, and consulting. We weren't actively selling the hardware, but NeXT would give us leads. When a potential customer contacted them, if the quantity of equipment was below NeXT's desired threshold, they would toss the business to us. Unfortunately, NeXT was selling their computers at heavily discounted rates, and by the time the lead reached us, NeXT would have already quoted a price, so we had no room to mark the equipment up. That meant that there was almost no margin for us from the sales. The good news was that most of the hardware sales were generating some revenue from custom software, training, and installation work. While it was not a large revenue stream, the margins were good.

On our books, that was all combined with our service management business. We knew that any potential investor would want to see our books and anticipated that what they would see the abrupt disappearance of the revenue from hardware sales and software/installation support. That would show a big dive in revenue. We envisioned spending our time dealing with this entirely legitimate drop in revenue, leaving no time or opportunity to focus on the service management software business or opportunity.

A Dancing Bear is Born

We asked our accountant to separate the NeXT hardware sales and consulting work from the service management work. That would create clean books that would allow us to focus entirely on the opportunity we wanted, specifically, the redevelopment of our software to license as a standalone product. The accountant took a couple of weeks to complete this process, and near the end, he asked what we wanted to name the NeXT business. A name was required so that he could do the taxes and officially close it down. We kicked around some comical possibilities since no one would ever see or know about this soon to be an abandoned business. Brian suggested "dancing bear." It was a play on words. First, the company was dancing bare, as there was no hardware or software to sell, and the market was nonexistent since NeXT had abandoned the field. Another wordplay was the bear vs. bare part. I have been called "Grizzly" most of my life. I would like to think it had to do with the name Griswold, but it just might have had something to do with my always being on the large size. The Dancing Bear name made both of us laugh, and the accountant thought it was funny as well. So our abandoned hardware and consulting business became "Dancing Bear Enterprises." We thought that would soon be the end of it.

A funny thing happened on the way to the corporate graveyard. Literally, within two hours of our informing the accountant of our decision, I got a call from Swiss Bank in Chicago. They told me that they had 5,000 NeXT Stations with a custom application running their trading floor. They had purchased the hardware directly from NeXT, and the various additional NeXT components, parts, etc. from a large national NeXT reseller. Both NeXT and their supplier were no longer able to support them. They were facing a potentially catastrophic problem. They had to keep the NeXT computers running while they redeveloped their application on a different platform.

Their question, almost a begging one, was can you support us, can you help us get the parts and the additional equipment we desperately need to keep these systems running? Being an entrepreneur, and having absolutely no source of income at the moment, I said we would absolutely be able to help. That day they placed an order for more than $40,000 in parts, disk drives, memory sticks, and a couple of printers if we could find them. So just two hours after we had officially named our deathbed hardware business Dancing Bear, it had become the *"oldest and largest NeXT reseller in the world."* We were, for a long time, the only NeXT reseller.

We knew where we could get compatible memory and disk drives, but actual NeXT hardware was another issue. We knew that NeXT had heavily targeted the education market, setting up sales through on-campus computer or bookstores at virtually every university in the US and Canada. When NeXT abandoned the hardware line, these school stores were stuck holding varying amounts of NeXT hardware. We started calling the school stores and offering to take their NeXT hardware and any other NeXT related items at their cost. No profit to them, but at least no loss. Educational reseller's costs were lower than what we had been paying as developers. Most were more than happy to unload and avoid the losses they were anticipating.

In parallel to our search for hardware, we started spreading the word. We developed a list of companies that had made significant investments in NeXT equipment and let them know that we were there to support them. Most of these companies faced the same challenge that Swiss Bank was dealing with, and most became our customers. Many of the universities that had sold us their remaining inventories actually had departments that were also NeXT users and they needed our support. In a few cases, we wound up selling other equipment back to the same schools.

First Online Store

The NeXT community was fairly well connected on the emerging Internet. Much of the early Internet browser development had been done on NeXT hardware. Even though the Internet was in its earliest (commercial) stage, a few universities and developers had rudimentary websites, and most NeXT developers were, at a minimum, using email. We grabbed the "dancingbear.com" domain name, and Brian set up a basic online catalog. We were among the very first to have an online store.

We quickly found that many of our best customers would access our website before contacting us. We didn't list prices, just availability. This was not an "online" store in today's terms; at that time all purchases were made using credit cards and by calling me directly. It was rudimentary but it was effective.

This was all taking place before any of the Internet scams started and so the credit card processing company never gave us any grief about selling over the Internet. I doubt they had any idea what we were doing. Most of our card purchases were quite large, $5,000 or more, but we never had a single chargeback, so the card processing company never balked.

Dancing Bear Logo 1994

The Dancing Bear name spread like wildfire. It was catchy and easy to remember. We soon had customers from all over the world. In Japan, the bear is a sacred animal, and so they always remembered our name. The NeXT was the only computer at that time with on-screen postscript. That meant that it was the only computer that could display Kanji, Mandarin, Hangul, and other non-Latin characters. That made the NeXT highly desirable in these markets.

We began getting rather strange requests, usually from someplace in Maryland or Fairfax County Virginia. They always wanted the same thing, a NeXT Cube with everything we could put on it. They wanted maximum memory, maximum disk size, and a 21" color monitor. The NeXT 21" color monitor was a repackaged Sony Trinitron. It was a huge beast and it was the maximum any computer had at that time. The NeXT Cube was unique in that it had a built-in digital signal processor. In plain English, that meant it could take a digital satellite feed and display it real-time on a nice big color monitor.

We were told not to ask questions. Just ship the machines to the addresses given. The Cube was NeXT's highest end system. Configured as they wanted, they could cost $30,000+. They always used credit cards and their cards were never declined. Think about a $30,000 credit card purchase way back in the

391

mid-1990s. Credit card daily limits, even today, are often $1500 or less. No individual could have a $30,000 daily credit line. They always gave a personal name, but we surmised we were shipping to either the CIA or NSA. They maintained a standing order for virtually all of the Cubes we could get.

Large companies seemed to have an insatiable need for NeXT equipment. At the same time, some small enterprises and individuals had equipment that they didn't need. Because NeXT was no longer in the hardware business, they often assumed the equipment had no value. Many companies would just box up their machines and ship them to us at no cost just to remove them from their inventory. Sometimes they would even pay the shipping. We always paid at least $1 so we could say we had legitimately purchased the equipment and held clear title. We would refurbish it, stack on memory and a bigger drive and sell the units at from 150% to 200% of their original new price.

The single best deal I made was for an unlimited-user Sybase license. A company "selling" their hardware tossed the Sybase license in the box when they sent it to us. Originally that license cost them more than $35,000. I bought it for $1 and sold it for $40,000.

— ■ —

Dancing Bear was a wild ride; the name proved to be a phenomenal asset. As I said above, everybody remembered it, and that was a great help to our business. It was a door buster. When I was making cold calls either trying to buy or sell equipment. I would call and ask for the IT Director's assistant. I never asked for the Director personally, if you do that, they will start asking all kinds of questions, and you will never get to speak to anyone. When I talked to the assistant, I would introduce myself and tell her (usually) that I was from "Dancing Bear Enterprises." Invariably that would be greeted with silence. I would pause for about two seconds and then say, "that's the animal, not the naked." It never failed. I would get a laugh, and they would ask me why I was calling. I would explain that we were the "oldest and largest NeXT reseller" and that I wanted to see if we could be of assistance by either providing needed hardware or by purchasing their unneeded equipment. It was rare when I didn't get connected. One IT Director started the conversation saying: "I never take cold calls, but I just had to find out what the hell Dancing Bear Enterprises was."

People would frequently ask if we were "dead heads." That would be Grateful Dead fans for those who might not know. In the beginning, I was one who had no idea what a "dead head" was; Brian had to explain. We found that people liked to assign various reasons that fit their imagination. In any case, the name worked. I sometimes played along, but in truth, Jerry Garcia's dancing teddy bears and the Grateful Dead had nothing to do with our name choice.

Honolulu Star-Advertiser 1995

The Honolulu Star-Advertiser newspaper came over to Maui and did an interview. They published a nice article on the company and had one of their cartoonists do a caricature of me with a bunch of Grateful Dead dancing teddy bears.

We pursued DBE full time. In reality, we didn't have the time to do anything

393

other than DBE. It was just Brian and me, but Sharon soon joined us to help keep the paperwork straight as we were scrambling to find machines, clean them up and find homes for them. We decided we wanted to move out of the LA area and chose to move the company to Vail Colorado. It was neat because we were making good money and we could work from our home using the garage to refurbish the equipment.

We continued the illusion of developing the Servare software, but in fact we never spent any time or money to redevelop the software. In retrospect, that was a big mistake on my part. Brian had developed an excellent system, and there was definitely a need, but we were too busy and having too much fun, so I failed to make the investment that was necessary.

— ■ —

When I first came back to California to work for Western Digital, we purchased a home in Coto de Caza. Katlin was born while we were living there. As I had said before, we had tried for several years to have another child and had finally given up when Sharon got pregnant. I think it was a stress thing that was preventing it. Once she stopped thinking about it, it just happened.

Katie was such a blessing. My first children were born during the era when fathers were relegated to the waiting room. They were never allowed in the delivery room, and they didn't get to see the mother until after she had given birth. Babies could only to be observed through the nursery window. That had all changed for the better by the time Katie came along. We had taken birthing classes, and so I was allowed to stay in the room even while they were performing a C-Section.

They kindly put up a belly-curtain so I couldn't see the actual surgery. I don't have any problem seeing my blood, but watching someone close to me bleed, like when they sliced Sharon's tummy, I would have probably made me pass out. They took Katie out and handed her to me seconds after she was born. I got to hold her and show her to Sharon, and then give her first bath. What a thrill!

Tim & Katie 1990

Raising Katie was so different from the other kids. I was not traveling so I was home every night. I made it a ritual to read to her every night from the day she came home. It didn't make any difference who was visiting or what else was going on. I would drop everything and spend at least ½ hour reading to her. Then I would sing her to sleep. You need to understand that I have a terrible singing voice; it is so bad that when we were singing in church, Sharon would nudge me and whisper that people could hear me. That's bad! To Katie, it

395

sounded good. Often I would tell her stories instead of reading. She had several favorites, but her first choice was always "Towser and the Cheese."

I mentioned the story in the earlier section about the summer of 1950 when Dad was trapping in the tri-county area west of Red Bluff. That took place when I was five years old. Dad was driving the Jeep up a steep dirt road in the mountains one day as he was working his trap line. It was very steep with lots of sharp turns. Over the winter and spring, storms and melting snow had sent a lot of water down the road and so there were deep ruts. That made for a very rough ride. Apparently, someone else had been on the same road fairly recently, as Dad spotted something that had fallen from another vehicle, probably a Jeep given the nature of our path.

It turned out to be a ball of cheese. Refrigeration was a rarity in those days, and so they preserved cheese by sealing it in a wax shell. The cheese was wrapped in cheesecloth, then a netting material and then dipped in hot wax so that it was completely sealed. At lunch time Dad got out his infamous knife and cut off several pieces so we could each have some. I was not a fan of cheese when I was a kid, but this was beyond any cheese any of us had ever tried. It wasn't just any cheese; it was Limburger cheese. The Limburger was so pungent that none of us could eat any of it. Towser, our black & tan hound, loved the stuff and wound up eating the whole thing which was probably a pound.

Things went along fine for an hour or so until Towser's stomach had a chance to chew up what Towser had swallowed more or less whole. When that happened, Towser got an atrocious case of the worst possible gas you can imagine. We were in an open backed Jeep with a canvas top, but Towser's farts were driving everyone crazy. Dad finally had to stop and make Towser get out and run beside the Jeep for a couple of miles until he was able to pass most of the gas and probably most of the cheese. Katie loved that story and would ask me to tell it over and over. I guess all kids like "gross" stories. Of course, I was the one who introduced the story in the first place, so I can't blame her.

By the time Katie was 18-months, she could read the stories with me. At first, I thought she had just memorized the words, but I would try having her read things and learned that she was able to follow the sentences.

There was a cute story called Soldier Soldier that Katie liked.

Oh, soldier, soldier will you marry me
With your musket fife and drum?
Oh, how can I marry such a pretty girl as thee
When I got no shoes to put on
Off to the cobbler she did go as fast as she could run,
Bought him a pair of the best that was there
And the soldier put them on

Oh, soldier, soldier will you marry me
With your musket fife and drum?
Oh, how can I marry such a pretty girl as thee
When I got no socks to put on
Off to the habber-dasher she did go as fast as she could run,
Bought him a pair of the best that was there
And the soldier put them on

Oh, soldier, soldier will you marry me
With your musket fife and drum?
Oh, how can I marry such a pretty girl as thee
When I got no pants to put on
Off to the tailor she did go as fast as she could run,
Bought him a pair of the best that was there
And the soldier put them on

Now, soldier, soldier will you marry me
With your musket fife and drum?
Oh, how can I marry such a pretty girl as thee
With a wife and a baby at home.

We started playacting it with me reading the soldier's part and Katie reading the maiden's part. After we practiced for several nights we called Sharon up to watch. Katie would dance around and sing her part with such emphasis. Sharon laughed until she cried.

When Katie was tiny, I would hold her on my arm while I would read the Wall Street Journal out loud to her, or while I was working on the computer with one hand. I had my old Fat Mac, and a bit later, at least one NeXT at the house at all times. She learned to boot up the Mac and open her games before she was 20-months old. When she tired of the games, she would shut down the Mac and power on the NeXT to play games there. Katie always loved computers.

One weekend we were at the Mission Viejo Mall for something. Sharon was shopping, and Katie and I were sitting out in the atrium. The local hospital had a computer display set up. Apparently, they were trying to recruit nurses or something. It had a massive black and white screen. They were demonstrating their sophisticated technology to prospects using X-rays: a snake, turtle, and dog.

Katie kept asking to go see the "puter," but I kept holding her back as I didn't want to interfere with the recruiting that was going on. Finally, all the people cleared away, and so I ask the guy if he minded if I let Katie look at the computer. He had no problem with my holding her on my lap while she explored.

She had never seen a rollerball mouse, but that only held her up for about 5 seconds. She had the pointer flying all over the screen clicking and dragging so she could zoom in on areas of the snake skeleton. After a few minutes, she had thoroughly examined the snake, and ran the mouse up to the corner and opened the turtle image. As she started clicking and dragging to look closer at the various parts, the guy asked how old she was. I told him 20 months. He just shook his head and said he has people that are 40 years old and couldn't understand how to do what she was doing.

— ■ —

Soon after they dropped the hardware line, NeXT conducted an auction to dispose of their remaining inventory of equipment. They wanted to get rid of any miscellaneous items that they thought anyone might be willing to buy. Brian flew to San Jose to attend the auction, and he faxed me a list of pallets with their content descriptions. I was busy trying to identify which ones we might want and the maximum we should pay for them while Brian was doing the bidding.

We were on the phone for hours and Brian wound up bringing home two U-Haul trucks full of NeXT stuff. We brought it to our offices in Laguna Hills and started inventorying and updating our website with all of the new goodies we had acquired. Among the items was a pallet with software from NeXT and other developers. It included 500 copies of a program called Mathematica developed by Wolfram Software.

Mathematica was a high-end math package that did fancy things with fractal geometry. I don't recall much about it other than that it was way past my math abilities. I do remember that it had a very cool demo that represented a spaceship zipping across the surface of the moon. It was fun to watch and play with, but otherwise useless for most mere mortals.

NeXT had done some deal with Wolfram, and they were giving a licensed copy away with each NeXT Cube that they sold. If I recall correctly, a full license cost something like $5,000. The copies we had were marked "Not for Resale." We didn't have any customers that would pay anything close to even $500 for a license.

Since we didn't see any possibility of selling any of these, we decided to use these packages as a promotional item. We started advertising that we would give a Mathematica package to anyone who purchased $500 or more. We just tossed the disk in the box when we shipped the stuff. I am sure most people found it about as useful as I did. We sent 50 or so copies over the next month. One day I got a call from NeXT's lawyer telling me we had to stop selling Mathematica. I laughed and said that we weren't selling it, we were giving it away. A few days later we got a letter telling us that we were violating the "Not For Resale" statement on the product cover. We checked with our lawyer, and he said that we were completely within our right to give it away. In fact, we had the right to sell it if we wanted. When you purchase something at an auction, it is sold "as-is, where-is," buyer beware. If you find it doesn't work, well that is too bad. If you find it is worth a million dollars, well you are lucky, and you don't owe the original owner a dime. Anything that restricted the original owner no longer applies to the new owner. So again we told NeXT to buzz-off.

What we discovered later was that Wolfram was the one that was pissed. People were getting our free copies, and some were trying to register them. Apparently NeXT had agreed to pay Wolfram some amount for each registration. Of course, we weren't obliged to make that payment, but NeXT was still on the hook. Furthermore, NeXT had violated their agreement with Wolfram by "selling" the product to us. Even though it was at an auction, NeXT had officially sold the product which it was not allowed under their agreement. So NeXT found itself obliged to pay Wolfram their fee for each one we gave away, assuming the recipient tried to license the software. NeXT intended to bully us into stopping our giveaways and thus ending the problem. We weren't cooperating.

Ultimately NeXT sued and we counter-sued. Brian had a college friend who worked for a large law firm in the Bay Area, and he took the case on a contingency basis. It didn't take long; NeXT lost and had to pay his fees, but they also had to buy back the remaining Mathematica packages that we had. I think the number was about 400 at that point. They wound up paying the lawyer's fee plus they paid us the equivalent of all that we had initially paid for everything that we purchased at the auction. All they got back were the 400 remaining Mathematica packages. We wound up with a lot of "free" stuff.

— ■ —

Living and working in Vail was fun. It seemed the snow always fell at night and the days were mostly clear but cold in the winter. It was expensive to live there, especially groceries. Everything is built around selling to the tourists. About every other month we would drive our VW Vanagon to Denver and fill it to the roof at Costco. That was usually $700 or $800, mostly food. These trips helped keep our costs down. Costco wised up and eventually put a small store near the Eagle County airport, but that was several years after we left Vail.

The house we rented was on a hillside, but then everything in Vail is on a hillside, or at the creek's edge. The house sat below the road with the garage up a short flight of stairs above the actual house. I had the NeXT computers shipped to the house, and we were doing all of the reconditioning work in the heated garage. One day, I was carrying a computer from the garage to the house when my left knee went out from under me. Fortunately, I didn't drop the computer, but it hurt like it was on fire.

I went to the Steadman Clinic in Vail. One thing I learned was, that if you are ever going to blow out your knee, the best place to do that is in a ski area. Skiers tend to destroy their knees at a phenomenal rate, and so a facility like Steadman's gets more practice than any large city clinic would ever get. Steadman was also the doctor for the Denver Broncos at that time, so he had a steady source of serious knee injuries. They did arthroscopic surgery on my knee and sent me home about an hour later.

I got to watch the process on TV while they were doing it. It was not torn cartilage as we had originally thought. It was a condition where I had grown some small pieces of cartilage that looked like grains of rice. There was at least one larger chunk, and that had lodged somewhere that was causing me all of the pain. All they had to do was vacuum the pieces out. They told me I would probably have to have it done again every five years or so. I made it 20 years before I had another vacuum done.

— ■ —

We were making a lot of sales into Asian markets, Japan in particular, and we got to thinking that it would work well to move the company to Hawaii so we could be closer, at least time zone wise, to our primary customer base. That move was the second huge mistake I made.

We discovered that Maui had a brand new National Laboratory with the world's 3rd or 4th largest massively-parallel supercomputer. It was a typical government thing. Senator Denial Inouye was on the Senate Appropriations Committee. That Committee is a license for graft in all forms and on a massive scale. Inouye used his position to ensure the development of a National Laboratory on the island of Maui, something that was completely unnecessary. The supposed logic was that a massive supercomputer was needed to process the image data coming off of the satellite surveillance telescopes that were located in the crater on the top of Mt. Haleakala. Of course, these telescopes had been there for years, and the data was being successfully shipped back to the mainland for processing. Never mind, a new National Lab was needed. Another part of the justification was that the supercomputer could be part of an economic development program for Maui. That is the part we fell under as they wanted to develop a software industry.

Lots of strings were pulled to get the National Lab. Knowing Hawaii, I am betting lots of palms got greased in the process, but Inouye got his supercomputer for Maui. Surrounding the Lab, they built the Maui High-Performance Computing Center in Kihei, a tech business park that had many of the "smart building" characteristics that TriQuest had been proposing nearly a decade earlier.

Initially, the Center was managed by the University of New Mexico, much to the irritation of the University of Hawaii, but ultimately it became a DOD High-Performance Computing Center. When we contacted them, we were warmly encouraged to move our company into the tech park. There were many incentives, but one of the main advantages was that they would provide free T1 connectivity at our desks. We were paying a lot for phone service at that time, and it wasn't anywhere close to T1 speed. They also kicked in 1 hour of access to the supercomputer per month. While we never took advantage of that particular benefit, on paper it was huge. The Lab billed their time at several thousand dollars per hour.

We moved to Maui and set up shop. It was a great place to live, but a terrible place to try to do business. We were still doing the Dancing Bear NeXT resales while we were trying to find a way to commercialize the service management software. DBE was paying the bills, but there wasn't enough left

401

over to do any serious development.

We were still looking for VC funding. I had looked at the demographics of the Maui residence and confirmed that there were a lot of high net worth individuals living there. What I didn't think through was the fact that most of them were retired there and used Maui as a second home. They kept their money on the mainland to minimize their taxes which were very high in Hawaii. More importantly, these individuals had finished their working and investing years. They were retired. They had no interest in risking the money they had spent a lifetime saving. If they did have any interest in investing in startups, they didn't want to manage the investments personally. They would give a small portion of their wealth to a VC firm, usually one located in California; they could just watch to see how they performed. So, while there was money on Maui, there were no startup investors on Maui.

The second problem proved to be finding employees. While my first thought was "who wouldn't want to live and work on Maui," the truth was very few of the right kind of tech folks wanted to do that. Most were working in Silicon Valley, and they had a network of friends that would pull them from company to company looking to find the one that would strike it rich so they could make their fortune. Moving to Maui might be a fun place to live and work, but it would take them out of the loop, and so they would miss their chance. They preferred to work 18-hour days while they were young in the hope that they would make enough so they could move to Maui to retire by the time they were in their 30s.

I must have interviewed 200 people during the time we were there. Universally, they were either dropped out, drugged-out, burned-out, or in the middle of a midlife crisis. All they wanted to do was make enough money so that they could lay on the beach, chase chicks, or guys, and smoke dope. I never did find one that wanted to work.

There was no university on Maui. The University of Hawaii is on Oahu, but it specialized in oceanography and astronomy, not computer science. That eliminated any feed-source of bright young minds that could help build the company.

Lastly, there were no customers in Hawaii. There were no significant prospects anywhere in Hawaii. We were either 6-hours from California or 6-hours from Tokyo. That worked for the NeXT systems as they sold themselves and we had no serious competition. However, it was not a good location from which to try to sell software or any other product.

— ■ —

Our time in Hawaii could only be called a boondoggle. We had a lot of fun, but it cost us a lot of money, and from a business standpoint, it was a dumb idea. I recognized some of the errors in my judgment fairly quickly and realized that while we could have some fun in Hawaii, it was unlikely to be our permanent home.

Sharon wanted to buy a home and settle in, but I resisted. The homes were expensive and even though many were ½ the price they had been only a few years earlier; I saw them as still overpriced. The Japanese economy had been super-hot throughout the 1980s, and as a result, land prices in Japan were completely irrational. Many business people in Japan had made a fortune, and they saw Hawaii as a place to buy a get-away or retirement home. The Japanese had bought land and built some incredible homes on all of the islands, but Maui in particular.

When the Japanese economy crashed in the early 1990s, many in Japan lost their fortunes and were forced to liquidate their Hawaii holdings. These properties were easy to spot because there were certain stylistic similarities. They almost all had extensive marble floor areas, sometimes, even upstairs. Hawaiian homes are very open to take advantage of the temperate climate and nearly constant Trade Winds. There are lots of spacious lanais and balconies, many of these were also marble covered. Pools were almost always part of the package. Most homes were furnished including linens, plates, and silverware. Some even had food and liquor in the cupboards. All of this was so the Japanese owner could hop over for a week or a month without bringing anything. Many were never occupied as they were completed just when the crash hit Japan.

Houses that had started in the $2 million range and were now selling just a little over ½ that. I was pretty sensitive to what was going on in Japan and saw these houses continuing to fall in price to roughly ½ of their current prices, about ¼ of their original price. At that price, they would truly be a bargain, but there were so many of these homes that it seemed likely to me. There was no way I was going to invest at the current prices. My predictions came true.

At first, we rented a townhouse in the Wailea area on the southwest coast of Maui. After about a year, we moved to a single family home in Sprekelesville which is the north shore area near Paia. It was one of the Japanese houses, about 2500 square feet, two level with the master suite on the second level. There were marble floors throughout. The house was for sale for $1.2 million, down from $1.8 million, but there were no interested buyers, so they rented it to us. We were in it for about a year when they finally sold it for $750K.

From Sprekelesville we moved upcountry above Makawao. It was a unique home on 8 acres high up on the side of Mt. Haleakala. The house was built for a radio disc jockey from Oahu back in the 1970s. Supposedly, it was his drop out drug house where he escaped on weekends. It was an all wood structure built mainly out of Hawaiian Koa Wood. The story was that he hired a Viet Nam veteran that was an artisan with wood and the guy spent several years living in and building the home.

All of the living area was on a single floor, primarily facing the north shore with a view of the harbor at Kahului, and out across the water to the island of Moloka'i, the leper's island. It sat on the boundary between the rain forest on the north side of the island, and the drylands on the west side. You could sit on the deck and have mist or rain falling on you while you had a blue sky above and a clear view north and west.

There were lots of fruit trees and some steep canyons where he could have easily grown all of the marijuana he might have wanted. That was the common crop in that area for a good number of years; it probably still is. The northwest side of the house was a wall of windows looking out on this spectacular view. The master bath shower had a sunken tub made with hundreds of small blue mosaic tiles. It had a full picture window on the west side, so you were standing in front of a big window looking out at the view while you were taking a shower. There was a big deck on the west side of the house so if anyone was outside they could easily be looking in while you were taking your shower. Beyond the deck, it dropped off sharply into the dense underbrush.

There was a balcony that ran from room to room on the east wall of each of the west facing rooms. We soon discovered that the wooden walls on the loft had a secret door that you could press and the wall would open to a hidden chamber behind the balcony. There was even a hay lift at one end of the secret back area; I suppose it was so he could lift the bales of marijuana into his stash.

We discovered this secret door while we were moving in. The movers dropped a box of books in a back bedroom, and when they did, an even larger box of what turned out to be vintage Playboy magazines, came crashing through the ceiling.

By following the books, we found the hidden doors. The owner had stashed all kinds of things up in this hidden storage area. He had not been too smart about how he had placed the boxes. Some were balanced on a single rafter. The shaking from the box drop below had tipped one off the rafter, and it fell through the ceiling. I can only imagine what would have happened if we had ever had an earthquake. The whole ceiling would have rained down boxes. I got a few boards to span over multiple rafters and rearranged his stash in a more secure fashion.

— ■ —

The woodwork was incredible. The archways built under the staircases that ran up to the loft were all fitted with shaped horizontal strips of Koa Wood. These ran from the floor, up over the top and then back down to the floor again. Each arch consisted a hundred or more 1" strips of Koa individually shaped to fit together tightly. Each stairway had several steps where the risers were made into drawers like you would find on a sailboat. Whoever had built this place obviously loved to do custom woodworking and the owner apparently just let him build to his heart's content.

— ■ —

The people who owned the place were in the music business. The guy had designed many famous album covers for some of the biggest recording artist: Elvis, the Beatles, and many others. There was a box in the attic with LPs personally autographed by the artists. They were probably worth quite a bit then, more today. Apparently, they decided to drop out and moved to Maui at some point, maybe as CDs replaced LPs. They later got "Island Fever." A disdain for living on an island where you cannot get away from where you are unless you get on an airplane. They decided to move to Hong Kong for a while. At some point either boredom or money caused them to move back to Laguna Beach to work in the industry to make more money. At this point, they rented the house.

When we rented the place, we asked for the key and discovered that the realtor didn't have one. The place apparently had been unlocked for years. We had them call a locksmith and make keys for us. Inside were all kinds of very expensive art, including a piano that was supposedly one of Beethoven's. I have no idea if it really was, but it certainly looked old enough to be. There was one locked room where they stored whatever they considered to be the most valuable items. I have no idea what was in there. We lived there for about a year before we moved back to the mainland.

— ■ —

The sky was so clear up on the side of the mountain that we had an incredible view of the stars and the Milky Way. The Hale-Bopp comet made its appearance while we were living there. You could sit on the back deck with the comet filling more than ½ of the sky. It looked like you could reach out and touch it. I happened to travel to Boulder, Colorado during that time and I was amazed by the difference in appearance. In Boulder, I had to search the sky to find the comet.

We enjoyed exploring the island while we were there, but I did get a bit tired of the confinement of island living. Fortunately, I traveled to the mainland fairly frequently, so I got a chance to break free of those constraints from time to time. One of my assignments, whenever I traveled through California, was to stop at Trader Joe's to pick up chocolate bars along with some other goodies that were unavailable on the island.

Costco opened a store on Maui while we were living there. People referred to things as "BC" and "AC" meaning Before and After Costco. Costco revolutionized shopping on the island. Before Costco, the little stores were ripping off the tourists with highly inflated prices. Costco put a large number of them out of business as well it should because they were gouging the tourists as well as the locals.

A lot of things were hard to find on the island. Everyday things were plentiful but expensive. Anything that was the least bit unique was almost impossible to find. That was before Amazon or any of the Internet stores, so it was not easy to get those hard to locate items.

— ■ —

Another thing we found interesting was the way they treated whites. Hawaii is one of the few places in America where whites are in the minority. There is a lot of, sometimes not so subtle, anti-white sentiment. There is even a "kill haole" day. Haole being the Hawaiian name for whites. Sharon was a light-skinned black, and she was often mistaken for either a Hawaiian or a Polynesian from some other island in the Pacific. When she walked into a store alone, she was served immediately. If I walked in separately, I would be completely ignored. We used to experiment to see which stores were the most obvious with their discrimination. We never experienced anything beyond the lack of service, but it was very apparent.

There was a lot of confusion as to the exact meaning of the word "haole." Even the native Hawaiians would disagree. The definition that I always liked was that the word meant "one without breath." Until the white man came along, the Hawaiians had no written language. Back then, when a Hawaiian met another Hawaiian, they would take a deep breath and recite their lineage almost like a chant. When the white man came along they would stick out their hand and give their name, hence the white man was referred to as "one without breath." I was never able to find out if it was the actual meaning, but it was the best story.

— ■ —

There was also a "screw the mainlanders" attitude that was prevalent everywhere. They referred to mainlanders as JOPs, "Just Off the Plane." Apparently in their mind that gave them the right to try to take them for anything they could. I suppose a lot of this had to do with the fact that Hawaii is primarily a playground for people who have more money than the native Hawaiians. That is a recipe for resentment.

There is a lot of corruption in the islands. Almost all power is in the hands of the 442 and 442 descendants. The 442 referred to the 442nd Infantry Regiment that was made up of Japanese-Americans during WWII. The 442nd went to Europe, and they were one of the most decorated units of the Army in the second world war. When they returned, they took over all important positions in Hawaii.

Senator Inouye was a 442 member. Spark Masayuki Matsunaga, a Senator from 1977 to 1990 was also a 442 member. If you looked at the Board of Directors members for companies or organizations, you would see that 442 members or their descendants dominated almost all business and political life in Hawaii.

I recall meeting a man who had struggled for years to try to develop a large tract of land on the northwest side of Maui. One mainland company had originally acquired the land and drawn up plans to build a beautiful resort hotel. After spending millions, and years in fruitless attempts, the company finally gave up and sold to another mainland developer. That company sent a Senior VP to live on Maui to try to get the project moving. He spent more

407

years and additional millions to no avail.

The second company had just about given up, and this guy was complaining to a friend that he feared he would have to sell the land and abandon the project. His friend casually mentioned that he might want to put so and so on the Board. That particular so and so was a 442 member. The company did, and there were bulldozers on the land within 48 hours. That is the kind of power and the kind of corruption that was everywhere. If you wanted to get something done, you had to scratch somebody with 442 connections. Even then, it would take twice as many people, and at least half of them had to be somehow related to the Queen Liliuokalani blood line. Liliuokalani was the last queen in Hawaii. All of this became quite frustrating.

Despite all of these frustrations, living on Maui was a fun experience. The weather was incredible, and the living was easy. The pace was slow, and no one got to stressed about anything. Katie started school at the Montessori school. One of the advantages of the Montessori system was that students could work at their pace. She was reading at 4th-grade level, so she attended reading with other students at that level. There was no holding her back.

Missed Opportunities

At that point, I had not yet learned one critical piece of business insight. Specifically: *Those who know why will always work for those who know how.* My BS in Business had taught me the mechanics, things like accounting. I had learned the "how" to run a business, but I needed to focus on the "why" side. I finally learned the why-how lesson before I studied for my MBA, and this insight radically changed my life. The MBA program brought the lesson home.

This lack of understanding brought about two serious misjudgments concerning my business. I did not have a real sense of how to leverage the assets that we had. More accurately to even recognize our true assets.

Abandoning Servare

I had let the service management software opportunity slip away. In truth, even at that point, there was still an opportunity for that business, and I should have redeveloped the software while we were on Maui. Unfortunately, I focused too heavily on the Dancing Bear NeXT resale side and didn't invest in the software.

Authorized Vendor List

Another big asset I didn't recognize was the value of our Dancing Bear customer list. DBE was a unique, once in a lifetime opportunity. Anyone who successfully develops a new company will tell you that the single hardest thing to do is to get in the door at large enterprises, to become what is called an "Authorized Vendor."

To get an order, you had to be cleared by their purchasing department and added to their Authorized Vendors (AV) list. In many cases becoming and Authorized Vendor is the most difficult part of selling. Big companies are very protective of their vendor lists. For the Purchasing Department, each vendor represents additional work, risks, and costs. Therefore, most companies will do some serious due diligence on any new supplier. Are you big enough to meet their need? Can you be counted on to be there if there is a problem? What are your financials? Do you have legal issues? Can you provide other references? And the biggest one, do they already have an Authorized Vendor who can provide this particular product or service? These are significant hurdles for a new company to get over.

Dancing Bear skipped past all of these barriers without a single question. We were the only ones providing the NeXT equipment and support, and our customers were desperate. Anyone who did look would only find DBE. When it came down to keeping 5,000 computers and the entire trading operation running at Swiss Bank, any risks that might have been associated with doing business with Dancing Bear were nothing compared to shutting down the trading floor. There was no alternative, so we were rubber stamped. Within a couple of months, we were "Authorized" at several huge companies and several Government agencies. We were soon Authorized at virtually every major university and pretty much everyone in between. We had customers all over North America, Japan, Korea, and Europe. We were an AV to a university on Madagascar off the coast of South Africa, and another school on Reunion Island in the middle of the Indian Ocean.

To sell to the Government, you have to be on the GSA list. We got there without even applying. Someone who needed a NeXT from us added us to the list as the only supplier. We never had to make a competitive bid as the Government knew we were the only supplier and they didn't have time to waste. Our customer list, those where we were an AV, would have been the envy of most Fortune 100 companies. It was unquestionably worth several million dollars to the right company.

As the NeXT resales activity waned, I failed to recognize and capitalize the value of our customer list. It is no excuse, but in many ways, the whole thing came too easy for us, and I didn't recognize how valuable it truly was. Also, I didn't know that once you are approved, expanding the products that you market to the company is relatively easy. We should have expanded our product line to include other technologies, software, services, and possibly even other hardware. We already had a solid reputation and a big Internet following. We were operating an online store and had a solid history of taking large credit card payments. Of course, this was long before an Internet presence had any obvious value. Even if I didn't want to expand our product line, I should have sought an acquisition/merger partner, either to buy into some new technology to sell to our list or to sell that company our brand and our Authorized list. Any of these would have been better than walking away from this asset. That is the mistake I made.

Ernestine Technologies

The NeXT resale business gradually tapered off as new products came online making the NeXT less desirable. As the NeXT sales wound down, we started working with Andy Kraftsow, a local who was also looking to build a technology startup. Together we started a new company called Ernestine Technologies.

We generated some funding from Bozell, a New York advertising company, and we brought in a couple of executives from the advertising world. Mel Newhoff became the president. There was another ad man who I liked, but he passed away shortly after he started working with Ernestine and so I never got to work with him.

PaperClick

Ernestine's primary product was an innovative technology we called "PaperClick." It created a link from a printed barcode to a web page.

What we wanted to do was to get advertisers to incorporate a small barcode in their print ads. Using a pen-scanner, users could link the ad to a web page. That would allow a person sitting on their sofa looking at a magazine to scan an ad to display the corresponding web page on their TV. The advertising aspect was the reason Bozell was interested in funding us.

We were way ahead of the market with our technology. Remember this was more than a decade before smartphones. We applied for a patent in 1995. Our vision did eventually come to pass. It was almost 20 years before the QR code linking process became standard, and that development was a direct outcome of PaperClick.

— ■ —

One of the challenges was to find or develop a small convenient barcode reader that would fit and work in a home environment. We sketched a design for a pen reader, and I worked with Welch Allyn to develop such a device. I traveled to WA's plant at Skaneateles, New York. It was an interesting trip. Skaneateles is out in the middle of nowhere New York. It was a cold winter with lots of snow. Coming from Maui where it never gets below 70 degrees, I nearly froze to death on that trip. It was worth it. They took me through their factory. Of particular interest was their development lab where they were working to develop the device we had designed.

Unfortunately, we never quite got to where we wanted as far as size and ease of use. There were two issues. The first was the communications technology needed to transmit the scan to a TV set-top box. Wi-Fi and Bluetooth had not been invented. We tried infrared, but it was not very satisfactory. Battery life was also an issue as the laser scanners of that day required more juice than a couple of AA batteries could provide. We settled for a PC-attached unit as an interim solution. It wasn't a good fit. Laptops were not yet common, and so there was not a real convenient solution for most home users. As I said, we were way ahead of the technology at that point.

I spent a fair amount of time working with AT&T at their Baskin Ridge NJ location to sell a license to the product. That process brought home our need to move back to the mainland. AT&T was a typical big company, and they seemed to want to meet almost every week. Living in Hawaii, that was a real problem. I was flying against the clock. I would take a 6-hour flight to LA or San Francisco and spend the night. Travel to New Jersey, the next day, arriving in the evening. I would meet AT&T the next day. Much like McDonald's, they never seemed to be able to make a decision so the only accomplishment would be to set a date for the next meeting. The next day I would fly back to LA and then the next day back to Maui. Every meeting took a week and cost $5,000. That was unsustainable.

— ■ —

When we all reached the conclusion that we needed to be back on the mainland, I tried to get everyone excited about Boulder Colorado; I even moved there briefly before everyone else finally made the jump back to the mainland. My campaign to get the crew to select Boulder was unsuccessful. Andy came to take a tour, and as luck would have it, he happened to arrive just as Boulder was experiencing one of its rare blizzards. We had close to two feet of snow and temperatures dropped to near zero. Andy had lived on Maui for a long time and the idea of coming to a place as cold as Boulder was for those few days, was just inconceivable. Mel Newhoff lived in the San Fernando Valley north of LA, and he didn't want to move. We ultimately relocated the company to Westlake Village, California. Of course, I had lived there before.

We did sell a license to AT&T. We then sold the company to NeoMedia. They were located in Ft. Myers FL at that time. NeoMedia continued marketing the product under the PaperClick brand name. They targeted industrial users initially where the link was more appropriate for things like parts catalogs or

412

chemical information. Over time, they developed the QR code reading technology that is standard on smartphones today.

As part of the sale, we each had to work for NeoMedia. The required duration was 24-months if I remember correctly. They wanted me to move to Ft. Myers, but I had no interest in relocating to Florida or continuing to work for them beyond the 24-month requirement. NeoMedia insisted that I at least move closer to their location. I talked with Sharon and we decided that we would try the Washington, DC area.

Sharon's sister Julia Tuzun lived in the area with her husband, and Washington met all of my requirements. I knew that I would only stay with NeoMedia the minimum amount of time required before I branched out again to start a new company. After experiencing all of the issues of trying to build a business on Maui, I was a lot smarter about my requirements. Any place we moved had to have a high tech community, VC industry, and an international airport. With those, I figured I could build a business or work internationally, whichever worked out. Ft. Myers, FL, aside from being too flat, too hot, too muggy, and too buggy, didn't meet any of my requirements. It is interesting that NeoMedia eventually relocated to Boulder Colorado, but this was much later.

Y2K

Before we moved to Washington, actually to Fairfax, VA, I had started working on my next venture. The Y2K (Year 2000 date processing) bug was the hottest topic in the tech world at that time. I explained the Y2K issue in some detail the early in my chapter on IBM; I won't repeat it here.

Several companies had developed what were called "remediation" applications. These programs were designed to, at a minimum, scan each application flagging suspected date fields that contained 2-digit dates. A few packages even had code that would attempt to create a workaround so that the application would comply with the 4-digit date standard.

I met a guy from Australia who lived in Westlake Village. His daughter and Katie were classmates. He was not a software guy himself, but he had a friend in Australia who worked for a company that had created a remediation application. They were looking for a way to market their software in the US. My friend had some money people lined up, but they lacked a technical lead to evaluate the application and to create sales and technical teams here in the US.

I flew to Sydney and spent several days evaluating the package and reviewing all of their stated claims. It looked to me like it would do most of what they were claiming, and we negotiated an agreement to represent them in the US.

That was my first and, at least so far, only trip to Australia. Sydney is a lovely city with a beautiful harbor. I took a boat tour of the bay and spent quite a bit of time in Royal Botanical Gardens which is 158 acres with all kinds of smaller venues within the Park. The famous opera house is at the edge of the Park, and of course, it is specular. One of the things I enjoyed the most was the abundance of wild birds and animals that I had only seen in zoos. Everywhere I looked I saw colorful and exotic birds flying around as common as sparrows.

There was an area in the Park with old trees that had grown over the walking path so that it looked almost like a tunnel. It was virtually silent walking along the path until suddenly this huge bat flew directly over my head. It had a wingspan of 4 or 5 feet. I was walking in silence, and suddenly there was a loud whoosh as it passed directly over me, probably no more than 2' away. It proceeded down this wooded tunnel until there was a break, then flew up and grabbed onto a branch where there were dozens of these huge bats hanging upside down the way bats do when they are on their perch. When it grabbed the branch, it locked on and swung over and around while it folded its wings. That shook the branch, and all of the other bats started squawking their complaint about the disturbance.

The locals call these "fox-faced" bats; technically they are called grey-headed flying fox bats. They are the largest bat in Australia. Their bodies are relatively short, about 15″, but their wings can get up to 6′. Like other bats, they don't have feathers, just a thin membrane that you can see light through them when they fly above you. They do have a reddish-brown collar of fur. They are fruit-eating and not nocturnal. They use normal eyesight and not the radar/sonar systems like smaller bats.

It was fun watching as a bat would come in for one of their crash-landings which caused all of the other bats to squawk, but I found it a bit creepy when you didn't hear a thing until suddenly the bat was right on top of you. Anything with a 5′ wingspan that suddenly appears a couple of feet above your head can be quite startling.

— ■ —

When I returned to California, we immediately moved to Virginia. We traded our old VW Vanagon off on a new Ford Windstar. The Vanagon had been a fun vehicle, and in many ways, I wish I could have kept it, but it had a bit over 100K miles, and it was showing the years. I remember driving our new Ford across the desert approaching Las Vegas, and the temperature outside was showing as 118°. There was no way the old Vanagon could have handled that kind of heat.

We rented a house in Fairfax, VA. I immediately started working to sell NeoMedia's products, mainly to AOL (America Online). I tried chasing government opportunities, but sales to the Feds is a 2-year minimum. You have to get them interested, you have to be on the GSA Schedule, and then you have to wait until they can get the purchase into their budget. Most companies can't afford to have a sales team waiting that long. I knew I wouldn't be around that long, so government accounts were not my primary target.

I also tried selling the Y2K software application. My Australian friend had somehow made connections with several people in the DC area who either had money or access to money and wanted to play in the Y2K opportunity. Unfortunately, they had all worked in and around the government, so none of them had any contacts in commercial accounts. It also turned out that their access to funding was more talk than reality, or at least quick access, and that was needed because we were coming late to the market.

I don't remember all of them, but one was Webster Lee "Webb" Hubbell, another was Judson "Jud" Gould. Webb Hubbell had just got back from a stint in prison, thanks to his friend Hillary Clinton. A few years earlier, then Governor Bill Clinton had appointed Webb, at age 36, to be the Chief Justice of the Arkansas Supreme Court. Webb had a distinguished career as mayor of Little Rock and Managing Partner of the Rose Law Firm in Little Rock. That is where he worked with Hillary.

Hubbell followed the Clintons to Washington and was a key member of the transition team, primarily involved in screening cabinet members. Hubbell's name was floated for the position of Attorney General. However, there were several controversies involving his previous positions in Arkansas. He was never nominated. He did serve as Associate Attorney General under Janet Reno. There, he managed the Civil Rights Division.

He eventually was forced to resign and was charged with overbilling clients during the Whitewater controversy in Arkansas. Ultimately he pled guilty to one count of wire fraud and one count of tax fraud in connection with his legal billing at the Rose Law Firm. Hubbell received a prison sentence of 21 months. Many people, myself included, assumed he "took the fall" to protect Hillary Clinton who was also deeply involved in Whitewater. Webb and I never talked about this, and he never said anything directly, but the few things I picked up didn't change my assumption.

Hubbell became one of the principal players in the Starr investigation on Whitewater. Starr and his prosecutors were convinced that Hubbell knew all of the Clintons' secrets that were under investigation. They believed that with sufficient pressure, he would tell all. On April 30, 1998, Hubbell and his wife were indicted for conspiracy, tax evasion, and mail fraud. That was ultimately thrown out, but it went all the way to the Supreme Court.

On November 14, 1998, Starr indicted Hubbell for the third and final time. The allegation was that he gave false testimony to the House Banking Committee and federal banking regulators. On June 30, 1999, the day Starr was required to step down as Independent Counsel, Hubbell entered into a plea agreement resolving the indictments and bringing Starr's pursuit of him to an end. Hubbell pled guilty to one charge of failing to disclose a potential conflict of interest. He received a sentence of one year of probation. In exchange, the prosecutor dropped all charges against his wife, his lawyer, and his accountant, and Starr agreed not to bring further charges against Hubbell.

I was working with Webb during most of this time. I wouldn't go so far as to call him a friend, I never got close to him personally. I saw him as a, maybe not so innocent pawn, caught in the greater war being played out by Kenneth Starr and the Clintons. Starr, as Independent Counsel was trying to break through the many walls built around what was believed to be extensive illegal activities conducted by the Clintons, mainly Hillary.

A lot of the actions taken against Webb and his wife were nothing more than pressure tactics to try to crack open a window into what until recently was one of the most controversial parts of Clinton's lives. I cannot imagine the pressure he and Suzy must have endured through all of this. Hillary owes them big time, but judging by the plethora of bodies under busses; Hillary is not one to pay these kinds of debts.

Working with Webb was an opportunity and a reason to start looking seriously at the history and actions of the Clintons. I concluded that they are both crooks of the highest order. Hillary being several orders of magnitude worse than Bill. She is an absolute con artist and a pathological liar, completely dishonest to the core. She expects unending loyalty from everyone but has zero loyalty to anyone. There is no one she won't throw under the bus.

One of the things that made it interesting was that while I was working with Webb, all of this legal maneuvering was being played out nightly on the national news.

— ■ —

I also had the pleasure of meeting and working with Jud Gould. Jud had retired from his law practice at that time, but he was still dabbling in legal matters for some startup companies. He may have been advising Webb, but as a friend. I don't believe he was ever officially Webb's attorney. Jud had been a very prominent K Street lawyer for years. K Street refers to a major thoroughfare in Washington, D.C. that is known for the offices of think tanks, lobbyists, lawyers, and advocacy groups.

Jud's father had been a prominent attorney in New York. He was the "Gould" half of the Shay & Gould law firm. Shay stadium was named after the Shay half of that firm. Jud's father had represented half of the influential people who founded and ran Israel from the 1940s to the late 1980s. Jud grew up knowing all of them. I was at Jud's house a few times, and there were pictures showing him as a child or as a young man, with people like Golda Meir, Arial Sharon, Chaim Herzog, and David Ben-Gurion.

I worked with Jud on the Y2K project, but also later when I was trying to raise capital for another venture I wanted to start. I remember on one train trip to New York to talk to some prospective investors; we were discussing the Clintons' problems, in particular, the issues that were coming up as Bill became a lame-duck president. Jud's summation was *"they are all whores; it is just a question of who is their pimp."* He was not limiting his comment to the Clinton's; he meant all politicians. That pretty much sums up my opinion of politicians.

We were able to sell the Australian software to a couple of small accounts, but by the time we got the money together and started selling, we were too late to the market. Most companies had already settled on their approach to solving the problem.

U.S. Check

I was working on the Y2K opportunity while I was simultaneously trying to sell NeoMedia's products. I made a good effort, but my heart wasn't in it. One of the VPs at NeoMedia had left the company and was trying to start a new venture involving tamper-proof financial instruments. His name was Robert, but I don't recall his last name. About the time it became apparent that the clock had run out on the Y2K opportunity, he asked me to work with him on pulling together the business plan for the check venture.

The opportunity centered around a special ink developed by a New Jersey company called U.S. Check. They had patented a unique magnetic ink that contained a secret formulation which had a combination of several rare earth metals suspended within the ink. That ink could be identified and uniquely traced to the specific batch when it was manufactured. They had also developed a module that was operational on production check sorting machines that could "read" this ink. That gave them the ability to electronically identify any document that had been altered, thus creating fraud-proof financial instruments. Mainly checks, but in fact, there were applications for this process on virtually every printed financial instrument: stocks, bonds, certificates of deposit, deeds, etc.

This opportunity tied back to my banking experience at IBM 20 years earlier; in particular, my industry as well as my equipment knowledge from my work on the 3890 Check Sorting program in the mid-1970s, later on, the Western Bancorp TIPS project, and still later with both CUFie and Gibraltar.

The founders of U.S. Check were getting older, and they wanted to sell the company as they had no heirs who were capable or interested in developing and marketing the technology. They wanted to cash out and retire to Florida. The opportunity was a bit of a boutique affair. Not something that was likely to become a huge company, but it could have been very profitable in that segment of the market where fraud was frequently in the 7-figure range.

I traveled to New Jersey several times to meet with the U.S. Check team. They were the ones I met at the Newark Train Station that I mentioned earlier. I wrote the Business Plan. Richard Arthur did the financials. He lived in Florida. I got to know Richard quite well, and we worked together on other projects over the years.

Unfortunately, in the process of searching for capital, Robert, who had initiated this opportunity, left our Business Plan with someone associated with NeoMedia. The plan listed me as one of the VPs. When that plan got back to NeoMedia, and they saw my name as an officer in the company, they claimed this was a conflict of interest and used it as an excuse to break my employment contract. In truth, there was no conflict as we were in an entirely unrelated field. The business at that point was not yet a business; it was just seeking funds to purchase U.S. Check. In any case, my agreement with NeoMedia had no restrictions on what I could do on my own time. I could have sued, but that would have cost more money, taken more time, and there was never a guarantee that I could have prevailed. I chose just to let it go. For me, the timing wasn't the greatest as I had not recovered financially from the moves, first from Hawaii to California and then to Virginia. Also, the NeoMedia stock I had acquired as part of the purchase of Ernestine Technologies was still restricted so I couldn't sell that for some time. In the end, it all worked for the better.

— ■ —

Robert was never able to raise the capital needed to buy U.S. Check, and so the deal ultimately fell through. As potential investors were doing their due diligence, they would naturally make inquiries about Robert's tenure at NeoMedia. I could never be sure, but I suspected that NeoMedia management had the same "doggie in the manger" tendencies that I had seen at NBI. They were vindictive about trying to keep any former employee, former executives in particular, from succeeding at anything, even if it was totally unrelated to their business. I could be wrong, but I think that they were instrumental in stopping Robert from raising money.

— ■ —

While I was with NeoMedia, I had started playing the stock market buying and selling stocks in the many Dot Coms that were hitting the IPO market. That opportunity lasted for a couple of years, and I only lost money on one deal. The stock market was paying my bills while Robert was chasing money, and then later while I was trying to put together and fund my venture.

When the U.S. Check deal fell through, I worked up another business plan, I don't even remember what it was about, but it was a Dot-Com venture. I included both Jud and Richard Arthur on the team. We started our search for funding, but our timing turned out to be all wrong. We were just starting our search when the whole Dot-Com bubble burst. It began to deflate in late 1999, but the real bust came in mid-2000. When that happened, the VC market dried up for Dot-Coms. There were no VC funds available for any Internet company for several years.

Another friend, Jerry Palmer, was also being considered for a position in the new startup. He was an executive with Verizon at that time. I had learned my lesson regarding listing people who were currently employed, so I did not include him officially on our management team. When we all realized that this was not the time to raise funds, Jerry suggested that I go to work for somebody for a few years while the market settled out. He had another friend, Jim Rutt, who was the president of Network Solutions. He called Jim and arranged a meeting.

Verisign

I met with Jim Rutt, the president of Network Solutions. At the time, Verisign was acquiring Network Solutions for the then record sum of $21 billion. Our meeting was supposed to be more of a meet-and-greet to explore possible opportunities to work together on some project. It was not meant to be an employment interview.

Jim was a large man, way overweight, but otherwise very energetic and full of ideas. His office was a scene of complete chaos. There was a long cafeteria style table piled at least a foot deep with papers in complete disarray. His desk was the same. There were Burger King wrappers and French fry containers here and there. It was unbelievable. He had two or three PCs on his desk, each with a huge monitor. I learned later that he had an entire server dedicated solely to his email. Supposedly, he had thousands of unopened emails in his inbox at all times. What amazed me was that in all the time I worked for him, he never failed to respond to any email I sent in more than 15 minutes. How he managed to stay organized amid all this chaos is beyond me, but he was certainly an organized, and in my mind, brilliant man when it came to business.

We talked about different experiences, and I mentioned my Ernestine experience and the PaperClick product. For some reason, that caught his attention, or maybe he was bored with it and wanted to change directions. He interrupted to ask me if I knew anything about the mobile Internet; I didn't. He tossed his phone to me which, unbeknownst to him, was a dangerous move because I have never been much good at catching things. Fortunately, I did catch his phone. When I did, he said, "go to any site on the Internet." I fumbled with it for a few minutes and finally got to the browser. I started to type very slowly using the multi-press typing system which was called "tap-coding." Predictive text typing was not yet standard on phones, and of course, it has never actually worked with URLs which tend to be several words with no spaces. At that time, and unbeknownst to me, you had to enter "wap" (Wireless Applications Protocol) instead of "www" to access mobile content. After several attempts, I mumbled something about this being impossible, probably with a couple of 4-letter expletives. He responded very simply. "Fix it!"

Jim talked about the need for companies to embrace new technologies and entrepreneurship, but I got the impression that his interest was more personal. He never said anything, but I think that in reality, he was more than a bit bored and turned off by his new status. Jim had expanded Network Solutions and successfully navigated the high-octane world of mergers and acquisitions. He now found himself working as a "division manager" rather than the head of a company. I think he was experiencing something akin to postpartum depression. He needed a new energy source; I believe my project was far more about him than anything else.

While I was technically an employee of what was now Verisign, I was to work independently. I had a contract that gave me a decent salary and a decent severance package regardless of the project's outcome. Of course, the package was weighted toward project success, but the clear understanding was that my destiny was not to become an executive inside of the ranks of Verisign. That worked for me because I had no desire to "rise through the ranks" of a big company.

I started immediately. Jim's instructions were pretty simple, "solve the mobile web navigation problem." Make it easy for people to reach mobile content. I reported directly to him and had his full support.

WebNum

From the beginning, I knew that we were stuck with phone's keypad. There was no way around it, as smartphones were not yet invented. Phones have always been about numbers; alpha was an afterthought. Assigning alpha values to numbers was just a klutzy way to allow text entry using an extremely limited keyboard. As a result, the instant you changed to alpha, things stopped being simple.

I also knew that numbers alone were not allowed as domain names. In part, this was an agreement between ICANN (Internet Corporation for Assigned Names and Numbers) and The International Telecommunication Union (ITU) to prevent companies from using their telephone number as their domain name. ICANN is a global nonprofit that administers the Internet. ITU is a similar organization, and part of the UN. It has authority over the global telephone system.

Despite the restriction on numbers as domain names, I kept coming back to the same answer. The key to any new system had to center on using numbers to address the Internet.

The challenge was keeping me up at 2 a.m. It turns out that 2 a.m. is the time of day when I solve most of my issues, design new things, invent new solutions, and just clear the decks. It has always been this way for me; it still is today.

Short codes looked like the place to start. Short codes often represent their alpha-equivalents. The number "8" represented T-U-V, "2" represents A-B-C, and "5" represents J-K-L. Therefore, the digits 825 could be a short code representing "UAL" for United Air Lines. Of course, those three numbers could represent a number of different alphabetic combinations.

Just to complicate things, the alpha/numeric relationship is not the same in all countries, for example in Australia; the "1" key represents the alpha values of Q & Z. The UK has yet another configuration. Also, there are a lot of countries that use something other than a Latin character set.

Creating short codes didn't solve the problem because ICANN still would not allow numeric-only domain names. To use any numeric navigation system, I would need a system that would translate the numbers into letters. I could create an application and a translation table on the handset, but it is not feasible to be constantly updating translation tables on every mobile phone in the world. I needed an off-phone directory.

Another concern was that short codes provided a very limited number of possible combinations.

— ■ —

Every approach I took kept circling back to the original problem; "how do I make it simple" for the user. That kept me churning all night. Finally, I hit upon a concept that appeared to have legs, but I needed to know more about how the Internet, or more correctly the DNS (Domain Name System) worked. I knew the basics, but not to the depth that I needed. The first thing that morning I sent Jim an email telling him I had an idea but I need a quick in-depth education on how the DNS worked. His response was predictable; one word, "come." I made it about ½ way through a brief explanation of my concept before he grabbed his phone and asked his Administrative Assistant to come in. He immediately told her to get some people together. When they arrived, he introduced me and had me go over the project and my thinking.

None of them had any prior knowledge of my project, but he told them to make themselves available for me at any time, on any subject. He reiterated to me that he wanted this pulled together quickly.

After our impromptu meeting, Jim gave me a list of people, most of whom I had just met, and he told me their areas of specialization. He also challenged me to come up with a name for the "service," one where the domain name was available. The rest of the day was a blur. I grabbed Bill Dutcher, one of the guys Jim had more or less assigned to work with me, and we brainstormed names while searching to see if the domain names were available. We came up with four or five and registered the domain names. I registered them so they couldn't be associated with Network Solutions.

By the end of the day, we had settled on the name we liked "WebNum" which of course, represented "web number," and registered the www.webnum.com domain. We had also sketched out a rough design of a separate registry that we would build to house WebNum registrations and the associated IP addresses.

Over lunch and between searches, Bill started my in-depth DNS training. Over the next few days and months, I had informal sessions from the experts who had built the .com, .net, and .org Top Level Domains (TLDs) and much of the DNS system.

Internet 101

Before we get too deep into WebNum, I needed to take a few minutes to give you an overview of how the Internet works. You may think that you already know, but I would be surprised if you really did.

Most people think of the Internet as a browser on your computer/tablet/phone, and an address line where you type in the name of the website that magically appears on your browser. In fact, that is not the Internet at all. The browser is an application running on your device. Like a game or a spreadsheet, it is just a piece of software that is your portal into the Internet. It gives you a window to request and view a site. The website is part of the Internet; the browser is just a tool to make it available to you.

The Internet is in fact, a massive number of computers hooked to a huge number of communications lines, scattered all over the globe. All of these computers are accessible, in varying degrees (controlled by security and encryption) to each other and to you. Most importantly none of them know what www.somewhere.com means. Every one of these millions of computers, including your own, only has a numeric address called an IP address.

In the early 1990s, when the Internet moved out of the nerd world, people realized that no mere mortal would ever be able to navigate the Internet using these IP addresses which, at that time, consisted of 32-bits of zeros and ones. IP addresses are difficult to remember, and companies could not build a brand around them. In short, they were not user-friendly.

To make it human-friendly, the Internet folks built and overlay system called the DNS which stands for Domain Name System. DNS sits on top of the Internet and acts as a translator (domain names to IP addresses) between your browser and the actual Internet. The role of the DNS is to allow user-friendly "domain" names to navigate to computers with unfriendly IP addresses. I suppose you could call it part of the Internet, but in reality, it is just a coat of paint that makes a small portion the Internet easy to access. In fact, there is a significant "other" part of the Internet; some estimate that it is 500 times the size of the www, or the "surface" Internet. The other part of the Internet is often called the "dark web." The dark web can only be reached by IP addresses. Without DNS, the Internet would have never become popular.

You could think of the DNS as a massive database. In fact, it is thousands of huge databases, but let's keep it simple for the moment. In that database is a large table that translates the "domain names" to the correct IP address for the actual computer where the target website lives.

Here, at the duckies and birdies level, is a brief explanation of the magic that makes this all works. You type a URL (Uniform Resource Locator), for example, www.somewhere.com into your browser's address line and you press enter. The browser sends that URL into the DNS. Your browser actually contains a small piece of the DNS software.

The DNS reads that URL from right to left looking for the first "." (period) it encounters. When it finds a period, it uses the data that came just before that period to tell it which database to look in to find the IP address. In our example, the letters "com" tells the DNS to pass that request to the .com database. That causes the database to lookup the IP address based on the next field, continuing right to left, in the address. In our example, that would be "somewhere." The .com database executes a lookup and comes back with the IP address of the actual computer where the "somewhere.com" website lives.

The DNS then sends that IP address back to your browser, along with a command called a "redirect." The browser replaces the "somewhere.com" portion of the original URL with the IP address, and the redirect causes the browser to send a new request directly to the computer where the "somewhere.com" website lives.

When the target computer gets that request, it usually returns the default "home" page. However, it can look at the entire URL to see if you want a particular page or another folder on that computer. The other fields to the right of the .com, or the left of "somewhere" will provide the information requesting a particular page or folder.

Incidentally, the http://www fields tell it that you want the "www" (World Wide Web) part of that computer. The http:// tells it to use the Hypertext Transfer Protocol. There can be other parts of the computer, and other formats or ways to transfer the data, but again we don't need to go that deep.

I should tell you that the actual process of getting the IP address of the "somewhere" computer is far more complicated than the simplified process I just outlined. Again, that is way beyond what I need to tell you.

– ■ –

Once I had defined the solution as numeric domain names, our next challenge was to develop a method of accessing the WebNum Directory that got around ICANN's prohibition of numeric domain names but did so in a way that simplified the user's Internet experience.

Initially, I considered having the user entering the WebNum as part of the URL. That would look something like WebNum.com/825. That would pass the ICANN roadblock, but to keep it simple I would need to have the browser automatically append "WebNum.com/" in front of whatever (WebNum) number the user entered. That meant modifying the browser. The browser modification would be a bit complicated, but the real problem was that it would require that we modify every current and future mobile browser. It also meant that we would potentially force the user to take additional actions whenever they wanted to access a website that did not have a WebNum. Any such modification, would "break the structure of the Internet." That would never fly, and it was doubtful that the mobile Operators would support this approach.

Finally, and most importantly, this solution would require a double redirect, first to access the WebNum database and second to access the target website.

That added time to the process which was a problem in itself, but the real issue was that it opened a huge security hole. Double redirects are a common way to "spoof," a website by redirecting the user to a fake version of a real internet site. Therefore, most browsers blocked double redirects. I had to find a better solution.

— ■ —

My ultimate solution, after a couple more sleepless nights, was to add a "WebNum Button" to the handsets. The IP address for the WebNum database would be hard-coded into the handset and associated with the WebNum button.

With a WebNum Button on the handset. The user would enter the WebNum using the keypad in standard numeric mode. That would be just like entering a phone number. Instead of pressing the "Send" button, the user would press the "WebNum" button. That would cause two actions. First, it would send that numeric "WebNum" directly to our database for a lookup, and second, it would launch the web browser on the handset if it were not already active.

The WebNum database would work just like a standard DNS database. It would use the WebNum to look up the corresponding IP address for the target website. It would then send that IP address along with a redirect command back to the browser on the handset. From that point onward, the browser would function exactly as it would if the URL had been entered directly into the address line of the browser.

With this approach, there was no double redirect, and we would not have to modify the browser. Of course, this solution would require the cooperation of the handset manufacturers, but we felt we could get that through pressure from the Operators (mobile carriers).

There was still only a limited set of short codes so there would be a limited set of high-value WebNums available, but I had two solutions for this. First, I was planning on setting up WebNum Registries for each country. That meant that each country would have a full suite of WebNums to sell to their customers. It also meant that the number 825 might link to the United Airlines site in the U.S., but a different site in France. That would allow United to build language-specific sites on a country by country basis.

Since the IP address of the WebNum database was hard coded based on the phone's "home" country, an American traveling in France would access the

US WebNum database while a French user standing next to her would access the French WebNum database.

My second solution was for the companies to use their phone number as their WebNum. The same phone number could be used to either dial a phone number or to access a website. As an example, Sheraton Hotels has used 800-325-3535 as their primary phone number for decades. They have invested millions establishing this number as part of their "brand." With WebNum, the user would be able to enter 8003253535 and either press "send" to call the hotel, or press "WebNum" to access their website.

That was an elegant solution, to say the least. No browser modifications would be required. No double redirects were needed. We would not "break" the Internet, and technically we were outside of both the ITU's and ICANN's reach ...at least technically. We could set up WebNum Registries in every country and code the appropriate IP address directly into the handsets. It was incredibly simple for the user; they did not have to understand anything about URLs or DNS or enter Latin characters just short-codes or phone numbers.

We felt that companies, as well as individuals, would love the idea of leveraging their existing phone numbers to access the mobile Internet, and Operators would love WebNum because it would drive Internet adoption, and hence data revenue.

WebNum was a highly visible grab for complete dominance of the mobile Internet. That was clearly going to piss off some folks. We knew that WebNum would make ICANN unhappy, but we were within the letter of the law if not the spirit so to speak. It would also piss off the ITU and the UN as it got around their probation on phone numbers accessing websites. However, if I were able to pull this off, Verisign would own the mobile Internet. WebNum was a huge play and only a company with the stature of Network Solutions, recently combined with Verisign, had the gravitas to pull this off.

That said, there were clearly political risks for Verisign. They were operating as a licensed monopoly as the only Registry for all of the major TLDs: .com, .net, and .org, and they were already receiving a lot of criticism because they controlled such a large part of the commercial Internet. In fact, Verisign would soon be forced to spin off the .org Registry to a nonprofit company to lessen the extent of their dominance in the industry.

Despite the elegance of the WebNum solution, we were facing a "double critical mass" problem. In other words, we had to build two separate critical masses to succeed. The first was to get enough Operators to buy into the program to attract Registrants (companies) to buy WebNums. The second was to get enough Registrants to make it attractive to users.

You might assume that the issue of getting the handset manufacturers to build WebNum-enabled handsets would be a third critical mass, but we felt the manufacturers would follow Operator demand. Most people assume that the handset manufacturers drive the innovation in the new devices. That is not the case, or at least not before smartphones. Mobile Operators were powering the Innovation. A manufacturer might come up with something they thought was slick, but if the Operator didn't want it, the manufacturers wouldn't put it into the phone. It all came down to revenue. If a feature generated revenue, the Operators wanted it. If not, then they didn't want to be bothered. It was as simple as that. We felt that the Operators would push WebNum because it potentially increased adoption of the mobile Internet, and that meant more data revenue.

Any marketing person will tell you that the biggest challenge of any startup is building a critical mass. Building a double critical mass is far more complicated than creating just one. Despite the challenges we faced, we believed that WebNum was sufficiently attractive solution addressing a big enough problem. We could get both the Operators and Registrants we needed to succeed.

– ∎ –

In essence, WebNum was a parallel DNS system operating outside of the ICANN-regulated DNS. I was not building a private Internet, but I was creating my private access method. We would have to develop our own WebNum Registry from scratch. As a regulated monopoly, Verisign had to erect a solid firewall wall between WebNum, this unregulated commercial venture, and the licensed monopoly portion of their operations. Once constructed, the WebNum Registry would have to continue to operate completely independent from the regulated Registries. These were not serious technical challenges, but they did require that I construct a "firewall" between Network Solutions' day to day operations and my WebNum project.

WebNum was Verisign's first such commercial venture and over time a good portion of my time was spent building the required firewalls, while simultaneously trying to find legal ways around the same walls I was building. Another exercise in politics. That required careful legal involvement.

$$- \blacksquare -$$

You may recall that I talked about IBM having to deal with the Department of Justice on a monopoly issue relating to the bundling of mainframe equipment, software, and service. That was way back in 1967 and 68. IBM had provided me with extensive training on the issue of monopolies. It was 30+ years in my past, but as with so many things in my life, I had now come full circle, and I was the one arguing with Verisign's legal department about what we could and could not do in the WebNum project. Verisign at one point had to hire outside council that specialized in monopoly law because I knew more about what could and couldn't be done then our internal council. I was once again rewarded, for IBM's investment in my training.

Taking on the World

Jim and I talked politics. We knew that as we began to roll out the WebNum service, the fact that we were creating this shadow DNS/TLD would be a major political issue with ICANN. The ITU would also be unhappy. In their mind, they would feel that I was messing with the global telephone numbering system. I wasn't doing anything with the actual system any more than I was altering the Internet or DNS; I was just using numbers in a different way. In any case, it was clear that WebNum would be crossing swords with two separate global regulatory authorities.

We would also upset individual countries as we would diminish the value of their Country Code (ccTLD) Registries. Years earlier, with Goshawk I was taking on significant parts of IBM. Now, with WebNum I was taking on the world. We would be eating a little bit of everybody's lunch. We knew that there would be more than a little discontent with our "land-grab."

www.washtech.com

Wireless's New Keys To the Net

VeriSign Technology Eases Web Surfing

By DINA ELBOGHDADY
Washington Post Staff Writer

Surfing the Web on your cell phone should be just as easy as dialing a phone number, according to VeriSign Inc.

That's the seminal idea behind the latest technology from the company that registers more than half the world's 28 million ".com," ".net" and ".org" Internet addresses and maintains the master list of Web sites.

A new technology for helping cell phone users surf the wireless Web is "all about quickness," says VeriSign executive Tim Griswold.

WebNum in Washington Post 2001

Around the World in 18-Days

I had invented WebNum, defined the system requirements, developed the marketing strategy and identified our initial approach and business challenges, all within the first week and a half. During this time, I was learning how the Internet worked and refined my solution on the fly. I was up to my eyeballs getting all of this designed and dealing with all of the technical, political, and legal issues. About seven days into this, Jim called me and told me that he had briefed his new boss, Stratton Sclavos, the president of Verisign.

Stratton was excited by what I was doing. He said that Verisign was sending a team on a world trip to talk to phone companies and handset manufacturers about encryption and certificates. He wanted me to join them and pitch WebNum. Ok, that sounded fine until I asked when are they were planning this trip. Answer: they were leaving Sunday to fly to London.

It was panic time. International patent laws are a bit inconsistent. In the U.S. you can talk publicly about something before you file for a patent. Outside of the U.S., if you publicly disclose something, you can no longer file for a patent. I had just started thinking about what might be patentable, but now suddenly, I had to complete the patent application before I took the trip, all in two days! In parallel, I needed to develop a professional presentation.

– ■ –

For those of you who haven't been through the patent application process, it is

435

not simple. You have to describe in detail your patent, laying out the specific claims you are filing, 65 in our case, but we also had to do searches to make sure we were not crossing over into some existing patent or patent application. That usually takes a minimum of two months, a lot of that time involving legal professionals. I couldn't accomplish all of this in 2 days, so I agreed to meet them in Finland in 4 days counting Saturday. I was able to extend it to 5 days by working Sunday.

Bill Dutcher and I went to work, and we grabbed Kevin Golden from the legal department to start the searches and the legal paperwork. We all worked straight through the weekend putting in 20-hour days, but we got an application in by Monday, actually two separate applications. Approval took many months of course but having the application filed meant that I was free to discuss WebNum with Operators and handset manufacturers around the world. United States Patents 7,536,639 & 7,543,227 Internet access architecture and methodology were granted sometime later.

– ■ –

In parallel to the crash program to get the patent applications in and the presentation developed, I needed to get tickets and reservations for the trip. I didn't know any of the details, and I didn't have time to spend working on it, so we had the travel department at Verisign set up my tickets and reservations to match their team. I did not even know who I was meeting or where I was going beyond Helsinki.

Another issue was my need for a corporate credit card. Getting one isn't instantaneous, HR orders it, and the bank sends it a week or so later. I didn't have a week. The finance people at first told me there was no way. Jim adjusted their thinking. I wound up carrying a Corporate Purchasing Card that they used to buy from vendors. I did have a few problems using it outside of the U.S., but it got the job done.

The final challenge was getting a laptop that would work. Network Solutions gave me a Toshiba. It was a good machine, but by the time you add the power cord and transformer, you are close to 10 pounds. It doesn't sound like a lot, but along with all of the other stuff I needed to carry, that can get to be quite heavy.

Verisign was using a special device that allowed secure remote access over an encrypted VPN (Virtual Private Network). The way it worked was that you carried a timer with a built in key-generator synchronized with the home computer. When you initiated the dial-in sequence, you had to enter the key that the timer displayed. That was transmitted to the host to identify you and let you log in.

I took my laptop home Sunday night, and it wouldn't dial in at all. I came to work Monday morning and immediately called the IT department to get some help. I told them I was leaving that afternoon for Finland and had to have a system that worked. I got the typical IT response …we will get to it later. Of course, I didn't have any later; I needed it now. I was standing at the door of the IT service center and not getting any response when a guy by the name of Shane Anderson walked up.

Shane is a large and very muscular black man that looked like he could break most anybody in half like a toothpick. He asked me what the problem was and I gave him a quick explanation. Shane invited me in. He grabbed his personal Toshiba, dumped all of his files onto a backup. Loaded my files onto his machine and handed it to me along with his work and home number. He told me to call if I had any troubles at all. Any hour, any day.

Of course, I had lots of trouble. Mainly that the secure key system seldom worked because of the time required to make the connection through the hotel system and then the international system, then actually connect to Verisign's computer, would exceed the 60-second window when the key would be valid. But even when I could establish the VPN, there were other problems. Shane and I worked on this as I traveled from hotel to hotel and country to country, around the world. I was calling him at all hours of the day and night because of the time difference. We never could get the system to work, so he shipped me another Toshiba. It met me at the hotel in Hong Kong. That one worked, but now I had two 10-pound Toshibas bricks to schlep through the airports.

Shane went on to become a lifelong friend. We have worked together on many projects, and I have mentored him in his private as well as professional life. I think of Shane as my son.

— ■ —

I was so busy and so tired that I didn't have time even to pack my suitcase. Sharon packed for me, but bless her heart; she packed for me like she was packing for herself, far too many clothes in a suitcase that was far too big. Guys pack light, or at least those who are experienced travelers. More than an overnighter, but not that much more. My bag was huge, and it weighed a ton. I got teased about my mega-case all the way around the world.

I caught up with the Verisign team in Helsinki. Our first joint meeting was with Nokia. I worked with Nokia quite a bit over the next ten years and visited Helsinki several times. Finland reminded me a lot of Maine. It has the same kind of landscape, lots of granite and low evergreen trees. It was late August, and the weather was beautiful for this trip, but we didn't have much time to look around.

I was in Helsinki on another trip a year later. It was during the Summer Solstice, with sunlight almost all day and night, only twilight for a couple of hours. The temperature was a balmy 72°, but the locals thought it was hot. Everyone was running around the park wearing nothing but underwear. There were a lot of snow white bodies in the park. It was a beautiful day, but for me, it wasn't all that warm, a light sweater wouldn't have been out of the question.

We left Helsinki on Friday afternoon, and I flew to Copenhagen, Denmark for the weekend. The Verisign team went to St. Petersburg just to sightsee, but the travel department had set me up in Copenhagen. That was one city I had not visited while I was with ITT, so I spent the weekend wandering around Denmark on my own. I particularly enjoyed the harbor area and all of the boats and houses. Mostly I slept as I had not had more than a couple hours sleep each night for about two weeks. I did make it to St. Petersburg briefly once, but that was on a different trip.

Monday we had meetings with the local Mobile Operator in Copenhagen then on Tuesday we drove over to Lund Sweden for a meeting with an Operator there. The Öresund Bridge is a 12-kilometer causeway that connects Copenhagen to Malmö Sweden. The Öresund had opened in July 2000, just a month before I crossed. It is the longest road/train bridge in Europe. There is an artificial island about halfway over. It was a beautiful drive in the summer. I never crossed in the winter, but I suspect it might not be so pleasant at that time of year.

Tim in Helsinki Finland 2000

The next stop was Paris and meetings with Vodafone as well as Orange, both mobile Operators. From there, we went to Germany, Austria and then Italy, meeting with Operators and handset manufacturers along the way. From Italy, we took the long hop over the pole to Hong Kong where we met with two Operators and a mainland (China) handset manufacturer. My new laptop caught up with me in Hong Kong. Fortunately, it worked, but I had a ton of email, mostly from Jim. I now had a mega briefcase with two 10 pound laptops, to match my mega suitcase.

We traveled to Tokyo for more meetings with DoCoMo and several handset manufacturers. DoCoMo was the primary mobile operator in Japan. DoCoMo is an acronym for Do Communications Mobil. From Japan, I traveled to Seoul Korea. We met with Korea Telecom, LG, and Samsung.

I learned a great deal about the mobile Internet on this trip, particularly in Japan and Seoul Korea, as both were light years ahead of the rest of the world when it came to the mobile Internet. A part of this was due to their development of more advanced handsets, but that was in response to demand. The cultures of the two countries, especially Japan influenced demand. The Japanese are very serious about not invading another person's space. I suppose this is a natural outcome from centuries of very close, crowded living in homes with paper walls. They go to great lengths not to disturbed those around them. For example, you cannot use a phone when you are out in public. Especially on a bus or train. If your phone rings while you are on the train, you must go and stand between cars to take the call.

At the same time, in Tokyo and most other Japanese cities workers have a very long commute. A 1½ hour train ride is not unusual. The "salarymen," a generic name for what we would call white collar workers, typically works at least 10-hour days. I would land at Narita International Airport in the late afternoon. After passing through Customs and getting my bags, I would take a bus to downtown Tokyo. That is roughly a 45-minute trip. It would be 6:30 or 7 p.m. by the time I reached the city. Most of the city roadways are elevated, so as I rode through the city, I could look in the windows of the office buildings. At 7 p.m. I would see rows and rows of salarymen sitting at their terminals in tiny cubicles. Each would be working away wearing what looked like identical dark suits, white shirts, and ties.

At some point, all of these men would get on a commuter train or bus for an hour and a half ride home. Since they could not speak on their phones during their commute, they would get on the Internet and read the news, send emails and texts their wives and friends. The next morning, they would repeat the process on the way to work. Because of the demand, DoCoMo had developed an excellent mobile Internet service and some sophisticated devices.

Korea didn't have the non-disturbance culture found in Japan, in fact, it is quite the opposite, but there is an extreme concentration of population in the city of Seoul, and so their commutes are onerous as well.

One other factor was that most individuals in both countries did not have personal computers at home. Apartments in both countries are tiny, and there was not enough room for a big system and monitor. Laptops were very expensive and tablets did not yet exist. Their work computers were limited to work. Personal use of the Internet was therefore restricted to mobile phones. Because of this combination of factors, the mobile Internet was several years ahead of the U.S. market in both of these countries.

— ■ —

Another thing that I noticed was that the young people were always texting. Of course, that is true today (2016) in the U.S. as well, but in 2000, nobody used text in the U.S. In Japan, you would see people walking down the street with their hand in their pocket typing texts in the blind. It was incredible to watch. I should note that the Japanese alphabet matches the standard handset keyboard better than English, but even with that, it was still something to see.

Texting was big all over the world, except in North America. That was due in part to the pricing structure and high call prices in most of the rest of the world. In the U.S., the billing system is "calling party pays," meaning the receiving party did not get charged. Furthermore, if the called party didn't answer, there was no charge to either party. In the rest of the world, even if there is no answer, both sides pay for a call. That would chew up your calling card minutes very quickly. It was far cheaper to send a text. Then you didn't have to worry about a no-answer. The other person would respond when they could.

In Finland, I would see several teenagers walking home from school. They would be side by side, but not talking. Instead, they would each be staring at their phones send or receiving text messages. It is that way in the U.S. today, but not 16 years ago.

— ■ —

By the time I got to Korea, I was exhausted. I had never quite recovered from the two-week endurance sprint leading up to the trip, followed by another 2½ weeks of constant moving from hotel to hotel, time zone to time zone, and spending every night working for hours with Shane, trying to get my laptop to link up with the mainframe. It had all taken its toll. After our meetings in Seoul, I parted company with the Verisign team. They were flying back to San

Francisco, and I headed to Washington DC, another 20-hour leg.

I had circumnavigated the globe in 18 days. The trip provided me with invaluable insight and exposure. I had met with almost all of the major handset manufacturers and Operators around the world, and I had received valuable feedback on the WebNum concept. I now understood how consumers around the world were using the mobile Internet and why. I knew how the Operators were dealing with the challenges and opportunities, and the relationship between the Operators and the handset manufacturers. Because I had piggybacked on the Verisign road trip, I also received an in-depth education on mobile phones and data security issues, how Certificates worked, Verisign's business model, and how encryption worked on the handsets. While certificates and encryption were not my immediate concern, or critical to my project, this insight, coming on top of what I had learned about the global telecommunications business over the years, helped me to gain a complete understanding of the overall industry. As it turned out, that knowledge proved precious, several years later in yet another startup venture, as well as in my later consulting work. What an education. There was absolutely no other circumstance where I could have gained so much insight and exposure in such a short time.

Time to Build My Team

I came home convinced that we were on the right path. The response to the WebNum service was universally positive. The small screens and challenging navigation were severely limiting mobile Internet adoption, especially in markets where users had access to home computers. Both Operators and manufacturers had questions and suggestions of course, but all saw the WebNum service as a way to make mobile Internet access simpler and to potentially drive adoption.

ARPU (Average Revenue Per User) is the Holy Grail for operators. Everything is measured against ARPU. Operators were seeing a continual erosion of voice revenues, in part because of the increasing use of text messaging, and they were desperate to drive data usage to compensate for that decline. Mobile Internet usage increased data volumes. WebNum would provide easier access. Therefore, WebNum = increased ARPU, therefore WebNum = good.

I spent the next month or two building a small team and laying out the project. I hired a long-time telecommunications salesman Mark Fruehan away from

CellStar and a telecommunications marketing guy Robert Pepper who had been with Iridium, the satellite communications company. I assigned Mark responsibility for sales in Europe, and Rob was my Marketing Director. I also hired Dennis Feely as my Operations manager and Chris Parente who worked for Rob in marketing. I brought a software developer over from another assignment inside of Verisign. We had a few others, including several part-time college interns who were bailing water or whatever was needed. These were working primarily for Dennis and the development manager. I took responsibility for sales in Asia.

I started traveling to Asia every month and spending two weeks on each trip. I concentrated on the Japanese and Korean markets, but also began to develop the markets in Singapore, Thailand, Malaysia, Hong Kong, and to a lesser extent China.

The business cultures in Asia are quite different from the American and European cultures. In America and Europe, sales tend to be based on functionality, reliability, and price. The personalities of the sales people are important of course, but the product ultimately takes precedence. In Asia, there is a much greater emphasis on developing a personal relationship. You may have the best product at the best price, but if you don't have a relationship with the buyer, you probably won't get the business. I spent many weeks and months building relationships.

I came to the conclusion that one of the most common mistakes American companies make when it comes to doing business in Asia, is not focusing enough on the relationships. They may start the process, but as soon as they have some success, they promote the salesman and lose all of their investment in relationship building.

Dongu Kim & Tim in Seoul 2001

In Korea, I found a small company, 7DC, that wanted to be the Korean Registrar for WebNum. The owner was a young guy by the name of Dongu Kim. Of course, in Asia, they always say the last name first so it would be Kim Dongu. He couldn't speak or understand English, but he had a partner Jahee "Jay" Yoon who was quite fluent in English. She worked as my interpreter.

In Japan, I collaborated with a company called J-Data and its owner Koji Sasaki. Koji spoke some English, but he had a young lady, Yumiko "Yumi" Yamamoto who worked as my interpreter.

I traveled to these two countries at least once a month. I got to know these individuals well. We ate many meals together, I visited their homes and got to know their families. I lost track of Dongu over the years, but 16 years later I remain personal friends with Jahee, Yumi, and Koji.

Doing business in Korea was quite educational. The Korean government mirrors the U.S. system. There are three main branches: executive, judicial and legislative. The legislative branch is slightly different, it is unicameral, consisting of a single large assembly with approximately 300 members. These are the ones you see on TV having knock-down-drag-out brawls every once in a while. Many of their laws and institutions are almost identical to ours. They have a Supreme Court, and they even have a "Blue House" equivalent to our

444

White House.

Jahee's family is well connected politically, and this came in handy as we tried to develop the WebNum business in Korea. Her uncle was the Chief Justice of the Supreme Court, and Jahee served for a couple of terms in the Assembly, but that was years after the WebNum project.

— ■ —

I quickly learned just how protective the Koreans are when it comes to introducing new technologies. Korea is a relatively small country and they traditionally feel inferior to both China and Japan. The three countries are called the "three kingdoms" with Japan at the top, China second, and Korea third. That goes back 5,000 years. Koreans are particularly sensitive about Japan. While the history of military occupations and invasions go back centuries, the Japanese occupation of Korea during WWII was particularly brutal; it is never far from the Korean mind. The Koreans remain very aware, and often bitter about that occupation.

— ■ —

The Korean's seemed to all use metal chopsticks. I will grant you that they are probably cleaner than wooden ones, but they are much harder to use. I asked several people why the metal chopsticks. I got many answers; it seems everyone has at least one version. One common one was that it dated back thousands of years as metal chopsticks were luxury items used by royalty. Another was that this was a reminder of the Japanese occupation. Supposedly, the Japanese confiscated virtually everything that was made of metal and melted it down to make war machines and weapons. After the war, the Koreans started making their chopsticks out of metal as a reminder of the occupation and confiscation. Another story I heard, was that it was a more recent adaptation necessitated by the total absence of trees after the Korean war. I have no idea if any of these are correct, but I do know that most Korean chopsticks were, at that time, metal.

— ■ —

Another indication of the ongoing resentment was the fact that they prohibited the importation of any Japanese cars. That was partially due to the remaining resentment about the Japanese occupation, but it was also in part to allow the Korean manufacturers time to develop their automobile industry. The interesting thing was how they chose to go about building their industry.

Rather than designing their cars, they would buy the previous model year's molds and presses from Japanese and American manufacturers and then set up factories in Korea using these last-cycle presses. They manufacture these vehicles under a Korean company's name. So you would see a car that looked like a Honda Accord, but it might have a Samsung, KIA, or Daewoo logo on the front. Some cars looked like Mercedes, Fords, and others. It was funny to see all of these look alike cars on the streets.

— ■ —

I ran afoul of Korean protectionism when I started to introduce WebNum. The universities and the technology portions of the government requested briefings on the technology and the process. The government then enacted legislation, actual laws, that expressly prohibited 7DC and Verisign from launching a WebNum Registry until a Korean company had a chance to develop a competing technology. Of course, that competing technology was just WebNum by another name. I am sure it violated the patent, but Verisign never pressed the issue.

The whole thing became quite political, and I got further into the Korean government then I had ever wanted or intended. Jahee's connections opened a lot of doors. I did television interviews on their equivalent to the Bloomberg network. I met with several professors, legislators, and the Technology Minister. I even had a meeting scheduled with the President of Korea. All of this was to try to get them to rescind the law that was delaying the implementation of WebNum. Interestingly, I was having almost as much trouble within Verisign. Senior management could not understand why it was necessary to get in the middle of Korean politics to launch the service.

— ■ —

My meeting with Kim Dae-Jung, the Korean president, was scheduled for September 12, 2001. On the morning of September 11th, I was at Narita Airport in Tokyo. Of course, that was across the International Date Line, so it was the evening of September 10th back home. I was scheduled to fly to Seoul, but there was a typhoon in the Sea of Japan, and so the flight was delayed until the afternoon. I finally arrived and took the bus to the Intercontinental Hotel in Seoul. I was unpacking and talking to Sharon on the phone when the second plane hit the World Trade Center.

We soon learned of the Pentagon strike, just a few miles from our home in Fairfax, VA. I was halfway around the world, and it was clear that our country was under attack. No matter what, I could not be home for at least 24 hours. As it turned out, it took nearly two weeks.

September 11th was not just a U.S. event. It turned the world upside down. No one was certain who had initiated the attack or if it was just the first wave. All flights were canceled, and all aircraft were grounded in the U.S.

Seoul was locked down just like Washington. They didn't know if they were next. Seoul is literally within artillery range of North Korea, and so they are always concerned about potential attacks. I found it a bit surprising to find trenches, and gun emplacements dug into the hillsides of various city parks.

My early morning meeting with the president was canceled, but I did meet with his press secretary for lunch. It wasn't so much a courtesy meeting as an interrogation. He wanted to know everything I was hearing, what I thought about the situation, and what the feeling was in Washington. Of course, I didn't know all that much. I had watched CNN, and I had spent most of the night on the phone with Sharon. I had her input, but I had nothing official that I could tell him. Not that what I knew was secret, I just didn't know much.

$$- \blacksquare -$$

I carried both a Japanese and a Korean phone along with my American phone. It was a matter of cost, convenience, and education. I was spending so much time in these two countries that it was much cheaper to have a local phone so I could contact people, and they could contact me more easily. I also wanted to take every opportunity I could to use their version of the mobile Internet. I couldn't read most of the sites, but I could get a pretty good feel for how their systems worked.

Naturally, before I could schedule a meeting with the Korean president, I had to pass their security screening, and a part of that included providing them with my local phone number. Because all flights to the U.S. were grounded, I couldn't get back home. I had intended to spend three days in Seoul, but I wound up spending six. I still couldn't get back to the U.S., so I flew back to Tokyo where I could meet with other people. Before I left Seoul, I had two more meetings with the Press Secretary. They were updates to the earlier meeting. We hit it off quite well. His English was excellent, and his son planned to attend a university in the U.S. He had a lot of questions about living in LA in particular. He ultimately took an assignment in the Korean Consulate in LA. I lost track of him after that.

447

Much later I asked him why he had taken the time to meet on what had to be a chaotic day at the Blue House. He told me that they were getting "official" briefings from the American Military and State Department but he and others wanted an "unofficial" channel to get a reading on American thinking. It seems that in some small way, I was helping to settle Korea's nerves.

While I was on the bus traveling out to the airport, I got a call from the press secretary wishing me a safe trip. I thought it was a nice gesture, but I didn't know the half of it. From then on, every time I would land at Incheon Airport after I passed through Customs, I would turn on my local phone. Without fail, I would get a call from him within 15 minutes. Obviously, they had some flag and location tracking on my phone number. I found it interesting, and more than a little Orwellian that I warranted such attention from someone so high up in the administration. There were a few occasions when I would leave my phone in the hotel just to make sure meetings were private. I don't think their surveillance went beyond the phone, but I will never know.

— ∎ —

When I flew back to Tokyo after 9/11, I was on a United 747 with only 70 people on board. There were 2 of us in business class; they bumped us up to first class, I think out of appreciation but also to make it easier to serve the few people that were in the two sections.

I finally made it back to the U.S. almost ten days after I had originally planned. The only flight I could get took me into Seattle. I had carried a small pen knife for years. It came in handy for a variety of things, and I never gave it much thought. When I went through the security process at Narita, they took the knife and instead of tossing it as they did with such items just a few months later, they put it in a box all by itself. The box was probably 12 x 12 x 4 inches, with my tiny little 1½" knife rattling around inside. I got it back in Seattle.

We arrived in Seattle around 2 in the morning. The passengers were primarily businessmen. We were all standing in line looking rather frumpy after being delayed for an extra week plus in Asia, followed by a 10-hour flight to Seattle. Because of the heightened security after 9/11, even the flight crews had to go through a full security and customs inspection.

There were bomb sniffing dogs being lead around checking everyone. I thought it a bit strange that they were checking for bombs after we arrived instead of before we got on the plane. Maybe they were drug dogs. In any case, they were more than a little bit obvious in their search. That, along with the closer general scrutiny, made the lines very slow.

While we were all standing there waiting in line, a Thai Air flight arrived. They were standing in another line 20 feet or so from ours. The Thai flight attendants were in line as well. If you have never seen Thai flight attendants, you would be amazed at how they look. I think they hire them at 18 and fire them at 21. They were all very young, and quite stunning in their beautiful Thai gowns. They looked like they were models at a fashion show, as fresh as if they had just dressed. United, as do all American airlines, let flight attendants select their routes based on seniority. International routes are the best duty, so you get the oldest stewardesses.

Standing there in need of a shower and some sleep, you couldn't help but notice the 8 or 10 beautiful young ladies in their brightly colored gowns looking fresh as spring. All the while, the whole room was stone silent other than the sound of the dogs' toenails on the tile. As the lines slowly inched ahead, someone back a few behind me said in a voice that was a bit louder than necessary: "You know, if you add up the ages of all of those stewardesses, they wouldn't equal the age of one of ours." Everyone in both lines burst out laughing.

— ■ —

Being out of the country during and immediately after 9/11 was a bit surreal. 9/11 had changed the world in some way. In the Washington area, there were a lot of people connected with the military and the Pentagon. The Metro was shut down, and as a result, many people had to walk many miles to get home. People became more connected. They talked to each other about that first week. There was no travel, and a lot of news was only about New York and the Pentagon. People rallied around the flag.

I missed all of that. My 9/11 experience was very different. The situation in Korea was in some ways the same; people did pull together and pulled inward, but I was not part of that. It was kind of like I was experiencing the whole thing on an elevated platform where I could see it all, but I could participate in none of what was happening. I wasn't in Korea, and I certainly wasn't in Virginia. I could talk with Sharon and Katie, and watch the endless news, but I couldn't be there physically to share the experience or support them. It wasn't depressing or anything like that, but it was just hard to relate to what the people in Washington had gone through.

— ■ —

Flying for the first 6 or 8 months after 9/11 was great. Many people were choosing not to travel and so the planes were only half full. The airlines were very appreciative of those of us who were flying, and so the service was excellent. Unfortunately, after about eight months everything went back to business-as-usual, overcrowded with poor service.

9/11 didn't impact my rate of flying at all. I tallied up my flights for the six months following 9/11. I passed through (in and out) Narita 18 times in that 6-month period. These were not all trips from the U.S.; many were to Hong Kong, Singapore, Bangkok, or Seoul. They just happened to pass through Narita on the way. Of course, a lot of those trips were times when I spent time in Japan as well.

— ■ —

Other than the roadblocks the Korean government put in front of WebNum, and the slightly creepy idea that the government was tracking me everywhere I went, I liked doing business in Korea. I met some nice people, and I had lots of opportunities to explore the city as well as the surrounding area. The response from the citizens after 9/11 was especially heartwarming. Korea is primarily a Buddhist country. There are many Christians, but it is still predominately Buddhist. There are many temples, shrines, and statues throughout the city. One was very close to the Intercontinental hotel where I usually stayed. Of course, it was pretty obvious that I was an American. For a few days after 9/11, whenever I was out in public, I had people come up to me and ask to pray with me. Many were Christian, but there were also Buddhist.

— ■ —

On one trip, I arrived in Seoul midweek. I planned to spend the weekend with several meetings on Monday before I flew home. There was another typhoon, this time in the Yellow Sea between Korea and Mainland China. The rain was coming down in torrents, and everybody was pretty much forced to stay in their homes on Friday and Saturday. I was stuck in the hotel and bored to the point where I was considering flying out Sunday instead of waiting until Tuesday. When I awoke on Sunday morning, the storm had passed. The sky was crystal clear, and the weather was perfect. That was a rarity; the sky is never clear, and the smog is perpetually horrid.

I decided to stay and spend the day at the Secret Gardens in Changdeokgung which is in the northern part of Seoul. I enjoyed visiting the Secret Garden because it was traditional ancient Korean, with little Western presences or influence. I went out there several times on weekends as it tended to be quiet with fewer tourists than the downtown areas.

Tim at Secret Garden Seoul Korea 2002

I enjoyed my morning in the gardens and early in the afternoon decided to find something to eat. I left the gardens and walked for a bit and found a commercial street full of stands and people milling around. It seemed that everyone was sick of being locked in their apartments, so this Sunday they were all out on the streets. I walked through the crowd, and as usual, I was the only "white guy" around. I was easy to spot as I stood a head taller than everyone around me.

Pumpkin Candy guy Seoul 2001

There was a crowd gathered around one stand and the guy was putting on quite a show. I could see over the heads that he had a wooden table, and on the table was a giant blob about 2' by 3' and about 6" thick. It looked like toffee. I listened and picked up that it was a type of pumpkin candy. He had an old wooden plane, and he was shaving off layers of the candy that he would grab with his hands, no gloves of course, and stick on the end of a bamboo skewer. The 10" kind that look like a long toothpick, sharp on one end so you can skewer vegetables.

The guy soon spotted me and began to try to get me to join him. I can't speak the language, but can usually get the gist of the conversation. He was good-natured and having fun, and the crowd was going with his program. I played along and came over to his table. He gave me the plane, and I started shaving candy for people while he was talking up the crowd. He may have been calling me all kinds of names, but it seemed to all be just good fun. I shaved for a few minutes and then bought one of his pumpkin-on-a-stick things for 90 won. That's about 7¢.

Now in my mind, I was thinking pumpkin, like pumpkin pie. Sweet with a slight "cinnamon" taste. I took a good-sized bite. The first thing I realized was this was not that kind of pumpkin. It was not sweet at all, more salt than cinnamon. Not like pie either, more like the vegetable. The real surprise was that it was so sticky I worried that I would pull a filling out if I forced my mouth open.

I walked along letting this strange tasting "candy" slowly dissolve. It didn't taste bad, just unexpected. I walked past some very aromatic vats of kimchee and others vats that smelled much worse. They were full of beetles and worms in soy sauce. The smell of these was quite prodigious. A beggar was asking for handouts, so I handed him the remains of my pumpkin-on-a-stick. He was happy to receive it, but not nearly as happy as I was to be rid of it. I finally found a stand selling Korean barbecue and enjoyed my lunch as I walked along.

— ■ —

On another trip to Seoul, I experienced a condition called the Yellow Wind. It is known as HwangSa in Korea. It is a seasonal occurring phenomenon sporadically during springtime. The dust originates in the deserts of Mongolia, northern China and Kazakhstan where high-speed surface winds kick up dense clouds of fine, dry soil particles. These clouds are then carried eastward by prevailing winds. They pass over China, North and South Korea, and even as far as Japan.

The dust is very yellow and very thick, but very fine, much like pollen. I couldn't see more than 10 or 15 feet. The streets and sidewalks are all covered. A car parked outside for 15-minutes would collect a thick layer. I couldn't help but think of the Dust Bowl in the Southwest back in the 1930s. The dust gets in your eyes, ears, and of course, your nose. Even with a mask, you just can't keep it all out. It can be overwhelming. I am not claustrophobic, but it did feel oppressive.

There are a lot of really nasty bugs and bacteria in this crap. I tried to stay out of it as much as possible, and I wore a mask every time I went outside. "Outside" was limited to the distance between the door and the car, but it still got to me. I lost my voice the second day. I couldn't speak at all.

Having no voice makes it hard to hold meetings. I was scheduled to travel next to Kyoto to give a keynote address at the inaugural Kaitai (Wireless) forum later in the week; having no voice presented a real problem. I went to a doctor in Seoul, and he gave me some medicine, but it didn't do a thing. I got out of town a day early just to get away from the yellow crud. I went to another doctor in Japan and their medicine worked so that I was able to speak at the conference.

That was one of the few times in all of my travels that I got sick. I credit that to growing up on well water and living in the country where most everything was not washed as clean as it might have been in town.

— ■ —

I almost always stayed at the Intercontinental Hotel in Seoul. It was an expensive hotel but centrally located with several good restaurants. One was a nice casual restaurant in the hotel. I would frequently meet people there for a business breakfast. I always marveled at how the cooks could make a perfect omelet using nothing but chopsticks. The hotel was quite nice, and I always had a suite so that I could hold meetings in my room whenever possible. People liked this arrangement because I could have a western-style lunch brought in and that was a treat for many of the people I was meeting. The suite was a bit more expensive, but I could use it like my Korean office, so it worked out ok.

When you came down the hotel elevator, there would always be a young lady (usually) waiting on the first floor. Her sole job was to bow to you as you got off of the elevator. Like many Asian countries, Korea had more people than it could normally employee. To solve the problem, they had hundreds of people whose sole job was to show respect by opening the door or bowing or some other menial task. I found it a little uncomfortable, but you become inured to these customs.

There was a department store close to the Intercontinental. I went in one Saturday to see if I could find some beautiful tea cups as a gift for Sharon. When I got off the elevator, there was a young lady to greet me and asked how she could assist. I told her what I was looking for and she immediately clapped her hands twice. Seemingly out of nowhere, at least half a dozen young ladies, all dressed alike in white blouses, and dark blue skirts appeared. The first young woman spoke quickly in Hangul. Koreans seem to always talk very fast, and to me, it sounds kind of like a machine gun, tat-tat-tat, tat-tat-tat, spoken in rapid flat succession. As soon as she stopped, all six young ladies started running, and I mean that literally, to try to find the perfect teacups. They returned almost as quickly carrying several samples. They wanted me to follow, and they seated me while they brought me tea to drink and showed me a variety of choices. None were quite what I was looking for, but how could I not buy one after all of this service. You find this in a lot of Asian cities, China in particular. In Shanghai I have been in stores where the clerks outnumber the customers by at least 3:1.

– ■ –

Verisign had one full-time employee in Seoul. His name was Jin Kim, and he was in his late 20s. He was a native Korean, but he had moved to the U.S. when he was 12 or 13. He attended school and completed college in the U.S. When he started working for Verisign; they made him the Resident Manager in Korea. Of course, he spoke perfect Hangul.

I took several Korea Telecom people out to dinner one night, and Jin Kim came along. I mentioned to them that they must find it easier to have Jin involved when they talked business because of his language skills. I was quite surprised when they said no, that he was more of a problem. At first, I thought they were teasing Jin because he was there, but they were sincere. I ask them what they meant. They responded that "when we talk to you, we know you don't understand our language, so we speak very carefully and chose our words to make sure you understand. When we talk with Jin, we see him as a Korean. He looks Korean; he speaks Korean, and so we talk to him like we talk to each other. The problem is that he doesn't 'think' Korean, he thinks like an American. So we believe we are talking on the same terms, but we are often completely misunderstanding each other."

Later that evening they showed me an example of Korean culture. Koreans are rightfully a very proud people with an ancient culture and traditions. Koreans are, or were at that time, still very traditional. For example, men and women were not supposed to talk to each other unless they had been formally introduced. In the modern world, this could make things dicey. They took me to a club designed specifically to bridge this gap. At the door, there was a male and a female greeter. When women came up, the female greeter would introduce herself and then escort the women to a table on the "female" side of the room. Men went through the same ritual. They sat on the "male" side of the room.

When a guy decided he wanted to meet one of the women, of course, it could never be the other way around; he would ask a waiter (male) to make the introduction. That man would get a female server to take him and introduce him to the woman of interest. After introductions, he would ask her to accompany him over to meet the man that had made the initial request. Tradition required that she protest such a forward proposal, so she would fuss while being bodily lead to be formally introduced to the man. It was all a charade of course, but it was necessary to "protect" tradition. It was like watching a comedy show.

Jin later wanted to marry a Korean woman. The problem was that her parents had to meet his parents before he could ask her to marry. That became complicated because, for some reason, her parents couldn't get visas to the U.S. and his father was too ill to travel to Korea. The resolution was to have her family fly to Canada, and Jin drove his parents up to meet them. It was all about tradition. Many of the old traditions didn't fit well in the 21st Century, but that did not relieve the obligation, they still must be followed.

— ∎ —

I had a few "formal" Korean dinners in Seoul. At a formal dinner, they would serve 15 or 16 different dishes. They would bring out tiny serving dishes one at a time. The first time, I had no idea how many of these dishes were going to appear. I was full by the time I got about ½ way through the meal.

Robin Pergament, my administrative assistant back in Virginia, and her husband, had a friend in Korea. His name was Ho Kim. He was probably in his 70s at that time. He had lived most of his life in the U.S. and was back in Korea working with their space administration. He was selling services for Hughes if I remember correctly. Mainly he was selling Korean military and communications companies space on launch vehicles. He had his hands in every satellite that Korea had launched up to that time. He was a very nice gentleman, and we became good friends.

— ∎ —

I worked with Dr. Yu-Ichiro "Tuk" Takagawa in Japan. Tuk was the uncle of a Japanese woman working at Network Solutions. She made the introduction. Tuk seemed to be involved in everything and know everyone in Japan. He taught at a university and was an adviser to virtually every company that had anything to do with technology or communications. Tuk introduced me to Koji Sasaki and J-Data.

J-Data had offices in Tokyo. But their headquarters was in Kyoto, about 300 miles south and west of Tokyo. When I came from the U.S., I usually flew into Narita (Tokyo) and took the train to Kyoto. I did sometimes travel between Osaka and Seoul as it saved time. I enjoyed taking the Tokyo-Kyoto bullet train as it gave me an opportunity to see the land. The line went right past Mt. Fuji and there were miles and miles of beautiful tea fields on rolling hills. It was a nice ride, much more pleasant than taking a plane.

– ■ –

Koji was very interested in becoming the WebNum Registrar for Japan. He needed Board approval to purchase the WebNum license which we had priced at $750,000. I did a presentation to his team in Kyoto, as a dry-run of the presentation I was to give to his Board of Directors the next day in Tokyo. Of course, we needed a translator for the presentation. Most Japanese do speak some English, but usually, men are reluctant to talk for fear of making a mistake and losing face.

Steve Burkholder was an American working for Koji. He had studied in Japan, married a Japanese wife, and spoke fluent Japanese. Koji wanted him to translate. When you work with translators, you learn to pace your presentation so that the translator can keep up. I would speak a couple of sentences and then pause while the translator spoke. With Steve as my translator, I didn't know quite what to expect, so I started talking then paused after a couple of lines as I normally would. Steve was supposed to translate, but instead, he just repeated exactly what I had said, in English, but very slowly. Not a word of Japanese, just very slow English. Everyone just looked at Steve and laughed.

The wife of one of Koji's team also spoke English, so we delayed my presentation, and he had her come in to translate for me. She did a good job, and she went with us to Tokyo the next day for the Board presentation. I tend to speak extemporaneously rather than from a script or even from notes. That proved to be a problem the next day. The translator was expecting me to give the same presentation as the day before. This time I was different. That was not the biggest problem. She had written down the numbers I had used, so she was prepared to translate them smoothly. It didn't quite work out that way.

During the first presentation, I got a lot of questions about the size of the .com Registry, so I added a few statistics regarding the scope of that operation to the Board presentation. That day, I discovered that most Asian languages have difficulty translating numbers because they don't count the same way we do. In Japan, for example, it is not 1 billion, 300 million, it is 130 thousand

thousand. So whenever I would give a new number, my translator would have to calculate the value so she could correctly translate it. When I threw in a bunch of additional numbers, it caused her to scramble. When she explained the confusion, I apologized and explained to the Board that I had added these new numbers which caused the problem.

I also learned that day why most translators in Asia are female. In large part this is because Asians don't think of women as having "face," so if they make a mistake and embarrass themselves, it is no big deal. I still felt sorry about the problems I had caused her.

From then on, I always told the translator the numbers that I would be using before the presentation. Even then, I always had to wait for the translator to make sure the numbers I was using were the numbers she was expecting.

There were a few times when I had a professional translator. That was only when I was talking with some government official. It was a bit spooky to work with those who did simultaneous translation. They would start speaking about ½ a heartbeat after I started and stopped when I did. Because I was accustomed to working with delayed translators, my tendency was to pause after a few seconds. With the professional translators, it would catch me off guard when they paused as well.

— ■ —

I mentioned earlier that I did some interviews on business television shows when I was in Korea. I remember one in particular. Jahee and I visited them the evening before, and we walked through the procedures for the next morning's interview. It was scheduled for just after the 7 a.m. news break. As in America, this was the prime morning business time slot. Pauses don't work well when you are doing a live television interview, so the interviewer gave me the questions in advance so that I could go through my responses with Jahee. That way she would be able to speak nearly simultaneously.

The next morning, we got to the studio early for makeup. Jahee was very nervous at the prospect of doing simultaneous translation. She felt reassured because she would be sitting next to me, and we had worked together enough so she knew that I could sense when she was getting behind and slow my pace accordingly. As we walked to the set, someone grabbed her arm and steered her behind a curtain and told her she was not to be on camera but she would be translating simultaneously. Her face went white. I felt sorry for her, but there was nothing either of us could do. I could still hear her speak, so I was

458

still able to pace my speaking accordingly. She did fine, but she cried all the way back to the office protesting that she had been a disaster.

— ■ —

I was asked to be the keynote speaker for the 2nd day of the inaugural International Kaitai (Wireless) Forum in Kyoto Japan. That was on the trip where I ran into the Yellow Wind in Seoul and lost my voice. There were guests from all over Asia, and so they had simultaneous translators in 4 or 5 languages. The guests wore headsets so they could select the language they wished to receive. I had given the interpreters a list of all the numbers that I was using in the presentation so that they could pre-translate them and maintain the pace. Fortunately, I couldn't hear the multilingual chatter, but it was still a bit nerve-racking as I wanted to make sure I didn't lose someone along the way.

The subject of my speech was the usability of the mobile Internet. That was the spring of 2001. The population of the world was about 6.5 billion at that time. Mobile phones were just starting to penetrate the 2nd level markets. There were almost none in the lesser developed countries.

I had my staff do some research in preparation for the speech. What we discovered was that, at that time, 80% of the people in the world, that is nearly 5 billion people had never heard a dial tone. In other words, they had never picked up a phone. What is so amazing is that today, only 15 years later, there are nearly 7 billion mobile phones in the world. That means that more than 90% of the people have not only used a phone, they now own a phone. The significance of such a massive shift is hard to fathom. From 80% who had never seen a phone to 90% now owning a phone, in less than two decades.

— ■ —

The point of my presentation was that navigation had to be simplified. It was one thing for users who are accustomed to having a computer and browser on their desks, to transition to having a browser on their phone. However, for someone who had never seen a browser or been on the Internet, to navigate the Internet on their phone would be extraordinarily difficult. Obviously, I was wrong, because 7 billion have somehow managed, and the mobile Internet certainly has not gotten any easier to navigate over the past 15 years.

After the presentation, a lady from Indonesia approached me. We talked about the situation in her country. Indonesia is a nation of hundreds of islands.

Running an underwater cable to each of these islands would be expensive. As a result, very few phones existed outside of the major cities. Up until the 1980s, only the rich and the government had phones. Phones became more affordable during the early 1990s, and hence more widespread in the cities. Still, the out-islands had few. With the advent of cell phones, it was relatively easy to put up a tower on even the smallest islands. Suddenly people had phones. She described what it was like to walk past a grass house and see someone inside reading the newspaper on the mobile Internet. Their quality of life was changing quite rapidly.

— ■ —

I loved working in Japan. The people were incredibly gracious and friendly. I was there during the cherry blossom season for two years in a row. The trees seem to be everywhere and the color, as well as the scent, was beautiful. If you ever get the opportunity to go, Kyoto, in my opinion, has better trees than Tokyo.

When I was in Tokyo, I usually stayed at the New Otani Hotel. I stayed at the Park Hyatt Hotel a couple of times, but it was too expensive, $500+ per night, and out away from areas where I could blend in with the locals. I tend to shy away from the traditional business areas as I like to experience more of what the local culture has to offer. The New Otani was a better fit. It was a bit older, but it was quite nice, and it had beautiful gardens. They held weddings in the gardens on most weekends. It was fun to watch. The New Otani is in an area fairly near the Imperial Palace. It is an area where a lot "real" Japanese people live and work. That allowed me to mingle and experience more of what the Japanese people and Japanese life was really like.

The hotel was still upscale, just not as ostentatious as the Park Hyatt. A lot of foreign dignitaries stayed at the New Otani. I remember once, the president of Pakistan was there at the same time.

Like the Intercontinental in Seoul, there was an abundance of service personnel to make sure you had an enjoyable stay. At several of the exits, there were double automatic doors that opened as you approached. The problem was that the taller westerners had a longer stride than the shorter Japanese. The doors were set to match the shorter Japanese stride; that meant taller folks had to hesitate as we walked up to the doors. That "inconvenience" was unacceptable to hotel management. To solve this problem, they stationed two young women at each set of doors, one inside, and one outside. Their job was to watch for anyone coming and to step over into the beam so that the door would be open when the person arrived. It is almost embarrassing to think of this, but to them, it was a sign of respect.

The New Otani had a casual restaurant that offered a fried oyster sandwich that was delicious. Tuk had introduced me to the New Otani, and he made sure to enjoy one of these unique sandwiches any time he was there to meet me. I sometimes thought the sandwiches was the reason he had introduced me to the hotel.

— ■ —

One thing that took getting used to in both Korea and Japan was having a woman open the car door for me. I suppose I am old-fashioned, but in my mind, I am the one who is expected to open the door for the woman. When Koji and I would walk in the street, Yumi would naturally fall in about 5' behind me. That drove me a bit crazy, and I kept insisting that she walk with us and not behind us. She would do it for me, but you could always tell that it made her a bit uncomfortable.

— ■ —

The mother of one of the guys who worked for Koji had decided at some point to shave her head and become a Buddhist nun. He told me the reason, but it was personal. Her son set up a meeting and dinner at the temple in Kyoto where his mother was the head of the temple. Her son, Yumi and I attended. It was a fascinating evening. The temple which had been built originally in the 13th or 14th century, had burned a couple of times. It was rebuilt, but it was still centuries old. It was small. This was where the emperor's courtesans were sent either after the emperor got tired of them or when he died.

Apparently, the deal was that when the Emperor or the Shogun had no further use for one of these young ladies, they had the choice of either beheading or spending the remainder of their life in a temple. They were not of the samurai class, so they were not permitted to commit seppuku (ritual suicide). There were women in the samurai class, but not these women, they were courtesans, and seppuku was not permissible. Beheading by a samurai was about as close as they would be able to come.

The logic for banishment or death was that the emperor didn't want any man to have these women. Many chose to be beheaded, but apparently, there were a lot of these young women, and so the temple was well stocked with ex-

461

courtesans. One requirement was that they shave their heads. I suppose that a shaved head is better than a missing head.

His mother brought out a scroll that one of these women had made using her hair. It was a poem dedicated to her emperor, and also an artwork. It was more than 300 or years old, and beautiful. I remember thinking that this woman must have had a lot of hair. His mother said we could hold the scroll. I hesitated because I felt that it should be treated with more reverence. His mother invited me to stay at the temple if I was able to bring Sharon to Japan. She showed us the few guest rooms which were traditional Japanese style, maybe 8' x 8', raised a foot or so off the ground, paper walls with a wooden floor. Gardens and koi ponds surrounded the rooms. The tatami mats might have been a bit hard to sleep on, but I profoundly regret that I was never able to bring Sharon to experience a night or two in that temple.

— ■ —

On one stay in Tokyo, Koji asked if I wanted to visit a geisha tea house. I had never thought about it before, and in my mind, probably based on false impressions from movies, it was a bit of a questionable venture. I wasn't particularly interested, but Yumi was adamant that I should go. I asked her later why she was so insistent. She told me that as a woman, she was not permitted to go to these establishments. She had always been curious to see a geisha tea house. I suspect that this is probably a common feeling among young Japanese women …it is a forbidden fruit kind of thing. If I went, that meant that she would be able to go as my interpreter. If I spoke Japanese, she would not be allowed to enter, and so this was probably the only time in her entire life that she would have this opportunity. I never ask, but I suspect she may have even suggested it to Koji. It wasn't something that Koji and I had ever discussed, and I don't think it was exactly Koji's style either, but it is not exactly something you would ask a Japanese man, so I have no way of knowing.

We did go, and while it was interesting, it was nothing like you might see in the movies or you might imagine. The geishas were all dressed in beautiful Japanese attire. Their role was to serve tea, to play traditional Japanese music, and to engage in conversation with the men. Of course, that was somewhat problematic in my case. That is where Yumiko came in. The tea was excellent, but my Occidental ear is not tuned for traditional Japanese music, so I had a hard time appreciating, or maybe even tolerating the music. These young ladies are schooled to be acutely aware of their guest's pleasures, or in my case lack of pleasure at listening to her music, and so she quickly abandoned that avenue. I think she was as interested in talking to Yumiko about this strange American as Yumi was to speak with her about her life. As I said, Yumi wanted to see, but to also understand the geisha's life and role. At the same time, this was also a once in a lifetime opportunity for this geisha; the young lady wanted to understand Americans better and how to relate to them. Yumi did a good job translating, but I think I only heard about 20% of what they were discussing. I had some great tea, a time to relax, and an experience that I would have never undertaken on my own. Even if I had, it would have been more frustrating than pleasurable.

– ■ –

I traveled to Singapore several times to start a search for a Registrar partner. I found Singapore to be very different from most Asian cities. Most were rather drab and gray. Tokyo was destroyed during the war, and it was rebuilt fast and cheap. A lot of it is very dull, not dirty, but just drab structures. The newer buildings are quite attractive, and we have all seen pictures of the Ginza District at night which is all bright lights and sparkle. During the day it is not so much bright as it is gray. Singapore and Hong Kong are quite the opposite. They are new and shiny. Singapore is a lot like Disneyland, absolutely spotless. You never see a piece of trash.

It may be clean and friendly, but the government has some strange ways of keeping it all shiny and new. Take cars as an example. Buying a car is expensive, a Toyota Camry would cost roughly twice what it did in the U.S. The annual license was the real killer. A permit can cost thousands each year. The curious thing is that unlike what we are used to, the fee goes up as the car gets older. When it reaches 10-years old, you must sell it back to the government and the government then exports these used cars and trucks to other Asian countries. You can pay a fee to keep a classic car, but the price is very high. The government simply doesn't want to have old cars on the streets.

Taxis and commercial vehicles at that time all had a blue light attached to their roof. The light was hooked into the speedometer. If they speed, the light starts flashing and the police will either pull them over or take their picture with the automatic cameras located on every overpass. Then they just mail the ticket.

You have probably heard that they don't allow gum in the country. The

463

government doesn't want people chewing it or dropping it or the wrappers on the street. If you are caught importing gum, you are in trouble. They have been known to flog (whip with a bamboo stock) people for having gum. Living in Disneyland has its drawbacks.

In other areas, they are very tolerant, maybe too liberal. It takes almost exactly 24 hours to fly from Washington Dulles to Singapore. There were no direct flights, so I usually flew from Washington to Chicago, to either Narita or Hong Kong, and then to Singapore. By the time I got there, it would be about midnight local time.

Many of the nicer hotels are located along Victoria Street so that I would pass them in my taxi on the way to my hotel. Invariably I would see several very elegantly dressed young ladies leaving these hotels at the time I was arriving. These were ladies of the evening. They would come to Singapore from all over Southeast Asia. They would work as prostitutes for a few years, sending money back to their families. That was a very rough and dangerous life. If they survived, and if they were not kidnapped and hauled off to some other country, after a few years, they would retire and go back home hoping to have enough money to eke out a life.

In many cases, their families sold the girls to the pimps. These unfortunate souls seldom lived to retirement age. In my travels, I have seen what many of the villages in Asia are truly like. Even knowing how they must have lived, I couldn't help but wonder about the poverty and desperation that would drive a family to sell their daughter or a young woman to do this voluntarily. As a father, my heart ached for the entire family. It was very sad to see.

— ■ —

I remember one time landing at the airport in Singapore. As usual, I was sitting in the upper deck business class area on a 747. The area was full of business people, mostly men, all frequent flyers like me. As we were letting down to land, the flight attendant came on the PA. Along with her regular announcements, she said that United Airlines wished to thank Mr. Smith who was completing 2.5 million miles on United.

There was silence in the upper deck for a couple of minutes and then someone said: "that's 25 years in the 100K Club." Someone else added, "I wonder how many wives he's gone through in that time?" Everyone chuckled at the last comment, but the truth is that travel can be hard on marriages.

464

I liked Hong Kong a lot. It is a clean city, but not sterile like Singapore. There was a lot to see and do. I was only there a few times, but I always enjoyed it. It was easy to get around, and English is spoken everywhere as a legacy of the decades under British management.

They now have an incredible airport that replaced their old death trap. There is a bit of a story that goes with the airport. When the British and the Chinese were negotiating the return of Hong Kong, one of the agreements was that the British couldn't raid the treasury on departure. The British didn't want to leave a lot of cash. They knew it would be transferred immediately to Beijing. Their solution was to build a grand airport using British construction companies.

They built and island for the airport and a very nice train from downtown. The terminal is on two levels, so the passengers coming in are on a different level than passengers leaving. It is both beautiful and efficient. The cost was something like $20 billion. Materials, engineering, and the profits all found their way into the hands of British contractors. Of course, Hong Kong got a specular airport in the deal.

— ■ —

I only went to mainland China a couple of times during my time with Verisign. My first trip was to Shanghai. It was at the end of a two-week swing through Asia, and I was exhausted by the time I got there. I had started at Tokyo then Seoul, then back to Tokyo, then to Singapore, then to Bangkok, and finally to Shanghai. I expected Shanghai to be like other Asian cities, gray and drab. In my imagination, maybe even a bit worse as we were talking about communist China. To my surprise, it was more like Paris, bright, clean, with tree-lined streets and wide boulevards. It was different from Paris in that it is full of beautiful new skyscrapers. Of course, that was in the city. I learned later that the suburbs are not like that at all.

There were a lot of bicycles, but even more Volkswagens and Buicks. It seemed like every taxi and police car was a Jetta and almost all the other cars were Buicks. It turned out there are VW and Buick factories nearby.

What surprised me was all of the super modern buildings. I went to the Bund; that is the street next to the Huang Pu River where the British, French, Americans and others had built their business headquarters and banks after the

First Opium War of 1842. That street looks very much like some city in Europe. But if you turn and look across the river you see the New Shanghai area called Pudong, which means "east bank," that is beyond modern. It looks like something out of a science fiction movie.

— ■ —

The history of the Opium Wars is a sad story of Western imperialism. It primarily involved the British, but the French and Americans were also there. The issue concerned the balance of trade and funding of exports. There was high demand for Chinese exports, tea being one of the main items. The British did not want to have to pay with gold or silver, and so they imported opium from India and Turkey to trade for the export items desired. Initially, the opium was for medicinal purposes, but it quickly became recreational, and the vast majority of Chinese population became frequent users of the drug.

That was a period of weak imperial rule in China, and the Emperor was unable to stem the widespread use of opium. His attempts resulted in two wars; the British won both. The first war led to a 155-year lease of Hong Kong as a Crown Colony of the British. It also opened China to Western trade. Shanghai became the primary center of commerce with the Bund as the headquarters.

— ■ —

When Hong Kong returned to Chinese control in 1997, the Chinese government was concerned that the people would compare Hong Kong with the drab Chinese cities. People would, therefore, conclude that the western system was better than the Chinese system. Their solution was to create two comparable cities, Shanghai and Beijing that would not embarrass the government.

That could not be achieved in the West. Companies would not erect buildings unless they were cost justified. In a capitalist economy, financing would depend on demand, tenants, and infrastructure. China is a "command economy." Since the government owns most everything and they control what they don't own, all they have to do is tell the company that they must build a building and it must look like this. No discussion, no options. Just do it as Nike would say.

There are a lot of issues in China, but the government can force almost anything.

Around the World[2]

On July 1, 1903, after a month-long voyage of 3,200 miles, Elizabeth McPhee, arrived in New York. At that time, ships were the only way to come to America. Six months later, on December 17th, the Wright Brothers made the first controlled flight, all of 120 ft.

In 1948, 45 years later, my Grandmother took her first and only trip back to Scotland. She traveled by train from California to New York, ship to London, and again by train to Edinburgh. The planning and scheduling took dozens of telegraphs and nearly two years to arrange. The trip cost a small fortune and required close to two months each way. Transatlantic air service was a decade old, but steamship remained the primary mode of global travel.

Fourteen years later I took my first plane ride. Twenty years after that, I found myself commuting twice a month, from New York to Brussels, about 8-hours each way. In 2000, less than a century after my Grandmother first came to America; I circumnavigated the earth two times in a single year; a distance of nearly 50,000 miles in a total of 36 days. A travel agent arranged my itineraries. Today I could do the same on my smartphone.

– ■ –

I did my second circumnavigation while I was with Verisign. I had my usual meetings in Asia, Singapore, Hong Kong, Seoul, and Tokyo, but I also had to attend a WAP Forum conference in Munich, Germany and a meeting in Stockholm, Sweden.

The WAP Forum was an industry group that was formed early in the wireless Internet era to establish and promulgate the various protocols and standards for the wireless world. It started big but quickly fizzled and ultimately disappeared. Verisign joined the Forum, and I attended their December 7-8, 2000 meeting in Munich. They held another conference in Sydney, Australia in May or 2001, but it was clear to me by then, that WAP was not going to prevail so I did not attend.

At that point, mobile devices used "wap" instead of the "www" to segregate mobile content. WAP (Wireless Application Protocol) supported only a subset of commands that severely limited content and images. Remember this was before smartphones, and before any phone had a touch screen, so it was not possible to zoom or drag to look at specific parts of a page. Mobile phones typically had a 1¼" by 1½" screen; they were useless when displaying all the content on a standard web page. The goal was laudable, but the content providers didn't want to have to develop this limited format content, so they pushed back. An alternate approach that allowed browsers to automatically strip out unnecessary data, and reformat the page for the mobile presentation was the first step. The results were often less than desirable, but far better than having to develop dual content streams. Remember that very few people outside of Korea and Japan were using the mobile Internet at that time. With time, larger screens and more powerful processors eliminated the need for WAP and it died an early death.

— ■ —

My trip was at the beginning of December. I started out immediately after Thanksgiving. James Walker the VP of Emerging Technologies at Network Solutions wanted to accompany me. I had been working with him and several of his team; Bill Dutcher reported to James. He had no real reason to make the trip other than that he was getting ready to retire and had never circumnavigated, so he wanted to come along for the ride. It was clearly a boondoggle for him.

Titles are important in international business. To maintain "face," especially in Asia, I used the title "Managing Director of WebNum Services." Managing Director means the top boss to anyone outside of the U.S. I was concerned that James would create a problem for me if he told them he was higher up the food chain than I was. He was a good guy, and he couldn't have cared less about rank. Wherever we went, he would tell people he worked for me. No one ever questioned it.

He accompanied me to all of the locations and the meetings, mostly he just listened. He particularly enjoyed our time in Tokyo. There is an electronics district in Tokyo called Akihabara Electric Town. It is a techie's Disneyland. I went there frequently to see the latest and greatest communications toys. I remember a wristwatch telephone. The mic was in the wristband, and the speaker was designed to radiate through your bone and tissue to your finger. Remember, this was 2001, 14 years before the Apple Watch. It was about the same size, but somewhat thicker. The face had tiny little buttons so you could dial.

To use the phone, you held one finger in your ear; this acted as the speaker, and you spoke into the wristband. It was more of a novelty than a useful device, but it did work. I used to tell people that you could tell when someone was talking to his boss by which finger he had placed in his ear. Visualize it; you will understand. James had a lot of fun visiting Akihabara; he was like a kid in a candy store. His suitcase was much heavier for the rest of the trip.

Tim & James Walker in Germany 2001

James didn't stay past the first night in Munich. He had no interest in the WAP Forum or accompanying me to Stockholm. He was tired and ready to take all his techie toys home for Christmas. The meeting was unimportant; he only had the leg back to Washington to fulfill his goal to circumnavigate

James was an excellent travel companion. He was enjoying the experience and didn't care much beyond that, so anything I needed to do was all right with him. James had been with Network Solutions since the beginning, even before they became the Registry. He told me a lot about the company, its history, and the personalities of various executives.

— ∎ —

James also told me an interesting story that should be a lesson for anyone dealing with sensitive information. He is a medium height, medium build, ordinary looking black business man. In other words, he can blend into almost any crowd when he wants. His looks are deceiving, as he is a sharp businessman and technologist. During the time when the U.S. Department of Commerce put out the RFQ (Request For Quotation) for organizations interested in running the Registry, James was on the Network Solutions team writing their response to the RFP. Once he traveled by plane from Washington to North Carolina. IBM was also preparing a response, and there were two individuals on the IBM team who were sitting with James in the same row. The IBMers spent the whole trip discussing in detail exactly how IBM would respond to the RFQ, pricing and all. By the time James landed, he had the complete inside story of IBM's RFP response. In the end, Network Solutions won the RFP. The lesson is clear; never assume you are sharing your seat with some insignificant nobody.

This is a good place to insert one of my favorite stories. "The Talking Skull." It is Nigerian folk tale, translated by Leo Frobenius and Douglas G. Fox

A hunter goes into the bush. He finds an old human skull. The hunter says: "What brought you here?" The skull answers: "Talking brought me here." The Hunter runs off. He runs to the king. He tells the king: "I found a dry human skull in the bush. It asks you how its father and mother are."

The king says: "Never since my mother bore me have I heard that a dead skull can speak." The king summons the Alkali, the Saba, and the Degi and asks them if they have ever heard the like. None of the wise men has heard the like, and they decide to send guards out with the hunter into the bush to find out if his story is true and, if so, to learn the reason for it. The guards accompany the hunter into the bush with the order to kill him on the spot should he have lied.

The guards and the hunter come to the skull. The hunter addresses the skull: "Skull, speak." The skull is silent. The hunter asks as before: "What brought you here?" The skull does not answer. The whole day long the hunter begs the skull to speak, but it does not answer. In the evening the guards tell the hunter to make the skull speak, and when he cannot, the guards kill the hunter in accordance with the king's command.

When the guards are gone, the skull opens its jaws and asks the dead hunter's head: "What brought you here?" The dead hunter's head replies: "Talking brought me here!"

No further explanation is required, but you should remember this story whenever you decide you want to post to one of the social networks.

— ■ —

On that trip, we got to see the sun rise and set two times in the same day. We got up in Seoul and flew to Narita in Japan. In midafternoon, we flew north over the North Pole; on the way north, we saw the sunset. We crossed over the pole, and as we were headed south toward Munich, we had another sunrise and then shortly after we landed it set again. Because we were flying with the clock this time, this all happened on the same day.

I took a two day trip up to Stockholm for another meeting. That was the weekend of December 9-10, and there were only about 2 hours of sunlight. The nights were cold, but not all that bad, and not all that dark. After my meetings on Monday, I flew to Paris, stayed overnight and then home. This circumnavigation was the same 18-day duration as my first round the world tour, but much easier than the first time. That said, it was still exhausting. I have flown so much and so many times across the pond, that I tolerate jetlag quite well. But there is no way your body can deal with traveling through 24 time zones, the international date line, a dozen or more flights and as many hotels in such a short period. It will take its toll no matter how accustomed you might be.

— ■ —

I made a few separate trips to Europe, but not nearly as often as I was in Asia. Europe was Mark's territory and the only time I went was to support his sales activities. Mostly to show my face as the boss when Marks prospects were getting ready to commit to WebNum. It wasn't necessary as Mark was a great salesman, much more experienced in both sales and mobile telecom than I was; mostly it was just political.

On one trip, there were a couple of trade shows that I wanted to attend. The first one was the Telecom show in Nice France. I wanted to see the show, but mainly it was a chance to meet all of the Operators as well as the handset manufacturers, in one place. Mark and Rob Pepper attended as well. Mark had worked in mobile telecom for many years, and he seemed to know everyone. Mark is a big guy, a former football player at Penn when they won the National Championship. He is outgoing and easy to talk with. I marveled that he could stand in any hallway and a dozen or more people would walk up and say high. He knew everyone, and usually their families. He was, and I am sure still is, a master salesman.

Mark and I went from Nice to CeBIT in Hannover Germany. CeBIT is a tradeshow that is similar to CES in Las Vegas. Every major technology company was represented. You can spend days and not see everything. We were there to see what mobile Internet devices were coming, but we got a chance to see a lot more. That was the only time I was ever in Hanover.

— ■ —

After J-Data had signed the Registrar Agreement, I took Mark with me on a trip to Japan. Mark had worked for the president of Mitsubishi America for a time, and they had become personal friends. If I remember correctly, his Mitsubishi friend was even his son's godfather. We set up a celebration with the J-Data team at the Hanezawa Gardens in Tokyo. Through his prior work in Japan, and relations with Mitsubishi, Mark was very familiar with Hanezawa Gardens and knew the elderly proprietress personally. We enjoyed a royal tour of the gardens and a very expensive feast. We even shared a few glasses of grappa with our J-Data friends.

I was very fortunate to have this unique experience as the Gardens no longer exist. Hanezawa Gardens was an old Japanese traditional estate on roughly 2.5 acres in Tokyo. It is almost impossible to imagine a private garden that large within the crowded confines of Tokyo. Forgetting the beauty and historical value, land in Tokyo was going for roughly $1 million per square meter. Hanezawa Gardens covered more than 10,000 meters.

Hanezawa Gardens was originally the home of Yoshikoto Nakamu who was a government bureaucrat, entrepreneur, and politician. At one time, he was even the mayor of Tokyo. That was in late Meiji period, from 1868 to 1912. That period corresponded with the reign of Emperor Meiji and represented the first half of the Empire of Japan period. That is the period during which Japanese society moved from being an isolated feudal society to its modern form. The Gardens survived WWII. They became a high-end traditional Japanese restaurant with extensive gardens. The proprietress passed away in 2005, and the restaurant closed. The Gardens, unfortunately, did not survive urban development. Mitsubishi owned the estate and soon began demolishing it to make way for a 6-story apartment house. The Hanezawa Gardens were completely gone by early 2012.

WebNum Rising

As we reached the end of our second year, we were making serious headway. I had signed J-Data and 7DC as Registrars for Japan and Korea respectively. J-Data paid their $750K license fee, but 7DC held off awaiting the government's final decision, and to allow them time to evaluate the competitive offering launched in Korea. Mark Fruehan had a group in northern Europe that was ready to sign for multiple Country Registrars.

We had the registry software working and in final testing. Several major mobile Operators were ready to promote WebNum access, and both Samsung and Nokia were developing prototype handsets with a WebNum Button. We had every indication that our patents would be approved, and they ultimately were. That would give us protection for the intellectual property represented by WebNum. We may have been in a position to force the Korean competitor to abandon their efforts, but even without Korea, we were in a great position to dominate the global market.

We were well on our way to developing both critical masses required for success. We were about to change the face of the mobile Internet. We were also on track to repay Verisign all they had invested up to that point. We were projected to reach the point of positive cash flow within the first half of year three. These were significant accomplishments for my very small team in less than 24 months. Our success was being noticed within Verisign, but also within ICANN; the Internet "police" were not happy.

The merger of Network Solutions into Verisign was completed. Jim Rutt, who had made something like $90 million in the deal had finished his 12-month obligation and departed. When Jim left, I knew WebNum was on borrowed time. In Star Wars terms, the Empire had won. The bean counters were now in charge. The critical question was timing; could we succeed before they killed us? Mark McLaughin became president of the Registry half of the company. A good executive, but not an entrepreneur, or if he was, he was not strong enough to stand up to the bean counters. He had his hands full, and little time or interest in the WebNum project.

They moved WebNum and Air 2 Web, a second venture that Jim had started, under the management of a young guy who had been Jim's deputy. This guy was the complete opposite of Jim. If he had any vision, it could not work where he kept his head stored. He also lacked both courage and character. He and I had not hit it off, and now I reported to him. Not a good development!

Jim had been something of a Wild Duck. His mind was going 20 different ways at once. He had a fire in his belly; he loved the challenge and didn't mind breaking glass. All of that left when Jim left. Timidity now reigned.

Jim's thinking was proactive. Spend a small amount of cash up front to drive technology in the direction you wanted. Use the Verisign/Network Solutions name and market position, facilities, management oversight, and money to advantage these ventures. He felt that in the end, that would significantly increase the odds of at least a couple of these ventures succeeding. In doing so, it would be far less expensive than waiting for someone else to develop them and then buying them. I think he was also interested in pushing what he saw as rather staid management within both companies. Of course, poking the eye of the establishment was frosting on the cake for Jim.

The bean counters attitude was entirely different. Their thinking was reactive, why risk any shareholder cash when you could wait and buy successful ventures using company stock. The net effect of that being to increase the value of the stock without spending cash.

While I adhere to the former mindset, I couldn't argue with the bean counters logic; both were correct depending on your perspective and role in the company. Of course, the impact of the bean counters on WebNum was predictable. They tolerated us for a time because they could see that we were succeeding. But in the end, they sacrificed us for what they saw as a greater opportunity.

International Domain Names

The DNS (Domain Name System) was originally an English-only system. More accurately, it was a "Latin character only" system. Remember the DNS is an overlay of the actual Internet so that we humans can navigate. As the Internet grew and expanded into Asia in particular, and the Middle East soon after, there was increased demand for "international" language support. In other words, to allow non-Latin characters in the address line.

– ■ –

Sorry but I need to get a bit into the technical weeds again, so bear with me. Computers talk in binary "bits" which are either a zero or a one. Those are

474

grouped into bytes which are 8 bits. Each 8-bit byte provides a total of 256 possible unique combinations. These 256 "characters" include the letters of the alphabet, the numbers 0 thru 9, and all of the standard special characters. Also, there are a few special and control characters defined in the ASCII Code set. That consumes all of the possible 256 unique combinations of zeros and ones in an 8-bit byte.

To represent non-Latin characters requires 2-bytes, in other words, 16-bits. As with the single-byte structure, there is a distinct code set accepted in the tech world. The problem was that the DNS address line did not support 2-byte characters and therefore it could not support non-Latin characters. A lot of folks around the world were pushing to fix this.

The 2-byte addressing change meant that the Registry had to be modified to store 2-byte, domain names. Of course, this represented both a challenge and an opportunity. As with the Y2K bug and IPv6, the software had to be modified on-the-fly without bringing the entire Internet to its knees. Once completed, there would be a new and huge market for these internationalized domain names. Verisign of course, wanted to continue to "own" the .com and .net Registries, and they were the only ones with the size and expertise to make all this happen.

The Death of WebNum

All good things must come to an end, and so it was with WebNum. It was quite unfortunate because I think that had we been allowed to succeed, and we were well on the path, we would have dramatically altered the trajectory of the mobile Internet. I believe that if WebNum had been allowed to continue on the course and trajectory I had plotted, today, you would see a WebNum button on every mobile phone and tablet. If that were the case, navigation of the mobile Internet would be far easier.

The mobile Internet was rapidly becoming "the" emerging technology, and I had become a recognized global expert. I was established with all of the major industry players and author of two patents in the mobile Internet addressing space. I was frequently asked to speak at various tech conferences throughout the world.

In August of 2002, I had just completed my "standard" monthly sweep through Asia. The trip had been a bit longer than usual; on most trips, I didn't visit Singapore or Bangkok, but with Japan and Korea ready to launch WebNum, I was starting to develop new markets. It was also longer as I had spent several days at CommunicAsia in Singapore where I was the keynote speaker for the second day's events.

I was preparing for an upcoming conference in Beijing. I was particularly looking forward to visiting Beijing. I had been pushing hard to establish a WebNum Registrar in China and had scheduled several private meetings with prospective organizations while in Beijing. I had visited most major Asian cities from Sydney to Seoul but had not yet made it to Beijing, so I was excited to see the city.

— ■ —

WebNum was winning, but there were powerful forces aligned against it. It was ok when we were struggling, and when Jim was defending us against internal adversaries, but it was now becoming a success, and that was threatening. As I was making final preparations for Beijing, my manager told me they had decided to shut WebNum down.

I can't say that I was surprised. As I said earlier, I recognized that we were on borrowed time as soon as Jim Rutt left the company. I tried to talk them into allowing me to complete the Beijing presentation. I argued that to drop out at this late date would be an embarrassment to Verisign. In fact, that was their objective; they were looking to send a strong message that they were abandoning WebNum and the mobile Internet navigation market, without actually making an official announcement. Dropping out of the Beijing conference was exactly the way to send that message.

Ultimately, Verisign chose to sacrifice WebNum in order to protect other business opportunities that were regulated by ICANN and the ITU. While personally, I would have loved it to have been otherwise, I can't say that I would have made a different decision if I had been a Verisign executive faced with that choice.

WebNum was a great ride; I learned an incredible amount in a very short time. I established myself in the mobile Internet space; I made some lifelong friends traveled around the world twice, and in the end, Verisign treated me very fairly money wise. Unfortunately, a genuinely disruptive technology was sacrificed for what Verisign felt was the greater good. The ride didn't last as long as I had hoped, and the mobile Internet will forever be harder to navigate without it, but I have absolutely no regrets.

Life after WebNum

A few months after Verisign had shuttered WebNum, Koji asked me to work with him on a funding situation. One of the members of the J-Data Board had co-written a book with former Vice President Al Gore. At that point, Gore was involved in the Venture Capital World, and Koji's Board member had talked to Gore about providing funding for a software product J-Data was developing. The project involved telephone search, and it had some characteristics similar to WebNum. Specifically, it indexed the data on the phone based on converting the alphanumeric characters to their numeric equivalents. That allowed the user to type in numbers and the J-Data's search engine would do a lookup of all data containing the transposed alpha equivalents.

Steve Burkholder, Koji Sasaki, Al Gore, Tim, Kaji 2003

While the concept was similar to the conversion done for WebNum Internet access, and my work on WebNum may have even inspired it, it was more like a predictive text look-up. There was no off-phone database or anything to do with website addressing, so there was no overlap.

Al Gore, or more likely Greg Simon, his former chief technology guru while Gore was VP, reviewed J-Data's history and saw several items about WebNum. They wanted to make sure that the current effort he was being asked to fund was not in violation of Verisign's WebNum patents. My name was on the patents, and he wanted my assurance that there was no violation.

Koji and his senior team flew to Los Angeles to meet with Gore, and Gore insisted that I attend as well so that he could ask me personally about any possible conflicts. Gore and his then wife Tipper were there, and we met for a couple of days. That was not the only work Koji did with Gore. I had several meetings with Greg Simon as well as with Gore over the years. We met in DC a couple of times and once at Kleiner, Perkins, Caufield, & Byers in Menlo Park. Each of these were in support of various funding projects involving Koji.

— ■ —

Gore is an interesting man, as you would expect given his history. We got to talk a lot about business, not always related to whatever Koji was pitching. His interests were broad given his involvement in the VC industry. We occasionally talked about politics, but I tended to avoid getting into that as I am opposed to his position on virtually everything, especially the whole "global warming" scam.

While he loves to get on TV and pontificate about the global warming/climate change thing, in private, I got the distinct impression that the subject never enters his mind. I see it as the perfect political opportunity for him. No one can prove it; any evidence can be spun to either support it or to refute it. If the facts don't match the projections, alter the facts and change the name. It isn't something that will happen during his lifetime, if it ever happens at all, and he has the perfect out. If it happens, he can claim people didn't pay enough attention. If it doesn't happen, he can claim credit for preventing it. And most important, vast sums of money are involved providing ample opportunity for an opportunist to make a killing. He won a Nobel Prize, an Emmy, and an Oscar for his efforts and his movie "An Inconvenient Truth." All of which served to enhance his image, prestige, and substantially increase his net worth. However, you should remember that the research for his campaign and the movie were done by his staff while he was VP, not even on his dime, we taxpayers paid the bill. Never mind, he rode that horse as if he had created the entire story. It is the perfect gig for a politician, and Al Gore is first, last, and always a politician.

— ■ —

I met with Greg Simon several times, primarily in the Washington DC area. Most of these meetings were related to Koji's funding projects. Greg had been Al Gore's Chief Domestic Policy Advisor and was deeply involved in technology. He led the effort for the passage of the Telecommunications Reform Act of 1996 as well as the development of the National and Global Information Infrastructure. He oversaw several key initiatives, including programs at the National Institutes of Health, the National Cancer Institute, the Food and Drug Administration, and the Human Genome Project.

When I first met him, Greg was leading a company founded by Michael Milken. Later he became a Sr. VP at Pfizer. Most recently he has become the Executive Director of the White House Cancer Task Force. I always liked talking with Greg. He is a very down to earth kind of guy, extremely sharp with a very broad perspective covering almost any subject. He is not at all full of himself like so many people who have moved in the circles he has.

– ∎ –

While I was at Verisign, I also got to know Jerome Glenn who was a futurist at the United Nations University. I didn't even know the UN had a university before meeting Jerome. Headquartered in Tokyo, few in America realize it exists. Jerome had the one job that I envied. He served as the director of the Millennium Project.

The Millennium Project connects futurists around the world. The goal is to improve global foresight. The Millennium Project collects and assesses judgments from over 3,500 futurists around the world. His role was to meet with some of the brightest people on earth, find out what they were working on, and get their feedback on the work of others in the network. The UN then publishes an annual "State of the Future" book. They look at issues that will be facing the globe 50 years in the future. The goal is to start people thinking about how to avoid unnecessary disasters. A sample question might be how the world will produce enough protein to feed the population?

I only met him a couple of times, but the discussions were always interesting.

MBA

I had learned while I was with ITT, that the best time to get more education was when you had someone else willing to pay for it. Even if you had no time, if you were committed, you would make the time. I had also learned that I could use the long hours on airplanes and in hotels more productively than staring out the window or drinking beer. Shortly after I joined Verisign, I decided that I wanted to get my MBA. I searched for the right school with the right Executive MBA program that I could fit with my travel schedule. Most

E-MBA programs required some time on campus at regular intervals; I couldn't do that. I was looking for a program that I could take 100% while traveling without any need to attend any campus classes. At the same time, I wanted it to be as close as possible to the on-campus courses. Finally, I wanted it to be from a fully accredited and recognized institution.

I selected Regis University located in Denver Colorado. Regis is a Jesuit school with at good reputation. I never had to visit the campus. I started their program in the fall of 2000 and completed 24 months later in 2002. I never attended a single day on campus, and I didn't even attend graduation.

For any of you who haven't been through an MBA program, they are all about case studies. The way Regis did it, each semester course was covered over a 7-week period, one at a time. A typical 2-week section would have 300-500 pages of reading on the particular subject for that module, followed by a related case study. The case studies were typically 8-10 pages covering some situation at some company. After you read the assigned subjects, you were to read the case study and then write a 4 to 6-page analysis/response/proposed solution. That corresponded well with the work I had been doing and also with my travel schedule. I would spend my air time and hotel time reading and then spend ½ a day doing my report. I loved the format and the subjects. The case studies were real situations at real companies. They always left a lot of information out, just like in the real world. It was a biweekly who-done-it. There were a lot of sleepless nights and exhausting trips where I would study for 18-hours in the air, get off the plane and go straight into meetings.

I left Verisign during the last quarter of the classes, but I was soon working on a consulting gig in Europe, so the pattern continued, the only change was that I was paying the bills.

Telnic 2002-2004

I often found it funny how one job would invariably lead to another. However, it was seldom along a straight path. Shortly after my work with Verisign ended I got a call from Benjamin Blumenthal with Telnic. I didn't know Ben, and I had never heard of Telnic. Ben wanted to meet me in New York for a consulting job interview.

A brief history of TLDs

The Internet first developed in the U.S., and many of the best domain names were taken by the time the rest of the world began to catch on to the value of this emerging communication phenomena. Countries and companies outside of the United States complained that the U.S. market had grabbed all of the good names.

ICANN's (Internet Corporation for Assigned Names and Numbers) solution was to release Country Code TLDs. There is one ccTLD for each country, more than 250 in total. ccTLDs are all 2-characters; ".us" is the ccTLD for the United States. That gave each country its complete set of possible names.

That only solved a portion of the problem, and it created a new problem; a brand and Trademark protection issue. At that time, Trademark laws for domain names had not been adjudicated. Companies felt that they needed to register every brand and Trademark in every one of the 250 ccTLDs. Many large corporations own thousands of names and Trademarks. As a result, their list of domain names became almost endless.

WIPO (the World Intellectual Property Organization), is the legal overseer of international branding and Tradename disputes. It took several years (1995-2000) and several trials before "case law" was established, and WIPO was able to enforcement issues relating to the Internet.

During that period the Internet continued to grow rapidly, and others organizations wanted to introduce more specific TLDs. That became a hot issue pitting companies that wanted to launch additional TLDs with companies who were already investing a lot of time and money acquiring, renewing and protecting their brands in all of the existing TLDs. ICANN was in the middle, and for a time they took the side of the companies who wanted less rather than more TLDs; they tightly limited the number of TLDs.

As the legal process began to show results, pressure grew for ICANN to release more TLDs. In 2000, seven new TLDs were introduced: .biz, .info, .name, .pro .aero, .coop, and .museum. An additional round of new TLDs was opened in 2003. Ultimately this round resulted in new TLDs for: .asia, .cat, .jobs, .mobi, .tel and .travel.

During this period, the process of acquiring a new TLD was a monumental task requiring years of preparation, ICANN fees, legal fees, document preparation, and politicking. I worked on the team that acquired .tel during the 2003 round. The company had tried to get that TLD in the 2000 round but failed. The process required more than ten years and reportedly cost nearly $10 million. The .tel Registry was approved in 2006 and launched in 2009.

Eventually, ICANN removed most of the barriers to starting a new TLD. By January 2016 there were more than 1200 TLDs. Of course, .com remains the dominant TLD with more than 125 million registered domain names as of January 2016. Most of the newer TLDs are unknown to all but a few.

— ∎ —

I met with Ben in New York and later flew to Paris to interview with the entire Telnic team. Telnic was a startup that had been around for several years. At that point, Telnic was overwhelmed with the process of preparing their second ICANN application; it was not going well.

Russell McHugh, a friend I had met while I was with Verisign, told me later that Telnic had approached him about doing the consulting. He told them "You are in deep trouble. You need someone much stronger than I am." He gave them my name.

— ∎ —

There were originally just two people in Telnic, both from the UK. Alan Price who lived in London was still with the company, but his original partner had passed away a year or so before I joined Telnic.

At some point, Alan and his partner had brought in financing from a Paris-based investor group. Kashayar "Kash" Madhavi became CEO. Kash is a very sharp businessman with a degree from Oxford. His family had money, and he had made more doing finance deals in Africa. His English is good but he lacked any understanding of the Internet, and he wasn't at all technical.

The rest of the company consisted of Ben Blumenthal, a young American with a fresh MBA, but little actual business experience. He was living in Paris with his wife. He was a decent writer, but at that point, he had only a surface-level understanding of technology and the Internet. Ben's day to day role seemed to be primarily to represent Kash to the rest of the team. Behind his back, they often referred to Ben as Kash's "mini-me."

Olivier Decrock, a Parisian, was a consultant and functioned as the Chief Technical Officer, but his expertise was more software than Internet specific. His English, while good, was not sufficient to write the needed documentation.

Telnic had contracted with Roke, a communications research company located south of London. Their role was limited to prototyping the planned services. Lawrence Conway worked at Roke. He was not involved in Telnic operations.

Telnic's headquarters remained in London, but with three of the four team members located in Paris, that was where the majority of the work took place.

NAPTR Records

Telnic's concept was to build an online business card using the .tel TLD and NAPTR records. Sorry, but I need to drag you back into the weeds with just one more piece of tech insight.

Going back to the WebNum chapter, remember that the Domain Name System is an overlay that sits on top of the real Internet. The DNS works as a translator converting user-friendly text "domain" names into computer-friendly IP addresses. In the vast majority of DNS transactions, that is all that is needed.

However, the DNS has some additional but lesser known and seldom used capabilities. One of the more fascinating and least understood capabilities is the Name Authority Pointer or NAPTR records. I was privileged to get trained on the NAPTR structure and functionality by Mark Kosters, the guy who invented them. I will try to explain them without getting too deep into the weeds.

When a NAPTR record is requested, it doesn't return an IP along with a redirect as the DNS normally does. Instead, it returns data that has been placed inside of the NAPTR portion of that domain's DNS record. I won't go into the structure of the data, or how a NAPTR record request is made, that is not important. The important thing is to understand that when you request a NAPTR record, you are not going to do a second access to a target website. You will only get whatever information has been stored within the DNS

NAPTR record.

In their implementation, Telnic did some magic so that additional information that is not part of the actual NAPTR record is returned. Even with this supplemental information, the data is still quite limited, so it looks like a single page website.

When your browser displays a NAPTR generated page, it functions as a standard internet site. An image of the Telnic.tel record is shown below. As you can see in this sample, the NAPTR record along with the supplemental fields Telnic allows can contain quite a bit of information, including clickable hyperlinked addresses for websites, emails, and telephone numbers.

The benefits of this NAPTR generated mini-website are that; it returns very fast; it does not require a separate computer to host a website on the Internet; it fits the mobile device display well, and an authorized user can easily update it without web developer knowledge.

Hopefully, this tutorial/history has been informative, and at least a little bit interesting. In any case, you needed to understand at least the basics, or you won't be able to comprehend the process or the significance of what Telnic was trying to do.

I was astonished by the absence of both technical and Internet expertise at the core of the company. That is no reflection on technological skills of either Olivier or Lawrence. They were technical, but neither were employees, and they both came to the company later.

As for Internet marketing expertise, none of the team came even close to understanding the Internet market. There appeared to be no market research to indicate there was demand for their proposed online business card. It was one of those "build it, and they will come" approaches. They were trying to solve a problem that, in my opinion, did not exist.

Despite all of this, they were spending vast sums of money to try to acquire a license that would allow them to set up a Top Level Domain that would use the DNS system in a way that had never been tried, and most likely had never even been intended to be used.

After the initial meeting in Paris, I told the entire team that I felt they were trying to solve a nonexistent problem. Companies do not want to publish or promote their phone number because they wanted users to contact them via email, not the phone. The Telnic team was convinced that their online business card was a highly marketable product. As a consultant, I was paid to do what the customer asks, and so I refrained from further debate regarding the wisdom of the proposed service.

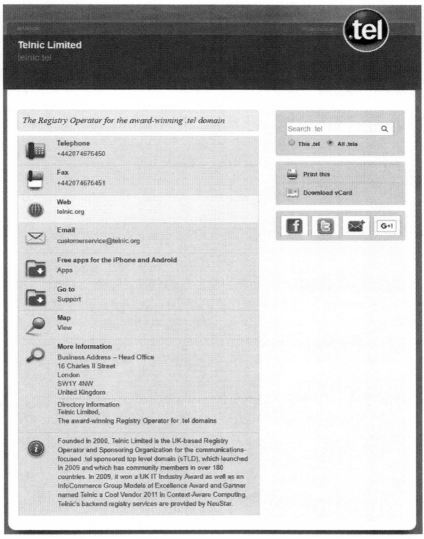

Telnic.tel

The most immediate challenge was to complete the ICANN Application. The Application consisted of an extensive set of complex questions the required the generation of massive amounts of technical and marketing documentation. Each was more like a "white papers" or essay rather than simple answers. In some ways the process was similar to building a business plan, only in this case it involved very specific questions, and would ultimately be presented to a group that had little business knowledge, so it had a lot to do with politics.

I spent the next two plus years commuting to Europe. Primarily Paris, but sometimes London where Telnic had some office space. I would typically stay in Paris two weeks, come home for a week, and then return. In 2003, I traveled to Europe 16 times. There were additional flights from Paris or London to Stuttgart, Helsinki, and a few to Munich. I moved between Paris and London so often I had a Euro Rail card with a lot of miles on it.

— ■ —

Kash had a strange way of approaching the new documentation areas. He couldn't visualize the desired outcome. I suppose that this was in part a reflection of his lack of technical as well as Internet knowledge; it certainly wasn't because he wasn't smart. He would say something like "I need you to give me a write up on XYZ." Naturally, I would ask what he had in mind. He never knew. So I would go figure out what I thought we should do, and write up a paper. At first, I would spend long hours completely researching and documenting the subject. I quickly learned that was a mistake. I would give whatever I had written to Kash, and invariably he would say that wasn't what he had in mind.

I came to understand that like a lot of people; he couldn't wrap their head around a subject or do any analysis unless he had a starting point. He couldn't deal with abstracts. You see a similar thing with people when you show them a blueprint; they cannot visualize what the house will ultimately look like, or even how it will flow. Once I would give him a starting point, then he could visualize, and refine. Without that first paper, his mind was just a blank.

The Nokia War

I never understood the logic behind the ".tel" name. In my opinion, "tel" implied telephony and yet the business card concept had almost nothing to do with telephony, it was all about the company name. Here again, my job was to do what the customer wanted, and fixing their business concept was not something they asked me to do.

Telnic had made an application for the .tel TLD in the first round, so the .tel name and their intended use was public knowledge. For the second round, they had made some adjustments, and enhancements. They were convinced that this would not only result in the .tel TLD being awarded, but it would also make it a smashing success that would revolutionize the entire Internet.

When I first came to work for Telnic, they were at war with Nokia. I don't know who or what started the war, or specifically what it concerned. I am not even sure that it wasn't an entirely fabricated and one-sided war. It looked very much like a "Mouse that Roared" scenario to me. Nokia was not particularly supportive or friendly toward Telnic, but they were the big dog at that point, and that was the way Nokia treated everybody. I saw nothing that was overtly anti-Telnic.

Nokia was also applying for a TLD. We knew that they were working jointly with Microsoft, but they had not announced any name or the intended use of the TLD. For whatever reason, it seemed that Telnic was afraid that Nokia would somehow block them this round. The general feeling was that Nokia was their arch enemy.

This went way beyond them simply being competitors, which in my mind, they weren't. It seemed pretty obvious that neither Nokia or Microsoft were stupid enough to try to build an online business card system. I don't know if Nokia had a hand in Telnic's failure in the previous ICANN round. Maybe it was just paranoia because Telnic was so sure that their concept was a winner, and therefore, they were afraid that Nokia would rip off their idea. It may have also been that they feared that Nokia would try to grab the .tel moniker for their own purposes.

It seemed pretty obvious to me that whatever Nokia planned, it most likely had something to do with the mobile Internet, most likely mobile specific content. Furthermore, since the ITU wouldn't allow telephone number registrations, the .tel designation seemed to be an unlikely name for their effort. I felt that conflict was unlikely.

They may have had a fear that there would only be a few new TLD licenses granted and that Nokia could get the last ticket and keep them out. To me, wasting energy fighting Nokia was a dumb way to win that battle. If resources or market power were the critical factors, Telnic could never win. The only solution was to build a better business case.

When I first started working with Telnic, Kash asked me to take charge of the relationship with Nokia. I suspect that he may have seen the whole idea of a Nokia war as a fool's errand. Shortly after that, we flew to Stuttgart, everyone but Kash, for a meeting with Nokia and Siemens. I don't recall the specific reason for the meeting, or why it was necessary for Olivier and Alan to attend. Ben seemed to be there to see that I didn't somehow sell the company down the river. In any case, they were all there as "good soldiers" in this stupid but ongoing war. When we got to the meeting, I discovered that I knew every one of the players in the room. They were all friends I had met and dealt with for years on the WebNum project, and so we spent the first 45 minutes talking about WebNum and why Verisign was killing the program.

As the meeting got going Ben started some antagonistic line of discussion and I quickly got him to be quiet. I asked some civil questions and tried to get Nokia to start an honest dialogue. Fortunately, my past relationships were strong enough to calm the waters, and we got to talk about what was needed. It seemed the UMTS (Universal Mobile Telecommunications System) Forum needed someone that was not an operator or a manufacturer to take responsibility for assembling the marketing requirements document for the next-generation (3.5G) of the mobile Internet. The UMTS Forum is the global industry group that consists of all of the Mobile Operators and Handset Manufacturers.

I suspect that Nokia and Siemens were trying to get Telnic to step up to this task, in part as an olive branch to calm the relationship. It was almost like they were throwing us a bone; give us something significant to do that would provide prestige and get us off of this silly war footing. Before this meeting, they were not aware that I was working with Telnic. My being involved was their best possible scenario. I was known to virtually every member of the UMTS Forum from my WebNum work, and I had a lot of respect from everyone. I fit the need as I was not an insider, and I had credibility with the members.

They needed an outside party because each of the UMTS Forum members was concerned that a member, e.g. Nokia, might have their finger on the scale during document preparation. They asked me personally if I would be willing to take on this responsibility. It was tempting because I could have easily made a lot more money than Telnic was paying, but I had made a commitment to Telnic.

It was clearly outside of the scope of work that Telnic had assigned me, and even somewhat outside of Telnic's line of business, but I saw an opportunity to not only end the war but to possibly neutralize Nokia. I considered asking the UMTS Forum to pay for my work directly but thought that Kash might find this to be a conflict of interest on my part. I also sensed that Telnic would be in a stronger position if they paid the tab. In any case, I knew that I could always make funding part of the deal later. I told them that I felt that Telnic would be willing to play that role, but that I would have to clear it with management as I was only a consultant.

Ben went ballistic. He excused himself from the meeting early so that he could call Kash and unload. Ben was perturbed that I had been civil with Nokia and that I had more or less accepted an assignment to work with the UMTS Forum and all of the Operators. Ben is smart and well educated, but at that time, he was still pretty wet behind the ears. It was also becoming apparent that Ben may well have been the instigator of the whole war, possibly with Alan's help or at least concurrence. When I came out of the meeting, he got Kash on the line again and handed the phone to me. Kash was overly dependent on Ben in many ways, but he was not blind to Ben's lack of experience.

Kash wanted to know my thinking. I told him that we were foolish to try to fight a war with the biggest handset manufacturer in the world. There was no way we could win and nothing to be gained even if we did. I recommended the old "keep your enemies closer" approach. By working with Nokia, we had an opportunity to learn more about what they were doing and, most importantly, we had a chance to gain stature with the other Operators and manufacturers, all of whom competed with, and universally resented Nokia's oft times insufferable arrogance. I felt it was better for Telnic to fund the work. That might at some point help to neutralize Nokia. In short, we had nothing to lose and everything to gain by declaring a truce with Nokia and assisting the UMTS Forum. Kash agreed. I returned to the meeting and informed Nokia and Siemens that Telnic would be glad to help with the assembly of the mobile Internet requirements document. I didn't ask for funding.

Ben was pissed; the war was over, but the peace was still shaky. Nokia sent me two of their newest handsets as a peace offering. Kash insisted on paying for them. That was a bit of a slap in Nokia's face, but they got over it.

The incident in Stuttgart brought a new balance in the Telnic team. Kash had allowed Ben to work far too closely with him, almost as his "chief of staff." As a result, the other team members viewed Ben as something of a spy in their midst. Kash had a rather harsh management style, and that didn't help. I don't think that either Ben or Kash felt that it was Ben's job to spy, but Kash tended to relay his directives through Ben. That not only heightened the appearance that Ben had Kash's ear, but it also provided Ben the opportunity to exert undue influence on those directives. Ben was quite young, in his late 20s at that time, and I am sure he did not realize that he was helping to create this distrust by flouting his access to Kash. As with most that age, he tended to be more than a little too sure of himself and more than a bit brash in his approach to things. The net effect was that it appeared Ben was working behind everyone's back.

Much later, when Nokia's application was made public, we learned that they were applying for .mobi, and, as I had anticipated, their intent was to use that TLD to identifying mobile content. However, the application group was far bigger than we knew. It included a who's who of the mobile industry: Google, Microsoft, Nokia, Samsung, Ericsson, Vodafone, T-Mobile, Telefónica Móviles, Telecom Italia Mobile, Orascom Telecom, GSM Association, Hutchison Whampoa, Syniverse Technologies, and Visa. ICANN approved the .mobi domain in July 2005.

I believe that Nokia's thinking was that the Mobile Operators would get more deeply involved in the mobile content market, selling .mobi domain names and possibly even hosting content. It didn't work out.

As it ultimately turned out, technology obsoleted the need for segregation of mobile content. It also became apparent that companies didn't want to invest in creating a separate mobile Internet brand under a different TLD. When it became possible for mobile users to display .com content on their phones and later on their tablets, it was a knife in the heart of the .mobi TLD.

ICANN at first rejected Telnic's second application, but after some adjustments and serious politicking, they were able to get then to reconsider and in 2006, they approved the .tel TLD. It was 2009 before Telnic had an operational Registry.

Today, most people have no knowledge of either of these TLDs. .mobi never really took off. .mobi registrations peaked at 1.2 million in January of 2014, but by April 2016, there were only 700,000. There are far fewer actual websites.

When .mobi was launched, they had a lot more money to spend on advertising, and with that gaggle of partners, they had global reach. In many cases, companies bought a .mobi domain just to protect their brand. As usual, some people decided to "squat" on a good name in the hope that it would one day be worth a fortune. The entire gambit was a losing bet.

Over the years, Nokia lost favor as a leading handset manufacturer, and in February 2010, Afilias acquired .mobi. Microsoft purchased Nokia's handset business in 2013. Thus effectively ending any hope of .mobi ever becoming a major TLD.

The .tel TLD group had fewer advertising dollars and almost no market presence. It never even reached the point of serious speculation. .tel registrations peaked at about 300,000 in 2011. They were at 100,000 in mid-2016.

.tel continues to hang on, but appears to have given up any thought of becoming a significant player. Given all of the ways to access Internet content, the proliferation of simple website design services, and the ongoing move away from telephone contact by companies as well as individuals, it seems unlikely that .tel will ever become a player. It can only be a matter of time until they also sell the Registry.

I have considered repurposing the .tel TLD. I know a way to turn it into a very valuable asset. I approached Kash about finding a new partner, but he showed little interest. Of course, I never disclosed the concept. It remains a viable business, but with the current management, it will not happen.

Private Slaves

Kash had a bad habit of treating people like slaves. His family was from the Middle East. I was told of his rather distinguished lineage, but I have no idea if what I heard was even accurate, so I will not repeat it. In any case, his was obviously a family accustomed to wealth and servants. In the Middle East, servants can be treated pretty much like slaves. Kash tended to slip into that mode with the team from time to time. When he did, it was not pleasant.

I pushed back whenever he treated me that way; it came to a head one time when I had just returned from a short trip home. I got back to London early Monday morning after flying all Sunday night. I put in a full day; by evening,

I was approaching 36 hours with no sleep. I had been writing one of his typical first-draft throwaway documents, the ones that never satisfied him. Kash got on the phone and started berating my work. I listened for about 1 minute until he started on my "screwing up" for going home. At that point, I said to him: "Shove it up you're a--. I am on the next plane home. You can find someone else to fuck over." I hung up and walked out to get a beer. Alan, who was sitting nearby, about had a cow! He came running after me and ask what the problem was. I told him very simply that I had had it with Kash thinking I was not doing quality work. I had other clients, and I didn't need him.

I went for a beer. Ben and Olivier joined me, and we all had a good laugh. I was relaxed; I was going home in the morning. Alan was usually pretty timid when it came to dealing with Kash, but apparently, he finally grew a set and told Kash for the first time how shitty he was treating all of the team. My departure would put them in a world of hurt. I was the only one capable of creating the necessary documents, and they all knew it. It was unlikely that they would be able to find a replacement in time to meet the filing deadline. Without me, they had millions at risk.

Alan came to the pub after we had another round. He asked me to return to the office so that Kash could talk with me. The beers had done their job, and even though I was bone tired, I knew that I had been a bit harsh. We talked, and Kash apologized, something I suspect he had never done before in his life. He said he was headed down to his home in Provence for the weekend and asked me to please join him and his family.

I took the train to Paris later in the week and then another train to Provence on Friday. He met me at the train, and he was a very gracious host. His home was beautiful, and of course, so was Provence. We drove around, and he showed me the sights. As usual, he had to have a cigar or two and so we stopped at a few little restaurants for lunch and wine. In one shop, I was admiring a vase that I thought Sharon would love and he immediately stepped in and bought it, insisting that I give it to her with his appreciation for all that he was putting her through.

That was a turning point in my relationship with Kash. Before that, he had played the king with his slaves. He continued to treat the rest of the crew poorly, but from that point forward he was very respectful and appreciative whenever he dealt with me. I know he was initially upset, but I think that Alan was finally strong enough to tell him that he was way out of line. Whatever

Alan said, or whether Kash came to his conclusions, I don't know, but from that point onward, we were friends. Having said that, I could tell from the brief conversation we had recently regarding the future of the .tel TLD, he has reverted back to his natural state. That is why I can assure you that there is no future for .tel under the current management.

— ∎ —

Telnic had no offices in Paris. When we needed to have team meetings, we would meet at a hotel, usually the Hotel Napoleon near the Arc de Triomphe. Occasionally, we would meet at Kash's apartment, but Kash preferred 5-star hotels where he could have a cigar and a nice glass of cognac.

Ben and his wife were living on a houseboat tied up near the Pont des Invalides on the Seine. The houseboat was a converted barge named the Mars. Ben quickly got over his ruffled feathers from Stuttgart, and we became good friends.

Alan Price, Tim, Ben Blumenthal & Olivier Decrock
On the Mars 2003

The Mars was small, but Ben had no children at that time, and so it was quite comfortable to work out on deck. Even on a chilly day, I liked sitting on the deck in the sun with the boat gently rocking from the wakes of passing boats; life was good. I could watch the passing boats and think about what I needed to write. The Eiffel tower was to the west, Notre Dame to the east, and the heart of Paris was just to the north. Life on Mars; what an office, what a way to earn a living.

— ■ —

Ben and his wife would frequently invite me to share Shabbat dinner with them on Friday nights on the boat. They had a lot of friends in Paris, but also from Brussels where his wife grew up. They often had other guests, and we would talk about a broad range of subjects late into the evening.

Ben's family was very well connected. His father was high up in the faculty at Emory University in Atlanta. He had two brothers, both living in Israel. I met his mother several times when she came to visit Ben. They seemed to know everybody who was anybody. I think that Ben's connection to Kash came through a friendship between Ben's brother Phillip and Kash. I never learned a lot about Ben's wife's family, but she was a remarkably accomplished person in her right. She had been involved in organizing art and music events as I recall, but more impressive to me was that she could speak something like 17 languages.

Ben and his wife invited me to a concert one evening. Itzhak Perlman was performing. He was incredible to see and hear in person. Ben introduced me to an elderly Jewish couple sitting with us. They were in their eighties and not in the best of health. Their names, of course, meant nothing to me. Ben has his own health issues, and during the performance, he needed to return to the Mars to lay down. He insisted that I escort the couple to a taxi and ensure that they were safely in to return home. Of course, I had no problem with that responsibility.

They were barely mobile, the man in particular. I got them on an elevator and eventually to a taxi and safely on their way. The next day Ben ask if I knew who they were. Of course, I did not. He said they were some of the major funders of the Guggenheim Museum in New York. It honestly didn't make a lot of difference to me; they were just a lovely older couple that I met along life's path.

— ■ —

Kash lived near the Mars with his wife and children. They had a beautiful apartment on Boulevard de La-Tour-Maubourg. Kash liked the finer things in life, cigars being one of his vices, along with a good cognac. His wife

494

wouldn't let him smoke in the house, so Kash would often invite me to meet him for a drink at the George V, the Four Seasons Hotel just off of the Champs-Elysées. It was a beautiful hotel, and it seemed to be his favorite place to sit and relax. He liked to have someone to talk with, and we had lengthy discussions about the .tel project, about life, and the various members of the team. The scotch was very nice; I am glad I was not picking up the tab.

Kash was pretty cheap on the wages side, but he was a generous host, and after our little tête-à-tête in London, he did appreciate my traveling and spending so much time away from my family. He would frequently invite me to his home for lunch on the weekend. Over time, I got to know his wife and children.

3.5 G Mobile Internet Requirements

In my nonexistent spare time, I worked at gathering the 3.5 G Mobile Internet requirements. I was fortunate in that most of the operators already knew me and the UMTS Forum made the introduction that refreshed all of the contacts. In most cases, I was able to work via the telephone and email gathering the necessary documents. I did visit with most of the UMTS Forum members in Europe, including one trip back to Finland.

It was slow, but enjoyable. In broad terms, each member was feeding their requirements to me and I was assembling a merged set of requirements. I would circulate interim versions which invariably generated modifications and more requirements to merge and recirculate. One of their major goals was to get to the point where they could all use the same cell towers. That meant getting to a standard wireless network radio technology. Of course, limiting the types of radios would also bring down the cost of handsets. The most popular radios (in the phones) at that time included: CDMA, TDMA, iDEN, EDGE, and GSM. Some rural areas still used the older analog systems as analog has much greater range.

The higher the Internet speed, the more bandwidth. The more bandwidth, the more cell towers required. With each tower costing up to $2 million. They wanted to get to a single radio type so that they wouldn't have to invest so much duplicating new towers. The problem was that each Operator had their reasons for choosing the type of radio they were using, and of course, they wanted everyone else to move to their type. While the requirements called for a single radio type, and everyone agreed and signed off on that, they never reached agreement, and so all of those radio types are still in use today.

The second major hurdle was that each Operator wanted some exclusive, but at the same time, they didn't want any of their competitors to have any exclusives. It became a cat-and-mouse game. As I would distribute different draft documents, each Operator would go through them looking for any sign that someone else had been able to slip in some exclusive. I was assembling the information and not being told exactly why one Operator wanted things that were very specific. Even if I had known, I could not have divulged their reason to another Operator. But that didn't stop them from calling me to ask who had added this or that requirement and why. So with each round, they would all try to play "hide the feature."

Another key objective was to get to the point where the Operators could participate in the retail marketing game. They were trying to do what is today called "Big Data" gathering and manipulation. The goal was to get to where they would know if you had gone on the Internet and looked at a pair of shoes on Amazon, and then two days later when you were in the Galleria Mall, they wanted to be able to pull these facts together and send you a text telling you that if you would stop by the such and such store just around the corner, they had that pair of shoes you were looking for and they would give you 15% off if you showed them this message. Of course, the Operators wanted a small slice of that business. Each Operator had their own vision of how this should work. Writing all of that up and getting everyone to agree was a complicated process.

This document had a final due date of course. As we got closer to the submission date, things got a bit hectic for me. It turned out that the drop-dead date was on a Friday night at midnight Paris time. I thought I had all of the pieces together and everyone in agreement so that I could submit it. I had traveled to New York with my family, and we were planning a relaxed weekend of sightseeing, starting with tickets to a Broadway play Friday night.

I was at the hotel ready to send the final document in when Ritva Siren at Nokia made a request for a change. Of course, that meant that I had to get everyone else to concur before I could add it to the document. I sent it around and got grudging approval. Ritva immediately followed with three more change requests. I was getting pissed. My theater time was rapidly approaching, and I had people all over the world up at all hours of the day and night, many on a Saturday, and Nokia was jerking us around. I sent a response to Ritva, copying everyone telling her that no more changes would be accepted. She came back with a BS answer whining about how she had been too busy and not had sufficient time to review and input her requirements. Of course, she had a full-time person involved all along. I responded, still in an open email that as unfortunate as her situation might be, that my refusal to accept any further modifications stood. If Nokia chose not to agree to the Requirements Document when it was reviewed in France the following month, then that would be her time to make her complaint. I started getting dozens of private "bravo" messages. Everyone was sick of Nokia's games.

– ■ –

I traveled to ETSI (European Telecommunications Standards Institute) headquarters at Sophia Antipolis, near Nice, France about six weeks later to formally present the Requirements document to the members of the UMTS Forum. They each had a copy of the document for several weeks in advance, so it was more of a formality than a real review. After I formally submitted the paper for acceptance, the chairman asked if there were any objections or questions. All eyes turned to Ritva to see what she would do. She remained quiet and voted to accept the document as written.

Of all of the political fracases I have had the opportunity to undertake, the 3.5 G Wireless Internet Requirements exercise tops the list. It was both fun and frustrating trying to get all of the Operators, and to a lesser extent the handset manufacturers to agree on anything. 3.5 G was also the first time the software companies began to flex their muscles. Google and Apple were not yet in the game, but Microsoft was starting to play. Of course, in the end, it was all for naught. I don't know that anyone ever so much as opened the document after that meeting. I am not aware of any effort to implement what they said were their requirements.

In all fairness, the "single-radio" challenge fell apart due to objections from the Chinese. I do know that there were at least a few discussions about trying to standardize on fewer if not a single radio, but just as they were beginning to talk, China Mobile and China Unicom announced that they intended to develop their own radio that was different from anything that currently existed. The single-radio initiative fell apart at that point.

The whole big data effort didn't happen. Outside events overtook it. I doubt that the concept was ever completely abandoned, just delayed. I am sure that they still want to get a piece of that action, but I doubt they will ever be able to get that coordinated.

Working in Paris

In Paris, I usually stayed at the Hotel de la Tulip at 33 rue Malar. The hotel was only a few blocks from the Mars and Kash's apartment. It was a small, absolutely authentic Parisian hotel. I stayed there so many times that I think I stayed in every room at one time or another. Sharon and Katie were able to accompany me on one trip, and they stayed there as well. The Tulip served a traditional breakfast of croissants and jam along with tea. I became good friends with the proprietor, and we often would sit, drink wine, and chat into the evenings.

Most evenings I would walk over to Rue Cler which is close to the hotel. Rue Cler is a two-block area of small shops of all kinds. It is primarily for locals. There were several small restaurants whenever the mood struck me, but most evenings I would buy a bottle of wine, a baguette, a bit of cheese, and head back to the de la Tulip where I would enjoy my dinner while working on more documentation. The wine would last a couple of days, but I would get fresh bread and cheese nearly every evening.

The de la Tulip was not a fancy place, it had more of a home-like atmosphere, especially since I got to be good friends with Bernard, the proprietor. It was probably the most pleasant living arrangements I have ever had in all of my travels.

Post Submission

I continued doing consulting with Telnic even after the .tel application was submitted. Fortunately, the pace wasn't nearly as frenetic, and I could do more of the work from home. We had concentrated most heavily on the materials required for the submission. Once that was complete, we started cleaning up and finalizing all of the necessary backup materials that would be needed once ICANN initiated its review process. That ran well into 2004.

Hotel de Tulip Courtyard Paris

Eiffel Tower near Hotel de Tulip 2004

The Transition Years

In January of 2004, I turned 59. It was no big deal, as I recall I was in Paris at the time. It was just another day, but that spring, for some reason, it hit me that I was approaching 60 years old. I couldn't, and still can't believe how fast the year's fly. I remember sitting at a desk in high school thinking that Thanksgiving was eons away and that spring would never come. Soon I was out of school and on my own; I had all of my life in front of me. Wasn't that just last week? Where had 40 years gone? Had I blinked?

I wasn't worried about death, I never have. I just figure that I will go to sleep one night and not wake up the next morning. I am a person of faith, so to me, even that will not be the end, just another beginning. I have always believed that I would live to 108, even as a young child. I don't know why I have felt that way or that particular age. I just accept that it is my destiny. But now I was approaching 60, and it struck me that I had passed the halfway point about five years earlier. Somehow I had missed that.

Maybe it was just that magic number, the approaching of the big six-oh! I didn't feel old or even older. I am 71 as I write this; I still feel like 35, well except for a few new aches and pains. But no matter how long you think you will live, reaching 60 is a time to reflect on how you have spent, hopefully, invested the decades that you have lived.

I knew that I was in a time of transition work-wise, but instinctively, I knew that it was also a transition time in my personal life, a time to think about how I wanted to structure the next phase of my life. I had finished my MBA program a couple of years earlier and saw no reason to try to acquire any additional diplomas. Now was the time to begin to harvest the investments I had made in both my formal and informal education. I wasn't harboring any regrets or trying to second guess my journey; it was more like savoring a good wine; I was just reviewing all that had gone before. I had and still have, no regrets. Mainly, I was looking forward to the next chapter, the next challenge.

The past few years of consulting had been good financially and personally satisfying. I was trying to decide if I should continue consulting, or should I start another company? I didn't relish the frustrations of chasing money to start a business, but chasing clients was often just as frustrating. My network of contacts was predominately in the technology arena, specifically at the intersection of the Internet and telecom worlds. They were broad and at high levels, but they were almost exclusively outside of the US. Even while I was working with Telnic and the UMTS Forum, I had done some odds and ends, small jobs. That was working primarily with Koji and J-Data and to a lesser extent with Omron in Japan, and with LG in Korea.

By early spring, as the Telnic work was winding down, I was starting to work more with Koji in Japan, but at the same time, I was looking for other long-term opportunities. Consulting is like that, some years are outstanding, some years are ok, and some are disasters, financially speaking.

Despite the cyclical financial aspects of consulting, there was a lot that I liked about the work. Remember I spoke of becoming a "corporate nomad" in the beginning of this book. I had certainly lived that life. I particularly, I liked being able to drop into new situations, to build or rescue a project or a program. I was seldom involved in the early stage stuff, trying to prove a project's value or fight for the money. In many ways it was similar to my CE days with IBM, dropping in to fix a computer when no one else could. There were also frustrations about consulting; you seldom got to reach the finish line. A consultant is like the hero's sidekick in the movies; I came, I saw, I conquered, and then rode away before the hero got to kiss the girl. That never bothered me because, for me, it was never about the glory, I didn't care who got the credit, as long as I got to fix the problem. You always moved on and let the company finish up and celebrate. It wasn't really about the money either; it was about the challenge, the living on the knife's edge. I love a challenge, but especially I loved that I didn't have to 'clean the filters' so to speak.

I also loved the "mobility" of consulting. I could work one day in one field on one problem, and another day in an entirely different field, on an entirely different problem, and often on an entirely different continent. I loved the travel, one week in France, one week in Japan, another week who knows where. I enjoyed working alone, but that meant that I didn't have someone else's income to cushion the economic swings. The only thing I didn't like was the uncertainty of finding the next job.

Telnic had provided a good stable income, not specular, but reliable, and for a long time, but as usual, I was worried about what would come next. I was kicking around the idea of starting my own business again, but I didn't have a killer concept in mind at that moment. We had saved some money to cushion any dry spell, but was it enough?

I can't say that I was relaxed; my mind was indeed spinning, but it was nice to take a bit of a breather and not spend three out of every four weeks outside of the country and away from my family.

— ∎ —

Sharon and I had been renting since we moved to Virginia in the summer of 1998. During that time, we had constantly been looking at houses to buy. The economy had gone up and down; the Dot Com bubble had burst. I had been extremely busy traveling, first with Verisign, and later with Telnic. A good deal of my time and a considerable amount of our money had gone into the completion of my MBA. All the while house prices kept going up and up. It seemed like we were chasing the market when we should have jumped in earlier. But schedules and funds had always gotten in the way.

I think that Sharon had looked at every home for sale and every open house from Washington DC to the West Virginia border, and from the Potomac River to Richmond. I am exaggerating of course, but she had looked at a lot of houses, and it felt like every time I was home she had some new subdivision with model homes she wanted me to see.

We were out looking late in the fall of 2003 when we came across a development called Ridings at Blue Springs. I remember thinking this was a natural because of the community initials, RBS, tied back 40 years to my Air Force days. It was a nice development done by Pulte Homes. There was a house that had fallen out of a deal. It was about ¾ completed which meant that we would not have to wait too long and that we could choose all of the decorator items like cabinets, flooring, and colors. I decided this is the one. Sharon was hesitant, but I liked the house and the community, and I was sick of looking.

We gave them our down payment and applied for what felt like, and was, an inordinately large mortgage. The home was $610,000. We had a decent income, and some savings. The banks were offering new "no docs" loans which meant that all you had to do was say you wanted a loan and they would give it to you. A stupid concept by any measure, but it worked for us given our erratic income and the lack of a traditional pay stub. The real estate market was crazy during that period; the price had already risen $100,000 by the time we moved in in April.

It was a 4500 square foot home on a ½ acre, so there was a lot of yard work to get done, trees to plant and rocks to move. When I wasn't working for Telnic, or trying to think up a new business, I would be busy in the yard or unpacking boxes. Of course, Sharon was right there with me hauling boxes and helping dig holes. We were busy but having fun creating our new home.

In retrospect, the house was way too big for our needs. We were making the mistake many people make. We had spent years building our family, my profession, my education, and moving with work. Now it was time to reap some of the rewards and what could be better than a beautiful big house. Unfortunately, that was very nearsighted. Katie was just a few years from heading off to college, and while I was at my peak earning period professionally, retirement and lower income were not all that far in the future, certainly not as far as the 30-year mortgage. Like many, we weren't thinking ahead; we should have picked something much smaller that was less costly to buy and to maintain. But we didn't.

Chaos: Thy name is cancer!

Everything changed in an instant. Looking back, I find that I do not measure Sharon's passing from the day she died, but rather from the afternoon of August 12th, 2004, the moment our world turned upside down.

In many ways, it was just a typical hot, humid summer day in Northern Virginia. I was busy at my computer working on some new plan. Katie was 14 at that time. Sharon decided she would take Katie over to Tysons Corner to pick up Sarah Faith, a school friend. There was some movie the girls wanted to see. Sharon wasn't interested in seeing the film, so she planned to hang out and do some shopping while the girls watched the movie. After it was over, she would take Sarah Faith home and then bring Katie home. She planned to be gone about 3 hours.

About an hour later, Sharon came home alone. I asked her what was up and she said her stomach hurt. I should have realized that if her stomach was just hurting she would have gone to Starbucks and relaxed with a cup of tea until it was time to pick up the girls. However, being a typical guy, it never dawned on me, and she didn't let on just how severally she had to be hurting to come home like that. We were in the process of moving, unpacking, planting and all those manual tasks that exercise seldom used muscles. I assumed she had merely pulled something, and told her to lie down while I picked up the girls.

Weeks later she told me that, on that afternoon, she had just walked into a store when suddenly a flood of pain had overtaken her. She had barely made it back to the car. By the time she told me this, we understood that this sudden onset of pain was the result of a rupture in her uterine wall as cancer burst through the soft tissue and formed a blister which immediately began to fill with blood. That minor breach of a small piece of tissue on the backside of her uterus was the tipping point. It was by no means the start of the cancer, but it was the point where, too late, it made itself known. That was the very moment when the chaos overtook our lives. It was called Leiomyosarcoma, an extremely aggressive form of cancer that is relatively rare and usually fatal.

On that day, unaware of any of what was happening, I got the girls and took Sarah Faith home and visited a few minutes with her parents who were friends. When I brought Katie home, I discovered that Sharon couldn't get out of bed, the pain was too severe. Within a couple of days, the blister had filled with blood, and she looked like she was 9-months pregnant.

505

For me, the realization of what we were up against came in an avalanche of diagnostic reports, EKGs, an emergency hospitalization for a pulmonary embolism, which evolved to a complete hysterectomy followed by that awful moment when the doctor confirmed that it was malignant. None of the news was good. We didn't know exactly what kind of cancer at that point, but she told us that Sharon had spots on her liver and lungs that were inoperable. Chemo, a poison so severe that it will burn your skin if a drop lands on it, became the dreaded but longed for salvation, a salvation that never materialized.

Sharon's cancer was sudden and unbelievable chaotic. She went from no symptoms whatsoever to being deathly ill in less than 2 hours. She had brief periods of mobility, even semi-normalcy, but they were all too brief, and they quickly became increasingly rare. She suffered great pain, and the medications left her groggy and disoriented. She was in and out of the hospital, enduring several surgeries along with chemo and frequent blood transfusions. During January and February of 2005, she received 22 transfusions.

The cancer quickly consumed her energy and her reserves. She could barely stay awake to hold hands or to talk. Our most intimate times were when I would gently rub her arms, legs, back or head so that she could sleep. Her temperature could shoot from 99 to 104 in less than 15 minutes. That resulted in several trips to the emergency room, which always led to yet another hospital stay, and more than once, additional surgeries. I had to give her medications throughout the night and always monitor her temperature. Over time I learned to manage the fever.

She hated going to the hospital. The staff took great care of her, but it was lonely and frightening; it was a graphic reminder of just how ill she was becoming. I arranged to give her all of the medications that I could so that she could stay at home as long as possible. At one point she was on 23 medications. It was a vicious circle. Most of these were to counteract the effect of other drugs she required.

They put a mediport on her shoulder so that I could hang IVs. A mediport is a small medical appliance that is installed beneath the skin. A catheter connects the port to a vein. She was losing a lot of blood and would quickly become dehydrated, so IVs were a twice-daily ritual.

I learned to recognize the indicators when a transfusion was needed, and I often conspired with her doctor to make sure she got the necessary tests even when they weren't scheduled. She would put on makeup before she went to the doctor. She thought it made her look healthier. She was hoping it would keep her out to the hospital or avoid yet another transfusion.

Sharon was kind, considerate, appreciative, and as gracious as she could have possibly been, but my exhaustion and worry never ended. I was reading every lab report and every piece of information that the doctor was giving me, and she was giving me everything. I am sure that I looked at her x-rays more time than all of the doctors combined.

Sharon had surgery to remove all of the tumors that they could in August, intense chemo followed that, but by late September the x-rays showed several new tumors as big as my fist. I searched the Internet endlessly for answers or information relating to her condition, to understand the drug interactions, and to try to comprehend the pathology and lab reports.

I grew up on a ranch where you see animals born and animals die all of the time. What I was seeing and reading told me everything; I knew early on, how this was going to end. Of course, that was something I could never discuss with Sharon; I had to pray that I was wrong, but to help keep her spirits up so that she could fight this monster within.

When her sister or her friends came to visit, I would have time to try to do a little work or get groceries. That was more to get my mind off of what was happening than to accomplish anything. Loyal friends came often, and they delivered more meals than we could eat. The downside was that Sharon would strive to put on her best face, but the visits drained what little energy she had. The hours following the visits were often accompanied by greater pain, sleeplessness and temperature spikes.

In early January she underwent her third major surgery. This one was emotionally devastating as they had to remove most of her colon and install a colostomy bag. Sharon was never a vain person, but she naturally wanted to be attractive like anyone would. The colostomy bag was emblematic of a transition in her life. It meant that even if she won her desperate battle, her life would never be the same. She could never go back. That was a terrible emotional blow to her.

I have lived through divorce, financial difficulties, job changes and job loss, major moves, losing a parent, and now I was losing my spouse. I can tell you that nothing compares to the challenges of being a caregiver to a terminally ill spouse. Your partner, the person you confide in, the person with whom you can discuss anything and everything, is suddenly the person you can't confide in, I couldn't burden her or even let her know that I was worried. I absolutely could not tell her that I knew how this would end. This was the most difficult and challenging period of my life. There were frequent visitors and a million things to do. It may be difficult to understand the nuance, but while I was not lonely, I have never felt more alone than during this period. Despite all of that, for me, taking care of her, loving her, and holding her hand as she died, was an honor and a privilege beyond measure.

Shane Anderson, my friend from Verisign, proved to be an incredible friend in my time of need. Many people would say things like "if you need anything, just call." They were sincere, but this is not the way men work. We don't call for help, or at least the way I was raised, you don't. You just lean into the storm and get it done. Shane never said, "call me." Instead, he would call on a Friday and say "I will be there first thing in the morning to mow. Don't you dare do it; I will bring the gas." That is how you care for the caregiver. You take away the option; you just roll up your sleeves and do whatever needs to be done. I will be eternally grateful for his incredible friendship.

I turned down several consulting opportunities and avoided all travel as I needed to be home to take care of my family. I was able to do a little work for some understanding clients who could tolerate my erratic schedule. The week before Easter I found myself in a situation where I had to attend a meeting in San Francisco. Katie was off from school, so I didn't have to drive her each day. Katie was very good at taking care of her mother, and I knew that she could handle almost any situation, but she was too young to drive if that became necessary. Sharon's sister Julie agreed to stay with Sharon in case anything happened.

I got up very early Thursday morning and caught a plane to San Francisco. I called Katie when I landed. Things were ok. Immediately after the meeting, one of the people who understood my situation rushed me back to the airport, barely in time to catch a return flight. I got home just after midnight; the house was in complete chaos.

Katie had been in the room with Sharon when Julie and her husband Ramazan arrived. Katie went downstairs to let them in. While Katie was downstairs, Sharon needed to use the bathroom and decided that she could make it without assistance. She did make it into the bathroom, but fell and didn't have the strength to get up. Katie and Julie came up and found her in the toilet area which was a small separate room. There was blood everywhere, and Sharon was in great pain. The room was small, and they couldn't get her up, so they called 911. An ambulance was dispatched. The attendants were able to get her up. They wanted to take her to the hospital, but Sharon refused. I know that she understood that if she went to the hospital at that point, she would never come home, and she wanted to die in her bed.

Sadly, this was the first time Julie had accepted just how sick her sister was. I don't know if she refused to see, or was just in a state of denial, but up to that point, she didn't accept the fact that Sharon was near death. I finally got Julie and Ramazan out and on their way home, and Katie calmed down. Katie was very upset and blaming herself for not being there to help her mother to the bathroom; it was not her fault at all.

My favorite picture of Sharon 1984

I sat with Sharon, and we talked. She was frail, and she would drift in and out, but she wanted to talk, to tell me that she knew what was happening and where she was. As the sun was coming up on Good Friday morning, she quietly said: "It's over." She had given up. She had no more fight left in her. She died less than 72-hours later.

— ■ —

I called Julie Sunday morning and told her that she needed to come over. She

509

asked why and I told her simply that Sharon was going to die today. Julie started crying. She had a hard time accepting the finality and couldn't believe the certainty in my voice. She asked me how I could know and I told her that Sharon had said early Friday morning that it was over; she had no more fight left in her. I told her I just knew.

For a person of faith, there is no day more meaningful than Easter. For me, Easter will always hold a very special meaning. At 4 p.m. Sharon was struggling to breathe, and I told her that she was free to go, that we would be ok. I was holding her hand and cradling her head at ten minutes after 4 o'clock on Sunday, March 27, 2005, when Sharon Tunisia Griswold my loving wife of nearly 26 years went home to be with the Lord. Her battle with cancer that had been both too short and too long, but she fought it as she had lived her life, with incredible courage, dignity, and grace.

— ■ —

My wife's needs were considerable, but I also had a 14-year old daughter to support. She attended a private all-girls school some distance from our home, and so we had time to talk and for her to decompress as I drove her to school every morning and picked her up each afternoon.

You could not live in the house and watch Sharon deteriorate without knowing what was happening and where it was going to end. I talked with Katie frequently about how she was doing and what was on her mind. Katie was an extraordinarily strong child and is now a remarkable young woman, married and studying for her Ph.D. She handled this situation with amazing strength and grace. Once, just before Christmas, I asked her how she was feeling about her mother. She replied that "Mother left last August." She meant no disrespect, merely that all of the things that "mother" used to do; her hair, shopping, girl talk, etc. all came to an end when Sharon got sick. Those things were no more.

One noteworthy outcome of our shared experience is that Katie and I are closer than we would have otherwise been. We share a unique bond and understanding. I know that she will look for enduring commitment in the man she married, and I know that if God forbid, she is ever in a situation where she has to give unselfishly of herself she will stand tall.

— ■ —

About 45 days after Sharon died, we had a Life Celebration. Sharon did not

510

want a funeral or anyone mourning her passing; she wanted everyone to remember the good things. Both families came together. I ask them to bring pictures and stories to share. To write them down so that I could place them in a scrapbook for her children and so that future generations could know about her remarkable life and what kind of person she was. There was a touch of sadness, as you would expect, but there was also great joy in remembering who she was. Several people told me that they hoped their families would do the same for them when the time came. I pray mine does for me.

— ■ —

In June of 2005, just three months after my wife's death, I was diagnosed with prostate cancer. In mid-August, I underwent a Robotic Prostatectomy using the da Vinci System, a blessed technological wonder that dramatically reduced the recovery time from months to weeks. I was extremely fortunate to have discovered the cancer early and aided by great doctors and remarkable technology the surgery was successful in removing the cancer completely.

There are several types of prostate cancer, some slow-growing, some faster. Some suggested that I watch-and-wait to see if I could "manage" the disease. I chose to get it out as soon as possible. I realized there were some risks associated with such surgeries, and it was possible that I could have waited years to deal with it, but my concern was more for Katie. She had just watched her mother die from cancer. I did not want her wondering if she was going to lose her father as well. For me, that was far more important than worrying about any possible side effects from the surgery. Fortunately, the side effects were minimal. I only spent one night in the hospital, and I didn't require any drugs or chemo, they were able to get it all. Eleven years later, I remain cancer free.

— ■ —

My story is not unique or particularly novel. It is in fact tragically common. It is at the heart of what I have come to see as the caregiver crisis in America. Looking back, I realize that I exhausted myself reinventing on-the-fly what others already knew. That was a tragic waste of both time and energy. Millions have walked the path I walked; millions more are walking it today. Now, as then there is no way to benefit from what others have experienced. There is no network to connect them with their fellow travelers, no way to leverage their knowledge, their successes, failures, or secrets of survival. While knowing their "tricks-of-the-caregiver-trade" would not have altered the outcome in Sharon's case, it would have made the journey much easier. It is in that vein that I established the Foundation For Caregiver, with a mission *"to care for those who care for others."*

Life after Cancer

We had insurance of course, but that didn't cover all of the medications, and some were super expensive. However, that was not the worst of the financial disaster brought on by double cancer. The biggest issue was that I had to quit working to support Sharon, and after my surgery and recovery, I could no longer pursue my profession, international consulting. I could not even do much domestic consulting if it required travel. I was now a single parent. I had to be home to take care of Katie. Her aunt and uncle were in the area, and they were certainly willing to help, but that wouldn't work if I went back to 3-weeks a month outside of the country. My career had to change.

Losing a spouse takes a while to wrap your head around. Immediately following that, having to go through my own cancer scare, as small as it was, by comparison, is another mental tumult. Compound that with the reality that I had to dramatically and immediately change my career. That was what you might call the "hat-trick" of bad things. Each one takes a bit of mental adjustment.

At 60, and having worked for myself the majority of the past 20 years, I didn't see myself as likely finding work with a company. Compounding that, having spent the majority of that period either on a different side of the country or a different side of the world, I didn't have any real network in the immediate area. It seemed the best option was to start another business, but doing what?

As I was recovering from my surgery, I formulated an idea for a business in the mobile Internet space. I started building my business plan. If you have never constructed a business plan, it is a lengthy and exhaustive process. It typically takes a minimum of 3 months. I have built a few for other people, and I charged a minimum of $30,000 for each project. It would cost twice that today. It is an exhaustive process. You must examine every aspect of the business. You have to do extensive and detailed research on competitive threats. Then develop your strategy to mitigate each risk. You need a complete financial plan that runs out five years. The first two years need to be in excruciating detail. There is a section called SWOT which represents Strengths, Weaknesses, Opportunities, and Threats. Any VC will have experts who will rip you up if you haven't crossed every conceivable "t" and dotted every "i." It takes 120% of your concentration to assemble a business plan that you can put in front of a VC.

By the summer of 2005, I had pulled together what I felt was a winning program. It was time to start the pain-in-the-ass process of chasing money. Just as I was ready to go after the dollars, Nokia and Microsoft announced that they had formed a joint venture to do exactly what I was proposing in my business plan. There was no way I would be able to raise capital in the face of that competition, and even if I did find a way to do it on my own, an impossibility at that point, there would be no way to convince potential clients to choose me over the Nokia/Microsoft offering. My business plan was just wasted time and paper. I had no choice; I tossed the plan in the trash and started over.

Foundation For Caregivers

All the time while I was trying to figure out how to restructure my life to make a living, in the back of my mind, I kept thinking that I needed to do something about the caregiver problem. I was busy, and my plate was full trying to figure out a way to make a living, so I kept pushing the thought aside. When the Nokia/Microsoft announcement crushed my plans, I was at a loss. I remember lying in bed and asking God what He wanted? The answer came that I needed to do something about caregivers.

Ok, so God wanted me to work on the caregiver problem, but what exactly did He have in mind? Eventually, I decided to launch a nonprofit foundation to work on the problem. I had never been involved in any nonprofit. I knew business, and so logically I thought of that organizational structure.

I found a legal firm that specialized in setting up nonprofits. I had established many companies over the years. I had no problem incorporating a new business, but knowing that a nonprofit had to file with the government to get their 501c3 status, I assumed that it would require a more comprehensive set of corporate documents. That assumption was correct. The bylaws needed to cover areas that are different from a for-profit corporation. The company I hired to do the paperwork knew the rules.

Of course, I needed a name to file the paperwork. I knew that one of the first things I would need, would be a website for the foundation and that would require a domain name. By 2005, all of the short names, and most all of good names had been registered long ago. I started brainstorming and searching using all of the combinations that I could. My "shorthand" name had always been the Foundation For Caregivers. It was simple and to the point but I thought I would have to get more complicated to find an available domain name. I was growing increasingly frustrated when someone casually asked: "what about initials?" That seemed like as good an idea as I was coming up with, so I searched on FFCG – Foundation For CareGivers and the ffcg.org domain was available. How could a 4-character domain name be available in 2005? There was no way; it was impossible. I remember thinking at the time, God moves in mysterious ways.

Foundation For Caregivers logo

We filed the incorporation documents and completed the 501c3 application by late September of 2005. The company told me that it typically took the IRS about six months to grant the 501c3 designation.

514

Before Sharon's illness, I had done a little work to develop a concept around a network security company in Tokyo. I didn't have enough information to do anything more than think about it. Dropping the Foundation filings on the IRS's desk meant I was free to work on the opportunity. It looked like I would have at least the next six months. In early December I flew to Japan to closely examine the security program. While I was there, I received a voice message from the law firm working on the Foundation. I assumed that they just needed some additional information. I didn't have any of the files with me, and I was halfway around the world on a different date and time zone. I put off returning the call until I came back to Virginia.

Soon after I got back home, I gathered all of my papers and called the firm assuming I would have to dig out some additional piece of information. When I got to the right person, I asked her what was up, and she responded simply "you got it." I wasn't thinking, so I asked her "I got what?" she laughed and said you are now a 501c3. I ask what was going on; I thought it would take six months. She said it normally does, and that they had never seen it come through so fast.

That forced me to take a serious look at which "opportunity" I should pursue. I liked the data security product; it was called TCP2, but there were a few issues. First, I wasn't in a financial position to do this on my own so that I would need some funding or a partner. My location was a bigger problem. The vast majority of the companies in the Washington DC Metro area were, in one way or another, working with the Federal Government. To break into this market would take a minimum of three years, and realistically five years. First, we would have to get on the GSA schedule. That would take months. Since we were dealing with data security, and we were dealing with a product developed outside of the U.S., we would have to get tested and certified. That would probably take 18 to 24 months, and lots of dollars for consultants and testing. After we were certified, we would have to get an actual order, and as I have said before that is a 2-year process at a minimum. The most significant issue, and the one that shut this opportunity down, at least for the foreseeable future, was that the Japanese company was in a legal battle over control of the technology. I never had a clear understanding of how it evolved, but apparently, two different people claimed ownership of the intellectual property. Until that issue had been resolved, we couldn't move forward.

All of that meant that I was not going to be able to take on the TCP2 product at this time. Even though I knew next to nothing about running a nonprofit, I figured that it was my best opportunity. Besides, I kept getting these nudges from God.

— ■ —

So now I had a Foundation, the $64,000 question was, what am I going to do with it? I know business, and so I started developing a business plan for the Foundation. Building a plan was not the issue, that I knew how to do. The challenge was figuring out how to fund the Foundation. I certainly couldn't afford to fund it myself; I would need outside money. I knew nothing about the nonprofit world, nothing about raising funds when you were not trading equity for dollars.

My initial concept for the Foundation was to build an online database to connected caregivers with support providers. A doctor or a nurse would register their patient's caregiver and indicate the medical situation of the patient. For example, a wife might be the caregiver for a husband with Alzheimer's. Once they were registered, the system would make the connection to the relevant resources that would be available to that caregiver. At first, it might be the Alzheimer's Foundation plus various state and local resources: adult day care centers, respite facilities, etc. Over time, I anticipated that it would grow to include more comprehensive services and we might even be able to get sponsorship from various pharmaceutical companies. Of course, that would not come until after the system was operational.

I had no interest in becoming involved in what I called "street-level" services. I didn't want to try and build a huge organization, or even a small storefront operation that was trying to help caregivers one at a time. My expertise was in business and technology. It didn't make sense to me to try to run a small "retail" caregiver operation, I was trained and equipped to work at a meta level, not a micro level.

The immediate problem was how do I get the funding to do this? I would need funds to run a small organization of 3 or 4 people, but considerably more to pay to have someone develop the software. Once that was in place, I would need to find a way to get both doctors to sign up caregivers and to get service providers into the database. I was back to the double-critical-mass problem I had faced with WebNum. Unfortunately, I wasn't under the wing of a big company that could provide both funding and credibility.

I talked with several doctors about my concept, and learned that I would need to get a billing code assigned to the caregiver registration process. In the medical world, insurance companies and various government regulations control everything. Everything a doctor does has to be "coded" so it can be classified and recouped. That goes clear down to the nuts-and-bolts level. If they hand a patient a piece of paper, there is a code for that. If there isn't a code, they won't do it, period, end of discussion. There was no code to hand a piece of paper to, or register a caregiver.

I had a friend who happened to be in the coding side of the business. She was a several steps above a coder, she worked as a professional coding auditor, reviewing the operations side of the major medical groups and hospitals. The coding system is so complex and convoluted that these organizations often miss codes on even the simplest procedures. When it comes to something complex like open-heart surgery, the missed codes can add up to tens of thousands of dollars. A typical audit might find several million in missed billings that could be recovered if filed in a timely fashion.

I talked with Mary Madsen, and she was excited about participating. She also knew the process required to go about getting the needed code. I invited Mary to join the Board of the Foundation where she remains to this day. Over the years, she has been a great help and encouragement as we have struggled to get the Foundation in a position to fulfill its mission.

– ■ –

The next challenge was to raise funds to sustain operations. Stepping into the not for profit world was a rude awakening. I had assumed that donors would be excited about the concept and at seeing a well thought out and documented plan. I was mistaken. One of the very first things I learned was that donors are loathed to give money for operations or infrastructure, the very things I needed at that point.

I had a conversation with Bob Korzeniewski, a friend from Verisign. Bob had been the Finance VP, so he was responsible for the budget allocation and review for the WebNum project. We had become friends in that process. Bob had made a good deal of money when Verisign bought Network Solutions. He had retired to run his own Family Foundation. We talked about the Foundation and my need for capital to get started. We also talked about the thinking of individuals and organizations that contributed to nonprofits. What I learned was that they universally preferred to donate to the end processes and not to operations and infrastructure. They wanted their money to go to the hungry,

517

the ill or whomever, not to the nonprofit's operation.

I offered this hypothetical situation. If a nonprofit was feeding the homeless at a cost of $1/meal, and it could show you that by investing $1000 for a PC and software, their costs could be lowered to 50¢, would you donate the $1000? His answer was no.

I was quite taken aback by this. Bob had worked in the high-tech industry, and he knew that technology (infrastructure) could provide significant productivity improvements. Even if 50% were wasted, he would still rather see his money go to meals.

I investigated the grant process and learned that you 'had to have done something significant, to qualify for the funds to do something significant.' These two insights forced me to rethink my plan. If I could not get a donor or a grant to provide funds to develop the needed system, then I either had to generate the funds myself or abandon the concept of providing the services.

I had to rethink the Foundation completely. However, it was clear that developing another service concept would only mean that I still needed funding to develop the infrastructure necessary for that offering, and that would bring me right back to the need of financing that was apparently not available. My only option was to develop my own funding stream. In essence, to self-fund a business. Funding continues to be a struggle for the Foundation.

— ■ —

On the personal side, not that my work and finances weren't personal, Katie continued to do well in school. Her grades had remained high, even while she was processing all that was happening with her mother. We spent the summer between her junior and senior year visiting colleges in the Northeast as well as on the West Coast. We flew to Portland, OR and took the time to visit my sister and brother with their families as well as my Dad who was living with my brother at that point. From there we drove to Boise, ID to visit another daughter and a new grandson. We drove to San Francisco, LA, and then flew home.

Dad was living with my brother in The Dalles, Oregon. He was 92 at the time and still doing very well. He had been an outdoor person all of his life, and that continued until he died. Tom and Linda lived on the edge of town and their property backed against the hills. Even at that age, Dad would hike up the mountain with his dog every day.

Dad was showing me around his garden. He loved to garden, and he had quite a prolific crop. He was pointing out the various things that he had done over the years since he had moved there and I suggested that he might want to do a particular thing for his garden the next year. He said, without hesitation, "Oh I won't be here next year." He wasn't planning on moving; he was planning on dying. There was no remorse or sorrow; it was just a statement, it was just Dad being Dad. His health was good, and he was still very mobile. His short term memory had slipped over the years so he might tell you the same story a couple of times the same day, but otherwise, he was in good shape. Somehow he had decided that it was time. He died the following year.

I have seen this many times in my life. Someone will simply decide it is time for them to go and go they will. Sharon had done that, Dad did that, and so have several others that I have met. That is in part, why I have always been so sure about my life span.

$$- \blacksquare -$$

Katie did very well on her SATs and graduated second in her class. She had several decent offers from some excellent schools. The best was a 'full ride' scholarship to Carnegie Mellon University.

Carnegie Mellon is one of the best schools in the country. To have a scholarship valued at close to ¼ million dollars over the four years, was unbelievable. There was no way I could have financed that education for her. She took that offer and graduated with a degree in Biology. She is now in a Ph.D. program at Washington University in St. Louis.

Dating

When Sharon passed away, I thought that I would not marry again. Ours had been a long and good marriage, and I was not looking to replace Sharon. I was looking forward to having time to "be alone." I had married at 19, become a father at 20, and for the next 40 years, there had been at least one child at home. I had never been on a real vacation alone in my life. I was looking forward to an empty nest, and downsizing my nest. Not only was the house too expensive, it was far too large for one person, even with a couple of pets. Just keeping it clean and the yard green was taking too much of my time and money.

I started dating if nothing more than to have some adult conversation. The last time I had done any dating was when I was a teen. At that time, it was 'boy pursues girl.' At 61, I discovered that the roles had completely reversed.

Tim 2006

I tried the various dating sites and found the dating scene to be insane. I remember putting my profile on one site; I think it was Match.com, that required 2 or 3 days to approve a new profile. I went on about my life and gave it no thought for about 4 or 5 days. When I logged in, I found some 200 messages waiting. I had stated in my profile that I was looking for someone local and someone closer to my age. There were messages from women all over the country and some in their 20s.

I was rather green at the online dating thing and thought I should be courteous and respond to each message. I quickly learned that my saying that I was not interested because they were too young or too far away, meant nothing. One woman, she was 28 and lived in Montana, replied that she would be happy to move in with me if I would send her a ticket. Starting with her, I learned just to delete and block the ones who weren't of interest.

The whole process was both comical and frustrating. Often simultaneously. A common ruse was the 10-year-old profile photo. It was so bad that sometimes I wouldn't even recognize the woman when we met. I quickly learned that it

520

was best to meet the first time at a Starbucks. That allowed for a short visit and quick exit, a common outcome. I also quickly learned why the majority of these women were no longer married. After 10-minutes of streaming complaints about their ex, I was already feeling sympathy for the guy.

— ■ —

Over time I began to realize that my thought about staying single wasn't what I wanted. I preferred to be married. I didn't like the artificiality or the temporary nature of dating relationships. I came to realize that when you lose a long-term spouse, you lose your memories. There are so many little memories, things that bind you together. The story about the turkey pan and the basset hound at Thanksgiving, the ham and cheese sandwiches in the middle of France. These are not big earth shattering events; they are tiny things that you shared, things that few others would understand. It turns out that you can tell them in your "life story," but otherwise, they get buried with your spouse.

Mostly I had a vision of myself sitting on the porch of an old folks' home telling some nurse who could not have cared less, about something that to me was a funny event in my life. The concept seemed rather pathetic. I wanted someone to share new memories, someone that would sit on that porch with me, laughing and telling me of events that she recalled. Dating was never going to achieve that goal.

That change of heart didn't happen instantly; it came over time and with the ever present frustrations of online matchmaking. I remember one woman. We never met, but her profile seemed interesting. She was, or at least claimed to be, an architect in DC. One of the things I noted on her profile was that she was "looking for a good-hearted do-gooder." That seemed like an interesting starting point. We exchanged a couple of emails, and I found her to be a bit pretentious and rather opinionated. I began to suspect that the 'do-gooder' line had been plagiarized. It just didn't fit with the way she stated things and asked questions. She was in-your-face and full of herself. After a few emails, I asked her "what about you makes you worthy of that good-hearted do-gooder you seek?" She responded that she thought my question was too difficult. End of story.

I did find one woman that I liked fairly well, and we got along alright, but I soon discovered that Katie didn't like her. I don't know why, she just didn't. One day the woman stopped by the house while her car was being serviced at a nearby dealer. I told her we needed to take a breather to see if Katie would get more comfortable. Her response was "you have to choose between Katie and me." I didn't say a word; I just escorted her to the door. As she was leaving, she asked what this meant. My response was "I have chosen." She called a few days later and said we need to talk. I said that we had already talked and there was nothing more to say.

Looking outside of America

That woman was the preverbal straw that broke the camel's back. I decided then and there that I would find a non-American wife. I had no doubt that there was a decent American woman out there that would be right for me, but I was just not willing to kiss any more frogs.

– ■ –

One of the things I had learned over the years was that there are significant differences in the way Americans, Europeans, and Asians see the world. You may recall my friend Jerome who worked at the UN University. He suggested that when faced with a problem, Americans respond: 'what technology do we need to develop, to overcome this problem?' Europeans respond: 'what laws do we need to pass to prevent this problem?' Unfortunately, we see the same attitudinal difference developing between conservatives and progressives. The progressive mantra is to demand government "solutions" to all problem, a very European approach.

I picked up another version of the differences somewhere along the way. I don't know if someone told me, or if I came up with it on my own. In any case, it goes like this. Four or five people are in a meeting. Someone says, 'we could do this.' If that meeting were at an American business, the immediate response would be "yes and." Others would agree and start expanding upon the initial idea. If that meeting were in Europe, the response would be "yes-but." People would immediately start finding reasons why it couldn't or shouldn't be done. If that meeting were taking place in China, before the first person had finished their statement, two people would be running for the door to make it happen. They have an "all-in" attitude.

– ■ –

So how does this apply to dating? I have little tolerance for yes-but people; that is not the way I choose to live. Unfortunately, this described the vast majority of the women I found on the American dating sites. I preferred the all-in attitude of the Chinese, so that was where I started looking.

I had spent lots of time in Asia, more in Korea and Japan than China, but I felt that what I was looking for was more likely to be available in China. There was a website called Asia Friend Finder (AFF) that appeared to have a decent system and selection process. I posted a complete bio, one that I felt represented who I am and what I was seeking. It was in English of course, and as with the American sites, shortly after I posted my profile, I was overwhelmed by the response. Unfortunately, the vast majority were in their 20s or 30s.

I know that a lot of middle-aged men dream of a 20-year old wife, especially a 20-something Asian wife, but I was not interested in anyone that age. I was looking for a woman who had experienced a bit more life, preferably one that had been married.

The Internet dating sites abound with players, and that includes AFF. It is not just the men; there are a lot of women who are playing games as well. I mentioned the 10-year old photos as an example. In the case of AFF, the game is a bit more serious as you can't simply meet at Starbucks. Many young women are desperate to escape the poverty of their village; others just want to come to America and the only way that could ever happen was to marry an American. Of course, after they have their Green Card or citizenship, they divorce. In some cases, they wait long enough for the husband to pay to bring their parents and then they divorce.

This "gold-digger" strategy was not limited to the young women, but they were easy to spot. The first contact email would be overly sweet, the second would be gushing, and the third would be a confession of eternal love. I was thinking that we have barely gotten past what town or city you live in and you are telling me I am the love of your life. Sorry, I don't buy that.

Of course, as with their American counterparts, some Chinese ladies were a bit better at the game, and it would take a little longer to see what their real motives were, but there were also some very nice and very sincere women that were worth getting to know.

— ■ —

When Kellie first responded, I looked at her picture and thought she was too young. She listed her age as 47. I thought it was a bit strange to say you were older than you were, so I didn't respond. A couple of days later, I got a much longer email, and it talked point by point, to what I had said in my profile. That was very unusual. Most of the emails I got were pretty generic. It was obvious that, since they had little or no English skills, they had someone who spoke English compose their emails. When that happened, in a strange way the English was too good for a non-English speaker.

I can't speak or write Mandarin, so I understood their dilemma. I would have to either send my text through a software translator, which in general aren't very good or have someone who knew the language compose my email. While cookbook emails didn't raise alarms, the fact that Kellie had taken the time to read my profile and then to respond directly to what I had said, caused me to take a second look. Kellie told me later that it had taken her two long days to understand my profile and write her email to me. She was the only person who made that kind of effort.

I kept looking at her profile picture and not believing the age she had listed. I figured it had to be a typo because there was no way she looked 47. I asked her, and she said that yes she was 47, but the camera always loved her and took off at least ten years. It turned out that she was correct, even today if you look at her picture, you would never guess her age. A part of it is the fact that she is a trained photographer, but mostly she just looks younger in her pictures.

We started corresponding both by email and with Skype. We could chat slowly on Skype, but for any serious discussions, we used email so that she could take the time to translate my message and then compose her answer, first in Mandarin which she then used a translation software package to translate to English. She would then try to retranslate back to Mandarin to see if it had come anywhere close to what she was trying to say. An email would often take a couple of days to answer. Even then, there were some messages that I would have to ask her what she meant.

Kellie had a dictionary (book), a handheld translator, and translation software on her computer. I would type a message to her on Skype, and I could see her typing, looking down at her translator, and often she would get out the dictionary. It was a slow process and a lot of work for her.

Through these ultra-slow conversations, over a few months, we got to know each other. The process was more about asking and answering questions than anything "romantic," but we came to have a far better understanding of who we both were and what we were seeking. After a few months, I suggested that

I should come to Shanghai to meet face to face. She found a hotel for me that was close to her apartment, and I arranged tickets.

Tim & Kellie in Shanghai 2008

I spent two weeks in Shanghai. I had been there a couple of times before, but always on business, and so I had not had a chance to get to know the city. Kellie, sometimes with her friend Natalie to help translate, showed me around the city. Kellie's Chinese name is Longying. We shifted that to become her middle name when she became an American citizen.

Most of the time we were on our own, except for the handheld translator to get us past the truly difficult words. I had worked with non-English speaking people so much that it was never a problem for me. I was accustomed to speaking slowly and using simple language. I found that while I couldn't speak Mandarin, we could understand each other quite well. We also discovered that we were very comfortable being around each other.

We talked about the future and the possibility of marriage which was the goal for both of us. Of course, we would have to go through the immigration process, and that would take some time. I told Kellie that two things needed to happen first. We would have to go somewhere for a few days. I told her that Beijing would be good; we could see the city but also see the Great Wall. I have always found traveling can bring out the worst in people. There are

525

always issues; the plane doesn't arrive on time; the hotel is overbooked; a meal is inedible. Something will go wrong, and some people just can't deal with it. In my experience, you will discover the real person when you travel with them. Camping is the best as it has the highest probability of including some mini disaster, two days of rain, no matches, or some other problem. Of course, camping in China is not an option, so I figured a week in Beijing would do the trick.

The second requirement was that I had to bring Katie to meet her and her daughter. I assumed that Yixin (pronounced ee-shin), she adopted the American name Ashley later on, would be living with us and I wanted to know how everybody got along. I figured tossing everyone together on a trip to Beijing would provide ample opportunity for stressful situations. Kellie said that it sounded like fun and that she wanted to meet Katie as well.

I returned home and started the paperwork for a Fiancé Visa. We could have married in Shanghai and then applied for her as a spouse, but that process usually takes far longer than the Fiancé Visa process.

— ■ —

I talked with Katie, and she was very excited to visit China and meet Kellie and Yixin. We went after Katie got out of school. We traveled by train from Shanghai to Beijing, about 800 miles. As I said earlier, I prefer trains because you get a chance to see the countryside, as well as the cities, towns, and villages. The land along our route, which is slightly inland, but follows the coast, is quite flat. It reminded me of the Mississippi delta area, wet and green.

One of the things that caught my attention was the trees. They tended to follow the roads and the small levees that separated most fields. There didn't seem to be any fences and very few animals. The thing that I found unusual about the trees was that they were all the same size. It looked like they had all been planted one weekend about ten years earlier. They all had a 5" diameter trunk. In the 800 miles, I don't think I saw a single tree that was larger or smaller. All the same kind, and all the same size.

Another interesting phenomenon were random apartment complexes. We would roll through miles of fields, and suddenly there would be a cluster of 10 or 15 high-rise apartments. No city or factory nearby, just a cluster of 16 to 18-story apartments. All brand new, and they all looked pretty much the same. I have seen many of these islands of apartments on other trips; they seem to spring up for no particular reason.

We toured around Beijing and visited several of the historical parks. Of course, we went to Tiananmen Square and explored the Forbidden City. One thing we noticed was that when you ask anyone for directions, they would tell us very authoritatively where the place was and how to get there. If we walked 10 feet and asked another person, we would get an entirely different set of directions; both were stated with equal authority. I think this was the result of "training" for the 2008 Olympics that were taking place the next year. The government had instructed everyone to be courteous and helpful to foreigners, and so they were.

Like Shanghai, Beijing had been rebuilt into a model city to compete with Hong Kong. Since the government doesn't have to be concerned with things like the profitability of a building, they built some incredible structures, far more expensive and far more buildings than any market could have realistically absorbed over such a short period. However, it did make for compelling viewing.

One of Kellie's brother's had a business associate in Beijing, and they were kind enough to act as our host for part of our stay. They drove us around Beijing one evening, and out to the Great Wall at Badaling, for a day trip. The Badaling trip was about 50 miles each way, but on the return leg, we took a side trip to visit the Thirteen Ming Tombs. It was so nice to have a car and a tour guide.

We were having dinner together when Katie suddenly got sick. Again it was fortunate to be with a local as they knew which hospital to take us to get Katie quickly examined. As I said, there is always something that happens while you are traveling.

We also attended a Chinese Opera. Not exactly a disaster, but definitely something I will not be repeating.

We returned to Shanghai on an overnight train. After a few days touring and visiting Kellie's family, Katie returned home, and I stayed for another week or so. Katie is only 11 months older than Yixin, and they were like long lost sisters. Everyone got along with no issues whatsoever and so Kellie, and I decided that we should continue the Fiancé Visa process.

— ∎ —

The only serious problems were that Yixin was starting her senior year of high school and it didn't make sense to move her until she had finished. Also, as is customary in China, her father had custody, and we would need to get his permission. Like most Chinese, she had taken English in school, and like most Chinese, her English was extremely limited.

The timing was a bit dicey. Any child that you include on a Fiancé Visa must be under 18 and single. Finally, an accompanying minor must come within one year from Kellie's arrival. It all depended upon her father granting permission, something that was questionable as he had worked very hard to keep mother and daughter apart over the decade since their divorce.

Of course, everything was dependent on Kellie's visa, and we knew from research that was far from a certainty. When I returned, we continued our low-speed dialogue over Skype, and we started gathering the materials required for her visa interview. There is a lot of information and stories on the Internet, even a diagram of the visa interview area at the Guangzhou Immigration Center.

We knew that there were three primary determinants. First USCIS (United States Customs and Immigration Service) wanted to make sure any applicant was not a security risk. Second, they wanted to make sure that this was a "real" relationship and not some Green Card scam. Finally, there had to be an opening, as there is an annual quota for immigrants from any country. We felt confident about our ability to present sufficient materials to pass the first two hurdles, but there was nothing we could do to know or influence the outcome of item number three.

The process is both complicated and expensive. On the American side it not only has to pass through USCIS, but the application takes a detour through the Department of Homeland Security. They do a thorough review of both the applicant and the American partner. Once the application clears that hurdle, it returns to USCIS. They send the entire package to the interviewing Consulate, in our case that was at Guangzhou which is west of Hong Kong. There are U.S. Consulates in most major cities in China, including Shanghai. Guangzhou was the only interview location for immigration visas.

The package delivery process is extremely slow. The packages are sent using public mail services, not as diplomatic materials. The Chinese tend to "hold them up" for a minimum of 30 days. They undoubtedly open the packets and photocopy the contents. One can only guess what else they might do once they have that information.

Once the package reaches the Consulate and completes their review, they send a packet to the applicant with instructions to obtain the necessary vaccinations, doctors certification, x-rays, etc. Once that is completed and returned, they review once again and finally send out an interview appointment.

All of this takes months, and from the time the application is submitted until the first packet reaches Kellie, there was almost no visibility of the process. The system is supposedly more transparent these days.

I could, and did call in to check the status from time to time, but that usually involved at least an hour on hold before I could speak to a real live person. At one point; I think it was in that black hole 30-day delivery delay, I told Kellie I was going to call USCIS to find out what was going on. That was before we knew about the "black hole" issue. Kellie panicked when I told her I was planning to call the government. Calling the government is something you just don't do in China. I told her not to worry, but this brought home the fact that our system, as incompetent and frustrating as it often is, is way better than the way much of the rest of the world works.

— ■ —

When it came time for the interview, I flew to Shanghai and then we flew to Guangzhou for the interview. We had a very organized and complete portfolio of everything we thought they might wish to see. We had every form and notice that we had submitted and received. We had photocopies of marriage and divorce documents, a photo book showing my first visit as well as our travels when Katie accompanied us. We had airplane tickets, and receipts for everything. We included a binder with nearly 200 pages of our emails and Skype communications. The assembled package was in a packet almost three inches thick.

Kellie was very nervous, but I was quite confident. To me, the only issue was the immigration quota. Was there a slot? Once she had signed in, I could not accompany her into the waiting room or to the actual interview. Like a bunch of expectant fathers, several of us waited at a café on the same floor. There were three of us at one table. We discussed our experiences as we sat waiting. One young guy had come to China several years earlier to teach English and had met and married a young woman in the village. This was their second time through the process. I don't remember why they didn't pass the first time, but as I recall, it seemed pretty trivial. This time he had even brought his parents to Guangzhou in the hope to sway the interviewer. She did get her visa. In fact, she was the first one out of the room, and we all celebrated their success.

The second guy was in his mid-50s, and this was his third trip to Guangzhou. His story illustrated the thoroughness of the process. His first time through he was the one that failed the application process. He lived in Chicago. After his divorce, he had taken in a roommate to help defray some of his housing expenses. His apartment was 2-bedroom, and he had chosen a female renter. DHS had discovered this and flagged him as someone who was probably in a relationship with this woman and therefore the Fiancé Visa was assumed to be a Green Card scam.

That meant that he had to get a different tenant and go through the whole process again. That took even more time because of these extenuating circumstances. Out of frustration, and in part to reassure the Consulate that this was a real relationship, he flew to China, and they got married. During the interview, one of the questions they asked was "are you married." She answered truthfully, and they tossed the application because it was no longer a Fiancé Visa that was required. He needed to process a request for a spousal visa. So here he sat drinking coffee in this café for the third time. The entire process had taken nearly four years. Needless to say, he was more than a little nervous.

After hearing these war stories, I was feeling slightly less confident in our application. About an hour after she had gone in, Kellie returned with a smile that told us she had passed. When they called her to the interview window, the person asked only a couple identity type questions. Kellie had her inches-thick portfolio setting on her lap. She was prepared to respond and to show anything the interviewer might ask. The interviewer asked when I had last visited. She replied that I was outside waiting for her now. The next question had to do with my family, and Kellie pulled out the photo album and handed it over. The interviewer scanned the various pictures and spotted one of Yixin and Katie together at the Great Wall. She asked Kellie who the girls were and Kellie told her that they were our daughters. You could tell from the photo that they were having a great time together. The interviewer handed back the photo album and stamped the acceptance paper. The entire process took less than 5 minutes. While Kellie was relating her experience, the other guy's wife came out and announced that she had also passed.

We had to wait over the weekend while the visa was processed and added to her passport. We were now able to relax, and we enjoyed our time in

Guangzhou. The food is quite different from Shanghai, more Middle Eastern and Indian influences. We flew back to Shanghai, celebrated Kellie's visa and her birthday. A couple of days later we flew home.

I had, as usual, packed very light. That was so that we would have the maximum room for Kellie to bring her stuff when we returned. We had to clean out her home, and get it rented. She had to either pack what she wanted in our suitcases, store it at relatives, or give it away. It is hard to think about divesting yourself of a lifetime's accumulation in just a couple days, but that is what we were doing.

The process of vacating her home was exciting but stressful. Everything in China requires a manual process. Disconnecting her Cable TV required visiting two separate locations. Her request was logged manually into a paper ledger. The telephone disconnect process was worse. That took three trips to the phone company, in part because she wanted to transfer the DSL and modem to her parent's house so that they would be able to chat over Skype. Of course, that required moving her computer, finding room in their tiny home, and teaching them how to boot up and log in. None of her family was very computer literate, and so the login process was soon lost, and Kellie had to revert to phone calls.

We were able to get all of this accomplished in 4 days, and we flew to Dulles with our bags each weighing within ounces of their maximum. They looked like they were ready to burst at the seams.

Kellie had only been on a few flights, and none longer than a couple of hours. The 16 plus hour trip, first to Chicago and then on to Dulles was all new for her. We had no problems getting her through Customs and Immigration, but the rolled up x-rays that USCIS had insisted she would need to turn over to the Immigration Service were greeted with disdain. They didn't want them.

There was nothing in the refrigerator at home, and so we went to Red Robin for her first meal in America. I figured that you really couldn't get more American than Red Robin, besides they had a restaurant near our house. I ordered of course, and Kellie couldn't believe the size of the servings. She barely made a dent in her burger, and so she also had her first "doggie" bag.

— ■ —

For Kellie, everything was new and exciting. It was early November, and the sky was clear, something you never see in China. Virginia in the fall when the leaves are a thousand shades of green, yellow, orange, and red is a photographer's delight. But the single greatest thing for her was the clouds. In Shanghai, you never really see the sky. Between the tall buildings and the smog, the sky is almost always gray and flat. Kellie was fascinated by the shapes and colors of the clouds against the clear blue sky; she took endless pictures of everything, but mostly the sky. Thank heavens for digital photography, I don't think I could have afforded to develop and print all of those pictures if they were on film.

Her handheld translator got a workout. After a few months, it died, and she had to become even more reliant on my helping her understand things. It was interesting to me as well. First, in answering and explaining virtually everything, I realized just how much we take for granted. I also quickly realize how much of my long ago civics training I had forgotten. That has been particularly apparent as she was studying to become a citizen a few years later. My spelling has always been weak, but translators don't work well with misspelled words. I had to step up my game so that she could access the words.

We married on my birthday in 2008. That meant we had to embark on yet another exercise with USCIS forms, this time to change her status from a visa to a Green Card. That is another months long process.

– ■ –

Yixin's father had agreed to let her join us; I think he was assuming Yixin would be able to act as an anchor to bring him to America as well. We were working on a hard date to bring her. We had to do more paperwork for Yixin, and she would have to have her physical, vaccinations, and consulate interview. That was somewhat complicated because Kellie could not travel outside of the U.S. until her Green Card was approved. She could leave, but there was no guarantee that she would be able to return. If she needed to provide additional information, she could be turned back at the point of entry.

As the clock ticked by the months, we were beginning to think that I might have to travel to Shanghai alone to bring Yixin back. She was 17, old enough to travel on her own, but a 17-year old in China is in no way prepared to travel across the world on her own. The date was rapidly approaching. Yixin's visa was finally approved, and at what seemed the last possible moment Kellie received her Green Card. We immediately flew to Shanghai, once again celebrated her birthday and flew back with Yixin just two days' shy of the 1-

year deadline.

Tim, Ashley, & Kellie 2009

— ■ —

Yixin had asked Katie to choose an "American" name for her. We had a neighbor where Katie regularly babysat. The woman's name was Ashley, and so Katie added that to a short list for Yixin to choose. Ashley was only two syllables, and it was relatively easy for a non-English speaker to say; Yixin

533

was now called Ashley.

Yixin had finished high school in China, but she was only 17, so she was able to enroll in the local high school. That was great as it gave her a full-emersion introduction to English as well as an opportunity to get to know some other people her age. Ashley would tell you that she has always been directionally challenged. The first day she rode the school bus. On the way home, she got on the correct bus but got off at the wrong location. There was a bit of a panic with us driving back and forth searching for her. Fortunately, I had given her a slip of paper with our name, address, and phone number. Ashley went into a small shop, and they called to let us know that she was there.

By spring, we decided it was time to move on with our lives. None of the various ventures were producing any significant income, and my huge mortgage payment had eaten all but the last of my savings.

The biggest issue was the house. As fast as the value had shot up, it came tumbling down as the housing bubble burst. By 2009, it was worth less that when we first purchased it. Any regular sale would have required that we put in additional money. I decided that our best option was a short sale. A short sale is where you get the mortgage holder to take less than the full payment for the property. We found a buyer willing to wait out what we anticipated would be a 6-month fiasco with the bank. We handed the keys to the bank and moved out. It took nearly two years for the bank to complete the deal but in the end, we were free of the house and the huge mortgage. Of course, we lost what I had put in as our down payment, but the bank took a haircut as well.

Moving West

I wanted to get back to the West. I always preferred life in the Western United States. I missed the more casual lifestyle, the lower cost of living, and I wanted to be closer to the family. Two daughters and one grandchild were living in Boise, Idaho. I had lived in the Nampa/Caldwell area about 20 miles west of Boise for several years when I was in the Air Force and thought that might be a good place to retire.

We rented a house in Caldwell and moved across the country for the fourth time. Katie was headed off to Carnegie Mellon, so it was just the three of us plus Drum our Golden Retriever and Oliver our Maine Coon cat. We were all stuffed into a VW Jetta. It was crowded, but not as bad as it might seem. Ashley is pretty small, and that helped.

We arrived in Caldwell the night before the truck with all of our furniture. It was late summer, and I was quickly reminded of some of the things I had not particularly enjoyed 40 years earlier. It was terribly hot and more humid than I remember. There was a farm with several horses and cows nearby, and they seemed to have attracted every fly within a 100-mile radius.

I found that either Idaho had not matured much in the preceding 40 years, or maybe I had just outpaced it, either seemed plausible. I found it was like a village. You can only imagine how Kellie and Ashley felt coming from a city of 24 million to a place where that was approximately the fly population. Idaho was just not the right place for us.

— ■ —

Ashley enrolled in the local community college which did not require her to pass the TOEFL (Test of English as a Foreign Language) exam. That was important because it would have probably required at least two years of intense study for her to pass that test. I took a look at it and thought that a good percentage of American high school graduates would struggle to get a passing grade. Our concern was that taking those two years before she could start college would put her way behind her classmates.

We carefully selected courses where her writing was a relatively small percentage of her course work. That would give her time to become more accustomed to the language and how American schools worked. She had to work hard, but she did quite well. By the time she completed her first year, we were looking for a different place to live.

— ■ —

I had decided to retire when I turned 65. I was still doing some consulting, just odds and ends, usually subcontracting sections of business plans or marketing plans for Ben Blumenthal. He was good at coming up with interesting projects, and often got himself more work than he could handle. He knew me and knew that I could write, so when he got overloaded, he would toss various pieces over the wall.

I was non-disclosed on most of these assignments, so for those, I can't even mention names, but I can outline the work. I did a marketing plan for an insurance company that was targeting expatriates moving to Brussels, Belgium. Belgium has universal healthcare, but it doesn't cover foreigners. Since Brussels is the headquarters of the European Union, NATO, and many international companies, there are a lot of expats coming to town for 2 to 5-year assignments. They required health insurance for themselves as well as their families. The problem was identifying them and reaching them, hopefully before they moved to the city. It was a challenging assignment. I knew nothing about the health insurance industry in general, and even less about a company that was uniquely targeting a niche market like this. It was a marketing challenge that was not all that specific to the industry. It took a while, but I came up with a useful concept and program.

— ■ —

Another company was developing an alternative payment program for the unbanked. The company was primarily in South America and Africa. They were trying to replicate PayPal's success, but targeting those who did not have a banking relationship or even a credit card. They could use their facilities to make online as well as in-store purchases. They had been in business several years and had a working product. They were looking for capital to dramatically expand. For that, they needed a business plan. Ben was doing the financial portion, and I was working on several other sections, primarily the competitive analysis, risk factors, and the SWOT (Strengths, Weaknesses, Opportunities, & Threats) table. I have a long history in the financial world, and it was fun going back and digging deep into how this company would be doing business, the competition, and risks they were likely to encounter as they grew their business. In the end, Ben and I developed a solid Business Plan.

As with most consulting assignments, once I finished my piece I was unable to track the success or failure of the project. In these two cases, the work was taking place out of sight and outside of the country. Since I was only working as a subcontractor, I didn't even have any inside contacts where I could check in to see how the project ultimately turned out.

— ■ —

I did a short and intense consulting assignment, again as a subcontractor for a Lamborghini marketing campaign. Lamborghini had decided that they wanted in on the brand licensing game. That is a typical revenue play for popular high-end brands. Companies like Porsche and Ferrari make a lot of money licensing their brand for any number of similarly high-end consumer products, things like watches, leather goods, and clothing. Someone at Lamborghini, or their marketing company, decided they wanted to play in this game as well.

536

Lamborghini considered themselves to be the ultimate in extreme driving and they thought it was logical to make arrangements with companies who manufactured extreme sports equipment. On the surface that seems reasonable, but when you dig a bit deeper, you realize that extreme sports items are by their very nature, low-volume businesses. Take sky surfing or air surfing as an example. Believe it or not, some people don't quite get enough thrill out of just skydiving. Instead, they want to strap an oversized skateboard looking device to their feet, and surf the air as they fall. Needless to say, there are not a lot of folks doing this, and there are even fewer companies manufacturing these specialized boards.

A high-end watch with the Porsche logo on it has a built in market that includes all Porsche owners, but they also have all those wannabe Porsche owners who may not be able to afford the car but will settle for a watch. There are very few skyboard owners and even few people who could be considered casual participants. No one is going to buy a board if they are not going to use it. Making it even worse, the kinds of folks who are into these extreme sports are the kind that will sleep in the back of their van to save up a few dollars for just one more ride. They are not about to pay a dime extra so that the bottom of their board will say Lamborghini on it. In short, the market for Lamborghini branded skyboards is at best tiny, but in reality, nonexistent. The same is true for pretty much any of the extreme sports categories.

I am a consultant and a subcontractor making me even further removed. It was not my job to tell Lamborghini that this is a dumb idea. It is my job to take the database of global extreme sports manufacturers by category and to contact them to determine their level of interest. I couldn't even use any term like "I am representing Lamborghini." Doing that would violate the terms of my agreement. I had to dance around that part of any discussion.

Skype is an excellent tool that lets you reach out all over the world for very little money. Unfortunately, it doesn't do anything to help the time zone issues, so I would have to get up in the wee hours of the morning to call manufacturers on the other side of the world. The response was both predictable and universal. After they had finished laughing, they would say that they had no interest in buying a license. They would, however, be interested in Lamborghini sponsoring their sport by paying a fee to have the privilege of placing their logo on the product in question. Of course, this was the polar opposite of what Lamborghini had in mind.

For obvious reasons, this was a temporary assignment. I placed a hundred or so calls over a three-week period. I wrote up a report showing company, contact, date/time, and result. It only took one report for Lamborghini to decide that this was not a line of business they wanted to pursue. Unfortunately, they paid me in cash, not with a car. Of course, the car I would have earned in those three weeks would probably come in a box with a tube of plastic glue. With my luck, the assembly instructions would have been in Italian.

Back to Henderson

Well not exactly, Henderson, NV not the old Henderson Place. We were looking to move from Idaho and Kellie left it pretty much up to me to choose. She had seen quite a bit of America in her short time here, but none of these were places where we wanted to live. I was looking hard at Washington State and Oregon, Bend in particular, but didn't like the prices or the taxes. I also see both states on the same idiotic path that California has taken and that can only mean more problems and more taxes as time goes on. It is truly a shame. California has screwed itself so profoundly that people moved to Oregon and Washington to escape, only to busily elect the same kind of pandering politicians who made the same kind of stupid decisions that are bankrupting California.

One day we were in the car, and they were talking on the radio about how Las Vegas real estate had completely crashed following an unprecedented boom in the early to mid-2000s. I jokingly told Kellie that we could always move there. The houses were cheap, and there were no state taxes.

There are only a few American cities that everyone in China has heard of: New York, Los Angeles, San Francisco, and Las Vegas. So while she knew nothing of the city, she at least knew the name. She asked what it was like and I told her it was a desert and that it was scorching hot in the summer. She asked where we could have a swimming pool. Las Vegas was the better choice for a pool, so we decided to drive down for a visit.

We came and spent a few days. Both Kellie and Ashley were more comfortable being in an area that at least seemed more like a city. I was ok as long as we were in the fringe areas, not in the middle of the actual city.

When we got to Henderson, we put most of our stuff in the garage so that we could redo the interior floors. We pulled all of the carpets on the lower level, and I started laying tile. We had scheduled a trip to Shanghai in late June, so we were only part way through the tile project when we flew out for a 7-week visit.

Shanghai

My interest in other cultures and my desire to explore the world began with my early interest in Mahatma Gandhi. That naturally led me to read about India; there I discovered a land and a culture vastly different from my small world in Shasta Valley. This early discovery fed the flames of my curiosity and my desire to see the world; it set my heart on Ithaka. Those flames have never abated.

Over the years, as I traveled extensively throughout the U.S. and Canada, I continued to read about other countries and cultures, Asia in particular. It took a long time but eventually I was able to explore much of the world. I have traveled outside of the U.S. more than 150 times, roughly ½ of those trips were to Europe and ½ to Asia. While it is a bit easier to travel in Europe, I have always been more curious about Asia, China and Japan in particular.

Tim at Chenghuang Maio in Shanghai China 2007

We seldom read about the Chinese journey to America, their contribution, or their life, but there are many similarities to the early African experience.

Like Africans, immigrants from China have made significant contributions to America, particularly to the early development of the West. In the 19th century, poor, often indentured, laborers were imported from China by the thousands. "Coolies" held the picks, shovels, and hammers that built much of the transcontinental railroad that first tied our nation together. They were also a major component of the Gold Rush. The evidence of Chinese influence is everywhere. The "China Ditch" that ran through our ranch in the Shasta Valley is but one example.

There was blatant discrimination against the "yellow peril," and the shameful Chinese Exclusion Act of 1882 was the only U.S. law ever enacted to prevent immigration and naturalization based on race. It wasn't until the 1940s that Chinese were again allowed to immigrate, to become citizens and eventually to intermarry with whites.

— ∎ —

I had never really thought about it until I was writing this section, but longstanding prejudice and the laws against interatrial marriage that were in place at the time I was born, would have prohibited two of my marriages, with Sharon because she was black, and with Kellie because she is Chinese. That represents yet another significant change that has taken place during my lifetime. We have come a long way.

— ∎ —

Despite their humble beginnings and a century of blatant discrimination: Chinese, Japanese, Koreans, Filipinos, and more recently, Vietnamese, have fused with the American melting pot, while remarkably maintaining much of their unique cultures. Chinese restaurant abound, and even the smallest cities typically have a "Chinatown," a generic name for all Asians, as most Americans have difficulty discerning one nationality from another.

While I feel comfortable almost anywhere, I have a particular affinity to China. I have long enjoyed the people, food, and art. When Kellie arrived, she was surprised by how much of the art and decorative pieces in my home were Chinese. We have now been married for nearly a decade and our home, as well as our family, is a blend of both cultures.

— ∎ —

Finally, consider the immense difference between where I started and where I am today. I was raised in the Shasta Valley, one of the most sparsely populated parts of America. Siskiyou County which is larger than the state of Connecticut, even today has barely 45,000 residents. My earliest years were in even more remote surroundings. By comparison, Shanghai is the largest city in the world. It has a population of more than 24 million, with 35 million in the metropolitan area.

With a large extended family in China, I consider Shanghai my second home. Ithaka has indeed given me a marvelous journey.

On our 7-week trip to China, I had been asked to travel to Anhui Province to do some consulting with the government in the city of Guoyang. They wanted me to work to develop a marketing plan to attract western companies to their newly developed business park.

We traveled by car to Guoyang. Traveling by car in China can be a terrifying experience. This trip definitely was. The vast majority of Chinese drives have less than five years driving experience. They tend to drive far too fast and not pay much attention to the road and other traffic. They will drive between cars or trucks, out on the road's apron, anywhere and anyhow to get there faster. Seatbelts seemed to be more ornamental than useful.

Mr. Yao, our host for the trip, had been seriously injured in an auto accident on this very route just two years earlier. He nearly lost his life but seemed unfazed by the crazy driving habits of the young man behind the wheel. That young man was himself killed in an accident just a couple years later.

Anhui is inland from Shanghai about 200 miles; the population is 60 million. It is mainly agricultural with a climate, geography, and size that is similar our State of Georgia. Of course, the population of Georgia is <10 million. There is lots of coal with navigable rivers, main rail lines, and red dirt; they do raise peanuts in that area. There is a very nice freeway that dissects the Province, but the minute you get off that highway, you discover that most of the roads are dirt. Cars and trucks were going in all directions, and far too fast. There seemed to be no concept of traffic lanes or staying on the correct side of the road. Like I said, it was terrifying.

We have all seen the pictures of the skyscrapers in Shanghai and Beijing, but those are the exception, not the rule. As soon as you leave either city, you drop into the 3rd World. The villages are indescribable. There is no automation as they have to keep the peasants employed. The water is undrinkable, but that is true in Shanghai & Beijing as well. Babies and toddlers do not wear diapers, usually no bottoms either, and just squat in the street when the urge hits them. That is still true in Shanghai once you get out of the core city area. Corruption is everywhere; the people are completely powerless. Life is short and brutal because the government places no value in individuals or lives. One less peasant means one less mouth to feed.

— ∎ —

Most "towns," even those with a million people, have pigs and chickens running loose in the streets. Guoyang is a smaller city with a population of just over 1 million. Bozhou, the county seat has 6.1 million.

544

Most of the wealth in China is concentrated near the coast. Most manufacturing of export goods takes place in either the Guangzhou area, inland from Hong Kong, or in the north near Beijing. The inland provinces such as Anhui do very little manufacturing for export.

Guoyang had developed a business park, and they were trying to attract companies to locate their facilities in that park. They had a great deal to offer, abundant water and coal, along with good rail and river transportation to the coast. There was even a land ownership option with some development deals.

The business park itself was well laid out, and it had the necessary infrastructure to support manufacturing. However, they lacked a skilled labor force, experienced supervisors, and much of the infrastructure that any western company would expect for their executives. As I said earlier, most of the area could only be described as 3rd world.

We spent several days meeting with officials and touring Guoyang as well as Bozhou. I got a lot of stares as we moved about; I think most had never, or at least seldom, seen a Westerner. You do grow accustomed to that.

At one point I brought up the fact that they would need skilled labor and experienced supervisors. I was a bit shocked by their response. They said that this was not a problem. Whatever they needed they could get. They went on to say that if they needed to build a city of 10 million they could do that. That is a city as big as Los Angeles. When I asked how they would get people, they said they would tell them they had to move there. It's hard to understand how a government can tell 10 million people that you must move to a different city.

— ■ —

The police chief was our chauffeur and tour guide. His wife accompanied us as well. I think in part because the Chief's police car was the nicest one in town. It was a Toyota Camry. We had a lot of fun touring. They are proud of their city and the area. Despite the 3rd world nature, it is attractive with a lot of history. They claim that Guoyang is the birthplace of Laozi (or Lao-tzu), in the 6th to the 5th century B.C.E. I suspect that other cities may make the same claim as it would be very hard to prove.

— ■ —

Since few Westerners will recognize the name Lao-Tzu or Laozi, I will try to give a short version of his background and significance, to put this in historical perspective. Laozi is the pinyin (pinyin is the Latinization for the

545

Chinese characters) name of a legendary Daoist philosopher. Laozi means "Old Master." He is also known as Lao Dan (which means "Old Dan") in some early Chinese documents. Laozi was the creator of the Daodejing. *"Dao"* means *"the way,"* and *"de"* means *"virtue."*

Laozi is believed to be Confucius' teacher and apparently admonished Confucius to stop promoting himself and making so many rules about living. Instead, he was to focus on finding the *dao* (the way). He called Confucius by his given name, Qui, which would have been incredibly disrespectful if Laozi were not his teacher.

Legend has it that at the age of 80, Laozi got fed up with the way the emperor was running things and immigrated west as far as India. At the western gate of the kingdom, he was recognized by the guard Yinxi. The sentry asked the old master to record his wisdom for the good of the country before he would be permitted to pass. Laozi wrote on bamboo sticks, 81 chapters in 5000 Chinese characters. That is the legendary origin of the Daodejing (in other texts it is called the Tao Te Ching). The religion called "Daoism" that arose during the later Han dynasty (25-220 AD) was organized around the Daodejing

In some writings, the "Old Master" journeyed all the way to India and was the teacher of Siddartha Gautama, the Buddha. Still, others claim that he was the Buddha himself. Some writings claim he lived to 160; others claim 200.

So as you can see, Laozi was at the very least, influential if not the actual founder of the three most important Eastern philosophies: Daoism, Buddhism, and Confucianism. In a sense, Guoyang is to these religions what Bethlehem is to Christianity.

— ■ —

We also visited Bozhou and toured the ancient tunnel system that lies under the city. The tunnels extend from the city center in all directions to the outside of the city. They were built at the end of the Eastern Han Dynasty (25 AD - 220 AD). They are sometimes called the "Underground Great Wall." Nearly 5 miles of tunnels are restored. The tunnels are small, particularly for someone my size. They have built in defensive features, things like dead ends, traps, and leg hindrances.

The tunnels were constructed to defeat the enemy when the city was under siege. The soldiers within the city would go through the tunnels at night and come out behind the surrounding enemy combatants. They could then slaughter the armies and break the siege. History does repeat itself, as they successfully used this tactic several times.

Bozhou Tunnels with Mr. Yao 2010

— ■ —

After the tunnel tour, we had a great foot massage. I had never had one before. They do poke and prod your tootsies pretty hard, so it takes a bit of getting used to, but boy does it feel good.

We were taken to a street market one evening. It was like a Farmers Market with hundreds of booths, mainly with various home prepared food items. Some enormous flying bugs were enjoying the evening as well. On several occasions, we would see the vendor quickly grab the bug off the food and drop it on the street by their feet. We respectfully declined samples.

On the way back to the hotel, the Chief turned on the red lights and siren. The locals paid absolutely no attention to the flashing lights or the siren's racket.

Bozhou Prisoners 2010

— ∎ —

It seems in China; all restaurants have private dining areas for family and business gatherings. They typically include these round tables that are 8' or 9' across. They put a lazy Susan in the middle, and there is a constant stream of great food rotating on it.

There is a local liquor brewed in the Guoyang area. Our host seemed to be a big fan, supposedly he drank a bottle every day, judging by what I saw, I think that is possible. We brought two bottles home and still have one.

You can't drink the water anywhere in China, and so beer is the usual substitute. Many seemed to like hard liquor as well. At all dinners, there were usually a couple of all-table toasts followed by a procession of individuals who then came to toast the guest of honor; that would be me. The rule, which I refused to follow, are that you must drink the whole shot-sized glass at each toast. There can be 2 or 3 tables with 8 or 10 people each. You can imagine how quickly the guest of honor would be passed out on the floor. I think that at least in part, they wanted to see how much I could hold and probably how I would act when I got drunk. I had seen this before, and I wasn't about to engage in this "game." I told them that I could only drink a small amount on doctor's orders. They protested, but I insisted, and of course, Kellie backed me up. Otherwise, these celebrations would have been just a forgotten memory.

— ■ —

We spent 5 or 6 days in Guoyang and Buozou, before returning to Shanghai and our vacation. When we got home I started outlining a plan to identify and talk with appropriate manufacturers. I needed to finalize financial arrangements. I also had some detailed questions that I needed to have answered. I don't know if my communications got lost in translation or just go lost, but they never answered my questions. However, they do keep telling me they want us to come back the next time we are in China.

I sometimes think it was all about having an excuse to eat, drink, and be merry. Having an American there was a great excuse to gather together and have some fun on the expense account. It probably gave our host something significant they could report in their monthly reports to the higher ups.

— ■ —

With seven weeks, we had time to take several side trips, a weekend in a small village with several members of Kellie's family, and a week in Nanchang which is a city of 2.5 million in Jiangxi Province. Kellie's sister lived and worked there for many years. She is retired now, but she still has a home there. Nanchang like most all of China has a long and rich history. It is known as the location of the first shot fired by the Communists against the Nationalists; that was in 1927. Nanchang is therefore considered to be the birthplace of the People's Liberation Army.

We toured many monuments and museums and visited with Kellie's sister's coworkers, many of whom have known Kellie for years. We also took a two-day side trip to Lushan Mountain, about 40 miles north of Nanchang. The mountain is only about 5,000 feet high but quite rugged. Since it sits on a flat plane that is barely above sea level, it appears much taller. It is surrounded by clouds nearly 200 days a year, and usually much cooler than the hot, humid areas below.

Lushan was supposedly one of Chairman Mao's favorite places to get away from the summer heat and humidity. Since Mao is viewed as a near-deity in China, every place he walked, slept or used the loo is considered a shrine.

There are beautiful trails out around the mountain top with some great vistas. Looking at the engineering of these trails was interesting. They often had stairways up or down and small retaining walls to hold up the trail. Incidentally, you never see wheelchairs in China, and there appears to be no effort to make any location wheelchair accessible. The stairs were constructed using pieces of granite that were roughly 10" square and 5' long. They probably weighed 400 pounds each. These were all hand carved, and hand carried out the trail and set in place.

The amount of labor to do this is staggering. It can sometimes be easy to forget that China has 1.3 billion people to keep employed. It is probably more like 1.7 billion, but nobody really knows. In America, we would use helicopters to haul cement to pour steps; they may use 200-300 men to accomplish the same thing and never consider automating anything. The scale of humanity can be staggering.

There is a constant stream of people walking these trails. Even after all my time in Asia and China, in particular, I sometimes find the sheer number of individuals to be a bit oppressive. There is just no place where you can stand quietly by yourself and view nature. I spotted a monkey in a tree; within a couple minutes, 200 people were amassed watching one single animal.

We took a short train ride down a canyon and then walked up a steep hill to a gap in the ridge. From there, we walked down 1500 stair steps, again made of hand carved granite. These went down the face of the hill to the bottom where there was a beautiful waterfall and pool. There were several shops and eating places and hundreds of people milling about. After a brief look, we had to climb back up the same stairs we descended. I suspect that from the air, it would look like two ant trails; one going down and one going up.

On the side of the stairs, there were dozens of porters with shoulder mounted sedan chairs. They would carry you up if you needed help. They charged a fee of course, probably by the kilogram of weight. Watching them watching the crowd made me think of vultures trying to figure out which critter would die first. You could almost hear them wagering on which ones would provide their daily income. I found it was harder to go down than back up, especially on my knees. I didn't need any assistance.

Our Henderson Place

A year or so after we returned from our China vacation, we had completed the upgrades to our Prosser Creek house. We decided that we wanted to buy a rental house to increase our retirement income and provide some financial security.

We had learned a little about Henderson, and an area called Townsite. Townsite is the original part of Henderson. Before WWII, there wasn't much here, maybe a couple of dozen people. Mainly it was a small watering station about half way between Las Vegas (population 8,000 at that time) and Boulder City. In those days, even on a short drive, most cars would boil over in the hot desert sun. They would need to stop to refill the radiators and buy a cold soda for themselves. That was about all there was to do at this wide spot in the road that would later become Henderson.

Boulder City is the closest town to Boulder Dam. That is where most of the workers and their families lived during the construction of Hover Dam. That began in 1931 and finished in 1936. At the peak of construction, Boulder City had a population exceeding 5,000. It was nearly as big as Las Vegas.

Just before America entering WWII, the Army ordered Basic Magnesium Incorporated (BMI) to construct a plant at least 250 miles inland. The location BMI selected was that wide-spot watering hole. There was some logic to the site as the Three Kids Magnesium mine was nearby. The new plant needed 25% of the electricity generated by Hover Dam to produce the magnesium. The process required lots of water, and of course, that also came from Hoover Dam. Over a period of 11 months and at the cost of $130 million (that is $2.2 billion in 2016 dollars), they built the largest magnesium processing plant in the free world. It came online in October of 1942. Just two years later, by November 1944, BMI had produced 166,322,685 pounds of magnesium at the Henderson facility.

There were approximately 14,000 BMI employees. As most of the men were off fighting the war, the workforce consisted mostly of women. There was no place for them to live, so a large tent city sprang up.

Someone realized that it wasn't very good to have 14,000 women plus children living in tents in the desert, and so the government commissioned to have 1,000 homes built in two areas called Townsite and Pittman.

In government speak, these were, called "demountable" houses. The intention was to take them apart and relocate them after the war. The house components were constructed off-site and then brought in and assembled. The homes are on raised foundations. They built the walls in 8' sections. The exterior walls used 2 x 4s. Everything was 24" on center. The roof sections were 4' wide and up to 16' in length. They were made by ripping 2 x 10s at a slight pitch to give a ¼" in 12" slope. These sat on the walls, and they were bolted together at the ridgeline. The center load bearing walls, in fact, all interior walls, were made with 2 x 3s 24" on center. All of these piece parts were just toenailed in place as they intended to take then down later. They are still standing 75 years later.

The interior walls were sheeted with ¼" plywood and the exteriors with 8" redwood lap siding. There was no insulation in the walls and only 4" of rock wool in the ceilings. Of course, none of this would even remotely pass code today, but back then there wasn't any code to regulate housing.

They built two models, a 2-bedroom 1-bath 650 sqft. version and a 3-bedroom, 1-bath version at 750 sqft. The streets were dirt with no curbs or sidewalks. Basically, they ran a grader across the desert and planted 1,000 houses.

After the war, there was such demand for housing that these demountable homes were never removed. Henderson was incorporated in 1953. It is the only city in America that was built by the government. Today Henderson is the 2nd largest city in Nevada with 250,000 people.

In the housing boom that hit the Las Vegas area beginning in about 2001, these tiny little houses increased in value; some were selling for $275,000 by mid-2007. When the crash came, the bottom fell out, and they dropped to under $50,000. Most of those who had financed or refinanced, based on the highly inflated values, eventually had to walk away from their homes.

We didn't buy at the bottom of the market, but close. We purchased a rental on Colorado Way, for less than $50,000. It was one of the 3-bedroom models, but at some point, someone had added a dining area which jumped the square footage up to about 850 feet. It was a mess. The roof was leaking, and the previous owner had cats that apparently thought the whole house was their litterbox. Someone had walked away with the roof A/C, and so there was a big hole. Structurally it was reasonably sound, but it was unlivable in its present condition. On the plus side, it was on a ¼ acre 2 blocks from City Hall.

Before & After

We had purchased the house under a HUD contract which meant that we had to live in it for a year before we could rent it. Our plan was to make the Colorado house livable and to rent our house on Prosser Creek for the year.

The yard was a mess. The fence was down, and the yard was overgrown with weeds, trash, and an abundance of what as kids, we had called puncher vines. They would flatten the tire on my wheelbarrow on virtually every pass across the yard. I ultimately got a solid tire replacement.

We continued to live in our Prosser Creek house while we cleaned up and remodeled. We tore out the carpet and padding and used only slightly diluted

555

bleach to mop the floors. Most of the stench was in the carpet and pad, and it cleaned up quickly.

Aside from getting the carpet and odor cleared out, we felt we had to redo the bathroom before we moved in. The original bathroom was tiny, 5' by 8', with an old cast iron tub replete with lots of chips and rust. The old tub must have weighed 300 pounds. The only way to get it out was to smash it with a sledgehammer and hauled out the pieces.

I wanted to put a small alcove on the side of the bathroom to house a shower. I cleared everything out and ripped up the floor, as I needed to reposition the plumbing and sewer lines. I soon discovered that the 70-year-old sewer stack, that is the breather line that ran up through the roof, was rusted through. I assumed it would be rusted all the way to the street. Better to replace it now than later, so I started digging.

There are alleys behind the property. In our case, on two sides as we are at the foot of a cul-de-sac. These alleys are primarily utility easements. The overhead power lines, as well as the sewer and water lines, run down the alleys. I called "Miss Dig" and told them I was getting ready to do some serious digging in the back yard. The gas company came out and said there is no gas line. NV Energy said no problem; the power lines are overhead. The City came and said the water line runs from the meter box in the alley to where I knew it came into the house, and they eyeballed the vent stack on our roof and said they thought the sewer must be right about here.

The community was built before permits, or even records were kept, so in fairness, the City folks had no better idea than I did. Of course, they have been managing these homes for nearly six decades. You would think that they would have the original construction techniques figured out by now. They didn't have a clue. Their estimation of the sewer line location was just a SWAG (Scientific, Wild-Ass, Guess). They assumed that the sewer line had taken the shortest route. That was a flawed assumption.

Not knowing that they were just guessing, I went to where they had indicated and started digging, and digging, and digging. Down about 7 feet, out a couple of feet on each side ...nothing. Out a couple more feet, still nothing. I had to build a ramp to get down into my pit. By now I had a hole big enough to bury a Volkswagen. Not really, but it sure seemed that way.

I finally decided to take a different approach. I came out about 5' from the back of the house, in the area where the sewer line had to exit. I dug down about 4' and then started trenching parallel to the back of the house until I found the sewer. I found the water line first, and the sewer line was directly below it. They had apparently used a single trench to lay both lines. That is strictly against code these days, but not back then. I went out to the fence where the water meter was just on the other side and dug down to discover both water and sewer lines as expected. I went back and filled in my VW burial pit.

I soon discovered that the sewer line changed from cast iron to fired clay pipe about 5 feet out from the house. While the cast iron was rusted out, the clay pipe looked as good as it did the day they laid it in 1942. None the less. I put an entirely new line clear to the fence. I wanted to put in a couple of sidelines for future use, and a new line was easier than trying to patch into the clay pipe multiple times. Also, the clay was a strange dimension and the couplings were very expensive.

Full Circle

As we were working on the house, we began to meet our new neighbors. We soon realized that Townsite was more like a village within the city of Henderson. Most of the people who lived here were 2nd or even 3rd generation residents. Some had been raised here, left for work or other reasons and then returned. It is a blue collar community, but the people were more open and friendly than in any town I have ever lived. A neighbor two doors away is 87. She has lived here since 1948 and she talks about standing out on the then dirt streets and watching the atomic bomb tests in Area 51 north of Las Vegas.

All of the houses were single story and spread apart so that there is room between the homes. Everything that was happening in the city emanated from Water Street which was just two blocks away. All of the parades, music festivals, farmers market, the largest antique auto show in Nevada, everything was right at out fingertips. It reminded me of the beach communities in California, a bit old and a bit funky, but a far more livable lifestyle. By the time we had the house ready to live in, we had decided that we wanted to make this our permanent residence.

We put the Prosser Creek place up for sale and moved into the Colorado house. Thus began our 2+ year house building adventure. I began life at The Henderson Place, and now we were building Our Henderson Place.

We crammed everything we could into the third bedroom. It was only 10' x 11', so it couldn't hold a lot. We stuffed boxes everywhere and rented a couple of storage units for what we couldn't fit in the house. I purchased a home design software package and started trying out different approaches.

I had some specific objectives from the beginning. I would ask Kellie what she wanted or what she thought, and her answer was always the same: "I follow you." That made designing and building so much easier. She was always there to help and occasionally would make a suggestion. With her artist's eye, her ideas invariably made more sense than my choice, but for the most part, she would just follow my lead.

First, we wanted to keep it under 2400 square feet, closer to 2000 if possible. Second, we wanted to have it fit into the community without looking like some monstrosity surrounded by 650 & 800 sqft houses. We kicked around the idea of adding a second level but ultimately decided against that because it would mean having stairs. We intend to live here the rest of our lives, so stairs didn't seem like a good idea. Also, it would tower over all the other houses, and that meant that it wouldn't fit in. On the plus side, we have a decent view of the Las Vegas Strip, but only from the roof. A second floor would provide a good view.

In the end, we rejected the 2nd story and settled on a design just under 2300 sqft. We designed it to be something close to ADA (Americans with Disability Act) standards. The main thing was to make it wheelchair friendly. In part, because we thought that Kellie's Mom might live with us after her father passed away, and in part, we saw it as an anti-wheelchair pill for us. If we built it to handle wheelchairs, maybe we would never need one. It turned out that Mom did come to live with us and the wheelchair accessibility proved quite convenient.

— ■ —

We are interested in having a motor home, so we wanted to build a garage that would accommodate that as well as at least one car. We came across a metal garage package the was 25' X 42' and priced to sell at what looked like it would be less than building an equivalent structure out of wood. In the end, the cost was probably about the same, but it is a much better structure.

Proving that the dirt is dirt 2013

Building code required that we have a soil test. That seemed like a rather foolish waste of money. Like I said earlier, the original construction consisted of grading the desert and planting the house. To me it was dirt, and it had been dirt for several million years. Why was it necessary to test to see if it was still dirt? But the code is the code and some things they just won't let you avoid. We hired a soils engineer, and they drilled a few holes in the back yard and my wallet. They produced a report saying that indeed it was still dirt. They did discover that we were over an ancient lakebed. I am thrilled to know that, but it was not exactly a cheap thrill. We said goodbye to our first $2,500.

When asked how he created David, Michelangelo supposedly said: "I started with a piece of marble and chipped away everything that wasn't David." In our case, this included nearly everything; a couple of slapped together outbuildings; a small laundry room addition that someone had kludged onto the back of the house; the roof, interior and exterior wall coverings, most of the walls themselves, and all of the electrical, water, and sewer system components.

There were a couple of wood screening fences that had to come out, and we found remnants of posts in several places throughout the yard. In the process, we discovered that one of the previous owners had decided the best way to get rid of their larger pieces of garbage was to bury them in the backyard. It was like a treasure hunt project finding and cleaning out these mini garbage dumps.

— ■ —

In my many diggings, I found a square coin. I had never seen a square coin, and it caught my eye. It is a 1920 1-cent coin from the "Straits Settlements." On the other side, it says "GEORGE V KING AND EMPEROR OF INDIA."

It turns out the Straights Settlements were a group of British territories located in Southeast Asia. Originally established in 1826 as part of the territories controlled by the British East India Company, the Straits Settlements became a British Crown Colony in 1867. It was dissolved in 1946 following the end of the Second World War. Most of these territories are now part of Malaysia.

What intrigued me was how that coin could have possibly landed in our yard. We have a neighbor who has lived here since 1948. I asked her if she remembered anyone who might have brought such a coin to our little street. She couldn't think of anyone.

— ■ —

I wanted to put the power line underground from the alley. I contacted NV Energy, and they sent a guy out to survey the property. He said that I would have to replace the transformer on the pole near our house. I looked at the rusted 70-year old transformer and asked why he felt I needed to replace it. It seemed that by my changing from a 100-amp panel to a 200-amp panel I would be exceeding the capacity of the transformer. I asked him by how much, and he admitted that the transformer was already over capacity, but I would be driving it even further. Of course, that is all theoretical assuming everybody was drawing their maximum amperage.

I told him in no uncertain terms that there was no way I was about to pay $12,000 to replace their old transformer. I said I would install a diesel generator before I paid for a new transformer. He left with no real resolution, but called back an hour or so later and told me not to worry; they would just replace the transformer if it blew out. Two years later and it is still transforming away.

While we were waiting for the structural engineers to finish their work, I completed digging out the crawl space for the house. The area was approximately 1500 square feet to a depth of 24". I then dug out the footings for the stem walls, so that was another 12" x 18" deep trench all the way

560

around. That amounted to nearly 130 cubic yards of dirt. At 3 wheelbarrows per yard, that is a lot of wheelbarrows to be moved.

As I was digging out the area for the crawl space, I came upon a gas line. It was running across the lot, instead of in from the street the way it should have been. I called the gas company, and they insisted that I must be mistaken. I sent photos, and they finally sent out a team to have a look. The crew scratched their heads for a while. It was clearly a wrapped gas line, but it should not have been there. Finally, they got a spray bottle with soapy water and a hack saw. They sprayed the pipe as they sawed away.

I stood back and watched, wondering what exactly they planned to do if gas started pouring out. Fortunately, it wasn't an issue. It was a gas line but apparently abandoned. I was talking to our 87-year old neighbor a few weeks later, and she told me that somewhere around 1950 a gas different company had laid gas lines down each block running from house to house, just like the one in my yard. In the late 1980s, the present gas company had bought out the other company and laid new lines down the center of the street. The original lines were just abandoned and left in place. Nobody remembered unless, like her, you had lived there a good long while.

When I got the dirt away from the back of the house, I discovered a very uneven back wall. The beams holding the floor were setting on individually cut 4 x 4 posts. After 70+ years, some were rotting away. In some places, the floor was down by as much as 2″.

Leveling back of house 2013

I bought a 20-ton jack and raised the floor beams and replaced the old blocks with 4 x 6 treated blocks. I went through the entire house and only found a couple of other places where the blocks were rotted out. All of the center area blocks were good; it was only on the exterior where dirt and water had been piled up against the wood. We don't have termites in this area, and the weather is dry 90% of the time. Wood rot is only a problem if you subject the wood to moisture.

— ■ —

The first task was laying out all of the new sewer lines. That was more than a bit nerve-wracking. I was setting pipes that would eventually come up through the floor. They had to be in the correct places, inside of walls and where things like toilets, tubs, and showers would eventually be. I have a reasonably technical mind, and I had designed the house and created all of the plans, so I knew what needed to go where, but I had no survey equipment or anything beyond a tape measure and a level. My only reference point was the back side of a house that was far from square. I wouldn't know if I measured correctly until after the walls were mapped out on the subfloors. I remember standing out in the vast expanse of dirt marking off where those walls should eventually be. It seemed like I was committing to something that was a long way off in the future.

Plumbing 2014

I hired a guy that specialized in concrete block work to construct the stem walls. I can handle a little concrete, but I wanted the walls to be in the right place, straight and level. Watching his team do the work, I was very glad I made that decision.

For the garage floor, I sent the plans over to a steel company for them to lay out and pre-bend the needed rebar and steel mesh. The structural engineer called for cross tied rebar every 6'. They delivered, what seemed to me to be an incredible amount of steel. As the concrete guys laid out the steel, we discovered that the supplier had misread the blueprints. Instead of providing materials for cross bar 6' on center, they provided enough for 6" on center. Instead of 8 pieces, they had sent 85. They weren't happy about sending a truck to pick up the pieces, but they knew it was there bad and so they did. I was delighted to get my refund.

— ■ —

I was just beginning to understand some of the games these various people play. They don't ever want to get sued, so if they think that a 12 x 18" footer with three pieces of #4 rebar would be sufficient, they will call for an 18 x 18" footer with five pieces of #5 rebar. They are covering their asses. If the thing ever did fall and they ever got sued, they would point out that the numbers called for the smaller footer with less steel, but they went on the safe side with the larger footer, more and heavier rebar. The fact is all of the costs are on my shoulders, so it costs them nothing to overstate the requirements.

One of the things you learn to hate is the obtuse way things are numbered. Wire gets larger the smaller the number; rebar gets bigger the higher the number. Bolts are measured in diameter, but they can be either Metric or Standard. The threads can be either standard or machine, but they can be course, fine or extra fine. Pipe threads are different from hose threads, which are different from gas line threads. Connectors to faucets are different from connectors to toilets, and on, and on, and on. Can't anybody make up their mind?

— ■ —

Initially, we were working the garage and the house in parallel, but by the time we finished the stem walls, it became clear that we needed to concentrate on one thing at a time. We opted to finish the garage first. It wouldn't take as long, and it would give us a place to store all of our stuff while we did the house.

The garage came as a series of 21 arches, which were 2' wide when assembled. Each arch consisted of 7 pieces of galvanized steel bolted together. Once they were loosely together, we had five people with ropes and pulleys to stand them up. We had two people up on scaffolding, one on each end of the arch, and one pushing wherever help was needed. As we stood them up, we would bolt them together. They overlap a few inches where the bolts went through. Keeping the first one or two up while we were pulling up the next arch was a bit tricky.

There were three rows of "L" brackets, one at the top center, one on each side where the side curved over to the roof. We soon discovered that these "L" brackets were the most important item. The instructions had not been very specific about when to install these. What we discovered was that when the arches were up and bolted to the slab, the weight of the arch would push down from the top and that would bend the sides out. That meant that the bolt holes on the next arch wouldn't line up. We had about four arches up before we realized we were digging a deeper and deeper hole for ourselves. We had to go back and use my 20-ton jack along with some 4 x 4 posts to lift up the center of the roof. That stopped progress for a while, but when we finally got it all aligned and elevated, we were able to install the arches fairly quickly.

Doug Wilder, a neighbor who lived a couple of doors down, and his brother Shane worked with us to do the assembly. Doug was a great help and a good worker. His brother worked hard, but you quickly learned that you never wanted to let him swing a hammer. He could bend a thumbnail if you let him have a hammer.

A young guy leaned over the fence one morning and asked if we needed help. We did, and I hired him on the spot. He was a young black kid named Leonard, must have been about 22 or 23; he looked 15. He had no idea what to do, but he was willing to follow directions. He lived nearby and went home for lunch but never returned. I owed him $35 for his hours, but he didn't come back. About three months later I was working in the yard, and he came walking down the alley and stopped to ask how we were doing. I went over to the fence to say hello. He started out by saying that he bet I didn't remember him. I told him to wait just a moment. I went inside and got the envelope with his name on the outside and his $35 inside. I handed it to him, and he started to cry. He couldn't believe that I had kept it for him and gave it to him with no questions asked.

It turned out that the police had picked him up on a drug charge and he had been in jail for the past three months. The woman and baby with him were his wife and child. They had no money whatsoever. The $35 was a lifesaver. I didn't have any other work for him at the time, and I never saw him again.

Doug was working with me, and he said nothing but watched all of this. After we got back to work Doug said something about how he couldn't believe that. I ask what he meant, assuming it had to do with Leonard's jail or his family at such a young age. He said he couldn't believe that I had held his money and immediately gave it to him. He said he didn't know anybody that honest. I guess I am just old-fashioned, but to me, there was no question. It was Leonard's money. If he had not come back, that envelope would still be sitting on my desk.

— ■ —

We had to tighten every one of the 2000 bolts. That meant one person on the outside with an impact wrench; someone else had to be inside with a wrench on the corresponding nut. It wasn't bad for the vertical parts, but the top was a little more of a problem. For that part, we put Doug in a harness and tied him to an eye bolt at the upper part so that he could walk around on the slope without falling off. It was a noisy process. Not only the rattle of the impact wrench but trying to communicate which bolt was next and to signal when everybody had their tool in place. As we progressed, we had to roll the scaffolding to a new position as Doug moved on the outside. One person, often Kellie, was up on the scaffolding. It was a bit comical to observe. I snapped a couple of photos of Kellie up on the scaffolding with Doug peering over the top. The combination made it look like she had a gun and he was hiding.

— ■ —

When we finished the garage, we moved all of the boxes from the house and the storage units. We knew we would need to take everything off of and out of the house. We were thinking about a place to live while we were redoing the house. We weren't quite up to residing in the garage. I had plumbed it for a toilet and shower, and we had water lines running to the garage as well, but with the coming summer heat and temperatures hitting 115° with no air conditioning, the garage was never a viable option.

We bought a 2-bedroom, 1-bath, 650 sqft. model that was on Idaho Way, the next street over. It was actually in excellent condition. There had been a severe storm a few months earlier, and wind had damaged the roof allowing water to get into the house. The owner had used the insurance money to repair and replace, including new roof and carpet throughout. We were able to move in immediately. We found that space was too small, we needed to do something to make it more comfortable.

We decided to convert the carport into a new master bedroom. That meant putting our Colorado house remodel on hold for four months while we did the addition to the Idaho house. The carport roof was already in place, but the front porch was sagging nearly 4" on the left corner, and the roof of the carport, which was on the left side of the house, was down an equal amount.

Technically, I was not allowed to do the remodeling. Owner/Builders can do their work, but only on their residence. I paid a licensed contractor to pull the permits and then I did the work. The contractor came by only one time. The City never seemed to be concerned that the contractor was never there for the inspections.

The first problem was the sagging front porch. Someone had poured a couple of inches of cement on top of the old boards and then put tile on top of that. I got out my, now well-used 20-ton jack and went at it. I figured that the porch would crack into a million pieces and I could just lift off the old chunks and do another pour-and-tile job.

I slowly jacked up the porch, letting it "rest" every inch or so, and wound up with only a few "character" cracks across the tile. I had several 4 x 4s from the Colorado house. Those were used to support the carport roof after I got it up and level. I had to splay them out at the base so that I could remove all the old posts and break out a 12" swath of the old concrete. The code required a 12 x 12 footer all the way around the exterior. That was a real bear. The old concrete was actually about 6" thick, and although it had no steel in the mix, it was very hard after all those years.

After the slab was in and set, I was able to put in new posts and start building the walls. It was an easy redo. I didn't add a bathroom, so no plumbing issues. Just electrical and piping in some of the air from the swamp cooler. It still took me more time than I wanted as I needed to get back to the Colorado house.

— ■ —

At the same time that we converted the carport, I extended the slab and built a laundry room on the back side of the house. These old houses all had outside laundry areas. Originally it was just a sink and a place for an old wringer washer. Over time, most everyone had put a small slab and had their washers and dryers out back. It was not pleasant going out to the washing machine that was sitting in the sun when it was either cold in the winter or 115° in the summer.

— ■ —

With the Idaho house now livable and the garage done, it was time to get back to our main remodeling task. We moved out everything that was no longer needed or that we planned to replace. That meant all the old sheetrock which had been installed on top of the even older ¼" plywood. In a few places, they had two layers of sheetrock on top of the plywood. As near as we could determine, there had been a leak. Rather than pulling down the bad sheetrock; they just covered it with a new layer. That is a great way to trap mold. Fortunately, we live in the arid desert. Next came the old roof. The first step was to drop the ceiling and pull out the dirt-laden rock wool. The dust and dirt were so bad, and so contaminated, that I had to wear a hazmat suit for the work.

Installing trusses 2014

Kellie and I were doing all of the work that we could, which was just about all of it. We had laid all of the floor trusses and rim boards on the new section, and we were almost through screwing and gluing the subfloor. As I said earlier, our lot has alleys on two back sides as we sit in the corner of the cul-de-sac. People walk up and down the alleys all day long, and men often ask if we need any help. They were looking for work. My answer was always the same. "I need a lot of help, but we are ok. Thanks for asking."

It was the Friday before Christmas 2014, and we were screwing down the last piece of subfloor. A guy and his girlfriend walked by with their two small dogs. I had seen them pass by on other days. He asked the usual question, and I gave the usual answer. He laughed and asked if I could use some volunteer help. I walked over and asked what he had in mind. He introduced himself, Matt Byron, and told me he was a builder, and they lived on East Pacific a block or so away. He said he had been watching our progress for the last year and he was happy to see someone improving the neighborhood. He said that he wanted to be a part of the project, and he would send his crew on Saturday to lend a hand.

Matt and his team were the perfect Christmas gift. They worked free for two days laying out the walls and completing much of the framing. We hired his crew to finish the rest of the framing, to roll the roof trusses and sheet the outside of the house and roof with the OSB. In total, it took them a couple of weeks. We could have done most of it ourselves, but it would have taken us months, and we wouldn't have done nearly as good a job.

— ■ —

I had long debated what siding to use. I have never been a fan of stucco, it collects too much of the blowing sand around here, and I don't like the way it looks. I looked at several alternatives, but most were either too expensive or would require painting every few years. We were trying to stay on a tight budget. We worried that we could easily overbuild for our area. We intend to remain in this house until we die, but I have always been of the opinion that you make money when you buy a house, not when you sell it. If you pay too much, you will never make your money back.

I ultimately decided that vinyl siding was the most cost effective and lowest maintenance option. It still wasn't cheap. I called a couple of companies. The lowest bid was $14,500 for installation and materials. The Lowe's quote for materials only was near $8,000; I felt that was still too high.

I searched the Internet for vinyl manufacturers located east of the Mississippi, specifically ones that did not have distribution west of the Mississippi. My logic was that if they had distributors, they would force me to buy through them and pay their markup. I found one company that agreed to sell it to me wholesale, with no returns. The price delivered was $3800. That we could live with, so we ordered from them and installed it ourselves.

— ■ —

Roofing was another battle. I had decided on metal roofing from the beginning. Primarily because of the endurance, low maintenance, and the esthetics. After much searching, I found that Lowe's sold Fabral steel roofing. It came in at about the same price as the siding. Several of the pieces were 24' in length. It was stacked and tied on the truck in a way that didn't support the long ends of the 24' pieces. As a result, 7 of these were slightly crinkled when they used the forklift to remove it from the truck. Of course, those would be highly visible on the front side of the house. Lowe's made it right and replaced them. I asked what they planned to do with the returns. They said they would send them to the dump. I offered them $100, and they sold them to me. I am not sure what I will do with them, but maybe I will build a covered patio at some point.

Installing Roof 2015

I had always planned on having the roof installed. I figured it might not be the brightest thing for a 70-year-old guy and his wife to be dragging 24' by 3' steel sheets around the roof. A gust of wind would send us sailing. A neighbor said he had a friend who had been an installer for years and was starting his own business. He came and took all the measurement and sent me a quote for $8300. I reminded him that this was labor only, I already had all of the materials. He told me he had already discounted it because I was a friend of Joe's. We decided to install it ourselves. It took us about a week and a half, but it wasn't all that difficult. We could have been faster, but we stayed off of the roof on any day that had even a slight breeze.

— ■ —

I wanted to use foam insulation. It gives better insulation and it virtually eliminated air infiltration. I wanted it sprayed on the underside of the roof deck so that we had a conditioned attic space. I opted for open-cell foam; it requires greater thickness but is much less expensive. It is amazing how much it takes. Doing 3½" in the wall cavities and the underside of the raised floor, plus 6" under the roof worked out to 27,000 linear feet. At any price per foot, that winds up being expensive.

570

I went back and forth between a couple of insulation companies and finally got one down to 21¢/foot. That was not all that much more than standard insulation, and it does a much better job.

We also installed our own A/C, sheetrock, flooring, and kitchen cabinets. We moved back into the house in July of 2015. We had several major pieces of work remaining, but the house was livable.

— ■ —

These old houses are unique, and I wanted to preserve a few reminders. The houses were originally sided with redwood. I had intended to salvage the siding and use it creatively somehow. Unfortunately, it was so dry and brittle after 70 years in the desert sun, that the boards would shatter like glass whenever I tried to remove them. The best I could do was salvage a few pieces to make window sills. I cut them to size, sanded off the old lead-based paint and shaped them with a router. They add a touch of class as well as a bit of nostalgia. I also salvaged about a dozen 1940 brass coat hangers. Cleaned and polished they look good along the inside wall of the master closet.

We had saved the old windows, and at Kellie's suggestion, I planted 8 treated 4 x 4s along the side of the garage and hung 4 of the old windows along with a few of the original shutters. We planted a tree plus shrubs along the base. Of course, it will look better as things grow in, but it changed the look of the side of the garage. One neighbor said it looks like a movie set.

— ■ —

Over the time we have been working on the house and yard, I had repeatedly had people ask if I was in the construction trades before I retired. Of course, the answer is no. Their immediate response is usually something along the lines of 'how did you know how to do all of this.' My answer is: 'I grew up in the country. If you didn't know how to do something, you had better figure it out, or it wouldn't get done.'

Stucco for front entry 2015

That was usually followed by something to the effect that they cannot believe that I would start such a massive undertaking at my age, and not having ever done anything like this before. That one was a bit harder to answer without sounding pretentious, but I can honestly say that I never considered my age or the size of the undertaking. I knew what I wanted to build, I knew what that would entail, I have a wife that never doubted that I could and would do it, and she was willing to stand beside me to make it happen. For us, it has been a great adventure.

— ■ —

Kellie's family, eight people from Shanghai, arrived for a two-week visit in late September 2015. We had to scramble to be even close to ready for company. With a lot of late nights on our part, we made it. Fortunately, they were willing to tolerate a lot of incomplete items, like the kitchen.

577

Faith & Religion

My story would not be complete without touching upon religion. That is a sensitive and personal subject that I suspect will upset people on all sides of the issue. None the less, faith and religion play an important part in my life and my American Dream. I would be remiss if I didn't address the subject.

My family was not religious. My parents did marry in a Baptist Church, but they were not members, and our family never attended any church. Given that upbringing, I had very little knowledge or bias concerning religion. At the same time, having read quite a bit, even at a young age, I was aware that religion had shaped civilizations as well as philosophies for the entirety of recorded history. When stationed at Kessler AFB in Mississippi, I began a serious quest to understand the major world religions. I wasn't seeking to join; I was trying to understand why virtually every culture throughout history had believed in some form of higher power. I wanted to know what was I missing.

I won't claim expertise beyond basic familiarity, nor will I explain what I found right or wrong about each, those are personal, and I neither wish to disparage nor to promote any religion. If the subject interests you, I suggest that you spend the time needed to educate yourself and make your own decision.

I will say that I found interesting and admirable aspects in nearly all religions. I believe that God has many names and that most religions believe in the same deity, regardless of the name. Ultimately, Christianity made the most sense to me, as it came closest to what I saw in the world around me.

I tend to be a bit cynical when it comes to "organized" religion. For me, organized religion is kind of like government. You need some but, in most cases, once they get started the inherent nature of any bureaucracy, and religious organizations are bureaucracies, is to grow and metastasize, to exist for their own purposes, and they bias their teachings accordingly. Just like living in the nanny state, over-dependence on a church leads to under dependence on self, and that is a mistake made all too often.

Why are we here?

I believe we are here to grow our soul. Our physical bodies are just a convenience to house our soul. For simplicity, I am using the words soul and spirit interchangeably. The body does influence the lessons the soul learns.

The difference between a man or a woman, black, white, Occidental, Oriental, short, tall, healthy, maimed, where we are born, etc., all shape our life experience and hence the lessons that our lifetime can offer.

Reincarnation and Karma

I believe in reincarnation as well as karma; to me, it is illogical to think that God would only give us one chance to get it all right, or that there would be no consequence for our mistakes. Life is just too complicated to be a one-shot, perfect-or-hell forever kind of thing. It is, therefore, logical that our soul will keep coming back over and over, to grow until it reaches the point where we enter Heaven. That point is not perfection, as we are deeply flawed and can never achieve that. It is the point when we have attained sufficient knowledge so that we can be of service to God. At that point, we stop returning, or at least not in the form of a living person.

I think the whole "game" is tied to the soul that we brought with us when we came. It is not about our bodies; they will return to dust; it is about our eternal soul. The paths we take reflect the mission of our soul; what we need to experience, what is to be learned, and therefore what path we must take to have those experiences. Our parents' DNA determines what our body looks like and our environment shapes how we start our life. Our soul guides us toward the path we must take to experience what we must experience in each lifetime. The opportunity for perfection is in every lifetime, but we have free will or "agency," and so we get to make choices.

— ∎ —

There are very mature souls and very immature souls, along with all gradations in between. Just look around you. If all souls began earthly life as complete equals, and only exist over a single lifetime, how can you explain the marked difference in the way people deal with life's challenges?

On more than one occasion, I have been asked: "why are you so different from your siblings?" That is a tough question to answer without considering the soul and reincarnation. Biologically we are of the same DNA, physiologically we had pretty much the same environment, psychologically we experienced pretty much the same "conditioning." So why such different outcomes? I believe the answer is that we each have souls that are at different points in our individual evolutions and that our souls are seeking to learn different lessons. Each lifetime is a classroom.

580

Evil

There is evil in this world. You cannot witness the depravity that some people exhibit, without acknowledging that there is some influence that is completely the opposite of love. Letting evil into your soul can lead to its degradation. I am not certain, but it seems possible that it can result in a permanent downward spiral that ultimately leads to an eternity of reincarnations.

Faith Makes Life Easier

Throughout history, wise men and women have: witnessed events, sought answers, gain wisdom, and reached logical conclusions. You can waste your lifetime trying to either repudiate or replicate their search and their knowledge. You can ignore what they can teach, or you can have faith. By standing on their shoulders, you can reach further.

I find it interesting that so many people readily accept, on faith, "facts" relating to non-spiritual matters. They are willing to stand on the shoulders of others without ever questioning the accuracy or the "wisdom" of those they follow, so long as no one mentions God. Though they act like sheep on some secular subject, they immediately claim their "intellectual independence" when the subject turns to spirituality.

For those who reject religion, I can only ask if you are proud of the life you are living? You will reach an end, and hopefully, you will have the opportunity to look back and decide if you lived a life of value. To me, it would be incredibly sad if the answer were no.

Inner Voices

I believe God talks to us quite frequently, maybe constantly. He speaks with a very soft voice, but we are seldom quiet enough to hear what He is saying. To align ourselves and our lives with God, we must learn to quiet our lives and our minds, so that we can hear Him speak.

Let God Lead

Finally, I know that there is too much Tim in Tim. Too often, I fail to let go and let God. I get in His way. I want to take charge, to make it happen on my schedule and in my way. God is not going to stop me, but He is unlikely to be pleased or supportive of the outcome when it is being driven by me rather than by Him. Try to let go and let God.

Griswoldisms 2.0

I realize that there are a few of life's lessons that I feel are worth giving but that did not fit conveniently into any of my prior discourse. Most are a bit more complicated than the Reader's Digest "isms" that profoundly influenced my upbringing. None the less, they are important lessons to consider.

Infovores

An "infovore" is someone who devours as much information as possible.

We live in the "Information Age." Put aside those things that waste your precious time and get excited about learning something new. Killing one more space alien, blowing up one more invader, or staring transfixed at yet another vacuous TV program or modern-age gladiator event, will not enhance your life or increase your knowledge one iota. Reading a book will.

Be acquisitive as well as eclectic in your quest for knowledge. You cannot read too much or explore subjects to far afield. Treasure knowledge. Get excited about learning something new. It doesn't have to be new knowledge, just new to you.

Fork In The Road

Yogi Berra was famous for his comically wise sayings which are known as 'Yogiisms.' My favorite is: "When you come to a fork in the road, take it."

Your choices will determine who you will become, how and where you will live, how your children will grow up, and who you will spend your life with; do not take these decisions lightly.

Remember three things:

1. The choices you make determine the outcome of your life.
2. Not to decide is a decision in itself.
3. You can never know the outcome of the road-not-taken; once decided, don't waste a minute thinking what might have been.

Towers vs. Pyramids

There once was a time when you could stay in the same job for your entire life. That is no longer the case. Most people will change careers 3, 4 or more times during their lifetime. The frequency will probably increase as technologies obsolete old professions.

If you build a single-skill tower, when you fall, and you will, there will be nothing between you and the ground. Build a pyramid. Learn as much as you can, about as many things as you can, across multiple fields. Let your career develop as you learn the appropriate skills. If your skill set becomes obsolete, or for whatever reason you want or need to change, you will have options.

It should not be about the money

Keep Ithaka on your mind. It should always be about the challenge, learning something new, doing something new, in particular, something that had not been done before. That is not to say that money is not necessary, but it is only money, and you can't take it with you.

Step-Up

I said this before, but it is worth repeating. Life is a matter of choice, not chance. Choose to be the hardest worker in the room or on the team. Be the first to step up, volunteer to do whatever needs to be done; no task should be beneath you, no assignment to trivial. Do the shit jobs, and you will be the one offered the sweet jobs. If you make the choices, you will get the chances.

Keep Standing Up

The difference between success and failure is the single decision to keep standing up. Everyone will get knocked on their ass from time to time. You can stay down, or you can stand up. The choice is yours, and the outcome is obvious.

Fact vs. Fault

Facts make a person stronger; faults make them weaker. If you can hear the facts, you can learn and improve. If you hear everything as "faults" (real or perceived), you will become defensive. When that happens, you will not learn.

Don't confuse them in either the giving or the receiving.

Be Intentional

The most important challenge in contemporary living is to be intentional. Intentional about what you do, about the choices you make, and most importantly, about being happy instead of miserable.

Integrity

I also said it before, but it is critical and worth repeating. Ultimately, all you have is your word. If you are not as good as your word, you are nothing.

Stuff

There is nothing quite as liberating as getting rid of most of your "stuff." Photos and music being the primary exceptions. What you discover is that you didn't own the stuff; the stuff owned you. If you have not used it in a year, get rid of it; lose it and be free!

Anger

Most anger is the result of unmet expectations. Moving back one level, unmet expectations are almost always the result of uncommunicated expectations. Therefore, the secret to any relationship, including a happy marriage, is to communicate your expectations. If you do that, you will find that most often the other person will meet your expectations or tell you up front that they cannot.

Guard against anger because "anger is a poor man's luxury." Few will deal with or trust a person who does not control their emotions. If you allow anger into your life, it will consume you and impoverish you.

Grievance vs. Gratitude

Attitude controls altitude. How high you go will be controlled, more by your attitude than your intellect.

As the bumper sticker says, "Shit happens!" How do you respond? Don't treasure your grievances. That is a waste of time and energy.

Chaos vs. Order

Order begets order and chaos begets chaos.

The environment you construct determines the life you will live. Put the trash in the trashcan, mop the floor ...choose to bring order to your existence. Even if you wake up to a dirt floor and a thatched roof, you can look for ways to bring order to your mind and other parts of your life.

Character Matters

Building character is a lifelong process; you can start with three simple rules: **"don't complain, don't explain, take the blame."**

At the risk of violating my second rule, let me explain why these three rules are fundamental to building character.

Don't Complain – Complaining makes you small! We all do it; some always do it. But it is wrong. At its root, complaining is expressing your feeling that you were not treated correctly. Someone did you wrong, a bad grade, a ticket, a stupid boss, and on, and on, and on.

No one cares. Furthermore, when you stop whining, you will still have a bad grade, a ticket, or a stupid boss. Getting it off of your chest won't make you feel better, and if the person listening to you, <u>parents I am talking about you here</u>, gives you a 'poor baby' response, all that does is reinforce your belief that life isn't fair. The truth is, life isn't fair, and the sooner you learn to deal with it, the sooner you can get past your self-pity and find happiness.

There is also the matter of perspective. As brilliant and honest as you might be, you can only see one side of the story. I can guarantee you that the dirty rotten scoundrel who did you wrong, sees things differently.

Don't Explain – Don't answer questions with unsolicited explanations. It is very hard to explain your actions without either complaining or sounding defensive. So don't volunteer explanations. If you are asked, keep your answers pithy.

Take The Blame – If you screwed up, step up! People are very tolerant, and we will almost always forgive the mistakes others make if they own them. On the other hand, if they have to conduct an inquisition to determine the truth, they will have little sympathy for the guilty party who tried to cover it up.

Stepping up will teach you humility, something that is woefully lacking in the world. Furthermore, if you know that you will have to step up and take the blame, there is a good chance that you will think twice before you do something stupid.

Things to Ponder

I leave you with a few things to ponder while you look forward to Volume II in another 35 years.

- Set worthy goals as results seldom exceed expectations
- A lifetime of integrity can be destroyed in one second
- Wisdom does not come from a book
- Character cannot be purchased
- Vision is not what you see
- Seek your own mountains
- Happiness is a choice
- Respect is not a gift
- Never settle
- Watch out for trucks
- Keep Ithaka always in your heart

If you have read this book in its entirety, you can see that anyone can start from anywhere and achieve success as well as happiness. You have been giving the incredible gift of birth and the opportunity to grow from wherever you started. It is not a matter of what others do to you; your outcome is controlled by what you choose to do to yourself.

My Journey To Ithaka

On August 20, 1986, Patrick Sherrill, a U.S. Postal worker in Oklahoma walked into his workplace; he shot and killed 14 co-workers, and injured six more before he killed himself. Several copycat incidents took place over the next few years. After months of searching, it was concluded that Mr. Sherrill and the others had cracked under the strain of constant repetitive labor without hope. The term "going postal" entered our lexicon.

I could never identify with Mr. Sherrill's methods, but I could certainly identify with his madness. My terror was never about the unfamiliar; it was about the familiar.

I could have never survived in a world where I went to the same job, met the same people, and did the same thing day after day. I sought the unknown; I needed to wake up not knowing what the day would hold.

My seven-decade journey toward Ithaka has been wonderfully long, full of adventure, and full of discovery. There have been many times when, with great pleasure and joy, I have come into harbors seen for the first time.

I have crossed swords with more than a few Laistrygonians and Cyclops, and on occasion, I have angered Poseidon. However, as Cavafy predicted, these were my failings, times when I did not keep my thoughts raised high.

My Journey is not over; a rare excitement continues to stir my spirit and my body. I am wiser now but in no hurry. By the time I reach the island, I plan to be timeworn with wealth beyond measure with all that I have gained, but Ithaka has already given me a marvelous journey.

Appendix – Milking the cows

These pages are excerpted, with permission, from Chuck Nelson's book called "Life at The End of a Dirt Road" ISBN: 1425922112. Chuck was a classmate and friend beginning in the 4th grade. His book is about his growing up in the Shasta Valley. What follows is a single chapter on the milking process. The entire book is definitely worth reading.

Milking the cows

Milking cows is an important part of ranch life. If you carefully studied the chapter about where milk really comes from, you should have a pretty good handle on the big picture involving ranchers, cows, bulls and milk. With this background, I think you are in a position to appreciate some of the particulars concerning that portion of the process known as milking the cows. In this chapter, you'll learn details that will add color and dignity to a process that might otherwise seem to be nothing more than the ruthless exploitation of the animal kingdom.

For most of my life on the ranch, we had a milk cow or two on hand. Before my brother Tom and I were old enough to milk the cows, we sometimes accompanied our father when he did the evening milking. During the winter it was almost always after dark by the time he got to the chore. While Dad was milking, Tom and I played on the bales of hay that were usually stacked high in the barn. It was cold, fun, dark and stickery. Sometimes we had flashlights to play with, but most of the time we played hide-and-seek in the dim light from the single light bulb in the corner of the barn where Dad was milking the cows.

Dad had an old electric radio that he plugged into the same socket that powered the light bulb. Battery-powered transistor radios were still waiting to be invented. The old radio rested on the sill just under the roof, and it was a raggedy thing without a case around it. When he turned the radio on, we could see the exposed tubes glowing in the dim light. Dad always listened to the radio while milking the cows. He said it settled the cows down, but I suspected it was just a way for a busy man to catch up on the news and to have some company in what was usually a big empty barn. It was a small luxury.

We had two cows on hand by the time Tom and I were old enough to start milking. We were assigned the chore as soon as we were big enough to sit on a stool and grip the applicable bovine appendages with enough strength to squeeze the milk out. The cow Tom milked was officially known as Patricia or Pat, but we always called her Bossy. The cow I milked was named Roamy, but for some reason, she was usually called Goldie. On occasion, for reasons that will become obvious shortly, I called her "@#%&@#%."

You will recall that we normally only named animals we didn't intend to eat. Naming animals you intend to consume just complicates things. For example, most people like to eat steak or hamburger, but not too many would like to eat Chester or Happy, the Cow. If you don't plan to eat your cat, dog or milk cow, go ahead and name them; but don't name your food. It's a good rule of thumb.

Pat, the cow that Tom milked, was older, gentler and gave more milk than Goldie. Goldie was less cooperative and tended to be cranky. As the older son, Tom got to milk the kinder, gentler cow, and I got the ornery one – go figure. Among siblings, might makes right, and that is the sum of all the rules between big and little brothers.

Tom and I began milking when we were about 7 or 8 years old. We still lived in the old Red House when we started and continued after we moved to the new house on the ranch. We milked Pat and Goldie until they died. As a teenager, I came to intensely dislike the chore, but I swear that the cows died of natural causes, and nobody can prove otherwise. Anyway, old cows don't die, they just "kick the bucket" one time too many.

The cows were always milked in the large, wooden, creaky barn, which many years before had been painted red like the Red House. For some reason we didn't call it the Red Barn; we just called it "the barn." The schedule was relatively simple. We milked the cows in the morning before going to school, and we milked them again before going to bed. Cows didn't have days off, so neither did we. If Tom or I wanted to stay overnight with a friend, the other brother had to milk both cows, or sometimes Mom or Dad would stand in for the missing brother.

The cows were kept in an irrigated pasture just south of the Red House and west of the barn. Normally, as milking time approached, the cows could be found standing near the barn door waiting for us to arrive. Our cows were golden-brown Guernseys, and they produced a lot of milk. Things got a bit "tight" and uncomfortable for them if we showed up late for the milking. If we were running unusually late, it was common to see milk spontaneously dribbling onto the ground beneath them. We always fed the cows hay and grain at milking time, so that gave them another incentive to look forward to our twice-daily visits. If the cows were feeling cantankerous, we had to go into the pasture and herd them to the barn, but that was the exception rather than the rule.

When we opened the barn door, the cows knew the routine. They walked right in and stuck their heads through the stanchions in their assigned stalls, where we had placed grain and hay for their dining pleasure. We locked them into their respective stalls by moving one of the upright boards of the stanchion lightly against their necks, where it was held in place by a locking block that dropped into place. Once locked in, they could move their head up and down, but they couldn't go forward or back out of the stall. It was necessary to lock them in because the milking process can take a while, and if the cow changes its mind about cooperating when you're in the middle of the procedure, things can get awkward. It's extremely difficult to milk a cow that's on the move, and, so far as I know, it's only done at rodeos.

Once the cow is locked in place and "manging" in the manger, we could go about the business of milking. The bovine milking appendages are located on the underside and toward the rear of the cow. They consist of a large udder from which four teats protrude. The job of milking is not finished until all four teats are dry, that is, until you cannot squeeze any more milk from the cow. The duration of the process depends upon the strength of your grip, the attitude of the cow, the attitude of the milker, whether the cow's calf escaped its pen and got to the cow's milk before you did, or whether you have a date later that night.

Normally the milking process takes from 10 to 15 minutes per cow, all things being equal. If you needed to get back to the house so you could clean up for a date, the milking could be accomplished in less than eight minutes, but with some slippage in quality control.

The job is accomplished while sitting on a low stool or, more often, an upside-down bucket so that your eyes and hands are at the appropriate level to engage the teats. After placing a clean bucket under the cow, you grasp two teats and pull down while squeezing at the same time. When done correctly, you can produce a substantial stream of milk. In practice, while you're using both hands, you usually only pull down on one teat at a time. While one hand is squeezing milk out of one teat, the other hand is repositioning its grip. With a bit of practice, you can keep a steady stream flowing – left, right, left, right, left, right -- and soon you learn how to fill the bucket without soaking your shoes.

Milking Complications

A number of complications can slow down the milking process. One of the worst is when the cow has had a close encounter with a barbed-wire fence and has managed to cut one of her teats. When this would happen, it would still be my job to milk the cow, but it became the cow's job to avoid pain at all costs. These jobs are not compatible. After washing the injured appendage, we would apply a substance called Bag Balm to the affected area. Bag Balm seemed to soothe the injury somewhat and speeded healing. Still, milking a cow with a cut teat was a lot like tap dancing in a minefield. About every fourth or sixth squeeze (you never knew for sure), the cow would signal the presence of pain by kicking you, knocking over the bucket of milk or both. If you were standing just outside the barn door, it sounded something like this: squirt, squirt, squirt, squirt, kick, slosh, clang, @#$%&@....squirt, squirt, squirt.

Bag Balm was something of a universal miracle ointment on the ranch. We used it on ourselves as well as the cows, although not in the same places we applied it on the cows. Bag Balm doesn't smell particularly good, and it's a little greasy, but the whole family used it to help sooth and heal our cuts and bruises, or just to smooth rough hands. When you live on a ranch, your hands are usually a bit gnarly, and Bag Balm makes them soft again. I even keep Bag Balm around my house in the city. I used it to help heal a serious ankle injury I incurred in the line of duty as a police officer. Bag Balm comes in a square green can just like it did 50 years ago. It has a picture of a cow's head on the lid and a cow's udder on the side – but it works for me.

Another complication that could slow the milking process had to do with the particular location where the cow had slept during the previous eight hours. Cows are not really fussy when it comes to personal hygiene, and it is not uncommon for them to sleep on top of a fresh cowpie. As luck would have it, the affected area would be, as often as not, the udder or teats; or, worse, the location on the side of the cow where the milker's head would be pressed while milking.

If you haven't milked a cow with your face in near contact with the remains of a fresh cowpie, you haven't missed much. The bouquet leaves much to be desired, but in the event of inadvertent contact, you will find that it's an excellent hair treatment. Once it dries, it will keep your hair in place all day better than that green stuff barbers keep in a jar. Milking a cow with your face hovering near fresh cow poop can be done if you are very careful, but I wouldn't recommend it unless you are an experienced milker. It's better to clean off the cow crap first, though that takes a minute or two and extends the total time it takes to milk the cows. Somehow cows must know when you have a date or are otherwise in a hurry because they seem to roll in a large, fresh cowpie in advance nearly every time you're in a rush.

A particularly bothersome complication that slows down the milking process occurs during fly season. When it comes to cows, the fly season lasts from spring thaw until the first hard freeze. I don't think there's ever been a fly that met a cow it didn't like. It's not that the fly likes the cow's personality so much as it is that the cow's body makes a great socializing platform for flies when they are between cowpies. Most of the time the rear quarter of a cow is smeared with what we euphemistically called "guacamole," and the flies surely seemed to appreciate this. Presumably, the guacamole was an ideal snack between cowpies.

The social relationship between cows and flies revolves around cowpies and is not particularly complex. When the cow deposits a "steamer" in the pasture, the flies quickly abandon the cow for a mating and feeding frenzy on the surface of the fresh cowpie. The relationship between cows and flies is sort of like the relationship between kids and an ice cream truck, except the cow's product, is hot rather than cold, it only comes in chocolate and it's free. I guess the analogy deteriorates rapidly, but the point is that flies tend to congregate around cows, and kids gather around ice cream trucks – and we'll leave it at that.

The problem with flies and cows is that during fly season, the cow is always transporting a few hundred flies wherever it goes. Cows are not particularly sensitive, but they do notice it when flies take off and land on their backs, especially if the fly is somewhat clumsy about it. The flies crawl around on the cow, some bite and that also adds to the cow's irritation. Cows respond to fly irritation by employing their built-in fly swatter. A cow's tail ends with a lot of long hairs, sort of like a frayed rope, and it makes an excellent fly swatter. From where the tail is attached on the north end of a southbound cow, it can swat flies at least halfway up the body toward the head. If the cow is so inclined, it can swing its head back and chase flies off of the forward portion of the body. The tail and head operating in concert make the cow a pretty effective fly-swatting machine.

But when we were milking, the cow's head was secured in the stanchion, and this put half of the cow's fly-swatting system out of commission. It also meant that the fly irritation factor was increased by 50 percent while we were engaged in the process of milking the cow. To compensate for the increased discomfort, the cow's brain sends a message to the tail instructing the tail to double its switching output. This is just fine for the cow, but it's bad for the flies, and it's really bad for the kid milking the cow. Cow tail switching is not a precise science; in fact, it's downright indiscriminate. The milker and the flies both get swatted on a regular basis.

Getting swiped across the face by the frayed rope attached to the cow's butt stings, but that is not really the worst part. The worst part relates to where the cow's fly swatter attaches to the cow. The proximity of the cow's fly swatter to the cowpie delivery system ensures that the tail is usually coated with guacamole. That's the worst part. A guacamole-coated fly swatter stings more than a dry one. I'm not saying the cow does it on purpose, but a well-aimed swish can wrap that tail around your head twice, with the guacamole-coated tip ending up in your mouth. You just can't spit enough when that happens.

Another complication that interferes with the milking process is when the cow kicks the bucket over or puts her foot in the bucket. Out of necessity, we developed procedures to handle each of these contingencies.

Cows will, on occasion, kick over the bucket. For some reason, this normally happens when you are almost done so that the maximum quantity of the milk is lost. The reasons cows kick over buckets can vary. Most often they are trying to kick you, and they simply miss and hit the bucket by accident. However, it could be because they are just shifting their feet or reacting to an itch. An experienced milker develops good reflexes and can see a lot of the kicks coming in time to grab the bucket and save the milk. But it's not possible to be 100 percent effective in this, so you have to expect to lose a bucket of milk from time to time.

Mom didn't like it when we came back from the barn with only half the usual milk because one of the cows had kicked over the bucket. When this happened, we normally got a "be more careful" lecture, so we did our best to save the milk to avoid the lecture. With any luck we could literally squeeze more milk out of the cow after she kicked the bucket over, so we would have something to show for our time and effort. If we could deliver some milk, this also shortened Mom's lecture.

When the cow puts her foot in the bucket, it's a different situation. The reason cows occasionally put a foot in the milk bucket varies, but mostly it's just because they're stupid. After they try to kick you or a cat, they have to put their foot somewhere, so it might as well be in the milk bucket. It doesn't seem to matter one way or another to the cow.

When this happens, your first challenge is to get the cow to lift her foot out of the bucket. Cows are not particularly agile and not particularly motivated to raise their feet high enough to clear the top of the bucket. I guess the foot feels warm and toasty in the milk, so the clumsy cow figures, "Why move it?"

So far as I know there's no method sanctioned by the People for Ethical Treatment of Animals to get a cow to lift her foot out of the bucket. Pleading, hollering and waving our arms had no noticeable effect, so we'd slap the cow on the butt and push on her until she lifted her leg and we could grab the bucket. As often as not, the milk was spilled in the process. This meant that we had to tell Mom that the cow kicked over the bucket and subject ourselves to another "be more careful" scolding.

If the cow managed to lift her leg out of the bucket without spilling it, I had two options. I could, and admittedly should consider the milk contaminated and throw it away, but then I would have to defend myself to Mom. On the other hand, if, upon inspection, the cow's foot didn't have as much crap on it as it usually did, I could consider the milk "salvageable." All I had to do was add a second filter to the strainer through which I poured the milk to bottle it, and I could rationalize that it was completely sanitized. Of course I myself wouldn't drink any milk until that batch was gone, but I figured what the rest of the family didn't know wouldn't hurt them. The important thing at the time was to avoid the "be more careful" lecture. In the process, it's entirely possible that the Nelson family developed antibodies to diseases that medical science has yet to discover.

Chuck Nelson: "Life at The End of a Dirt Road" ISBN: 1425922112.

Made in the USA
San Bernardino, CA
14 June 2018